D1480469

# Correspondence of James K. Polk

VOLUME VII, JANUARY–AUGUST 1844

JAMES K. POLK

*From an engraving by the Gravure Company of America, 1901*

# Correspondence of

# JAMES K. POLK

*Volume VII*
*January–August 1844*

## WAYNE CUTLER
Editor

## JAMES P. COOPER, JR.
Associate Editor

1989
Vanderbilt University Press
Nashville

LIBRARY OF CONGRESS CATALOGING IN PUBLICATION DATA (Revised)
Polk, James Knox, Pres. U.S., 1795–1849.
   Correspondence of James K. Polk.
   Vol. 7 edited by W. Cutler
   CONTENTS: v. 1. 1817–1832.—v. 2. 1833–1834.—v. 3. 1835–1836.—
v. 4. 1837–1838.—v. 5. 1839–1841.—v. 6. 1842–1843.—v. 7. 1844.
    1. Polk, James Knox, Pres. U.S., 1795–1849.    2. Tennessee—Politics and
government—To 1865—Sources.    3. United States—Politics and
government—1845–1849—Sources.    4. Presidents—United States—
Correspondence.    5. Tennessee—Governors—Correspondence.    I. Weaver,
Herbert, ed.    II. Cutler, Wayne, 1938–
   III. Title
E417.A4      1969      973.6'1'0924      75–84005
ISBN 0-8265-1225-9

Copyright ©1989 by Vanderbilt University Press
Printed in the United States of America

*Sponsored by*

Vanderbilt University

The National Historical Publications and
Records Commission

The National Endowment for the Humanities

The Tennessee Historical Commission

*To*
*William H. Goetzmann*

# PREFACE

Defeated in his 1843 gubernatorial race in Tennessee, Polk hoped to place himself on the Democratic party's 1844 ticket with or without Martin Van Buren in the top position. Holding the Old Democracy's North-South alliance together would require of the party a new and bold strategy for achieving victory in the forthcoming presidential election. Van Buren loyalists could not easily detach themselves from the only man who had ever led the northern wing of the party. Nor were there any "safe" states in their half of the Union, for the nomination of John C. Calhoun or a northerner of southern persuasions would diminish prospects for winning state and local elections. For their part southern Democrats would face equally certain defeat should the party run Van Buren a third time.

In his 1843 gubernatorial race Polk had made the forthcoming presidential contest a major issue and had endorsed Van Buren without reservation; Polk's failure to win the governorship demonstrated in part that Van Buren could not carry Tennessee. In November of 1843 the pro-Van Buren faction in Tennessee lost control of the State Democratic Convention. Tennessee Democrats could agree to support Polk for vice-president; but they could not unite behind either Van Buren or a candidate of nullification persuasions, for the latter choice would prove unacceptable to those Jacksonians not yet displaced by the rising power of the "Young Democracy." The Tennessee splits likely would occur throughout the South and undermine party strength at the grass roots.

Sectional divisions between the northern and southern branches of the Old Democracy begged for a western candidate, but the party's three most prominent westerners could offer little chance of reuniting Andrew Jackson's fractured coalitions of 1828 and 1832. Missouri's Thomas H. Benton and Kentucky's Richard M. Johnson might gain northern acceptance because of their antislavery sympathies, but for the same reasons neither could carry the cotton South. Michigan's Lewis Cass might win the support of southern cotton producers because of his low-tariff views, but the same would defeat him in the protectionist states of the North. In 1844 the discordant Democracy divided against all of its prominent leaders; and had it not been for the dreaded fear of a Henry Clay presidency, the contentious factions might never have compromised on an "available," that is, an electable candidate.

The letters in this the seventh volume of the series may raise as many questions of fact and interpretation as they settle. For example, Polk's 1844 vice-presidential bid invites particular attention because at first glance it would appear to be a grasping attempt to salvage a failing political career; closer scrutiny suggests that Jackson's protégé aimed at a higher mark and that party elders agreed in advance of the convention to look for a compromise candidate. Benjamin F. Butler's visit to the Hermitage in April of 1844, Hendrick B. Wright's proposal of the two-thirds rule in the nominating convention, and Andrew Jackson's espousal of a pro-annexation candidate from the Southwest argue for a second look at Polk's "dark horse" nomination. Van Buren's failure to support the immediate annexation of Texas no doubt separated him from Jackson's further support for the nomination, but the Texas question did not operate so forcefully on most of Van Buren's northern friends, some of whom defected on the critical decision to adopt the two-thirds rule. A majority of delegates to the nominating convention wanted to vote for Van Buren on the first ballot; yet the same majority did not support convention rules that would have assured a Van Buren nomination. Perhaps Van Buren's hedging on the question of Texas annexation facilitated defection on the two-thirds rule, but that is not to say that the test of "availability" would have operated any less forcefully in setting up conditions for a deadlocked convention. As expected, the delegates adopted the traditional two-thirds rule and after eight ballots turned to a pro-annexation candidate from the Southwest.

Polk's presidential campaign strategy followed the same conciliatory lines as his earlier bid for the vice-presidential nomination. In his behalf convention managers offered second place on the ticket to Silas Wright, Jr., of New York; unwilling to compromise his deeply felt loyalty to Van Buren, Wright quickly declined the offer, which next went to and was accepted by George M. Dallas of Pennsylvania. Upon learning officially of his nomination, Polk pledged in his acceptance letter to Henry Hubbard et al., June 12, 1844, that in the event of his election, he would not run for a second term. By rendering the 1848 nomination open to all branches of his party, he hoped to bring the disappointed factions together behind his one-term candidacy. On the Texas annexation issue he let stand his unequivocal support for the "re-annexation" of Texas and the establishment of the United States' authority and laws in both Texas and Oregon. Again, he anticipated that the divisiveness of Texas annexation would be composed by including Oregon in his determination "not to permit Great Brittain or any other foreign power to plant a colony or hold dominion over any portion of the people or territory of either." (Polk to Salmon P. Chase et al., April 23, 1844)

Strongly committed to reestablishing an Independent Treasury system, as opposed to a national bank, and equally committed to reducing the general government's debt, Polk embraced traditional Jeffersonian dogmas and advocated a strict preservation of the Union's decentralized system of governmental powers. Indeed, Polk's expansionist views reflected his deep belief that the westward line of settlement would further the goals of political and economic democracy, for the addition of new states to the Union would diffuse the older states' influence and thus would retard the tendencies inherent in all governments to foster economic privilege through political consolidation. Government created and protected monopolies undermined the will of the people to govern themselves free of special interests; and apart from the virtue of a disinterested citizenry, democracy had no moral claim superior to that of monarchy and other forms of authoritarian rule. The question was not whether all races would enjoy the civil liberties of self-government, but whether the Union's experiment in democracy, limited as it might be, would survive.

Polk did not take the Union of states for granted, and for that reason he resisted the notion that the general government could or should be made sufficiently powerful to advance or balance sectional interests. The constitutional settlements of 1787 had compromised those difficult conflicts that in and of themselves denied resolution above the state and regional orders of political, economic, social, and religious action. Time and experience had intensified those strains upon the bodies politic, and the presidential campaign of 1844 brought into sharp relief the full measure of the Union's essential fragility. Polk defined very carefully his position on tariff protection, the formula for which had been accepted by northern and southern Democrats since Jackson's first administration. Polk would accept incidental protection occasioned by the general government's revenue requirements, provided that the government was economically administered and that the protection afforded was distributed fairly "to all the great interests of the whole Union, embracing agriculture, manufactures, the mechanic arts, commerce and navigation." (Polk to John K. Kane, June 19, 1844) Polk's endorsement of a "revenue tariff" defused the most explosive issue of his day. Without tariff protection northern manufacturers would be forced to reduce their labor costs through the importation of cheap foreign labor. The prospect of massive immigration, largely from Catholic countries, posed a serious threat to those native Americans who might find themselves displaced in both the work place and the city hall. The rise of the Native American party in New York City and anti-immigration riots in Philadelphia signaled growing sectional discontent with southern opposition to tariff protection, with the expansion of slavery in the West, and with the republican ideology of the aging Democracy. Thus the tariff question required careful formulation to avoid igniting collateral disputes over immigration, popery, and slavery.

Perhaps Polk's most difficult campaign problem was not that of defining a conciliatory platform, but that of preventing his candidacy from acquiring a more sectional identity than was prudent. Leaders of the Tennessee Democracy proudly issued a call to party faithful in all parts of the Union to rally in Nashville on August 15; however, their invitation coincided with extremist declarations in South Carolina urging "Texas annexation or disunion." Polk became alarmed that northern voters would perceive the Nashville meeting as a vehicle for promoting a filibustering expedition to Texas, or worse. Whig editors across the Union denounced the "disunion" threat and argued that the organization of Texas Volunteers in Nashville proved that Polk's election would lead to war, or worse. Urgent instructions went from Columbia to Nashville on measures to counteract the "disunion" issue. The formation of additional uniformed militia companies in Nashville received little notice from the Democratic nominee, for the objectives of the Volunteers were entirely political, not military.

Probably no aspect of American history has received so little attention as the linkage between bugles and ballots in the antebellum period. Perhaps rightly enough, military historians have played down the contributions of the local militia muster to the training of combat-ready troops. That the militiamen organized their volunteer companies and elected their officers along partisan lines cannot be ignored without prejudice to a fuller understanding of how the second party system was structured and maintained. The Democratic mass meeting in Nashville brought together 35,000 armed militiamen from Tennessee and neighboring states. The *Nashville Union* of August 17, 1844, described the gathering of the participants in the following terms: "On Wednesday Nashville was from sunrise to sunset as a *Military Camp.* On every road to the city was to be seen approaching companies, battalions and regiments, mounted and on foot, with their bands of music, their banners and their mottoes, on their way to this great *encampment* of the sovereign people." The Democratic "volunteers" and "delegations" paraded through the city and then marched to "Camp Hickory," where they bivouacked and heard numerous speeches designed to energize them for political action in their home counties and states.

The designation "volunteer company" referred to those county militia units that required special duty, the burden of which was to perfect more difficult drills. To be certain, wearing colorful dress uniforms and demonstrating parade skills did attract the public's attention and often inspired admiration; more importantly, the peacetime volunteer companies—organized as they were on a strictly partisan basis—displayed which worthies of the community belonged to which party. Militia laws in most states provided for the formation of volunteer units, and membership excused participants from duty in the district militia companies. Regular militiamen also attended the mass political meetings, although they generally went as members of their county's combined militia force. County delegations operated outside the official chain of command but within the same regulations as were observed at company and regimental musters. During the summer months volunteers and delegates of both parties traveled extensively to do political things; unfortunately their operations were not always limited to political action. The national Whig rally, which met in Nashville on August 22, heightened partisan feelings, and ensuing confrontations led to several street fights and three deaths, despite the best efforts of militia officers of both parties to prevent violence. On August 25 Daniel Graham of Nashville urged Polk to leave Columbia for safety's sake when the Whigs held their rally there later in the week; the Democratic candidate chose to ignore Graham's warning.

Contrary to his customary practice of stump speaking in earlier congressional and gubernatorial contests, Polk declined to appear in public during the 1844 campaign. Although he assisted in drafting a career sketch for publication purposes and corresponded extensively with political leaders throughout the Union, he made no systematic effort to manage campaign activities outside Tennessee; each state conducted its own presidential campaign in its own fashion and with its own money. Common counsel from every quarter urged the candidate not to answer interrogatories from either friend or foe; and except for his tariff letter to John K. Kane of June 19, 1844, Polk let his record and the convention platform answer all inquiries, however urgently or sympathetically put forth. Throughout the early months of the campaign, observers reported that the level of party unity had not been higher since the 1832 election and that the Whig leadership had not been successful in generating much enthusiasm for Clay's candidacy. It was generally agreed that Polk's prospects in Kentucky, North Carolina, Ohio, New Jersey, and Massachusetts were at best marginal; his chances of carrying Pennsylvania and New York were good, but far from certain. Negotiations leading to John Tyler's withdrawal from the contest required great delicacy, but his support did not add greatly to Polk's voting strength in any of the closely contested states. Polk's nomination caught the Whig leadership off guard, and that advantage led many Democrats to expect an easy victory in November. By summer's end the dangers of that expectation had become clear to Polk and a worried Democracy.

### This Volume

Since the issuance of the sixth volume in 1983, the Polk Project has changed host sponsors and joined the Andrew Jackson and Andrew Johnson projects in forming the Tennessee Presidents Center, sponsored by the University of Tennessee, Knoxville. The Polk editorial staff relocated Project offices to Knoxville on August 1, 1987, and moved into the new Presidents Center on June 15 of the following year. Project reevaluations, sponsorship negotiations, office relocations, technological innovations, and personnel changes have delayed preparation of this present volume. After several false starts, the editors have adapted the TEX microcomputer software to their needs and have utilized the new technology in typesetting in house the whole of volume seven. With past difficulties overcome and new beginnings well begun, the editors look forward to more timely publication of the remaining volumes of the Correspondence series.

Always concerned that the reader's primary focus fall on the text of the document, the editors have limited their annotations to textual criticism and identifications. Persons, subjects, and oblique references have been noted on the occasion of their first mention in this volume; for the full name of persons mentioned subsequently in the text only by surname, the reader will want to consult the index. The editors have transcribed the text faithfully with a strict regard for original spellings, punctuation, and text placement, except for the following rules of normalization:

1. initial words of sentences have been capitalized and ending punctuation marks have been supplied when the syntax is clear (uncertain constructions are noted and rendered without normalization);

2. conventional spellings have been followed except when misspellings have been clearly written;

3. conventional upper and lower case usage has been followed when the writer employed multiple and/or irregular forms of the same character, thus indicating no discernible meaning behind the writer's use of capitals;

4. interlineations, cancellations, and unintentional word repetitions have been ignored unless something more than writing errors may have been indicated;

5. short dashes on the base of the line have been transcribed as commas or periods as the syntax may suggest;

6. redundant punctuation and random flourishes or ink marks have been ignored;

7. superscripts have been brought down to the line, and markings beneath or beside superscripts have been transcribed as single periods;

8. punctuation marks following the abbreviations *st, nd, rd,* and *th* have been deleted;

9. regardless of their position in the original manuscript, the salutation, place of composition, and date have been set on the line or lines immediately below the document's heading;

10. place of composition and full date, if omitted but known to the editors through content analysis, have been supplied in brackets and noted, and misstatements of place and date have been corrected and supplied in brackets with the misinformation noted;

11. the complimentary closing has been omitted, and the omission of same has been indicated by an ellipsis if the closing was written as part of the ending paragraph;

12. the author's signature has been rendered in capitals and small capitals at the end of the text (or supplied within brackets if unwritten or clipped);

13. the inside address has been omitted, but the information has been stated in the head note, along with the document's classification and repository location;

14. textual interventions (words supplied within brackets) have been made only to complete probable meanings (garbled texts have been transcribed without intervention and so noted); and

15. bracketed ellipses have been added to indicate that a portion of the text has been obliterated by ink blots, sealing wax, or some other kind of damage, and the nature and extent of same has been noted.

The editors' identification and explanatory annotations often have been assembled from standard reference and monographic sources that are so well known and reliable as to obviate the need for citation. These considerations, coupled with a desire to ensure that the endnotes do not overwhelm the presentation of the textual material, have persuaded the editors to forego the naming of sources in their endnotes.

## Acknowledgments

It is the editor's great pleasure to dedicate this seventh volume of the series to William H. Goetzmann, his mentor in the graduate history program at the University of Texas at Austin. By good example and with genuine concern, Professor Goetzmann brought fledgling students into the vitality and flow of historical investigation, and that experience gave purpose to even the most flawed efforts of youthful inquiry. In addition to teaching the mechanics of sound scholarship, he insisted upon a respectful attention to the "so what?" questions of the story at hand and its sources; and in so doing he led his charges gently through the fear of new and challenging ideas. The editor takes the occasion of this dedication to express his deep appreciation to a teacher who taught the whole person as well as the course of instruction.

Several young and very able historians have contributed their talents and energies to the preparation of volume seven. James P. Cooper, Jr., associate editor, shared all of the major editorial tasks that shaped the contents of this volume, such as document selection, research, and annotation; during his year with the Project, NHPRC Fellow David R. Hoth brought renewed vigor to the tasks of compiling research materials and searching for new documents; Cecilia S. Cornell served the Project as a part-time research associate for two years and inventoried thousands of additional Polk documents in the National Archives; and Robert G. Hall II and Jayne C. DeFiore, assistant editors added to the staff since the Project's relocation, have begun their editorial training by proofing and indexing the present volume. No editor ever owed more to his staff for keeping "our project" alive than the one who acknowledges this debt with great gratitude.

Together we express our sincere thanks to those librarians and archivists who have assisted us in our labors at the Jean and Alexander Heard Library, the Tennessee State Library and Archives, the University of Tennessee Library, the National Archives, and the Library of Congress. We are equally grateful to the members of the

National Historical Publications and Records Commission, the National Endowment for the Humanities, and the Tennessee Historical Commission and to the staff personnel of the above-mentioned agencies. We also acknowledge with appreciation the valuable assistance of John W. Poindexter and Jane C. Tinsley of the Vanderbilt University Press and of William Taylor of Technical Typesetting Inc., of Baltimore, Md.

The relocation of the Polk Project would not have been possible without the generous support of the administrative officers of the University of Tennessee, Knoxville; and we thank most particularly Chancellor Jack E. Reese, Provost George W. Wheeler, Dean Lorman A. Ratner, and Associate Dean Charles O. Jackson. To Harold D. Moser of the Andrew Jackson Project and Leroy P. Graf of the Andrew Johnson Project we say a special "thank you" for sharing your sponsor and making room for the Polk Project in the new Tennessee Presidents Center.

Nashville, Tennessee                                           WAYNE CUTLER
*January 1989*

# CONTENTS

Contents

# Contents

# SYMBOLS

*Document Classification*

| | |
|---|---|
| AC | Autograph Circular |
| ACI | Autograph Circular Initialed |
| ACS | Autograph Circular Signed |
| AD | Autograph Document |
| ADI | Autograph Document Initialed |
| ADS | Autograph Document Signed |
| AE | Autograph Endorsement |
| AEI | Autograph Endorsement Initialed |
| AES | Autograph Endorsement Signed |
| AL | Autograph Letter |
| AL, draft | Autograph Letter, drafted by writer |
| AL, fragment | Autograph Letter, fragment |
| ALI | Autograph Letter Initialed |
| ALI, draft | Autograph Letter Initialed, drafted by writer |
| ALS | Autograph Letter Signed |
| ALS, copy | Autograph Letter Signed, copied by writer |
| ALS, draft | Autograph Letter Signed, drafted by writer |
| ALsS | Autograph Letters Signed |
| AN | Autograph Note |
| ANI | Autograph Note Initialed |
| ANS | Autograph Note Signed |
| C | Circular, authorship attributed |
| CI | Circular Initialed |
| CS | Circular Signed |
| D | Document, authorship attributed |
| DI | Document Initialed |
| DS | Document Signed |
| E | Endorsement, authorship attributed |

| | |
|---|---|
| EI | Endorsement Initialed |
| ES | Endorsement Signed |
| L | Letter, authorship attributed |
| LI | Letter Initialed |
| LS | Letter Signed |
| N | Note, authorship attributed |
| NI | Note Initialed |
| NS | Noted Signed |
| PC | Published Circular, authorship attributed |
| PD | Published Document, authorship attributed |
| PL | Published Letter, authorship attributed |
| PN | Published Note, authorship attributed |

*Repository Designations*

| | |
|---|---|
| CSmH | Henry E. Huntington Library, San Marino |
| CSt–V | Stanford University, Nathan Van Patten Library, Stanford |
| DLC–AB | Library of Congress, Andrew Beaumont Papers, District of Columbia |
| DLC–AJ | Library of Congress, Andrew Jackson Papers |
| DLC–AJD | Library of Congress, Andrew Jackson Donelson Papers |
| DLC–GW | Library of Congress, Gideon Welles Papers |
| DLC–HC | Library of Congress, Henry Clay Papers |
| DLC–JKP | Library of Congress, James K. Polk Papers |
| DLC–Johnson | Library of Congress, Andrew Johnson Papers |
| DLC–LW | Library of Congress, Levi Woodbury Papers |
| DLC–Misc. Coll. | Library of Congress, Miscellaneous Collections |
| DLC–MVB | Library of Congress, Martin Van Buren Papers |
| DLC–WLM | Library of Congress, William L. Marcy Papers |
| DNA–RG 15 | National Archives, Records of the Veterans Administration, District of Columbia |
| DNA–RG 28 | National Archives, Records of the Post Office Department |
| DNA–RG 42 | National Archives, Records of the Office of Public Buildings and Grounds |
| DNA–RG 45 | National Archives, Naval Records Collection of the Office of Naval Records and Library |
| DNA–RG 46 | National Archives, Records of the United States Senate |
| DNA–RG 49 | National Archives, Records of the Bureau of Land Management |

| | |
|---|---|
| DNA–RG 56 | National Archives, General Records of the Department of the Treasury |
| DNA–RG 59 | National Archives, General Records of the Department of State |
| DNA–RG 60 | National Archives, General Records of the Department of Justice |
| DNA–RG 75 | National Archives, Records of the Bureau of Indian Affairs |
| DNA–RG 77 | National Archives, Records of the Office of the Chief of Engineers |
| DNA–RG 92 | National Archives, Records of the Office of the Quartermaster General |
| DNA–RG 94 | National Archives, Records of the Adjutant General's Office, 1780–1917 |
| DNA–RG 99 | National Archives, Records of the Office of the Paymaster General |
| DNA–RG 107 | National Archives, Records of the Office of the Secretary of War |
| DNA–RG 156 | National Archives, Records of the Office of the Chief of Ordnance |
| DNA–RG 217 | National Archives, Records of the United States General Accounting Office |
| GU | University of Georgia, Athens |
| ICHi | Chicago Historical Society, Chicago |
| IHi | Illinois State Historical Library, Springfield |
| Ia–HA | Iowa State Department of History and Archives, Des Moines |
| IaU | University of Iowa, Iowa City |
| InHi | Indiana Historical Society, Indianapolis |
| KyLoF | Filson Club, Louisville |
| MB | Boston Public Library, Boston |
| MHi | Massachusetts Historical Society, Boston |
| NHi | New-York Historical Society, New York |
| NN–Kohns | New York Public Library, Kohns Collection, New York |
| NcD | Duke University, Durham |
| NcU | University of North Carolina, Chapel Hill |
| NjMoHP–LWS | Morristown National Historical Park, L. W. Smith Collection, Morristown |
| NjP | Princeton University, Princeton |
| PHi | Historical Society of Pennsylvania, Philadelphia |

| PPAmP | American Philosophical Society, Philadelphia |
| T–ARW | Tennessee State Library, A. R. Wynne Family Papers, Nashville |
| T–GP | Tennessee State Library, Governor's Papers |
| T–JPH | Tennessee State Library, John P. Heiss Papers |
| T–JKP | Tennessee State Library, James K. Polk Papers |
| T–Misc. File | Tennessee State Library, Tennessee Historical Society File |
| T–RG 5 | Tennessee State Library, Internal Improvements Papers |
| T–RG 80 | Tennessee State Library, Secretary of State's Papers |
| Tx | Texas State Library and Historical Commission, Austin |
| WHi | State Historical Society of Wisconsin, Madison |

*Published Sources*

| AHR | *American Historical Review* |
| ETHSP | *East Tennessee Historical Society's Publication* |
| NCHR | *North Carolina Historical Review* |
| THM | *Tennessee Historical Magazine* |
| THQ | *Tennessee Historical Quarterly* |

# CHRONOLOGY

| | |
|---|---|
| 1795 Nov. 2 | Born in Mecklenburg County, N.C. |
| 1806 Fall | Moved to Maury County, Tenn. |
| 1812 Fall | Underwent major surgery by Dr. Ephraim McDowell in Danville, Ky. |
| 1813 July | Began study under Robert Henderson at Zion Church Academy |
| 1816 Jan. | Entered University of North Carolina as sophomore |
| 1818 June | Graduated from University of North Carolina |
|     Fall | Began reading law in office of Felix Grundy of Nashville |
| 1819 Sept. | Elected clerk of the Tennessee Senate |
| 1820 June | Admitted to the bar |
| 1823 Aug. | Elected to the Tennessee House |
| 1824 Jan. 1 | Married Sarah Childress of Murfreesboro |
| 1825 Aug. | Elected to the U.S. House |
| 1827 Aug. | Reelected to the U.S. House |
|     Nov. 5 | Death of his father, Samuel Polk |
| 1829 Aug. | Reelected to the U.S. House |
| 1831 Jan. 21 | Death of his brother Franklin, aged 28 |
|     April 12 | Death of his brother Marshall, aged 26 |
|     Aug. | Reelected to the U.S. House |
|     Sept. 28 | Death of his brother John, aged 24 |
| 1833 Aug. | Reelected to the U.S. House |
|     Dec. | Chosen to chair the U.S. House Committee on Ways and Means |
| 1834 June | Defeated by John Bell for Speaker of the U.S. House |
| 1835 Aug. | Reelected to the U.S. House |

|  |  |  |
|---|---|---|
| | Dec. 7 | Elected Speaker of the U.S. House |
| 1836 | Aug. 6 | Death of his sister Naomi, wife of Adlai O. Harris |
| 1837 | Aug. | Reelected to the U.S. House |
| | Sept. 4 | Reelected Speaker of the U.S. House |
| 1839 | Aug. | Elected Governor of Tennessee over Newton Cannon |
| 1840 | May | Withdrew candidacy for the Democratic vice-presidential nomination |
| 1841 | Aug. | Defeated in gubernatorial election by James C. Jones |
| 1843 | Aug. | Defeated in gubernatorial election by James C. Jones |
| | Nov. | Recommended by the Tennessee Democratic State Convention to be the party's 1844 vice-presidential nominee |
| 1844 | May | Nominated for the presidency by the Democratic National Convention |
| | Nov. | Elected President of the United States over Henry Clay |
| 1845 | Mar. 4 | Inaugurated President of the United States |
| 1849 | Mar. 4 | Yielded office to his successor, Zachary Taylor |
| | June 15 | Died in Nashville of cholera |

# Correspondence of James K. Polk

VOLUME VII, JANUARY–AUGUST 1844

# JANUARY 1844

## FROM SAMUEL H. LAUGHLIN[1]

Post office, Monday morning

My dear Sir,                                    Nashville, January 1, 1844

I have just received yours of Saturday night,[2] having been out of town from early yesterday morning until 10 o'clock at night. Yesterday Mr. H. L. Turney and myself rode up to Maj Donelson's,[3] dined there, and spent the afternoon at the Hermitage. The old chief[4] had been told we would be there by Donelson who was in town on Saturday.

The Gen. wrote a pressing letter,[5] modestly couched, so as to be disarmed of all appearance of dictation, to Col. Medary,[6] in which he urges your claims warmly, but with proper deference to the judgment of the democracy and the claims of others. He also wrote letters introducing Turney to Mr. Dawson and Parson Burke,[7] and authorizing Turney to confirm to the former the facts of a letter the General had lately written him correcting a falsehood in relation to your present position on the Bank question.

Mr. Turney remains here to-day in the Supreme Court. Donelson cant go with him—neither can Cheatham.[8] Donelson has to leave for Mississippi, and poor Cheatham has his property under execution. Gen. Armstrong[9] and myself will try to get some suitable coadjutor to go during this day. If we fail, we will send some decent young man along for company, as Mr. Turney is in hourly danger of being knocked up by sickness. He and some one will go.[10]

Since Friday, Dr. Kenney[11] and myself have put under cover and sent nearly 250 copies of the Committee's Address,[12] to friends out of the state, all over the Union. I sent a packet of them to A. A.

*3*

Kincannon and J. Percy Brown[13] at Jackson, Mississippi. Turney will take a packet of them with him.

I wrote the agreement between myself and Hogan and Heiss,[14] just as approved by Armstrong & Heiss, signed it, and left it with H. & H. to sign and deposite it with Gen. Armstrong. I dont believe they have done it yet. I have not heard of the other paper,[15] but suppose all will be right. Nothing, however, in this world is certain, till accomplished.

S. H. LAUGHLIN

P.S. Gen. Jackson's health is just as usual, confined mostly to his chamber, full of life and spirits, judgment and zeal clear and strong. [A ha]ppy New Year to you.[16]  L.

ALS. DLC–JKP. Addressed to Columbia and marked "Private."

1. A McMinnville lawyer and farmer, Laughlin served three terms as a Democrat in the Tennessee Senate, 1839–45.

2. See Polk to Laughlin, December 30, 1843.

3. Hopkins L. Turney and Andrew Jackson Donelson. A lawyer from Winchester, Turney served four terms in the Tennessee House, 1825–31 and 1835–37; three in the U.S. House, 1837–43; and one in the U.S. Senate, 1845–51. He was Polk's political friend and spokesman in the Mountain District. Donelson, a nephew of Rachel Jackson's, served as private secretary to Andrew Jackson during the period of his presidency, 1829–37. Donelson later guided negotiations for the annexation of Texas and served as U.S. minister to Prussia during Polk's administration.

4. Andrew Jackson.

5. Jackson's letter not identified further.

6. Editor of the Columbus *Ohio Statesman,* Samuel Medary was a powerful political figure in the Ohio Democracy.

7. Moses Dawson and William Burke. Dawson, an ardent Irish nationalist, was forced to flee his native land; he worked in Philadelphia before moving to Cincinnati, where he edited the *Advertiser,* a Democratic newspaper. A strong Jacksonian, Burke served as postmaster from 1832 until 1841.

8. A Nashville lawyer and prominent Democrat, Leonard P. Cheatham was president of the Democratic State Convention that met in Nashville on November 23, 1843.

9. Robert Armstrong served as Nashville's postmaster from 1829 until 1845. An unsuccessful candidate for governor in 1837, he remained politically active and coordinated Polk's three gubernatorial campaigns. An officer in the War of 1812, Armstrong commanded a brigade of Tennessee militia in the Second Seminole War.

10. Reference is to a proposed trip by Turney to Columbus, Ohio, where the Democratic State Convention was scheduled to convene on January 8, 1844. Turney did not make the journey.

11. Daniel Kenney, a Jonesboro physician and merchant, served a single term in the Tennessee House, 1843–45, for Greene, Hawkins, and Washington

counties.

12. The Address of the Democratic State Convention of 1843 has not been found. See Polk to Laughlin, December 4, 1843. Attended by approximately 230 delegates, the Tennessee Democratic State Convention met in Nashville on November 23, 1843, elected delegates to represent the state at the Democratic National Convention in May 1844, endorsed Polk for the vicepresidential nomination, and resolved to support the choice of the party's national convention.

13. Andrew A. Kincannon and J. Percy Brown. While a resident of Tennessee, Kincannon served as sheriff of Lincoln County and as a member of the 1834 Constitutional Convention; in the late 1830's he moved to Columbus, Miss., and served in the Mississippi House in 1844. Polk appointed him marshal for the northern judicial district of Mississippi in March 1845. Brown, a resident of Bolivar County, served in the Mississippi House from 1842 until 1844.

14. Thomas W. Hogan and John P. Heiss had published the *Nashville Union* since April 1842. Reference is to an agreement that set forth the terms under which Laughlin would serve as editor of the Nashville *Star Spangled Banner,* a Democratic campaign newspaper to be issued from the *Nashville Union* office from May through October 1844. For Polk's difficulties in retaining control of his principal party organ in Tennessee, see Polk to Laughlin, December 4, 1843; Laughlin to Polk, December 7, 1843; and Laughlin to Polk, December 25, 1843.

15. Reference is to a legal instrument securing payment of a cash loan to be used to finance the Nashville *Star Spangled Banner.* Use of *paper* to mean *note* was commonplace. See Laughlin to Polk, December 25, 1843.

16. Writing obscured by ink blotch.

## FROM WILLIAM H. POLK[1]

Dear Brother                                          Nashville Jan'y 1st 1844
I received your letter last night by Elias[2] after I had written to you. Turney & Laughlin returned from the Hermitage late in the evening, having obtained letters from Genl. Jackson to *Medeary*[3] and *others* at Cincinnatti & Columbus. I called to see Col Turney after reading your letter. He has been willing and ready to go,[4] but the difficulty has been to induce some one to accompany him. When I left him last night he told me he would go & I will to day, if *Cheatam*[5] is not in the City, *ride* out to his House and if possible prevail on him to go. If he will not, we *must* and *will* get some intelligent, good Democrat who can be relied on to accompany Turney. Turney says he is willing to leave to night in the Stage. I will write you by to nights mail. In Haste.

WILLIAM H. POLK

ALS. DLC–JKP. Addressed to Columbia.

1. James K. Polk's only surviving brother, William H. Polk, practiced law in Columbia and served three terms in the Tennessee House, 1841–45 and 1857–59, and one term in the U.S. House, 1851–53. He went to Naples for two years as U.S. minister to that court, 1845–47; he attained the rank of major during his service in the Mexican War.

2. Elias, a slave, attended Polk as his personal servant.

3. Samuel Medary.

4. See Samuel H. Laughlin to Polk, January 1, 1844.

5. Leonard P. Cheatham.


## FROM WILLIAM H. POLK

Dear Brother                                        Nashville Jan'y 1st 1844

I have been laboring all day to prevail on some Democrat to accompany *Turney* to Columbus.[1] The best I could do was to have Genl Jackson's letters sent by the mail to night, with a clear promise from *Turney* that he will leave in the Stage to-morrow night (Tuesday) direct for Columbus. Going by stage he can be there by Saturday night. The letters will be there on Friday night. The letters of Genl Jackson were accompanied by one, written by *Turney* to *Medeary*,[2] covering all the points, and stating that he would be in Columbus in a few days. This latter move was recommended by *Laughlin, Humphreys, Donaldson & Armstrong*.[3] I myself doubted the propriety of the move. I will write you again by the next mail.

Enclosed I send you a letter from *Eastman* and *Crozier*,[4] relating exclusively to myself. Read it. Send it back with your views and my answer will be *framed* according to your directions.

WILLIAM H. POLK

ALS. DLC–JKP. Addressed to Columbia. Polk's AE on the cover states that he answered this letter on January 2, 1844; Polk's reply has not been found.

1. See Samuel H. Laughlin to Polk, January 1, 1844.

2. Samuel Medary.

3. Samuel H. Laughlin, West H. Humphreys, Andrew Jackson Donelson, and Robert Armstrong. A lawyer from Somerville, Humphreys won election to a single term in the Tennessee House, 1835–37; served as state attorney general and reporter, 1839–51; and presided over the U.S. District Court for West Tennessee from 1853 until 1861, in which latter year he accepted the position of C.S.A. judge for Tennessee.

4. E. G. Eastman and Arthur R. Crozier. Eastman established the Knoxville *Argus,* a Democratic newspaper, in 1839; he edited the *Nashville Union*

from 1847 until 1849. Crozier was the son of John Crozier, Knoxville's postmaster from 1804 until 1838. Eastman and Crozier's letter has not been found.

## FROM DANIEL KENNEY

House of Representatives
Dear Sir                              Nashville Jany 2nd 1844

Last night I received from you a letter,[1] and send you the following reply. Col. Laughlin, and my self have been attending to sending off the addresses.[2] On Saturday night we sent off a great many as per List sent me, going over it in regular order. To night we expect to finish the list sent. We have even sent to many other Gentlemen not named. We have been careful to attend to Ohio and Mississippi.

We have no news from Washington since you left of any importance. Have you any? Nothing of any importance in the Legislature is being transacted.

I send you the Phamphlet form of the address,[3] as requested. The Democracy speak of doing something here on the 8th.[4] If so you will know it, and must come over.

DANL. KENNEY

ALS. DLC–JKP. Addressed to Columbia.
1. Letter not found.
2. See Samuel H. Laughlin to Polk, January 1, 1844.
3. No copy of the Address of the Democratic State Convention, November, 1843, has been found.
4. On January 8, 1844, Nashville celebrated the anniversary of the Battle of New Orleans with the firing of cannons and a parade of the Nashville Blues in full uniform. A large number of citizens paid their respects to Andrew Jackson at the Hermitage.

## FROM J. G. M. RAMSEY[1]

My Dear Sir                        Mecklenburg Jany. 4th 1844

By this days mail I received yours of the 29th Ult.[2] We had a meeting on Tuesday of our Central E.T. Comtee.[3] at which I was directed to correspond with you & other leading friends in W.T. on several points & I was preparing to carry that direction into execution when the mail arrived. I think with you that from all the indications every where that Mr. V.B.[4] will be nominated by the Baltimore Convention.[5] But I am far from being sanguine that its nomination will be responded to by the whole Democratic party. Two important considerations render

that whole matter doubtful, to say nothing of the mode of organizing
that body. I think that the action of the present Congress & especially
of the V.B. members of the H. of R. upon the Tariff will have a momentous bearing upon the harmony of our party. The vote upon Mr.
Rhetts resolution if not countervailed by the subsequent action of the
Northern Democracy[6] must & will destroy V.B. south of the Potomac.
I do not believe it will prevent his nomination, but that it will defeat
his election I very much fear. (Most heartily do I rejoice to notice the
votes of the Tennessee members on that resolution. If your friends use
that vote right they can essentially further your claims by doing so.
It furnishes me a new lever which I have already been using & will
continue to use wisely with my correspondents in several quarters altho it might not do any good to put it in a public journal. I shall press
it in the Carolinas & Virginia by letter.)

The other consideration that may prevent our harmony after the
Baltimore nominations is the nominee that may be associated with
V.B. for the Vice-Presidency. It cannot be concealed longer that
Richie[7] if not against you is certainly not for you. His quid pro quo
is Stephenson[8] for Van Buren & Van dare not refuse to ratify the
Bargain. The Enquirer[9] in republishing the Arkansas nominations[10]
stops at the Presidency. Nothing said of you. These indications are
pretty strong that the pretensions of Tennessee & all other States are
overlooked by Va. & N.Y. It will be the worst move possible (excepting
perhaps Col. Johnson[11]) & will make irreparable breaches & result in
defeat to us all around. To prevent this most disastrous policy should
be the aim of every one of our friends & at no point can more good
be effected in that way than at Richmond[12] during this very month. I
shall write myself to morrow to Col. Goodson[13] again reminding him
of a pledge he cheerfully made to me at Greeneville in Sep. to take
care of you this winter at Richmond—also to L. F. McMullen[14] with
whom I have heretofore corresponded at length.

The Editors of the Mecklenburg Jeffersonian expressed last year a
very high regard for your claims & if they had not been so sensitive
about Mr. Calhouns[15] fortunes would as Hampton assured me by letter
have at that time run up your flag.[16] That reason can no longer have
much weight & I will in a day or two bring the subject directly &
pointedly to their attention.

I felt no disappointment in not being delegated to Baltimore. My
only regret is that with one fragment of the party & that a very honorable & influential & virtuous one I occupied such a position as no
other Tennessean did & could have, I sincerely believe, most essentially contributed to promote the pretensions of yourself. I know I

could. But I shall put the existing delegate[17] in possession of the same position so far as it is transferable & enable him to the fullest extent possible to carry into effect the same object. I supposed before your letter, how he was delegated. But I must condense a little or leave a good deal unsaid. My correspondents all prefer you to Stephenson—King—Johnson[18] & several of them since Mr. Calhouns prospects for the nomination begin to wane are disposed to drop Woodbury.[19] You are their choice. I think from their letters your prospects are 100 fold better than before the meeting of Congress. I expect a letter from a reliable source in a short time. If its tenor is different from this view I will write you.

You know the late Convention at Nashville appointed the three central Committees to nominate the 2 electors for the State. It will of course be done by means of letters from the several Committees. It is now certain that the Whig Electors will be nominated soon.[20] They will be instantly in the field. Our electors are not to be nominated for some months to come. In the mean time we ought to have active & strong men in every District to engage at once in the canvass. My own opinion is that we ought now to know who our electors will be & request them to meet their competitors from the start. This E.T. Comtee. has taken the same view but we are not well enough acquainted all over the State to make the proper selection. Your Brother Wm. & Col. Nicholson[21] are both mentioned & also Coe & Staunton.[22] Which two of these would make a summers business of it & do us the most service? I know no one in E.T. that will answer well for this important service. Please write me *freely* on the subject. It shall reach the eye of no one. It is an important selection & we need advise. You can give it.

My ink was frozen last night. I hope this part of my letter will not be illegible before it reaches you.

J. G. M. RAMSEY

ALS. DLC–JKP. Addressed to Columbia.

1. A Knoxville physician, railroad promoter, and banker, Ramsey wrote one of the early landmarks in Tennessee historiography, *The Annals of Tennessee to the End of the Eighteenth Century.*

2. Letter not found.

3. The Democratic State Convention of November 1843 resolved that the president of the convention, Leonard P. Cheatham, should appoint three central committees, one each at Nashville, Knoxville, and Jackson. Each five-member central committee would organize party affairs in its grand division of the state, including the creation of corresponding committees and Democratic Young Men's Associations in each county. Reference is to the Knoxville com-

mittee, which was composed of Ramsey, E. G. Eastman, Robert B. Reynolds, Arthur R. Crozier, and William Lyon.

4. Martin Van Buren.

5. The National Democratic Convention assembled in Baltimore on May 27, 1844, and concluded its deliberations five days later.

6. On December 11, 1843, Robert Barnwell Rhett of South Carolina moved a suspension of the rules of the House and resolved that the Committee of Ways and Means inquire "into the expediency of reporting a bill repealing the tariff act passed in the year 1842, and in lieu thereof imposing a maximum rate of duty of 20 per cent, ad valorem on imports, discriminating below this maximum in the duties imposed on the principle of producing revenue only." All members of the Tennessee delegation except Joseph H. Peyton and William T. Senter voted in favor of the rule suspension; however, that motion failed 108 to 77. Many Northern Democrats voted with the majority of the House against the rule suspension, thereby preventing Rhett's resolution from coming to a vote.

7. Thomas Ritchie, editor of the *Richmond Enquirer* from 1804 until 1845, unofficially directed the affairs of the Virginia Democracy.

8. Andrew Stevenson, a lawyer, served several terms in the Virginia House of Delegates before winning election to the U.S. House, where he served from 1821 to 1834. He presided as Speaker of that body during his last four terms. Stevenson served as minister to Great Britain from 1836 until 1841.

9. *Richmond Enquirer.*

10. On December 5, 1843, the Arkansas Democratic State Convention nominated Van Buren for the presidency and Polk for the vice-presidency.

11. Richard M. Johnson, a Kentucky lawyer and hero of the War of 1812, served in both houses of Congress before election by the U.S. Senate in 1837 to the vice-presidency.

12. The Virginia State Democratic Convention met in Richmond for three days, February 1–3, 1844. Harmony was restored between the Van Buren and Calhoun factions of the party. The Virginia Democracy declined to endorse specific contenders for the presidential ticket, but did agree to support the candidates of the National Democratic Convention.

13. Samuel E. Goodson, a Jacksonian Democrat, represented Washington County, Virginia, in the Virginia House of Delegates from 1838 until 1847.

14. L. Fayette McMullen, a teamster, farmer, and banker, served as a Democrat in the Virginia Senate, 1839–49, and sat in the U.S. Congress, 1849–57. He was governor of the Washington Territory from 1857 until 1861.

15. John C. Calhoun.

16. In a letter to Polk dated February 26, 1842, Ramsey mentioned that he had written to Joseph W. Hampton, editor of the Charlotte *Mecklenburg Jeffersonian,* and had urged support for a Calhoun-Polk ticket in the 1844 election. ALS. DLC–JKP. For Ramsey's brief of the answer that he received from Hampton, see Ramsey to Polk, April 18, 1842. See also Ramsey to Polk, May 10, 1842.

17. Alexander O. Anderson represented East Tennessee at the National

Democratic Convention of 1844. A lawyer and Calhoun Democrat, Anderson supported Polk in his 1839 gubernatorial race; in 1840 Polk appointed Anderson to the U.S. Senate in place of Hugh L. White, who had resigned in opposition to instructions from the Tennessee legislature. In 1849 Anderson moved to California, where he served in that state's Senate, 1850–51, and on its Supreme Court, 1851–53.

18. Andrew Stevenson, William Rufus King, and Richard M. Johnson. King was U.S. Senator from Alabama 1819–44 and 1848–53, and U.S. minister to France, 1844–46. Elected vice-president of the United States in 1852, he took his oath of office in Cuba and died shortly after returning to Alabama in early 1853.

19. Levi Woodbury headed the U.S. Treasury Department from 1834 until 1841. Earlier he had served as governor of New Hampshire, Democratic senator from that state, and secretary of the navy. In 1841 Woodbury returned to the U.S. Senate and served until his appointment to the U.S. Supreme Court in 1845.

20. Whig conventions met in Nashville and in Knoxville on February 22, 1844, to form an electoral ticket for the state and to appoint delegates to the Whig National Convention.

21. William H. Polk and A. O. P. Nicholson. A Democratic member of the Tennessee House from Maury County, 1833–37, and of the Tennessee Senate, 1843–45, Nicholson served an interim appointment in the U.S. Senate from December 1840 until February 1842. He moved to Nashville in 1844 and edited the *Nashville Union* before being named president of the Bank of Tennessee in 1846.

22. Levin H. Coe and Frederick P. Stanton. A popular lawyer and Democrat from Somerville, Coe sat two terms in the Tennessee Senate, 1837–41, and presided over that body as Speaker during the latter part of his second term. A Memphis lawyer, Stanton served as a Democrat in Congress, 1845–55, and as governor of the Kansas Territory, 1858–61.


## FROM ROBERT ARMSTRONG

*Sunday* night
Dear Sir                              [Nashville, Tenn. January 7, 1844][1]
I have been so engaged in my office it being the last of the year and the last of the *quarter* that I have not had a moment.

You have been informed of Turney['s] failure to visit Columbus.[2] I did not confer or understand the reason why he did not go. The letters went under my frank to Col. Medary. I am of opinion to[o] Old Dick[3] will let his friends in Ohio understand that he is up for the second place. The managers in Washington may have other views—for King or Stephenson[4] perhaps.

The Union affair is not settled,[5] but I think will be. I have been doing all I can and will after Tuesday *next* have more leisure to devote to it.

Write to me any news you get from abroad &c &c.

R. ARMSTRONG

[P.S.] Atkinson[6] says he will pay next week, or as soon as Majr. Allison[7] pays him for the new ware house, *he will do it.*

ALS. DLC–JKP. Addressed to Columbia. Polk's AE on the cover states that he answered this letter on January 8, 1844; Polk's reply has not been found.

1. Letter dated by its postmark and Polk's endorsement.
2. See Samuel H. Laughlin to Polk, January 1, 1844; and William H. Polk to Polk, January 1, 1844.
3. Richard M. Johnson.
4. William Rufus King and Andrew Stevenson.
5. For details of Polk's problems with the *Nashville Union,* see Samuel H. Laughlin to Polk, January 1, 1844.
6. Polk's slave, John, was in the hire of a Mr. Atkinson, for which service Robert Armstrong was the financial agent. Atkinson is not further identified.
7. Possibly Alexander Allison, who served as mayor of Nashville from 1847 to 1848.

## FROM LEVIN H. COE

Dear Sir             Somerville Jany 7th 184[4][1]

You will be somewhat surprised to find I am here to night instead of being at Jackson.[2] I went to H. Springs[3] at the beginning of the week to the chancery court where I have a suit to which I am a party & save $4,000 or loose that amount by the result. But I had succeeded on Tuesday evening in getting it so arranged as to be able to leave it when I met with a man[4] now resident of Missi., a defaulting Administrator from this state to the tune of $12,000 & for whom my Father & John C. Cooper[5] were securities. Cooper & myself took charge of him & by sticking close to him succeeded by taking property in part & by giving time on getting security in closing an arrangement on Friday.

Whilst at H. Springs I saw leading Democrats from all parts of Mississippi. They have but one opinion. That is that the North of the State is en-masse for you & that your nomination is certain. Even the Calhoun men seem delighted at the arrangement made at Washington & go with zeal into the support of V. Buren.[6] I wrote to my acquaintances in the Legislature & the Convention urging a direct nomination of V.B. & Polk & warning them of the probable effect of throwing away the might of the state in an idle compliment to Walker.[7] Judge Chalmers[8] (a Calhoun man) wrote letters of the same kind urging all to vote at once for V.B. and P. I procured others also to write, and I have no doubt that all is done that I could have done by being present. I find Walker is sinking in the state. There is a powerful party among the Democracy displeased with him. Marshall, Tippah & others of the Northern Countys instructed their delegates to vote for V.B. & P. even before it was known that Calhoun had in fact stepped back.

Roger Barton[9] is in Jackson. He will aid our views as far as his position will justify. He is a candidate for U.S. Senate against McNutt[10] & will be elected if McNutt yields to the will of a majority of his party. All the danger is that McNutt may sell himself to the Whigs. Barton will have 37 Democrats upon first ballot in caucus. I cannot learn that this race which will probably come off on the 10th will have any effect on the action of the Convention.

I wrote also to Judge Adams,[11] of the Columbus circuit, who is in Jackson, and a devoted friend of yours to stir himself.

We have nothing new here. More than 150 negroes have changed hands in this county[12] at forced sales & at heavy advanced prices in the last 20 days. This puts the County nearly out of debt. The pressure with us may be said to be past, land & every thing is advancing.

The signs here look right for the struggle next summer.

L. H. Coe

ALS. DLC–JKP. Addressed to Columbia.

1. Erroneously dated "1843."

2. Reference is to Jackson, Miss., where the Democratic State Convention was scheduled to convene on January 8, 1844.

3. Holly Springs, Miss.

4. Not identified further.

5. Joseph Coe and John C. Cooper. A native of Maryland and a Jacksonian Democrat, Coe represented Fayette, Hardeman, Haywood, Madison, Shelby, and Tipton counties for one term in the Tennessee Senate, 1833–35. Cooper was a Somerville merchant.

6. Martin Van Buren.

7. Pennsylvania born, Robert J. Walker moved to Natchez, Miss., in 1826 and practiced law. He served in the U.S. Senate from 1835 until 1845, when he became Polk's secretary of the Treasury. Subsequently, he served as governor of the Kansas Territory and as U.S. financial agent in Europe during the Civil War.

8. A former resident of Jackson, Tenn., Joseph W. Chalmers moved in 1838 to Holly Springs, Miss., where he practiced law and served as vice-chancellor for the northern part of the state. A Democrat, he represented Mississippi in the U.S. Senate from 1845 to 1847.

9. A lawyer, planter and jurist, Barton was born in Knoxville and removed in 1827 to Bolivar, where he practiced law, won election to a single term

in the Tennessee House, 1829–31, and held the post of attorney general for the Eleventh Judicial District from 1831 until 1836. In the latter year, he removed to Holly Springs, Miss., where he subsequently won election to two terms in the Mississippi legislature.

10. A native of Virginia, Alexander G. McNutt moved to Mississippi in 1824, held a seat in the state Senate in 1835, and by appealing to strong anti-bank sentiment won election as Democratic governor two years later. For two terms he opposed corruption in Mississippi's banking institutions. In his legislative message of January 1840, McNutt detailed abuses in the banking system and recommended repeal of all bank charters.

11. Born in Franklin County, Tenn., Stephen D. Adams represented Franklin and Warren counties in the Tennessee Senate, 1833–35. Later he removed to Aberdeen, Miss., where he practiced law. He served as a Democrat in the U.S. House, 1845–47, and as a Union Democrat in the U.S. Senate, 1852–57.

12. Fayette County.

## FROM CAVE JOHNSON[1]

Dear Sir,                                      Washington, 7th Jany 1844

Yours of the 30th Dec. I recd. this morning.[2] I do not shew *your letters* to any *body* for reasons which I will explain to you when we meet, & rarely mention having recd. any from you to my most *intimate* friends because I doubt *every* body almost, and think that *any thing* I say or do will have a better effect, coming from *me alone* unadvised *by you.* I wrote you a long letter last week.[3] The apprehensions I then expressed still continue. I wrote fully to Mr. Medare & Brown wrote Medill.[4] I have seen Judge C—tron[5] & mentioned all the difficulties I thought in the way. He promised to see B—ton, Bu—an[6] & all, & talk freely with them on the subject and he says *he can remove all difficulties* as to the course *of the convention* and also as to the succession. I have several times throwed myself in the way of those gentlemen & gave opportunities for them to renew the subject but they have not done so, seem studiously to avoid it. S.W. Jr.[7] talks to me with great freedom & the opinion I expressed in my last as to the New Yorkers I still believe.[8] We shall spare no pains here.

We are thrown into great confusion about the 21st rule, & the Tariff.[9] And the *Southern men* & the Whigs & abolitionists play into each others hands just as they did several years ago. I labored day & night to bring about harmony in the organization & perhaps did as much as any body & hoped we should have no further trouble. Rhett started by moving to suspend the rules & instruct the Com. of W & M to re-enact the Compromise Tariff[10] succeeded by various propositions from other quarters all designed to make the Van Buren Tariff men vote, so that they might make capital of it, knowing too that the subject was before a democratic anti tariff Committee. Then Adams reports the rules *leaving* out every one that tended to expedite business (Wise & Dromgoole at home, J. W. Davis[11] joining him) particularly the 21st rule.[12] Black assumed the former position of Wise, was most inflamatory & ungovernable.[13] And we have been in a state of great confusion four or five days.

I contrived to get a caucus last night. We appointed a com. to confer with Senators and I brought up the rule. Tried to compromise upon *Athertons resolution.*[14] The southern gentlemen kicked at every thing, would yield nothing, whilst the north was generally disposed to do every thing if the petitions *could be received.* They say, the only difficulty at the north now is, *the Reception.* Many honest men, not abolitionists vote with them & for their ticket on that ground alone. That *the reception* being allowed all those honest deluded men acting with abolitionists would not act with them further, and the hypocrisy & villany of the abolitionists exposed. I proposed to *receive & lay on the table without debate.*[15] Rhett made an inflamatory speech agt it. Harrolson of Georgia &c.[16] We came to no conclusion & adjourned to meet again on tuesday night. Beardsly,[17] pretending to be a Van Buren, did us more harm than Adams himself. Upon some such proposition as mine, I think we shall finally rally a majority. I have to kick out of our ranks *southern hot heads* and a few of *the silk stocking democrats* of the North. We greatly need some body familiar with the rules & parliamentary law. Dromgoole is always d—k[18] when we need aid. Beardsly, Adams, White & Wise[19] do not desire to do us good but to embarrass Jones,[20] & He is *so anxious* to do *what is right & hear everything,* that he does nothing. If he would decide & act, we would make him run rough shod over them. I never have turned my attention to the rules & yet am compelled to play a part in the business of the House & am compromising for which I am little suited & have less inclination. Among the new members we have some excellent debaters & generally men of firm sense and great providence but none familiar [with] the rules.

If we can get a favorable ticket, I will fight the next summer with you with more energy than ever if I keep my health and *then I am done whatever may happen.* I must attend to my boys.[21] I think you should have certain orators appointed in every district to aid the Electors & they too should be *immediately* appointed, that we might supply them with all necessary documents before we leave here. I think if we are organised we can beat them. We are talking of corresponding regularly with our Editors but I do not see how I can have time. My duties on the Indian Com. are likely to be very laborious & you know I am besides Uncle Sam's "unpaid atto." and my wife & child [are] with me at night.[22] I have scarcely an hour for myself unless my wife goes to Church on Sunday alone as she did to day, so that I might bring up my correspondence. The Tyler & Calhoun men will go agt us.

We have now no Whig officer left in the Capitol & we are still in doubt whether we can get Langtry[23] an office. We shall be deceived I fear on our Ohio Clerk & also the Sargeant at Arms.[24] They are good & true but I fear inefficient. The clerk has not decided on our application for Langtry.

I was severly afflicted for two days with my old complaint.[25] It seems to have passed off tho I am constantly threatened. I fear that my colleage Jones[26] is *ultra radical* & obstinate & will yield nothing. I know nothing of A.J.[27] yet. Brown & Jones are now with us at Missi's 4 1/2.[28] Cullom is with Cross[29] & S. Carolinians at Hills[30] but will unquestionably be good & true. A.J. is with a mess back at Dowsons.[31] I don't know who is with him.

C. JOHNSON

ALS. DLC–JKP. Probably addressed to Columbia; marked *"Private."* Published in C. L. Grant, ed., "The Politics Behind a Presidential Nomination as Shown in Letters From Cave Johnson to James K. Polk," *THQ,* XII (June, 1953), pp. 157–58.

1. One of Polk's closest friends and political allies, Cave Johnson practiced law in Clarksville and served in the U.S. House as a Democrat, 1829–37 and 1839–45. Polk appointed him postmaster general in 1845.

2. Letter not found.

3. See Cave Johnson to Polk, December 30, 1843.

4. Samuel Medary, Aaron V. Brown, and William Medill. A resident of Pulaski, Brown was Polk's former law partner and longtime friend. He served in the Tennessee Senate and House, 1821–33, in the U.S. House, 1839–45, and in the governorship, 1845–47. From 1857 until his death in 1859, Brown was postmaster general in the administration of James Buchanan. An Ohio lawyer, Medill served as a member and Speaker of the Ohio House, 1835–38, before winning election in 1839 as a Democrat to the first of two terms in the U.S. House. He subsequently held a position in the Post Office Department, 1845, and served as commissioner of Indian affairs, 1845–50, before winning election to one term as governor of Ohio in 1853.

5. One of Polk's staunch political friends, John Catron was appointed to the U.S. Supreme Court in the last days of the Jackson administration. A Tennessean, Catron helped the *Nashville Union* financially and occasionally wrote editorials for it.

6. Thomas Hart Benton and James Buchanan. A strong supporter of Jackson and hard money, Benton represented Missouri in the U.S. Senate for thirty

years.

7. Silas Wright, Jr., U.S. senator from New York from 1833 until 1844, backed Martin Van Buren for the 1844 presidential nomination, declined the second place on Polk's ticket, won election to the governorship of New York in 1844, and served in that post until 1846.

8. Johnson believed that although his New York friends favored Polk's nomination for the vice-presidency, they preferred to "follow the great body of the Democrats instead of taking the lead."

9. On December 4, 1843, the House organized itself under the rules of the previous session; on December 22, 1843, the House Select Committee on Rules voted to delete the 21st rule, popularly known as the "gag resolution," which prohibited formal receipt of petitions calling for the abolition of slavery. The Tariff Act of 1842 returned duties to their higher levels of 1833, which had ranged from 23 to 35 per cent ad valorem; later attempts to lower tariff schedules proved highly divisive in both houses of Congress.

10. Robert B. Rhett's resolution, introduced on January 3, 1844, called on the Committee of Ways and Means to report a bill reducing all import duties over 30 per cent ad valorem and providing for a final reduction to 20 per cent ad valorem within two years. His resolution failed by a vote of 57 to 112.

11. Henry A. Wise, George C. Dromgoole, and John W. Davis. Wise, a lawyer from Virginia, sat in the U.S. House from 1833 until 1844. Originally a Democrat, he broke with Jackson over the U.S. Bank issue; in 1841 he became leader of the Tyler Whigs in the House. Wise subsequently served as governor of Virginia from 1856 until 1860. Dromgoole, a Virginia lawyer, served five terms in the U.S. House, 1835–41 and 1843–47. An Indiana Democrat, Davis served four terms in the U.S. House, 1835–37, 1839–41, and 1843–47; and he presided as Speaker during his last term.

12. John Quincy Adams, sixth president of the United States, served as a Whig member of the U.S. House from 1831 to 1848. On January 2, 1844, he reported for the House Select Committee on Rules; the House tabled his report and ordered it to be printed; members did not take it up for debate until January 5, 1844.

13. Edward J. Black, a Georgia lawyer, served as a States Rights Whig in the U.S. House, 1839–41; he won election as a Democrat to that body and served from 1842 until 1845. On January 5, 1844, he moved that the House Select Rules Committee be instructed to include the 21st rule in its report; he argued that abolitionist petitioners should be "deterred from intruding upon them their incendiary doctrines, the effect and operation of which were most damnable."

14. Charles G. Atherton's resolutions of December 11, 1838, provided for the reception of abolition petitions, but denied them any further consideration on grounds that Congress lacked power to legislate the abolition of slavery, either directly or indirectly.

15. Johnson's proposal of January 5, 1844, to lay the motion for reconsideration on the table followed considerable debate on the 21st rule.

16. Hugh A. Haralson, a lawyer, served several terms in the Georgia leg-

islature before winning election as a Democrat to the U.S. House, where he served from 1843 until 1851.

17. A lawyer and judge from Utica, N.Y., Samuel Beardsley won election to four terms in the U.S. House, 1831–36 and 1843–44. On January 5, 1844, Beardsley attempted to have the gag resolution question laid on the table and wished to know on what date the subject would be brought up on the House calendar. Later in the debate he noticed the absence of certain members of the Select Committee on Rules, including that of Dromgoole; the chair ruled Beardsley out of order. Beardsley continued, however, and argued that though Congress was bound to receive and give a respectful hearing to abolition petitions, they were not bound to grant the prayers contained in them. "There was," he claimed, "no country in which the right of petition did not exist."

18. An abbreviation for "drunk."

19. Samuel Beardsley, John Q. Adams, John White, and Henry A. Wise. A lawyer from Kentucky, White sat in the commonwealth legislature in 1832 and won election as a Whig to five terms in the U.S. House, 1835–45; he was elected Speaker of the House in 1841 and served in that post for a single term.

20. John W. Jones, a lawyer from Virginia, won election in 1835 to the U.S. House, where he served five consecutive terms. In 1839 House Democrats nominated Jones to succeed Polk as Speaker of the House; but several Nullifiers refused to support the caucus nominee and thus defeated Jones' bid. He won election as Speaker in 1843 and served one term in that post.

21. Cave and Elizabeth Dortch Brunson Johnson had three children who survived infancy. James Hickman and Thomas Dickson Johnson were born in 1840 and 1842, respectively. Polk Grundy Johnson was not born until November 2, 1844.

22. Johnson served as chairman of the House Committee on Indian Affairs; reference to his legal practice has not been identified.

23. A Columbia merchant and director of the Bank of Tennessee's branch at Columbia, Hillary Langtry assumed the postmastership of Columbia on January 9, 1844, and served in that post until June 1845.

24. Caleb J. McNulty and Newton Lane. McNulty, a resident of Ohio, defeated Matthew St. Claire Clarke for the office of House clerk on December 6, 1843, and served until January 18, 1845, when he was dismissed from office. For the clerk's election, see Cave Johnson to Polk, December 11, 1843. On December 7, 1843, Lane of Kentucky defeated Eleazer M. Townsend to become sergeant at arms of the House.

25. Johnson suffered from neuralgia.

26. A native of Virginia, George W. Jones followed a saddler's trade in Fayetteville, Tenn. He served two terms in the Tennessee House, 1835–39, and sat one term in the Tennessee Senate, 1839–41. An unsuccessful candidate for presidential elector on the Van Buren ticket in 1840, Jones first won election to the U.S. House in 1843 and served as a congressman until 1859.

27. Andrew Johnson, seventeenth president of the U.S., served in the Tennessee House, 1835–37 and 1839–41, and in the Tennessee Senate, 1841–43, before winning election as a Democrat to the U.S. House, where he held a

seat from 1843 until 1853. He served as governor of Tennessee, 1853–57, and subsequently won election to the U.S. Senate in 1857.

28. Aaron V. Brown and George W. Jones resided at an unidentified boarding house on 4 1/2 Street in the capital.

29. Alvin Cullom and Edward Cross. Cullom, a lawyer and a Democrat, represented Overton County for one term in the Tennessee House, 1835–37, and served two terms in the U.S. House, 1843–47; he sat on the bench of Tennessee's Fourth Judicial Circuit from 1850 until 1852. Cross, a native Tennessean, moved to Arkansas in 1826. Having served as U.S. judge for the Arkansas Territory, 1830–36, and as U.S. surveyor general for Arkansas, 1836–38, he won election as a Democrat to the U.S. House and served from 1839 until 1845.

30. Hill's boarding house, located on Capitol Hill, had been the residence of several Tennessee congressmen, including Cave Johnson.

31. Reference is to Dowson's No. 1 or Dowson's No. 2, both popular boarding houses on Capitol Hill.


## FROM LEONARD P. CHEATHAM

Nashville, Tenn. January 9, 1844

Cheatham reports that the Whigs have selected Bell and Henry to be electors-at-large.[1] Several East Tennessee Democrats want their party's at-large electors to come from Middle Tennessee and to be selected promptly. Sentiment is rising in behalf of Nicholson for one of the posts. Cheatham solicits advice on the choices and indicates his reluctance "to pass by Coe."

ALS. DLC–JKP. Addressed to Columbia. Polk's AE on the cover states that he answered this letter on January 10, 1844; Polk's reply has not been found.

1. John Bell and Gustavus A. Henry received their appointments from the Whig convention that assembled in Nashville on January 8, 1844. Bell served a partial term as Speaker of the U.S. House, 1834–35, but was defeated by Polk in his bid for reelection to that post in 1835; he headed Hugh Lawson White's Tennessee presidential campaign in 1836 and subsequently became one of Tennessee's most powerful Whigs. A Kentucky lawyer, businessman, and Whig, Henry served one term in the Kentucky legislature, 1831–33, before removing to Clarksville, Tenn.; he won election to the electoral colleges of 1840, 1844, 1852, but lost bids for a seat in the U.S. House in 1841 and for the governorship in 1853.


## TO SAMUEL H. LAUGHLIN

My Dear Sir.                                    Columbia Jany. 9th 1844

I did not know until I recevd a letter from *Armstrong,*[1] on yesterday, (in which it was incidentally mentioned) that *Turney* had declined making his contemplated visit. I suppose it was unavoidable. I shall be disappointed[2] if the news from Columbus is not unfavourable. My latest advices from Washington render it probable that a *few managers* there, against the manifest wishes of the mass of the party, will for reasons personal to themselves unite on Col. K.[3] If I am right, orders have gone forth, and will appear in the action of the Ohio Convention.[4] It is barely possible that the counteracting influence from *another quarter,* may prevent any action at all. From all the information now before me, I have upon full deliberation resolved that as my name has been kept thus long before the country without any agency of mine, *it shall not by my agency be withdrawn.* I will go before the Convention[5] and whatever motives may influence the decision of that body, I will abide by it when made. If *ruled out* by the Convention, I will continue to fight as earnestly and as valiantly *in the ranks* as I have heretofore done. It will not be the first time that I have performed *hard service* & made immense sacrafices in the cause, whilst others who have enjoyed their ease have been rewarded with the *Honours. Johnson* in a late letter[6] thinks the course of *certain leaders* will be that which I have indicated. The matter was still in some doubt.

I have written to *Armstrong* a pressing letter[7] about the *Union*[8] and think he will attend it without delay. Will you adjourn on monday next? If so write me by return mail[9] and I will come in. I *must see* our Democratic friends before you disperse.

Request *Mr Kizer*[10] to procure and enclose to me a copy of the "Constitution of the Democratic Association" of Davidson.[11] Our people are forming a similar association here, and will desire to do so in Marshall[12] also, where I will be at Court on the 4th monday in this month.

                                                    JAMES K. POLK

ALS. NjP. Addressed to Nashville and marked *"Private."* Laughlin's AE on the cover states that he answered this letter on January 11, 1844, and requested Polk "to come to Nashville by next Monday."

1. See Robert Armstrong to Polk, January 7, 1844.
2. Archaic usage of *disappointed* for *surprised.*
3. William Rufus King of Alabama.
4. The Ohio Democratic State Convention convened at Columbus on January 8, 1844. The Convention instructed its delegates to the Democratic National Convention to support Martin Van Buren for the presidency and Richard M. Johnson for the vice-presidency.
5. Polk's reference is to the Democratic National Convention scheduled to meet at Baltimore in May.
6. See Cave Johnson to Polk, December 30, 1843.
7. Letter not found.

8. *Nashville Union.*

9. See Laughlin to Polk, January 11, 1844.

10. Timothy Kezer, a Nashville merchant and hatmaker, was Laughlin's son-in-law and a member of the Democratic State Central Committee at Nashville.

11. On March 11, 1843, delegates from the civil districts of Davidson County met in convention at Nashville, nominated candidates for the Tennessee General Assembly, and appointed a county committee to oversee the forthcoming campaign. Similar committees or associations were formed in other counties.

12. Marshall County, Tenn.

## FROM J. G. M. RAMSEY

My Dear Sir                              [Mecklenburg, Tenn.] Jany. 10, 1844[1]

My letters from abroad recd. since I last wrote you contain nothing very important only that "Tennessee stock is looking up since her Representatives voted for Rhetts resolution."[2] I have written letters (of which I send you hereon a copy which I have had made) to Goodson & L. F. McMullen at Richmond, [to] the editors of the Jeffersonian[3] & to Harold Smythe Esq. of Wytheville Va. who is just starting there a new paper.[4] I have made myself a subscriber to day & told him that your nomination as V.P. would widen his circulation. I have varied each a little from the copy, but you have the substance. In those to Richmond I left out the allusion to Calhoun but enlarged on the nomination of Johnson.[5] I shall write to morrow to Elmore[6] & other S. C. friends. Will thank you for such additional suggestions as have escaped me. We had a good celebration of the 8th.[7] The best spirit prevails.

J. G. M. RAMSEY

ALS. DLC–JKP. Addressed to Columbia. Polk's AE on the cover states that he answered this letter on January 18, 1844; Polk's reply has not been found. Ramsey penned his note to Polk in the margins of a circular letter written for southern newspaper editors; he began his text at the foot of page four and concluded at the head of page one.

1. Ramsey's address taken from postal cancellation.

2. Ramsey's source concerning Robert Barnwell Rhett's tariff resolution is not identified further.

3. Joseph W. Hampton's editorial colleagues on the Charlotte *Mecklenburg Jeffersonian* are not further identified.

4. Harold Smyth, a lawyer and newspaperman, served as the first editor of the Wytheville *Republican and Virginia Constitutionalist,* a Democratic weekly founded January 1, 1844.

5. The document on which Ramsey penned his letter to Polk probably was a copy of a letter Ramsey had written to Hampton on January 6, 1844; in that letter he discussed the Democratic party's presidential and vice-presidential nominations. Ramsey, who regretted that John C. Calhoun probably would not head the ticket, voiced great concern that Richard M. Johnson might secure the second slot. Resigned to the presidential nomination of Martin Van Buren, Ramsey promoted Polk as the vice-presidential candidate most able to balance the ticket. C, copy. DLC–JKP.

6. Franklin Harper Elmore, South Carolina lawyer and supporter of John C. Calhoun, sat in the U.S. House, 1836–39; presided over the Bank of the State of South Carolina, 1839–50; and served briefly in the U.S. Senate in 1850.

7. The celebration on January 8 commemorated Andrew Jackson's victory at the Battle of New Orleans.

### FROM ARCHIBALD YELL[1]

Dear Govr                                        Little Rock 10th January 1844

I droped you a few lines after the adjournmt of our State Convention[2] and then promised to write you more fully when I had leasure.

So far as I am able to Judge there is little or no doubt of the Nomination of Mr Van Buren for the Presidency, and the struggle will be between *yourself* and Col Johnson for the Vice Presidency; how that may terminate I am now wholy unable to determine. The friends of Johnson in the Convention will press the claims of the old Hero to run the old tickett which was defeated in 1840. They will urge his claims with more of feelings of pride than sound policy. I Judge it will depend very much upon the course of the N York Delegation, for I am inclined to believe that you will recieve the support of the Southern States (Mr Calhouns frinds) N Carolina Virginia and posibly Pensylvania. If so You will receive the Nomination. I feel confident that Mr Van Buren would himself prefer you to Johnson but I suppose he will indicate no preference.

Your *prominence* is such now, as to render your success more doubtful than I am willing to allow myself to believe, I mean for the V Presidency. The reason of my *doubts* of your Nomination arises from a fear that the candidates for the Presidency in Expectency may take it in their head that you might become a troublesome costomer for the Presidency some 4 or 8 years hence. You are growing in popularity and young enough 12 years hence. How they may calculate the chances between you and Johnson I can not tell, but *Self* will have more to do in their decision than *Patrotism*. I have learned much in the last ten years that but few Politicians of either party a[ct][3] altogether from

love of country. You are both *aspiring* men and will not be content
to be Vice President. We know that is so with Johnson & you have
such prominence before the American people as to *flatter into life* all
that *modesty* which we know you to possess, and once in the "line of
safe presidency" you may be hard to *choke off*. At least I fear that Bu-
chonon Cass Benton Woodbury King and posibly Calhoun may think
so.[4] If they should you may rest assured that their influence *secretly*
will be used aganst you. However all this is my own conjecture. You
no doubt understand their feelings and inclinations much better than
I do.

This state is well pleased I am sure with the Nominations for President & Vice President & perticularly the latter. Here you can beat
any body for any office. I am sorry to say that the Convention made
Nominations for Gov & Congress that is not altogather acceptable to
the party. Genl Conway has invited an other Convention as the last
was not fully attended.[5] He has taken the proper ground. I do not
believe they can get up an other. If they should it may & I hope will
tend to harmonise the party, let who may recieve the Nomination.
I believe I wrote you that I had determined to return to the "Wax-
haws"[6] and get *married*. Please say to Madam Polk[7] that I cancel all
my former frindly feelings for her & that I am not certain that I shall
not carry it into the next Presidential election for the *Vice* Presidency
perticularly. Through her *Negligence* I have lost the *Genls Widdow*
which was a matter of much more interest to me than any Election.[8]
Since the arrivle of our good friend Genl Maclin[9] he has promised to
do somthing with a relative of his, Mrs Taylor[10] of this state late from
Tennessee. She is nearer my age than Mrs. F.,[11] and is nearer home
too which is no small matter these hard times. I hope I am provided
for!

I am dilighted with your friend Genl Maclin. He settled at this place
and will I hope do well. He will in a few years become a prominent
man and a leader of our party. He has many or all the qualities
nessesary for a politition.

I have appointed him a special Judge in the 3d Judicial Circuit in
the Northern part of the state, the backbone of Democracy. He will
hold courts in 5 or 6 counties, which will give him an introduction to
the people. Besides the Whig N Papers will abuse me no doubt for
appointing him so soon and that will also give him some notoriety at
least. All your old Ten friends are warm for you.

My respects to Mrs P. and believe me as ever ....

                                                        A. YELL

ALS. DLC–JKP. Addressed to Columbia. Polk's AE on the cover states that he answered this letter on February 1, 1844; Polk's reply has not been found.

1. A close personal and political friend of Polk's, Yell practiced law in Fayetteville, Tenn., until his appointment as U.S. judge of the Arkansas Territory in 1832. He won election to several terms in the U.S. House, 1836–39 and 1845–46, and served as governor of Arkansas from 1840 until 1844. Yell died at the Battle of Buena Vista in 1847 during the Mexican War.

2. On December 5, 1843, Yell wrote Polk to inform him of the results of the Arkansas Democratic State Convention. ALS. DLC–JKP. See J. G. M. Ramsey to Polk, January 4, 1844.

3. Ink blurred.

4. James Buchanan, Lewis Cass, Thomas Hart Benton, Levi Woodbury, William R. King, and John C. Calhoun. A lawyer, Lewis Cass served as governor of the Michigan Territory, 1813–31; U.S. secretary of war, 1831–36; U.S. minister to France, 1836–42; U.S. Senator from Michigan, 1845–48 and 1851–57; and U.S. secretary of state, 1857–60. In 1848 Cass ran unsuccessfully as the Democratic candidate for president.

5. The convention that nominated Elias N. Conway for governor and Daniel J. Chapman for Congress represented only sixteen of Arkansas' forty-six counties. A second convention, held in May 1844, nominated Chapman for governor and Yell for Congress. Conway, born in Tennessee, removed to Arkansas in 1833, where he served for many years as state auditor, 1835–49, before becoming governor of Arkansas in 1852.

6. Named after his birthplace in North Carolina, Yell's plantation was located near Fayetteville, Ark.

7. Sarah Childress Polk.

8. Yell's correspondence to Polk, 1842–43, often contained humorous entreaties to Sarah Polk to procure for him a suitable marriage partner. See, for example, Yell to Polk, June 25, 1842; and October 31, 1843. The widow mentioned here is not identified further.

9. A Democrat, Sackfield Maclin represented Fayette, Hardeman, and Shelby counties in the Tennessee Senate, 1841–43.

10. Not identified further.

11. Not identified further.

## FROM SAMUEL H. LAUGHLIN

Senate Chamber
My dear Sir,                                    Nashville, Jany. 11, 1844

I have received yours of the 9th. I supposed that you had been earlier advised that Mr. Turney did not go to Columbus. In the matter, I was overruled, and he declined under the advice of others, his own impressions, and against my urgent advice. He wrote to Medary, and enclosed to him a strong letter from Gen. Jackson. I wrote previously to Medary, enclosing the Editorial ground taken by the Columbia Democrat,[1] which he immediately republished and sent me his paper.

When Turney declined going, I also wrote a strong letter for the State Corresponding Committee, the Committee of five,[2] which they signed and sent to Medary. It was a private letter, but strong, pressing and respectful in its terms.

I do not think we will adjourn on Tuesday, but possibly we may. I wish you would come up. All will want to see you. We will have the result at Columbus.[3] Jones has written to Ross[4] that, at Washington among the politicians, the question is between you and King. That King voted for the Bank of 1816[5] which was a drawback on him.

The Union matter[6] is not consummated, though, relying on providence and the fidelity of friends, I have hired a man to live at my home at $200, and have rented a room here. I am, now, in for it, let other things go as they may. When you are here, all will be consummated. I am not in situation to press the *signing* by Hogan & Heiss; or any other signing or matter. Come by Sunday.

S. H. LAUGHLIN

ALS. DLC–JKP. Addressed to Columbia and marked "(Private)." Polk's AE on the cover states that he answered this letter on January 13, 1844; Polk's reply has not been found.

1. Edited by C. J. Dickerson, the Columbia *Tennessee Democrat* was owned jointly by Polk, A. O. Harris, A. C. Hays, and A. O. P. Nicholson; editorial in the *Democrat* has not been identified further.

2. The Nashville Democratic Central Committee, appointed at the Democratic State Convention of November 1843 by convention president Leonard P. Cheatham, was composed of Felix Robertson, Andrew J. Donelson, Willoughby Williams, Joseph B. Southall, and Timothy Kezer.

3. See Polk to Laughlin, January 9, 1844.

4. George W. Jones and William T. Ross. A Fayetteville criminal lawyer, Ross served as a Democrat in the Tennessee Senate, 1841–45.

5. The Second Bank of the United States.

6. See Laughlin to Polk, January 1, 1844.

## FROM CAVE JOHNSON

Dear Sir,                                   Washington January 13th 1844

I recd yours of the 3rd[1] this morning. We have just heard from the convention at Columbus[2] tho. the proceedings have not yet reached us. Private letters say that Van was unanimously nominated & no nomination made for the vice-presidency tho. one of the M.C. (Weller) told me they expressed an opinion favorable to R.M.J. but refused to instruct.[3] Weller expressed an opinion decidedly favorable to King and attributed the loss of the State to your refusal to call the Legislature & elect Senators[4] & that you was too timid &c. The piece which you will see in the Globe[5] I consider conclusive as to the course of Benton & his friends & it is confirmed by the opinions expressed by Weller. Upon the appearance of the article in the Globe I & Brown cast about to get it answered I addressed Doct. Martin,[6] who replied to day that he was too much the friend of both to interfere & Brown is now engaged in the preparation of a reply which he will submit to me tomorrow & we will have *if we can* in the Globe of Monday evening.[7] There is already a good deal of talk of setling the controversy between you & King by giving it to R.M.J. Our *strong hope* now is, that when the fact is known that K—g[8] *voted for* the *old* USB[9] the Democracy will hardly take him up. Yet we must be so modest with Kings friends as not to incite them agt. you. It will take you both to beat old Dick.[10] He has withdrawn, come out for Van & looks to the second office & will be pushed for that. I have been this evening with Judge C—tron who takes the same view of the course of B—ton & B—on[11] that I do. I am satisfied that Van's northern friends prefer you, yet policy will prevent their taking the lead. Penn will go for K—g if B—on can carry it. Strong demonstrations are making for R.M.J. in some parts of the state.

Van's cause is not esteemed so flattering as at the commencement. The abolition & Tariff will both injure him. They will give up the 21st rule & the utmost I hope for now, is to fall back on the Atherton rule.[12] The select Com. having charge of the Mass Resolution for altering the basis of Representation (the Hartford Convention Res) has been under examination in the Com.[13] A Journal[14] has been kept, which Gilmer[15] says will arouse the South &c. They have postponed the Report[16] to the 1st of Feby waiting no doubt the action of the House on the Rule,[17] lest the Report might [have] an influence on the decision upon the Rule. Beardsly consented to *strike out the rule & leave all open.*[18] He plays the part on Van that Bell did on Jackson. I am compelled to take a greater part than is agreeable to me. McKay[19] stands back, Dromgoole is always d—k[20] when needed, the speaker[21] inefficient and none of the rest knows more of the rules than I do. We are of course bad off.

Upon the Tariff we shall *be compelled* to make the Whig Tariff the basis of our action. Reduce the heavy duties, tax many of the free articles (excepting Coffee & Tea) & increasing those on luxuries. We cannot carry a new tariff advalorem & for Revenue at this time & if we did it would be rejected by the Senate. I say we can not carry it because every body but myself thinks so. My opinion is we could carry it by 8 or 10, yet I think it better for the present *to attempt reduction,* so that we may do some good. It is said here upon the authority of a letter from Judge Porter,[22] that Clay says, the exchanges have regulated themselves beyond his hopes & the country is prosperous & probably will not require the incorporation of a USB, another Harrison trick.[23] Rives[24] has come out for Clay. I have not read his letter.[25] He is a disgraced man on all sides. Hopkins[26] says, he will carry with him two men & that neither of them can carry another vote. Gilmer attends our caucuses &c. Spencer is said to have been nominated for the place of Thompson.[27] It is believed that Henshaw will be certainly rejected as will Porter unless he & the Governor[28] pledge themselves to Clay. It is thought arrangements are on hand to renominate Wise & then Sargeant[29] that a confirmation may be secured. Very doubtful. We are without a leader from N.Y. & but little or no assistance. The nullifyers keep up the old game with the abolitionists & northern Whigs and they are strugling to use the Tariff in the same way. I think the leaders will stand off from us tho. they can not vote for Clay. Tyler & friends will go for Clay.

My health continues very good. I was much scared ten days ago for fear of a return of my disease.[30]

C. JOHNSON

ALS. DLC–JKP. Addressed to Columbia and marked "private." Polk's AE on the cover states that he answered this letter on January 30, 1844; Polk's reply has not been found. Published in *THQ*, XII, pp. 158–60.

1. Letter not found.

2. Reference is to the Democratic State Convention of Ohio.

3. Martin Van Buren, John B. Weller, and Richard M. Johnson. An Ohio lawyer, Weller served three terms in the U.S. House, 1839–45, and represented California in the U.S. Senate from 1852 until 1857. He fought with the rank of colonel in the Mexican War, won election to one term as governor of California, 1858–60, and went as U.S. minister to Mexico in 1860.

4. During his governorship, 1839–41, Polk had refused to call a special session of the Tennessee Assembly to elect U.S. senators, one to serve a full six-year term and the other to complete the unexpired portion of Felix Grundy's term. Grundy had died in December 1840 and A. O. P. Nicholson had served an interim appointment lasting until the end of the 1841–42 legislative session. With the failure of the Twenty-fourth General Assembly to fill either position, Tennessee was without representation in the U.S. Senate from February 7, 1842, until October 16, 1843.

5. The Washington *Globe* of January 8, 1844, printed a letter from "Amicus," which discussed the Democratic party's vice-presidential nomination. After comparing the qualifications of King and Polk, the author concluded that the Alabama senator was the superior choice for the position. This letter was the first salvo of a political war of words waged in the *Globe* by the friends of each man.

6. An experienced writer, Jacob L. Martin of North Carolina had previously served as chief clerk of the State Department in 1840 and 1841. In 1838 he had declined an offer to edit the *Nashville Union*.

7. Brown's defense of Polk's claims to the vice-presidential nomination appeared in the Washington *Globe* of January 15, 1844; he signed his letter to the editor, "A Tennessee Democrat."

8. William R. King.

9. Second Bank of the United States.

10. Richard M. Johnson.

11. John Catron, Thomas Hart Benton, and James Buchanan.

12. See Cave Johnson to Polk, January 7, 1844.

13. On December 12, 1843, John Quincy Adams introduced in the U.S. House resolutions passed by the legislature of Massachusetts to amend the U.S. Constitution. Those resolutions called for apportioning direct taxes and representation in the House on the basis of the numbers of free inhabitants in each state. A similar proposal had evolved from the Hartford Convention of December 1814. After an extended debate Adams' resolutions were referred to a nine-member Select Committee on the Massachusetts Resolutions.

14. For the text of the Journal of the Select Committee on the Massachusetts Resolutions, see House Report No. 404, 28 Congress, 1 Session, pp. 115–19.

15. Thomas W. Gilmer served several terms in the Virginia House before being elected governor in 1840. A year later Gilmer resigned the governorship to serve as a Whig in the U.S. House. Gilmer won reelection to the House as a Democrat in 1843 and served until February of 1844, when he became secretary of the navy. Prior to his resignation from the House, Gilmer served on the Select Committee on the Massachusetts Resolutions. He died in an explosion aboard the U.S.S. *Princeton* on February 28, 1844.

16. Six separate reports finally emerged from the Select Committee on the Massachusetts Resolutions. See House Report No. 404, 28 Congress, 1 Session, pp. 1–114.

17. Reference here and in the next sentence is to the rule adopted by the U.S. House governing the reception of petitions on slavery. Commonly referred to as the 21st rule, or "gag rule," this regulation was actually number 25 of those adopted at the commencement of the 28th Congress. See Johnson to Polk, January 7, 1844.

18. A member of the Select Committee to Revise the Rules and Orders of the House, Samuel Beardsley had voted in committee on December 22, 1843, to delete the rule concerning petitions on slavery.

19. James I. McKay, a lawyer and Democrat from North Carolina, served in the U.S. House from 1831 until 1849; earlier he had won election to several terms in the state senate and had served as U.S. attorney for the district of North Carolina.

20. An abbreviation for "drunk."

21. John W. Jones.

22. Probably Alexander Porter, an Irish immigrant who eventually settled

in Louisiana. A lawyer, he served as judge of the state supreme court 1821–33 and as a Whig in the U.S. Senate 1833–37. Elected to another term beginning March 4, 1843, Porter failed to take his seat for reasons of poor health and died on January 13, 1844.

23. Reference is to formation of a new national bank and William Henry Harrison.

24. A Virginia lawyer and planter, William C. Rives served several terms in the U.S. House and Senate. Originally a Democrat, he subsequently became a Whig. He twice served as U.S. minister to France, 1829–32 and 1849–53.

25. A copy of Rives' letter in support of Clay's presidential bid was printed in the Nashville *Republican Banner* on January 22, 1844.

26. A lawyer and Democrat, George W. Hopkins of Virginia won election to seven terms in the U.S. House, 1835–47 and 1857–59.

27. John C. Spencer and Smith Thompson. A former legislator, congressman, and secretary of state of New York, Spencer served as U.S. secretary of war from October 12, 1841, until March 3, 1843, when he became secretary of the Treasury. He resigned from the latter post on May 2, 1844. Thompson, a lawyer from New York, was U.S. secretary of the navy, 1819–23, and associate justice of the U.S. Supreme Court, 1823–43. His death on December 18, 1843, occasioned a prolonged contest between Tyler and the U.S. Senate. Tyler offered the seat on the Supreme Court to Martin Van Buren, who declined. Tyler then nominated Spencer on January 8, 1844. Ardently opposed by the Clay Whigs, Spencer's appointment was rejected by the Senate on January 31, 1844. Subsequently, Tyler offered the appointment to John Sergeant, Horace Binney of Philadelphia, and Silas Wright, Jr., each of whom rejected the offer. On February 4, 1845, Tyler nominated Samuel Nelson of New York; ten days later the U.S. Senate approved the appointment.

28. David Henshaw, James M. Porter, and David R. Porter. A prominent Democrat from Massachusetts, Henshaw had previously served as collector of the port of Boston prior to his service as ad interim secretary of navy from July 23, 1843, to February 19, 1844. The Senate overwhelmingly rejected his nomination to the permanent post on January 15, 1844. In a similar vote on January 30, 1844, the Senate rejected the nomination of James M. Porter, as secretary of war. David R. Porter, an iron manufacturer, served as governor of Pennsylvania from 1839 until 1845.

29. Henry A. Wise and John Sergeant. In the previous year John Tyler had placed Wise's name before the U.S. Senate to be minister to France, in place of Lewis Cass. First nominated on February 27, 1843, Wise was rejected by the Senate on March 3, 1843. Tyler reappointed Wise a second and third time on March 3, 1843; Wise was twice more rejected. On January 18, 1844, Tyler nominated Wise to be minister to Brazil, an appointment the Senate approved on February 9, 1844. A Philadelphia lawyer, Sergeant served seven terms in the U.S. House, 1815–23, 1827–29, and 1837–41, as a Federalist, a National Republican, and a Whig, successively. He served as chief legal and political adviser to Nicholas Biddle, president of the Second Bank of the United States.

30. Johnson suffered from neuralgia.

## FROM JOHN W. CHILDRESS[1]

Murfreesboro, Tenn. January 14, 1844

Unfavorable weather has prevented gathering a third of this year's corn and cotton crops. Childress cannot move his slaves to Mississippi without sustaining a considerable loss. He has decided to plant another crop in Rutherford County and move south after the harvest. He asks about a possible arrangement for the use of Polk's Mississippi lands,[2] "to take effect after this year," if Polk does not dispose of them earlier.

ALS. DLC–JKP. Probably addressed to Columbia.
1. A younger brother of Sarah Polk, Childress lived in Murfreesboro where he practiced law.
2. Polk owned a plantation in Yalobusha County, Miss. On December 5, 1843, Childress wrote that he was determined to sell his Rutherford County lands. However, he had come to the conclusion that it was imprudent for him to "buy land at a high price, and incur all the expense of removal and provisions for the first year." Rather, he would rent land for a year or two, unless he could buy at a very low price. ALS. DLC–JKP.

## FROM ADAM HUNTSMAN[1]

Dear Sir                                    Jackson Jany 15th 1844

Your communication upon the subject of getting Laughlin to Edit the Union has been recd[2] and duly attended to by the Central Committee.[3] I drew up the address,[4] gave it to Ewell[5] to copy and put on Signatures &c and send it on by next mail. I have no doubt now that old Dick Johnson is playing for the V. Presidency in a covert manner under the assumed garb of one of the Presidential Candidates. I am fearful he will succeed in the Free States where his family associations are not so obnoxious as in the South. If he does obtain the nomination of V.P. for our party it will destroy our prospects in Tennessee in more objects than one. First he may supersede us in our choice of V.P. and secondly I think it will put it out of the power of the democrats to carry the state next November. My reasons are these. Neither Clay[6] nor Vanburen can carry the full strength of their respective parties. But as they are both in the same predicament we can fight one against the other. But we all know the prejudices we had to encounter in 1840 in relation to Johnsons family affairs[7] and how it was handled against us, much to our disadvantage and it will be so again. Now Sir if we have this weight to carry also I do not believe we can succeed. I have written to some of our friends in other states to this effect in a confidential way in order to prevent it. I hope it may not be so, but I believe it. It is the business of wise politicians to look the worst of evils in the face, and to provide as far as practicable the most honourable retreat (if retreat we must) from those contingences which we can neither avoid nor controul. If Johnson is the nominee as Webster[8] says *Where are you to go.* As a friend I speak candidly. You will have to take the place of one of the State electors and attend to your Trusty Couzin John Bell in his campaigns and if we carry the next Legislature, as I verily believe we shall then you must supercede the immortal Eph[9] which will be a kind of resting place untill better times.

Who can we get to compete with Bell and Henry?[10] The Whigs has put forth their heaviest metal. I have not one earthly doubt but we will succeed in electing VB & the V.P. But to be beat in Tennessee is mortifying.

A. HUNTSMAN

ALS. DLC–JKP. Addressed to Columbia. Polk's AE on the cover states that he answered this letter on January 19, 1844; Polk's reply has not been found. Published in Emma Inman Williams, "Letters of Adam Huntsman to James K. Polk," *THQ,* VI (December, 1947), pp. 356–57.

1. Born in Virginia, Adam Huntsman had moved by 1809 to Overton County, where he practiced law and engaged in extensive land speculations until 1821. He sat three terms for Overton County in the Tennessee Senate, 1815–21, and later represented Madison County in the Senate for two terms, 1827–31. A loyal Jacksonian Democrat, he defeated David Crockett for a seat in Congress and served one term in the U.S. House, 1835–37.

2. Letter not found. See Samuel H. Laughlin to Polk, December 7 and 25, 1843, and January 1, 1844.

3. The Jackson Democratic Central Committee, appointed at the conclusion of the Democratic State Convention of November 1843, was composed of Huntsman, James Caruthers, A. W. O. Totten, Thomas Ewell, and George Snider.

4. The address of the Jackson Central Committee has not been found.

5. Thomas Ewell, a Jackson lawyer and Democrat, ran unsuccessfully for a seat in the Tennessee House in 1843.

6. Henry Clay of Kentucky was the Whig presidential candidate in 1844.

7. Richard M. Johnson's most notorious political liability was his earlier relationship with Julia Chinn, a mulatto woman by whom he fathered two daughters.

8. Daniel Webster.

9. Ephraim H. Foster, a Nashville lawyer and one of the founders of the Whig Party in Tennessee, served three terms in the Tennessee House, 1827–31 and 1835–37. Appointed to the U.S. Senate following the resignation of Felix

Grundy in 1838, Foster won election to a full six-year term beginning March 4, 1839. Having pledged to resign should a Democratic majority be elected to the next legislature, he redeemed his promise in November of 1839; the Tennessee General Assembly elected Grundy to the vacancy; and Grundy served from November 19, 1839, until his death on December 19, 1840. Polk appointed A. O. P. Nicholson to the vacant seat; and he served until February 7, 1842, when the Assembly adjourned without electing a successor and thus terminated the interim appointment. The seat remained vacant until the Assembly elected Foster to the place in October of 1843; Foster finally completed the term on March 3, 1845.

10. See Leonard P. Cheatham to Polk, January 9, 1844.


### FROM JAMES M. HOWRY[1]

My Dear Sir                                         Oxford 17 Jany 1844

Our State convention has been held and the nomination of Van Buren & Polk has been made by decided majorities.[2] Thus Mississippi has turned right side up at last. The opposition that was made to you in the southern part of the state by many of our *leaders & would be great men* I was fearful would present a similar state of things as in Alabama,[3] & result in the nomination of R.J.W.[4] for the V. Pres. But it seems Mr. Walker had more prudence & foresight than his friends, & *he withdrew*. The Southern presses too, were against you. The VB & Calhoun organs at Jackson & Vicksburg were opposed to you. Gov. McNutt controls two of them. V. Buren in Convention beat Calhoun 3 to 1.[5] You beat R. M. Johnson nearly 2 to 1.

Now if we had the advantage of your *real strength* in Alabama in the Convention on the first ballot it would be a strong force to begin with from home. I do not now entertain much doubt of your nomination. I think if Pennsylvania goes for you, it is sure as N York is now safe. Our Convention was presided over by Hon Powhattan Ellis.[6] The Delegates were appointed to attend the convention and Electors were appointed. Jos. W. Matthews & J. Davis[7] of Warren for the State. Henry S. Foote, Col Boone, Col Bell & Arthur Fox[8] for the Congressional Districts. You will have seen that our friend Jas. L Totten[9] was elected Speaker of the H of Reps.

Our Senatorial Election is over and although a Northern Man elected yet the North is badly whipt. Roger Barton was our man & the whole north with a very few exceptions presented an unbroken front for him. The race this fall was run with his name, and the north demanded his election. This thwarted Gov McNutts views, and he declined, but evidently piqued. The whigs "lay in wait" determined to join any party that could by their aid succeed in defeating the popular Democrat. They ran Pinckney Smith,[10] Bond Democrat, first ballot. The discontented McNutt Dems. ran Gen Speight.[11] The Whigs dropped Smith although the foremost man and took up Speight and elected him by a large majority on the 2 Ballot. Speight you know, and he does not stand here as any sort of a man, He being betwixt the Heaven & the Earth on the Bond Question[12] & finally settled down Anti-Bonder. He was first V.B. then Calhoun. Then V.B. & finally wrote a long letter in favr. of Calhoun. He was a "marvellous proper man"[13] for the Whigs to *tinker* with.

It seems Mississippi will carry on some sort of swindling and when they cant find enemies to swindle they will swindle each other. Speight will first aspire to the Presidency *pro tempore* of the Senate. Next, *not known*. If you get there I know he will envy you your seat.

I like your incipient organization and if carried out, I think you must beat Clay next fall. We will try & do it here.

I think your name on the ticket will add strength in this state.

I fear the Whigs in Tenn. will have the strongest electoral Ticket.

We've no local news here. All well. Present my respects to your Lady.

J. M. Howry

P.S. When convenient give me the prospect in the north & north western states. The only question in the convention will be as to the V.P.[14]

ALS. DLC–JKP. Addressed to Columbia.

1. Formerly a resident of Hickman County, Tenn., Howry moved in 1836 to Oxford, Miss., where he continued to practice law. In 1840 he lost a special election for judge of the circuit court, but in 1841 won the regular election for that post.

2. The Democratic State Convention of Mississippi was held in Jackson on January 8, 1844; Van Buren and Polk were nominated for the presidency and vice-presidency, respectively.

3. The Alabama Democratic State Convention met on December 4, 1843, and nominated Martin Van Buren for the presidency and William R. King for the vice-presidency.

4. Robert J. Walker.

5. A test vote to substitute the name of Calhoun for that of Van Buren failed by a vote of sixty-three to twenty.

6. A Mississippi lawyer, Ellis served on the state supreme court, 1823–25; in the U.S. Senate, 1825–26 and 1827–32; and on the U.S. district court in Mississippi, 1832–36. Ellis went to Mexico as chargé d'affaires in 1836 and served there as minister plenipotentiary from 1839 until 1842.

7. Joseph W. Matthews and Jefferson Davis. A member of the Mississippi legislature, 1840 and 1844–48, Matthews won election as a Democrat to the

governorship in 1847; he served in that post from 1848 until 1850.

8. Henry S. Foote, Reuben H. Boone, Joseph Bell, and Arthur Fox. A Mississippi lawyer and 1844 Democratic presidential elector, Foote won election in 1847 to the U.S. Senate as a Unionist; he resigned from the Senate in 1852 to become governor of Mississippi. Reuben H. Boone, a farmer, lawyer, and collateral descendant of Daniel Boone, lived in Tennessee before moving to Tishomingo County, Miss., in 1835; elected to the lower house of the legislature in 1839, 1840, and 1843, he also served in the Mississippi Senate for four years, 1846–50. Bell, a native of Tennessee, settled in Winston County, Miss., in 1833; he served both as a state representative, 1839–41, and as a state senator, 1842–44. Fox represented Lawrence County in the Mississippi House in 1821, 1823, 1830, 1837–38, and 1840–41, and in the Mississippi Senate, 1842–44, 1846, and 1848; he served as president of the Senate, 1843–44, and as a vice-president of the 1844 Democratic State Convention; and in 1845 he succeeded John A. Quitman as major general of the second division of the Mississippi militia.

9. James L. Totten, a lawyer, represented Marshall County in the Mississippi legislature from 1844 until 1846; he served as Speaker of that body during both legislative sessions.

10. Cotesworth Pinckney Smith, a lawyer and Whig, served one term in the Mississippi House, 1826, and one term in the Mississippi Senate, 1830. He was elected to the bench of the Mississippi High Court of Errors and Appeals in 1833 for a four-year term; returned to the High Court for a few months in 1840, by appointment; and won election to a full term in 1849. In 1851 he became chief justice of the High Court and held that post until his death in 1862.

11. A native of North Carolina, Jesse Speight served in the North Carolina legislature during the 1820's and in the U.S. House, 1829–37; he moved to Lowndes County, Miss., which he represented in the state legislature in 1840; he served twice as president of the Mississippi Senate, 1842 and 1844; and in 1844 he won election to the U.S. Senate, where he served until his death in 1847.

12. See James M. Howry to Polk, April 19, 1843. McNutt had wanted to repeal the charters of those state banks that had suspended specie payments. In 1841 he proposed repudiation of state bonds issued in behalf of the Union and Planters banks; but both houses of the legislature refused and resolved that the state was "bound to the holders of the bonds of the State of Mississippi, issued and sold on account of the Planters and Mississippi Union banks, for the full amount of the principal and interest due thereon; that the State of Mississippi will pay her bonds and preserve her faith inviolate; that the insinuation that the State of Mississippi would repudiate her bonds, and violate her plighted faith, is a calumny upon the justice, honor and dignity of the State." McNutt vetoed that resolution and in his last legislative message, submitted in January of 1842, called for the repudiation of $5 million in state bonds delivered to the Mississippi Union Bank.

13. Quotation is from William Shakespeare's *King Richard III*, act 1, scene

2; reference is to Richard, Duke of Gloucester, afterwards King Richard III.

14. By a vote of 51 to 29, the Mississippi State Democratic Convention preferred Polk to Richard M. Johnson for the vice-presidential nomination.

## TO SAMUEL H. LAUGHLIN

My Dear Sir: Columbia Jany 20th 1844

I send to my brother[1] an additional list of names, and have urged him to multiply copies of the letter[2] for the committee to sign. The address of Genl. *T. A. Howard*[3] *is Rockville Parks County Indiana.* Send him one of the committee's letters & write him a private letter yourself. All these letters should be dispatched forthwith. Do not fail to have the list I left with you as well as that sent to my brother filled promptly. The Pennsylvania Convention[4] sits on the 4th of March. *Mr Buchanan* will make great efforts, undoubtedly, to pressure the nomination of his favourite at it. That State therefore should be attended to, with special care, and at the earliest possible day. *The Hon. Henry Horn*[5] of Philadelphia is the controlling spirit in that state. Send one of the first letters of the committee to him. I think it very important too, that you should write a full and strong private letter to him, explaining the action of our convention to him, and the importance of the nomination, so far as this and the South-Western states are concerned. He is my personal and political friend, and a letter from you, stating to him who you are, that you are a Delegate to the Baltimore convention, & that you are for Van-Buren, would have a fine effect. *Mr Horn* is the devoted friend of Mr Van-Buren, and was for him and against Buchanan before the latter declined. I fear if he is not excited to active exertion in time, that Mr *Buchanan,* operating from Washington, may carry the nomination of that State, according to his wishes. I fear Pennsylvania more, because of Mr Buchanan's influence than any other part of the ground. Will you write to Johnson and Brown to correspond immediately, with their acquaintances in that state. It is very important they should do so. Do not fail to procure from *Mjr. Heiss* the names of the Democratic committee at Pittsburg & let our committee address a letter to them. Will you take a leizure moment and write to *Van-Pelt*[6] at Memphis to take more interest and stronger ground than he has heretofore done.

A letter received by Dr. Hays[7] to day from Jackson Mississippi states the vote in Convention: For *Van-Buren* 62—against him 20; *For Polk* 59—against him 29,[8] but does not state to whom the opposing votes were given. This must give a great impetus to my prospects, and if properly used must overcome the schemes at Washington to defeat me. Have a prominent notice taken of it, in tuesday's Union.[9] For the future I think the Union should devote more space to this subject. Let the Cincinnatti proceedings[10] and all others that may appear have a prominent insertion.

JAMES K. POLK

ALS. DLC–JKP. Addressed to Nashville and marked "*Private.*" Published in Joseph H. Parks, ed., "Letters From James K. Polk to Samuel H. Laughlin, 1835–1844," *ETHSP,* XVIII (1946), pp. 165–66.

1. William H. Polk. See Polk to William H. Polk, January 20, 1844.

2. See Samuel H. Laughlin to Polk, January 11, 1844.

3. Born in South Carolina, Tilghman A. Howard practiced law in Tennessee and won a single term in the Tennessee Senate, 1827–29. In 1830 he moved to Indiana and served as U.S. district attorney for Indiana from 1833 until 1837. He went to the U.S. House in 1839, but lost his gubernatorial race in 1840. Howard served briefly as chargé d'affaires to the Republic of Texas in 1844.

4. The Pennsylvania State Democratic Convention assembled in Harrisburg on March 4, 1844. On March 6, the Convention nominated Martin Van Buren for the presidency and by a unanimous vote chose Richard M. Johnson for the vice-presidency.

5. A Philadelphia hardware merchant, Horn served as a Democrat in the U.S. House for one term, 1831–33.

6. Henry Van Pelt, who began his editing career with the Franklin *Recorder* in 1821, assumed direction of the Democratic *Memphis Weekly Appeal* on April 21, 1841; he remained with the *Appeal* for some ten years.

7. John B. Hays, a Columbia physician, was the husband of Polk's youngest sister, Ophelia Clarissa Polk.

8. See James M. Howry to Polk, January 17, 1844.

9. The *Nashville Union* of Tuesday, January 23, 1844, carried a brief mention and a letter noting the vote of the Mississippi State Democratic Convention.

10. Reference is to the Ohio State Democratic Convention.

## TO WILLIAM H. POLK

Dear Sir:                          Columbia Jany 20th 1844

A letter received by Dr. Hays to day, from Jackson Mississippi, states the vote in Convention as follows, for *Van-Buren* 62, against him 20; for *Polk* 59, against him 29,[1] but does not state who the other persons voted for are. This will give a great impulse to my prospects and if improved promptly will overpower the scheming at Washington to defeat me. I write you to night, to urge you to loose not an hour in multiplying copies of the letter from the committee,[2] and let Laughlin and Cheatham see that they are signed and despatched without delay. A few weeks at most will settle the question, & to have effect my friends must *act now.* I beg you to suffer nothing to prevent a sufficient number of copies from being made out and sent off. I give you on another page a list of names to whom among others they should be sent. Laughlin may have a part of these names and by conferring with him, you can learn which they are.

JAMES K. POLK

[ATTACHMENT]

1. His Excellency Hugh J. Anderson,[3] Governor of Maine
2. Hon. Franklin Pierce, Hilsborough, N. Hampshire
3. Hon. Thomas P. Moore,[4] Harodsburg, Kentucky
4. Hon. Tilghman A. Howard, Rockville, Parke County, Indiana
5. Hon. Gorham Parks,[5] Bangor, Maine
6. Hon. Ransom H. Gillett,[6] Ogdensburg, St. Lawrence County, New York

See Laughlin's list for others. None of the above are included in his list.

ALS. DLC–IlHi. Addressed to Nashville and marked *"Private."*
1. For the vote of the Mississippi State Democratic Convention on January 8, 1844, see James M. Howry to Polk, January 17, 1844.
2. Reference is to the Nashville Democratic Central Committee.
3. A lawyer, Anderson won election as a Democrat to two terms in the U.S. House, 1837–41; subsequently, he served as governor of Maine, 1844–47, and as commissioner of customs in the U.S. Treasury Department, 1853–58.
4. A Democrat from Mercer County, Ky., Moore sat three terms in the U.S. House, 1823–29; served as minister to Columbia, 1829–33; and ran unsuccessfully for Congress in 1833.
5. A lawyer, Parks sat two terms in the U.S. House, 1833–37; served as U.S. marshal for the Maine district, 1838–41; became U.S. attorney for Maine in 1843; and resided as U.S. consul at Rio de Janeiro, 1845–49.
6. A Democrat, Gillet won election to two terms in the U.S. House, 1833–37; during Polk's administration he served as register of the Treasury, 1845–47, and as solicitor of the Treasury, 1847–49.

## TO THOMAS W. HOGAN AND JOHN P. HEISS

Gentlemen:                                                       Columbia Jany 21st 1844
I neglected when I was at Nashville to suggest to you the propriety of placing *Mr Van-Buren's* name at the Head of your column in your paper, as well as mine. It is now certain that *Mr Van-Buren* will be the candidate, and some of my friends out of the State, do not understand,

why it is, that my name is at the head of the column of the Union and *Mr Van-Buren's* is not. Some of my opponents, or rather some of those who urge the nomination of another for the Vice Presidency, are attempting to use the fact that *Van-Buren's* name has not been hoisted in your paper to my prejudice. If you see no objections therefore, I hope you will run-up his name, subject of course to the decision of the National Convention.[1]

JAMES K. POLK

ALS. T–JPH. Addressed to Nashville and marked "*Private.*" Published in St. George L. Sioussat, ed., "Papers of Major John P. Heiss of Nashville," *THM*, II (June, 1916), p. 141.

1. The *Nashville Union* endorsed Martin Van Buren's candidacy on February 8, 1844.

## FROM CAVE JOHNSON

Dear Sir,                                        Washington Janry 21st 1844

I recd your two letters[1] several days ago and delayed a day or two that I might see what would come of Brown's reply to the article agt you.[2] It created a good deal of feeling among some of the friends of Col K.[3] and a rejoinder was prepared which the Globe refused to publish for several days & great efforts have been made I learn by Blair & Bagby[4] to suppress it, but all efforts were unavailing as the author would publish if not in the Globe in the Madisonian.[5] The Globe then yielded. The piece you will see in the paper of the 20th,[6] which only shews great malignity in the author whose name is not known. The Article signed a Ten. Democrat,[7] compared your course in Congress with that of Col. K. & said the Col. tho here during the War could scarcely be found except by a minute search of the records. The author affects to consider it an attack upon the personal courage of Col. K. & then launches out a commendation of *his courage* & says the Col. K. never submitted to insult &c to be waylaid & insulted & called a petty tyrant of a party, using Wise's language.[8] An answer will be in the Globe of tomorrow, a full & ample vindication.[9] I suspect Buckhanon[10] for writing the first article whoever may assume the paternity. It is like his style manner &c.

It is spoken of with regret on all hands & if we get into a bad temper, quarrelling &c the danger will be, that the nomination may be given to old Dick,[11] to avoid the controversy but then *he is for Clays Bankrupt Bill*[12] & that may be made a more formidable objection than Col K.'s Bank notions.[13] These two give us great advantage over both & if I am not mistaken will tell more before the Country than they do here among politicians. You will be defended here whatever Consequences may ensue. I was glad to find A.V.B.[14] so zealous in your defence. Many friends here begin to *fear* that we may be beaten—talk of some new man who can run better—the impossibility to elect Van &c which may do us some harm & excite hopes in the Southern wing of our friends, who seem inclined at present to look to Cass. This feeling has grown up out of the 21st rule & the Tariff, but by moderation & firmness I think we can over come all such scruples. I think we shall finally settle on the Atherton resolution upon which we may all safely stand. Our Ways & Means will probably make the Tariff of 1842 the basis of our action, reduce on each article as much as we can safely do & save our northern friends & increase the Revenue, without coming down the Southern ad valorem Revenue Standard, & thus make a favourable *contrast with the Whig Tariff.* As yet there has been no action of the Com. of W. & M. further than seeking information & of course my opinion is conjectural. McKays Bill[15] [will] reduce about six millions & if we can sustain them will reduce our expenditures to about $16,000,000. If we can do these things & come home in May which we will attempt, I do not think we need to fear the result of the elections next faul.

We could do these things without any difficulty but for the Calhoun men. I had a long talk today with Burt[16] (a relation of Calhoun) who talks very well & gives me some hopes that all will yet be well.

We had a violent bitter contest between Stewart & Weller[17] on which the former was much worsted, & I suppose all ends with the debate— the first presidential squabble we have had. Hopkins will take an active part for you & write to Va. I fear the Ohio men will go agt. you, simply from the fact that they evade expressing any opinions in my presence & because I have recd no reply from Columbus.

Mangum gave a diplomatic dinner—Webster, Botts[18] & many of the discontented who gave in their adhesion to Clay were present & I suppose there is but little doubt that Tyler & the few he can control will do so likewise. The latter has not as yet given up the hope of getting a third candidate.

Gilmer declines going into the Navy[19] & we have no idea who will. Some suspicions are entertained that he[20] will not be allowed by the Senate to make another Cabinet, hoping that he may be driven to resign; yet I think such a result is not possible. Wise's fate, Spencer's for Judge, Porter[21] —still unsettled & doubtful. Chances seem to be agt. all without the adhesion of certain leading men to support of Clay.

I am troubled every day with my old complaint tho not enough to keep me out of the House. My wife & child keep very well.[22]

C. JOHNSON

ALS. DLC–JKP. Addressed to Columbia. Published in *THQ*, XII, pp. 160–61.

1. Polk's letters not found.

2. For prior reference to the anti-Polk article, published by "Amicus" in the Washington *Globe* of January 8, 1844, see Cave Johnson to Polk, January 13, 1844. Aaron V. Brown's reply appeared in the Washington *Globe* of January 15, 1844, under the pseudonym, "A Tennessee Democrat."

3. William Rufus King.

4. Francis Preston Blair and Arthur Pendleton Bagby. Founder and editor of the Washington *Globe* from 1830 until 1845, Blair became one of the leading spokesmen among Jacksonian Democrats. A lawyer, Bagby served as governor of Alabama, 1837–41; U.S. senator, 1841–48; and minister to Russia, 1848–49.

5. Established in 1837 with Thomas Allen as editor and publisher, the Washington *Madisonian* backed conservative or "soft-money" Democrats. In the spring of 1841 the newspaper suspended publication, but in September of that year John Tyler revived it with Allen retained in his post as editor.

6. The rejoinder submitted by William Rufus King's friends appeared in the Washington *Globe* of January 19, 1844.

7. Reference is to Brown's article of January 15, 1844.

8. The unidentified author of the pro-King article of January 19 refers to Henry A. Wise's verbal harassment of Polk during Polk's first term as Speaker of the U.S. House. The author wrote, "King has never been insulted day after day, and, above all ... never caught roughly by the arm, when escaping from the Capitol, pulled round, and told that he was the '*contemptible tool* of a petty tyrant!'"

9. On Monday, January 22, 1844, the Washington *Globe* published a second pro-Polk article, which was also signed by "A Tennessee Democrat." This second letter answered the pro-King communication printed in the *Globe* on January 19, 1844.

10. James Buchanan.

11. Richard M. Johnson.

12. Passed in August of 1841, the second federal bankruptcy law permitted voluntary bankruptcy, but allowed creditors to proceed against debtors; Democrats repealed this law in 1843. An earlier bankruptcy law, passed by Congress in 1800, had been repealed in 1803.

13. See Cave Johnson to Polk, January 13, 1844.

14. Aaron V. Brown.

15. Reference probably is to the draft of a bill introduced in the U.S. House on March 8, 1844, by James I. McKay, chairman of the Committee of Ways and Means, to modify and amend the tariff act of 1842. McKay's tariff bill failed to pass the House during the 1843–44 session.

16. A lawyer and farmer from Abbeville, S.C., Armistead Burt served in the U.S. House, 1843–53; his kinship to John C. Calhoun is not identified

further.

17. Andrew Stewart and John B. Weller. A Pennsylvania Whig, Stewart was appointed U.S. attorney for the western district of Pennsylvania by James Monroe, 1818–20; Stewart served nine terms in the U.S. House, 1821–29, 1831–35, and 1843–49.

18. Willie P. Mangum, Daniel Webster, and John M. Botts. A North Carolina lawyer, Mangum served in the U.S. House, 1823–26, and in the U.S. Senate, 1831–36 and 1840–53; he held the post of president pro tempore of the Senate from 1842 until 1845. A Virginia lawyer and farmer, Botts won election in 1839 as a Clay Whig to the first of three terms in the U.S. House, where he served from 1839 until 1843 and from 1847 until 1849.

19. On February 15, 1844, Tyler nominated Thomas W. Gilmer as secretary of the navy; the U.S. Senate immediately confirmed Gilmer in his post; and less than two weeks later, on February 28, the new secretary of the navy died in an explosion aboard the U.S.S. *Princeton*.

20. John Tyler.

21. James M. Porter, a Pennsylvania lawyer, jurist, and brother of David R. Porter, served as ad interim secretary of war from March 8, 1843, until January 30, 1844.

22. Cave and Elizabeth Dortch Brunson Johnson took both of their children, James Hickman and Thomas Dickson, to Washington during the sitting of Congress; Johnson's reference to "child" probably is used inclusively.


## TO CAVE JOHNSON

[Dear Sir,]                 [Columbia, Tenn.] January 21, 1844

I have read the article in the Globe of the 8th inst. signed "Amicus."[1] I learn from *Turney* and *Laughlin* that an article in reply to it, has been prepared, and forwarded by *Turney* to *Mr. Blair,* under cover to for insertion in the Globe.[2] Blair surely cannot do me the injustice to exclude it from his columns. It is very important that it should appear in time to reach Richmond for the Convention in Va. on 1st February. If he refuses, or is likely to delay its publication, have it struck off in pamphlet form and sent to our friends. If published in time in the Globe, —mark the article and send copies of the Globe to Richmond. Indeed even though *Blair* shall publish it in the Globe or whether he does or not, it will be important to have several hundred copies published in pamphlet, and sent to leading friends and newspapers in every part of the Union. Let a copy in pamphlet be directed to every Democratic member of Congress, and to every Democratic member of the Pennsylvania Legislature now in Session. You can learn their names from some of the Pennsylvania gentlemen. Forward a copy too to each Delegate to Baltimore, who has been appointed, as far as you can learn their names. Some members of Congress from each State can give you their names and Post office. They can give you the names also of the Democratic members of their respective State Legislatures. I deem this of such vital importance at this moment, that I hope you will not fail to attend to it. I fear *Mr. Buchanan's* influence upon the Pennsylvania Convention which meets on the 4th of March; and therefore I think special and prompt attention should be given to that State. The *Hon. Henry Horn* of Philadelphia is the leading spirit of the Van Buren party in that State. He was warmly for Van Buren and against Buchanan before the latter declined, and can do more to counteract his influence upon their convention than any other man. It is important I think that you should write a full and strong letter to him, fully explaining the action of our State convention and the causes of it, our true position in Tennessee, and the importance of the Vice-Presidential nomination, to our success, —not only in that State, but some others of the Southwestern States. *Mr. Horn* is my personal and political friend, and such a letter from you, would undoubtedly stimulate him to the most active exertions. If he goes into it, as I know he will if you will write him such a letter, he will overpower the schemers at Washington, who seek to direct public opinion and thereby to defeat me.

A letter received by *Dr. Hays* of this place to day, —from Jackson, Mississippi, —states that the nomination vote in the Mississippi State Convention on the 8th of January was—For Mr. Van Buren 62, against him 20; For Polk 59, against him 29, but does not state for whom the opposing votes were given.[3] This must give a powerful impulse to my prospects if properly improved upon. Will the Globe publish the proceedings?[4] If he does will he give it as prominent an insertion as he did the proceedings of the Alabama Convention? Or will he suppress it, or stick it in an obscure corner as he did the Tennessee and Arkansas nominations? Will you attend to this? I know, My Dear Sir, that I give you much trouble, but I have no one else upon whom to rely, unless it be Brown. What is the matter with Brown? He has not written me since the 9th of December. I have written him so often without an answer, that I almost despair of getting one from him. I saw today a short letter from him to *Mr. Thomas*[5] of this place on the subject of the Post office, in which he desires him to say to me that the article in the Globe signed "Amicus" shall be attended to.[6] If it has been answered before Turney's communication reaches you, still from what I learn of that communication I much desire to have it published also, —both in the Globe and in pamphlet. I understand that it is probably fuller that[7] any notice, you would have time to take of

"Amicus" would be. Have it published and circulated as suggested—*by all means and without fail,* —no matter what may have been published upon the same subject before it reaches you.

I repeat what I said to you in my last. I am satisfied the popular voice of the party is for me, and I am resolved to contest the nomination with the leaders at Washington who would have it otherwise. They have not done me justice. If they shall be able to control the convention, I will yield like a true party man should, and will fight on for my principles. My friends at Washington will be stimulated I hope to action, and will not give way to a feeling of despondency, because a few powerful leading men at Washington have undertaken to direct the public sentiment of the party. These leading men at Washington constitute but a small portion of the party, and unless my friends at Washington become desponding of success and yield, they cannot carry out their designs. These remarks are not make[8] in reference to yourself, far from it, but that you may impress them on others, and stimulate my friends to active exertions to counteract them in their plans.

[JAMES K. POLK]

P.S. My friends at Nashville and here are much excited at the appearance of "Amicus" in the Globe more than I have ever known them upon any subject of the kind. Turney's publication, it was thought best by my friends to have inserted first in the Globe and printed in pamphlet. When it appears it will be copied into the Union.[9] Laughlin's services as Editor of the Union and the extra—to be called *"The Star Spangled Banner"* will be secured.[10] He will take charge of the paper as soon as the Legislature adjourns, which will be in about ten days.

PL. Published in St. George L. Sioussat, ed., "Letters of James K. Polk to Cave Johnson, 1833–1848," *THM,* I (September, 1915), pp. 232–34. Addressed to Washington City and marked *"Confidential."*

1. See Cave Johnson to Polk, January 13, 1844.

2. Dated January 18, 1844, Hopkins L. Turney's communication appeared in the Washington *Globe* on February 5, 1844. Refuting the "Amicus" letter to the *Globe* of January 8, which contained claims of seniority and superior service for William Rufus King, Turney defended Polk point by point. He explained that the Tennessee State Democratic Convention's refusal to make a presidential nomination or to instruct Tennessee's delegation to the Baltimore Convention had prudently avoided "even the slightest division in the party in the state, in advance of the action of the national convention."

3. For the vote of the Mississippi State Democratic Convention, see James M. Howry to Polk, January 17, 1844, and Samuel H. Laughlin to Polk, January 20, 1844.

4. On January 26, 1844, Francis P. Blair, editor of the Washington *Globe,* carried two letters concerning the meeting of the Mississippi State Democratic Convention of January 8, 1844. The first was an extract of a letter, dated January 9, 1844, giving the vote of the Convention. The second was the text of Robert J. Walker's letter of November 20, 1843, which requested that the Mississippi Convention pass over his name in selecting a vice-presidential nominee.

5. Reference probably is to James Houston Thomas, a Columbia lawyer and district attorney, 1836–42, who prosecuted the state's indictment of William H. Polk in 1839 for the murder of Robert H. Hayes. A law partner of James K. Polk's in 1843, Thomas won election as a Democrat to three terms in Congress, 1847–51 and 1859–61.

6. See Cave Johnson to Polk, January 21, 1844.

7. Polk probably intended to write the word "than."

8. Polk probably intended to write the word "made."

9. Publication of Turney's article, signed "A Tennessean" and printed in the Washington *Globe* on February 5, 1844, has not been found in the *Nashville Union.*

10. Samuel H. Laughlin became editor of the *Nashville Union* and the *Star Spangled Banner* on March 12, 1844.


## FROM AARON V. BROWN

(at table)

Dear Sir                    H. Rep. [Washington City January 22, 1844][1]

I received your last[2] full of complaint for not writing more frequently to you. My perpetual never ceasing engagements, are my only excuse. I have not however failed to communicate every thing that has occured not likely to reach you through the papers.[3] "A Tennessee Democrat"[4] has not only proved fatal but has created considerable excitement here. His second appearance is *moderated* by the universal wish of friends to put an end to this family quarrel especially as *another*[5] is the formidable competitor for the vice presidency. Blair hesitated long before he would admit the 2 Correspondent in favor of Colo. K.[6] I doubt whether the matter will be carried any further. But "a Tennessee Democrat" having now put the matter on the most *liberal* footing, asks no odds in the future. There are two important points to be attended to—not to give enemies an opportunity *to profit* by these discussions & not to incur the displeasure of *friends* by too much severity. I received a letter from Madill[7] stating his opinion that Colo. Johnson was evidently the first choice & you the second choice of Ohio.

In short all that I have now time to say is that I believe with you, that as it is the interest so it is the purpose of a few aspiring politicians here to postpone you as long as possible. The correspondence about it, so far, has done you no harm, especially the last publication against you—the *fling* about the Wise case,[8] either escaped observation or excited contempt. So soon as this shall be closed I shall prepare a series of publication in your favor, if no one of more leisure shall prepare them in Tennessee & send them here for publication.[9] I cannot do it well under my engagements on two troublesome committees[10] & other responsibilities in the house beside my correspondence. No night finds me in bed by 12 O'ck & often 2 O'ck. Johnson[11] is hard to get to do any thing in such matters—*all* our delegation (Democrats) seem to take a lively interest in your behalf.

A. V. Brown

[P.S.] You will find the 2nd reply of "a Tenessee Democrat" in todays Globe[12] with a few typografical errors easily corrected.

ALS. DLC–JKP. Addressed to Columbia and marked "*confidential.*" Polk's AE on the cover states that he answered this letter on February 1, 1844; Polk's reply has not been found.

1. Date identified through content analysis.
2. Letter not found. See Polk to Cave Johnson, January 21, 1844.
3. On January 14, 1844, Brown wrote Sarah Childress Polk a "confidential" letter relating political news of the day in Washington City. Of recent efforts to promote William Rufus King's vice-presidential prospects, Brown wrote, "Mr. Buchanon looks gloomy & dissatisfied & so did *his better half* until a little private flattery & a certain newspaper puff which you doubtless noticed, excited hopes that by getting *a divorce* she might set up again in the world to some tolerable advantage. Since which *casual* event, which she has taken for real and permanent overtures, *Aunt Nancy* may be now seen every day, triged out in her best clothes & smirking about in hopes of seeing better times than with her former companion. You will however see in the Globe of tomorrow that she is presented to the world 'as no better than she should be.' This however is what every prude deserves who sets herself up for more than she is worth." On the presidential race Brown commented, "I was amused today at hearing of a little incident affecting our friend Genl. Saunders. He is a warm Calhoun man you know & in the presence of Mr Buchanon and *his wife* & some others [he] advanced the opinion that neither Mr Calhoun nor Mr Van Buren had any chance to be elected, & being asked by some one 'who then can be,' he forgot himself & said that Colo. Polk could run better than any other man in the nation. This of course was hig[h]ly indecorous toward *Mrs B.* to whom the Genl. found much difficulty in making the necessary apology. I am exactly of that opinion. That is to say Colo. Polk is now encountering the very identical difficulties as to the *Vice* that he would have to do for the first office of the governmnt & if he can overcome the one he could have done the other." ALS. DLC–JKP. William Rufus King, for many years James Buchanan's roommate and special friend, received his nickname,

"Aunt Nancy," from Andrew Jackson in the early 1830's.
4. See Cave Johnson to Polk, January 13 and 21, 1844.
5. Richard M. Johnson.
6. For the second article promoting William Rufus King for the the vice-presidential nomination, see Cave Johnson to Polk, January 21, 1844.
7. William Medill.
8. See Cave Johnson to Polk, January 21, 1844.
9. See Polk to Cave Johnson, January 21, 1844.
10. Brown chaired the House Committee on Territories and served as a member of the Committee on Elections.
11. Cave Johnson.
12. Washington *Globe,* January 22, 1844.


## FROM ROBERT ARMSTRONG

Sunday night
Dear Sir                                    [Nashville, Tenn.] 28 Jany [18]44
The Legislature will adjourn on Wednesday night. I think you should come in on Tuesday. Humphreys told me Genl Pillow would be here.[1] Expecting him, I did not answer his letter. Please say so to him and bring him with you. Very cold.

R. ARMSTRONG

ALS. DLC–JKP. Addressed to Columbia. Polk's AE on the cover states that he answered this letter on January 30, 1844; Polk's reply has not been found.
1. West H. Humphreys and Gideon J. Pillow. A Columbia lawyer and general in the militia, Pillow played a key role at the 1844 Democratic National Convention. He later served as a general officer in the Mexican War and commanded a Confederate brigade during the Civil War. Pillow's sister, Amanda Malvina Pillow, married West H. Humphreys in 1839.


## FROM CAVE JOHNSON

Dear Sir,                                    Washington 31st Jany 1844
I recd yours of the 21st last evening. I recd also a letter from Turney with an article signed the Ten. democrat which I handed to Blair two days ago & certainly expected its appearance this morning.[1] I understand it will appear tomorrow & we shall distribute it according to your suggestions. It is one of the best written articles that I have read & withal in a good spirit & is calculated to do much good. I have had a good deal of talk with members on the subject of the vice presidency & it is rare to meet one who would not prefer you to either of the others.[2] We are occasionally met with "but how can we get

rid of old Dick?"[3]  Amicus has not hurt you in the least here but K. will feel the force of Browns defense.[4]  I find it the opinion of some of the I[ndian]a members that it will be decidedly for you. We shall take much pains in distributing Turneys article. Brown promises assistance & is no doubt very cordial for you but he has been talking in a round about way of Vans not being available & talking indirectly for Cass & Jones is in the same way tho rather stronger than B.[5]  Yet I think they both will cheerfully sustain Van under the belief however that we shall be beaten. B. & myself talked more warmly to day on the subject at dinner than ever before. He talks of New York politicians, their hypocrisy &c just as the nullifyers are constantly in the habit of doing & attributing their conduct & sentiments to Van. The question of the Tariff produced it.  Beardsly[6] (who now plays upon Van, the game that Bell played upon Jackson) & a few others from N.Y. are agt. touching the Tariff. So is Wilkings & Ingersol & therefor Van & Wright[7] is playing double &c. This was the cause of more feeling than was exhibited.

I have written Henry Horn & shall also enclose him the article of Turney. I see a boost given you at Cincinatti which if we could get followed up in Pennsylvania with the late impetus from Mississippi will help us.[8]  Hopkins & Coles & Lucas will aid me in Va. & so would Steenrod if he is not controled by Allen & Weller[9]  The weather has been so bad of late that I rarely get out except to the Capitol where I have not much chance amidst the confusion of business to have much talk. I have acquired lately a very unenviable notoriety about the city that annoys me exceedingly. No scamp has a claim or interest in any Bill or measure but hunts me up & annoys me morning, noon & night; until I have come to the conclusion to tell every fellow "I oppose your Bill if you talk to me about it." I have no hour to myself scarcely except when I run to my Committee room in the morning & remain there until the House meets.

We are to be greatly troubled about the Tariff & I begin to fear we shall do nothing with it.  Jones[10] has been very unfortunate in his Committees not only on Rules but on *the Ways & Means.* They are said to be equally divided except a new man Chappel,[11] a Whig from Georgia who holds the balance; 4 for not touching it unless to raise it & but little is known of Chappel & McKay fears he will not be able to get such a Bill as is desirable. Seymor of N.Y. [is] *a Democrat* & a thorough Tariff man almost as bad as Beardsly.[12]  McKay, Rhett, Lewis, Weller, Seymor, are the Democrats.[13]  The Chairman[14] lacks energy. He begins tomorrow on the appropriation Bills.

I think serious efforts are making to force us to give up Van Buren

& more earnestly by those who have recd the greatest favors from Van Buren than any other & on the ground, that they have had so many favors that they may & probably will have to stand aside for others. This added to the Calhoun & Tyler influence will give us yet great trouble. I had to say in strong terms to day, if that game was to be played by a fraction of our party I should Play the part I did in Jones election when defeated by eight nullifiers, that 9/10 of the party would never yield to the other tenth even to secure success.[15]

The Senate has rejected Henshaw, Porter &c & to day refused to confirm the nomination of Spencer in the place of Thompson.[16] Tomorrow they will confirm Wise as Minister to Rio in the place of Profit,[17] simply to have him out of the country next summer. There is some talk of Gilmer succeeding Waddy Thompson.[18] He declined the Navy. Mallory[19] is now spoken of for it. Hiram Ketchum it is thought will be now recomended in the place of Mr. Judge T.[20] (not half as good as Spencer). There is no intimation yet who will be Porters successor.

The Weather has been very unfavorable to my health & I am looking out daily to be thrown on my back. The pains in my face now come daily & often unfit [me] for business tho I have kept in the House every day but one. Redding of New Hampshire lost his wife[21] & we attended the funeral to day. He has taken her to N.H.

Genl Anderson is still here, business unknown. Finly Gillespie also, who keeps half his time drunk & has lost much of the money gambling, that he has collected for Cherokee Claimants[22] (as rumor says). He is very angry with me, because I will not sanction a law that the certificates of Eaton & Hubly Cheroke Com. be paid at the Treasury.[23]

C. JOHNSON

ALS. DLC–JKP. Addressed to Columbia and marked *"private."* Polk's AE on the cover states that he answered this letter on February 10, 1844; Polk's reply has not been found. Published in *THQ*, XII, pp. 161–62.

1. Hopkins L. Turney signed his article, "A Tennessean." See Polk to Cave Johnson, January 21, 1844.

2. Richard M. Johnson and William R. King.

3. Richard M. Johnson.

4. William R. King and Aaron V. Brown. For more on the pro-King articles signed "Amicus" and published in the Washington *Globe,* see Cave Johnson to Polk, January 13 and 21, 1844; and Aaron V. Brown to Polk, January 23, 1844.

5. Martin Van Buren, Lewis Cass, George W. Jones, and Aaron V. Brown.

6. Samuel Beardsley.

7. William Wilkins, Charles J. Ingersoll, Martin Van Buren, and Silas Wright. Wilkins, first president of the Bank of Pittsburgh, served in the U.S. Senate, 1831–34; went to Russia as Jackson's minister plenipotentiary,

1834–35; sat in the U.S. House, 1843–44; and headed the War Department under Tyler, 1844–45. Ingersoll, a Pennsylvania Democrat, served five terms in the U.S. House, 1813–15 and 1841–49, and three terms as U.S. district attorney for Pennsylvania, 1815–29.

8. References are to the state Democratic conventions of Ohio and Mississippi, which met on January 8, 1844, and to the Pennsylvania convention scheduled for March 4, 1844. Ohio Democrats, who convened at Columbus rather than Cincinnati, praised Richard M. Johnson but made no nomination for the vice-presidency. Mississippi Democrats nominated Polk by a wide margin over Johnson.

9. George W. Hopkins, Walter Coles, William Lucas, Lewis Steenrod, William Allen, and John B. Weller. Coles, a farmer who served several terms in the Virginia House of Delegates, won election as a Democrat to five terms in the U.S. House and served from 1835 until 1845. Lucas, a lawyer and farmer from Virginia, served two terms as a Democrat in the U.S. House, 1839–41 and 1843–45. Steenrod, a Democrat and lawyer from Wheeling, Va., won election to three terms in the U.S. House, 1839–45. A lawyer, farmer, and stockman from Chillicothe, Ohio, Allen won election as a Democrat to one term in the U.S. House in 1833 and sat in the U.S. Senate from 1837 until 1849.

10 Speaker of the U.S. House of Representatives, John W. Jones.

11. References are to the House Committee on Ways and Means and to Absalom H. Chappell. A lawyer from Macon, Chappell served in both houses of the Georgia legislature prior to his election as a states' rights Whig to one term in the U.S. House, 1843–45.

12. David L. Seymour and Samuel Beardsley. A New York lawyer, Seymour served two terms as a Democrat in the U.S. House, 1843–45 and 1851–53.

13. James I. McKay, Robert Barnwell Rhett, Dixon H. Lewis, John B. Weller, and David L. Seymour. An extreme advocate of states' rights and a South Carolinian loyal to John C. Calhoun, Rhett served in the U.S. House from 1837 until 1849; he succeeded Calhoun in the U.S. Senate in 1850, but resigned his seat two years later. Through his newspaper, the *Charleston Mercury,* Rhett espoused the right of secession and inveighed against the South's reliance upon the Democratic party; he led South Carolina out of the Union in late 1860. A Montgomery lawyer and member of the Alabama House, 1825–27, Lewis sat in the U.S. House from 1829 until 1844, when he resigned to fill the U.S. Senate seat vacated by William R. King.

14. James I. McKay chaired the Committee on Ways and Means.

15. Johnson's reference is to the election of the House Speaker in December of 1839. In that contest, five members of the South Carolina congressional delegation ran Dixon H. Lewis for the speakership against Virginia's John W. Jones, nominee of the Democratic caucus and favorite of Thomas Hart Benton. Unable to elect Jones and unwilling to support Lewis, eleven Democrats, including Tennessee's Cave Johnson, Hopkins L. Turney, and Julius W. Blackwell, voted with the Whig minority to elect Robert M. T. Hunter, a nullifier from Virginia.

16. See Cave Johnson to Polk, January 13, 1844.

17. Henry A. Wise and George H. Proffit. A Whig congressman from Indiana, 1839–43, Proffit had received an interim appointment from Tyler to be U.S. minister to Brazil; on January 11, 1844, the Senate rejected his nomination.

18. Thomas W. Gilmer and Waddy Thompson, Jr. A South Carolina lawyer, Thompson won election to Congress in 1835; he joined the Whig party and served in the House until 1841. He served as U.S. minister to Mexico from February 1842 until March 1844.

19. A physician and farmer from Elizabeth City County, Va., Francis Mallory won a seat in the U.S. House in 1837, lost his bid for reelection to Joel Holleman in 1839, regained his old seat upon Holleman's resignation in 1840, and carried his district for a second full term in 1841. From 1853 until 1859 Mallory headed the Norfolk and Petersburg Railroad Company.

20. Hiram Ketchum and Smith Thompson. A lawyer and Whig politician in New York City, Ketchum shared a close personal and political friendship with Daniel Webster.

21. John R. Reding served as a Democrat in the U.S. House, 1841–45, and later as the mayor of Portsmouth, N.H.; his wife is not identified further.

22. A Madisonville lawyer, John Finley Gillespy served three terms in the Tennessee Senate, 1829–33 and 1839–41. Johnson's reference is to Gillespy's service as legal counsel to persons seeking indemnity for losses covered by the Treaty of New Echota, signed in December 1835. That agreement provided for the forced relocation within two years of those Cherokees unwilling to accept U.S. citizenship and for the payment of $5 million to relocated tribesmen for property losses and travel allowances.

23. John H. Eaton and Edward B. Hubley served as commissioners to adjust and settle claims under the provisions of the Treaty of New Echota. A strong supporter of Andrew Jackson, Eaton resigned his Senate seat in 1829 to become secretary of war in Jackson's cabinet. Washington society's refusal to accept Eaton's second wife, Peggy O'Neale, led to his resignation two years later. Eaton received appointment as governor of Florida Territory, 1834–35, and then as minister to Spain, 1836–40. Hubley, a Democrat from Pennsylvania, served two terms in the U.S. House, 1835–39. Johnson opposed legislation that would have given the commissioners greater authority in the settlement and payment of claims.

# FEBRUARY

## FROM AARON V. BROWN

Dear Sir                    H. Rep. [Washington City] Feby 2nd 1844

You may be a little supprised that the reply to "amicus" *from Tennessee* has not yet appeared.[1] It has been in Blairs hands a week under a promise to publish it. He says as it is written in good temper he will admit this one but no more on either side. I think it an excellent answer, but it may elicit a further reply on the other side. If so, let it come say I. Colo K.[2] & myself have met casually several times but he seemed not [to] be acquanted. He hardly suspects how very indifferent I am on that subject.

Since the publications[3] the question has subsided & but little is saying about it, under the frequent suggestion that "whilst P. & K. are disputing about it old Dick[4] may carry of[f] the prize." This however to my mind is by no means certain, as it is still publishd. that he does not withdraw as a candidate for the first office. I have no idea that the case will be settled before the Convention. Then it will be between you & Johnson. King I take it is effectually used up by his vote for the Bank in 1816.

I am by no means satisfied with the state of things here. The course of Beardsley Davis & others from N. York on abolition[5] will weaken us some, & the course of the N.Y. & Pa. democrats on the Tariff will injure more. I have conversed with Buchannon C. J. Ingersoll & Judge Wilkens[6] who protest against touching the subject at all & if at all they will not vote for reductions on many points. Davis of N.Y. & I have no doubt Beardly[7] too are the same way & I fear Mr Wright

*51*

concurs with them. If so, the *votes* & *speeches* & party criminations during its pendency before Congress will weaken us much if they do not withdraw the Tariff altogether from the list of party questions, which cannot be done you know in Tennessee without prejudice to our cause. In short I fear much from this quarter. You will see Mr. Calhoun's letter.[8] You can judge of his future course. My own opinion is that if not *hostile* he will be quite *indifferent,* producing such effect on his friends as to do us much harm. In Virginia the loss of but few will loose the state & so in some other places. You notice Duff Green's new position in N. York.[9] He is said to have large means & may do more good or harm than is commonly supposed.

From all I can learn the Virginia State convention will give the vice the go by. But we shall soon know. I am a little supprised that neither the N. Union nor the Columbia paper,[10] notice even the simple *fact* that I had argued the question on the Jackson fine[11] question of the 8 & 10 Janry. I am too proud to complain to them of such apparently studied avoidance of my participation in debates here, & so soon as I am informed that it is *intentional* I shall seek the Banner or the Whig[12] for the publication of those days proceedings, with such explanations as I may choose to make. The Difficulties which delay the Texas question are not known to the public, but I fear they arise from the head of that goverment. Every precaution however has been taken to influence him favorably on the subject & you have no doubt noticed what is going on in the Texian Congress.[13]

The house has this moment adjourned on the announcmt of the Death of Senator Porter[14] of La. Present my best respects to Mrs. Polk & other friends.

A. V. Brown

ALS. DLC–JKP. Probably addressed to Columbia.

1. Reference is to Hopkins L. Turney's reply to the communication in the Washington *Globe,* January 8, 1844, signed "Amicus," expounding the merits of William R. King for the vice-presidency.

2. William R. King.

3. For dates of the polemical exchanges between "Amicus" and "A Tennessee Democrat," see Cave Johnson to Polk, January 21, 1844.

4. Richard M. Johnson.

5. Samuel Beardsley and Richard D. Davis. A lawyer from New York, Davis served two terms as a Democrat in the U.S. House, 1841–45. Beardsley and other Democratic congressmen from New York maintained that Congress had a constitutional obligation to receive abolition petitions.

6. James Buchanan, Charles J. Ingersoll, and William Wilkins.

7. Samuel Beardsley.

8. John C. Calhoun decided in December of 1843 to terminate his candidacy

for the 1844 Democratic presidential nomination. On December 21, 1843, Calhoun informed the Charleston Central Committee of his decision; and on January 3, 1844, the Charleston Committee published Calhoun's letter in the *Charleston Mercury.* The Washington *Globe* of February 2, 1844, carried Calhoun's withdrawal letter.

9. A journalist, politician, and industrial promoter, Duff Green was editor of the Washington *United States Telegraph* from 1825 until 1836. Green followed Calhoun in his break with Jackson and supported Clay for the presidency in 1832. From 1842 until 1844, Green was an unofficial representative of the United States in England and France. Returning to the United States in January 1844, he established the New York *Republic* and in its columns advocated radical free-trade policies and reform of the civil and postal services.

10. *Nashville Union* and Columbia *Tennessee Democrat.*

11. On February 10, 1844, the U.S. Congress approved legislation refunding a contempt-of-court fine levied on Andrew Jackson in New Orleans on March 31, 1815. The appropriation included payment of the original one-thousand-dollar fine, plus six per cent interest compounded from the date of imposition by the U.S. district judge, Dominick Hall.

12. The Nashville *Republican Banner* and *Nashville Whig* were both of the Whig persuasion.

13. Sam Houston, president of the Republic of Texas, refused for a time to allow the signing of an annexation treaty; however, renewed pleadings from Abel Upshur and Andrew Jackson, together with strong pro-annexation sentiment in the Texan Congress, persuaded Houston to send a special representative to Washington to sign a treaty.

14. Alexander Porter died on January 13, 1844.

## FROM CAVE JOHNSON

Dear Sir,                                         Washington 6th Feby 1844

I should have written you several days ago but wished to delay until I could see Turney's piece in the Globe[1] which was delayed five or six days on account of several other articles which were ahead of it as Reeves[2] told me to day. The delay induced me to believe that they had declined publishing it & two days ago I wrote Blair to return it to me that I might have it published else where, & it appeared in the paper of last evening. There has been but little said as to it. We shall have four or five hundred coppies struck in pamphlet & placed in hands we think the likeliest to use them to advantage. There is a very general impression prevailing here, that in the conflict between you & King the chances are, that it will be given to R.M.J.[3] and that is the part to which our attention should now be directed. I have intimated this danger several times to the MC's of Alabama & to day Chapman[4] spoke to me of that danger & proposed that your friends & Kings should act in concert to defeat it. The Democrats from Alabama & Tennessee should unite in a letter to the Southern delegates in the Baltimore convention & urge upon them to meet, compare notes as between you & King & all unite upon the strongest agt. old Dick,[5] which I thought your friends would agree to & he will converse with Kings friends & I with yours & try & so arrange it. I think there can be no doubt of your success over him in the South. Indeed I look upon it as certain, and I think this is the only way we can get it over R.M.J. In my opinion the Northern democrats will be inclined to yield the nomination to the Southern delegates. They are certainly in favor of you, if left free to act from other political considerations. I enclose you a letter from Henry Horn which you will be glad to see.[6]

The V–a convention[7] is over but have sd. nothing so far as I can learn about the vice-presidency. The Calhoun men had a caucus the evening before & met our friends in the convention—made liberal advances for a reconciliation, which was met by a noble speech from old Tom. R.[8] which was applauded beyond any thing of the kind. The old man is in ecstacies, pronounces the future harmonious action of the parties and victory as certain in that State. Calhouns letter[9] *will ruin him* tho treated mildly by our friends now. Old Dick's letter[10] does him some credit when compared with Calhoun. Parmenter[11] is inclined to think the Democrats of Mass. are inclined to favor R.M.J. tho he is for you. I am fearful that my course here agt. the navy & mismanagements of Henshaw may do you some harm there. If we can act in moderation with Kings friends & keep every thing smooth, we can beat R.M.J. & rely upon it K's[12] vote on the old Bank will keep him off. An old man from NC told me to day that in a conversation with Col B–ton about the vice-pres., he told the Col. that K.[13] would not do because of *that vote.* The Col replied, "Oh! that made no difference, we all were for it in 1816." These & similar occurrences incline me to fear that he is not for you. I board with Senator Atchison & Hughes[14] & I think they are both inclined to favor you but do not like to commit themselves until more is known of matters at home.

I am fearful that the feelings of Brown & Jones towards Van[15] will do us little good at home next summer unless they can be rectified in some way. They both think him unavailable & talk so, & talk occasionally of Cass & both seem leaning a little toward Calhoun, but principally on this Texas question. Tyler moved upon the subject hoping to gain for himself & become prominant whilst the Calhoun men think, whatever influence it may have will redound to his benefit, &

hence great efforts are making to have the question presented in such an aspect as to have an influence in the approaching election and under the hope, that Van Buren men enough here will take ground agt. it to justify them in charging upon Van hostility to their favorite measure, just as they do upon abolition & the Tariff. Brown is overzealous upon that subject and has persuaded himself *that now or never is the time.* The leaders of Calhoun here show a bad spirit in every thing. Belser took grounds to day agt. the MC's representing the general ticket states[16] & we think he will go to the whigs & shall not be surprised nor regret if he should be followed by Holmes, Jno. Campbell & Beardsley.[17]

I think Gilmer will go into the War office & shall not be surprised if the navy should be offered to Genl. Saunders.[18] Wise will be confirmed for Rio. We took up yesterday the contested elections of the General ticket States, & will end the debate next Tuesday or Wednesday unless the debate is over which seems likely from indications to day. We have agreed to give it six days to keep them from quarrelling about stopping debate & to sit until 5 O'clock every day.

The weather has become mild & damp & it is with much difficulty I have kept up the last two days. My wife & child keep very well.[19]

C. JOHNSON

ALS. DLC–JKP. Probably addressed to Columbia; marked *"private."* Published in *THQ,* XII, pp. 162–63.
1. See Polk to Cave Johnson, January 21, 1844.
2. A shrewd businessman, John C. Rives shared the ownership of the Washington *Globe* with Francis P. Blair from 1833 until 1845. Rives reported congressional debates in the *Congressional Globe* for the period 1833 to 1864.
3. William R. King and Richard M. Johnson.
4. Reuben Chapman, a Democratic congressman from Alabama, served in the U.S. House from 1835 until his election as governor of that state in 1847.
5. Richard M. Johnson.
6. In his letter to Johnson, written from Philadelphia and dated February 2, 1844, Henry Horn praised Polk and promised to promote him for the vice-presidency. He indicated that Polk's support in the area surpassed that of William R. King and Richard M. Johnson.
7. Reference is to the Virginia State Democratic Convention.
8. Thomas Ritchie.
9. See Aaron V. Brown to Polk, February 2, 1844.
10. In a letter to the editor of the Washington *Globe,* dated January 28, 1844, and published in that paper on February 5, 1844, Richard M. Johnson reviewed his political prospects. Emphasizing his devotion to the Democratic party and to its principles, Johnson announced that he would accept the party's presidential or vice-presidential nomination or a "position among the rank

and file, if such be the pleasure of the convention, without a murmur."

11. A pioneer in the glass industry and president of the Middlesex Bank, William Parmenter served in the Massachusetts House in 1829, the Massachusetts Senate in 1836, and the U.S. House, 1837–45; he held the post of naval officer for the port of Boston from 1845 until 1849.

12. William R. King.

13. Thomas Hart Benton and William R. King.

14. David R. Atchison and James M. Hughes. A lawyer and farmer, Atchison served in the Missouri House prior to his appointment in 1843 to the U.S. Senate upon the death of Lewis F. Linn; Atchison subsequently won election to Linn's seat and served two terms, 1843–55. Hughes, a lawyer and businessman in Liberty, Mo., served one term, 1843–45, as a Democrat in the U.S. House.

15. Aaron V. Brown, George W. Jones, and Martin Van Buren.

16. A Montgomery lawyer, James E. Belser served a single term as a Democrat in the U.S. House, 1843–45; he subsequently joined the Whig ranks and supported Zachary Taylor for president in 1848. References here and below are to House debates over congressional elections in Georgia, Mississippi, Missouri, and New Hampshire. Those states chose their representatives in the U.S. House by state-wide or "general" elections rather than by district-level balloting, which had been mandated by the reapportionment act of June 25, 1842. Belser argued that Congress had the constitutional power to require district elections and that members from those states, not having been elected in accordance with the law, were not entitled to their seats.

17. Isaac E. Holmes, John Campbell, and Samuel Beardsley. A Charleston lawyer, Holmes served several terms in the South Carolina House, 1826–33, before winning election as a Democrat to the U.S. House, where he served from 1839 until 1851. A South Carolina nullifier, Campbell served five terms in the U.S. House, 1829–31 and 1837–45.

18. Thomas W. Gilmer and Romulus M. Saunders. A lawyer active in North Carolina politics since 1815, Saunders lost his bid for the governorship in 1840; having previously served three terms in the U.S. House, 1821–27, he returned to that body and served two more terms, 1841–45.

19. Cave and Elizabeth Dortch Brunson Johnson had two young sons, James Hickman and Thomas Dickson; Johnson's reference to "child" is not identified further.

## FROM SAMUEL H. LAUGHLIN

My dear Sir,                                 Nashville, Tuesday, Feb. 6, 1844

After a good deal of persuasion, I have now got a small article in type, putting up Mr. Van Buren's name at the head of the Union.[1] I thought to have gotten it in last Saturday, but it failed on that and to-day. There has been no particular objection to [the] thing, but both

Hogan & Heiss doubted about this being the *proper time*. I have now got it agreed to, and will go home tomorrow to arrange for my return here, which will be as soon as possible. The time stipulated is 1st March, but I wish I was ready tomorrow.[2]

Poor Hogan is unable to do anything, and has made me promise to-day to write you that his sole reason for not answering your last letter has been physical inability. He is, poor fellow, almost wholly helpless. I have been to his House to-day to see him to insure the insertion of the short article on hoisting the Van Buren Flag.

I was going to Gen. Jackson's on Saturday to get him to write the letters you mention[3]; but hearing that he was much feebler than usual, I forebore to trespass upon his quiet. I have, however, written him a most respectful letter, begging him to write if it meets his views of propriety at his earliest convenience. I have no doubt of his having written, or, that he will write almost immediately. I have stated my impressions of the unjust necessity, and of the cruel and unjust course of a portion of the southern democracy towards Mr. Van Buren.

There is no new thing here since the adjourn[m]ent.[4] I have taken a room, and the moment I return will lay my hands to the plough with no intention of looking back.

N.B. I wish you would write to Dr. Ramsey, and tell him to write or for himself and the Knoxville Committee[5] to write to me at McMinnville, pressing me to consent to take Editorial charge of "Star Spangled Banner" and Union during the Canvass, and to assure me that I can well do it, thus temporarily, without *removing to Nashville or changing my residence.* I find that it will behoove me to be well fortified on this point.

I have written too[6] of my most pressing and circumstantial letters to Gen. Howard of Indiana, and Henry Horn of Philad.[7]

For the next fortnight, address me at McMinnville.

S. H. LAUGHLIN

[P.S.] On going to the Post office to put this letter in the mail, in company with James H. Thomas, I met Mr. Humphrys[8] and Gen. Armstrong, and learn that Eastman, Crozer[9] and some other one of the Knoxville Committee have written to Mr. Nicholson (he got the letter last night) that they have chosen him at Knoxville as the Candidate for the state at large, or one of them.[10] N. showed the letter to Armstrong. Now, how comes this? The resolution conferring the appointing power on the Committee requires their *joint action.* No one committee can appoint. This is the work of Crozier, who, you know, moved for Cass in the Dem. Association at Knoxville. I will ask Humphrys to write to Reynolds.[11] I told Nicholson on the day of our adjournmt, that I understood the Committees were in correspondence on the subject of the two candidates for the state at large. I said not a word, however, of our preference. Powell, Kenney, Torbett[12] &c all wish for Turney for one.

Have letters written to [the] District.[13] I will write to Huntsman by to-night's mail, and Armstrong, Cheatham and Humphrys must regulate the Committee here.[14] I have told Armstrong & Humphrys that they *must* see to it as I *must* go home. S. H. LAUGHLIN

ALS. DLC–JKP. Addressed to Columbia and marked "Private." Polk's AE on the cover states that he answered this letter on February 10, 1844; Polk's reply has not been found.

1. On February 8, 1844, the *Nashville Union* placed Martin Van Buren's name at the head of its editorial column and in a brief notice endorsed the former president for a second term, subject to his being nominated by the Democratic National Convention.

2. Laughlin did not become editor of the *Nashville Union* and of the Nashville *Star Spangled Banner* until March 12, 1844.

3. See Polk to Laughlin, January 20, 1844.

4. Reference is to the adjournment of the Tennessee General Assembly on January 31, 1844.

5. Reference is to the Knoxville Democratic Central Committee; following previous campaign organizational patterns, the state central committee divided itself into three branches, one for each of the state's grand divisions, and centered its operations in Knoxville, Nashville, and Jackson. See J. G. M. Ramsey to Polk, January 4, 1844.

6. Misspelling of the word "two."

7. See Polk to Laughlin, January 20, 1844.

8. West H. Humphreys.

9. Arthur R. Crozier.

10. Reference is to the appointment of two "at-large" delegates to the Democratic National Convention scheduled for May in Baltimore, Md.

11. Robert B. Reynolds, a lawyer and key member of the Knoxville Democratic Central Committee, served as attorney general for Tennessee's Second Judicial District from 1839 until 1845.

12. Robert W. Powell, Daniel Kenney, and Granville C. Torbett. A native of Maryland, Powell practiced law in Elizabethton and represented the counties of Carter, Johnson, Sullivan, and Washington in the Tennessee Senate for two terms, 1841–45. Torbett, a Monroe County lawyer, served one term in the Tennessee House, 1841–43, and sat two terms in the Tennessee Senate, 1843–47; in 1852 he moved to Nashville where he practice law and in association with E. G. Eastman published the *Nashville American*.

13. Reference is to the Western District of Tennessee.

14. Reference is to the Nashville Democratic Central Committee.

TO SILAS WRIGHT, JR.

My Dear Sir:                                   Columbia Tenn. Feby. 9th 1844

I had the pleasure to receive your letter of the 27th ultimo,[1] two days ago. I had observed the embarrassment in which our party in Congress were involved in reference to the 21st Rule and the tariff, and deeply regretted it.[2] The abolition agitation is now as it has ever been, political in its object and design, and being so, the Southern portion of the party as well as the Northern, might well have compromised upon the *Atherton rule,* as proposed in caucus by my friend *Johnson.*[3] The refusal to accept that proposition manifests I fear a willingness, if not a deliberate purpose, to keep up the agitation in Congress, with a view to its effect upon the approaching Presidential election. This and the usual question of the tariff will unquestionably be used by our opponents, and [by] the impracticable and secretly dissafected portion of our own party, more with a view to control the result in that election than to effect a satisfactory adjustment of either. The opposing extremes, prompted by no other or higher motives, will, it is to be feared, act their respective parts in the present Congress. This course of party warfare both you and I have witnessed in former times. It is much to be regretted that there is a necessity for a revision and reduction of the tariff at the present Session, but it is unavoidable and indispensible. It is demanded, not only in reference to the revenue, but to the interests of the Southern and planting states, which are so prejudicially affected by the present exorbitant rates of duty. I hope, My Dear Sir, that the party may have a safe deliverance from these perplexing questions before your adjournment. The course of my old Congressional acquaintance *Mr Beardsley,*[4] does not surprise me. It is what I have always suspected of him, and is in full keeping with the part he acted when I was with him in Congress. That he was in heart and feeling with Tallmadge, Rives & Co.[5] when they left the party a few years ago, I never doubted. It would be much better to have such men openly in the ranks of our opponents. They could do less harm. *Mr Beardsley's* relations to *Mr Van-Buren* and the party in New York as you describe them are precisely those of *Mr Nicholson* to myself and the party in this state. The latter has given us much trouble, and yet claims to be [one] of us, and occasionally, when he calculates his personal advancement is to be promoted by it, becomes zealous. It was the capital error of my public life, as his subsequent course has proved, when I appointed him to the Senate to fill the vacancy occasioned by the death of our lamented friend *Mr Grundy.*[6] Just before the meeting of our state convention in November he set to work *secretly* and without publickly committing himself, to get up a *Cass party* in the state. I was absent at the time in the state of Mississippi. To this movement is mainly to be attributed the course which was pursued by the convention, as in my former letter[7] I explained to you. Recently I understand he is making earnest professions of a willingness to support Mr Van-Buren if he is the nominee & I suspect is seeking to worm himself into a place on the Electoral ticket. Like Mr B.[8] he possesses respectable talents, but is governed in his course solely by his view of his own personal interest. I think it proper that *you* should understand his true position, as I learn he is in correspondence with some of our friends at Washington.

I regret extremely to see the reluctance with which a small portion of the leading men of the Southern wing of our party seem disposed to yield to the clear and undoubted indications of the public sentiment of the party, in favour of *Mr Van-Buren.* Seeing however, as they must see, that they cannot without the most glaring inconsistency, as well as abandonment of all principle, coalesce with the Federalists against whom they have been so recently fighting, I hope they may yet come into his support. I agree with you that we are to have a fierce and most excited contest in the Union, but I have confidence of success. Some of our friends at a distance seem to have yielded Tennessee up to the enemy. This I re-assure you need not be. It is true that upon no part of the ground will the fight probably be harder, or the field bloodier but I am as confident as I can be of any future event that, if harmony shall prevail, in the General Convention at Baltimore, and we shall have an acceptable ticket,[9] that we will carry the state. Such is the opinion of our whole party in the state. I have never known a more fixed and resolute purpose, than now prevails with the Democracy here to fight the battle of principle once again. The majority against us at the last state election was less than 4,000 out of a poll of more than 112,000 votes and all here know that local causes & state questions, which can have no bearing upon the Presidential contest, weakened us more than that majority. I sincerely regret with you, the appearance in the Globe of the recent communications to which you allude, on the subject of the V.P.[10] It is no time now for controversy among friends. All our energies should be directed against the common enemy. The personal claims of *men* of our own party, when they come in conflict, are subordinate to the success of the party, and should be so regarded by all. Least of all should there be any acrimonious feeling indulged in among friends. In reference to the communications alluded to, I of course could have had no agency, and at this distance knew nothing of them, until they appeared in the Globe. I have been for some years past the object of vituperative and calumnious attack from the Federal press in this part of the Union, but have never before been assailed by a professed member of my own party in so cruel, unjust and ungenerous a manner. For myself I attribute it, I have no doubt to the proper cause, to the over-zeal and indiscretion of at most but *a few* individuals, and care therefore nothing about it. The Federal press here have seized upon the circumstances to make the most of it, and many of my friends were at the moment much excited. I have received since, many letters from *without* as well as from *within* the state in reference to it, complaining of the injustice done me & expressing surprise at the articles in the Globe, to all of which I have replied satisfying them as far as I could that it was not the act of any considerable portion of the party, and that so far as their insertion in the Globe was concerned, the columns of that paper were I presumed open to all respectful communications, from any member of the party, whatever the particular views of the writer might be. My friends were perhaps more sensitive than they would have been from the fact, that they had observed that no notice had been taken by the Globe of the numerous expressions of the popular opinion of the party in which my name had been mentioned in the primary meetings of the people which have taken place within the last four months in *Illinois, Missouri, Arkansas, Louisiana, Mississippi, Alabama,* this and other Western states; whereas special notice seemed to have been taken of similar expressions of opinion in reference to others who have been mentioned for the V.P. Of this I cared nothing, & have not certainly complained and only now mention it because I desire to communicate to you *frankly,* the views which many of my friends had taken upon the subject. My great desire is for the success of the party, and whatever nomination may be deemed most [useful] to promote that object, I desire to be made. My name was brought before the country by my friends four years ago, and after the failure of the Baltimore convention to make any nomination, in order to preserve the harmony of the party I voluntarily withdrew it, and gave to another my support. It has again been brought before the country by my friends without any agency of mine in reference to the nomination to be made at Baltimore in May next, and will not be withdrawn. My friends would not consent to its withdrawal, if I desired it. It will be presented by them to the convention and I need scarcely say to you that I will cheerfully acquiesce in whatever nomination may be there made. Whoever may be nominated I will as earnestly and zealously labour in our cause as I have heretofore done. My desire is, that upon full consultation of the party, some one may be nominated on the ticket with *Mr Van-Buren,* who will bring most strength to it; and that as the party fell with *Mr Van-Buren,* they may now rise with him and triumph in his person. The victory will be vastly greater to elect him, than it would be to succeed with any other man in the nation. It is due to him as well as to our cause, that nothing shall be permitted to cause to weaken him, or to embarrass us in the coming contest.

I am aware that it is perhaps, not in good taste, to say so much in reference to matters connected with myself. Having however in your letter opened the subject by alluding to the articles in the *Globe,* I could not, having regard to that frankness and freedom from all reserve, which was due to you, say less. There are but few men living to whom I would express myself with equal freedom. I know however that what I have said will be *safe* in your hands. I shall be much pleased My Dear Sir, to hear from you as your leisure may permit, during your session.

JAMES K. POLK

ALS, draft. DLC–JKP. Addressed to Washington City and marked *"Confidential"* and *"Copy."* Polk's AE on the cover states, "This copy, instead of the original, was sent to the P. Office, by mistake & was afterwards taken out Feby. 10th 1844."
1. Letter not found.
2. See Cave Johnson to Polk, January 13, 21, and 31, 1844.
3. See Cave Johnson to Polk, January 7, 1844.
4. See Cave Johnson to Polk, January 13 and 31, 1844.
5. Nathaniel P. Tallmadge and William C. Rives. Tallmadge served as a U.S. senator from New York from March 4, 1833, to June 17, 1844, when he resigned to become governor of the Wisconsin Territory. Rives broke with regular Democrats over the Sub-Treasury plan, for several years led Virginia's soft-money or conservative Democrats, and eventually joined the Whig party; Tallmadge also moved into the Whig party over the issue of creating a new national bank.
6. Mentor for Polk's legal training and early political career, Felix Grundy served as chief justice of Kentucky's Supreme Court prior to moving to Nashville in 1807. He won election as a War Democrat to two terms in the U.S. House, 1811–14; sat in the Tennessee House for two terms, 1815–19; and served in the U.S. Senate from 1829 until 1838, when he resigned to become U.S. attorney general. Grundy returned in 1839 to the U.S. Senate and served until his death in December of 1840.
7. Polk's letter not found.
8. Samuel Beardsley.
9. At this place in the text Polk cancelled the words, "for the second as well as the first office."

10. See Cave Johnson to Polk, January 13, 21, and 31, 1844; Polk to Johnson, January 21, 1844; and Aaron V. Brown to Polk, January 22, 1844.

## FROM JOHN P. HEISS

Union Office

Dear Sir                                    [Nashville, Tenn.] Feby 14, 1844

I am extremely anxious that the contemplated [change] in the Editorial department of the Union[1] should take place as soon as possible, for this reason: I want the specimen No. of "The Star Spangled Banner" to go out under the superintendance and in the name of Laughlin at a very early day. Hogan has been confined to his room for ten days and has not done anything during that time for the paper.[2] I think it important that Laughlin should take charge early not only for the benefit of the "Union" but of the party.

I percieve by the McMinnville Gazette[3] that he intends remaining in Warren until after the 22d and my object in writing to you is that you will request him and at the same time urge him to assume the Editorial duties of the "Union" as soon as he conveniently can.

I recieved a letter from Harris[4] a few days back. He expects to be home in April.

JOHN P. HEISS

ALS. DLC–JKP. Addressed to Columbia. Polk's AE on the cover states that he answered this letter on February 22, 1844.
1. See Samuel H. Laughlin to Polk, February 6, 1844.
2. Thomas W. Hogan suffered from tuberculosis.
3. A Democratic newspaper in Warren County, the McMinnville *Central Gazette* was edited by John W. Ford from 1835 until 1842. In 1844 Leonidas N. Ford was editor of the paper.
4. A staunch New England Democrat, J. George Harris had been associated with the New London *Political Observer* (Conn.), the *New Bedford Daily Gazette* (Mass.), the Boston *Bay State Democrat,* and the Boston *Morning Post* before assuming the editorship of the *Nashville Union* on February 1, 1839. In March 1843, Harris received a commission from Secretary of State Daniel Webster to be a commercial agent of the United States, with special regard for American tobacco sales in Europe.

## TO THOMAS W. HOGAN AND JOHN P. HEISS

Gentlemen:                                    Lawrenceburg Feby. 18th 1844

Some of the friends of Hon. A. V. Brown are disposed to complain that his two speeches on the *Jackson fine* and *abolition questions,* have not been republished in the Union.[1] I myself thought they had been published, though I may be mistaken. If they have not been I hope you will give them an insertion in your paper as early as practicable. *Brown* is a prominent member of our party and may feel *wounded* (and I have an intimation that he probably does so) at the failure to republish what he says in Congress, in the Tennessee Democratic papers, and especially in the Union. If you have omitted it, in this instance, I have no doubt it has been accidental.

I am here attending Court, but expect to visit Nashville in about a week from this time.

JAMES K. POLK

P.S. There being a Whig Post master here[2] & my hand-writing being known as well as my face, I will send this, under cover to Genl. Armstrong. J.K.P.

ALS. T–JPH. Probably addressed to Nashville and marked *"Private."* Published in *THM,* II, pp. 141–42.
1. See Aaron V. Brown to Polk, February 2, 1844.
2. Stephen Busby was appointed postmaster at Lawrenceburg on August 30, 1839.


## FROM WILLIAM TYACK[1]

Dear Sir                                     New York Febry 19th 1844

You have no doubt long ere this Expected some information from me in regard to the very important trust committed to my charge. On my arrival at Louisville I called upon the Democratick Editor[2] & gave him all the information of the prospects below. He at first was strongly in favour of Col Johnson as the Vice, but finally admitted that Governor Polk was the strongest and safest man we could put with Mr Van Buren, and said he would feel around carefully and raise his name as soon as possible—for that state, Kentucky, will not be saved at any rate. I called upon the editor at Lexington,[3] and after consulting some time he came to the same conclusion that Gov Polk might bring a much greater suport to Mr Van Buren than Col Johnson. But as yet he dare not hoist the Polk Flag. But I think if Col Johnson resided in any other state he would not hesitate A Moment.

I spent one Night with the old soldier Col. Johnson. He recvd. me with Kindness. He spent an hour with me, from 8 untill 9 Evening. His time he says is so much occupied in his correspondence. He spends the days on his Plantation & the Evenings from 8 untill 12 or so he is engaged in replying to his numerous correspondence. Therefore he retired to his office and would not be seen untill 9 in the Morning. He says he is A Candidate for the Presidency, Vice P. or nothing at all. He promised to be satisfied with whatever the People do with or for him, and will find no fault if he gets Nothing. I regret extremely to find his Plantation Buildings do all appear to have been so much Neglected. He says he has been Engaged in Publicke Business for forty years which is the cause of this apparent Neglect to his Estate. I called upon Moses Dawson Esq. Cincinnati and Communicated my views. He fully agreed with me and said he should use all his Exertions to Bring it about, first at the Wards and then at A Mass Meeting. No other Man, as Vice President.

We yesterday recvd the glorious News that Congress has at last thrown off its shamefull Coverings and rendered Justice to the greatest and Best of men, *Andrew Jackson.*[4] I believe every Member of Both Houses and Both Parties were gratified at the result. Great enthusiasm prevails among not only Democrats but among all Classes. Major Davezac,[5] a worthy member of our Legislature from the City, An ardent friend of Genl. Jackson & A Companion in Arms, has done himself as also the Legislature Much Honor in the cause he has taken up of his friend *Genl. Jackson.* He thinks soon of visiting that good man next season. In all places and at all times are the People inquiring of me how is that good old man *Genl. Jackson.* And when Informed of his feebleness, his aparent declining state of Health, their Eyes will glisten with tears, and their Hearts swell with grief. But again when Informed of the pious state of his mind, his Hope and Confidence in his Redeemer, the Calmness & Serenity of his aged Brow, his Constant watch for the call to give up his Breath, then will their tears flow with Joy and lament to part with him.

I regret the result of the Baltimore Election,[6] although there was no reason to hope or Expect a different result. They are so Divided by local Difficulties that they cannot succeed. But that is nothing. Everything works well around us. The Federalists always have their Victories first, and we often gain it on the same ground, and in the same Battle afterwards, when truth takes Command. It will be extremely Difficult for me to correspond with all those Highly Respectable gentlemen with whom I had the Honor of an Introduction During my Visit at Nashville. And I must ask you my Dear sir[7] to Express to them my warmest thanks for the very Kind and friendly attention which they rendered me during my stay.

And Beg of them as also yourself to accept of my sincere regard for the future Prosperity and Happiness of *yourselves, Families,* and *Friends.* I shall write the Venerable Patriot[8] in A few Days, at the Hermitage. And sir should you think there is anything Contained in this Letter that in the least would be pleasing to him, you will please to send it to him, and after reading it, use it as you think proper. You will please to forward it to Ex-Governor Polk as early as Convenient, and with as little Delay as you may think Necessary.

WILLIAM TYACK

ALS. DLC–JKP. Addressed jointly to Polk and Robert Armstrong in Nashville. Polk's AE on the cover states that the letter was "Handed to J.K.P. by Genl. Armstrong," and answered by Polk on March 1, 1844; Polk's reply has not been found.

1. William Tyack, associated with the "Hunker" faction of the New York Democracy, resigned his post as master warden for the Port of New York to campaign for Polk in 1844; he served as president of the Polk and Dallas Association of New York City and spoke at the Democratic mass meeting in Nashville of August 15, 1844.

2. Reference probably is to John H. Harney, editor of the *Louisville Democrat* from 1844 to 1868; Harney formerly had served as president of Louisville College.

3. Reference is to Daniel Bradford, editor of the Lexington *Kentucky Gazette.*

4. See Aaron V. Brown to Polk, February 2, 1844.

5. Auguste D'Avezac, a Creole emigrant from Santo Domingo and brother-in-law of Edward Livingston, served as Andrew Jackson's aide-de-camp during the War of 1812; interrupting a successful legal practice in New Orleans, D'Avezac served consular and ministerial appointments to the Netherlands and to the Kingdom of Two Sicilies during the 1830's; in 1839 he settled in New York City; and in 1843 he won election to the New York legislature. D'Avezac returned to the Netherlands as chargé d'affaires for five years, 1845–50.

6. Congressional elections under Maryland's new system of district voting were held on February 14, 1844; winning in every district, the Whig party also carried Baltimore County under the banner of Henry Clay and protective tariffs. Democratic candidates endorsed Martin Van Buren for the presidential nomination and supported free trade policies.

7. Here Tyack speaks to Robert Armstrong, through whom this letter was directed to Polk. Tyack headed his letter with the following inside address, "To The Honble James K. Polk"; the author closed his letter with a second inside address, "To Genl. R. Armstrong, Post Master, for His Excellency James K. Polk, Ex-Governor, State Tennessee, Columbia."

8. Andrew Jackson.

## TO JOHN P. HEISS

My Dear Sir:                              Columbia Feby. 22nd 1844

On my return home from Lawrence Court on yesterday I received your letter of the 14th Instant.[1] I will write a pressing letter to

*Laughlin* to night, urging him, to take charge of the Editorial Department of the Union at the earliest practicable day. He wrote me two weeks ago, that he would certainly do so on the 1st of March.[2] The specimen No. of the "Star-Spangled Banner" should [be] an able paper, and his first attention should be given to the preparation of matter for it. I am sorry to learn that our good friend *Hogan's* hea[l]th continues so bad.

I wrote you from Lawrenceburg[3] suggesting the propriety of your publishing *A. V. Brown's* speeches on *abolition* and the *Jackson fine* in the Union. *Brown* himself has some feeling because it has not been done sooner. Insert them with suitable Editorials calling attention to them. I will be at Nashville next week.

JAMES K. POLK

ALS. T–JPH. Addressed to Nashville and marked *"Private."* Published in *THM,* II, p. 142.
1. See Polk to Samuel H. Laughlin, February 22, 1844.
2. See Laughlin to Polk, February 6, 1844.
3. See Polk to Heiss, February 18, 1844.

## TO SAMUEL H. LAUGHLIN

My Dear Sir:                          Columbia Feby. 22nd 1844
I returned from Lawrenceburg Court on yesterday. The earliest practicable day on which you can take charge of the Editorial Department of the *Union* the better. Our good friend *Hogan* continues sick, and I learn has been confined to his room for the last ten days.[1] The cause is suffering much for the want of Editorial talent in the paper. It is time too, that the specimen No. of the *"Star-Spangled Banner"* was out. I will be in Nashville on tuesday and wednesday next, and hope to meet you there.

My latest accounts make it certain that the only contest for V.P. will be with *Col. R.M.J.*[2] My friends at Washington are satisfied that they can defeat him, in the convention.

JAMES K. POLK

ALS. DLC–JKP. Addressed to McMinnville and marked *"Private."*
1. See John P. Heiss to Polk, February 14, 1844.
2. Richard M. Johnson.

## FROM AARON V. BROWN

Dear Sir                                               Washington Feby 25th 1844

Not a single incident has occured worthy of communication. Every thing is profoundly still here. Not a word saying about the Vice Presidency amongst the members of Congress. In the meantime Johnson and myself are sending off "a Tennessean" into the different states to the Delegates & others which we suppose is the best [that] can be done.[1] Our fate is wrapped up in the next few weeks. If the negro question[2] is settled wrong (& we are now setling it) & if nothing can be done with the Tariff We are a lost & doomed party. If these however can be adjusted *pretty well* we may make a good fight. We have no enthusiam amongst us—if we do not *quarrel* we do not *love* one another. Your good friend Cullum[3] was with me this afternoon & thinks from appearances, you ought not to court any alliance with the Van Buren ticket, but he is truly your friend & so is Andrew Johnson & Jones. They all seem but little taken with Benton on account of his supersilious & haughty bearing & his supposed jealousy of you. You must not misconstrue my silence. Since the World began no man ever performed more labor than I am doing. For instance during the past Week I have been on committee from 11 to 12 every day & from candle lighting to 11 OCk every night. Besides I have a vast deal of business in the departments, more from Mississippi than Tennessee. Add to this some letter writing & franking speeches which had you know previously to be written out & you can have some idea of my engagements. But be assured that we are neglecting no matter here in which you are interested nor failing to say & do any thing which we suppose to be serviceable so you must pardon a want of that frequency of letters which you might otherwise have expected. I see that my only "confidential" has been treated as I suppose it deserved with silent contempt.[4]

You & Thomas & the Maj.[5] must not neglect my speeches. I could do no better for although I have begd for one none of you have furnished me with a list of names.[6] Col. Dew writes that old Mr Voorhies complains of me for Langtry's appointment.[7] This is unjust. I acted in good faith & did all I could in justice to L. to appoint Voorhies[8] but I have kept all the letters & bid defiance to imputations. Tell Wm. H. to write to me on that & other subjects.

                                                        A. V. BROWN

ALS. DLC–JKP. Addressed to Columbia. Polk's AE on the cover states that he answered this letter on March 5, 1844; Polk's reply has not been found.

1. See Polk to Cave Johnson, January 21, 1844.
2. Reference is to the adoption of the 21st rule or "gag resolution," which prevented official notice of abolition petitions to the U.S. House of Representatives.
3. Alvin Cullom.
4. See Brown to Polk, January 22, 1844.
5. William H. Polk.
6. On February 23, 1844, Brown stated that he had sent 200 franked documents to Polk, William H. Polk, and Jonas E. Thomas for distribution in Maury County. ALS. DLC–JKP. Brown addressed his letter jointly to Polk and William H. Polk. A successful lawyer and farmer, Thomas represented Maury County in the Tennessee House, 1835–41, and sat for Maury and Giles counties in the Tennessee Senate, 1845–47.
7. John H. Dew, William Voorhies, and Hillary Langtry. A Wilson County lawyer, Dew served as a Democrat in the Tennessee House, 1831–35; he moved to Columbia in 1836 and represented Maury County for a single term in the House, 1841–43. Voorhies, one of the early settlers in Maury County, was a saddler by trade. A Columbia merchant and bank director, Langtry assumed the postmastership on January 9, 1844, and served in that post until June 1845.
8. William Van Voorhies, son of William Voorhies, applied for the Columbia postmastership in 1843; became William H. Polk's law partner in 1844; went to California early in 1849 as a special U.S. postal agent; and in 1850 won election as California's first secretary of state.

## FROM CAVE JOHNSON

Dear Sir, Washington Feby 25th 1844

I recd two letters[1] from you since I have written & if I had any thing worthy of troubling you with I should have written earlier. We are progressing rather badly here. Indeed we are in great confusion & I see no way of getting out of it. The interminable abolition has been up all day, yesterday, & we are now father[2] than ever from agreeing. The rule *must go* & whether we can get any other in its place is very uncertain.[3] The Whigs found 14 of our men sick & 5 of theirs, & *moved* the previous question. Our friends moved to lay the whole subject on the table, which would have left us with the *rules* of the *last* Congress as adopted at the Commencement including the 21st Rule. After an hour or two calling the House, we took a vote and was beaten by a majority near 20. We then refused to second the previous question, & the question then came up on Drumgooles amendments, changing *nearly all the rules* & adopting the practice of the Senate on abolition petitions, upon which a debate arose.[4] Believing there was no chance of getting Drumgooles I moved the adoption of the rules of

the last Congress & Atherton's resolution in the place of the 21st Rule
& so the matter now stands.[5]  My amendment will not be voted for by
most of the South because they wish to get Drumgooles amendment;
nor will the Whigs because they wish to get clear of the hour rule
& the power of the majority to take a Bill out of Committee & to go
into Committee. So it will be rejected. Drumgooles will be rejected &
so we shall be without any rule. This state of things produces great
confusion. The Southern Whigs generally voted *agt. laying on the table*
as did the Maryland members whose aid we expected & delayed action
until this time to obtain.[6]  The question will not again come up until
tuesday & I hope to settle our difficulty.

If Drumgooles proposition was rejected mine would pass because
the Southern democrats would consider it generally as the next best,
but the vote on mine must be first taken, being an Amendment to
the Amendment. Drumgoole has taken the stand & will not let his
precede mine, which we could do by changing positions & so we stand.
We can never get a vote except under the previous question, so that if
I withdraw, mine can never come in & his will be rejected & we shall
be left without a rule, & so we adjourned.  I think much of all this
difficulty grows up out of a secret wish to supersede Van Buren in the
Convention in Baltimore. Many from the South hope, if the 21st rule
is rejected it will produce so much discontent at the South (with the
Tariff) that all the South will unite agt. him on *account of the course
of his friends*—then Calhoun may have a chance or Cass or old Dick.[7]
There is a secret movement going on *here* & *elsewhere* to effect that
object at the Convention and I suspect an effort is making to start
the ball in Tennessee & Indiana, & this is to be done by satisfying
the Convention that *Van has no chance*. Woodbury is talked of in
Pennsylvania on old Dicks ticket and an effort is making there to
effect that object. You & Col King are occasionally talked of on Cass'
ticket. These things are talked of to produce discontent & to incite
the impression that Van has no chance, but you will find 9 out [of] 10
for him in the Convention. I have scattered Turneys letter throughout
New England & Pennsylvania & Missouri & some in Louisiana, &
Brown took the directories & has sent to all the old members who
knew you here as far as we could learn. We have had 1200 pamphlets
struck & will continue to distribute so as to put them in the hands of
the delegates.

I had occasion to write Ritchie & send him a pamphlet as I did to
most of the Democratic printers north. He will take no part for the
Vice-presidency because of the difficulties for the first office. He is
for Stephenson[8] but neither he or Stephenson expects it.  Burke &

his paper in N.H. have come out for King & Norris is probably with him.[9] Redding[10] & his brother's paper[11] have come out for you & I think Hale[12] will probably go with him. I sent 50 of the letters to Henry Horn. I have not time to write as many letters or take as much pains as I could wish. I have a great deal to do on my Indian Committee as well as much to do in the House and am so wearied by the time I get to my room that I am unfit for any thing. Had I been aware of the state of things here I would not have come back. McKay is sick half his time, Drumgoole not reliable as a leader & New York would be better unrepresented, so that we are litterally without leaders, no concert about any thing, and judging from what we are likely to do, it would have been better never to have come here. The Tariff Bill is ready to report & only delaying for some Treasury statistics. McDuffie[13] & most of the Southern members agree to it. Rhett, & Lewis & Belser & I fear Woodbury, Burke & a few others will stand out agt. it, but I think we can pass it in the House. You are not perhaps aware that Woodbury & a few followers are considered rather more identified with Calhoun than Van Buren; yet they act with us very well. Gov Van Ness[14] is here beging the Mexican Mission, & so is Genl Anderson, who is likely to be successful. Carrol[15] has no chance. Wise, Minister plenipo. to Rio Janeiro—Profit & Watterson[16] both there! None to France, no Judge of the Supreme Court. Genl Howard here (a Calhoun man). Packenham & Almonte figured largely at the birth night ball, and two monkeys Capt. Bertrand & Barney (son of Commodore).[17]

C. JOHNSON

N.B. S.W.[18] told me he recd a letter from you in good spirits but complained of the course of the Globe. I am *now thoroughly identified with Northern democrats* & may be of *some service to you.*

ALS. DLC–JKP. Addressed to Columbia. Published in *THQ*, XII, pp. 164–65.

1. Letters not found.
2. Misspelling of the word "farther."
3. On February 24, 1844, the U.S. House discussed the majority report of the Select Committee to Revise the Rules and Orders of the House. The committee recommended 102 rules to govern the operations of the House, but did not propose a rule to cover the reception of abolition petitions. That omission sparked a heated debate and the procedural maneuvers described by Johnson. For the text of the majority report dated January 2, 1844, and dissenting minority reports, see House Report No. 3, 28 Congress, 1 Session.
4. Dromgoole's amendments included a rule that prohibited the reception of abolition petitions in any manner.

5. Johnson's amendment provided that abolition petitions be received and tabled without debate.

6. Maryland's congressional elections were not held until February 14, 1844, due to a delay in districting the state by the legislature.

7. John C. Calhoun, Lewis Cass, and Richard M. Johnson.

8. Andrew Stevenson.

9. Edmund Burke, William R. King, and Moses Norris, Jr. Burke, a lawyer and journalist, edited the Newport *New Hampshire Argus and Spectator* until his election to Congress in 1839; he served three terms in the U.S. House, but did not seek reelection in 1844. He was appointed commissioner of patents by Polk and served in that post from 1846 until 1850. A New Hampshire lawyer, Norris represented that state in the U.S. House as a Democrat from 1843 until 1847 and in the U.S. Senate from 1849 until 1855.

10. John R. Reding.

11. Not identified further.

12. A lawyer from New Hampshire, John P. Hale sat in the New Hampshire House prior to his service as a Democrat in the U.S. House, 1843–45. He served several terms in the U.S. Senate, 1847–53 and 1855–65, and ran for president as the nominee of the Free Soil party in 1852. Appointed minister to Spain in 1865, he held that post until 1869.

13. George McDuffie, a lawyer, won election to seven terms in the U.S. House, 1821–34; served as governor of South Carolina, 1834–36; and went to the U.S. Senate for parts of two terms, 1842–46.

14. Born in Kinderhook, N.Y., Cornelius P. Van Ness moved to Vermont where he served in the lower house of the legislature, 1818–20, and presided as chief justice over the State Supreme Court, 1821–22, prior to his tenure as governor, 1823–26. He served as minister to Spain during the Jackson administration and as collector of the Port of New York, 1844–45.

15. Reference probably is to William Carroll, an elder statesman of the Tennessee Democracy and state governor for six terms, 1821–27 and 1829–35; Carroll remained active in party affairs until his sudden illness and death on March 22, 1844.

16. Henry A. Wise, George H. Proffit, and Harvey M. Watterson. A lawyer and founding editor of the Shelbyville *Western Freeman,* Watterson served one term in the Tennessee House, 1835–37, and two terms in the U.S. House, 1839–43. He was sent on a diplomatic mission to the Republic of Buenos Aires by John Tyler in March 1843. On February 16, 1844, Tyler appointed him chargé to the Republic of Buenos Aires; that appointment was rejected by the U.S. Senate on June 5, 1844. Elected to one term in the Tennessee Senate, 1845–47, he presided over that body as its Speaker. From 1847 until 1851, he edited the *Nashville Union;* in 1851 he became editor of the *Washington Union.*

17. Sir Richard Pakenham, Juan N. Almonte, and probably Napoleon Bertrand and John Barney. A career diplomat, Pakenham served as British minister to Mexico, 1835–43, to the United States, 1843–47, and to Portugal, 1851–55. Almonte, a general officer in the Mexican army, served as Mexican

minister to the United States from 1842 until 1845, when he was recalled
following the United States' annexation of Texas. Bertrand was the son of
Henri-Gratien Bertrand, a famous French general and long-time comrade of
Napoleon Bonaparte. Young Bertrand accompanied his father on a celebrated
tour of the United States in the fall of 1843 and remained there during the
following winter. Barney, a member of the U.S. House from Maryland, 1825–
29, was the son of Commodore Joshua Barney. Reference here is to the festive
celebration of George Washington's birthday.

18. Silas Wright, Jr.


## FROM SILAS WRIGHT, JR.

My Dear Sir,                                            Washington 27 Feby. 1844
Your very acceptable letter of the 9th int. came to me several days
since, but the pressing calls upon my time have prevented an earlier
acknowledgement. Even now I have little more than time to say I
have your letter and thank you for its frankness and confidence. It
would truly grieve me to believe that I had done any thing to forfeit
your esteem, or kind feeling, and you certainly needed no apology for
expressing yourself to me as freely and fully as you have done.

Remembering as distinctly as I do the circumstances under which
you left Congress, the considerations which induced you to leave, and
the real reluctance which I know you felt to exchange the positions, I
have watched the hard and unfortunate course to which that change
has subjected you, with an anxiety as deep as has been my admiration at the manly and patriotic manner in which you have met your
formidable duties. I use the term unfortunate, not as so much ap-
plicable to yourself as to our party, as I doubt whether any amount
of success could have given you so firm a hold of the democracy of
your state as the self denying and self sacrificing labours you have
performed leave you in.

I am sorry to be compelled to say that I cannot materially improve
the picture of the state of things here, which I gave you in my last
letter.[1] We do not yet seem to approach a state of organization, or of
action, but, on the contrary, the House appears to me to have become
settled down to an exclusive consideration of the 21st rule,[2] and of each
others abstract propositions as the few friends of Mr. Calhoun and old
Mr. Adams choose to entertain it with. I was surprised to learn that,
yesterday, upon an attempt to consider a resolution, fixing the 30th
May for the adjournment of this present session, upon two separate
efforts, members enough could not be induced to rise to order the ayes
and noes.[3] I mention this, because it will be to you indication of the

temper of the body, very few working men, an unusual number who enjoy themselves with the amusements they can find here, when the House is not in session, and almost none anxious to get through and go home. And this state of feeling exists in the face of the declarations of the Whigs that the longer we stay here the better we shall please them.

It is said that a new hope has sprung up, within the last few days, that there is yet a possibility of defeating the nomination of Mr. V.B.[4] and it is manifest that the efforts at distraction have revived and extended for a short time. In addition to the names of Cass and Johnson, it is said that vigorous efforts are now making here to bring out Stewart[5] again, with new dresses and decorations, as the play actors say. Indeed I do not now hope to see these efforts cease until after our nominations are made in May, and whether they will cease then, or be continued for the benefit of Mr. Clay, time alone will tell. I have felt most strongly the force of a remark made by a correspondent of mine, residing in the Western part of my state, in a letter lately received. He says "our party is more extensive than our principles, and that the complaints of the unpopularity of Mr. V.B. do not proceed from personal objections to him, or from any belief in his unpopularity, but from a dislike to the principles, which are certain to be restored to the administration by his re-election; and hence that any body else is prefered to him and the lesser the politician, the more to be prefered the candidate." I fear there is too much truth in this, and time alone can tell whether these dislikes of our principles are strong enough to induce those harkening them to prefer Mr. Clay to Mr. V.B. I do not believe that will prove to be true to an extent sufficient to defeat us, and one evidence of that I think is the extreme anxiety of these [...][6] brethren to get rid of Mr. Van Buren. If they were ready to take Clay, it appears to me they would be willing to have Mr. V.B. nominated and make that the apology for defection.

It appears to me, however, that these base feelings are making rapid advances in favor of the nomination of Col. J.[7] again for V.P. In Pennsylvania that seems to be peculiarly true, while the evidences of the same character seem to be multiplying in other quarters. What will be the result of all this I confess I cannot foresee.

You will notice by the papers that our folks at Albany are about relieving us from your and my peculiar friend Beardsley. One of the Judges of our Supreme Court died a few days since,[8] and B. has been already appointed to supply the vacancy, and I am, at this moment, informed that he takes his leave of the House on Thursday next.[9] I hope his absence may improve the condition of our friends in our delegation there; and yet, by that singular tenacity which some men have to serve their friends, whether they wish to be served or not, I am told that he intends that the matter of the rule shall be finally disposed of before he leaves.

I am afflicted at what you say of Nicholson. During the short time he was here, his warm manifestation of attachment to you made me like him, and since he left us he has written to me occasionally, and though I have not liked his letters, I have had every confidence in his integrity and political soundness. Such disappointments we constantly meet, and they are to me one of the worst features in a political life.

My time is consumed and I must leave you, having written what is written, under constant interruptions, and carrying on one or two conversations at a time, while writing, and without time to re-read. Please excuse, therefore, my disjointed manner, and all other errors, and believe me, as ever ....

SILAS WRIGHT

ALS. DLC–JKP. Addressed to Columbia.

1. Wright's letter to Polk of January 27, 1844, has not been found.
2. See Cave Johnson to Polk, January 7, 1844.
3. On February 26, 1844, David L. Seymour offered a resolution calling for the adjournment of the U.S. House "on Tuesday, 30th day of May next"; having submitted his adjournment resolution, Seymour asked for the previous question. Dixon H. Lewis inquired if the House would second Seymour's call for the previous question; the House refused by a vote of 74 to 51.
4. Martin Van Buren.
5. Charles Stewart achieved a distinguished record while commanding the U.S.S. *Constitution* during the War of 1812; both he and his frigate earned the nickname, "Old Ironsides." George M. Dallas of Philadelphia backed Stewart for the presidency in 1844 as well as earlier.
6. Word illegible.
7. Richard M. Johnson.
8. Justice Esek Cowen of the New York Supreme Court died on February 12, 1844; the New York legislature observed customary obsequies in his honor on that same day in Albany, N.Y.
9. Samuel Beardsley resigned from the U.S. House on Wednesday, March 6, 1844.


## FROM AARON V. BROWN

Wednesday night

Dear Sir                                    Washington Feby 28th 1844

That counfounded new steam ship the Princeton has played the wild to day.[1] Her big gun bursted killing Sec. Upshaw & Gilmer & Com-

modore Kennon[2] on the spot & a good many of the hands. Wounding
Colo. Benton badly & Capt. Stockton.[3] Benton seems to have been
hurt by the jar as he has none of his limbs broken. They have brought
him up into the city in his senses & greatly affected by the absence
of his family. I suppose as most others do that he will get over [it].
A Dozen or more of members with their wives & a vast concourse of
ladies were on at the time but I suppose none of them were seriously
hurt. A few days ago the *whole house* nearly were on her.

A. V. BROWN

ALS. DLC–JKP. Addressed to Columbia.
1. The U.S.S. *Princeton,* the first warship driven by a screw propeller, carried a 12-inch gun, which was nicknamed the "Peacemaker" and which was
developed by Robert F. Stockton. About two hundred government officials
and guests, including John Tyler, were aboard the steamer for a demonstration cruise down the Potomac River.
2. Abel P. Upshur, Thomas W. Gilmer, and Beverly Kennon. A justice
of the Virginia Supreme Court, 1826–41, and secretary of the navy, 1841–
43, Upshur succeeded Daniel Webster as secretary of state on July 24, 1843.
Kennon was chief of the navy's Bureau of Construction and Equipment.
3. Thomas H. Benton and Robert F. Stockton. A career naval officer,
Stockton declined appointment in 1841 to be secretary of the navy; assisted in
the construction of the steamer *Princeton* and served as her first commander,
1843–45; conveyed to the government of Texas the U.S. Congress' resolution
of annexation; saw action in the War with Mexico; and won election as a
Democrat to the U.S. Senate, where he served from 1851 until 1853.

# MARCH

## FROM ADAM HUNTSMAN

Jackson, Tenn. March 1, 1844

Huntsman relates information obtained from political friends and discusses selection of electors at-large. Hannegan[1] thinks that the Democratic party will carry Ohio, Indiana, and New Jersey, and that the party will select King or Polk for the vice-presidential nomination. Cave Johnson fears that the fight between King and Polk might result in Richard M. Johnson's nomination. Huntsman thinks that Polk will receive a cabinet appointment from Van Buren should Polk be left off the ticket. The Knoxville Central Committee is divided over the choice of electors. Reynolds, Crozier, and Eastman want to pair Nicholson with a person chosen by the Jackson Central Committee. Ramsey and Lyon favor Coe and Turney, but Coe declines the nomination.[2] Turney is acceptable to the Jackson committee, but they have reservations about Nicholson. Huntsman solicits Polk's advice on this matter.

ALS. DLC–JKP. Addressed to Columbia and marked "confidential." Polk's AE on the cover states that he answered this letter on March 8, 1844; Polk's reply has not been found. Published in *THQ*, VI, pp. 358–59.

1. An Indiana lawyer, Edward A. Hannegan served in the state legislature; in the U.S. House, 1833–37; and in the U.S. Senate, 1843–49. From March 1849 until January 1850, he was U.S. minister to Prussia.

2. J. G. M. Ramsey, William Lyon, Levin H. Coe, and Hopkins L. Turney. Lyon, a Knoxville Democrat, is not identified further.

## FROM ROBERT ARMSTRONG

Gov.                                    [Nashville, Tenn. March 4, 1844][1]

You Must be here on the 15 Inst. We a[re][2] Making arrangements for a La[rge] Meeting. Make an Editorial for th[e] Democrat[3] and

Invite all our friends [in] Maury and adjoining Counties to Com[e] in.
See and urge all our friends to Join us. Jonas Thomas ought to bring
a Regiment. We will have the old Chief here.[4] Laughlin will take
Charge of the union on Monday.[5] He arrived last night.

R. Armstrong

ALS. DLC–JKP. Addressed to Columbia.
1. Date identified through content analysis.
2. Part of this word and those on succeeding lines have been obliterated by
a tear in the manuscript.
3. Columbia *Tennessee Democrat.*
4. Reference is to Andrew Jackson's attending a Democratic mass meeting,
which was scheduled to coincide with his birthday celebration on March 15,
1844.
5. Samuel H. Laughlin resumed editorial work on the *Nashville Union* on
Thursday, March 7, 1844; he published his first issue as editor on March 12,
1844.

FROM CAVE JOHNSON

Dear Sir,                                    Washington 6th March 1844
   It has pleased heaven to take from us Upshur & Gilmer[1] & I trouble
you with a few lines because I think it is destined to have an important influence on our public affairs at least in our elections. Calhoun
was nominated & confirmed today as sec. of State without opposition.[2]
Gov. Shannon as minister to Mexico[3] & it is sd. James M. Mason will
go into the Navy.[4] It is generally believed Calhoun will accept. His
presence here is destined to have great influence in some way, but
what is a mere guess. My own impression is, judging alone from his
position, that after maturely weighing Tylers prospects, it will be settled that he has no hopes & that Mr. C. will go *thoroughly for Van.*[5]
Having gone so, of course he must be certain in the Department of
State—*the slippery stone* & if he acquires Texas & Oregon or makes
himself the leader upon both or either, he *will calculate* not to be set
aside for *either* or *any other in 1848.* These are my surmises. A serious
& earnest movement secretly to supplant Van & nominate Cass is now
on hand & is injuring us now by producing despondency among our
friends in the country, delaying action here of the public business as
well as keeping us unorganized. It is obliged *to fail altogether* & will
be worse than *a failure,* if Calhoun takes the course which his apparent interest indicates. In our own state,[6] the movement is probably

based on *your popularity,* & because it is said you are *to be rejected at Baltimore,* your friends should [go] for Cass & you.

Whatever may be the action of the Baltimore Convention (& none of us have any grounds to guess further than I have written you) no such step ought to be *permitted under any circumstances,* & I am decidedly of opinion, if such a ground be take[n] publicly for you, you should not *permit* your *name to be used in that way.* We can have no hope of democratic principles ever being sustained except thro. the democratic party. That our leaders from N.Y. are decidedly friendly to you under all circumstances I·have not the slightest reason to doubt, whatever may be the feeling of some Western leaders. If Van Buren should decline or be withdrawn there would be several others whose claims would be far beyond those of Genl. C.,[7] & he would have no more chance than I would have. If Van was withdrawn or declined our party would be irretrievably lost. Calhoun, Benton, Buchanan neither would yield to Genl. C. & several others of our leaders have equally as good, if not a better chance than him. Our unity, our safety depends upon Van & in my judgment *your only chance* for the position we wish arises from the continuance of Van. My great fear now is that the division among your & Kings friends may throw it to R.M.J.[8] & I doubt whether any harmonious action can be effected. Benton was injured by the bursting of the gun[9] & has not yet resumed his seat. Silas Wright has been offered a place on the Supreme Bench—Thompsons place which he has rejected.[10] We have had several meetings of the Democratic M.C. & have finally agreed to have an Executive Committee which I as Chairman have to appoint by tomorrow. This gives me great trouble as it is a delicate as well as an important matter.

I have written you freely for reasons which you will appreciate in a few days, that you may see as clearly as I think you ought the whole ground. Whilst I esteem Genl. C. very much I cannot but think any movement such as I am sure is now in contemplation cannot but injure him & his friends & *ruin them* should Mr. C—n's friends take the course I have suggested as probable.

The evening of the funeral[11] the Pres. horses, with him & daughter in the carriage & prince John[12] with the driver, descending the Capitol hill took fright & dashed at full speed up the avenue filled with carriages, horsemen, footmen, drays, &c and were stopped before the turn at the Treasury building. No damage. The Pres. says he was cool all the time, had no apprehensions, that providence had charge of him & would preserve him for some important ends yet.

We are much encouraged by the news this evening from New Orleans, of beating the Whigs in New Orleans in a special election so soon after Clays great convention.[13]

C. JOHNSON

[P.S.] I cannot boast much of my health tho I keep up.


ALS. DLC–JKP. Addressed to Columbia and marked *"private."* Polk's AE on the cover states that he answered this letter on March 18, 1844; Polk's reply has not been found. Published in *THQ*, XII, pp. 165–67.

1. Reference is to the deaths of Abel P. Upshur and Thomas W. Gilmer, both of whom were killed in an explosion aboard the U.S.S. *Princeton* on February 28, 1844.

2. Calhoun accepted the office of secretary of state with the expressed understanding that he would be at liberty to retire immediately upon conclusion of his best efforts to resolve the Texas and Oregon questions; he assumed the duties of office on April 1, 1844, and continued to serve until March 10, 1845.

3. Governor of Ohio, 1838–40 and 1842–44, Wilson Shannon served as minister to Mexico, 1844–45; won election to a single term in the U.S. House, 1853–55; and removed to Kansas Territory, where he served two years as governor, 1855–56.

4. James M. Mason, a Virginia lawyer, sat one term in the U.S. House, 1837–39; having filled a Senate vacancy in 1847, he won two terms in his own right and served until 1861, when he withdrew to become a delegate to the Provisional Congress of the Confederacy. John Y. Mason, however, was appointed secretary of the navy by John Tyler. Mason served as a member of the U.S. House, 1831–37; as U.S. district judge for the eastern district of Virginia, 1837–44; as secretary of the navy, 1844–45 and 1846–49; and as U.S. attorney general, 1845–46.

5. John C. Calhoun and Martin Van Buren.

6. State of Tennessee.

7. Lewis Cass.

8. Richard M. Johnson.

9. Reference is to the explosion of the *Princeton's* 12-inch gun, the "Peacemaker."

10. See Cave Johnson to Polk, January 13, 1844.

11. The funeral for those killed aboard the *Princeton* was held in Washington City on March 2, 1844.

12. John Tyler, Letitia Tyler Semple, and John Tyler, Jr. Letitia Semple, second daughter of the president, married James A. Semple, a navy purser; she assisted her father as White House hostess from March 1844 until his marriage to Julia Gardiner on June 26, 1844. John Tyler, Jr., served as his father's private secretary.

13. Reference is to the election of mayor and corporation officers of New Orleans on March 1, 1844. Henry Clay visited New Orleans from January 22 until February 2, 1844, while touring the South for the Whig party.

## TO SAMUEL H. LAUGHLIN

My Dear Sir:                                                    Columbia March 7th 1844
I did not receive your letter from Manchester[1] until to day. I learn from Genl. Armstrong that you have reached Nashville.[2] I hope in the next Union to see that your name is at the head of its Editorial columns. Your aid is much needed to make the paper such as I have no doubt you will make it. The specimen Number of the "Star-Spangled Banner"[3] should be issued as soon as possible; still it is of more importance that it should be *a good paper,* than that it should be issued with undue haste. *Huntsman* in a letter received to day,[4] says *Coe* will not serve as an elector for the state at large. Who is to supply his place I am at a loss to know. *Turney* must be one. It would be better to have the other from one of the *ends of the state,* but who is there that will do. If both are taken from the middle Division, who is the second man to be? Who do you think he should be? Write me. *Armstrong* insists that I must be at Nashville on the 15th.[5] I will come if I can.

*Cullom's* apprehensions, that R.M.J.[6] will be nominated, are I think without good foundation. I had a second letter from *Silas Wright*[7] two days ago, as also letters of late date from Johnson & Brown.[8] My own opinion is that Col. J.[9] cannot get the nomination. Much however will depend upon the exertions which are made by my friends between this time and the meeting of the convention at Baltimore, as else upon the efficient action of the Tennessee Delegates in that convention.

JAMES K. POLK

ALS. DLC–JKP. Addressed to Nashville and marked *"Private."*
1. Laughlin wrote to Polk from Manchester on March 1, 1844; he stated that he would arrive in Nashville on March 3, expressed concern for the Democratic electoral ticket's two at-large nominations, and noted that Leonidas N. Ford had raised Martin Van Buren's name with that of Polk's to the masthead of the McMinnville *Central Gazette.* ALS. DLC–JKP.
2. See Robert Armstrong to Polk, March 4, 1844.
3. A sample issue of the weekly Nashville *Star Spangled Banner* was published on April 8, 1844.
4. See Adam Huntsman to Polk, March 1, 1844.
5. See Robert Armstrong to Polk, March 4, 1844.
6. Richard M. Johnson.
7. See Silas Wright to Polk, February 27, 1844.
8. See Cave Johnson to Polk, February 25, 1844, and Aaron V. Brown to Polk, February 28, 1844.
9. Richard M. Johnson.

## FROM THEOPHILUS FISK[1]

Sir,                                          Washington March 9. 1844

I address you *in the strictest confidence,* and I trust that I am sufficiently well known to you to be believed implicitly when I affirm that
your answer shall be regarded in that sacred character to its fullest
extent.

I desire to be permitted to inquire as to your views and feelings with
regard to the President of the United States; and whether it would
meet with your approbation to be tendered a place in his Cabinet.[2]
He is fully determined to organize his council entirely of Jeffersonian
Republicans; the appointment of Mr. Calhoun to the post of Secretary
of State, of Mr. Wilkins to the War Department, the tender of the
vacant judge-ship of the U.S. Supreme Court to the Hon. Silas Wright
give an earnest of what the country has to expect at his hands.

The office of Secretary of the Navy has become vacant, as you already know, by the melancholy death of Gov. Gilmer. Will you consent
to take it if tendered to you without any pledge, shackle or trammel
being asked of you, other than is already guaranteed by your exalted
character and standing?

I am not at liberty, perhaps, to say by whose authority I have ventured to ask these questions. You know me too well, I hope, to suspect
for an instant that they are asked to gratify an idle curiosity merely,
or upon slight authority; the idea was suggested first by myself and
allow me to say it has been received by the warmest enthusiasm by the
*two* or *three* most deeply interested in your acceptance, and they are
the only ones who are at all acquainted with the matter. There is on
their part the deepest solicitude that your services should be secured
to the country at this critical juncture. Texas and Oregon need such
a champion as yourself at this emergency, & the country would look
upon your acceptance of this office as an act of exalted patriotism.

No one doubts that Mr. Calhoun will accept the office of Secretary
of State. He has been written to by all parties urging his acceptance,
as you would be were it known the office was about to be tendered to
you.

I write in great haste and perhaps incoherently. I have such an
exalted opinion of your peculiar fitness for the station, and such an
anxious solicitude that the country should receive the aid of your wisdom and experience at the present crisis of our affairs, that I am
beyond expression desirous that you should say, *"I will accept."* That
your friends here will advise you to that course I have not a doubt.

It was only last night that the idea was forced upon my mind. This morning after visiting the _____ White House, the secret is out. I ventured to hint it in the strictest confidence to the Hon. A. V. Brown, who declared his belief that you ought to accept and could do so, if the appointment was offered.

I know that your generosity will excuse any seeming officiousness on my part in this matter. You are in no possible way responsible for any thing I have done. What I have said has been entirely on my own individual responsibility, induced alone by the admiration and respect in which I hold your talents and character. What I have done will forever remain a profound secret from the world if you should desire to decline the profer, which, may heaven forbid. You are not asked to commit yourself to any body or anything but to the great interests of the nation. Let me hope that no consideration will induce you to give a negative answer.

Please allow me the privilege of begging that you will write me at once on the receipt of this, and believe me ....

THEOPHILUS FISK

ALS. DLC–JKP. Addressed to Columbia under the frank of Aaron V. Brown and marked *"Private and confidential."*

1. Theophilus Fisk and A. F. Cunningham published the Portsmouth and Norfolk *Chronicle and Old Dominion* from 1839 until 1845. At the time he wrote, Fisk held a congressional clerkship, which Aaron V. Brown had helped him obtain.

2. Reference is to John Tyler's cabinet realignment, which was occasioned by the deaths of Abel P. Upshur and Thomas W. Gilmer.


## FROM AARON V. BROWN

Dear Sir                               Washington March 10th [18]44

I have just franked and directed a letter to you the contents of which may somewhat surprise you.[1] I did not read it & I judge of its contents from the communication with Mr. Fisk the Writer. He has communicated to me several interviews which he has had with the President & informed me last night, that he was about to write to you. It is proper to say to you that Mr. Fisk has been in the City during the Winter & for some time has been acting as clerk to the Committee on elections a situation which I was chiefly instrumental in getting for him. He is now esteemed as he was when you were familiar with him a gentleman of respectability and veracity & I should not doubt or distrust any of his statements or purposes in a correspondence with him. He seems very intent on the subject & will expect an early answer. His communication with me was for the purpose of asking my opinion of what would be your reply & if necessary what would be my *advice* to you if it were asked. This induced me to ask permission to mention the subject to Colo. Johnson[2] (without giving names & particulars) in order to have his views on the subject. I called on Johnson accordingly & he does not hesitate to give it as his opinion that if Calhoun accepts, you ought not to hesitate if the Navy Department is tendered to you. The current of opinion here is that he will, but I believe no one is well informed on the subject. A few days will show. If he accepts the Cabinet would then stand 3 to 2 Democratic & those two you know not very Whiggish.[3] But how would such an acceptance affect you in the future? No worse than Mr. Calhoun at all events, & if he accepts it will be because he cannot see how it is to injure *him*. Would it affect your nomination at Baltimore? The Democracy would take no *umbrage* at it. This is proven in the case of Gilmer & Wilkins. There are no persons here who insist that *Democrats* ought not to take office under him. If you were to accept & Democracy were to succeed in the next election (you not being vice) you would no doubt be continued in that or other department. If the Whigs succeeded you would of course have to *walk*. That every body else would have to do & even *then* you would only be where you now are.

One thing more I will add because I think of it. How would it affect our State elections. The most that could be said would be, that having often said you were determined to rise *from* the people & *by* the people, you have now taken office under Tyler. Well what of that? Ones enemies can allways say as much as that. We should loose by your *absence* or for the want of your speeches &c but I do not think in any other way.

You must however distinctly understand that no one of your friends here has directly or indirectly moved in this matter, nor has one word been said *before the public* on it. No one suspects it (of even our delegation but Johnson & myself). Now if the probability of your getting the nomination at Baltimore is to have any influence on your course, I can only say that since the nomination of Johnson in Pennsylvania[4] I have thought it more doubtful than formerly, but even with that I do not think *he* can possibly succeed. Nor do I think the result at Baltimore would be affected by your having become Secretary of the Navy.

One thing more I will add because I think of it. How would it affect our State elections. The most that could be said would be, that having often said you were determined to rise *from* the people & *by* the people, you have now taken office under Tyler. Well what of that? Ones enemies can allways say as much as that. We should loose by your *absence* or for the want of your speeches &c but I do not think in any other way.

On the whole I know of no better way than for you to reply to Fisk by refering the matter to myself & Johnson with whom he or the President can confer if he desires it & if we shall recommend or counsel its acceptance, that you will accept. I will suggest that in your letter you ought to assure Fisk of your personal kind feelings toward the President & that you have often felt it your duty as well as inclination to sustain his course on the Bank & some other subjects of great importance against the rude & violent assaults of his enemies. Something of this sort would be proper & strictly true & so I have often told the President the facts were. I know persons have intimated to him last session to the contrary but I have set his mind at rest on that subject.

This course of reply to Fisk will relieve you from any delicacy which you might feel in corresponding too freely with him, but you must at the same time let Johnson & myself know exactly what to say & do in case of the nomination by the President or his consultation preparatory to a nomination. Well, & last, for I have just thought of it. Would there be the least doubt of confirmation? None I think. Johnson thinks none. Could Foster & Jarnagin[5] unite all the Whigs against you? I should think it altogether unlikely if they were to try it. Nor do I think that King or Benton or Allen or any of the Clique could be foolish enough to do any thing in that way.

If howev[er] it was done I think it would rouse a feeling in the country by which *you* could be nothing looser. Well you see my sheet is run out. I have rambled over, all over the subject & so leave you to your better judgement & feelings on the matter.

A. V. BROWN

[P.S.] Now how much trouble might I have saved if I had cut all this short by asking "What will Mrs Grundy say to this"[6] for after all I know *where our orders* come from.[7]

ALS. DLC–JKP. Addressed to Columbia. Polk's AE on the cover states that on March 20, 1844, he answered Theophilus Fisk's letter of March 9, 1844; Brown had franked and sent Fisk's letter to Polk, probably under separate cover.

1. See Theophilus Fisk to Polk, March 9, 1844.
2. Cave Johnson.
3. William Wilkins, secretary of war, and John Nelson, attorney general, were Democrats, while John C. Spencer, secretary of the Treasury, and Charles A. Wickliffe, postmaster general, were Whigs. Nelson, a Maryland lawyer, served in the U.S. House, 1821–23, prior to his service in the cabinet, 1844–45. A Kentucky lawyer, Wickliffe served as a member of the U.S. House, 1823–33; lieutenant governor, 1836–39; governor, 1839–40; and postmaster general, 1841–45.
4. Reference is to Richard M. Johnson. See Polk to Samuel H. Laughlin, January 20, 1844.
5. Ephraim H. Foster and Spencer Jarnagin. Jarnagin studied law under Hugh L. White and practiced in Knoxville until 1837, when he removed to

Athens, McMinn County, and became a leader of the Whig party. A presidential elector in 1840, Jarnagin failed in his efforts to win a seat in the U.S. Senate in 1841. Two years later, however, the Tennessee legislature elected him to that body; and he served from 1843 until 1847.

6. "Mrs. Grundy," a character in Thomas Morton's play, *Speed the Plough* (1798), became the symbol of conventional propriety in nineteenth-century England.

7. Brown's allusion is to Polk's wife, Sarah Childress Polk.


## FROM CAVE JOHNSON

Dear Sir,                                        Washington March 10th 1844

I have just been informed by Mr. Brown that a letter will be addressed to you this evening by Th. Fisk[1] (formerly Editor of the Old Dominion) who says he does so by the authority of the Pres[2] desiring to know, if you would go into the Navy department. Thinking it will come upon you by surprise & that you would like to hear the opinions of some of your friends, B & myself concluded to write[3] —not that we would expect to have any influence on your better judgment but because we are here & see perhaps more of the workings of party than you possibly can at home. Calhoun it is generally believed will be the Sec. of State, & you could have no difficulty in council with him, Nelson, & Wilkins & perhaps but little with Spencer & Wickliffe. If Calhoun comes in it is thought, he will identify himself with the Texian & Oregon question & become if he can the leader in the South & West & to make himself acceptable with the friends of Van,[4] will probably act with them thoroughly in the presidential election, so as to be retained by *Van or necessitate* in that position as a stepping stone in 1848. Others think, he will thoroughly identify himself & friends with the efforts now making for Tyler, get up a third party, hold the balance & take their chances.

My own opinion is, that he & friends will take the former course, act thoroughly for Van *to kill Clay* & then make battle with Benton Buckhanan Cass[5] &c for the succession. Should this be his course I can see no objection to your acting with him & them for the present. Should they take a different course then you could not with propriety have any thing to do with them. There could be no objection to your taking the office if the world could be satisfied that you were merely performing the duties of the office & not engaging in any of these political movements, but you cannot know before you will be required to act who is to be the premier or his course. Calhoun may decline. A non-descript may then come in with whom you could not act. Under

such circumstances, would it not be advisable to write a very civil reply, which will of course be shewn, referring the Pres. to a consultation
with Brown & myself & authorising a nomination if we concurred in
it. I mention Brown & myself because I know of nobody here that you
could more safely trust, & besides I do not know enough of Fisk to say
how far he should or could be trusted with any such communication
as he would expect from you and besides we could see all the ground,
understand the motives & would consult with Silas Wright in whose
judgment I have more confidence than all of them together. He was
offered the Judge of Supreme Court in place of Thompson but declined,
because he thought the policy was to weaken Van Buren. It will be or
has been offered to Ingersol of Connecticut [6] & possibly with the same
view that Shanon [7] was appointed to Mexico, to weaken if practicable
Van in the Convention. And it is very probably, the offer to you will
be made with the same view.

I fear some secret movements are making here so as to bring up the
Texas question more prominently before the Convention meets & to
make it operate if practicable agt. Van in the Convention & agt. Clay
in the election. If it can be brought up fairly & properly & with a
reasonable prospect of getting it I should have no objection but if it
is designed merely as a political question to operate in the ensuing
canvass then I shall deplore it. An effort no doubt will be made to unite
the destinies of Oregon and Texas so as to unite the South & West.
May you not be identified with these movements if in the Cabinet? &
if unsuccessful what follows?

Your present position as I have informed you created some suspicion,
whether you was not ready to go for *any man* who would take you
on his ticket, arising mainly from the omission of our convention [8]
to nominate a president & this was to some extent confirmed by the
movements of some persons in Ten. for Genl C. [9] connected with your
name. The acceptance with Mr. C. [10] of a cabinet appointment might
tend to identify you still further with the discontents and therefore
also, no steps should be taken without a full understanding of all
our leading friends from the North. If you were here, fully & properly
understood by our Northern friends & with their approbation, I should
think your prospects for the Vice presidency would be increased rather
than diminished but let me repeat what I said in one of my last, do
not let your name in anyway be connected with the movement in Ten.
for Genl. C. Such a movement in Ten. would destroy us there & loose
all confidence in us elsewhere.

I have written these remarks hastily & such as present themselves
to my mind upon the first suggestion. As to the influence of such a

movement in Ten. in our next election, you can judge better than I.

C. JOHNSON

[P.S.] The Tariff Bill is reported.[11] We will send it to the Senate early in April and I think adjourn the last of May. I do not well see how we could spare you in Ten. next summer.

ALS. DLC–JKP. Probably addressed to Columbia and marked *"private."*
Published in *THQ,* XII, pp. 167–68.
1. See Theophilus Fisk to Polk, March 9, 1844.
2. John Tyler.
3. See Aaron V. Brown to Polk, March 10, 1844.
4. Martin Van Buren.
5. Thomas H. Benton, James Buchanan, and Lewis Cass.
6. A New Haven lawyer, Ralph I. Ingersoll served in both the Connecticut House, 1820–25, and in the U.S. House, 1825–33; in 1846 Polk appointed him U.S. minister to Russia, where he served until 1848.
7. Wilson Shannon.
8. Reference is to the Tennessee State Democratic Convention that met at Nashville on November 23, 1843.
9. Lewis Cass.
10. John C. Calhoun.
11. On March 8, 1844, James McKay of the House Committee on Ways and Means reported a bill proposing to modify the tariff act of August 30, 1842.


## FROM SAMUEL H. LAUGHLIN

Nashville, Tenn. March 12, 1844

Laughlin advises that he has taken editorial control of the *Nashville Union.* The first issue of the *Star Spangled Banner,* held back waiting for new type, will be published soon and will report "Friday's Jubilee"[1] and Johnson's anti-abolition speech.[2] He plans "to give two more constant columns to politics and news" in the tri-weekly *Union* and wishes to speak with Polk about the matter. Laughlin urges Polk to attend the mass meeting on Friday.

Democrats have made recent gains in Rutherford County, where on March 11 Currin ably debated with Caruthers.[3] Coe probably cannot serve as an elector, although he may have been appointed already.

ALS. DLC–JKP. Addressed to Columbia and marked "Private."
1. See Robert Armstrong to Polk, March 4, 1844.
2. Cave Johnson spoke on the Atherton Resolution and the 21st Rule during the House debates of February 27, 1844.
3. David M. Currin and Robert L. Caruthers. A Murfreesboro lawyer and Democrat, Currin ran as the Democratic candidate for elector in the Seventh Congressional District in 1844; he later moved to Memphis and served one term in the Tennessee House, 1851–53. A Whig lawyer in Lebanon, Caruthers

represented Wilson County for one term in the Tennessee House, 1835–37, and
sat in the U.S. House for a single term, 1841–43.


## FROM THEOPHILUS FISK

Sir,                                                    Washington March 13. 1844
   I regret more than I have language to express that matters here have
turned out so differently from what I had any reason to expect, when I
wrote you on Saturday last.[1]  It was then universally believed by the
leading friends of the President that Judge Mason would not accept the
Secretaryship[2] which had been proposed to him to take; intimations to
that effect had been received and the President promised that in case
his positive declination came as was then expected, that the wishes of
your friends should be complied with most promptly.  Since then Judge
Mason has concluded to resign his judgeship and he has consequently
been nominated to the Senate today.
   I beg you to rest assured that the President appreciates your talents
as they deserve; the time will come at no distant day when he will
manifest that appreciation in some tangible form.  Although (greatly
to our mortification and regret) this post has been unexpectedly filled
by a change of views on the part of Judge Mason, there are other
stations now vacant and others that soon will be, where your services
may be required; situations equally honourable, and more profitable,
than the one we had hoped so earnestly to see you occupy.
   I shall be grateful if you will allow me to hear from you at your
earliest convenience.

                                                    THEOPHILUS FISK

ALS. DLC–JKP. Addressed to Columbia.
1. See Theophilus Fisk to Polk, March 9, 1844.
2. Reference is to the post of navy secretary in John Tyler's cabinet.


## TO CAVE JOHNSON

[Dear Sir,]                          [Columbia, Tenn.] March 18, 1844
   I wrote you hastily from Nashville two or three days ago,[1] in answer
to your letter of the 6th inst. I said enough in that letter to show you
clearly that I entirely and fully concurred with you in all the views
expressed in your letter. The movement which you say is on hand,
to profess publicly to support Mr. Van Buren, with a secret intention
to attempt to nominate Genl. Cass in the Convention, can receive no

countenance from me. I agree with you that "it is obliged to *fail altogether.*" You say "in our State the movement is probably based on *your popularity,* and because it is said that your are to be *rejected at Baltimore,* your friends should go for Cass and you." If any such movement is being made in this State, it has not come to my knowledge. Should any such be made *my name shall not be used in that way,* and I will take the earliest opportunity to discover any such attempted use of it. It is now settled that the preference of a large majority of the party is for *Mr. Van Buren,* and the whole party should yield to his nomination and make it unanimous. Such men as *Duff Green,* and the discontented in our ranks, may attempt to produce confusion by resisting the popular choice of the party, but their movements can receive no countenance or support from me. In regard to the *Vice* as I have repeatedly informed you I am in the hands of the party, and will cheerfully acquiesce in the decision of the Convention. I see from the Intelligencer[2] received to day, that Col. R.M.J. has been nominated at Harrisburg.[3] This I was prepared to expect. Still it can scarcely be possible that he can receive the nomination at Baltimore. If he does, (and I speak not from any personal or selfish views) you may rely upon it that the success of the party is put into imminent jeopardy. In this State we would be hopelessly lost. Such a result should therefore be opposed by all fair and honorable means. All our Delegates will attend at Baltimore. They feel and know the incubus which *Col. J.'s* nomination would be to us, and they believe that the State can and will be redeemed with the aid of the nomination which they desire. It is important I think that the correspondence of which I have heretofore spoken should be kept up at Washington. As the period approaches the greater vigilance is required, to prevent a few politicians at Washington from giving a false direction to the popular sentiment in favour of *Col. J.* You will see the importance of this, and will I know give the proper attention to it. A few active men and especially at Washington may make that appear to be public sentiment which is far from being so. If this central influence can be counteracted, I have the fullest confidence that the Delegates to Baltimore "fresh from the people," can never consent to *Col. J's* nomination. *Majr. Donaldson*[4] and one or two other of our Delegates will go on early in May, will be at Washington and will be ready to co-operate with you in all proper measures to carry out the wishes of my friends. *Laughlin* is now at the head of the Union at Nashville. He is *true and reliable.* You should keep him advised of all that he ought to know, and he will make a prudent and proper use of the information in his paper.

Mr. Calhoun's appointment to the Department of State is well received here, and the general wish is that he may accept.

Have you written the letter to Genl. Jackson which I suggested two or three weeks ago.[5] Such a letter would induce him to act with all his energy.

[JAMES K. POLK]

PL. Published in *THM*, I, pp. 234–35. Addressed to Washington City and marked *"Confidential."*

1. Polk's letter has not been found.
2. A leading Washington City newspaper from 1800 until after the Civil War, the *National Intelligencer* was edited by Joseph Gales, Jr., and William W. Seaton.
3. Reference is to Richard M. Johnson. See Samuel H. Laughlin to Polk, January 20, 1844.
4. Andrew J. Donelson.
5. Polk's letter has not been found; however, Cave Johnson did write to Andrew Jackson on March 15, 1844, estimating Polk's prospects for the vice-presidency. ALS. DLC–AJ.

## TO THEOPHILUS FISK

My Dear Sir:　　　　　　Columbia Tennessee March 20th, 1844

I have received your kind letter of the 9th Instant. The information which it conveys, as well as the proposition made,[1] I need not assure you was wholly unexpected. In responding to your inquiries I am frank to say, that my personal feelings towards the President are as they have ever been of a friendly character. Knowing him personally as I do, I have often felt it to be my duty, as well as inclination, since he has occupied his present exalted station, to vindicate and sustain him in his course on the Bank, and some other subjects of great public importance, against the rude and violent assaults of his political enemies. You desire me to intimate to you, whether it would meet with my approbation to be tendered a place in the Cabinet, and whether I would accept the office of Secretary of the Navy, made vacant by the late melancholy and lamented death of *Gov. Gilmer.* I have implicit confidence in the sincerity of the declaration which you make, when you say that this inquiry is not made to "gratify an idle curiosity merely, or upon slight authority." A situation in the Cabinet is one which I have never sought or desired under this or any preceding administration. If I believed that I could by accepting, render any great public service, which others could not more ably perform, it would be my duty not to hesitate. Believing however that there are many others, whose services the President can command, who could render more service to the country than I could, I must express my disinclination to yield to the wishes, which you so earnestly express, and my sincere desire that some other may be selected. Declining therefore the proffered honour, I have to express my acknowledgements to the President, and other friends who may have thought of me for so distinguished and important a station. I may add that all the public preferment which I have at any time enjoyed, I have received directly from the hands of the people, and since I have been in retirement, I have often declared to my friends, that if I ever again filled any public place I expected to receive it from the same source. This is well known to my friends *Mr. A. V. Brown, Mr. Cave Johnson,* and others of the Representatives in Congress from this state.

I most anxiously desire that *Mr. Calhoun* may accept the Department of State, which has been tendered to him by the President and Senate. Entertaining the most exalted opinion of *Mr. Calhoun's* talents and patriotism, I am quite sure that there is no citizen who could better, if so well, fill the important station to which he has been called, in the present posture of our foreign affairs, and especially in reference to the Texas and Oregon questions. Were I to occupy a place in the Cabinet, there is no man in the country with whom I would be more happy to be associated. I hope the country may have the aid of his great mind in bringing these questions to a favourable settlement. Should he undertake the task and be successful, as I have great confidence he would be, it would add to his already just claims upon the public consideration, and would entitle him to the lasting admiration and gratitude of his countrymen. Hoping that the President may have no difficulty, in filling the office of Secretary of the Navy, by the selection of some other than myself....

JAMES K. POLK

ALS, copy. DLC–JKP. Addressed to Washington City in care of Aaron V. Brown and marked *"confidential."* Published in Lyon Gardiner Tyler, ed., *The Letters and Times of the Tylers* (3 vols.; Richmond and Williamsburg, Va., 1884–96), III, pp. 133–34; and in *THM,* I, pp. 235–36.

1. Reference is to the post of navy secretary in John Tyler's cabinet; see Fisk to Polk, March 13, 1844.

FROM ROBERT ARMSTRONG

Dear Sir,                                     Nashville March 21. 1844
     Doctr. McNeill[1] died this morning at 8 Oclk, and Govr. Carroll cannot live untill Morning.[2]

In relation to the Washington Letter,[3] I would prefer to see you advanced by the *people* and I would say "take not, touch not." Their is something in the offer to *you*, that I do not understand.

I would like to see you in the Cabinet but not as things *now* stand.

R. ARMSTRONG

ALS. DLC–JKP. Addressed to Columbia.

1. William McNeill, a physician and successful merchant, resided in Maury County for nearly half a century before removing to Nashville; he died shortly thereafter on March 21, 1844.

2. William Carroll died in Nashville on March 22, 1844.

3. Reference is to the letter of Theophilus Fisk to Polk, March 9, 1844.

## TO CAVE JOHNSON

[Dear Sir,] [Columbia, Tenn.] March 21, 1844

This letter is intended for *Brown* as well as yourself. In a hasty note addressed to you jointly last night,[1] I informed you that I had answered *Mr. Fisk's* letter—declining to accept.[2] Without anyone here with whom to counsel, I concluded it was better to decide promptly and for myself, than to keep the question open by referring it to *Brown* and yourself, as both of you suggested in your letters I might do.[3] I took this course because I had really no wish to fill the place, and because my acceptance might have left the impression on the minds of some that I was among the discontents of the party and towards *Mr. Van Buren* especially who might possibly have been thereby weakened. I did not intend that by any act of mine, my motives or position should be questioned. My acceptance too would probably have been regarded as a retreat from anticipated defeat before the Baltimore Convention. By declining my true position in the party and before the country will be preserved. By remaining at home I may continue to render some service to our cause, and shall at all events be freed from all supposed participation in the political schemings and intrigues at Washington, for which I profess to have neither taste nor talents. I had reason to believe too that the influence of *Tyler* and his administration, —as far as they may have any, would continue to be hostile to *Mr. Van Buren,* and I should have been placed in a false position, to have been compelled to hold confidential relations with him and his advisers. True I was informed that in the event of my acceptance, no pledges as to men or measures were required, but that I should be left free and untramelled, to act as my own judgment might indicate as proper. My answer to *Mr. Fisk* was of course a civil one, but was at the same time decisive as to my declination of the proffered honour. I had the utmost confidence in the judgment of yourself and *Brown,* and of *Mr. Wright* of New York, whom one of you informed me you would consult, in the event my decision was left open and referred to you. I could not however foresee any possible state of things that could arise at Washington, which could change my opinion, and therefore I preferred to act myself, rather than to delay action and cast the responsibility upon you. *Mr. Calhoun's* appointment is well received here. If he accepts, I think it probable that he will see that it is his interest to co-operate thoroughly with the Democratic party, so heartily for *Mr. Van Buren,* harmonize his friends at the South, and make a great effort upon the Texas and Oregon questions, —to place himself if not at the Head, in a very prominent position in the party. Placed as he is, this would undoubtedly be the sensible course. It is hard to tell however how far his feelings may control his judgment.

The *Union* of to day you will see has a strong article against the course of the discontented in our ranks, who continue to make efforts to produce division by still talking about *Genl. Cass.*[4] Laughlin will follow it up by articles of a like character, and you may have no apprehension that any scisme [*sic*][5] can be produced in the party in this State. There are a few who would desire it, but their numbers are too small to enable them to effect it.

I see *Col. J.* has been nominated in Pennsylvania.[6] Without speaking in reference to myself personally, you and all others in this State know, that if the same nomination be made at Baltimore, our defeat in this State is inevitable, and the success of the party in the Union is put in imminent jeopardy. Let me hear from you on receipt of this.

[JAMES K. POLK]

PL. Published in *THM,* I, pp. 237–38. Addressed to Washington City and marked *"Confidential."*

1. Note not found.

2. See Theophilus Fisk to Polk, March 9, 1844; and Polk to Fisk, March 20, 1844.

3. See Aaron V. Brown to Polk, March 10, 1844; and Cave Johnson to Polk, March 10, 1844.

4. The *Nashville Union* of March 21, 1844, lamented efforts by those wishing to promote the presidential nomination of Lewis Cass, since "an overwhelming majority of the whole democratic party of the Union" favored Van Buren. The Tennessee Democracy, in particular, was urged to disallow "the demon of division and discord again to enter and mingle with our councils and actions as we did in 1836."

5. Bracketed word previously supplied.

6. Reference is to Richard M. Johnson's nomination for the vice-presidency by the Pennsylvania Democratic State Convention.

## TO CAVE JOHNSON

[Dear Sir,]                                             [Columbia, Tenn.] March 21, 1844

That *Brown* and yourself may be in possession of the precise contents of my letter to *Mr. Fisk,* I send you herewith a copy.[1] In my letter of today which is intended as you will see for both of you, I have made no mention of sending you a copy, —for the reason that I thought it possible that you might think it useful to show the letter *without the copy,* to Mr. Wright. By showing my letter to him *confidentially,* the Northern Democracy will know through him, what I have done and the true position which I occupy. You will of course exercise your discretion in this respect. My determination heretofore communicated to you is unchanged. I calculate my friends will make the best showing they can at Baltimore whatever the result may be. I shall not believe it possible until I see it that the party are mad enough to place *Col. J.*[2] again on the ticket. If the Democracy of the North and especially of N. York, take ground against him in the convention, he cannot possibly be nominated. *Mr. Wright* has too much sense not to see, that his nomination[3] could bring no strength in any State in the Union, whilst in several of the States it would be a *positive incubus,* and probably be the means of defeating the party in the *Union.* You are sufficiently intimate with him to talk with him as freely as you please, and I think it would be advisable to do [this][4] in time. If *Mr. W.* resolves to prevent his nomination, I am satisfied he can do so, in spite of the power of the two *B's.*[5] *Col. K.* I presume from all that I see, has been wholly lost sight of.[6] Am I right in this, or has he a few who still press him.

[JAMES K. POLK]

PL. Published in *THM,* I, pp. 236–37. Addressed to Washington City and marked *"Confidentially."*
1. See Polk to Theophilus Fisk, March 20, 1844.
2. Richard M. Johnson.
3. Reference is to Richard M. Johnson's nomination.
4. Bracketed word previously supplied.
5. Silas Wright, Jr., Thomas H. Benton, and James Buchanan.
6. Reference is to William R. King's prospects for the vice-presidential nomination.

## FROM ROBERT ARMSTRONG

at Night
Govr.                                              Nashville March 22 [1844][1]
    Genl. Carroll died this evening at 7 ock. Can you come in by Sunday *morning* with any of his old officers & soldiers?
    You see that Mason is Confirmed to the Navy Dept. Their is some shuffling and deception at work. In haste....

R. Armstrong

[P.S.] The old Genl[2] was well this morning. We had no mail East of Cincinnati to *night*. Of course no news. RA

ALS. DLC–JKP. Addressed to Columbia.
1. Date identified through content analysis.
2. Andrew Jackson.

## FROM WILLIAM H. POLK

Dear Brother                              Nashville March 26th 1844
    Enclosed I send you the "deeds" you forwarded to me,[1] properly certified by the Clerk of the County Court. Belinda[2] is just alive. She was taken *very* severely last night about 1 or 2 o'clock, and has been very ill ever since. She cannot live through the night without some great change. It is now three o'clock. I will write to Mother[3] to night before the mail closes.

William H. Polk

[P.S.] Mrs Polk died a quarter before 3 ock this afternoon in the full possession of her intellect perfectly tranquil & happy. R. C. K. Martin[4]

ALS. DLC–JKP. Addressed to Columbia. Postscript is in the hand of and signed by Robert C. K. Martin.
1. Enclosure not found.
2. Belinda G. Dickinson Polk of Franklin, Tenn., married William H. Polk in April 1837.
3. Jane Knox Polk, widow of Samuel Polk and mother of James Knox and William Hawkins Polk, resided in Columbia.
4. Robert C. K. Martin, a former resident of Columbia, practiced medicine in Davidson County.

## FROM CAVE JOHNSON

Dear Sir,                                   Washington 29th March 1844

I recd your letter on yesterday & also to day yours addressed to Brown & myself.[1] I am truly glad that you was so prompt in declining[2] & S.W. Jr[3] to day expressed himself much gratified tho he said he knew it would be so. We wrote you[4] in the way we did from an apprehension that but little reliance was to be placed upon the *means* of communication resorted to by the *Pres.* & because we knew, that any other disposition of the office would be made, if by so doing any advantage could be obtained.

The Cass movement to which I alluded[5] was *certainly contemplated* & I hope has been put down by *recomendations from this place. Advice* as well as *co-operation* was sought from this place, and based upon the idea, that your co-operation, at least your acquiescence was necessary to a successful prosecution of the project in Tennessee. I hope it may have been given up. The signs here are too strong to allow much equivocation. We shall soon know whether we act harmoniously in future. Calhoun reached the city to day & I suppose it will not be long before we know whether he will unite with Tyler in the effort to make a third party. My own impression is that he will go in for the nominee & commence the battle for 1848. If he dont he has no common sense. There is no doubt I presume that a treaty for the annexation of Texas is prepared & ready for the signing of the parties. Genl Henderson[6] it is said reached the city to day, with full powers. Many fear however, yet, that it is *all a trick* to create a new fever to operate *on the Baltimore Convention* and after that is over, action on it will be postponed to the next session & the fever kept up until after the presidential election. It is thought by those most zealous for the acquisition that it will be made to operate agt. Clay & Van Buren both. Webster is already spoken of as *the candidate* on that question & will break down Clay in the North, whilst Calhoun and the Admn. will play a similar game upon Van[7] in the South, and thus the election be thrown into the House. There is a good deal of feeling in the House upon Texas & Oregon questions & an effort to unite them.

We hear but little as to the vice-presidency; the subject is seldom mentioned. All seem to wish to avoid it. Benton is now able to attend the Senate, made a great Tariff speech on Monday & Tuesday & goes tomorrow to Kentucky for his wife.[8] McKay went after his to day.[9] We shall commence the Tariff upon his return about the 9th of April & I think we shall pass it in the House in ten days after. Pennsylvania will go agt. us in a body & probably New Jersey & about five in N. York & 2 in Mass & possibly one or two in Ohio. We can not yet calculate certainly; I think our majority will be 20 in the House. We are reducing the pay of the army about 500,000 & will probably do as much or more for the Navy.[10] *I have to hold our retrenchment* men back a little to keep from doing too much.

I fear B. & Jones[11] are greatly dissatisfied with every thing here. The latter talks with great freedom & in a way to do us no good, if he keeps it up on our return. I fear, to say the least of it, he will be neutralized in the next election. Holmes & Black of G–a are substantially Whigs in their course here & really do us more harm than they could as open & avowed Whigs. We shall adjourn I think the 27th May, tho we may postpone acting on the resolution of the Senate until May—such is the impression now.[12] It is thought the Whig Senators wish to evade any questions on the Oregon or Texas and the probable application of Florida & Iowa to be admitted into the Union, as well as the Tariff. The Whigs of the House are equally pressing & such a number of democrats too, that I fear we shall not be able even to postpone the adoption of the resolution until May. We have an excellent party, good materials—if we had a leader.

My health continues better than usual & I shall fight this battle out. Then I am done. I think if you should not be nominated at Baltimore that you should go upon the ticket as an Elector. I fear the prudence of Turney & Coe. If Connecticut & Virginia repudiates Clay by strong majorities as we believe here, I think Clay will be dropped at Baltimore.[13]

As far as we can learn his trip to the South has done him no good.[14]

C. JOHNSON

ALS. DLC–JKP. Addressed to Columbia and marked *"private."* Published in *THQ,* XII, pp. 168–70.

1. Johnson probably received Polk's letter of March 20, 1844, on March 28; this brief letter, which stated only that he had declined the post of navy secretary, has not been found. On March 21, 1844, Polk wrote two explanatory letters to Johnson and Aaron V. Brown and probably sent both under a single cover, which Johnson received on March 29.

2. See Theophilus Fisk to Polk, March 9, 1844; and Polk to Fisk, March 20, 1844.

3. Silas Wright, Jr.

4. See Aaron V. Brown to Polk, March 10, 1844; and Cave Johnson to Polk, March 10, 1844.

5. See Cave Johnson to Polk, March 6 and 10, 1844.

6. A brigadier general in the Texas army and an experienced lawyer, James P. Henderson served as attorney general, secretary of state, and agent to

England and France for the Republic of Texas prior to his appointment in 1844 as a special minister to negotiate a treaty of annexation with the United States. Elected governor of Texas in 1846, he fought in the Mexican War with the rank of major general; later he served part of one term in the U.S. Senate, 1857–58.

7. Martin Van Buren.

8. Thomas H. Benton's wife, Elizabeth McDowell Benton, was the sister of James McDowell, who served as governor of Virginia, 1842–46, and as a member of the U.S. House for two terms, 1846–51.

9. James I. McKay was the husband of Eliza Ann Harvey McKay.

10. A report dated March 25, 1844, and submitted to the House by James A. Black of the Committee on Retrenchment, recommended salary reductions for army personnel totaling approximately $522,000. See House Report No. 373, 28 Congress, 1 Session.

11. Aaron V. Brown and George W. Jones.

12. On March 25, 1844, the Senate passed a resolution that called for the adjournment of Congress on May 27, 1844.

13. Reference is to state elections in Connecticut and Virginia held on April 1 and 25, 1844, respectively, and to the Whig National Convention, which convened in Baltimore on May 1, 1844. Whigs gained a decisive victory in Connecticut by winning majorities in both houses of the legislature. In Virginia, Democrats won a majority of ten seats in the upper house, and Whigs gained a majority of twelve in the lower house; thus on joint ballots of the legislature Whigs commanded a majority of two.

14. Henry Clay began his tour of the South at New Orleans and returned by way of Washington City to his home in Lexington, Ky., on April 26, 1844.

## FROM SALMON P. CHASE ET AL.[1]

Sir,                                                  Cincinnati March 30th 1844

We have the honour of transmitting to you a copy of the proceedings of a very large meeting of the Citizens of Cincinnati, assembled, without distinction of party, on the 27th inst, to express their settled opposition to the annexation of Texas to the United States.

The State of Ohio has, heretofore, through her legislature, protested against this measure. A vast majority of her citizens, it is believed, are irreconcilably opposed to any enlargement of the domain of Slavery, and feel it to be a sacred duty to resist its extension to any new territory. Nor, would they, we think, be willing, however desirable the acquisition of Texas, were slavery abolished within its limits, might seem to many of them, to purchase that acquisition at the expense of a broken treaty & a violated constitution.

You will perceive that we are required by one of the resolutions of the meeting which we represent, to solicit from each of the distinguished individuals, whose names have been brought before the people by their respective friends as candidates for the Presidency & Vice Presidency, an explicit expression of opinion upon this question of annexation. We, therefore, respectfully ask for such an expression from you, & hope to be favoured with your reply at as early a period as your other engagements will permit.

S. P. CHASE

P.S. A copy of Cin. Gazette[2] containing proceedings is forwarded by this mail. Apl. 2, [18]44.[3]

ALS. DLC–JKP. Addressed to Nashville and forwarded to Columbia. Polk's AE on the cover states that he received this letter on April 21, 1844, "having been absent to the state of Mississippi from the 1st April '44 to this date," and that he replied on April 23, 1844.

1. This letter is addressed to Polk by a Committee of Cincinnati Citizens and signed by Salmon P. Chase, Thomas Heaton, T. Finkbine, Gamaliel Bailey, Jr., and Samuel Lewis.

2. The *Cincinnati Gazette,* Whig in its political orientation, was one of Ohio's major newspapers.

3. Enclosure not found.

# APRIL

## FROM CAVE JOHNSON

Washington City. April 10, 1844

Johnson notes that King has been confirmed as minister to France and Shannon, as minister to Mexico. King's appointment to France should be favorable to Polk's nomination at the Baltimore Convention. Most congressmen think that Richard M. Johnson will receive the vice-presidential nomination, but "it is rare to find a member for him." Johnson states that he has never seen such discord among members of the Congress as presently exists. Dromgoole refused to delay the vote on the tariff bill until after the Connecticut elections, which the Democrats lost. Now Dromgoole seeks its passage before the Virginia elections. Votes on two successive days have failed to call up the bill; every southern Whig except Chappell of Georgia voted against bringing up the bill. Attempts to force another vote have failed, and the bill may be lost to the "clear anti Tariff majority in the House." Foster has informed Johnson that Calhoun will not vote for Van Buren. "Rumor says" that a treaty with Texas has been signed.[1]

ALS. DLC–JKP. Probably addressed to Columbia. Published in *THQ*, XII, pp. 170–71.

1. A Texas annexation treaty, written by John C. Calhoun, was signed on April 12, 1844, and submitted to the Senate ten days later; however, on June 8, 1844, the Senate rejected the treaty decisively by a vote of 35 to 16.

## FROM WILLIAM TYACK

Dear Sir                          New York April 13th 1844

Your highly esteemed favour is duly Receivd,[1] for which I return you my most sincere thanks. I am extremely Hapy to learn you are well as also that Democracy is looking up in the Chivalrick State of Tenessee. I am doing all that is possible in A quiet way to Bring Influence to bear at the Convention to secure your Nomination, and am hapy to say it looks well.

You see the result of our Election here—*20,000 Democrats to 5,000* Whigs. The Whigs abandoned their own Regularly Nominated Candidate for Mayor & Charter Officers to put down old Tamany. They gained the Election. But they are ashamed of their own Business. They know not what to say—*20,000* to 5,000 looks very Bad. Our last Corporation appointed most all of the City Officers from the Irish. This so displeased the Natives that about 3 or 4,000 left us and joined with the Federalists & Beat us.[2] This whole Ruse will greatly help us in the fall you may rely upon it.

The Honble B. F. Buttler will be with the Venerable Chief[3] at the Hermitage from the 18 to the 20. I hope you will see him without fail. I sincerly thank Mr President Tyler for Providing for Mr King.[4] He is out of our Way. It will now remain I think between yourself & old Tip,[5] and the result cannot fail to favour the wishes of A very large Majority of the Democracy of the Country.

I thank you for the Information in regard to the Health of our Beloved Jackson. Although enfeebled as he is yet he had the great Kindness to write me on the 25th Instant. May God in his Mercy spare him to Behold his Beloved Van Burren[6] & Polk Placed in the seats Prepared for them by the Allmighty God and the Democracy of the American people. I intend if possible to be at the Baltimore Convention.

Should you visit the Hermitage you will Please Present my most gratefull Respects to the *Genl, Mrs* Jackson, Mrs Adams, Col A. Jackson and all the children.[7]

WILLIAM TYACK

ALS. DLC–JKP. Addressed to Columbia.

1. Letter not found.

2. Reference is to New York City elections held on April 9, 1844. James Harper, candidate of the American Republican or Native American party, won the mayoral contest with 24,606 votes. He defeated both the Democratic candidate, Jonathan I. Coddington, and the Whig candidate, Morris Franklin; the losing candidates received 20,726 and 5,207 votes respectively.

3. Benjamin F. Butler and Andrew Jackson. A former law partner and close confidant of Martin Van Buren, Butler served as U.S. attorney general, 1833–38, and twice as U.S. attorney for the southern district of New York, 1838–41 and 1845–48.

4. Reference is to William R. King's appointment as minister to France.

5. Richard M. Johnson's more familiar sobriquet was that of "Old Tecumseh."

6. Martin Van Buren.

7. Andrew Jackson, Sarah York Jackson, Marion York Adams, and Andrew Jackson, Jr. Sarah York Jackson was the wife of Andrew Jackson, Jr., and the sister of Marion York Adams. The Jacksons and their children, Rachel, Andrew III, and Samuel, resided at the Hermitage, as did Marion Adams, a widow, and her three sons.

## FROM CAVE JOHNSON

Dear Sir,                                    Washington April 15th 1844

We have been again defeated on taking up the Tariff Bill.[1] Again 27 demo. absent & only 9 Whigs. It was probably defeated because many of the Western Democrats are determined to have the River Bill[2] pass & refuse to take up the Tariff until the other is finished lest it be smothered.

The Texian question is exciting deep feelings here & Clay & Van are both in a quandry.[3] Many believe that Van & Clay are both opposed to it but my opinion is they will both take ground for it. Possibly Clays friends in the Senate, may postpone any action on it until after the election & he will play hide & seek with the Abolitionists. It is understood, that Calhoun has taken such high ground on the Oregon that Packenham[4] will have to await instructions from his Gov. or the attempt to treat is at an end. I see to day a call for a meeting of the friends of Texas signed by a large number of the members of Congress. Upon the news of the treaty having been formed Willis Green[5] left here to meet Clay in N.C., no doubt for orders. It is not improbable, that Benton of N.Y.[6] visited N.Y. with a view of seeing Van also upon the same subject but we have learned nothing tho Benton has returned. The Vice Presidency is lost sight of here. Texas & Oregon are all in all.

To day F—k[7] who wrote you took me out (as Mr. B.[8] is not here) & went into a long explanation of his letter, its origin, & your reply. The nomination had been tendered to J. Y. Mason but it was expected he would decline. That caused the letter to you. To day he informs me that it is by no means improbable, that there will soon be a vacancy *in the Treasury* and in the *mission to England* & wished to know my opinion whether you would accept either. I told him you took a deep interest in the Tennessee elections & I thought it doubtful whether you would like to be absent from the State during the Canvass but expressed the opinion *for myself,* not knowing any thing about your feelings or wishes, that you ought to accept the mission to England. Everett[9] *will be recalled* as well as all *other friends of Webster.* I express what I thought & still think, a years absence, with your oeconomy might get you out of debt and I think you should authorise me to say, if it should come *from a proper source* that you would accept & that a nomination might be sent in. I think it probable, that such is the wish of Mr. C.[10] From the ground he has taken on the Oregon & Texas question, he would wish a minister at that court whose views coincided with his own & upon whom he could rely. He has no confidence I am sure in Everett. If you trust me with any such authority I would not of course let *anyone know,* except at head quarters & then not without a proper application & proper assurances. I met Calhoun this morning for the first time[11] on the street, but had but little conversation with him.

We are much troubled in all our movements here. We have some fifteen or twenty men, who wish *some other,* than Van, and they have got it into their heads *if the Tariff* Bill is postponed or could be defeated, that it will induce a belief of his want of popularity & produce the nomination of some other. This feeling has much influence upon all movements connected with the Tariff & upon several other important party questions. Vans friends from N.Y. (a portion of them) are as prejudicial to his interests as ever Bell & Co. were to Jackson. I shall hear more upon these subjects soon & will advise you. My health is better than usual.

C. JOHNSON

ALS. DLC–JKP. Probably addressed to Columbia and marked *"private."* Published in *THQ,* XII, pp. 171–72.

1. The tariff bill was scheduled for consideration on April 15, 1844, but a quorum of the House could not be raised. J. W. Davis moved that the sergeant-at-arms be dispatched to collect those in the city who had not been excused; however, by a vote of 107 to 64 the House suspended further proceedings for the day.

2. A bill appropriating funds for selected western harbor and river improvements was introduced in the U.S. House on February 15, 1844, by Robert McClelland from the Committee on Commerce; following considerable debate the bill passed the House on April 20, 1844, by a vote of 108 to 72.

3. Henry Clay and Martin Van Buren. See Cave Johnson to Polk, April 10, 1844.

4. Sir Richard Pakenham, British minister to the United States.

5. A Kentucky Whig, Willis Green served three terms in the U.S. House, 1839–45.

6. Charles S. Benton, a New York lawyer and journalist, served two terms as a Democrat in the U.S. House, 1843–47; he removed to Wisconsin in 1855

and subsequently became editor of the *Milwaukee News*.

7. Theophilus Fisk. See Fisk to Polk, March 13, 1844, and Polk to Fisk, March 20, 1844.

8. Aaron V. Brown.

9. Edward Everett, a Harvard professor, sat five terms as an Independent in the U.S. House, 1825–35; served as Whig governor of Massachusetts, 1836–39; went to Great Britain as U.S. minister to the Court of St. James, 1841–45; presided over Harvard College, 1846–49; served as U.S. secretary of state, 1852–53; and sat in the U.S. Senate, 1853–54.

10. John C. Calhoun.

11. Johnson's point of reference was the first meeting since Calhoun had become secretary of state.

## TO SALMON P. CHASE ET AL.[1]

Gentlemen.                                Columbia Tennessee April 23rd 1844

Your letter of the 30th ultimo, which you have done me the honour to address to me reached my residence during my absence from home,[2] and was not received until yesterday. Accompanying your letter you transmit to me, as you state, "a copy of the proceedings of a very large meeting of the citizens of Cincinnati assembled without distinction of party on the 29th Inst. to express their settled opposition to the annexation of Texas to the United States." You request from me "an explicit expression of opinion upon this question of annexation." Having at no time entertained any opinions upon public subjects, which I was unwilling to avow, it gives me pleasure to comply with your request. I have no hesitation in declaring that I am in favour of the immediate re-annexation of Texas to the territory and Government of the United States. I entertain no doubts as to the power or the expediency of the re-annexation. The proof is clear and satisfactory to my mind that Texas once constituted a part of the territory of the United States, the title to which I regard to have been, as indisputable as that to any other portion of our territory. At the time the negotiation was opened with a view to acquire the Floridas, and the settlement of other questions, and pending that negotiation, the Spanish government itself was satisfied of the validity of our title, and was ready to recognize a line far West of the Sabine, as the true Western boundary of Louisiana, as defined by the Treaty of 1803 with France under which Louisiana was acquired. This negotiation which had been first opened in Madrid, was broken off, and transferred to Washington, where it was resumed and resulted in the Treaty of Florida by which the Sabine was fixed upon as the Western boundary of Louisiana. From the ratification of the Treaty of 1803 with France, until the Treaty of 1819 with Spain the territory now constituting the Republic of Texas belonged to the United States. In 1819 the Florida Treaty was concluded at Washington by Mr John Quincy Adams (then Secretary of State) on the part of the United States, and Don Louis de Onís[3] on the part of Spain, and by that Treaty, this territory lying West of the Sabine and constituting Texas, was *ceded* by the United States to Spain. That the Rio del Norte or some more Western boundary than the Sabine could have been obtained, had it been insisted on by the American Secretary of State, and that without increasing the consideration paid for the Floridas, I have not a doubt. In my judgment, the country West of the Sabine and now Texas, was most unwisely *ceded* away. It is part of the great valley of the Mississippi, directly connected by its navigable waters with the Mississippi River, and having once been a part of *our* Union, it should never have been dismembered from it. The government and people of Texas, it is understood, not only give their consent, but are anxiously desirous to be reunited to the United States. If the application of Texas for a re-union, and admission into our confederacy, shall be rejected by the United States, there is imminent danger that she will become a dependency, if not a colony, of Great Brittain, an event, which no American patriot anxious for the safety and prosperity of his country could permit to occur, without the most strenuous resistance. Let Texas be re-annexed and the authority and laws of the United States be established and maintained within her limits, as also in the Oregon Territory, and let the fixed policy of our Government be, not to permit Great Brittain or any other foreign power to plant a colony or hold dominion over any portion of the people or territory of either. These are my opinions, and without deeming it to be necessary to extend this letter by assigning the many reasons which influence me, in the conclusions to which I come, I regret to be compelled to differ so widely from the views expressed by yourselves and the meeting of citizens of Cincinnati whom you represent. Differing however with you & with them as I do, it was due to frankness, that I should be thus explicit in the declaration of my opinions.

JAMES K. POLK

ALS. NjMoHP–LWS. Addressed to Cincinnati, Ohio. ALS, draft marked *"Copy,"* in DLC–JKP.

1. Polk's letter is addressed to S. P. Chase, Thomas Heaton, T. Finkbine, Gamaliel Bailey, Jr., and Samuel Lewis, a committee representing numerous citizens of Cincinnati, Ohio.

2. Polk was absent from Columbia on an inspection of his plantation in Yalobusha County, Miss.

3. Luis de Onís was appointed Spain's minister in 1810.

## FROM SAMUEL H. LAUGHLIN

My dear Sir,        Nashville, Tenn. April 24, 1844

Learning from your letter to Gen. Armstrong[1] that you have just reached home, and some things having transpired here lately, and since you left, which you would perhaps like to know, I hasten to address you a line.

The Hon. B. F. Butler has been on a visit to the Hermitage. When he arrived here, he made no stay in town, but proceeded forthwith to Gen. Jacksons. After remaining there some days, he returned to town late yesterday evening, and left in the stage at 3 o'clock this morning, intending to cross Kentucky so as to visit the Mammoth Cave in company with his son, to go to the Ohio at Maysville, leave it at Wyandotte,[2] going by Monticello, & Richmond, Virginia. He is in great haste, as he must be in New York by the 8th or 9th of May at the Supreme Court of that state.

I saw him and Gen. Jackson together yesterday in company with Gen. Armstrong, and again had a more particular interview with him in town late last night, after he had taken leave of most of the friends who met him here. From all I can comprehend of the posture of affairs, and the prospect before us, I think matters wear a favorable aspect. Kings removal narrows the contest down to two competitors, yourself and Col. Johnson.[3] As New York, Virginia, and Ohio, or perhaps any two of them will hold the balance of power probably, I must think that your nomination must be carried. The Northeastern democracy, if only true, secures your nomination anyhow.

That the whole matter has been *conned* over, counted, and prospectively adjusted *in posse*[4] by Gen. Jackson and Mr. Butler, I can have no doubt, and that their conclusions and calculations are favorable for you, from a number of expressions dropt yesterday, both Gen. Armstrong and myself believe. The last word of Mr. Butler last night was charging me to present his sincere and most cordial respects to you.

You will see that on Saturday the 4th of May we are to have a *mass* Texas meeting here,[5] and you and others be invited to attend which you must do if possible. We have the enemy in a world of trouble here on the Question. Blair, Wilkins &c speaking out,[6] and Linn Boyds Letter[7] are the best political articles we have had for some days. We look with intense anxiety to the Virginia election.

Maj. Donelson got home from New Orleans yesterday Evening. I have not seen him; but hope he will be in town tomorrow, and that he will be making ready for his departure to Baltimore. Mr. Powell of Carter has just gone home, and is going to Baltimore. I must get ready and be off in a few days, just at the close of the Texas meeting at farthest, and in the meantime I wish to see you before I leave. Write me. Can you come here by Thursday or Friday of next week, or sooner.

The appointment of Johnson and Brown, as suggested in your letter to Gen. Armstrong, is an excellent arrangement.[8] I hope Mr. Brown is about to return to the city.[9] While here, as he is on his way, he must be furnished with credentials for himself and Johnson. I will see to their preparation. I informed Gen. Jackson that it was proposed to appoint them, and he highly approved of it. Possibly Blair[10] may go to Washington, but still they will all have seats for the state, or as alternates.

S. H. LAUGHLIN

NB. I wish Maury would send in liberally for the Banner[11]; 22 subscribers names come to-day from Greene Co., Mo.

ALS. DLC–JKP. Addressed to Columbia. Polk's AE on the cover states that he answered this letter on April 25, 1844; Polk's reply has not been found.

1. Polk's letter has not been found.
2. Misspelling of "Guyandotte."
3. William R. King had accepted an appointment as U.S. minister to France, thus leaving Richard M. Johnson and Polk the field for the vice-presidential nomination. See Cave Johnson to Polk, April 10, 1844.
4. A Latin phrase used in law to designate that which is "in potential" as opposed to that which is "in essence."
5. A mass meeting of the friends of Texas annexation was held at the Court House in Nashville on Saturday, May 4, 1844; Felix Robertson presided over the meeting, which issued resolutions favoring annexation and praising John Tyler's efforts in that direction.
6. Francis P. Blair and William Wilkins. Blair, editor of the Washington *Globe,* published a lengthy editorial on April 15, 1844, earnestly advocating the re-annexation of Texas. Also in that issue Blair printed a pro-annexation circular addressed by Secretary of War Wilkins to his former constituents in Pennsylvania on April 13, 1844.
7. Linn Boyd, a Democrat from Kentucky, served several terms in the U.S. House, 1835–37 and 1839–55. His letter, written in answer to an inquiry from Walter Coles and George W. Hopkins, members of Congress from Virginia, renewed and extended the 1825 charge of "corruption, bargain, intrigue and management" between Henry Clay and John Q. Adams. Dated March 29, 1844, Boyd's letter was published in the Washington *Globe* of April 13, 1844.
8. Apparently Polk wished Cave Johnson and Aaron V. Brown to be named delegates to the Democratic National Convention.
9. Aaron V. Brown had returned to his residence in Giles County to attend

his ill wife; Laughlin expected Brown to visit Nashville en route to Washington City and thence to Baltimore for the Democratic National Convention.

10. A merchant, manufacturer, and lawyer in Washington County, John Blair served as a Democrat in the U.S. House from 1823 until 1835; he lost his bid for reelection in 1834 to William B. Carter. Blair subsequently sat for one term in the Tennessee House, 1849–51.

11. Reference is to possible subscriptions to the Nashville *Star Spangled Banner* by Democrats in Polk's home county.

## FROM SAMUEL H. LAUGHLIN

My dear Sir,                                        Nashville, April 26, 1844

I am duly in receipt of your letter of the 24th.[1] The evening of the day before I received it, was, I believe, the date of my last to you,[2] informing you of my visit to the Hermitage, my interview with Mr. Butler and his departure. Having written that letter, I did not answer yours on yesterday as I otherwise would have done. You see by the papers how we are getting on here. The Texas question is doing us essential good in many parts of the state as I sincerely believe, and I am pleased that you have determined to come out openly and boldly upon it. C. Johnson writes me under the date of the 18th (I received his letter last night) that he will support immediate annexation. The quotation you will see in the Union[3] of tomorrow morning, printed this evening, as to the conditions of the Treaty as understood at Washington, is from his letter.

I wish [to know] how soon you may be able to come up here. I will be obliged to go to Warren before I leave for Baltimore, and I must have some money. Not a cent has been paid or tendered to me here yet. I considered the money I was to have as a sure fund, and did not think of drawing on it in March when it was to have been paid, reserving it to keep my debts easy, by renewing a debt in bank and paying calls, and discharging every pressing obligation, so as to be free and easy, and looking to my own means for current personal expenses, and going to Baltimore. But nothing has been said to me about [money] nor have I spoken to a human being except Gen. Armstrong from whom I have had to borrow $20. Want of the money, however, has compelled me to submit to a protest, when I ought to have paid and expected to pay.

These matters all being to rectify, and my instructions for Baltimore having to be concerted, I wish you would come up soon in the coming week, or in the week and stay to Saturday, the day of the Texas meeting to which you are invited. I wish to go to Warren by Thursday or

Friday of next week, where I must go, and with some money, before I leave. I must leave here before the Texas meeting, as I have indispensable business of my own with Warren County Court on Monday the 6th of May.

I saw Maj. Donelson to-day. He says he doubts not that Gen. Jackson and Mr. Butler fully talked matters over. You should come up soon in order to see Gen. Jackson before myself or Donelson leave for Baltimore.

My respects to Gen. Pillow. I hope to hear of him, Mr. Childress and Donelson being off for the City and Convention.[4] Now is the time of trial. No man must look back.

S. H. LAUGHLIN

ALS. DLC–JKP. Addressed to Columbia and marked *"Private."*
1. Polk's letter has not been found.
2. See Samuel H. Laughlin to Polk, April 24, 1844.
3. *Nashville Union.*
4. References are to Washington City and the Democratic National Convention at Baltimore.

## FROM CAVE JOHNSON

Washington City. April 28 [1844][1]

Johnson states that upon reading Clay's public letter opposing Texas annexation,[2] he became convinced that Democrats would ride "roughshod" over Clay in the South. However, Van Buren's anti-annexation letter, which appeared "in this morning's Globe,"[3] has lowered Democratic spirits. Party discontents are now at a great advantage and probably will seek a new presidential nominee at the convention. He thinks that they will take up Cass as a tactic to promote the candidacy of another.

The House has been unable to bring McKay's tariff bill out of committee, and the failure to act will prove disgraceful. Twenty-seven Democrats opposed an attempt yesterday to place the bill on the House calendar for May 6.

The vice-presidential nomination commands little attention. Although Polk seems to be the decided favorite among congressmen, Richard M. Johnson probably will be chosen should Van Buren get the presidential nomination.

Neither Fisk nor any other of Tyler's intimate friends has renewed the subject of future vacancies at the Treasury post or the Court of St. James.[4] Dixon Lewis will succeed King in the Senate and "rumor says" that Spencer will go to Russia.

ALS. DLC–JKP. Probably addressed to Columbia. Published in *THQ*, XII, pp. 172–73.

1. Date identified through content analysis.
2. Henry Clay's letter, dated April 17, 1844, and written from Raleigh, N.C., appeared in the Washington *National Intelligencer* of April 27, 1844. Clay stated that by treaty with Spain in 1819 the United States had alienated its title to Texas and was thus bound by that prior commitment. He assumed that Texas' annexation would mean war with Mexico. Adding additional states would undo the balance of political power between the two sections of the Union and thus would lead to the Union's dissolution. Also the United States would become liable for Texas' $13 million debt, an obligation that it could not afford to assume.
3. Martin Van Buren's letter, dated April 20, 1844, and addressed to members of Congress, was published in the Washington *Globe* on April 27, 1844. Van Buren stated that he would support Texas' annexation provided that the state of war between Texas and Mexico were resolved first. He did not think, as did some, that a European power would annex Texas if the United States failed to do so; however, as president he would resist any such encroachment by a European power. Van Buren argued that immediate annexation would render an injustice to Mexico; yet if Mexico attempted to reconquer Texas and if Texas then requested annexation, he would submit the question to Congress.
4. See Cave Johnson to Polk, April 15, 1844.

## FROM WILLIAMSON SMITH[1]

My Dear Sir,                                    Washington City 29th April 1844
I reached here 4 days ago, in bad health and have been pretty much confined since my arrival, but have found out enough, to know that our people here, are all in confusion distraction & despair. The appearance of Mr. Van Buren's letter upon the Annexation of Texas,[2] has thrown every thing in confusion. I have conversed with very many of the southern Democrats, since the appearance of Mr. Van Buren's letter, and I have not seen one but is determined to drop him. Genl. McConnel[3] of Ala., G. W. Jones, Ten., John Blair of E.T.[4] is here, two of the delegation from Miss., Thompson & Roberts,[5] and a number of others are determined to drop him. What is to be the consequence God only knows. There was a strong disposition to drop Van Buren before the appearance of his letter that gives now a good excuse, and I believe he will not be nominated. Cass & Johnson[6] seem to be now spoken of. Cass is decidedly the favourite, and with him your name for the Vice Presidency is very favorably spoken of. How that will terminate I am not able to say. I have not seen Cave Johnson. I called at his room this morning but he was not in. Would have been glad to see him before the writing of this letter.
The Whigs are in as much confusion as we are, for doubtless before this reaches you, you will see that Clay and Van Buren are both out

against annexation. That question will absorb all others in the south, and my own opinion is, that neither of the two will get the south.

I would suggest, (and trust you will pardon me if it does not meet with your views, and would not even make the suggestion, if you did not know it was from a *sincere friend,* who has never forsaken you,)— That you write to some friend here, giving your views upon the annexation of Texas, should you be favourable to that measure. It might be of great service to your friends, should Van Buren be droped and some other man taken up. Of all this however I have no doubt you will be the better judge, or rather I have no doubt you will be more ably advised, of what is going on here than I am able to do—So far as I have been able to form an opinion since I have reached here. If Van Buren is nominated Johnson will be for the Vice Presidency. Of [...][7] I am not fully informed. I must again repeat I have [not seen] such confusion & splitting up among our people before. It looks to me like defeat is inevitable if we cannot unite upon some other man than Van Buren.

My own business I have done nothing as yet but think I will be able to make a start in a few days but every-thing is in such Confusion I much fear [I] will get not much if anything done. My health is improving and I hope in a few days, will be able to attend to business. I should have delayed writing to you a few days longer, and waited for the smoke to blow over a little, but was fearful a letter would not have time to reach you, and for me to hear from you before the Democratic Convention.

Please let me hear from you on the reception of this.

WILLIAMSON SMITH

ALS. DLC–JKP. Addressed to Columbia. Polk's AE on the cover states that he answered this letter on May 8, 1844; Polk's reply has not been found.

1. A lawyer and former resident of Columbia, Smith completed the unfinished term of Terry H. Cahal in the Tennessee Senate, 1836–37, and won election to one term in the Tennessee House, 1839–41. In the early 1840's he moved to Mississippi and eventually settled in Canton.

2. See Cave Johnson to Polk, April 28, 1844.

3. Felix Grundy McConnell, an Alabama lawyer, was a member of the Alabama House, 1838, and Senate, 1839–43, before winning election as a Democrat to two terms in the U.S. House, 1843–46.

4. East Tennessee.

5. Jacob Thompson and Robert W. Roberts. A Mississippi lawyer, Thompson served six terms as a Democrat in the U.S. House, 1839–51; subsequently he served as secretary of the interior during the administration of James Buchanan, 1857–61. A lawyer and farmer, Roberts served several terms in the Mississippi legislature, 1838–44, before winning election to two terms in

the U.S. House, 1843–47.

6. Richard M. Johnson.

7. Fading of the ink has rendered illegible two or more words on this and the following line.


## FROM CAVE JOHNSON

Dear Sir,                                         Washington 30th April 1844

I wrote you two days ago,[1] giving you a sketch of the embarrassments prevailing here and I am sorry to inform you that matters are no better if they are not worse, though there is rather more of calmness to day than yesterday. Clays & Van Burens letter[s] in opposition to Texas appeared Saturday & Sunday mornings. Bentons appeared this morning[2] coinciding with Van Burens. Buckhanons[3] will appear tomorrow in favor of Texas unless dissuaded from so doing to night. The friends of Texas had a meeting last night in the Capitol at which R. J. Walker presided. Many speeches were made but I have not been able to learn the particulars further than there was a good deal of feeling & a general & setled hostility to Van Buren. I learn there was 20 or 25 present & I think this small number has to some extent diminished the feeling to day & upon this we get returns to day from V—a that the Whigs have probably a majority in the Legislature, which increases the dissatisfaction or gives encouragement to our despondency. The discontents claim a hundred members now in opposition to Van Buren but I cannot count more than twenty five or thirty who are active & zealous & perhaps a few other timid men who think we could run some other better than Van Buren. The most of the discontents are looking to Cass, some few to Stewart,[4] but nearly all secretly for Calhoun. Rhett & Lewis take the lead. G.W.J.[5] seems furious & I am sorry to say but little forbearance. A.J.[6] concurs with him, but is moderate in his feelings & seems inclined to do right. Cullom & Blackwell I understand agree with them in the main but take no part as far as I can learn. Hopkins is for Stewart & Polk & some of the Pennsylvanians & New J. members go with him. Most of the Indiana delegation led on by Genl Howard are very zealous for Cass. Genl H. has disappointed me greatly, a tricky man not to be relied on & secretly for Calhoun. Several from Illinois take the same course & one from Ohio (McDowell)[7] & Dick Davis swears that Van Buren cannot get a Congressional district in the Union. Rumor says this morning, that all these discontents are to write letters to several parts of the Union & have answers here ready to exhibit to the convention to prove that Van Buren cannot be elected, & there is a further talk of address-

ing him & if possible induce him to withdraw. Of course this State
of things puts an end to all business. Most of us sit still & endeavor
to calm the excitement but tell them firmly, if they choose to divide
the party, the responsibility [will] be on themselves, that we can bear
defeat, the oppressions of the Bank & tariff &c as well as they can, but
never hint at yielding. Drumgoole[8] & the Virginians, McKay & most
of the N.C. & most of the northern democrats, stand firm for Van. No
yielding, but avoid every thing like irritation. We take ground for Van
& Texas as soon as it can be safely & honorably done. Bentons letter
& a reperusal of Van Burens has shut up a few & most of them will
not let their names be known as advocating any other than Van, but
will prevent us from doing any thing.

Buckhanon makes the decision agt. Benton & Tom Benton as you
see assails Calhoun, & will prove, that he pressed the treaty of 1819
fixing the Sabine thro. the Cabinet in *opposition to the remonstrances
of J Q Adams* who *will come out* & declare it the first chance.[9] If
Van Buren is to be thrown over which I do not believe possible we
must have an *entirely new man.* Throw Cass, Buckhanon, Calhoun all
overboard with him. But this cannot, will not be done & in my opinion
a third candidate will be run on Texas. Cass is the first choice (if he
will yield), of a majority as they *talk publicly* but secretly Calhoun is.
I expected as much & told Rhett so when they opposed the Convention
last fall & had it postponed. If that course is taken, its tendency is
*to divide parties* by *Mason & Dickson's line,* & the Texian candidate
must be defeated & Texas inevitably lost. There is but one chance of
electing *any democrat,* to beat *the Whigs & Calhoun men* together. I
write you frankly & confidentially about men, *for yourself alone.* In
my opinion we are broke up *here* & I see *no hope* of mending matters,
but prudence & forbearance & moderation may do much.

                                                          C. JOHNSON

ALS. DLC–JKP. Addressed to Columbia. Polk's AE on the cover states
that he answered this letter on May 9, 1844; Polk's reply has not been found.
Published in *THQ,* XII, pp. 173–74.

1. See Cave Johnson to Polk, April 28, 1844.

2. Thomas H. Benton's letter, addressed to members of the Texas Congress
and published in the Washington *Globe* on April 29, 1844, objected to the
immediate annexation of Texas in the same spirit as Martin Van Buren's
public letter to members of Congress of April 20, 1844. Benton's letter was
followed by a "postscript" in the *Globe* on May 2, 1844.

3. James Buchanan's letter on the annexation of Texas has not been found.

4. Charles Stewart achieved a distinguished record while commanding the
U.S.S. *Constitution* during the War of 1812; both he and his frigate earned

the nickname, "Old Ironsides." Stewart's name had been mentioned for the presidency as early as 1841, particularly by George M. Dallas of Pennsylvania.

5. George W. Jones.

6. Andrew Johnson.

7. An Ohio farmer, merchant, and lawyer, Joseph J. McDowell served in the Ohio House, 1832, and the Ohio Senate, 1833, before winning election as a Democrat to two terms in the U.S. House, 1843–47.

8. George C. Dromgoole.

9. The Adams-Onís Treaty, which was signed on February 22, 1819, provided for a boundary delineation along the Sabine River from the Gulf of Mexico north to the 32nd parallel, thence north to the Red River and along same to the 100th meridian.

# May

## FROM CAVE JOHNSON

Friday night
Dear Sir,                                     Washington. May 3rd [1844][1]

I have only a moment before the mail leaves to acknowledge the receipt of yours on your return & to express my gratification that you have taken ground for the annexation. Clays letter[2] has had no influence on Southern whigs. Vans opponents & the friends of Texas are outrageous & the chances now seem to be, that his nomination will be defeated.[3] Heaven & earth will be moved for that purpose—Calhoun's friends of course in the lead. For this they have been at work, like moles all the winter. Penn & New Jersey seem likely to present Com. Stewart. Arkansas (Sevier, Fulton & Cross)[4] is fully & openly agt. Van. Indiana, Illinois, part of Missouri & Miss are openly agt. Van & for Cass. Ritchie introduced resolutions before the Dem. asso. at Richmond which passed unanimously recomending a withdrawal of the instructions given to her delegates to vote for Van or that new instructions be given to vote for a Texas man. The Globe & Spectator[5] came out yesterday evening about the same hour, the one denouncing Calhoun & the Treaty and the other Van Buren & Benton & their letters.[6] So the war has commenced for the succession. I shall be the last to leave Van tho decidedly for the annexation. The treaty is in itself well enough, but the documents accompanying are horrible—beging, entreating, coaxing, threatening, lying as all say here, & placing the ground for annexation on the slavery question.[7] Our Ten. Whigs, will take ground with Clay. Mr. Brown[8] says he will support it under *no circumstances*. Jarnegan[9] is loud in his denunciations. Foster is still *on the fence*. The others I have heard nothing from.

The Dem. from Tenn. all go for annexation & myself & B.[10] for Van.
The others I understand prefer Gen. Cass. The course of Arkansas,
kills old Dick[11] I think if Van is nominated. Your name is used in
connection with the old commodore.[12]   There is no body thought of
for Cass's Lieut. Benton *is furious.* He went to Hanegan, Fulton (two
active men) & his colleague[13] & began most abruptly about the 11
traitors that nominated White[14] & talking of the same game now &
exposing it. Atchison was much provoked. I try & keep cool but must
say I have never before seen such discord and the chances I now think
are that we shall have three candidates or throw Van overboard.

The correspondence shows that this work was commenced & pressed
forward for the purpose of having it completed before the Baltimore
convention & in all human probability, was the cause of postponing
the convention until May.

I can make no calculations for the future movements of any body.
I shall remain steady & stand by N.Y. until they surrender Van & I
think they will stand by us.

I hear this evening that Calhoun has instructed the S.C. delegates
to say that he will have nothing to do now with the convention.

I have sd. to Laughlin this evening, that I thought our true policy in
Ten. was to go *for annexation* & the *nominee* relying upon the prudence
of the convention to adjust the difficulties at Baltimore. Hanegan says
this evening, the Cass men are for you & Cass. I fear that will not
go down both being in the west. We will do the best we can. I regret
that Coe does not come on & I learn that Dewitt[15] will not.

I fear we shall not be able to pass McKays Bill. We take it out of
Com. & stop debate on Wednesday next the 8th. We hope Brown[16]
will be here. We still hope to adjourn the 27th. I keep unusually well.

Freelinghuysen[17] you know was the able advocat of stopping the
mails on Sunday & is believed to be an abolitionist. The South nominated him.

C. JOHNSON

ALS. DLC–JKP. Addressed to Columbia. Polk's AE on the cover states that
he answered this letter on May 13, 1844, "whilst at Nashville"; Polk's reply
has not been found. Published in *THQ*, XII, pp. 174–76.

1. Date identified through content analysis.

2. See Cave Johnson to Polk, April 28, 1844.

3. Reference is to party reactions to Martin Van Buren's public letter rejecting the immediate annexation of Texas. See Cave Johnson to Polk, April
28, 1844.

4. Ambrose H. Sevier, William S. Fulton, and Edward Cross. A native Tennessean, Sevier served as delegate from Arkansas Territory from 1828 until
1836; he won election as a Democrat to the U.S. Senate in 1836 and served

until 1848. Fulton, a Tennessee lawyer and military aide to Andrew Jackson in the 1818 Florida campaign, moved in 1820 to Florence, Ala., where he served seven years as county judge until his appointment in 1829 as secretary of Arkansas Territory. Fulton became governor of that territory in 1835, won election as a Democrat to the U.S. Senate upon Arkansas' admission to statehood in 1836, and gained reelection to the Senate in 1840.

5. Washington *Globe* and Washington *Spectator*. In March 1843, friends of John C. Calhoun acquired the financially troubled *Spectator* and published it as his national newspaper until its demise in late 1844.

6. For Martin Van Buren's letter see Cave Johnson to Polk, April 28, 1844. For Thomas H. Benton's letter, see Cave Johnson to Polk, April 30, 1844.

7. Perhaps the most controversial document accompanying the Texas annexation treaty's Senate submission was John C. Calhoun's letter of April 18, 1844, to Richard Pakenham. Calhoun condemned Great Britain's diplomatic efforts to link Mexico's recognition of Texas independence to the abolition of slavery in that republic; he informed the British minister that a treaty had been concluded and would be submitted to the U.S. Senate without delay.

8. Born in Ohio, Milton Brown moved to Tennessee and lived in Nashville and Paris before settling permanently in Jackson. A member of the Madison County bar, he served as chancellor of West Tennessee, 1837–39, and sat in the U.S. House for three terms, 1841–47.

9. Spencer Jarnagin.

10. Aaron V. Brown.

11. Richard M. Johnson.

12. Charles Stewart.

13. Edward A. Hannegan, William S. Fulton, and Benton's colleague from Missouri in the U.S. Senate, David R. Atchison.

14. Reference is to the eleven members of the Tennessee congressional delegation who nominated Hugh L. White for the presidency in 1836.

15. Washington J. DeWitt, a practicing physician, took a prominent part in political affairs in Paris, Tenn.; he later removed to Texas.

16. Aaron V. Brown.

17. A New Jersey lawyer, Theodore Frelinghuysen won election as a National Republican to the U.S. Senate, 1829–35. Subsequently, he was mayor of Newark, 1837–38; chancellor of New York University, 1839–50; unsuccessful Whig candidate for vice-president on the ticket with Henry Clay in 1844; and president of Rutgers College, 1850–62. Frelinghuysen also served as vice-president of the American Sunday School Union, 1826–60, and vice-president of the American Colonization Society.

## TO CAVE JOHNSON

[Dear Sir,]                                    [Columbia, Tenn.]  May 4, 1844

I went to Nashville on the day I last wrote you,[1] was there and at the Hermitage on yesterday and returned today. I found *Genl. Jackson* in better health than I have seen him for years. He manifests great anxiety about the approaching contest, and particularly about the nominations to be made at Baltimore. He avows his preference to all who visit him and declares publicly that *Col. J.*[2] is too heavy a weight to be carried by the Democracy. He says he has written to many of his friends to this effect and assured me that Mr. B.[3] who lately visited him entertained similar opinions.

*Col. Laughlin* will leave for Baltimore on tomorrow, and will join *Blair* and *Powell* at Jonesborough and travel from there via Richmond to Washington. *Majr. Donaldson*[4] and *Genl. Pillow* will leave Nashville about the 10th or 11th and will travel via Cincinnati and Columbus. I hope there will be a full attendance of Delegates from the State, and that they will be at Washington some days before the meeting of the Convention. You will find *Pillow,* as soon as he learns how the land lies, a most efficient and energetic man. The managing politicians at Washington will have everything arranged to their liking at Washington, before the Convention meets if possible. It will require some activity and vigilance to counteract their movements. This can and should be done by my friends; otherwise the true choice of the party may be defeated.

I received today the Arkansas Banner (*Democratic*)[5] of the 24th ultimo, containing the proceedings of the second Democratic State convention[6] in that State. So far as President and Vice-president is concerned they have confirmed and reaffirmed the nominations made at the first convention held in December last,[7] and have appointed their Delegates to Baltimore to carry out their expressed wishes. Among the Delegates, you will see from the paper which I will forward to you with this letter,[8] are Messrs. *Sevier* and *Fulton* of the Senate and Mr. *Cross* of the Ho. Repts. The appointment of the former of the three was perhaps a little unfortunate, though I suppose none of them will disregard the wishes of the Convention. It may be well however for you to see *Fulton* and *Cross* before the other Delegates from the State reach Washington. I send you the paper containing the proceedings of the convention; I received another letter from *Brown* this morning. His wife[9] is worse and therefore he could not leave. There is no certainty when he can do so.

*Clay's* anti-Texas letter[10] reached Nashville last night. If Van Buren will now take ground for annexation as I hope and believe he will, and the Convention shall make a proper nomination for the *Vice,* the Democracy will certainly and beyond all doubt be again in the ascendancy in this State, as I have no doubt it will be in all the Southern and Southwestern States, unless it be Kentucky, and even there the contest will be doubtful. I have not in my letters disguised from you the fact, that I feel an interest (I hope a proper one) in the result of the deliberations at Baltimore. I hope you will write to me often after you get this letter, giving me all the movements, developments and prospects as you may learn them. One thing I repeat in conclusion and that is, that my name will in no event be voluntarily withdrawn, but I desire it to go before the convention, whatever the result may be. It is better for me that this should be so, though it was certain that I would be defeated. My interests are committed to my friends and mainly to yourself. I hope you may be able by a proper appeal to Genl. Anderson of Knoxville, if he attends as a Delegate, to prevent him from doing mischief. Farquharson[11] of Lincoln who was the only other of our Delegates who was impracticable, will not go on as I learn. Your credentials as the Delegate for the State at large in *Coe's* place were made out, and Cheatham told me they would have been sent on, but he had been waiting for *Brown* to pass on, by whom he had intended to send them. They will be forwarded by mail.

[JAMES K. POLK]

PL. Published in *THM,* I, pp. 238–39. Addressed to Washington City and marked *"Confidential."*
1. Polk's letter not found.
2. Richard M. Johnson.
3. Benjamin F. Butler.
4. Andrew J. Donelson.
5. The Little Rock *Arkansas Democratic Banner,* edited by Solon Borland, was one of the leading Democratic newspapers in the state.
6. On April 24, 1844, the Arkansas Democratic State Convention nominated Dan Chapman, a physician, for the governorship and Archibald Yell for the state's lone seat in the U.S. House of Representatives. Sam Adams succeeded Yell upon his resignation from the governorship on May 20, 1844.
7. See J. G. M. Ramsey to Polk, January 4, 1844.
8. Enclosure not found.
9. Aaron V. Brown was married to Sarah Burruss of Giles County.
10. See Cave Johnson to Polk, April 28, 1844.
11. Robert Farquharson, a Lincoln County merchant, farmer, and lawyer, won election to three terms in the Tennessee House, 1839–41, 1843–45, and 1851–53, and sat one term in the Tennessee Senate, 1853–55; a major general in the state militia, he saw action in the Mexican War.

## FROM CAVE JOHNSON

Sunday evening
Dear Sir,                                 Washington May 5th [1844][1]
I know you will be anxious to hear from me often and therefore write, rather than from any thing I have to tell other & different from

what I have before told. So many members of Congress becoming dissatisfied. The loss of Connecticut & Virginia[2] & old Tom Ritchie coming out agt. us,[3] has disheartened many of us. Drumgoole replied to Ritchie in last evenings Globe,[4] & the papers tomorrow, it is said, will bring out forty or fifty members in reply to the charges of "traitors &c" in the Globe[5] & we shall have an exterminating war. I with a few others kept it down at the commencement & suppressed most of our difficulties for a while, but now *the disease* is beyond *remedy*. A split, a fatal split has taken place. Rhett, Lewis, Burke, Woodbury &c go with the Calhoun clique. C. J. Ingersoll (with a commission in prospect for St. Petersburgh as rumor says) leads another set. Sevier & Fulton another. Indiana & Illinois & part of Missouri, most of Ten. & Ky., all departments. Much of this was exerted before the Texas question, but now it is all attributed to it. It grows out of the hostility between Benton & Calhoun.[6] Benton is furious & Silas Wright not much better. More mild, equally as firm. There is no hope unless the convention has firmness enough to do the will of the people *without regard to Congress*. Johnsons friends *now, will all* go agt. Van.[7] I have today lost all hope of reconciliation & shall make no more efforts for that purpose until the delegates come on. In Congress nothing can be done. I shall of course stand by Van to the last as the most worthy. Benton provokes & irritates every man friend or foe who converses with him & Allen is still worse more domineering & dictatorial than even Benton. The treaty will be discussed with open doors in a day or two. Calhoun has requested of the chairm[an] of the Com of Foreign affairs[8] as I hear to delay discussion for forty days until the return of a messenger from Mexico with the *assent of Mexico*. Rumor says the proposition will be ten millions with *a guaranty to her of the Californias against* all other nations. Benton says the treaty *when understood & sifted* is more damnable than the correspondence. I can see but little objection to the treaty as published. The whole patronage of the Government is at work upon the electors, some nominated, others promised offices, missions &c and it is now believed that Van will be *defeated in the convention,* or that the departing states will not go into the convention. I have heard it whispered that delegates will be ready from the Calhoun states & if upon counting noses *he can* be defeated they will *go into the convention.* If not, they will hold back. I wish you *could send certainly* all our prudent & discreet men. Commodore Stewart is out for Texas. Cass's private letter is here from which one set claims him as the advocate of Texas, the other places him on the same ground of Van Buren.[9] Buckhanon is at Harrisburgh, and it is expected every mail will bring out his letter for annexation[10] (rumor says to get the nomination to the bench in the place of Baldwin).[11]  J. C. Spencer has resigned & rumor says will be out in a day or two for Clay.

We should in Ten. carefully distinguish between *the treaty & annexation.* The treaty *is dead,* but *annexation* as soon *as practicable* & Van upon the principles of his letter, the *best man to secure it,* is the position many of us assumed, & I think the true principles for our State, until a nomination is made. Many of us will strugle to get away the 27th, but I fear we shall not be able to accomplish it. I shall advise you often. The coming week or two will be stirring times here.

C. JOHNSON

ALS. DLC–JKP. Addressed to Columbia and marked *"private."* Polk's AE on the cover states that he answered this letter on May 14, 1844. Published in *THQ,* XII, pp. 176–77.

1. Date identified through content analysis.
2. See Johnson to Polk, March 29, 1844.
3. Thomas Ritchie, chairman of the Central Committee for the Virginia Democracy, issued an address withdrawing prior instructions and urging convention delegates to vote for men favoring the annexation of Texas.
4. George C. Dromgoole's letter to Thomas Ritchie, dated May 3, 1844, appeared in the Washington *Globe* of May 4. Dromgoole rejected Ritchie's making the immediate annexation of Texas the sole basis for selecting a presidential nominee and for abandoning his former commitments to Martin Van Buren. Dromgoole argued that the search for "some more available candidate" would create "new rivalries, strife, and discord" in the party.
5. Several pro-annexation letters appeared in the Washington *Globe* on May 6, 1844; included were communications from Romulus M. Saunders, the Indiana congressional delegation, and the Mississippi congressional delegation.
6. See Cave Johnson to Polk, May 3, 1844.
7. Martin Van Buren.
8. William S. Archer, a Virginia lawyer, served in both the U.S. House, 1820–35, and in the U.S. Senate, 1841–47.
9. Reference to an earlier "Texas letter" from Lewis Cass has not been identified. In a letter to Edward A. Hannegan, written on May 10 and published in the Washington *Globe* on May 16, Cass declared in favor of the immediate annexation of Texas. He argued that the unification of the two countries was natural, for they shared common borders and like origins. From a military point of view, Texas' weakness posed a threat to the United States; annexation would block British power and influence on the southwestern frontier.
10. No "Texas letter" by James Buchanan of Pennsylvania has been found.
11. Henry Baldwin, a Pennsylvania lawyer and congressman, was appointed associate justice of the U.S. Supreme Court in 1830 by Andrew Jackson; Baldwin served on the Court until April 21, 1844, when he died in Philadelphia of a stroke.

## FROM J. G. M. RAMSEY

Mecklenburg, Tenn. May 6, 1844

Ramsey relates that he has written Ritchie and urged him to support Polk rather than Johnson for the vice-presidential nomination. Polk's position on Texas, as revealed in his Texas letter,[1] would strengthen the ticket in the South, Southwest, and West. Ritchie probably will agree unless Benton dissuades him. Ramsey will send copies of Polk's Texas letter to Stuart and Hampton[2] and to others if time permits. All Democratic newspapers in the state should print this letter, for it will popularize the treaty of annexation and promote the Democratic cause in Tennessee and elsewhere in the country.

ALS. DLC–JKP. Addressed to Columbia.
1. See Polk to Salmon P. Chase et al., April 23, 1844.
2. John A. Stuart and Joseph W. Hampton. A supporter of John C. Calhoun, Stuart was the editor of the *Charleston Mercury.*

## FROM ROBERT ARMSTRONG

(night)

Dear Sir                                             Nashville 7 May [1844][1]

We have a party of men that seem to me determined to destroy Van Buren before the meeting of the Convention. Men who say they are democrats &c. Will it do to put the Union in such hands during Laughlin's absence—you had better look to this.[2] Laughlin is yet here. He recd. your letter directed to him at McMinnville.[3] When he will go I do not know.

Donelson says he will go next week. He is in bad spirits and mortified.

I will not go. On the whole Van Buren is nearer to us on the Texas Question than any northern man and our southern Democrats friendly to Texas can surely support him if the Whigs of the south friendly to Texas support Clay. But it is not so. Our Democrats are not satisfied. [They are] discontented and ready to fly, go any where, want a new man &c &c. In haste.

R. ARMSTRONG

ALS. DLC–JKP. Addressed to Columbia. Polk's AE on the cover states that he answered this letter on May 9, 1844; Polk's reply has not been found.
1. Date identified through content analysis.

2. Reference is to editing the *Nashville Union* while Samuel H. Laughlin attended the Democratic National Convention in Baltimore.

3. Letter not found.

## FROM LEONARD P. CHEATHAM

Dr. Sir:                               Nashville, May 7th 1844

I have received your letter[1] advising me of the increased illness of Brown's wife[2] & the uncertainty of time when he will arrive here. My movement eastward depended much on his opinion &c.[3] Without counselling him & taking into view my *daily* oppressed situation, I do not know whether I will go at *all* this Session. I see Armstrong wants me to go, though knowing as he does my situation, he is modest in pressing it & leaves perhaps *too much* to my own *judgement* or *feelings*.

On Saturday we had a most glorious meeting, & though attempts were made to thwart & weaken the effects, *we* had the lever fixed; but behold that night in comes V.B.'s letter & leaves us no ground to stand on, or *but little too little for the mass!*[4] And what a day I had on yesterday; *Armstrong Williams*[5] & others gone to the Hermitage, *others* hid. I of course [walked] all through the streets, *Democrats* & Whigs friendly to *annexation* calling on me & asking what shall we *do?* I would parry soften & reason, but both sides, meaning the common people not the leaders, would say *we must* have a third candidate. Most of them said *Calhoun,* many said *Polk,* & a few said *Tyler!*

If V.B. had have modified his answer a little stronger *we* could have carried this State. We are rather down in the mouth; ought you not to come on direct & spend a few days with us?

*Old Jackson's* voice is still for *Texas—good.*

Should you not come in, which I prefer, I will write to you as soon as I determine to go on, should I go. Donelson is here to day, at first doubting whether he would go, but I believe now he *will.* I tell him he must, extreme cases require the more boldness; I think you had best come in. *All* this is private except so far as your judgement decides otherwise. In haste....

L. P. Cheatham

ALS. DLC–JKP. Addressed to Columbia.

1. Letter not found.

2. Sarah Burruss Brown, wife of Aaron V. Brown.

3. Cheatham contemplated a journey to Washington City and to Baltimore for the Democratic National Convention.

4. References are to a mass meeting in Nashville on May 4, 1844, in support of the annexation of Texas and to Martin Van Buren's Texas letter.

5. Robert Armstrong and Willoughby Williams. A prominent Nashville lawyer and former sheriff of Davidson County, Williams became president of the Bank of Tennessee in 1842.

## FROM CAVE JOHNSON

Wednesday evening
Dear Sir,                                               Washington 8th May [1844][1]
My former letter[2] will excite your curiosity to know how we are getting on here I know & I write now to gratify that rather than any additional information I have. I know of no change in the feeling of the House except *there is less said* than during the last week. The feeling is setled & strong but calm & quiet, the malcon[t]ents meeting with more powerful opposition than they expected. They begin to look upon a dissolution of our party *with* horror but seem determined. The Globe has become more mild, as Blair is begining to write for himself & Benton & Wright tho firm more mild & forbearing. Yet I do not see how we are to get through with safety. I called yesterday to see S. Wright because several of the malcontents had said to me, that they were willing to go with us for any body else & some of them even proposed S.W. Jr. in the place of Van B.[3] I had a long & free conversation with him. He will not allow himself to be substituted in the place of Van & was sure they would not yield to it, when it was known that his sentiments corresponded with those of Van B. & assigned many reasons why Genl C.[4] would not do or the old Commodore[5] & sd. that you was the only man he thought the Nothern democrats would support if Van B. was set aside because you was known *to be firm & true* to the cause.

We had a free conversation as to the course of the Globe & his good sense, you will see in the editorial of the Globe this morning & the former articles are attributed to Col B. or Mr Senator Allen.[6] Yesterday Fisk again called on me & inquired of me as to Browns return, & then said the nominations for Sec. of the Treas. & Minister to England was under consideration and that your name was among the number and wished to know what Genl J. thought of the Admn. (I understood him to mean as to the selection of Mr. T. for our candidate).[7] I replied truly that I knew nothing of the Genls. sentiments further than they had been made public but that I was sure nothing would be more agreeable to the Genl than your selection for any office. He only talks to me because Brown is absent. My course is so well setled, that they do not like to say much to me. I repeated to Mr. W. Jr.[8] what had been intimated to me & written to you and your response declining any such position, which seemed to gratify him exceedingly.

I gave it as my opinion to him that if Van was nominated there would be a third candidate for Texas, which would of course break us up & that as they were more alarmed than we, *we might in my opinion* have the selection *of a new candidate* & thus save the *party & our principles.* They will never agree to Van, simply because they believe that the benefit of his election would inure to Benton, and if they can get another they may have better prospects for J.C.C.[9] in future. This undercurrent existed long before Van's position as to Texas was known. Your letter to Cinncinatti[10] is in the morning papers & gives great satisfaction to the Texas men.

We reported the Tariff Bill from the Committee to day & will settle it in a day or two. The chances are agt. its passage. When we were voting to day in Com. on proposition after proposition, upon which the fate of the Bill depended Saunders & Rhett were on the sofas fast asleep. The Bill would have been cut to pieces but the opposition persued a most singular course, in voting down all amendments. If they had resorted to their usual tricks 60 of them could have made the Bill in Com. what they pleased, & yet they did not, possibly because they think the defeat of the Bill certain. We shall give *about one million* to the Rivers & Harbors by a combination of the Western democrats with the Eastern Federalists & the Senate to day sent us a Bill for near half a million for the Cumberland road. Jarnigan[11] voted for it & Foster was *non est inventus.*[12] I slipped into the Senate chamber whilst the vote was being taken & Foster was sitting behind the seat of the President of the Senate. Without reflection, for you know I always feel a deep interest in the defeat of such Bills, I said are you not going to vote agt. that Bill? He made some apology that he was not well enough to vote for any thing & that he ought to be at home. Seeing that it was a plain case of dodging, I said no more. Crittenden[13] was also absent, so that if we defeat the Bill we are to loose Indiana & Illinois & if we pass the Bill we are to be abused for reviving the system of Internal Improvements.

Dickson Lewis[14] took his seat in the Senate on yesterday loosing us a vote for the Tariff, because it was expected the Texas treaty would come up.

I shall write you again soon.

C. JOHNSON

ALS. DLC–JKP. Probably addressed to Columbia.
1. Date identified through content analysis.
2. See Cave Johnson to Polk, May 5, 1844.

3. Silas Wright, Jr., and Martin Van Buren.

4. Lewis Cass.

5. Charles Stewart.

6. References are to the Washington *Globe,* Thomas H. Benton, and William Allen. After the publication of Martin Van Buren's letter on the annexation of Texas, the *Globe* defended the former president and attacked his opponents. Its editorial columns castigated those who sought to prevent Van Buren's nomination for president, including John Tyler, John C. Calhoun, and Thomas Ritchie, who had reversed his support for Van Buren. In an editorial in the *Globe* of May 7, 1844, which was not distributed until the following morning, Francis P. Blair penned a lengthy explanation of his newspaper's recent course. Conciliatory in tone, Blair maintained that his obligation to inform the public had been his guiding principle.

7. References are to Andrew Jackson and John Tyler.

8. Silas Wright, Jr.

9. John C. Calhoun.

10. See Polk to Salmon P. Chase et al., April 23, 1844.

11. Spencer Jarnagin.

12. Latin expression meaning "not to be found."

13. A Kentucky lawyer and prominent Whig politician, John J. Crittenden held several governmental posts at the state and national levels during his public career, which spanned several decades. He served in the U.S. Senate, 1817–19, 1835–41, 1842–48, and 1855–61; the U.S. House, 1861–63; the U.S. attorney generalship, 1841 and 1850–53; and the governorship of Kentucky, 1848–50.

14. Dixon H. Lewis.


## FROM SAMUEL H. LAUGHLIN

at night

My dear Sir,                                 Nashville, May 8, 1844

I have seen yours of to-day to Gen. Armstrong,[1] and precisely the difficulties you apprehend have existed here, which is one main reason why I am still on the spot. Notwithstanding pecuniary troubles, I would have been off, though I have a sore knee, but for the bad state of things produced by Mr. Van Buren's letter[2] and the disinclination of Maj. Heiss to insert any thing in mittigation or explanation of Van Buren's course. He even had the Globe editorial which accompanied Benton's letter[3] left out after I had sent it in marked to be published with the letter. I had so marked it and put it in copy drawer, but he directed the foreman, without consulting me, to leave it out and it is left out. He also caused to be left out Van Buren['s] paragraph near the end of his letter, where he says that if Mexico persists in a fruitless war, that then he would go for annexation at all hazards. This I had put at the end of a paragraph about Benton's letter in tomorrows paper. The remainder of what I said is published, but he left that out.[4] To-day, he says to me, that he approves the ground I have taken, but accompanied it by no excuse for leaving the extract I had made out, except that he was pressed for room. Mr. Humphreys has informed Gen. Armstrong and myself of the letter to Nicholson[5] to put us on our guard. Heiss, I know consults Nicholson, and has inserted things written by Nicholson once or twice without submitting them to me. This I cared not for however, as I had asked Nicholson to write any thing and every thing as a war on Whiggery which he really believed proper for the purpose. Heiss, I think, is an applicant for office to Tyler, or has an application for a partnership lying over.

All these things together, caution must be used, and care taken to prevent the evils here you speak of. The paper here must be left by me under care of Humphreys, Mosely, Armstrong and Southall.[6] Nicholson will write, but I will get Heiss to pledge himself to let no stand be taken for any name until the nominations are made, other than it has taken. Humphreys can write, and Moseley[7] copy for the press. Nicholson will write. I will, as he has written at my request heretofore, make him promise, that no step is to be taken but for the nominees, or to interfere with the nominations. Possibly I may be forced to stay here, and go on with Gen. Pillow. We have been in a terible drive. V.B.'s letter has been both misunderstood and misrepresented by persons who ought to have known better. Humphreys understands its whole *why and wherefore,* just as Gen. Armstrong, Esselman,[8] myself and a few others understood its interpretation before he (Humphreys) arrived.

I have never been in so much trouble. I have had no peace or quiet for days and nights. Yet I feel confident, that in some respects the letter may operate for our good, and as tending to strengthen your prospects.

If I go with Gen. P.[9] I will certainly return by Richmond, and so on down through Tennessee, ready to speak or do any thing in the way of work that offers on the road.

I would feel safer, if you could come with Pillow, and take new pledges, and give advice to Heiss, as he will be guided by you if you talk to him, and show him how he might even unintentionally injure and possibly ruin your prospects.

S. H. Laughlin

ALS. DLC–JKP. Addressed to Columbia and marked "Private." Polk's AE on the cover states that he answered this letter on May 9, 1844.

1. Letter not found.
2. Reference is to Martin Van Buren's letter on the annexation of Texas.
3. The editorial in the Washington *Globe* of April 29, 1844, called Thomas H. Benton's letter on the annexation of Texas a "plain, direct, straight forward expression of facts and opinions."
4. In his editorial in the *Nashville Union* of May 9, 1844, Laughlin explained the stance of Henry Clay and Martin Van Buren on the annexation of Texas. Clay was unalterably opposed to the proposition, wrote Laughlin, while Van Buren merely opposed annexation as long as "certain temporary obstacles" existed.
5. Not identified further.
6. West H. Humphreys, Thomas D. Mosely, Robert Armstrong, and Joseph B. Southall. A Democrat, Mosely had unsuccessfully sought election in 1843 to the Tennessee House from Davidson County. In 1841 Southall, a Nashville Democrat, considered running for a seat in the Tennessee House, but declined the race; he was appointed to the Nashville Democratic Central Committee by action of the Democratic State Convention in November 1843.
7. Thomas D. Mosely.
8. A well-known Nashville physician, John N. Esselman was married to Anne Campbell, sister of George W. Campbell.
9. Gideon J. Pillow.

## TO SAMUEL H. LAUGHLIN

(night)

My Dear Sir:                                        Columbia May 9th 1844

Your remaining a few days at Nashville, was not only necessary, but perhaps indispensible. The appearance of Mr Van-Buren's letter[1] required it. I am glad to learn that *Majr. Heiss* has consented to yield to your views. The Union will be in safe hands, during your absence, when it is under the control of such men as Humphreys and the other gentlemen you name at Nashville. *Genl. Pillow* will be at Nashville on saturday night on his way to Baltimore. I think all things considered that you had better abandon the Virginia route, and go on in company with *Donaldson, Childress and Pillow.*[2] You would find the Virginia route very fatiguing, and might have to travel the whole distance alone. *Williamson Smith* (who is a Delegate from Mississippi) is now at Washington, & writes me that *John Blair* was already in the City, and I suppose will not return before the convention is over. You should write to *Powell* by the next mail not to wait for you, but to meet you as early as possible at Washington. I hope *Donaldson, Childress* and *yourself,* will be ready to leave with *Pillow* in the Louisville stage on sunday morning, or at furthest on monday morning. Will you write to

*Childress* and *Donaldson* to meet *Pillow* and *yourself* at Nashville at that time. You should not delay longer. *Jno. W. Martin (Childress's* son-in-law)[3] will convey a note to him forthwith, if you desire it. I am very anxious that you should all leave as early as practicable. From what *Cave Johnson* writes, I think the recent occurrances, on the chess board, have decidedly improved my prospects. The presence of my friends from Tennessee, at Washington for a few days before the convention meets is not only vastly important, but may decide the action of the convention.

I have been constantly and incessantly engaged in Court during the whole week, in labouring to save our Democratic Clerk of the Circuit Court.[4] Late this evening the case was closed & the decision pronounced in his favour. It was a just & righteous decision, but was resisted with great energy by the Att. Genl. & five lawyers to assist him.[5] The case is however over and the Clerk will be inducted into his office in the morning. I mention this as one reason why I could not come to Nashville. I will now have some leisure and will attend to the subscription for the "Star Spangled Banner" and the other matters which I mentioned to Armstrong and yourself. Tell Armstrong to write to *Daniel Turner*[6] of Huntsville, that he must not fail to go on. I shall expect to be regularly advised of any thing of interest which may transpire in your absence.

JAMES K. POLK

ALS. DLC–JKP. Addressed to Nashville and marked *"Private."* Laughlin's AE on the cover states that he answered this letter on May 10, [1844]. Published in *ETHSP,* XVIII, pp. 166–67.

1. Reference is to Martin Van Buren's letter on the annexation of Texas.

2. Andrew J. Donelson, William G. Childress, and Gideon J. Pillow. A resident of Williamson County and a cousin to Sarah Childress Polk, Childress served one term as a Democratic member of the Tennessee House, 1835–37, and ran unsuccessfully for the U.S. House in 1839. In 1844 he attended the Democratic National Convention as a delegate from Tennessee.

3. Not identified further.

4. Prior to succeeding Pleasant Nelson as circuit court clerk in Maury County in 1844, James O. Potter served as postmaster at Spring Hill.

5. A resident of Maury County, Nathaniel Baxter served as attorney general of Tennessee's Eighth Judicial Circuit, 1841–47, and later as judge of the Sixth Judicial Circuit, 1852–58. His assistants, the particulars of the case, and Polk's involvement in the dispute are not identified further.

6. A native of Virginia, Daniel B. Turner moved early in life to Huntsville, Ala. He served as sheriff of Madison County, postmaster at Huntsville, and state senator, 1839–42; in 1844 he attended the Democratic National Convention as a delegate from Alabama.

## FROM ROBERT ARMSTRONG

Friday night

Govr., [Nashville, Tenn.] 10 May [1844][1]

I send you a note from Donelson.[2] It is Important you should be here. Start on receipt of this and you may reach the Hermitage *Sunday night.*

I fear Van Buren has used himself up with the lights before him. I believe he is for annexation but he did not *say so.*

We will find the Convention in great difficulty to Harmonize. I believe they will not be able to effect it. I cannot see how the South & West who have declared for annexation can support him. He ought to have saved us, as we have here expressed ourselves. He ought to have paid some little respect to the Old Chiefs[3] opinions. He has pearced him badly, and he feels it. Dick *Johnston* & *Cass*[4] will be pressed. Buchannan will also & will be out in favor of annexation in *next* Globe.[5]

I told you when here my views. They are not changed. Others think so *now.* Turner is here and believes with me, that you for the Presidency & Woodberry[6] for the Vice, we could redeem ourselves. *Come in.* In haste.

R. Armstrong

ALS. DLC–JKP. Addressed to Columbia and marked *"Private."*
1. Date identified through content analysis.
2. See Andrew J. Donelson to Polk, May 10, 1844.
3. Andrew Jackson.
4. Richard M. Johnson and Lewis Cass.
5. No letter from James Buchanan concerning the annexation of Texas has been found. On June 8, 1844, Buchanan counseled the U.S. Senate to ratify the treaty of annexation; he declared on that occasion that he had not previously expressed his views publicly on the Texas question.
6. Levi Woodbury.

## FROM ANDREW J. DONELSON

Dr Sir, Nashville 10th May [18]44

It is important that you should see us here without delay. The division in our ranks threatened by conflicting views about the annexation question must be obviated in time for the convention at Baltimore.

I am particularly anxious that the ground occupied by the Genl[1] should be thoroughly understood by you. What he may now say if

not modified by disclosures recently made will produce important results. If the Texas question is urged as it doubtless will be by Tyler
& Calhoun, and Genl Jackson gives the weight of his name to sustain
their views, making it the leading question in the south, the sooner
we know it the better. Come and talk over the matter with the Genl
and our friends generally. I feel deeply mortified that our wise men
should differ so much; and particularly that a measure of such vast
consequences should have been kept so long in the dark and precipi-
tated with so much haste.

A. J. Donelson

[P.S.] Come directly to Genl Jackson's.[2]

ALS. DLC–JKP. Addressed to Columbia and sent under cover of Robert
Armstrong to Polk, May 10, 1844.
1. Andrew Jackson.
2. Postscript written in the left margin of the page.

## FROM CAVE JOHNSON

Dear Sir,                              Washington May 12th 1844
I recd yours of the 2nd[1] & also one from Brown the same day, with
the news papers containing the Ten. resolutions.[2]  I regret to find
that so many members of our convention will be absent. Without the
exercise of great forbearance & wisdom we are blown to the devil.
Indeed I do not see how we are to get out of it in any way.  I do
not see that *Benton & Van's*[3] *N.Y. friends are likely* to yield to any
*force* that can be brought nor is it likely that the Southern Calhoun
Texas men *will yield.* They all talk well, both believing *they will have
the majority in the Convention.* I see no hope unless some man can
be found disconnected with both these fragments of the democratic
party & who will yield to the annexation of Texas. We are greatly
disheartened, almost without hope, & many of us have determined to
adjourn on the 27th & the balance of our party perhaps a majority
held a caucus last night to drive us from our determination & agreed
to postpone until the 10th of June. Those for adjourning refused to
attend the caucus or be bound [by] it & many of us will vote for the
adjournment happen what may and if the Whigs stand firm to the
adjournment, we shall carry it agt. a majority of Democrats. Many
of us feel so much disgraced by the conduct of our party here that we
think we will be serving the country most effectually, by seperating
us as soon as possible. The Western Democrats have united with the
Eastern Federalists & passed a River Bill, over a half million & will

pass another in a few days for as much more.[4] The Northern Tariff Democrats have united with them & defeated the Tariff[5] by a majority of six, but the latter was lost by the inefficiency of McKay. A few *immaterial amendments* & which he was *willing to accept,* would have secured the vote of *New Jersey & Connecticut* & passed the Bill. They were shewn McKay. He agreed to them, but refused to offer them in Committee & was too damned lazy to get up in Committee & tell them that they ought to pass & they were of course rejected. When we came in to the House, he was willing to offer them but could get no chance because we could never get a vote until after the previous question was called. I told him in Committee & begged him *to offer* the amendments, to say that he was willing to them but he sat still like a block never moved, took no part. I went to Drumgoole[6] who seemed equally indifferent, had not examined. Knew nothing about them. I saw the Bill was lost & give up, before we got out of Committee. McKay lacks energy beyond any man I ever saw of his talents. We are beaten in every thing & so I think we should come home. My opinion is that Van Buren will not be nominated, & if he is, there will be certainly a *third candidate* probably Cass & in addition Capt Tyler will run on his own hook. The Madisonian says, that Stewart & Cass must not use *the Capt's thunder* that *Tyler & Texas* must go together & will beat the field. Benton says "he never felt more victorious than now" & will push Van & every thing to the Devil rather than yield a inch.

I noted one thing which I ought not to omit to tell you as an evidence of the spirit prevailing among us. During the strugle to get the amendments to satisfy New Jersey & Connecticut after my efforts with McKay, I walked in dispair almost around the hall, & Genl Saunders was lying on the sofa, hankerchief over his face apparently asleep & on the next sofa lay *Mr. Rhett fast asleep.* I went to my seat & never opened my lips again about the Tariff. In this state of things the best thing we can do for the country & the party is to go home. I ought to mention another thing—Dickson Lewis[7] took his seat in the Senate *the day before* the final action *on the Tariff.* Black of G—a at home practising law. I am sick of this place & these things & am almost tempted to resign in disgust & come home & quit politics forever.

We hear nothing of the Vice presidency unless it be now & then used, to bring some strength in aid of the discontents.

C. JOHNSON

ALS. DLC–JKP. Addressed to Columbia and marked *"private."* Published in *THQ,* XII, pp. 177–78.
    1. Letter not found.

2. Reference probably is to a resolution passed by the Nashville and David-son County Democratic Association at its meeting on April 20, 1844. The text of that resolution, printed in the *Nashville Union* of April 27, 1844, called for a mass meeting of the friends of Texas annexation to convene in Nashville on May 4, 1844.

3. Thomas H. Benton and Martin Van Buren.

4. Known as the western and eastern "harbors and rivers" bills, those two measures passed the U.S. House on April 20 and May 16, respectively; the U.S. Senate approved both bills on June 1, 1844. Appropriating a total sum of $655,000, the western bill became law on June 11, 1844. Tyler, who distin-guished between the purposes of the two bills, vetoed the eastern legislation, which would have appropriated a total sum of $439,000. He returned the bill with his objections to the House that same day, and the House sustained his veto.

5. By a vote of 105 to 99 on May 10, 1844, the U.S. House laid the tariff bill on the table.

6. George C. Dromgoole.

7. Dixon H. Lewis.

## TO CAVE JOHNSON

Monday Night

[Dear Sir,]                              [Nashville, Tenn.] May 13, 1844

At the urgent solicitation of *Maj. Donaldson,*[1] *Genl. Armstrong,* and one or two other friends who wrote to me, I came to this place on yesterday. Today *Genl. A.*[2] and myself visited the Hermitage. On our way up we met *Donaldson* with a letter from *Genl. J.*[3] for publication in the Union, reiterating and reaffirming his views upon the sub[j]ect of the annexation of Texas. He urges immediate annexation as not only important but indispensible. He speaks most affectionately of *Mr. Van Buren,* but is compelled to separate from him upon this great question, and says both he and *Mr. Benton* have by their letters cut their own throats politically. He has no idea that *Mr. V.B.*[4] can be nominated or if nominated that he can receive any Southern support. He is not excited but is cool and collected, and speaks in terms of deep regret at the fatal error which *Mr. V.B.* has committed. He says how-ever that it is done and that the convention must select some other as the candidate. The truth is and should no longer be disguised from yourself and other friends, —that it will be utterly hopeless to carry the vote of this State for any man who is opposed to immediate an-nexation. The body of the Whigs will support *Clay,* regardless of his opinions, but hundreds, indeed thousands of them will abandon him, and vote for any annexation man who may be nominated by the Balti-more Convention. If such a man shall be nominated we will carry the

State with triumph and with ease. If an anti-annexation man is nominated, thousands of Democrats and among them many leading men will not vote at all and *Clay* will carry the State. The Texas question is the all-absorbing one here and swallows up all others at present. It is impossible to arrest the current of the popular opinion and any man who attempts it will be crushed by it. What you can or will do at Baltimore God only knows. My earnest desire is that you shall harmonize and run but one man. *Genl. J.* thinks that *Mr. V.B.* becoming sensible that his opinions are not in harmony with those of the people will withdraw and hopes he will do so. For myself I attribute *Mr. V.B.'s* course to *Col B—ton.*[5] *Genl. J.* says the candidate for the first office should be an annexation man, and from the Southwest, and he and other friends here urge that my friends should insist upon that point. I tell them and it is true, that I have never aspired so high, and that in all probability the attempt to place me in the first position would be utterly abortive. In the confusion which will prevail and I fear distract your counsels at Baltimore, —there is no telling what may occur. I aspire to the 2nd office and should be gratified to receive the nomination, —and think it probable that my friends may be able to confer it upon me. I am however in their hands and they can use my name in any way they may think proper. *Genl. Pillow* and *Col. Laughlin* left here last night. *Wm. G. Childress* leaves tonight and *Majr. Donaldson* on tomorrow night. They can give you more in detail the state of things here. I repeat that I wish my friends to place my name before the convention, —no matter what the result may be.

I deplore the distraction which exists in the party. It has all been produced by at most half a dozen leaders, who have acted with a view to their own advancement. Add to this the Texas question and I have great solicitude for our safety as a party. Surely there is patriotism enough among these leaders yet to save the party. This can only be done by uniting upon *one* candidate, and he must be favorable to the annexation of Texas. I have stood by *Mr. V.B.* and will stand by him as long as there is hope, but I now despair of his election—even if he be nominated.

The idea which has been suggested of running three candidates, —*Mr. Clay,* the Whig, a Texas annexation Democrat in the South, and an anti-Texas annexation Democrat in the North—ought not to be entertained for a moment. If that is attempted it insures *Clay's* election. We would have triple tickets in almost all the States, which would enable a plurality—less than a majority—to give the electoral vote of the State to *Clay.* I shall expect you to write me daily after the receipt of this, until the convention is over.

[JAMES K. POLK]

P.S. I learn that *Genl. Jackson's* letter will not appear in the Union of tomorrow, —the paper having no space for it. It will appear in Thursday's paper unless he changes his mind about its publication and withdraws it, which is not probable.[6] *W. G. Childress* can give you its contents in detail.

PL. Published in *THM*, I, pp. 239–41. Addressed to Washington City and marked *"Strictly Confidential."* Also published in Tyler, ed., *Letters and Times of the Tylers,* III, pp. 136–38.
  1. Andrew J. Donelson.
  2. Robert Armstrong.
  3. Andrew Jackson.
  4. Martin Van Buren.
  5. Thomas H. Benton.
  6. Dated May 13, 1844, Andrew Jackson's letter to the editor appeared in the *Nashville Union* of May 16, and the Washington *Globe* of May 23, 1844.

## TO CAVE JOHNSON

[Dear Sir,]                              [Nashville, Tenn.] May 14, 1844
  I wrote to you last night. I learn that *Donaldson* took the letter back to *Genl. J.* for further consultation.[1] He will be down again today and will take the stage for Washington tomorrow morning. My opinion is that the Genl. thinks his reputation requires its publication at this time. If I am right in this, it will appear in the next Union. He is as kind to *Mr. V.B.*[2] as to his manner of expressing himself as he can be, to differ with him so widely as he does upon the Texas question. If the letter appears, it will reach Washington on the Thursday evening before the meeting of the Convention. It will require care on the part of my friends to prevent *Mr. V.B.'s* friends from becoming excited at the letter and withdrawing from my support in the Convention. *Genl. J.* says that *Mr. V.B.* had *his* views before him when he wrote his letter. He says he has been misled and ruined unless he can find some plausible ground to modify his opinions. Even then the public mind has taken such a direction that it would be almost impossible to rally the Democracy for him. Judging at this distance, and from the additional lights given by your letter of the 5th which I received here after I had mailed my letter to you last night, the opinion of *Armstrong* and other friends is that I may receive the nomination, and that I will do so, unless *Mr. V.B.'s* friends should abandon me. *Genl. J.* has

written a private letter to *Mr. V.B.* and also to *Blair* in which he has spoken frankly and plainly. He is of opinion that *Mr. V.B.* seeing the impossibility of his election even if nominated, will and ought to withdraw. He has great confidence in his patriotism and thinks he will do so. He regards this step of *Mr. V.B.* (his opinion on Texas) as the only great and vital error he has committed since he has known him. He thinks this single error however must be fatal to him. He thinks the candidate for the Presidency should be an annexation man and reside in the Southwest, and he openly expresses (what I assure you I had never for a moment contemplated) the opinion that I would be the most available man; taking the Vice-Presidential candidate from the North. This I do not expect to be effected. Nothing could effect it, but the state of confusion which exists in the party. The much greater probability is that a new man for President if one be taken up will hail from the North, and in that event I would stand in a favorable position for the nomination for the second office. Should *Mr. V.B.* be withdrawn his friends will probably hold the balance of power and will be able to control the nominations for both offices, and therefore the great importance of conciliating them. It will never do for the Convention to break up in confusion or without a nomination. Any and every sacrifice should be made to effect a nomination in harmony. This done and we are safe. It will never do to break up in confusion and thus force the party upon *Tyler*. This the Democracy can never do. In a word nothing can prevent *Clay's* election but a reunion of our party, and a harmonious support of the nominations to be made at Baltimore. I have but little hope that union or harmony can be restored among the members of Congress, but I have hope that the Delegates *"fresh from the people"* —who are not members of Congress—and have not been so much excited can be brought together. Let a strong appeal be made to the Delegates as fast as they come in, *to take the matter into their own hands, to control and overrule their leaders at Washington, who have already produced such distraction, and thus save the party.* The Delegates from a distance can alone do this. I suggest as a practicable plan to bring them to act, —to get one Delegate from each State who may be in attendance to meet in a room at Brown's Hotel[3] or somewhere else, and consult together to see if they cannot hit upon a plan to save the party. If you will quietly and without announcing to the public what you are at, undertake this with energy and prosecute it with vigor, the plan is feasible and I think will succeed. If the preliminary meeting of a Delegate from each State can egrea[4] upon *the* man, then let each one see the other Delegates from his own State, and report at an adjourned meeting the result. This is the only way to secure efficient action when the Convention meets. In this way let the few men at Washington who would break us up, be controlled. Something of the kind must be done to save us. I make these suggestions because I deem them important. Some one has to take the lead and no one can do it with more prospect of success than yourself. Show this to Genl. *Pillow confidentially* who will be a most efficient man in carrying out such a plan. My old friend *Williamson Smith* of Miss. is a delegate and will do any and every thing he can. So will *Turner* of Alabama. In setting on foot such a movement, of course you should keep your own counsels, —for if known to *all* there would be troublesome spirits who would set to work to defeat it. I am on the eve of starting home and have written in great haste.

[JAMES K. POLK]

PL. Published in *THM*, I, pp. 241–42. Addressed to Washington City and marked *"Confidential."*

1. Andrew J. Donelson and Andrew Jackson. See Polk to Cave Johnson, May 13, 1844.
2. Martin Van Buren.
3. Reference is to Brown's Hotel in Washington City.
4. Possibly an error in transcribing the word "agree."

## FROM HOPKINS L. TURNEY

My Dear Sir                           Winchester May the 14th 1844

What is to become of us? May I flatter myself that the darkest hour of the knight is just before the day. Vans Letter[1] has played Hell with us. What is to be or can be done? If He had answerd wright our majority would have been verry large; in fact in this section we would have taken all. But alas all was blasted by that fatal and I might add foolish Letter. I again ask what is or can be done? Are we to submit to be sacrifised now and perhaps forever when every thing can and ought to be saved by runing another man. If the convention should in the face of all that is now apparrant before us nominate him what remaines to be done? To make battle for him is death to our cause in Tennessee if not in the whole south. I hope he will not be the nominee. But if he should be, then we ought to start a third man and one from the south, who is known to be sound on this all important question. By this course we save Tennessee from Federalism. This is one important object accomplished, and secondly we will finally Elect our man. The election will go into the House of course, and our candidate will go into the House with an eaquil if not a Larger vote than either of his opponants. His friends can under no circumstances vote for either of the Others. The house is Democratic, and the friends of Van must settle the contest. Will they take us with Texas, or Clay with his Federalism? If they prefer the Latter, then they would rather sever the union than to receive Texas and thereby give strenth to the south.

All is despondancy here. The prominant democrats sware they will not vote for Van, that they will not vote if him and Clay are the only candidates. The confusion and devisions prodused by this d—le[2] & foolish letter is indescribable, and if we have to run Van, I fear our party in Tennessee will be anihilated. The Whags can and will rally for Clay unless we bring out some one else, whereas we never can rally for Van. He I think is done forever. I will meet you at Marshal court.[3] Let me hear from you ....

H. L. TURNEY

N.B. Vans Letter prevented my writing as you requested except to C. Johnson, to whom I wrote fully my views &c. H.L.T.

ALS. DLC–JKP. Addressed to Columbia.
1. Reference is to Martin Van Buren's letter on the annexation of Texas.
2. Probably an abbreviation of the word "damnable."
3. As provided by law, the Marshall County Court convened the first Monday of each month.

## TO CAVE JOHNSON

[Dear Sir,] [Columbia, Tenn.] May [15], 1844[1]

All that I have said in the enclosed letter[2] is strictly true and expresses the opinions which I honestly entertain. I have however omitted to embrace in it some things which I design for your *own eye alone.* I thought it possible that you might think it useful to our cause or to myself individually, to show the enclosed (*confidentially* of course if you do so at all) to *Silas Wright,* and in that event I desire not to embrace in it what I am now about to say. It is this and is for yourself alone. *Mr. Wright's* declaration to you, in the conversation which you detail in your letter of the 8th that I was "the only man he thought the Northern Democrats would support if Van Buren was set aside, because I was known to be firm and *true* to the cause," is precisely the opinion which *Genl. J.*[3] expressed to me when I saw him two days ago. The General had previously expressed the same thing to others. He thinks the man should come from the Southwest. You know that I have never aspired to anything beyond the second office, and *that* I have desired. Until recently I have regarded the nomination of *Mr.*

*V.B.*[4] as certain, and the contest for the Vice Presidency, to be between *Col. J.*[5] and myself. The recent explosion at Washington, and
the incurable split in the party there and elsewhere, puts a new face
on things. "Fortuna is in a frolic,"[6] occasionally and in the midst of
the confusion which prevails, there is no telling what may happen.
In view of *Mr. V.B.'s* withdrawal by his friends, —which is not only
possible, but I think probable, —his friends will undoubtedly hold in
their hands the controlling power in the selection of *the candidate,*
and therefore it will be very important to *consolidate* them before the
event occurs. Among the Texas annexation delegates opposed to him I
will undoubtedly have many friends, and if they and the friends of *Mr.
V.B.* can unite, the whole object will be effected. It will require judgment and delicacy in managing the matter. If however it shall be first
settled that *V.B.* is to be withdrawn, I see no reason why my friends
should not make the effort. If the feeling of the Northern Democrats
continues to be such as *Mr. Wright* expressed it to be, in the conversation with you, —they would probably yield to a compromise, —if my
friends in the South and Southwest would propose it as a *compromise.*
These speculations, arising out of the unexpected events of the last
few days, may turn out to be very ridiculous. If so, they are committed to *yourself* alone. If a new man is to be selected, my friends at
Nashville think that my position and relations to the party give me
more prominence than any other. You will be on the spot and will
be best able to judge. Whatever is desired to be done, communicate
to *Genl. Pillow.* He is one of the shrewdest men you ever knew, and
can *execute* whatever is resolved on with as much success as any man
who will be at Baltimore. Lead him therefore into all your views. He
is perfectly *reliable,* is a warm friend of *V.B.'s,* and is my friend, and
you can do so with entire safety.

After all however, I think it probable that my chief hope will be for
the second office, and if so, I wish my name to go before the Convention
at all events. I have made up my mind that it would be better for me
to be defeated by a vote, than to be withdrawn. Whatever is done
will undoubtedly be settled upon at Washington before you assemble
at Baltimore, and everything will depend upon the vigilence of my
friends and their prudence in conciliating the Delegates who may be
there [assembled].[7] I calculate that this letter will reach you on the
*Friday* before the meeting at Baltimore.[8] If any new suggestion comes
to me I will write to you by tomorrow's mail. I hope you will not fail
to be a Delegate at Baltimore yourself.[9]

Our friend *A. V. Brown* cannot be back in time. The rumor here to
day is that his wife is dead.[10] I think it probably true. Two days ago

she was extremely ill, and her recovery had been despaired of by her physicians and friends.

[JAMES K. POLK]

P.S. I conclude to send the letter which purports to be enclosed in this, under a separate envelope, so that this will be seen by *no one but yourself.*

N.B. If you think it best not to show the letter *confidentially* to *Mr. Wright,* retain it and do not do so. You will be the judge.

PL. Published in *THM,* I, pp. 242–44. Addressed to Washington City and marked *"Highly Confidential."*
1. Date identified through content analysis; copyist dated this letter May 14.
2. See Polk to Cave Johnson, May 14, 1844, and Polk's postscript to the present letter.
3. Andrew Jackson.
4. Martin Van Buren.
5. Richard M. Johnson.
6. Quotation not identified further.
7. Bracketed emendation made by copyist, who indicated that Polk had written the word "assembly."
8. Polk thought that his letter would reach Johnson on May 24, 1844.
9. Johnson attended the Democratic National Convention as an at-large delegate from Tennessee.
10. Although Sarah Burrus Brown died in Pulaski on May 14, 1844, Aaron V. Brown reached Baltimore in time to serve as a delegate to the Democratic National Convention, which opened at noon on Monday, May 27, 1844.

## FROM CAVE JOHNSON

Dear Sir,                          Washington May 16th 1844

I recd yours of the 9th this morning.[1] I met Col Smith shortly after. He, you will have seen, united in the Mississippi card, signed by the M.C.s[2] who are all delegates. They had him thoroughly imbued with all their feelings & ready to desert Van.[3] We had a long talk this morning & I think he will act moderately & prudently hereafter. They had made him believe that you & Cass would be the nominees & under that impression the card was signed. The arrival of some of the delegates—Govr. Miller[4] of Miss. & Judge Ellis of Mississippi & a few others, who are fore-decided have quieted to some extent the excitement tho. the feeling is not less deep nor their action less certain. They will *defeat Van* or run *another candidate.* Old Dick's brother[5] is here & told Smith, that old Dick would not run on the same ticket with Van. *The only thing* in my opinion which will prevent a breaking up will be to run Silas Wright & you and I am inclined to think the Calhoun men will unite in that way, if Wright should not take too strong ground agt. Texas, which is now in secret session, under discussion.[6] Some of them have said so & urged it because they think we will have the power & fear we will nominate Van. The secret of all this disturbance is in the fact, that the friends of C.[7] think that if Van is elected, the Admn. will use its influence to advance T.H.B.[8] & that it is safer now to assail both than trust coming events in their hands. At the same time T.H.B. has the most implacable hostility to C. & would upset heaven & earth rather than see him advanced. In this state of things I see no hope in agreeing except in a *third man* if any thing like compromise & union. A Joint resolution for annexation upon the conditions of the treaty is now ready to present to the House[9] and was delayed (by Tibbats)[10] at my urgent request, until the decision of the Senate on the Treaty could be had.

Benton, Wright, Allen & Tappan[11] Dem. are said to oppose & that Tappan *will renew the Missouri squabble* & on that acct. it is said, the discussion was not had in public.[12] Genl Jackson has written a letter to W. B. Lewis which creates a good deal of sensation, in which he says in substance that any Senator voting agt. the treaty is a *"traitor to the best interests of the Country."*[13] An extract from the letter is read about the House & creates more feeling than I could wish. It is a private letter & its publication refused but will soon be *in substance* in the letters from this place. I understand, that the Dem. Senators are in favor of annexation but oppose the treaty, the grounds upon which it is made, the means used to effect it and the whole Executive Action, ordering the army to the Sabine and the Navy to the Gulf of Mexico.[14] The documents were yesterday ordered to be published & we shall have them in a day or two & I will send you a copy.[15]

Almonte has taken up his residence in N.Y. where he will remain until the decision of the Senate.

We have adjourned over until monday under the pretext of removing the carpets—really to attend the races.[16] Lucius[17] is here. Genl Anderson also, who is said to be a Tyler man, *denounces Van* in strong terms. Defeated in his application to go to Mexico & in his contract for removal of the Choctaws,[18] he will I reckon be content with the Capts.[19] old breeches.

Our old friend Frank Thomas is writing the most provoking & insulting letters to T.H.B., charging that Mrs. T. had been seduced before marriage, that T.H.B. knew it & brought about his marriage with her aided by Mrs. B. & copying the letters & sending them to M.C.s[20] He is certainly deranged.

My boy[21] has been sick several days but is better to day.

C. JOHNSON

ALS. DLC–JKP. Probably addressed to Columbia; marked *"private."* Published in *THQ,* XII, pp. 178–79.

1. Letter not found.

2. Dated May 4 and written from Washington City, the card, which appeared in the Washington *Globe* of May 6, 1844, was addressed to the Mississippi Democracy. The writers, including Williamson Smith, announced that they would only support for the presidential nomination someone who favored the immediate annexation of Texas.

3. Martin Van Buren.

4. Governor of Missouri from 1825 until 1832, John Miller won election as a Van Buren Democrat to the U.S. House, where he served from 1837 until 1843.

5. Probably Henry Johnson, Richard M. Johnson's brother, who was a delegate from Kentucky to the Democratic National Convention of 1844.

6. Reference is to the treaty for the annexation of Texas, which was being considered by the U.S. Senate in executive session.

7. John C. Calhoun.

8. Thomas H. Benton.

9. A joint resolution for the annexation of Texas was not introduced in the U.S. House at that session of Congress.

10. A Kentucky lawyer, John W. Tibbatts was elected as a Democrat to the U.S. House, where he served from 1843 until 1847.

11. Thomas H. Benton, Silas Wright, Jr., William Allen, and Benjamin Tappan. A lawyer in Steubenville, Ohio, Tappan served as judge of the Fifth Ohio Circuit Court of Common Pleas in 1816 and as U.S. district judge of Ohio in 1833; he won election as a Democrat to one term in the U.S. Senate, 1839–45. He opposed slavery; but unlike his brothers, Arthur and Lewis Tappan, he rejected the abolition movement.

12. The U.S. Senate had decided not to discuss in open session the treaty for the annexation of Texas; after rejecting the treaty, the Senate voted on June 8, 1844, to remove the injunction of secrecy on those deliberations.

13. An extract of Andrew Jackson's letter of May 3, 1844, to William B. Lewis has been published in John Spencer Bassett, ed., *Correspondence of Andrew Jackson* (7 vols.; Washington, D.C.: Carnegie Institution, 1926–35), VI, p. 282. Johnson's quotation is a close paraphrase of Jackson's words. Jackson's neighbor and longtime friend, Lewis had resided in the White House during Jackson's presidency and had been a member of the "Kitchen Cabinet."

14. John Tyler notified the U.S. Senate on May 15, 1844, that he had dispatched U.S. forces to protect Texas pending ratification of the treaty of annexation. He sent naval vessels to the Gulf of Mexico and army troops to Fort

Jessup near the Texas border.

15. On May 15, 1844, the U.S. Senate voted to remove its injunction of secrecy on the text of the rejected treaty and on all documents related to the question. The next day the Senate authorized printing 20,000 copies of the treaty and its related documents.

16. The National Jockey Club races, held in Washington City over a four-day period, had commenced on May 14, 1844.

17. Possibly Lucius J. Polk, the son of William Polk of North Carolina and Polk's cousin. Owner of a large plantation in Maury County, Lucius Polk served in the Tennessee Senate, 1831–33; his wife, Mary Eastin Polk, was Rachel Jackson's niece.

18. Although most of the tribe had been removed to the Indian Territory in the 1830's, thousands of Choctaws still remained in Mississippi. Alexander O. Anderson, who had served in 1838 as a federal agent for removing the Indians from Alabama and Florida, apparently solicited a contract for transporting the Mississippi Choctaws.

19. John Tyler.

20. Francis Thomas, Thomas H. Benton, Sally Campbell McDowell Thomas, and Elizabeth McDowell Benton. A leading lawyer from western Maryland, Francis Thomas won five terms as a Democrat in the U.S. House, 1831–41; he served as governor from 1841 until 1844. In 1841 he had married Sally Campbell McDowell, twenty-year-old daughter of James McDowell of Virginia and favorite niece of Thomas H. Benton. On May 20, 1842, Cave Johnson had reported to Polk that the couple had become estranged over "some foolish jealous fit of his, for which there was not the slightest cause." ALS. DLC–JKP.

21. Either James Hickman or Thomas Dickson Johnson.


## FROM GIDEON J. PILLOW

Dear Govr.                                          Cincinatti May 16, 1844

I arived in this city this morning. I have seen Messrs Dawson and Foran,[1] the last a Delegate to the Baltimore convention. They are both for you for V.P.

I have heard from Washington. Our party is in great distraction. A powerful effort is being made to get clear of V.[2] & to bring up Tyler. This measure, if carried, would certainly defeat your prospects. This whole country is for annexation,[3] except a small portion of the Whig party about the cities. Ohio is for V.B.[4] over any body, & you are the choice for V.P. and feel confident of getting the support of the Ohio Delegation. These opinions are formed from my conversations with the Delegates from this city[5] and Dawson.

I have only time to say, I understand the game playing at Washington & if I do not then I shall for once be deceived.

Dick Johnson, having his hopes revived for the Presidency in the Distraction of our party, has gone on to Washington. This will kill him off.

My boat is about to leave & I must conclude. I will write you again as soon as I reach Washington.

GID. J. PILLOW

ALS. DLC–JKP. Addressed to Columbia.

1. Moses Dawson and James J. Faran. A lawyer, Faran served in the Ohio House, 1835–39, and Senate, 1839–43; sat in the U.S. House as a Democrat, 1845–49; and served as mayor of Cincinnati, 1855–57. From 1844 until 1881 he was associate editor and proprietor of the *Cincinnati Enquirer*.

2. Martin Van Buren.

3. Reference is to the annexation of Texas.

4. Martin Van Buren.

5. Reference is to James J. Faran and Nicholas Schoonmaker.

## FROM GIDEON J. PILLOW

Dear Govr.                    Washington City May 22nd 1844

Myself & Col. Laughlin reached this city yesterday evening. Since that time we have been busily engaged examining into the condition of things here and though I had expected to find much confusion & excitement among our friends, yet I confess myself much surprised at the extent of the *distraction* and the bitterness of feeling which exists between the Van Buren men & the disaffected portion of the party. This last party I am satisfied is daily gaining strength by the arrival of Delegates from regions of the country which have been lost by V's letter.[1] I have spent a good portion of this day in confidential consultation with Gov. Bagby & Wright. Last night I was with Cave J.[2] The *two former,* who are the leaders of the V. forces (Benton being excepted) and who represent the feeling & determination of the V.B. Democracy, say they are unable to suggest any remedy for the existing state of things. They say the Northern Democracy will never yield up their preferences for V. & that his name will in no event be withdrawn.

The Democracy or rather the Delegates of the south west & west are making an extraordinary effort for Cass. Many of them are going so far with their opposition to V. as to declare they won't go into convention if he is to be the nominee & that they won't support him in any event. If they continue to occupy that ground, they will breake up *the party* & will leave no hope of reconciliation. Among the very worst of these *aggitators* is your friends Geo. W. Jones & Gen. Anderson. The last is doing us great mischief.

He wants an office from Tyler & is violent in his abuse of V. & is
for Tyler or any body else.  I have gone to work to try & get the
northern & southern branches of the party to agree to meet in convention & to try who is the strongest man & to agree to submit to
the decision of the convention.  I have to night had Powell, Blair,
Jones, Blackwell at my room, talking & consulting about the plan to
be adopted.  We have fixed upon Tomorrow night for general meeting of our Tennessee delegation to shape our course of action with an
eye single to the restoration of the re-union of the party & of your
nomination.  I think we shall be able ultimately to get the division
of the party together in the convention, but there [are] some serious
difficulties in the way.  The disaffected say they won't go into convention unless Two thirds of the convention shall be necessary to make a
nomination.  Understanding what would be the result of such a principle, the other party refuse to make any such agreement, insisting
that a majority only shall make the nomination.  In this attitude the
parties now stand, abusing each other most bitterly.  I do not dispair
of reunion yet, but I confess the prospect is most gloomy.  Both parties
seem to look to you as the probable V.P.  There is however so much
distraction & division & difficulty about the *first,* that but little is said
of the *second* & I think it now best to use all our influence & power
to *heal the* wounds of the party & re-unite it if possible & until that
is done, say but little about the V.P.

If we do not unite *all is lost.*  If we do unite we will then I feel
confident get your nomination, although *old Dick*[3] is here & pressing
himself strongly upon the party & actually electioneering with all
his might.  You see we have trouble enough.  We are certainly in
Deep water.  My great effort shall be to *conciliate* & to hold things
in attitude to secure your nomination no matter which party may
succeed.  S. Laughlin & myself act together in this view of the case
& I think we will be able to get all the Tennessee Delegation to co-
operate in a silent acquiescence in the action of the convention except
Anderson & possibly Jones.  No effort shall be left *undone.*  If the party
should not be totally broken up I think we will get you the ticket.  We
are pretty certainly to have a *sort of ticket for* Tyler, & we are much
afraid the disaffected will *secede* from the convention & join the Tyler
convention.

You see Gov. we are at *sea* & upon a boisterous one at that.  I hope
to succeed & you may rely upon all my exertions being used for that
purpose.  I have a good deal I should like to explain connected with
Tylers game here to *use* up the Democracy & buy them off from V. but
I can't do it in this letter.  I will write you again soon & make Laughlin

do so to. You shall be kept constantly advised of every movement of interest & when you do not hear from us it will be because things have assumed no new aspect. Childress arrived this evening.

GID. J. PILLOW

ALS. DLC–JKP. Addressed to Columbia. Published in Jesse S. Reeves, ed., "Letters of Gideon J. Pillow to James K. Polk, 1844," *AHR*, XI (July, 1906), pp. 835–37.
1. Martin Van Buren's letter on the annexation of Texas.
2. Cave Johnson.
3. Richard M. Johnson.

## FROM SAMUEL H. LAUGHLIN

My dear Sir       Washington City May 23, 1844

You must pardon my seeming remissness in not writing earlier, as I have been influenced in waiting by no other wish than a desire to learn and ascertain something definite, and something material and interesting to communicate. All yet, however, is chaos and darkness, and no man knows any thing definite. I was in a meeting of friends last night at Gadsby's[1] with Cave Johnson, Dromgoole, Gen. Fine of N.Y. Gov. Morton of Mass. Col. Medary, Gen. Pillow[2] &c. &c. but no definite count could be made. Some of our friends find fault with some of our delegates for talking too much. I cannot attach blame to good and true motives and zeal to serve the cause and you. But every word that any of us utter, and especially Gen. Pillow from your own district, is told again, misrepresented, lied about and may do harm. Our position is, as pressed and agreed by Johnson, Blair, Powell and myself, to stand for Union, harmony, and opposed to dividing, splitting and destroying the party—a position of firmness, dignity, reserve, and which is necessarily aloof from the several factions.

A scheme is on foot, and Blair and Powell favor it, to adopt a rule that it shall require 2/3 two-thirds to nominate. This is a plan of the southern factions, and intended to enable them to try strength, and possibly succeed themselves, but if *they* cannot, they will try to know before hand that Van Buren cannot. They wish to play with his friends for the crown with stacked cards—*they* may win, *he* cannot. Powell thinks it will produce harmony. That some good man will in the end get two thirds, and that the other third then, will not dare to secede. I have great doubts at present of the efficacy of the plan. They are all enemies of Van Buren, and no special friends of yours who propose it, except Cullom. He says if Van Buren is nominated, that you ought not to go on the ticket with him, because it will destroy you forever, especially in the south. I told him you would be before the Convention, in its hands, must be your judge and guardian, and that it would be a high honor to be nominated with any body nominated for the first office by the voice of the regular democratic Convention. He is a fool, boards with James A Black[3] (the best man from South Carolina) and others from S.C. and Georgia. Geo. Jones, Andy Johnson, and Gen. Anderson are all rabid, wild, mad.

I am sorry that Coe has written to Gen. Anderson (he received the letter to-day) that if Van Buren is nominated, he will retire from the ticket. Austin Miller[4] has written despondingly to A. V. Brown, and Geo. W. Jones has the letter. I saw it to-day.

Two or three New Yorkers seem to-day, to be pleased with Gen. Jackson's last letter.[5]

Benton told Childress to-day, that Gen. Jackson is exactly and perfectly right as to Texas, the Texas we sold and ceded in 1819, but not as to *the* Texas about to be ceded to us, which includes a large country we never owned, and never ceded, and that never has been reduced to the possession and occupancy of Texas. On all the facts Gen. Jackson has formed his opinion upon, his opinions and course he says are right, but not upon the facts now disclosed by the documents and Treaty. There is much truth in this *inter nos.*[6]

The count we could make last night, showed that Van Buren will loose 2 votes in Maine, some in Massachusetts, New Hampshire, Connecticut, &c. because he is for annexation. The anti Texas folks understand his letter[7] better than we Texas folks.

Williamson Smith, Col. G. R. Fall,[8] and Mississippi are sticking to us like brothers.

Ohio is mad and rabid for Van Buren. Two of the five Michigan men are against Cass.

Old Dick[9] is going it like a man electioneering for a clirkship before our Assembly, for either place. His brother[10] says he will not go on a ticket with Van Buren. His other friends say *he* has never said that. To night I will go with Cave to see the Capt. Wright and Benton.[11]

May God give us a safe deliverance! Blair has gone up to Baltimore to-day to complete some mercantile matters of business.

S. H. LAUGHLIN

P.S. A. Johnson has given me some franks—you will see by this letter.[12] Rashly, he abused the Ohio men in the House yesterday for their card.[13] What was it to him? He has no discretion. S.

ALS. DLC–JKP. Addressed to Columbia under the frank of Andrew Johnson and marked "Private."

1. Gadsby's was a popular hotel in Washington City.
2. Cave Johnson, George C. Dromgoole, John Fine, Marcus Morton, Samuel Medary, and Gideon J. Pillow. A New York lawyer, Fine served as judge of the Court of Common Pleas for St. Lawrence County, 1824–39, and 1843–47, and as a Democrat in the U.S. House, 1839–41. Morton, a lawyer, represented his Massachusetts district in Congress for two terms, 1817–21, and sat on the State Supreme Court from 1825 until 1840. Elected governor as a Democrat in 1840, he narrowly won reelection in 1842. In 1845 Polk appointed him collector of customs in Boston, where he served until 1849.
3. A veteran of the War of 1812 and banker from Columbia, S.C., James A. Black won election as a Calhoun Democrat to the U.S. House, where he served from 1843 until his death in 1848.
4. Austin Miller practiced law in Bolivar; served as judge of Tennessee's Eleventh Circuit Court, 1836–38; and won election as a Democrat to three terms in the Tennessee House, 1843–47 and 1861–63.
5. See Polk to Cave Johnson, May 13, 1844.
6. Latin phrase meaning "between us."
7. Reference is to Martin Van Buren's letter on the annexation of Texas.
8. Williamson Smith and George R. Fall. An Englishman, Fall served at various times from 1835 until 1850 as editor and/or publisher of the influential Jackson *Mississippian,* which he and his brother, James S. Fall, owned. He also served three terms in the Mississippi House, 1844, 1861, and 1862.
9. Richard M. Johnson.
10. Probably Henry Johnson.
11. Cave Johnson, John Tyler, Silas Wright, Jr., and Thomas H. Benton.
12. Laughlin wrote his postscript in the left margin of his last page.
13. In a card dated May 1 and published in the Washington *Globe* of May 3, 1844, the Democratic congressional delegation of Ohio advised their constituents that a secret intrigue, with which they were unconnected, was underway in Washington City to prevent Martin Van Buren's presidential nomination. Alarmed, they predicted that "disastrous consequences" would result if the conspiracy succeeded. During a May 22 debate in the House on naval appropriations Andrew Johnson disavowed knowledge of any movement identified by the Ohio delegation and criticized them for their allegation.

## FROM CAVE JOHNSON

My Dear Sir,                           Washington Friday 24th May [1844][1]
I recd two or three letters[2] & had intended to have written you oftener but have had no time for any thing & besides have nothing to tell you good. Confusion is worse counfounded. A large number of delegates has been here & most of them yet here. It is doubtful whether Van Buren has a majority of the convention. His friends count from 145 to 150 including Tennessee. The discontents have no

man yet fixed on. The Calhoun portion are secretly working the wires to prevent any nomination so as to have a new convention, in Augt or Sept. The first question will be the 2/3 rule. If that is adopted no nomination will be made. If it fails, the discontents will probably secede. There is but little talk of the Vice-presidency. A rumor to day in the House that excited some feeling was, that the Ten. delegation had bargained with the Ohio & N.Y. for you & Van.[3] Some of your friends (Jones & Johnson)[4] talk publicly that you ought not to suffer yourself to be put on the ticket with Van. Old Dick[5] is looking out for the first but will take any. I think if Van Buren is nominated that it is now the intention of his friends to place you on his ticket. At least Judge Fine & Col Young[6] think so. Ralph Ingersol[7] is here, who would like you for the first. Gov. Morton is for you & he thinks the Massachusetts delegation.

The difficulty & I feel it sensibly is this. We go into the convention. If the South secedes & runs a *Texas candidate,* we will be in a bad box. Shall we secede with them? Or shall we remain & our nomination & ourselves [be] run over at home? We have talked it over but not decided. My impression is & I have so stated to Pillow & Powell that Ten. will have to *vote for a new man,* tho I have kept it from Johnson & Jones lest they should talk about it among the discontent. I shall say so to Silas Wright to night or tomorrow. I have recd so many pressing letters from Turney, Coe, Fitzgerald, Humphreys, Cheatham,[8] & meetings in Paris & Bolivar besides others from my other counties[9] that I am driven to the conclusion that our friends want another candidate, tho. I shall give such a vote, if I do at all, with the greatest reluctance. I am sometimes hesitating whether I should *even go*—let my colleagues do it. I have promised Powell to go to Baltimore on Sunday. Genl Saunders &c are leaders in the South & will be there & a bold push made for a majority. In[10] Van's friends have the power they will adopt the majority rule. We have 11 delegates here from Ten.[11]

C. JOHNSON

[P.S.] I shall write you every evening.

ALS. DLC–JKP. Addressed to Columbia.
1. Date identified through content analysis.
2. Polk had written to Johnson on May 13, 14, and 15, 1844.
3. Martin Van Buren.
4. George W. Jones and Andrew Johnson.
5. Richard M. Johnson.
6. John Fine and Samuel L. Young. A lawyer and political supporter of Martin Van Buren, Young had a lengthy career in state government, including

service as a member of the New York Senate and as secretary of state.

7. Ralph I. Ingersoll.

8. Hopkins L. Turney, Levin H. Coe, William Fitzgerald, West H. Humphreys, and Leonard P. Cheatham. Fitzgerald served as circuit court clerk in Stewart County, 1822–25; sat one term in the Tennessee House, 1825–27; and held the position of attorney general of Tennessee's Sixteenth Judicial Circuit before winning election in 1831 to a single term in the U.S. House. He moved to Henry County in the late 1830's and in 1841 became judge of the Ninth Judicial Circuit.

9. Johnson's congressional district included the counties of Robertson, Montgomery, Stewart, Dickson, Humphreys, Benton, and Henry.

10. Johnson probably meant to write the word "If."

11. As listed in the Washington *Globe,* June 4, 1844, thirteen delegates attended the convention. Apparently Johnson had not included himself in his count; and Aaron V. Brown had not reached Washington City.

## FROM GIDEON J. PILLOW

Dear Govr. Washington May 24 [18]44[1]

Since my last letter to you our troubles have *increased.* The anti-Van Buren party are becoming *stronger* and though Van can get, agreeably to the best estimates, I can make, about 145 votes in convention, yet I fear the Two thirds rule will be *adopted* by the aid of the vote of Pennsylvania & that of a part of the Tennessee delegation who cant be controuled upon this question. Cass can get, as his friends think, about 80 votes on the first ballot & Johnson[2] will get the ballance. On the 2nd ballot Cass' friends think he will take the vote of Pennsylvania from V.[3] which will give him about 106 votes. These estimates, if correct, you will see render the result exceedingly doubtful. The Johnson votes, will go for Cass, which will give him a majority, but whether he can get *two thirds* so as to nominate him, under that rule is very doubtful.

The breache between the V's & anti-V's has become impassible. The parties will never meet except upon some other man than Cass, unless Cass should have strength enough to carry him through under the 2/3 rule. The Tennessee Delegation had a meeting night before last. Jones & Andy Johnson *were there* & were ready to *sacrifice* you, to get clear of V. They both profess to be your friends & have been kind enough to say that they are unwilling for your name to go on V's ticket. So says Collum, & *some other* of your friends, also.[4]

Upon the subject of the Vice Presidency, not much has been said until to day. To day the report has been busily circulated that your friends were looking to Benton's & Van's friends for support for you,

& with some it was even said that a distinct understanding existed
&c. Having been called upon as your immediate representative by
Several of the disaffected I disclaimed in the most positive terms any
such understanding. They then pressed me & hard for our position, &
said that if Polks friends voted for V. they would not vote for P.[5] These
were part of the Mississippi & part of the North Carolina delegation.
I took the position that as we intended to place your name before the
convention, we thought it our duty to be modest and not to be *active*
in arraying the parties, that I thought we ought not to interfere &c
but that we would cast our votes without reference to the V.P. &c
and when we had determined upon our course as we would before the
convention met, it would be known &c. The object you will easily
understand is to *force* me as your friend to commit myself against V.
& to compel all your friends to do so to. What this ever will result in
I cannot tell. I do not think V. will get the nomination. I think he
will be cut off under the 2/3 rule, & I much fear the loss of strength
to you, in Alabama, Miss, North Carolina & Virginia by the position
we will be obliged to take with reference to the Presidency.

I am now satisfied that it is contemplated to run Stephenson[6] for
the V.P. on Cass' ticket. This the disaffected deny, but the thing is
sure to work out that way. If it were not for the present organization
of parties here and the embarrassment which is brought upon you by
this *Conspiricy,* you have more strength with the Democracy than any
man whose name has come before the country and though by these
movements I regard every thing as thrown into confusion and uncertainty I would not still be surprised if a compromise were finally made
by both parties taking you up for the P.[7] This I give as a *possability.*

Jones & Anderson are wholly *rabid,* & we do not now consult with
them atall. I saw your letter to C.J.[8] & noted its suggestions. Medary
& his Ohio people we think will certainly go for you, for V.,[9] though
we can only judge from the intercourse we have. Govr. M[o]rton of
Massachusetts is for you & he says his Delegation he thinks will all
go for you. The Illinois & Indiana delegation are friendly to you.
Some of them particularly of the first mentioned state are clear for
you. It is said *Benton* now prefers you. He keeps silent on the subject
however. It is impossible for me to give you even a brief outline of
one half I want to wright. You may consider every thing, even the
fate of the party, as at *sea.* Every thing is *doubtful.* The foundations
of party are all broken up here, & I do not believe they will ever be
reconciled. You know I am not in this state of things *idle.* There are
so many *aggitators* and reckless men who are looking to their own
aggrandisement & care nothing for the party or the country, that is

impossible to controul the *moving mass.*

We will spare no effort to get things *quieted.* C.J. & *all* our friends are almost in *dispair* of *every thing.* We shall go to Baltimore tomorrow, [...]¹⁰ Saturday.

GID. J. PILLOW

ALS. DLC–JKP. Addressed to Columbia. Published in *AHR,* XI, pp. 837–38.
1. Pillow wrote over the date, "23d."
2. Richard M. Johnson.
3. Martin Van Buren.
4. Alvin Cullom. Several members of the Tennessee delegation met with Pillow on the evening of May 22 and scheduled a meeting of the full delegation for the following night.
5. Reference is to Polk and his bid for the vice-presidential nomination.
6. Andrew Stevenson.
7. Reference is to the presidency.
8. Cave Johnson.
9. Vice-president.
10. Word illegible.

## FROM WILLIAM G. CHILDRESS

Dr Sir                                          Washington May 25th 1844
Agreeable to promise I write you upon the subject of our Convention. I have been here some days and as yet am unable to say what will be the result. All seem to be unwilling to make a move fearing the consequences. We are in a most deplorable condition. You are the favorite with the North for the second office but we dare not form any open connexion with them for in that event we loose the south. I dread the organisation.¹ The Vanburen men are for a majority, his opponents for two thirds to nominate. If the former prevails there is great danger of the South seceding & join[in]g Capt. Tyler & in that event we would be greatly injured in Ten. I shall go for the two third rule with the hope & belief that the North will stand firm & we will retain our strength in the South. You will have seen ere you recd. this the construction as also the manner of reception of Gen. J['s] letter by the Vanites.² His opponents construe it differently. There is a possibility & a faint probability of Vans being out of the way & in that event as far as I can learn his friends will be for you. But Sir I have never seen as much caution & circumspection before.

W. G. CHILDRESS

ALS. DLC–JKP. Addressed to Columbia.

1. Reference is to a probable floor fight over the rules for organizing the Democratic National Convention, which was scheduled to begin in Baltimore on May 27.

2. Reference is to Andrew Jackson and to supporters of Martin Van Buren.

## FROM CAVE JOHNSON

Saturday evening

Dear Sir                       [Washington City] 25 May 1844

The day has passed, with groups of democrats in every part of the House in close & earnest consultation & with great anxiety depicted on every countenance. Pickens[1] is here a delegate from the State of South Carolina. Whether he takes any part in the convention or not is uncertain. Most have gone to Baltimore. I go in the morning.

Van[2] will probably have a majority not 2/3 & we have had a plan on hand to day to compromise from which we hope much. First vote for Van. The discontents will scatter on Stewart, Buckhanan, Johnson, Cass &c.[3] Then Van's friends to say to them, now, if you cannot take ours, present us your candidate. Agree upon some one, Cass or any other & present him as a compromise. They cannot agree. The Calhoun men will not probably yield to him nor the Johnson men & they will try to break up the convention & postpone & call a new convention. A majority will probably fall on Silas Wright who is right on the Tariff & will be right on Texas, agt. *the treaty* but for immediate annexation by law. If the South presents Wright, the friends of Van in the North will yield & take him. This is the only hope of any thing like unity of action. Wright will yield to no such thing but we must force him.

I say he is right on Texas, because I have seen a resolution prepared by him to be offered by the North & passed at Baltimore & besides he & Benton will reject the treaty but pass a law to annex upon the conditions of the treaty & with the assent of Texas. This is the best position for us & for you. You scarce hear a word as to the Vice presidency. If Van is dropped, RMJ[4] will be of course. This project seems to take well so far as we can learn. We have been urging the discontents to agree upon their man & if they do agree upon one whether Wright or any other (except R.M.J.) I verily believe we shall be able to induce the North to yield & unite & make a nomination. I therefore have finally settled to go in the morning to Baltimore. It is probable that Donelson Pillow & myself will scarcely yield Van whilst he is kept up by his friends. We have not as yet fixed upon an action as a delegation. Weller told me to day that Ohio would go for R.M.J. with reluctance. If Van is nominated we shall pass the Texas resolution in Convention & he will of course accept upon the terms proposed. Van Buren is censured in the North by Whigs for having yielded too much to the South in the late Texian letter. Every thing is in motion here day & night. In haste.

C. JOHNSON

ALS. DLC–JKP. Addressed to Columbia. Published in *THQ*, XII, pp. 179–80.
1. Francis W. Pickens, a South Carolina lawyer and planter, first won election to Congress as a nullifier and sat from 1834 until 1843; a member of the Nashville Convention of 1850, he served as governor of South Carolina from 1860 until 1863.
2. Martin Van Buren.
3. Charles Stewart, James Buchanan, Richard M. Johnson, and Lewis Cass.
4. Richard M. Johnson.

## FROM GIDEON J. PILLOW

Dear Sir, Washington City Saturday 25th May [18]44
A better feeling prevails to day & I think there is now a prospect of ultimate union. I regard it almost certain Van Buren cannot get the nomination & I think his friends at the north so consider it. Some of them say if the Democracy cannot get along with him at the south and will fix upon a man upon whom the south will *unite,* that they will support him, & the Disaffected say if the North will withdraw V.[1] that the north may name the man. These concessions indicate a better feeling & will I hope, result in harmonious action. The chief difficulty in getting together under this state of feeling grows out of the rival claims of Johnson, Cass, Woodbury[2] & others. The south may not be able to agree on any man & in this way, we may still have difficulty & it may even be possible, that when the disaffected find themselves unable to agree upon any other man, they may some of them come back to V. If V. should be withdrawn or beaten in convention, the chances are strongly in favour of Cass, unless V's friends should take you up & unite with your friends of the south to defeat Cass.

You have more friends here than any man in the field & if your name had been brought before the country for the *first* place, we would have had far more unanimity. I am satisfied you are the choice of 2/3 of the convention for the Vice, & almost every one of your friends say they would prefer you for the Presidency. Things may take that turn yet. We of the south cannot bring *that matter* up. If it should be done by the north it will all work *right,* but if we were to make such a move it would in all probability injure your prospect for the Vice. Almost all the Delegates composing the convention have been here. I have made it my *special business* to become acquainted with them & to find out as well as I could, their preferance for the *Vice,* and I think it is next to impossible to defeat your nomination if the convention ever comes to any conclusion at all. You are the choice of both branches of the Democratic family beyond all doubt for the Vice, & I do not believe if Stephenson[3] should be brought out, that he can defeat your nomination. He certainly cannot unless there should be a very extraordinary change in the feelings of the convention. Our delegation, that portion of it which we can manage are *Still & silent,* urging harmony & peace & abstaining from all active interference in arraying the parties against each other. Powell, Anderson, Jones, & Blair & Taylor[4] are all determined to go for Cass. Johnson, Loflin, myself, Donalson & Childress[5] are still waiting for further developments and light before we act or determine what we will do. As far as I know or believe or am informed, all V's friends are for you. We have carefully avoided saying or doing any thing to alienate their feelings. If we can retain their strength & your own in the south & west you are safe.

The Ohio Delegates & the new england Delegates, I think are all or nearly so for you. So are New York, but they are very silent. C. Johnson is in low spirits about our prospects & seems to have lost his energy. I feel confident of your success unless the convention should breake up in a r[ow].[6] The Ultra-discontents, who care but little about Texas & only use the power of the measure as a lever to turn out Van & to kill off Benton as his successor, are understood now to play their game with the view of preventing any nomination, & have proposed to have another one in July. But they cannot affect their object. I received yours of the 17th. Inst today.[7] We will give you Two annexation men I think. The North has become allarmed at the excitement about Texas in the south & say we shall have Texas &c. We shall go to Baltimore this evening. I will write you regularly & daily if I can.

Gid. J. PILLOW

[P.S.] I do not think you have lost a particle of strength by the report of which I wrote you in my last.[8] It will endear you to the friends of V. & will recoil on the head of those who started it as slander & falsehood. I have not heard it mentioned for nearly 2 days. G.J.P.

ALS. DLC–JKP. Addressed to Columbia. Published in *AHR,* XI, pp. 839–40.
1. Martin Van Buren.
2. Richard M. Johnson, Lewis Cass, and Levi Woodbury.
3. Andrew Stevenson.

4. Robert W. Powell, Alexander O. Anderson, George W. Jones, John Blair, and George T. Taylor. Taylor, a prominent Democratic operative from Tipton County, represented Tennessee's Tenth Congressional District at the Baltimore Convention.

5. Cave Johnson, Samuel H. Laughlin, Andrew J. Donelson, and William G. Childress.

6. An ink blot has obscured part of one word.

7. Polk's letter has not been found.

8. See Pillow to Polk, May 24, 1844.


## FROM CAVE JOHNSON

(Monday night)

Dear Sir                                     Baltimore May 27 [1844][1]

We met to day *Genl. Saunders 20* minutes before the hour (12) called the convention to order & nominated Mr. Wright of Pa[2] chairman pro. tem. Of course we could not resist it. He then introduced a resolution adopting the rules of 1832 including the 2/3 rule. This led to a debate and a variety of propositions of but little importance. We finally organized by the appointment of Wright & 25 Vice presidents, S. Carolina not being there. *Wright* is said to be a Porter, Tyler man, claiming to be a democrat.[3] A debate sprung up upon the 2/3 rule which lasted most of the evening. Saunders & Walker for the rule and B. F. Butler agt. it. We vote on it tomorrow & will probably adopt the 2/3 rule. Ten. delegation will vote for it. The movement regarded to day as most formidable agt. Van Buren is for Buckhanon & Johnson.[4] Hence the selection of Wright. Ten. takes her stand for the present for Silas Wright. From what we can learn, public opinion will not justify us in giving our vote to Van.

There is so many rumors, so much excitement, that it seems impossible to come to any correct conclusions for the future. Every thing is in doubt.

There are near 400 delegates in attendance, all full except Louisiana, only two & Alabama three. As far as I can judge, there is a greater collection of talents & character than we have had at any time before. We have had an immense crowd all day in front of the Odd fellows hall. I have been entertained by speeches all day.

The Tyler Convention met & nominated the Capt. and adjourned over until tomorrow.[5] Their policy seems to be, to have Van Buren nominated so that they can have Tyler & Texas without a division. McDuffie has introduced a Joint resolution for the immediate annexation,[6] which we understand all the Democratic Senators will vote for.

I will write you as soon as we have any thing worthy.

C. JOHNSON

ALS. DLC–JKP. Addressed to Columbia. Published in *THQ*, XII, pp. 180–81.
1. Date identified through content analysis.
2. A Pennsylvania lawyer and Democrat, Hendrick B. Wright served first as temporary and then as permanent chairman of the Democratic National Convention of 1844; he was a delegate to six of his party's subsequent national conventions, 1848–76. Wright served four terms in the U.S. House, 1853–55, 1861–63, and 1877–81.
3. David R. Porter, an iron manufacturer, served as governor of Pennsylvania from 1839 until 1845.
4. James Buchanan and Richard M. Johnson.
5. The Tyler Convention convened at Baltimore on May 25, 1844, and declared a preference for John Tyler for president and Richard M. Johnson for vice-president.
6. On May 23, 1844, George McDuffie offered a joint resolution in an executive session of the U.S. Senate; his resolution called for the annexation of Texas "as soon as the supreme executive and legislative power of Texas shall ratify and confirm the said compact of annexation."

## FROM GIDEON J. PILLOW

My Dear Sir                                   [Baltimore, Md.] May 28th [18]44
We have been all day engaged balloting for Candidate for President. We commenced at 149 for Van & 82 for Cass.[1]  After 6 Ballotings we now stand 99 for Van & 116 for Cass, 32 for Johnson & 35 for Buckhannon.[2]  We have for 2 hours past had the most extraordinary excitment in convention. The whole convention had well-nigh got into a general pel-mell fight. The Ohio Delegation produced it all. At this moment the excitment is still wholly ungovernable by the chair. If the balloting continu[e]s the chances will be for the nomination of Cass judging from the present vote. The V.B. men will not go for Cass and the Buckhannon men say they must. I doubt very much if Cass can ever get 2/3 of the votes. I have within the last few minutes received a proposition from a leading Delegate of the Pennsylvania & of Massachusetts to bring your name before the convention for President.

I said to them that your name was subject to the will of the convention, that I would not at present bring it before the convention, that if it was the will of the convention the name should be brought out by the North.

There is, I think a strong probability of your name ultimately coming up for President. I do not think it prudent to move in *that* matter now. I want the North to bring you forward, as a *compromise* of all interests.

Time will alone tell what will be done. You shall hear from us. We are about adjourning & it is night.

GID. J. PILLOW

ALS. DLC–JKP. Addressed to Columbia. Published in *AHR,* XI, pp. 840–41.

1. The first ballot's official tally was as follows: Martin Van Buren, 146; Lewis Cass, 83; Richard M. Johnson, 24; John C. Calhoun, 6; James Buchanan, 4; Levi Woodbury, 2; and Charles Stewart, 1.

2. The sixth ballot's official tally was as follows: Van Buren, 101; Cass, 116; Buchanan, 25; Johnson, 23; and not voting, 1. On the seventh ballot Van Buren had 99; Cass, 123; Buchanan, 22; Johnson, 21; and not voting, 1.

FROM BENJAMIN B. FRENCH[1]

House of Representatives U.S.

Dear Sir,                                              [Washington City] May 29 1844

Permit me to congratulate you on the selection just made unanimously by the Baltimore Convention of yourself as Candidate for the Presidency of the United States.

That Convention assembled under somewhat gloomy auspices and for a time the unfortunate breach in the Democratic ranks seemed rather to widen than to heal. At lenth, the name of Mr. Van Buren having been withdrawn, the entire convention rallied upon you & the name of James K. Polk is now, & hence forth is to be, the watch word of the Democratic Party!

No man rejoices in this result more sincerely than I do, and no man will do more and with a more hearty good will, than myself, in the sphere in which I can operate, to promote your election to the high office which I believe you are destined to honor.

This is no mere effervescence of the moment; for more than ten years I have enjoyed the high satisfaction of your acquaintance, and I dare believe your friendship. In all that time I have met no man, who to my notions of Democracy, came nearer *the perfection of a democrat* than yourself, and I cannot but believe that that Providence who has thus far most evidently watched over & controlled for good, the destinies of this Nation, has caused you to be selected, that this country may not be cursed with the misrule of that would be Tyrant Henry Clay.

I expect your old friend Governor Hubbard[2] here this evening. He is to make my house his home while in the city. I understand that after Mr. V.B.[3] was withdrawn he used all his influence to effect your nomination & was very instrumental in bringing about the happy result which seems to be so satisfactory to every democrat I have yet seen.

I renew my ardent wishes for your success, & wish you health & happiness.

B. B. FRENCH

[P.S.] 1/2 past 6 o'clock p.m. We have now in operation between the R. Road depot in Baltimore & the Capitol, Mr. Morse's Electric magnetic telegraph which gives any item of news between this & Baltimore in less than a second.[4] About 10 minutes since it announced Mr. Wright as the nominee for V.P. Mr. Wright immediately returned an answer by telegraph that he would not accept. An answer was returned from Baltimore requesting Mr. Wright to enter into a communication with a gentleman at Baltimore by telegraph, & they are at this moment *holding a conversation with each other.*[5] Mr. Wright positively declines & it is probable Mr. Woodbury will be nominated.[6]

ALS. DLC–JKP. Addressed to Columbia under the frank of Caleb J. Mc-Nulty. Polk's AE on the cover states that he answered this letter on June 20, 1844; Polk's reply has not been found.

1. A Democrat from New Hampshire, French served as clerk of the U.S. House of Representatives for several years prior to becoming treasurer of the National Democratic Committee in 1848.

2. A New Hampshire lawyer, Henry Hubbard sat in the state legislature for several terms before serving in the U.S. House, 1829–35, and the U.S. Senate, 1835–41. He also saw government service as governor of New Hampshire, 1841–43, and as U.S. subtreasurer at Boston, 1846–49.

3. Martin Van Buren.

4. A congressional appropriation of $30,000 in March of 1843 enabled Samuel Morse to establish his experimental telegraph line between the two cities.

5. On instructions from the convention, John Fine handled the telegraphic communications with Wright.

6. Unable to persuade Wright to accept the vice-presidential nomination, the convention unanimously selected George M. Dallas to complete the Democratic ticket.

### FROM HENRY HUBBARD ET AL.[1]

Sir,                                                     Baltimore May 29 1844

At a Democratic National Convention of Delegates from the several States of this Union, convened on the 27th inst. & now sitting in the City of Baltimore, for the purpose of nominating candidates to be supported for the Presidency & Vice Presidency of the United States at the ensuing election, the Hon. James K. Polk of Tennessee having been designated by the whole number of votes given, to be the candidate of the Democratic party for President of the United States, was declared to be unanimously nominated for that office.

The undersigned were appointed by the Convention a Committee to request your acceptance of the nomination thus unanimously tendered to you; & they cannot forbear to express the high gratification which they experience in the performance of this duty, & the hope which they confidently entertain, in common with their colleagues of the Convention, that the devotion to the cause of Democratic principles which has always characterized your conduct, will not suffer you to turn a deaf ear to the call of your country, when in a manner so honorable to yourself, she demands your distinguished services.

HENRY HUBBARD

LS. DLC–JKP. Addressed to Columbia and enclosed in Robert Rantoul, Jr., to Polk, May 29, 1844. ALS. DLC–JKP.

1. The names of the Convention Committee, which included Henry Hubbard, William H. Roane, Benjamin H. Brewster, Romulus M. Saunders, and Robert Rantoul, Jr., were signed by Rantoul, secretary of the committee. A grandson of Patrick Henry, William Henry Roane of Virginia served both in the U.S. House, 1815–17, and in the U.S. Senate, 1837–41. A Philadelphia lawyer and Democrat, Brewster was appointed in 1846 a commissioner to examine claims arising under the Cherokee Treaty of 1835; subsequently, he became a Republican and served as U.S. attorney general under Chester A. Arthur. Rantoul, a Massachusetts lawyer and Democratic legislator, served as U.S. district attorney for that state from 1845 until 1849.

## FROM CAVE JOHNSON

Dear Sir,                                    Baltimore 29th May [18]44

Your nomination for the presidency unanimously upon the second ballot[1] was made today. Never was there such unanimity & such enthusiasm. Even Pickens & Elmore delegates from S.C. came in, made eloquent speeches & gave the vote of S.C. on your behalf. But I must delay until another time the particulars. Silas Wright was nominated for the Vice presidency upon the first ballot with every vote except 8 from Georgia which was given to Woodbury. We closed the labors of the day with more harmony and unanimity than I ever witnessed in such an assembly. Immense crowds are now assembled in different parts of the city, listening to the democratic thunder of our noble orators, & already songs are made & sung throughout the city. Such confidence in our success I have never before witnessed. All feel confidence & think of nothing but victory.

Such an assemblage of men, so much patriotism, so much talent, so much honesty of purpose and integrity of character, has not been found in any assembly of its size since the formation of the federal constitution, & I will add such unanimity never existed before in so large an assembly. Your frnds did their duty nobly.

C. JOHNSON

[P.S.] Flags are already flying Polk immediately over Jackson Wright and Jefferson.

ALS. DLC–JKP. Addressed to Columbia. Polk's AE on the cover states that he answered this letter on June 8, 1844. Published in *THQ,* XII, p. 181.

1. Polk's name was brought forward on the eighth ballot of the convention, and the vote was as follows: Martin Van Buren, 104; Lewis Cass, 114; James K. Polk, 44; and not voting, 4. The initial tally on the ninth ballot was as follows: Polk, 231; Cass, 29; and not voting, 6. Votes were changed at the conclusion of the roll call, and Polk was chosen unanimously by the convention's 266 delegates.


## FROM GIDEON J. PILLOW

Dear Govr:                              [Baltimore, Md.] May 29th 1844

On this morning we brought your name before the convention for the Presidency. On the first ballot you received 42 votes—on the 2nd you received 266 votes, being every vote in the convention. The delegates of South Carolina, then made their appearance and pledged the State of South Carolina to support and sustain the nomination. Never was there such *unanimity.* Never was there such *enthusiasm* before seen or witnessed in *any body.* I held you up before the convention, as the *"Olive Branch of peace,"* and all parties ran to you as to *an ark of safety.*

I was up nearly all night last night in bringing about *this result.* I had many *difficulties* to *encounter.* But I *faultered not,* & this day I had the proud satisfaction of witnessing the *glorious result*—glorious beyond the expectations of any of our delegation or friends.

Silas Wright will be your *Vice* with almost as much unanim[i]ty as you were. What a *ticket.* How *pure,* & *elevated* & *Herculian* in intellect. I cannot in this letter give you an account of anything but the result. It is *glorious.*

We will Sweep every Whig strong hold in the land. We will raise the shout all over the land.

GID. J. PILLOW

[P.S.] Wright is nominated by a vote of 258 votes on first Ballot. All's well & Glorious & all is *enthusiasm* & union & Harmony. G.J.P.

ALS. DLC–JKP. Addressed to Columbia. Published in *AHR,* XI, pp. 841–42.


## FROM GIDEON J. PILLOW

My Dear Govr,            Baltimore May [29th] 1844[1]
I wrote you to day giving you the result of the proceedings of this day in the Democratic convention. I wrote under the influence of great excitement on my part, and in the convention. I did not then and cannot now give you a full account of the effort made & the means used to bring about a result so astounding to every body. It was all done last night after my letter was written[2] though I had laid the foundation for it yesterday. As I said in my letter of to day I was at it nearly all night. I entered into no combination. I used *no improper* or *dishonorable* means. It was the *result* & *force* and *power* of *circumstance,* which I seized hold of & wielded, as I think with *no little skill* & judgment.

I had good help in some *true men* in the North who understood the whole *game* and whose names you shall in due *season know.* I got no help on the work which was done last night from our home people. I communicated the plan & prospect to some of them & they had *no faith* in the *thing* & so expressed themselves. I was fully convinced it would *work out right,* and I worked on until nearly day this morning and this morning the *boys* did not know what *"hurt them."* The fatal blow was given, but it was not *seen* nor known what produced such a result, nor where the blow came from.

I never saw such enthusiasm, such *exaltation,* such *shouting for joy.* One spirit, one Soul animates the great party, leaders and all. No one doubts the success of the *Ticket.* Victory is all ready hovering over our banner, which has been spread to the breezes under the lead of *Polk & Wright.* Some of our own *faithful* delegation, to whom I have referred several times in my letters—who have done all they could in their secret, assassin-like manner to destroy your prospects & sacrifice you, are overwhelmed with astonishment at this strange result. I shall defer giving you particulars until I can see you in person.

Laughlin has been sick for 2 days & not been able until this afternoon to be in the house.

C. Johnson says "I am a *great General* & that the first war we have I shall command the Malitia of Tennessee *By God."* I decline the honor of the compliment, but as it comes from so stale & *sedate* an old gentleman & is so much *out* of character with him, I could not help telling you of it.

This morning just before we went into the Ballotting, my movements during the night had been discovered by a few & powerful efforts were made to defeat it by some of your—*now*—would be friends. Oh Govenor how much good it did me to see the boys over-reached, out-done & *whipped* into the ranks. Every man in the convention is *now* your *warm friend.* If you were here you would imagine yourself the most popular man in the world & you would be sure you *never had* an enemy in the convention. You cannot know how much pain they take to give in to me *their adhesion* to you, & to impress me with the *great merit* of their *conduct.* I am almost ready to conclude that *your success* has made *me* a *great man.* Every body wants *my "address,"* and desires me to present *them* & their *services* in the proper point of view to *you.* I laid the foundation for last nights work during the day yesterday. I have written to you freely, fully & without the least reserve & desire that *all my letters* shall be considered *confidential.* I desire this as I do not want to create *enemies* about the matter resulting so *gloriously* as it has.

I shall leave here in the morning for Philadelphia and New York & will be at home about 15th June.

GID. J. PILLOW

ALS. DLC–JKP. Addressed to Columbia. Published in *AHR,* XI, pp. 842–43.
1. Pillow mistakenly dated his letter "May 30th 1844"; corrected date identified through content analysis.
2. See Gideon J. Pillow to Polk, May 28, 1844.

## FROM WILLIAMSON SMITH

My Dear Sir,                                        Baltimore 29th May 1844
Permit me to congratulate you, not upon your Nomination for the Vice Presidency, upon a Nomination still more gratifying to me and more Honl. to you. Yes Sir, It is for the *President* of *these United States,* and what is still more pleasing it was done with a unanimity and enthusaism which I never before witnessed in all my life nor never expect to again. We had balloted on yesterday 8 times, without

being able to unite.[1] This morning we met again, and the very first balloting that we made you received the *unanimous vote* of *the whole convention*[2] and at the result such a continued and heartfelt burst of enthusaism of gratulations and heart cheering speeches I have never before witness in any assemblage of People. You who was at home in retirement quietly attending to your own private vocations, to be called by one voice by seventeen millions of *Freemen* to preside over their destiney, will create in your bosom a sensation which falls to the lot of but few men to experience.

This is one of the proudest days of my life, and the feelings of your friends from Ten who are here are well paid for their trip to Baltimore, Just to see her *favorite Son* elevated to so high & honourable a station. Yes to see him who has laboured so faithfully for the great cause Democracy, now so amply compensated for his Toils, his Labours, & his privations.

The Convention is now in session for the purpose of nominating a Vice President, which I think will be Silas Wright. I will not trouble you with any more news at present, and if the Postage would have cost you one cent, would not have troubled with this, as I know you have other and many other Friends who can give you more satisfaction than I have been able to do. I trust it will be at least worth reading as you know at least it is from a Friend, who has never deserted you in the hour of knead.

WILLIAMSON SMITH

P.S. I cannot designate among your friends from Ten, but I will say, set Cave Johnson a post of honour. W.S.

I must be permitted to record one other result from the time it was acertained that you was certainly nominated, until we got done balloting as we had many cheering speeches during the time, the news was Telegraphed at Washington City, and returned to us, and at the moment the Chairman[3] was in the act of announcing the final result, A messenger appears, with a response from Washington, that the Democracy of Washington City have assembled in the Representative's Hall of the Capitol and give their full entire apporbation to the Nomination and send three cheers for James K. Polk of Ten. At the two results, such long & contin[u]ed cheers and shouts I have never before witnessed. This however you will get more fully detail[ed] by your friends &c. W.S.

ALS. DLC–JKP. Addressed to Columbia and mailed under the frank of William H. Hammet.

1. Seven ballots were recorded on May 28, 1844.

2. For details of Polk's nomination on the second ballot taken on May 29, 1844, see Cave Johnson to Polk, May 29, 1844.

3. Hendrick B. Wright.

## FROM AARON V. BROWN

At Table

Dear Sir [Washington City] May 30 1844

I write as I have opportunity. Do not doubt all that you read about the universal harmony of your nomination. No discontent any where. No heart burnings & not a single friend of one of the aspirants thinks hard of the Tennessee delegates. Their course gives universal satisfaction—well enough on that except, I hear that even Benton is content & says you will get Missouri by 15,000 votes. This is hearsay but I believe it.

Now to another point. In your acceptance you must some way or other express your self in favor of the one term system. This is important. I might say all important & you will know exactly *how* it will be highly useful. I need not say who & how many of our friends expect it. The thing is right *per se* & under all the circumstances I think you ought not to *hesitate* to do it.

Now to another point of not less importance. Sit down in your library, let nothing interrupt you, & write out your own biography— your birth place, your ancestry, your education, your progress through College, any honors awarded you, noting every thing striking about yourself or your ancestry—*when* you went to college, the state of your health &c rendering it impossible to have been in any of the war campaigns &c. Then your study of Law, your success in the practice & allusion to any very striking criminal cases in which you appeard or were associated with Grundy &c &c.

Then go through your career in the legislature of Tennessee, your movements there on the occupant law &c, & then your election to Congress—your career throug[h]out, as Chairman of Ways & Means, Speaker, noting every important incident to which your mind adverts with pride & satisfaction. In this point[1] notice something of the appropriations reported by you as chairman of ways & means *for* the Cumberland road & any thing you may have said in *support* of such items (this for Ohio Indiana & Illinoise). You may insert on the different subjects now at issue, extracts from your best speeches on them.

Now all this (enough for 1 or 200 pages) must be furnishd *privately* to me & I will furnish them (as my material) to *Bancroft,* Kendall, Rantoul[2] or some one else, for a well compiled Biography, beautifully printed in large type on good paper, with an *elegantly engraved likeness.*

We shall adjourn on the 19 Inst & you *must* have all this ready by the time I get home. If I can do any good on the adjournmt, I shall go north thro Philadelphia New York, The lakes &c., to see that the matter is started well in all that region & suppress any wrong ideas that may get up.

Well another thing. At Baltimore the Son of Louis McLean[3] the old Sec called on me with a message from his father, that he had seperatd from the democracy for years but he should now heartily support the nomination bearing the fullest testimony to your personal character, your industry & entire capability for the high office to which you have been nominated. Of Mrs. Polk he was also pleased to speak in terms for which I very sincerely thanked him.

Yet another thing. Much is said here by *some* as to continuing the Globe as the Polk Organ. This we will manage with sound discretion. The Globe will change its *tone* & perhaps take back much that it has said, & go in *warmly* if not heartily. If so, well. But we will not commit ourselves to it *after* the election. I write under most unfavorable circumstances & have not time to copy.

A. V. BROWN

ALS. DLC–JKP. Addressed to Columbia.

1. Here Brown cancelled two and a half lines and rephrased his language about appropriations for the Cumberland Road.

2. George Bancroft, Amos Kendall, and Robert Rantoul, Jr. Historian and diplomat, Bancroft was influential in securing Polk's nomination to the presidency and subsequently served as his secretary of the Navy. A newspaperman and member of Andrew Jackson's "Kitchen Cabinet," Kendall served as postmaster general from 1835 until 1840. In 1842 he edited a Washington biweekly, *Kendall's Expositor.* The following year, Kendall issued a prospectus for a biography of Jackson, which was never published.

3. Louis McLane and Robert Milligan McLane. A lawyer and Democrat, Louis McLane served five terms in the U.S. House, 1817–27, before winning election to the U.S. Senate in 1827. He served as minister to England, 1829–31 and 1845–46; as secretary of the Treasury, 1831–33; and as secretary of state, 1833–34. McLane's son, Robert Milligan McLane, a Baltimore lawyer and Democrat, won election to the U.S. House in 1847, where he supported Polk's war policy against Mexico. In 1853 he became U.S. commissioner to China and served in that position through the following year; in 1859 James Buchanan named him minister to Mexico.

## FROM ROBERT J. WALKER

Dear Sir                                    Baltimore May 30, 1844

I write to you in haste to say that there is but one question which can by any possibility defeat your election. It is the tariff. We must have the vote of Pennsylvania in order to succeed. Now you know my strong antitariff notions, but I represent *one state;* you are to be the representative of the democracy of *the union.*

You then must not destroy us. The Texas question will carry the *South;* you must then go as far as your principles will permit for incidental protection. Could you not say that being *now* the representative candidate of the democracy of the whole union you go 1st For such a tariff as will supply the wants of the Government economically administered; 2d That within this range you go for such just & fair measure as will embrace all the great interests of the whole union & as will be calculated to afford *equal* & adequate protection to American industry in all its branches of agriculture, manufac[turing], commerce, & navigation. (This is the doctrine of Benton's last speech.)[1] An out & out Free trade candidate *cannot* receive the vote of Pennsylvania. This is *certain,* & without her vote we are beaten.

This doctrine (which is in fact Van Burens) will insure the vote of *Pa* & make our triumph certain. Mr. Clay must not be elected & you must take no course to produce such a result. Dallas' nomination[2] will help you much in *Pa.*

In our Mississippi Convention of the 8th of Jany. last I declined the nomination of vice Prest. that you might receive her vote. On this occasion I strained every nerve to unite the Texas democrats & friends of Cass in your favour. I have at all times declined any nomination myself for any of these offices, altho strongly urged before & during the sitting of this convention, but I take the ground that if I should run now for *any* office, it would be said I had got up the Texas question for my benefit & thereby injure the cause. In fine if we can steer clear of the tariff difficulty, all will be safe, & you must recollect that you now belong not to *one* state, but to the *union.*

R. J. WALKER

ALS. DLC–JKP. Addressed to Columbia and marked "Confidential." Polk's AE on the cover states that he answered this letter on June 8, 1844.

1. On March 25, 1844, Thomas H. Benton called for the repeal of the Tariff of 1842; he urged the U.S. Senate to return to the concepts and structures of the pre-1812 tariff laws, which began with revenue as their object, admitted protection of home industry as incidental, discriminated between necessities

and luxuries, and appraised imports at their true value.

2. A Philadelphia lawyer, George M. Dallas served as mayor of Philadelphia, 1829; U.S. Senator, 1831–33; minister to Russia, 1837–39; vice-president under Polk, 1845–49; and minister to Great Britain, 1856–61.

## FROM ANDREW J. DONELSON

My Dr Col                                        Philadelphia May 31st 1844

I have just seen Mr. Dallas who accepts the nomination, and has no doubt of the approbation of the people of Pena.

You are aware, that the hobby which will be used against you, in this region, is the Tariff. It therefore becomes important before you answer calls upon you for information on this subject, that you should deliberate carefully, and be sure to give your enemies no advantage which can be avoided.

Mr Clays position before the south is calculated to shake the confidence of Penna in his consistency and sincerity. He is for a Tariff[1] adequate to the production of a revenue sufficient to defray the economical administration of our Government, and for discrimination, only, where the duties thus imposed do not decrease revenue but may promote the manufactures of our own citizens. On this whole subject it would be well to look over the Genls.[2] messages and see the ground on which he stood, as well as the language he employed. He stood up all the time against Clay, and yet conciliated the good feeling of both sections of the union. It was however the most difficult task of his administration. I have been already asked by many of your friends if your views were not directly at war with the principles of the existing Tariff. My answer has been that there was much evil in that Tariff which you would remove if you had the power. But in the main that you agreed with Genl Jackson as was proved by your cordial and public support of his administration; and that even where as the representative of an anti Tariff people you had spoken decidedly and firmly their wishes on the subject; you would doubtless feel yourself at liberty if elected President, to pursue that course which would be best calculated to meet the expectations and harmonize the interests of all the sections of our diversified union.

What I aim at here is to give you notice that you will be interrogated; and I wish you to be able to keep your advantage over Clay. There is nothing but enthusiasm and confidence in the ranks of our friends and a general expression of the belief that you will be triumphantly elected. Pillow is admirably suited to the task of responding to the applause which every where welcomes your nomination: He does so in fine style and is happy and joyous. Last night the masses hurrahed around him for half an hour before he could proceed to speak.

I tell you your success is certain if your ground on the Tariff is wisely chosen. Do not be in a hurry in taking it.

I shall be on my way home as soon as I see my son[3] at West Point, and will be happy to communicate with you more freely after I reach home. Pillow as well as myself can tell yet much to laugh about, and something to make you serious.

A. J. DONELSON

ALS. DLC–JKP. Addressed to Columbia.

1. Here Donelson indicated an aside and wrote in the left margin: "In the South, & in the north he used to [be] understood as the pillar of an exclusive protective system."

2. Andrew Jackson.

3. Andrew J. Donelson, Jr., attended the U.S. Military Academy at West Point from July 1, 1844, until June 1, 1848, when he was graduated and appointed to the rank of brevet second lieutenant in the Corps of Engineers.

## FROM THEOPHILUS FISK

My Dear Sir,                                    Washington May 31 1844

I feel undoubting confidence that you will not look upon it as a mere idle compliment when I say, that I congratulate you and the country upon your *unanimous* nomination as the Democratic candidate for the Presidency of the United States. It is hailed with enthusiastic approbation from every quarter with the single exception of Mr. Benton's organ, the Washington Globe. That paper I believe is unsound in its advocacy of pure democratic principles and ought to be driven over to the Whigs where it properly belongs. So omnipotent, however, is the potency of public opinion, that even the Globe has been compelled to give your nomination its support.

It is not a little singular that you should have been selected *by the President* as Minister to England, or as the Secretary of the Treasury, and *by the people* as a candidate for President, at the same time. He had promised me to make the nomination immediately after the Baltimore Convention, little dreaming of the result. It serves to show the high estimation in which he holds your talents and past services.

Since your nomination I have exerted myself with unremitting industry to preserve a good understanding between your friends and those of President Tyler, wishing to be able to induce Mr. Tyler to withdraw in your favour. I have found however that to press his withdrawal, *at this moment,* any farther, would be only to sacrifice myself without being able to benefit you hereafter. We are therefore proposing as a medium ground on which to compromise for the present, that only one electoral ticket shall be run in each State, that the friends of each candidate shall manifest their preference at the polls, and the highest number of votes shall be instructions to the electors how to vote. You need not fear the result as *all* Mr. Calhoun's friends in the Tyler Convention have gone home with the unalterable determination to support your nomination. I have spared no pains to inform them of the unflinching friendship which you have ever entertained for Mr. Calhoun. I have repeated to them the expressions of kindness I have at all times heard you use in relation to his character and talents, and they will fight under your banner until victory shall crown our efforts. That you will be elected by an overwhelming majority, I doubt no more than I do that the sun will rise tomorrow. I look upon the selection of your name as an act of special, particular Providence, at this momentous crisis. You are the only man who could reconcile all the conflicting elements at this juncture. You are the *only one* upon whom the friends of John Tyler could unite with their whole souls. In nominating and supporting your nomination, your friends have no vices to palliate, no faults to conceal.

Your kindness will pardon me for the liberty I am about to take in very respectfully suggesting one idea for your consideration. It is this. You are aware that there are a number of prominent candidates for the Presidency before the people. If these gentlemen could be assured that you would only serve *one* Presidential term, they and their friends would support you[r] nomination with infinitely warmer zeal, than if that matter was left in doubt. By setting the example of declining a re-nomination, by avowing this determination in advance, you would not only ensure your election, but would place your name in the highest niche of fame in the estimation of posterity. I know you will pardon the suggestion, as it is made from the purest motives of sincere friendship and respect.

We hold an immense mass meeting in front of the Theatre this evening, to ratify your nomination.[1] It will be a rouser. We look upon it as the nomination of Gen. Jackson, jr. and the blood will be up to fever heat all over the land in less than three weeks. The cause is safe.

I hope most earnestly, that a democratic organ will be established here by your friends to supersede the Globe. It is a perfect incubus upon our party and has been so for months.

I beg leave to assure you that while I have strength to wield a pen or wag my tongue, nothing shall be left undone on my part to ensure the overwhelming success of the nominee of the Baltimore Convention. In great haste.

THEOPHILUS FISK

ALS. DLC–JKP. Addressed to Columbia.
1. A Democratic rally, described by the Washington *Globe* of May 31, 1844, as "the largest political meeting we ever saw in this District," assembled in front of the National Theater, which was located on Pennsylvania Avenue.

## FROM CAVE JOHNSON

Dear Sir                                  Washington 31st May 1844

The nomination is universally admitted the best we could have made. All factions will unite, & the party will be more united than at any time since Jacksons last election. There yet remains slight discontent in Indiana & with a few members from N.Y. Calhoun friends are decided & sincere & the Spectator takes the lead. Benton & the Globe fall in but not with so good a grace as we expected. We have already proof *positive,* that you was a private soldier in the battle of N. Orleans & was badly wounded and that you are now a leading member of the Methodist Church. Your life will appear in two days. Bye the bye materials must be furnished by you very soon for an extended life. Several M.C. from Illinois desired me to say that you should answer no address from *Joe Smith,*[1] which you may soon expect. I need not say to you, that the less said is the easiest word. You will be compelled to omit answering letters addressed to you. That we shall triumph I have not a doubt. So many old friends desire me to remember them to you with promises of support that it would take a sheet to put down their names. Some of them beg my interference with you to save *certain* friends of theirs now in office.

Silas Wright declined the Vice because he was fearful that he would be suspected of being connected with the intrigues to overthrow Van.[2] What a wonderful thing, that Wright has been offered in *one month,* the nomination for Gov. of N York, a seat upon the supreme bench of the U.S. Court, the nomination with certain assurances of success of President & Vice President & *rejected them all,* and all on account of his friendship for Van Buren.

Dallas will accept as Wilkins informs me & is perhaps a *better Vice* than Wright & will add more to our strength. The Tylerites have now a project on hand, to unite upon the Democratic Electors in the different States & let the voters endorse on their tickets *Polk* or *Tyler* to shew how the vote should be given. This is a mode of getting easily off the tract. Calhoun expresses *entire satisfaction* with the nomination & Benton says you will get Missouri by 20,000.

C. JOHNSON

ALS. DLC–JKP. Addressed to Columbia.

1. In 1830 Joseph Smith, a resident of Seneca County, N.Y., organized the Church of Jesus Christ of Latter-Day Saints; in that same year he published *The Book of Mormon*, which formed the basis of his religious teachings. He moved his followers westward to Ohio, then Missouri, and in 1839 to western Illinois, where he gained control of the small village of Commerce and re-named it "Nauvoo." The community prospered and grew rapidly; on February 15, 1844, its leader announced his candidacy for the U.S. presidency. Public hostility to Smith's political, business, and religious practices led to his incarceration and murder at Carthage, Ill., on June 27, 1844.

2. Martin Van Buren.


## FROM SAMUEL H. LAUGHLIN

My dear Sir,                                          Washington City, May 31, 1844

While I knew others were keeping you constantly informed of every step attending our daily affairs here and at Baltimore, I have been every leisure moment engaged in writing letters in every direction to our friends. But now, in reference to the affair Mr. Brown has written you about to-day,[1] I must also trouble you with a hasty letter. No false modesty must prevent you from sitting down and writing as much in detail as possible the materials for the work in question. Brown's first suggestion was for me to write it; but happily I had met Bancroft before going to Baltimore at Blairs, and had ascertained his attachment to you, and his willingness and wish to write a new and complete life of Jackson, for which I promised him certain materials. He is the best Historical writer of the age in any language, and no doubt will, as he has been, be equally successful in Biography, especially biography connected with our current political History. I suggested him to Brown. I know he can be got at a word to do the work. He and old Morton are the men who did most to wheel old Massachusetts and the Yankey states into your line in Convention. He will esteem it a great honor. To write History of Jackson's Administration, a part of which you was, he has procured from Blair, or Blair promised to furnish him all the Debates and Congressional proceedings from 1824. He will therefore have the original of Congressional proceedings and debates to refer to. All your local speeches, inaugural, messages, and all our democratic addresses, written by you, or in relation to you, and your circulars must be collected. I have most of them, and we can get all.

But you must select and copy out all necessary extracts at length, with references. You must write out all the facts, and add what you please of embelishment and Commentary. The danger is that you will write too little and not enough or too much. It is agreed with myself and Brown, that when I come home, I will make a fair copy, adding perhaps some things with your consent, so as to make the whole a full and easy rough draft of ample materials for Bancroft to write off quick, and almost at a heat, in his polished style a work creditable to him, and useful to all persons. It is agreed that no human being but Brown, Cave[2] and myself are to know any thing of the manner of getting up, or that you have furnished a single fact. Brown, or Brown & Cave will furnish Bancroft, or Brown will do it for and of himself. It must be done.

In five minutes from the date of the vote of your nomination, communicated from Baltimore here by Telegraph (Morse's electric Telegraph)[3] and your portrait was hung up in a nitch in the Rotunda of the capitol as the Democratic nominee for the Presidency. They are now thick in this city and Baltimore.

I have seen many people, and have heard and seen ten thousand men shouting for you in the last three days. The ticket, judging from the press, and from information of papers from the cities, and from Steamboat and Railroad travellers, is running like wildfire. The whole party has most abundant cause to thank God for our safe deliverance.

I think you should reflect well before you insert the *one term* suggestion which Brown tells me he put in his letter to you to-day.[4] Perhaps all in all it may be best, and will be making assurance doubly sure, and put us on an equality with the Whigs on that question. Your nomination is wormwood to some persons here who affect to be greatly for it. Not one of these is John H. Eaton, who tells me to-day that he is *for* the ticket decidedly.

Gov. Morton asked me what sort of lady Mrs. Polk was—did she make her butter like Mrs. Clay.[5] I will not say what account I gave of her, only that I made her any thing else to the old frugal Yankey, who has taught his accomplished daughters good House-keeping, than a dashing, extravagant, proud southern woman. The old fellow said, without my telling him, or supposing that he knew any thing, that it was a remarkable fact that all our best Presidents, and you among them, were men who have had no children.

McDuffies Bill was rejected to-day, on a direct tariff vote, made on an amendment of Allen.[6] Buchanan & Sturgeon[7] both voting against it. Jonakin[8] voted against it. Foster being absent, having relapsed in his sickness since your nomination.

Bancroft will write most of our address. I am of the Address Committee.[9] As soon as I can, I shall leave, *via,* Richmond to see old Ritchie, having promised his son and son in law Green[10] at the convention to do so. My respects to your democratic better half, and am, as ever....

S. H. LAUGHLIN

P.S. I wrote letter yesterday to Heiss, of considerable length, seven or eight pages, for publication, and also one to Ford.[11] I have no time to correct. Pillow has gone to Philadelphia, the happiest man I ever saw. He is a *friend indeed.* S.H.L.

ALS. DLC–JKP. Addressed to Columbia and marked "Private."

1. See Aaron V. Brown to Polk, May 30, 1844.
2. Aaron V. Brown and Cave Johnson.
3. See Benjamin B. French to Polk, May 29, 1844.
4. See Aaron V. Brown to Polk, May 30, 1844.
5. In 1799 Henry Clay married Lucretia Hart, daughter of Thomas Hart of Lexington, Ky.; renowned for her domesticity, Lucretia Clay reared six sons and five daughters.
6. The Senate Committee on Finance reported a resolution postponing indefinitely any further consideration of George McDuffie's tariff bill; the Committee argued that all revenue bills must originate in the U.S. House. William Allen offered an amendment asserting that "the duties imposed on importation by existing laws are unjust and oppressive and ought to be repealed." Allen's amendment was rejected by a vote of 25 to 18; the Finance Committee's resolution then was approved by a vote of 33 to 4.
7. James Buchanan and Daniel Sturgeon. A physician, Sturgeon won election to several terms in both the Pennsylvania House and Senate, 1818–30; served as state auditor general, 1830–36, and as state treasurer, 1838–39; and sat two terms in the U.S. Senate, 1839–51.
8. Spencer Jarnagin.
9. Laughlin, along with twenty-five other delegates, had been appointed to the committee on resolutions of the Democratic National Convention. That committee was empowered to prepare and publish an address to the American people.
10. Thomas Ritchie, William F. Ritchie, and Thomas Green. William F. Ritchie, son of Thomas Ritchie, was co-editor of the *Richmond Enquirer* with his father after 1843 and represented the Abingdon district of Virginia at the 1844 Democratic National Convention. Thomas Green was married to Thomas Ritchie's daughter, Mary Roane Ritchie.

11.  John W. Ford, a Polk supporter, edited the McMinnville *Central Gazette* from 1835 until 1842; he served as postmaster at McMinnville during that same period.

# June

## FROM CAVE JOHNSON

Saturday night

My dear Sir                                   Washington 1st June [1844][1]

I take pleasure in giving you the information that the democratic party seems well pleased with your nomination & we still believe will be more united than at any time since the last election of Genl Jackson. We have a few of the friends of Cass yet grumbling from Indiana (Hannegan & Smith & Howard[2] seem the leaders). The Madisonian of this evening says that you will decline & that Dallas has declined, that you are too honorable to use the Capts.[3] thunder. There is yet one danger. The South was zealous in the nomination. The Spectator has taken ground in the same spirit. The Globe has taken ground with not so much zeal but they fear that the influence of the incoming admn. may be thrown into the old channels & if so they will not look so well. There is a strong feeling for a new Organ. We have been so constantly occupied in the House that I have had no chance of seeing F. P. Blair. I had a long conversation with Elmore to day & will again see him tomorrow.

I have seen many N Yorkers to day & some of the leaders from the City will take ground thoroughly tho. the Evening Post[4] has taken strong ground agt. the procedings of the Convention. *N.Y. & Penn. & Louisiana* are deeply interested in your position on the Tariff, particularly on Wool & Sugar. Van Buren's position in his Indiana letter[5] & Silas Wrights speech[6] is as far as the north can go at present. You will be soon called on by *Slidel*[7] of La about the sugar duties, & see his speech[8] which he will send you. The exposition of Revenue principles, made by McDuffie & Calhoun quoted in his speech[9] will give satisfaction. McKays Bill (drawn by Silas Wright) will give the north general satisfaction with a slight increase of the duty on the Wool. I need not remind you of the importance of not saying too much & writing too often. We shall leave here on the 17th June (probably to be recalled) without a ratification of the treaty.[10] We shall organize an Executive Com. in the Senate & one also of members of Congress to spend the summer here & in the northern cities to frank, &c. The Convention appointed a committee for tract publication. Every thing you ever said or done is now the subject of whig scrutiny & will be probably brought out in the civil & diplomatic Bill in the next two weeks.[11] You must consider well the propriety of leaving home. Doct Duncan[12] will want you in Cincinatti to pass through Ohio &c. There is great bitterness between the Calhoun party & the friends of Van Buren Benton &c. & to move along straight without being subjected to the suspicion of influence from one or the other will require great skill & more judgment than I possess.

I write in great haste.

C. JOHNSON

ALS. DLC–JKP. Addressed to Columbia.

1. Date identified through content analysis.

2. Edward A. Hannegan, Thomas Smith, and Tilghman A. Howard. A tanner, Smith served in the Indiana House and Senate prior to his service in the U.S. House as a Democrat, 1839–41 and 1843–47.

3. John Tyler.

4. A major Democratic paper, the New York *Evening Post* was edited by William Cullen Bryant.

5. In his Febuary 15, 1843, reply to interrogatories posed to him by the Indiana Democratic State Convention, Martin Van Buren endorsed a tariff for revenue with incidental protection to American manufacturers.

6. In a lengthy speech in the U.S. Senate, begun on April 19 and carried over to April 23, 1844, Silas Wright, Jr., expounded his views on the tariff. He favored a tariff to provide revenue for the needs of government economically administered, with incidental protection to American industry.

7. A native of New York City, John Slidell removed to New Orleans, where he practiced law and participated in politics. Elected as a States Rights Democrat to the U.S. House, he served from 1843–45. In 1845 Polk appointed him minister to Mexico, but that government refused to receive him. Later, he served in the U.S. Senate, 1853–61, before undertaking diplomatic service for the Confederate States of America. See John Slidell to Polk, June 1, 1844, for his inquiry about the tariff.

8. In his speech of April 27, 1844, before the U.S. House, Slidell defended the sugar interests of Louisiana and argued that the duty on sugar and molasses should not be reduced.

9. To buttress his argument for the maintenance of existing duties on sugar and molasses, Slidell quoted George McDuffie to the effect "that a revenue duty must be the lowest possible duty that will yield the largest, or the required, amount of revenue." He also cited John C. Calhoun's statement that "I can agree, however, to no duty but such as the revenue may require, and none so high on any article as will push it beyond the highest rate of revenue that can be derived from the article." Slidell contended that the existing duties on molasses and sugar met these tests.

10. Reference is to the treaty for the annexation of Texas.

11. Johnson anticipated that Polk's stance on salient issues would be aired during deliberations over the civil and diplomatic appropriation bill.

12. Alexander Duncan, a Cincinnati physician, sat for several terms in both the Ohio House and Senate, 1828–34; he served three terms in the U.S. House, 1837–41 and 1843–45. Many Democrats celebrated Duncan's congressional speeches for their forceful attacks on Whig principles.

## FROM JOHN SLIDELL

Washington City. June 1, 1844

Slidell writes to Polk about the tariff on sugar, pointing out its significance in Louisiana. While Democrats in his state oppose the protective system, says Slidell, they support "a revenue tariff with discrimination." The duty proposed by the House Committee on Ways and Means[1] would be sufficient to their interests. Slidell solicits a letter from Polk setting forth his views on the sugar duty; he wishes to use the statement in upcoming state elections.[2] He urges the importance of the contest, being the first election after Polk's nomination for president. Slidell encloses a copy of his recent speech on the subject as well as a paper that contains articles about the tariff.[3]

ALS. DLC–JKP. Addressed to Columbia and enclosed under cover of Aaron V. Brown to Polk, June 1, 1844. ALS. DLC–JKP.

1. Reported favorably by the Committee on Ways and Means but defeated by the full House on May 10, 1844, the tariff bill proposed a reduction in the duty on sugar. On raw sugar the levy would have been lowered from 2.5 to 2 cents per pound.

2. On July 1, 1844, voters in Louisiana elected congressmen, legislators, and delegates to a state constitutional convention.

3. Enclosures not found, but see Cave Johnson to Polk, June 1, 1844.

## FROM FERNANDO WOOD[1]

Dear Sir New York June 1, 1844

As one of your early admirers & friends, permit me to congratulate the Democracy and yourself upon the results of the Baltimore convention. Though in favor of Mr. Van Buren for Presdt. & yourself for *Vice,* under the circumstances I am more than pleased with the Selections. We will carry our *little* State beyond doubts. To a man we rally for the ticket, as it is. You know "regular nominations" are our watch words and though a great majority of our voters are devoted to the Ex Pres and looked for his nomination yet they will one and all sustain the ticket. Besides, we will receive the aid of thousands who for the sake of appearing consistent would not have voted for him. In fact it is the opinion of many our oldest heads that before victory was doubtful, but now it is certain.

As a friend allow me to advise that as far as is compatible with your present position all expression of opinion be avoided. The great body of the party know you to be sound upon the cardinal principles and none but a few enthusiasts upon certain points or those who are enemies will attempt to call you out. One chief merit of the selection of your name as the candidate is that you have been in no way identified with the struggle which has for some time been going on between the friends of the different candidates. Yours has been a negative position and without refusing to give any opinions upon all public questions when called upon in the right way and for proper objects it appears to me it would be well to retain the same position before the country that has been before the party.

FERNANDO WOOD

P.S. Presuming you may not at once recolect me, I will add that I had the honour of making your acquaintance during your last visit to Washington when I was as one of the members of the House from this city. F.W.

ALS. DLC–JKP. Addressed to Columbia. Polk's AE on the cover states that he answered this letter on June 25, 1844; Polk's reply, which Wood read as June 26, has not been found.

1. A shipping merchant in New York City, Fernando Wood won election as a Tammany Democrat to one term in the U.S. House, 1841–43. He held the post of dispatch agent for the State Department at the port of New York from 1844 until 1847. After serving as mayor of New York City, 1855–58, 1861, and 1862, he won nine terms in the U.S. House, 1863–65, and 1867–81.

## FROM CAVE JOHNSON

Sunday Night

Dear Sir                                   Washington.[June 2, 1844][1]
    Every thing looks well—unanimnity & enthusiasm pervade every where. Dallas has accepted. Rumor says, that 60 of the nothern dele-

gates went in the evening cars headed by Walker arrived at Philadelphia at 3 Oclock, marched in procession to the House of Dallas. Walkers voice being *known* excited alarm lest some mishap had befallen the daughter in Washington.[2] Dallas rushed down in his night cloths & was addressed by Gov. Fairfield[3] *in that fix.* We shall carry every thing with a sweep. I send you to day Wrights speech.[4] It is desirable to place yourself as near as you honestly can on Van Burens platform. Allow me to suggest for your reflection one other idea that I think the presidential candidates have not sufficiently adverted to. The Pres. has nothing to do with the Tariff except sign the Bill. He would veto no Bill that Congress might pass. As the Tariff is now sufficiently if not too high for revenue you would of course approve any Bill that Congress might pass reducing it to increase the Revenue. *Revenue with incidental protection* is all now claimed. Upon this point is the danger. Examine well. The Hartford times approves heartily as does the N.Y. Plebeian.[5]

Louis McLane of Balt., McMahon[6] & another distinguished Maryland Whig have taken ground agt. Clay.

Old Cramer[7] has been with me & pretends great anxiety for your success.

C. JOHNSON

ALS. DLC–JKP. Addressed to Columbia.

1. Johnson mistakenly dated his letter June 3; corrected date identified through content analysis.

2. George M. Dallas was the father of six daughters: Julia, Elizabeth, Sophia, Catherine, Susan, and Charlotte. Charlotte married Charles H. Morrell, a Cuban merchant; Catherine married wealthy Bostonian FitzEugene Dixon; and Elizabeth married David H. Tucker, a Richmond doctor. The other three daughters never married. Which of his daughters may have been in Washington in 1844 is not known.

3. A Maine lawyer, John Fairfield was elected as a Democrat to the U.S. House where he served from 1835 until 1838, when he resigned to become governor of Maine, 1839–43. Fairfield resigned the governorship in 1843 and filled the seat of Reuel Williams in the U.S. Senate from 1843 until his death in 1847.

4. See Cave Johnson to Polk, June 1, 1844.

5. The *Hartford Times* was a leading Democratic newspaper that began publication in 1817. The New York *Daily Plebeian* was published for three years, 1842–45, before it was merged with the New York *Morning News.*

6. A Maryland lawyer and historian, John Van Lear McMahon served several terms in the Maryland House of Delegates. An ardent Jacksonian, McMahon broke with the Democratic party over Jackson's fiscal and commercial policies; in 1831 he published his *Historical View of the Government of*

*Maryland.*

7. A lawyer from Waterford, N.Y., John Cramer sat in both houses of the state legislature and served two terms in the U.S. House, 1833–37.

## FROM GIDEON J. PILLOW

Dear Govenor                              Philadelphia June 2d 1844

I have been in this city several days. I have been present at two meetings of the Democracy of the city. The great mass meeting held last night far exceeded in the vastness of the immense multitude any thing I ever witnessed. There must have been 12 or 15 thousand people present. Such *enthusiasm,* such unanimity of feeling I never saw. There is even here in this city, supposed to be as strongly for V.B.[1] as any portion of the whole country, but one feeling upon the subject of your nomination, and that is a universal feeling of joy and approbation. It is admitted on all hands that you are stronger than V. ever was. This state is divided (I mean the Democracy) into several parties—the Porter party, the Mulenburgh[2] party &c. All these parties unite in your nomination & will heartily support you.

My object now however is not to give you an account of the glorious prospects ahead & of the relief felt by Mr V's friends from all apprehension of defeat, but it is to suggest to you the propriety of withholding any farther expression of your views from the public until I reach home. I have to day had a long conference with Mr Dallas—the *Vice* on your ticket. He is very talanted and popular & most captivating in his address &c.

You will be pressed on all hands for your *opinions* upon different questions now before the country. I think I have acquired a knowledge of the *feeling* & condition of parties in this country which may be of service to you & I am fully in possession of Mr Dallas' views also. It is important that you go to work & prepair or have prepaired as early as possible, a *full* & *just* Biography of your life & services. You can yourself embody the facts & incidents of both and if you can get no abler *head* at the *work* I will fill it out myself.

So great is the enthusia[s]m here that when it was ascertained that I had arrived in this place and that I was from your District I was literally dragged to a large gathering of the Democracy & forced to address the people giving them an account of your life—purity of character, public service &c. and if I were allowed to form my opinion of the *speech* from the *applause,* I should say I had made a distinguished popular effort; but it was the very popular *theme* which drew forth such bursts of applause. We will carry this state by from 15 to 20 Thousand votes.

I have heard 2 of the New York Speakers—Mr Chamberling & Gov. Dickerson[3] address the people in this city. They both sustain your nomination as the very best that could have been made & place you upon high ground. They were delegates in the convention and devoted V.B. men. I shall not go further East than this place, and expect to leave here for home on Tuesday 4th Inst. We will in the coming election re-organize the old *Jackson Party* & sew up the nation by majorities in 18 & possibly 20 states. You see Govr. I write confidently. I have the *data* upon which to predicate this *opinion*.

GID. J. PILLOW

ALS. DLC–JKP. Addressed to Columbia.

1. Martin Van Buren.

2. David R. Porter and Henry A. P. Muhlenberg. With his eyes on the vice-presidency, Porter had used his influence and patronage to promote the political fortunes of John Tyler. Porter's efforts in 1843 secured the nomination of his brother, James M. Porter, to be secretary of war; but the governor's advocacy of Tyler provoked strong opposition among regular Pennsylvania Democrats. In January 1844 the U.S. Senate rejected Tyler's nomination of James Porter. Muhlenberg was elected as a Jackson Democrat to the U.S. House, where he served from 1829 until 1838. He declined appointments by Van Buren as secretary of the navy and minister to Russia in 1837, but served as minister to Austria, 1838–40. Muhlenberg, a friend to both Polk and Andrew Jackson, was nominated by the Democratic Party for the governorship of Pennsylvania in 1844, but died on August 11, 1844, before the election.

3. Churchill C. Cambreleng and Daniel S. Dickinson. A party stalwart and member of Van Buren's inner circle, Cambreleng was engaged in mercantile business in New York and served as a Democrat in the U.S. House, 1821–39. Van Buren appointed him minister to Russia, 1840–41. A lawyer from Binghamton, N.Y., Dickinson was a delegate to the Democratic National Conventions of 1835, 1844, 1848, and 1852. He was a member of the state senate, 1837–40, and lieutenant governor and president of the Court of Errors of New York, 1842–44. Appointed to fill the seat of Nathaniel P. Tallmadge in 1844, Dickinson was re-elected to a single term in that same year.

## FROM SILAS WRIGHT, JR.

My Dear Sir,                        Washington 2 June 1844

I have waited purposely, since the adjournment of the national convention before writing to you, that my correspondents, from whom I doubted not I should hear immediately, might inform me whether I had misjudged, in promptly declining the nomination tendered to me as Vice President upon the ticket with yourself. You will probably, before you receive this, have learned enough of the proceedings to know that the nomination was a surprise as well upon the convention, as upon myself, and that I was compelled to decide and act instantly, to prevent a dissolution of the convention, without making a second nomination.

The only instant hesitation upon my mind, or feelings, was the appearance to your self and your friends to which so prompt a declination would subject me. Yet I could not doubt what was my duty, and I resolved to make the necessary explanation to yourself, so early as to prevent any painful, or mischievous misunderstanding. Still the delay of which I have spoken, upon reflection, seemed advisable, and I have waited until I have received letters as far north as Albany in my State.

Let me say, then, what I am sure you will believe, that an association upon the ticket with yourself, so far from being an objection with me against being a candidate, was, both as a matter of feeling and principle, a strong inducement to accept the nomination. You must believe me, when I make the further declaration, that our respective positions upon the ticket constituted, with me, no inducement to decline the place offered to me. If I had myself had the formation of the ticket, its collocation would have been as the convention made it. I say this on account of what I have already seen in the public papers, and what you will doubtless see often repeated, upon this point.

My declination was dictated by two considerations, separate from those of a private character, of which I have said and am required to say nothing.

*First.* The democracy of my state will feel most deeply the injustice done to itself, in the person of Mr. Van Buren, by the course of the convention, and the circumstances which preceded, surrounded, and manifestly influenced, its action. It will feel that not merely the want of brotherly party feeling, but positive bad party faith, was exercised towards it and its favorite candidate, and that the seat of both and their strongest manifestation is in the South. And as the fruit of these untoward influences was the nomination of a Southern candidate for President, had I consented to go upon the ticket for the second office, I should have been looked upon as compounding the offence against that noble party, which has so generously sustained me for twenty years, and winked at the injury to my best friend, to elevate myself. The indignation thus engendered against me, and against the convention for permitting me to become the instrument of such a proceeding would, as I was satisfied, have made the ticket perfectly obnoxious with our democracy, and destroyed every hope of its success in the state. I did not feel that any obligation rested upon me to sacrifice myself to a proceeding so grossly unjust, and certainly not when I should sacrifice the ticket with myself.

Upon every principle of democracy, Mr. Van Buren was nominated upon the first ballot, and if, after that, he was to be got rid of, a moments reflection will satisfy you that to attempt to appease the feeling which could not fail to be excited in the minds and hearts of our democracy, either by taking another name from among themselves for the same place, or for a subordinate one, should be felt by them to be an aggravation to the injustice. It could not fail to destroy forever, with them, the fellow citizen of their own who would consent to be made the instrument of such double disappointment, the rejection of the one they had prefered, and the selection of one they had not.

Beyond their brethren of the State, they had not, and have not, any right to make these points, any further than to demand the rejection of the intriguers, through whose exertions the injustice has been brought upon them and their candidate. That was done by the convention in selecting yourself, and so far as the course of the Tennessee delegation was concerned I have no complaint to make, though had they been able to vote against the 2/3 rule, as the thing has resulted, I should have been glad of it.

Yet I hope we shall be able to give to the ticket a fair, and a successful support; but I have no hope that it can be done in any other way than, by exposing and denouncing the intrigues and the intriguers, and showing that you had no part, in feeling or action, with them, and that you owe your nomination to that fact, and to the votes of the delegates in the convention who were true to them and to their candidate, and was selected by them to defeat the leaders in the foul plot, which was perfectly accomplished by the movement. In this way I hope to rouse the pride and patriotism of our democracy, and to induce them to give a faithful and ardent support to the ticket. If it cannot be done in this way it certainly cannot in any. They must do it under the proud feeling that, for their principles and their country, they will consent to return good for evil, without the semblance of reward beyond the merit of the cause, and not because a compromise is tendered to them.

I am relieved in being able to tell you that every letter yet received from any republican of the state fully coincides with me in this opinion, and in the course I have pursued.

*Second.* The assumption, in the Convention and before the public, is that Mr. Van Buren is set aside in consequence of his Texas opinions;

and, although we have too much evidence here that this has been and is, with the intriguers, a mere pretense, and that the question has been raised, at this precise point of time, on purpose to form the pretext for either getting rid of him, or dismembering our party, yet it is all important that it should be believed in the North that this is the real ground for the defection of the South. To have placed me upon the ticket would have been to give the lie to this assumption, as every body knew that my opinions upon the subject of annexation were, at least, not more favorable than his, and that I must and shall vote against this Treaty, if called to vote upon it. Under these circumstances, to have rejected him and placd me upon the ticket would have been a declaration to our democracy that the Texas question had not set him aside, which would have greatly aggravated the result to them. I could not consent to become the instrument of this declaration, and retain any hope that the ticket could be supported in New York, because all would have said, with justice, that I could not have been ignorant that the Texas question was a mere pretense, when offered a place on the ticket for myself.

My declination has been without reasons given, and if compelled to give them hereafter in self defence, as I hope I shall not be, I shall be at liberty to presume that the convention expected me, if I accepted, to meet their rule upon that point, though I repeat that Mr. Walker, who brought forward my name, and nearly all the convention with him, knew what my course had been, and was to be, upon that question, and a letter of mine was in the hands of a member of our delegation to prevent any use of my name for the first office, in which it was expressly stated that my opinions as to annexation were identical with those of Mr. V.B.'s letter, as certainly not more favorable, and that I should vote against the Treaty.

I did not intend to trouble you so far, and will not go into further detail at present. I expected to have seen Major Donaldson[1] yesterday and hope to see him tomorrow, or certainly before he returns to Tennessee. I am anxious to talk very freely and fully with him, that he may be able to communicate my views to you more fully than I shall have time to write them.

In my deliberate judgement our Union was never so much in danger as at this moment. The course of Mr. Calhoun and his clique in all the Southern states, and the success they have had upon this occasion, together with the course of our friends at Richmond, with Mr. Ritchie and the Enquirer and the Course of the Southern delegations in the late convention, with the single exceptions of a solitary vote from Alabama and the vote of Missouri, and almost all given for a candidate notoriously rotten in democratic principle,[2] has given a fatal shock to the confidence of the northern democrats in the faith and fidelity of their Southern brethren, which it will take much time and good conduct to lose; and the consequences likely to arise form this state of things have, to my mind, more importance than a hundred tim[es][3] what the Texas question has now, or can ever have. Upon that subject, time will show you that no free State will go farther than Mr. V.B. has gone, and the danger is much greater that he has, in expressing, as a statesman should under such circumstances, his honest opinions, overstepped the boundary for that portion of the Union, than fallen short of it.

If we reject the Treaty, and have no more Texas, we hope we may save the North and the Union, but if that thing continues to be treated as the convention has treated it, as the only one in our instrument, the votes will be those of defeat, before November comes.

I am anxious to be at home, that I may devote my time and humble exertions to the support of our ticket, and both shall be given as cheerfully and faithfully as they would have been, had Mr. V.B. been nominated. Still I must not disguise the fact that we must enter the canvass under every possible disadvantage, and my only hope is in rousing our party to the high and patriotic determination of showing to their Southern brethren that, when they abandon the Union for sectional issues, mischievous intrigues, and sudden excitements, they will take the charge of the Democratic Ark of safety, and, in the face of ingratitude and injustice, will preserve it from rash destruction, and from the grasp of federalism, until time and opportunity shall be allowed for passion to subside, and for that sense of justice to return, which appears now to be almost wholly lost.

I have marked this hasty letter "private," because I have intended it only for yourself. I hope it will not appear unkind to you. Not one word of it is so intended, nor is there a feeling of unkindness towards yourself, among those which have dictated it.

If I do not see the Major,[4] as I hope to do, I may write you again before I leave here. I took the liberty a day or two since, to address to you a speech upon the tariff.[5] I doubt not you will soon be interrogated upon that subject, as it is already apparent that the great assault upon you in the North is to be made upon that point, and upon annexation; and I desire that, hereafter, you should write with full reflection, and a survey of the whole ground, upon both.

SILAS WRIGHT

ALS. DLC–JKP. Addressed to Columbia and marked *"Private."*
1. Andrew J. Donelson.

2. Delegates from only three southern states voted for Martin Van Buren on the first ballot at the Democratic National Convention: Alabama, 1; Missouri, 7; and North Carolina, 2. Lewis Cass received 57 votes from six southern states: Alabama, Georgia, North Carolina, Tennessee, Virginia, and Mississippi. Twenty-four southern votes were cast for other candidates by four states: Georgia, 1; Louisiana, 6; North Carolina, 5; and Kentucky, 12.

3. Two letters of this word are covered by the binding of the volume.

4. Andrew J. Donelson.

5. No cover communicating Wright's speech has been found; but see Cave Johnson to Polk, June 1, 1844.

## FROM ROBERT ARMSTRONG

at night

Dear Sir                                                     Nashville June 3d [18]44

The Northen mail is in and brings us nothing more than you will find in the Globe.

The Convention settled on the two third rule, a stage passenger says. They balloted all day on *tuesday* and done nothing. *This* is one day later than the mail.

I fear all is Confusion and want of union. Dick Johnston[1] joined his forces to Buchanan with some Disafected Democrats and passed the two third rule and it is said Dick is trying to kill you off by the move. Buchannan & Johnston against Wright & Polk.

My Impression is that the delay and postponement is made to *kill time*, that Van Burens letter of withdrawal may be received.[2]

It is said Cass is pressing and his friends urging him without a state to back him. It is a bad state of things and I have no hope any good is to come of it, at least to us, to the south, to Tennessee.

I am glad now that I did not go on. See part of Laughlins letter in the Union.[3] Our friends here are *down* and Dispirited. Others in our ranks are *pleased* at the troubles that are upon us. In a word Govr. their is now but little honesty or Dependance on some of the *friends* of the party, as they are called. In haste (12 Oclk).

R. ARMSTRONG

ALS. DLC–JKP. Addressed to Columbia and marked *"Private."*

1. Richard M. Johnson.

2. On the ninth ballot Benjamin F. Butler encountered difficulties convincing his fellow delegates from New York to support Polk; for the first time Butler disclosed that prior to the convention's meeting he had received from Martin Van Buren a letter authorizing him to take such action as might be necessary to bring the meeting to an harmonious decision; at length the New York delegates agreed that Butler could withdraw Van Buren's candidacy.

3. The *Nashville Union* of June 4, 1844, carried an unsigned letter from Washington, dated May 25, 1844, saying that it was "highly probable" that Martin Van Buren was "out of the way with the full and entire assent of the Tennessee delegation ...." The letter argued that in the selection of a presidential nominee party unity must be placed ahead of personal preferences. Silas Wright, Jr., and Polk had been mentioned along with Lewis Cass, Levi Woodbury, and James Buchanan; however, part of Indiana, Michigan, and the whole of Ohio opposed Cass' nomination.

## FROM GRANVILLE S. CROCKETT[1]

Dear Sir                                     Washington June 3rd 1844
I have been here ever since the Convention adjourned, and have made it my business to hear and see all I could, and I do not suppose there are many who have heard more than I have. At Gadsbys, Browns and Fullers[2] there are great crowds, and there is scarcely any thing talked of but the nomination. The excitement has somewhat subsided and the people are talking coolly and dispassionately. I have seen and conversed with men from every section, and nearly every state in the Union, and among the Democrats there is but one opinion, they all agree that the very best selection has been made, and that our success is certain. Dallas seems to be more acceptible than Wright and places Penna. beyond a doubt. Every body admits Va and Geoa. to be ours now beyond a doubt by larger majorities, before they were exceedingly doubtful for Mr V.B. Ohio and Ky are the only western States claimed by the Whigs and even they admit Ohio to be uncertain. The truth is if Butler[3] is elected in Ky. of which his friends have no fears Mr Clay will not get a State South of the Potomac. Texas and Oregon are as popular to the North with the democracy and a large portion of the Whigs as they are to the South & So. west, and these questions are killing Mr Clay. I understand he complains of his friends for having deceived him on the subject of annexation, and that he has a right to complain I have no doubt.
The Whigs are biting their lips, and are now lavish in their praises of Mr V.B. and hope to sour the minds of his warm friends by inducing them to believe he has been badly treated. But this you know is all stuff and wont begin to take. Their own disappointment and the enthusiasm with which the nominations are received is what galls them, which added to the scores which are daily falling off and quitting their ranks gives them certain evidence of defeat.
They are raving mad because all the vile slander and abuse which is piled up in bushels ready to be scattered against him to every district

in the whole country must now be lost and thrown away. It is said and truly too, that thousands of bushels of gold spoon and standing army speeches are now piled up,[4] ready franked to be sent out and flood the Country so soon as he was nominated, and now these very men have become loud in praises of the man they were ready to devour.

To day the Appropriation Bill[5] came up in Com. of the whole and an animated discussion took place and continued all day. Nothing was talked of scarcely but the candidates for the Presidency. Your friends marched up boldly and fearlessly to the scratch, and met every question firmly.

The Tennessee Delegation have as yet taken no part in the debate, but are waiting for Mr Clays friends from Kenty. to begin. Mr A.V. Brown told me this evening that he should say nothing until the Lexington Rep. Mr Davis[6] came into the fight when he felt himself fully prepared to define your position and Mr Clays also and place you both fairly before the Country on all the great subjects which are now agitating the public mind especially the Tariff. Col Johnson and the rest of your friends from Tenn, are constantly in their seats watching all the turns and you will see some good speeches reported on this bill.

I write for you only and would not wish to create any false impression on your mind, and state nothing but what I see and hear. I repeat again the whigs are greatly troubled and scarsely know what to say or do. The general impression is that Congress will adjourn on the 17th and I heard this evening at Browns Hotel that there would be an extra Session called this fall. What for I could not learn.

G. S. Crockett

ALS. DLC–JKP. Addressed to Columbia.

1. Granville S. Crockett, a Rutherford County farmer, served as sheriff, 1834–36, and sat for one term in the Tennessee House, 1835–37; he attended the Democratic National Convention, but was not one of Tennessee's official delegates.

2. Gadsby's Hotel, Brown's Hotel, and Fuller's Hotel. Located on the northwest corner of Third Street and Pennsylvania Avenue, John Gadsby's establishment later came to be known as the Washington House. Brown's Hotel, also known as the Indian Queen, was located near the northwest corner of Sixth Street and Pennsylvania Avenue. Fuller's Hotel, also called the City Hotel, later took the name of a subsequent proprietor, Henry Willard; it was located on the northwest corner of Fourteenth Street and Pennsylvania Avenue.

3. William O. Butler fought in the Battle of New Orleans, served as an aide to Andrew Jackson, 1816–17, and sat in the Kentucky House, 1817–18; twenty years later he returned to political life and won election as a Democrat to two terms in the U.S. House, 1839–43. He ran for governor in 1844, but lost to

William Owsley, nominee of the Kentucky Whigs. During the Mexican War, Butler held the rank of major general of volunteers; he ran unsuccessfully for the U.S. vice-presidency on the Democratic ticket of 1848.

4. In the 1840 presidential contest Whig orators frequently charged that Martin Van Buren was a man given to extravagant tastes and devoted to dangerous schemes for subverting the republican traditions of militia organization and governance. The "gold spoons" were part of a White House silver service purchased by James Monroe; and the "standing army" was a militia reform proposal by Secretary of War Joel R. Poinsett, who wanted basic militia training placed under the supervision of regular army officers.

5. The annual civil and diplomatic appropriations bill was taken up in the U.S. House on June 3, 1844. Discussion on the bill moved quickly to the questions of free trade, tariffs, Texas annexation, and presidential politics.

6. Garrett Davis, a lawyer, served one term in the Kentucky House, 1833–35; sat as a Whig in the U.S. House, 1839–47; and won election to the U.S. Senate as a Whig in 1861 and as a Democrat in 1867.

## FROM ISAAC G. McKINLEY[1]

Democratic Union Office
Dear Sir,                                                    Harrisburg June 3 1844

I last addressed you on the 1st of March, 1838, soliciting as a Reporter for the "Globe" a seat in the House of Representatives, & I now have before me, in my letter file, your note assigning me a place in Box No 3,[2] and I shall ever remember with pleasure the scenes that passed in review before me during the time that I occupied said Box, by the leave of the House & its then amiable, gentlemanly & dignified speaker. Little did I then suppose that in the short period of six years I should witness that speaker selected, almost by a dispensation of providence, I may say, as the standard bearer of the great Republican party of this Union. About the time that you left Congress I returned to this my native place, purchased an interest in a newspaper, & have since been honored by our Legislature in being elected State Printer. After the disastrous campaign of 1840 we presented a candidate of our own in the person of Mr Buchanan, with a view of getting clear of another battle under Mr. Van Buren, which we always regarded as hazardous. We however were not seconded & our candidate withdrew, before the meeting of our State Convention. We were then either compelled to go for Mr. Van Buren or permit our Delegates to be instructed in favor of Gen. Cass. This I never could consent to because I resided in Washington City at the time of the Removal of the Deposites by that Great & good man Gen Jackson, & knew the course that Gen. Cass then pursued, & I knew the course he had pursued in regard to the United States Bank question subsequently.[3]  We therefore without hesitation went for Mr Van Buren & our Delegates were accordingly instructed for him, although we would have preferred seeing some other true Democrat nominated.  I attended at Baltimore, in company with your old friend Jesse Miller,[4] & some twenty other gentlemen from our neighborhood & when we saw that our candidate was out of the question Col. C. Johnson, & the balance of the Tennessee Delegation will be o[u]r witness that we went among the very first for your nomination because we knew you to be a Democrat of the right stamp & we did not trust Gen. Cass, & we knew that by taking the Tennessee Delegation from Gen. Cass [that][5] he could never be nominated, and I do most seriously believe that this movement was suggested by a special Providence which guides & directs the affairs of men.  In proof of this I may refer to the fact that the very moment that that gallant old Democrat Governor Hubbard, led off the New Hampshire Delegation for James K. Polk, a new spirit of enthusiasm infused itself into the Convention.  The "Egyptian tombs" in which they had assembled rung with applause,[6] the fire communicated itself to the thousands & tens of thousands that crowded the streets of Baltimore & all went on the way rejoicing.  The intelligence was conveyed to Washington, instantaneously, on the wings of the forked lightning, & the greetings of the people of Washington were returned & announced in the Convention, before the final result was announced by the Secretaries.  On my way home I found every Democrat inspired with new vigor & every thing now looks cheering.

The only thing that the Whigs expect to work upon in our State is the Tariff & I trust that you can occupy such position on this question as to satisfy our tariff Democrats in Penna.  All we ask in Penna is a *Revenue tariff,* so adjusted as to afford protection to our iron, coal, & manufactures, & as you live in an iron region we will at least contend that your interests are nearly similar to ours.  In the South I take it that *annexation* is to be the all absorbing question & therefore in that region they need not bring their views on the tariff so much in conflict, in the Presidential canvass, with the views of our people.  This may be a suggestion worthy of consideration, & whatever you may say or write on the subject give us at least as fair a chance on this question as you do the other extreme of the Union, & I trust the time will soon arrive when our manufactures will still need less protection.  I shall forward you a copy of the Union during the campaign so that you may see how we conduct the Canvass, & I can assure you that we will spare no effort to achieve a glorious victo[ry] in November next.

ISAAC G. MCKINLEY

ALS. DLC–JKP. Addressed to Columbia. Polk's AE on the cover states that he answered this letter on June 24, 1844; Polk's reply has not been found.

1. McKinley was an owner and editor of the Harrisburg *Democratic Union,* a powerful Democratic newspaper in Pennsylvania.

2. Letters not found.

3. Lewis Cass, Andrew Jackson's secretary of war, opposed the president's removal of government deposits from the Second Bank of the United States.

4. Jesse Miller sat in both the Pennsylvania House and Senate prior to his election as a Democrat to the U.S. House, where he served from 1833 to 1836. Appointed first auditor of the Treasury Department in 1836, he served in that post until 1842.

5. Ink smears here and below have obliterated portions of the manuscript.

6. A large but dimly lighted facility, the Egyptian Saloon of Baltimore's Odd Fellows' Hall housed the Democratic National Convention of 1844.

## FROM HENRY A. P. MUHLENBERG

My dear Sir                                        Reading Pa. June 3 1844

Permit me to congratulate you most warmly & sincerely upon your nomination as the candidate of the Democratic party for the Presidency. The nomination was somewhat unexpected but not the less agreeable. It was received here with bursts of applause & new life and energy at once pervaded the whole party, shortly before considerably depressed.

You are aware that I have always been very friendly to Mr. Van Buren. If he had been nominated we should have sustained him in this County, the Banner County of the Keystone[1] & given him a very large & decided majority, but *I doubt very much* whether we could have carried the State for him. This impression had become so general that the party began to despond & as far as he was concerned, showed neither life energy nor enthusiasm. He had been the mark at which the shafts not only of the Clay men, but of the friends of all the different candidates of our own side had been levelled without intermission. All cried out: "he cannot be elected—it is labor lost," & the consequence of this incessant cry from all sides was prejudice, disaffection & luke warmness. He certainly could not have received any thing like the whole democratic vote. Now however the case is different. There is not only new life, there is enthusiasm. Those who left the party in '40 & voted for Harrison are rapidly returning & hourly giving in their adhesion. I have *no doubt* of your getting the *overwhelming majority which* this County (old Berks) is in the habit of giving & of your carrying the State by a very decided vote.

We have however one difficulty to encounter in this State, and the Clay men will give us much trouble upon that point. You are no doubt aware that Penna. is a decidedly tarif state that is to say, in her usual moderate way. She is not for a high protective tarif, a tarif exclusively for protection, but one which will yield sufficient revenue for the necessary wants of the Government & at the same time by means of *discriminating duties* give usefull *incidental protection.* The great mass of our people believe that this can be done without exclusively favoring any particular class or sensibly injuring any portion of the Union—nay that it must in the end conduce to the benefit of the whole. They are great sticklers for their favorite Jacksons "judicious tarif." I believe all the candidates on our side of the house had in some way made declarations more or less favorable to discriminating duties & incidental protection. You are however a new-man & as yet the mass of our people know but little of your opinions but this subject. I notice an attack already made on you thro' Genl. Irwine of this State & J. J. Hardin,[2] a member from Illinois in the National Intelligencer of the 31st of May.[3]

As a *warm & sincere* friend, who will *under all circumstances zealously* support you I know you will pardon my calling your attention to this subject & advising you to be *cautious & prudent* in regard to it, as it is, as far as Penna. is concerned, a dangerous one. God forbid that you should offend the South in any way. But the President of the U.S. stands in a different position from that of a mere Representative of Tennessee. If therefore you could devise some mode of giving us in Pennsylvania some moderate declaration respecting a revenue tarif adopted to the wants of the Government embracing the principle of discriminating duties & incidental protection it would do much to give the Whigs a complete Waterloo with us in this State at least. Mr. Van Buren being a northern man, stood so straight that he bent a little towards the South. May not a Southern man, to show his impartiality, lean a little towards the North. Such I always predicted would be the consequence if we should get a southern President &, candidly speaking, I was always enclined to favor one believing that it would tend greatly to promote union & harmony.

You must not give too much attention, sub rosa, to what the Philadelphians say respecting our State. They do not exactly understand it, and too often look upon the City as the State itself whereas it is compared with the State only what a single letter is to the whole alphabet. Very often an entire different atmosphere is found outside of its circumference.

I rely greatly upon your well known prudence & discretion & firmly believe that, as respects the tarif, if you cannot give us Pennsylvanians a helping hand in our moderate views, you will at least not give us a knock-down law. A little concession often produces a great good. [Be][4] pleased to present my respectfull regards [to your] good lady & tell her that Pennsylvania will fully stand by James K Polk & certainly give him a majority, more or less. The greater the majority the more we shall all be gratified, and that as far as we can judge in this section of the Union, "all will be well" in the Union.

Excuse this long letter & believe me....

HEN. A. MUHLENBERG

ALS. DLC–JKP. Addressed to Columbia. Polk's AE on the cover states that he answered this letter on July 10, 1844; Polk's reply has not been found.

1. Muhlenberg was from Berks County, Penn.

2. James Irvin and John J. Hardin. A Pennsylvania Whig merchant and manufacturer, Irvin won election to two terms in the U.S. House, 1841–45; he lost his bid for the governorship of Pennsylvania in 1847. An Illinois lawyer, Hardin was a member of the state house, 1836–42, before winning election as a Whig to a single term in the U.S. House, 1843–45; a major general in the Illinois militia, he was killed in the Mexican War.

3. On May 31, 1844, the Washington *National Intelligencer* published a letter from John J. Hardin to James Irvin in which Hardin concluded that Polk's strong anti-tariff views had made him a viable compromise candidate acceptable to John C. Calhoun and his southern friends.

4. A tear of the letter's seal has mutilated at least one word on this line and one on the line below.

## FROM AARON VANDERPOEL[1]

My dear Sir                                      New York 3d June 1844

Permit me most cordially, to congratulate you on your nomination for the Presidency. You know I am an *out-and-out* Van Buren man; that we are natives of the same town[2] and that his son married my brothers daughter.[3] His defeat at the convention was to me very mortifying! Yet this feeling was soon overcome by the fact that the nomination had fallen upon one so entirely acceptable to me as *yourself*. Since you were here in 1842[4] I have been placed on the Bench of our Superior Court. I can not, therefore, be quite as *noisy* as in days of yore, But I trust that though a *Judge*, I am not without some influence & efficiency as a politician. You will have the support of Mr Van Burens friends in this State, and I would not be surprised, if, within one week from this time, Mr Van Buren should indicate to the Public his entire acquiescence in the nomination. On tuesday, we shall have an immense gathering in the Park, in front of the City Hall (which you visited with me in 1842), to respond to the nomination.[5] *We mean to carry New York for you.* At all events, a most vigorous effort shall be made, and I doubt not, we will succeed.

The whigs say, they mean to have Catechisms *"polked"* at you about the tarriff, and other issues, which they suppose will help them at the North. I see they are already publishing in all their papers your anti-tarriff speech in 1843[6] and the letter of Hardin of Illinois. I am a free trade man *to the hub,* but there are thousands in the northern & eastern States, who generally vote our ticket that are a little *tariffish.* If I dared to give you advice, I would say "write as few letters for publication as possible, and do not come out stronger on the tarriff, than you have already done." Our friends here are in fine spirits, and will go the ticket in blood earnest. I have seen the Editor of the E. Post.[7] He will go the nomination & will daily run stronger & warmer. I have advised our papers immediately to republish the article about you which appeared in the Democratic Review in 1838.[8] The Whigs here are, evidently, alarmed. I think the defeat of Mr Clay is pretty certain.

A. VANDERPOEL

[P.S.] I have enclosed this to our friend Johnson for *his frank.* A.V.

ALS. DLC–JKP. Addressed to Columbia under the frank of Cave Johnson and marked *"Private."* Polk's AE on the cover states that he answered this letter on June 25, 1844; Polk's reply has not been found.

1. A lawyer, Aaron Vanderpoel served in the New York Assembly, 1826–30; in the U.S. House, 1833–37 and 1839–41; and on the Superior Court in New York City, 1842–50.

2. Martin Van Buren and Vanderpoel were born in Kinderhook, Columbia County, N.Y.

3. John Van Buren, James Vanderpoel, and Elizabeth Vanderpoel Van Buren. A New York lawyer and politician, John Van Buren was active for many years in state and national politics. As a member of the radical wing of the New York Democracy he won a single term in 1845 to the office of attorney general. In 1841 he had married Elizabeth Vanderpoel, the daughter of James Vanderpoel, a prominent lawyer in Albany and the owner of considerable land in Kinderhook.

4. In June and July of 1842 Polk traveled to Washington City, Philadelphia, and New York for purposes both political and financial.

5. A large number of Democrats met in City Hall Park in New York City on the afternoon of June 4, 1844, to respond to the nominations made at Baltimore. Invited to preside over the gathering, Martin Van Buren declined that honor but expressed his satisfaction at the nominations in a letter read to the crowd. See Martin Van Buren to Gansevoort Melville, et al., June 3,

1844. Copy by Martin Van Buren, Jr. DLC–MVB.

6. Reference is to Polk's gubernatorial campaign speech delivered at Jackson, Tenn., on April 3, 1843. See Polk to George W. Smith et al., May 15, 1843.

7. A native of Massachusetts, William Cullen Bryant practiced law prior to becoming assistant editor of the New York *Evening Post* in 1826. In 1829 he became editor of the paper and ultimately became a major voice in Democratic ranks. Though public affairs consumed much of his time, Bryant also achieved considerable recognition for his poetry.

8. The *United States Magazine and Democratic Review,* vol. II (May, 1838), pp. 197–208, carried a biographical sketch of Polk. Published and edited by John L. O'Sullivan and Samuel D. Langtree, the *Review,* which focused largely on public affairs, also received acclaim for its literary merit.

## FROM ROBERT ARMSTRONG

at night

Dear Govr,                           [Nashville, Tenn.] 4th June [18]44

The news recvd. to night and enclosed[1] is like that of last night which proves to be correct. One day ahead of the Mail. It is True. There is no doubt of it. You had better remain at home a few days. I saw your note promising to be in on Thursday to Humphreys. I have already told Heiss that nothing must go in the Union but what is *"proper"* untill Laughlin comes Home.

We will Succeed. All seems Harmony in the Convention. The Whigs here in deep distress and others furious. The Democracy are in high Spirits and the happiest fellows alive. It is now for us to do or die. I will write you tomorrow. In haste.

R.A.

ALS. DLC–JKP. Addressed to Columbia. Polk's AE on the cover states that he answered this letter on June 6, 1844; Polk's reply has not been found.

1. Enclosure not found.

## FROM WILLIAM E. CRAMER[1]

Albany, N.Y. June 4, 1844

Cramer informs Polk that the press of New York has come out vigorously in Polk's support, that the immediate annexation of Texas has not proven very popular in New York, and that local Democrats are "decidedly *in favor of letting the Tariff alone."* Cramer notes a recent attack upon Polk's tariff position by John J. Hardin in the *Intelligencer*[2] and requests copies of Polk's recent speeches on the question.

ALS. DLC–JKP. Addressed to Columbia. Polk's AE on the cover states that he answered this letter on August 3, 1844; Polk's reply has not been found.

1. William E. Cramer, son of Polk's former colleague in the U.S. House, John Cramer, became associated with the *Albany Argus* in March 1843. Cramer's letter was enclosed in Cave Johnson to Polk, June 5, 1844. ALS. DLC–JKP. In his cover letter Johnson communicates John Cramer's assurances that "the Argus under the control of his son will be kept straight...."

2. See Henry A. P. Muhlenberg to Polk, June 3, 1844.


## FROM ROBERT ARMSTRONG

Wednesday night

Dear Sir                              [Nashville, Tenn. June 5, 1844][1]

Childress arrived in the stage to night. He confirms all, says Wright declined, and that G. M. Dallas was nominated in his place. All well and good.

I was out to give the Old Chief[2] the news this morning. He is pleased beyond measure and happy. Says we will succeed. Has no fears of the result. Your name I see is at the head of Mr Calhouns paper, the Spectator. It will put every thing in a blaze and we must keep it so. Genl Jackson says Tyler will withdraw and the whole Democracy will be united.

The Genl had letters today from Washington. Some persons "trying to get back where they once was."

You must come in but *in the proper way* and at a *proper time*. We will see. In haste.

R. ARMSTRONG

ALS. DLC–JKP. Addressed to Columbia.
1. Date identified through content analysis.
2. Andrew Jackson.


## FROM J. GEORGE HARRIS

My Dear Sir                              Near Nashville, June 5, 1844

Permit me to congratulate you on the result of the deliberations of the late democratic convention at Baltimore. It is truly most glorious, and it affords me no little pleasure to perceive that the ball was put in motion by my old friends of New England.[1]

I hope you received the letter[2] which I sent the other day enclosing the reply[3] of one addressed to my friend Greene, antecede[n]t to my departure for New Orleans. On the way to Smithland I wrote three others, one to Croswell of the Argus,[4] another to Pratt of Baltimore,[5] who are not less efficient in primary movements than my friend Greene.

I shall be most happy to lend my poor hand to any point where it may be considered serviceable.

J. GEO. HARRIS

[P.S.] I was at the great Texas meeting in N. Orleans[6] at which Plauché, Houston[7] & others of both parties took leading parts. All that feeling will be cordially turned to you.

N.B. Since the 15th of March I have travelled through the country from New York to New Orleans, rather leisurely, and have had a fair opportunity to confer with your friends and more especially to sound public opinion on the proposition to annex Texas to the Union. I was well satisfied, and so expressed myself here repeatedly, that if Van Buren was run a great many democrats would oppose him on the score of his half way position on the Texas question. And I was also satisfied that with an unexceptionable candidate like yourself, and with your views of annexation we would not only combine all the strength of the democratic party, but about one third or one quarter at least of the whigs. It is still my opinion formed from actual observation, that such must and will be the result.

I shall be much disappointed if Tyler and Calhoun do not cordially give you their support. Indeed, Clay's prospects were never more hopeless. J. Geo. H.

Col. Childress has just arrived bringing intelligence that Wright declined and Geo M. Dallas of Pa. was nominated for V.P. on the eighth ballot.

ALS. DLC–JKP. Addressed to Columbia. Polk's AE on the cover states that he answered this letter on June 7, 1844; Polk's reply has not been found.

1. Reference probably is to Henry Hubbard, head of the New Hampshire delegation; Hubbard placed Polk's name in nomination on the convention's eighth ballot. Reference may also be to Harris' political mentor from Massachusetts, George Bancroft; throughout the previous evening Bancroft, Gideon J. Pillow, and Benjamin F. Butler had labored to bring northern and southern delegates to a compromise choice for the presidential nomination.

2. On May 24, 1844, Harris wrote to Polk, enclosing a letter addressed to Harris by Charles G. Greene on May 14, 1844. An influential leader in the New England Democracy, Greene founded the *Boston Morning Post* in 1831 and remained its editor for some forty-eight years. In his letter to Polk of May 24, Harris related that Greene had "more influence in a movement of this primary character than any other one man in all New England—and I

have no doubt we shall see the effect of his efforts in the National Convention."
ALS. DLC–JKP.

3. Greene's letter to Harris of May 14, 1844, promised his full support for the vice-presidential nomination of Polk at the Democratic National Convention. ALS. DLC–JKP.

4. Edwin Croswell edited the *Albany Argus* from 1823 to 1854.

5. Pratt is not identified further.

6. On May 10, 1844, a meeting was held in New Orleans in support of the annexation of Texas, that territory located between the Sabine River and the Rio del Norte. The meeting resolved that in the event of the Senate's rejecting the Texas treaty, Louisiana would form a compact with the Republic of Texas "to extend the boundary of Louisiana to her ancient limits," subject to the approval of the U.S. Congress required by Article I, section 10 of the U.S. Constitution.

7. Jean Baptiste Plauché and Felix Huston. Plauché commanded a battalion of city militia directly under Andrew Jackson's command during the Battle of New Orleans. A successful New Orleans merchant and cotton broker, Plauché strongly supported the annexation of Texas. On June 2, 1844, he wrote Jackson that he considered the present as being an opportune time to annex Texas, "and if we do not seize upon Texas, it is lost to us for ever." ALS. DLC–AJ. Plauché won election as lieutenant governor of Louisiana in 1850. Huston, a lawyer from Natchez, Miss., raised and equipped an army of 500 men, at a personal expense of $40,000, to fight in Texas in 1836. Commissioned a general in the Texas army, he served briefly as its commander-in-chief in 1837; in 1840 he commanded Texas volunteers in battle against the Comanches at Plum Creek. Huston returned to Louisiana in 1840, continued to espouse the cause of Texas, and renounced his Whig ties in favor of Polk's presidential bid in 1844.


## FROM THOMAS P. MOORE

My dear Sir                                    Harrodsburg June 5h, 1844

We have just recd full confirmation of your Nomination as a Candidate for the first office in the World, & meet on the 8h to respond to it. I need not tell you that I ardently desired the nomination of Mr Vanburen & yourself, but that I have fully as much confidence in your integrity & capacity & your fitness for an executive station as I have ever had in his, & much more attachment to you personally. I hope the nomination may lead to Union, harmony, & energetic action; if so, we shall triumph & save the country. Here we are all Texas men & mean to make a vigorous effort to astonish the country.

A few words of advice & I have done. Vanburen conferred too little with his friends; an opposite course discreetly exercised is best under our institutions. Letters without number will be poured upon the country from Ten declaring that you cannot get your own state. Let this be vigorously counteracted. We have a few Duff Greens[1] in our ranks; give them no power to do mischief. From this day forward I shall be found constantly engaged, ready for any labor or responsibility, & prepared to go to any point where there is most danger.

Heartfelt regard to Mrs P.

T. P. MOORE

[P.S.] The exclusive Dick Johnson clique see now that their denunciation of me has done me no harm, him no good.[2]

ALS. DLC–JKP. Addressed to Columbia. Polk's AE on the cover states that he answered this letter on June 26, 1844; Polk's reply has not been found.

1. Duff Green, originally an ardent supporter of Andrew Jackson, played a leading role in the quarrels that led to John C. Calhoun's break with the president and the Democratic party.

2. Moore wrote his postscript in the left margin of his sheet.

## FROM JAMES M. PORTER

Dear Sir                                      Easton Penna June 5, 1844

Although I have not the pleasure of a personal acquaintance with you, yet I believe we have heretofore held some intercourse by letter.[1] In the position however which you now occupy before the people of the United States I should have no hesitation in addressing myself to you on the subject of this letter, were we totally unacquainted, with each other.

In common with nine tenths of the people of Pennsylvania I am interested in the protection of the domestic industry of our country. As a citizen of the United States I hold however that the interests of no one section of the country or class of inhabitants should be fostered or protected at the expense of another. That the *general* good should be the object of the Legislation of the general government. It will no doubt often happen in effecting this, that from temporary causes occasional injustice may be done to certain parts or portions. This, insofar as it can be done, should be remedied as the evils occur, without deranging the general system. It happened in the formation of the old union under the articles of Confederation, and again in adopting the constitution of the United States, that different sectional as well as political views and interests had to be reconciled, for the general good of the whole. Hence the federal constitution is one of compromises and concessions.

It seems to me that the *administration* of the Government under it should always partake of the same character, whilst none of the cardinal principles should ever be yielded. In this view of the subject I have thought that the agitating questions of protection, tariff & revenue could and ought to be adjusted upon like considerations. Those interested in domestic manufactures would stand in their own light by the advocacy of high protecting duties, because their imposition would be constantly exciting the hostility and attacks of their Opponents; Whilst those duties would produce unhealthy action in the business, by leading so many to embark in it, as to introduce ruinous competitions. Their true policy, in my judgment is to have a regular & certain system adopted not subject to frequent changes and fluctuations, which must render their business precarious.

I think the friends of domestic industry in this region & indeed everywhere else, where they do not seek to mix up the question with politics, are satisfied that the amount of revenue required for an economical administration of the government shall be raised by the imposition of duties upon goods imported into this country from abroad, provided that in the imposition of the duty, there be such a discrimination made as will give incidental protection to the products & manufactures of our own country. I speak of things as they are, taking the systems of other nations as they have them in operation.

My own opinion always has been that upon principles in a republican government, all taxes should be direct and immediate, so that every man could know exactly what he paid to the support of Government, each one paying his proportion according to his means. In that event he would be likely to look much more carefully to its due application and expenditure than he would, where he paid what he contributed indirectly and without knowing its amounts. But with the system in existence both here and elsewhere, it will be utterly impossible to carry this theory out and as I am more of a utilitarian than a theorist, I must be content to take man, the governments of the world and their systems as they are, if I wish to arrive at practical results.

Your political opponents here charge you with being an out & out anti-protectionist or free trade advocate. From the insight which I have been able to obtain of your views, as evinced in your career in Congress I have supposed that you were disposed to take the middle ground of compromise to which I have referred. If I am right in this conjecture I should be pleased to learn so, from yourself, in such manner that I may be able, if necessary, to state your views to others. I am an old fashioned democrat and desire to see the principles of democracy in the ascendant. I believe that a knowledge of your views on this question of revenue &c would be of essential service to you in this commonwealth in the ensuing canvass.

Under these impressions I have taken the liberty of addressing you in the spirit of friendship. I shall probably not take any very active part in the details of politics during the coming contest, as I am now a private citizen and shall probably remain so, having returned to a full practice of my profession. Still, however, enjoying as I do the confidence of my neighbours and fellow citizens I am often called upon for information in relation to leading topics and am always happy to have it in my power to correct erroneous impressions and to convey correct information to them.

J. M. PORTER

ALS. DLC–JKP. Cover sheet not found.
1. No prior correspondence between Porter and Polk has been found.

## FROM EDWIN CROSWELL

My dear Sir,                                              Albany, June 6, 1844
The republicans of this State every where congratulate themselves upon the result of the Baltimore Convention. Next to Mr Van Buren, towards whom, as you know, the attachments of our friends in this State are strong, no one c'd have been presented who w'd have been more acceptable to our Democracy than yourself. Altho in some quarters disappointment may be manifested because their own candidate was not the nominee, the feeling is in no respect directed towards yourself. Beyond an occasional remark in the N.Y. Eve. Post (which upon the Texas & Abolition questions is not in accordance with the views of the democratic masses) the feeling and expession are cordial, & auspicious of the best results.

Before this will reach you, the indications in the South and West will have been such probably, as to enable you & our friends in Tennessee to form an estimate of the Campaign. In this State, the tone is already admirable. The great meeting in the City of New York, on Tuesday afternoon, at which Mr V.B.'s letter was read,[1] was an earnest of what our friends can & will do there. The Ratification meeting to-night in this city,[2] called by several of our democratic citizens (some of whom you will recognise) and concurred in by the Gen. Committee, will be in the same temper, unless we entirely mistake the indications. Every where in the State, as you will perceive by the Argus, the Democracy not only spontaneously & enthusiastically respond to the nominations, but are awakening at once to the contest with unwonted spirit & energy. Already the whigs, so ready in gasconade, quail before these manifestations.

The Tariff Question will be the chief Whig topic, for the Bank they dare not assume openly, & long before we come to the polls, Texas annexation will be a question they will scarcely care to meet. The great body of the democracy of the State are in favor of a revenue Tariff, with Protection as an incident of revenue. There are sections of the State, however, in which the Tariff feeling is stronger & which require a cautious handling of the subject. In Pennsylvania also, undoubtedly, that interest is more or less prevalent. So far, however, there is nothing in yr. speeches & reports on this question on which the democracy of this State, in all sections, cannot stand & maintain their ground. Upon all the other issues, the argument & feelings are immeasurably with us. And we shall arouse the State by such efforts as have rarely if ever been put forth.

In relation to our local politics, Gov. Bouck, Gov. Marcy[3] & their friends are, as I believe, impregnable, whatever may be the occasional & partial efforts in a few localities. The tide will roll on down to our nominations in Sept.,[4] & I have the utmost confidence that we shall carry the State, upon the National & State tickets, triumphantly.

The intermediate State Elections (in Aug. & Sept.) will be of far more importance than their actual electoral vote. As an index to the popular sentiment, the result in Louisiana, Indiana & Maine, will be material.[5] Indiana is debateable ground. Our friends write favorably, but it cannot be too much attended to. I have no fear that we shall not carry Maine, altho the whigs will struggle hard. Of Lou. we know nothing.

Personally, I need not assure you with what gratification & alacrity we take the field with yr. name; nor how cordially I remain ....

E. CROSWELL

ALS. DLC–JKP. Addressed to Columbia. Polk's AE on the cover states that he answered this letter on June 24, 1844; Polk's reply has not been found.

1. For Martin Van Buren's letter see Aaron Vanderpoel to Polk, June 3, 1844.

2. The Democrats of Albany assembled at the state capitol for their mass meeting to respond to the nominations.

3. William C. Bouck and William L. Marcy. A farmer from Schoharie County, N.Y., Bouck served as a canal commissioner for nineteen years. Defeated in his first attempt in 1840, Bouck, a leader of the Hunker faction of the Democratic party, won election as governor in 1842 and served a single term. A lawyer and politician, Marcy served as state comptroller, 1823–29;

associate justice of the state supreme court, 1829–31; U.S. senator, 1831–32; and as Democratic governor of New York for three terms, 1833–39. Polk appointed him secretary of war, a post he held from 1845 to 1849; he later served as secretary of state, 1853–57.

4. The Democratic State Convention of New York convened in Syracuse on September 4, 1844, to make nominations for state offices.

5. State elections were scheduled for July 1 in Louisiana, August 5 in Indiana, and September 9 in Maine.

## FROM PHILEMON DICKERSON[1]

Dear Sir                                    [Paterson, N.J.] June 7, 1844

Permit me to congratulate you upon your nomination, and to express the hope, and belief too, that in due time we may also congratulate you upon yr. Election as President of The United States.

It cannot however be concealed that to insure success will require evry proper Exertion on our part. The Whigs have been Elated with their prospect of success, arising from dissentions in our ranks, but since they have noticed the unanimity & Enthusiasm with which the nomination has been recd. I think their prospects begin to fade. As to our little State, we have a hard battle to fight and altho we cannot promise success, we shall certainly try to deserve it at least. Our State is essentially a Tariff state & deeply interested in manufactures, and particularly in this District. I am aware that your views have been generally adverse to the Tariff but do not know particularly what those views are. Our opponents charge that you are an ultra free trade man, and opposed to the protection of our domestic manufactures in any form, as well upon constitutional ground as Expediency. If such be your views, It could be of no service here to make them more public. But if your views are more favourable to our manufactures—If you think that Congress in adjusting the duties upon imports, should discriminate in such manner as to afford favourable protection to our manufactures, without raising a greater amount of revenue, than should be necessary to meet the current expenses of government administered upon the most Economical plan, it would be of great service to us here to know it, as a great proportion of our people of both parties have those views.

For myself I have no fear for the success of our manufactures provided we are saved from a National Bank, and with such an institution our manufactg. establishment would be liable to constant fluctuations & embarrassments, even under the operation of the most favourable tariff. But without a National Bank we can get on with the aid of a

Revenue Tariff with all our principal manufactures Except perhaps in the case of Iron, which is the most important, and may require, and I think should recive, as much protection as may be found necessary, to establish it firmly & permanently, the consequence of which wd. be that very soon it would be furnished to the consumer cheaper than it has been ever before or would ever be without being thus protected.

I should be happy to hear from you upon this subject, but I wish this letter to be considered private, as I should consider any answer which you may please to make, as I do not wish to interfere publickly in the Elections. But your answer may lay the foundation of a more formal request for your sentiments upon this subject.

Present my best respects to Mrs Polk and say to her that my wife[2] sends her love, and altho she cannot come to Tennee, yet she declares that if you get into the white house you may look out for a visitor.

PH. DICKERSON

[P.S.] When you see Genl Jackson you will please present him my best respects.

ALS. DLC–JKP. Addressed to Tennessee. Polk's AE on the cover states that he answered this letter on June 26, 1844; Polk's reply has not been found.

1. A New Jersey lawyer, Dickerson won election as a Democrat to the U.S. House in 1833 and served until 1836, when he resigned to become governor of New Jersey. He was re-elected to a single term in the U.S. House in 1839, but lost his bid for re-election. Dickerson was appointed judge of the U.S. District Court for New Jersey in 1841 and filled that post until his death in 1862.

2. Dickerson was married to Sidney Stotesbury, daughter of John Stotesbury of New York.

## FROM SAMUEL H. LAUGHLIN

My dear Sir,                     Washington City, Friday, June 7, 1844

For the first time in my life, for the last three weeks I have suffered more from temporary (I hope) ill hea[l]th than I have ever done in the same time.[1] Still I have been able to work, and since the 29th ultimo, have wrote more than I perhaps ever before wrote in the same space of time. I am doubly sorry to be unwell, and mostly, from advice remaining in my room, adjoining the appartmints of our good friends Blackwell and Linn Boyd at Browning's, (a few doors from the Grove now occupied as a private residence).[2] I do little else but write letters to accompany Linn Boyd's speech, corrected, enlarged and revised, in reply to John White.[3] They do the franking, and every speech I send to a man in Tennessee known to me I have accompanied with a letter. I repeat that I am sorry to be unwell for if ever man was surrounded

by scenes and events which ought to rouse his blood into action like
the sound of trumpet, it is myself. I see the goal in view which I have
prayed and hoped for for many years, and it is in sight without that
long militant waiting-for, which myself, and those who thought of you
as I ever did, expected to have to submit to. In view of *certain success*
I am as happy as a man can be, the success of whose best friend is as
dear to him, as far as human infirmity will permit, as his own. You
know I called and presided at the first public meeting in Tennessee,
some years ago, which first nominated you, on resolutions drawn by
myself, as a candidate for the Vice Presidency.[4] Since that day, I have
ever looked, at a future time, to the accomplishment of the event which
now under providence, and the promptings of patriotism, is about to
happen sooner than your best friends anticipated. It is, however, what
I ardently hoped for from the moment I read Mr. Van Buren's letter.
His Texas letter. If he had been an "enemy," and written a book, it
could not have been more promotive of what has happened.

I need not remind you of what you will see in the New York,
Philadelphia, Richmond, Ohio, and other papers, and by packet upon
packet of letters which I know you will receive, of the enthusiasm with
which the nominations are everywhere received.

The Whigs are in perfect consternation here. They were alarmed at
first, but the daily news coming in here has panic-struck the stoutest
of them. Green of Kentucky has left, post haste, for Kentucky. The
Senate will, it is understood, ask to rescind the adjourning resolution
now standing for the 17th. The truth is, they are like a frightened
army of raw militia here, with no General. They are weak in counsel-
lors. They have in caucus now, no Clay, Bell, Granger, J. C. Clarke[5]
and others as in 1840. The dirty little attack[6] on you the other day
by Schenk Hardin, Peyton, &c.[7] for which they were well scourged by
Douglas, Payne, Belser, McClernand, and last and severest by Henley
of Indiana,[8] at the request of Tilghman A Howard (who is here) myself
and others who intreated him to do it, it being his first speech. He
is a leading man, *was* a Cass man, and we wanted him to bury his
first discontent in a public committal. Douglas of Il. a smart fellow
suggested the propriety of it. This attack shows their weakness in
means of attack. Andrew Johnson tried to get at Peyton but failed.[9]
He and Hardin are poor puppies. A. Johnson did scourge Hardin's
letter giving your views of tariff.[10] Milton Brown uses him. I have
noticed these things in my letters home. Besides Louis McLane, J.
V. L. McMahan, who it is understood did more to carry Baltimore to
Whiggery when he deserted as a member of the Maryland Legislature
than any one man, it is understood is *flat out for our* nominations.

The Ratification glorifications at New York, Boston, etc. has employed Butler and Bancroft so much, and to good purpose, that our Address[11] is delayed; but it is all well, and it can now be made stronger and better. Dromgoole, with whom I am intimate, and Gov. Fulton, as well as myself, are disposed to commit most of it to Butler and Bancroft. We then will have strong southern principles, and strong eulogies of the southern candidate from northern pens.

You will see a note from A. V. Brown to Rathbun, a noble New York democrat—he who whipped White[12] or would have done it—contradicting the lie of your being a duelist and having shot a man.[13]

Alex. Anderson, the poor devil, has been pressing upon Williamson Smith to write you that Van Buren, Wright, and others were cold, that neither they, Ohio, or any of their men would support you heartily. He said he had it from true sourse. It is a bare lie. Since he urged Smith to write, Van Buren's letter, Butler and Melvilles and Cambreling's speeches[14] have appeared, and Medary's great shout at Columbus Ohio. I heard Wright say yesterday, that though the wishes of his heart had been disappointed, he would support the nominations, heart, hand and soul. Anderson dont talk to me of his secrets. We meet frindly but I have not consulted or confided in him and never will. Blackwell, though he has not been consulted as much as he ought to have been by Brown and Cave,[15] has ever been of their mind and yours and mine, and against the mad folly of Geo Jones, A Johnson, and Cullom.[16] Cullom lives with some South Carolinians and Colquit.[17] Black of S.C. is a noble fellow, and been always moderate and right.

By being here, I have given information anxiously sought by hundreds of our warm frinds from various states and to many members of Congress. As I have been partly obliged to stay, I have watched men and events, for I have visited messes and delegations continually, and by writing to the Union, I have done and [....][18]

[SAMUEL H. LAUGHLIN]

N.B. There were some very improper things in the Union of 23 and 28th of May, and if they had gotten to Baltimore in time, small as they were, they would have ruined us—destroyd us. You know what your advice and mine was to Heiss. I thank God we escaped. Save us from friends sometimes is a wise prayer.[19] L.

ALS. DLC–JKP. Addressed to Columbia and marked "Private."
1. On June 10, 1844, Laughlin wrote Polk from Washington City that since returning from the Baltimore Convention he had been too unwell to travel; he explained that chronic diarrhea had forced him to limit his diet to "milk, corn bread, and crackers and coffee." ALS. DLC–JKP.

2. Browning's boarding house is not identified further.

3. See Laughlin to Polk, April 24, 1844. On April 13, 1844, Linn Boyd published in the Washington *Globe* a letter renewing the "corrupt bargain" charge against Henry Clay and John Q. Adams. On April 23, 1844, John White of Kentucky attempted to refute those allegations in an address to the U.S. Senate; he demanded proof of a claim by Boyd that Clay had written a highly incriminating letter to Francis P. Blair on January 8, 1825. On April 30, 1844, Boyd replied on the Senate floor to White's speech of April 23; he invited White to make a public call on Clay to answer whether or not he had written Blair on January 8, 1825. White declined to make any such inquiry.

4. Democrats of Warren County, Tenn., met publicly on September 2, 1839, appointed Laughlin chairman of the meeting, and adopted resolutions nominating Martin Van Buren for reelection and Polk for the vice-presidency. See Laughlin to Polk, September 6, 1839.

5. Henry Clay, John Bell, Francis Granger, and John C. Clark. A New York lawyer and Whig, Granger served two terms in the U.S. House, 1835–37 and 1839–41, before resigning to accept an appointment as postmaster general in William H. Harrison's cabinet. He served in that post from March until September 1841, when he returned to the House to fill a seat vacated by John Greig. Also a New York lawyer, Clark served two terms as a Democrat in the U.S. House, 1827–29 and 1837–39. Opposed to Van Buren's sub-Treasury system, Clark became a Whig and served two additional terms in the House, 1839–43.

6. On June 3 and 4, 1844, a partisan debate in the U.S. House arose after John Wentworth of Illinois resolved that "for the purpose of economizing the public time, and stopping of political discussions ... all members of the House, who have made speeches at this session, against Mr. Van Buren, have permission to erase the name of Mr. Van Buren therefrom, and substitute instead the name of James K. Polk; and that the officers of the House be requested to buy those anti-Van Buren speeches of the Clay club for wrapping paper, when they can be bought as cheap as other wrapping paper."

7. Robert C. Schenck, John J. Hardin, and Joseph H. Peyton. An Ohio lawyer, Schenck won election as a Whig to four terms in the U.S. House, 1843–51. He went to Brazil as U.S. minister, 1851–53; served in the Union army during the Civil War; and returned to the U.S. House as a Republican for three terms, 1863–71. A Sumner County physician and Whig, Peyton served one term in the Tennessee Senate, 1841–43, before winning election to a single term in the U.S. House in 1843.

8. Stephen A. Douglas, William W. Payne, James E. Belser, John A. McClernand, and Thomas J. Henley. An Illinois teacher and lawyer, Douglas served as a member of the Illinois House, 1836–37; as Illinois secretary of state, 1840–41; and as a judge of the state's highest court. He went to the U.S. House as a Democrat for two terms, 1843–47, before winning election in 1847 to the first of three terms in the U.S. Senate; northern Democrats nominated him for the presidency in 1860. Payne, an Alabama planter and state legislator, won election as a Democrat to three terms in the U.S. House, 1841–

47. Belser, a Montgomery lawyer, served a single term as a Democrat in the U.S. House, 1843–45; he subsequently joined the Whig ranks and supported Zachary Taylor in 1848. An Illinois lawyer, McClernand served several terms in the state legislature, 1836–43, before winning election as a Democrat to four terms in the U.S. House, 1843–51; he was returned to the House again in 1859 and served until October 1861, when he resigned to accept a commission in the Union army. Henley, an Indiana lawyer and banker, served in the state legislature, 1832–42, before winning election as a Democrat to three terms in the U.S. House, 1843–49. He moved to California in 1849, where he served in that state's first legislature, 1851–53.

9. On June 6, 1844, Andrew Johnson and Joseph H. Peyton exchanged sharp words in a U.S. House debate on direct taxation.

10. For John J. Hardin's letter, see Henry A. P. Muhlenberg to Polk, June 3, 1844.

11. See Laughlin to Polk, May 31, 1844.

12. On April 23, 1844, George Rathbun and John White of Kentucky had a personal altercation on the floor of the House. At the time of the confrontation, White was concluding his speech in answer to Linn Boyd's letter, but wanted more time than allowed by the hour rule of the House.

13. Brown's note has not been found.

14. Martin Van Buren, Benjamin F. Butler, Gansevoort Melville, and Churchill C. Cambreleng. A New York Democrat, Melville was appointed secretary of legation to Great Britain in December 1845. Reference is to speeches made by Butler, Melville, and Cambreleng at the New York Democratic meeting of June 4, 1844, and Van Buren's letter, which was read by Melville to the gathered thousands. See Aaron Vanderpoel to Polk, June 3, 1844.

15. Aaron V. Brown and Cave Johnson.

16. See Jacob Thompson to Polk, June 7, 1844.

17. A Georgia lawyer, Walter T. Colquitt won election as a Whig to the U.S. House, 1839–40; refusing to support Harrison for president in 1840, he resigned and subsequently stood for the seat as a Democrat; he won and then went to the U.S. Senate for one term, 1843–48.

18. Binding has obliterated two lines written in the right margin of the letter's fourth page.

19. Laughlin wrote his postscript in the left margin of the letter's first page.

## FROM LUCIUS LYON[1]

My Dear Sir,

House of Representatives
Washington, June 7 1844

Among the thousands of congratulatory letters which are pouring in upon you from all parts of the Union, permit me to send mine.

I rejoice to see the flattering prospect which you now have of reaching so soon the most exalted political station in the world; and I also rejoice to see the union, harmony, zeal and determination which every where prevail in our ranks, and to know that our party is better united now than it has been for many years.

I attended the Baltimore convention as a friend of General Cass, who but for unfair management on the part of friends of Mr. Van Buren would have been the nominee of the convention. I supported him because I knew him to be thoroughly democratic in all his views and feelings; and because I thought he would be more likely to unite the different sections of our party than any other man. When your name was mentioned as a candidate, and it became evident that the convention could unite on you, even better than on Genl. Cass, we gave him up most cheerfully and went for your nomination; and I can assure you that the General himself and all his friends will give you a warm and zealous support.

I believe you will get many more votes than Mr. Van Buren could, even in the northern States, and in the South we expect you will sweep all before you. But let other States go as they may, we shall endeavor to give you the vote of Michigan, and I beg you to present my compliments to Mrs. Polk, and to tell her that I expect to have the gratification and honor of paying my respects to her at the "White House," from and after the 4th of March next.

LUCIUS LYON

ALS. DLC–JKP. Addressed to Columbia. Polk's AE on the cover states that he answered this letter on June 26, 1844; Polk's reply has not been found.

1. A Michigan land surveyor, Lucius Lyon won election as a Democrat to a single term in the U.S. House, 1833–35; sat in the state constitutional convention of 1835; served in the U.S. Senate, 1837–39; again won election to the U.S. House, 1843–45; and held the post of surveyor general for Ohio, Indiana, and Michigan for five years, 1845–50. He was a delegate to the 1848 Democratic National Convention, which nominated Lewis Cass of Michigan.

## FROM JACOB THOMPSON

House of Reps
My Dear Sir                    [Washington City] June 7th 1844

While in the Baltimore convention I thought I would write you immediately a congratulatory letter on your very complimentary nomination for the first office in the gift of our people. This result was effected by great courage and decisive action of many of your warm friends. It is true when we set out we knew not what port we were to enter. But we felt the people called for a fresh standard bearer and to convince the convention of this truth required no little nerve and firmness. In the first place a portion of your delegation came nigh overturning and destroying every thing by their obstinate adherence to our old friend Mr Van Buren. But you had some gallant spirits such as Cullom, Jones, A. Johnson who worked and stood forth like patriots who saved the vote of the State & opened the way for a compromise candidate. Your nomination is the result of no trick, no manouver. It was done fairly and openly. The little efforts at management served but to embarrass the whole proceeding, and retard the happy and fortunate conclusion. In your nomination all ill-feeling was buried & forgotten. And the convention adjourned in the happiest state of feeling. All division is healed, all dissention quieted, and all you have to do is to remain at the post of private duty. Go on as though your name had never been mentioned beyond the precincts of your own quiet village. The utmost confidence is felt among your friends. Bets to a large amount are making on the final result. Congress adjourns on 17th inst and every member of our party flies to the field eager for the thickest and hottest part of the fight. I promise a glorious campaign for our little but gallant State,[1] and a still more glorious result. The news from New York, Pennsylvania & Ohio is most cheering. Col Benton still embarrasses us, but he does not take open ground against us. This annexation and his unfortunate position will keep him cool for some time. But the force of public opinion will drive him into proper position. Genl. McDuffie will enter the arena like a valiant knight. He has given us assurances to travel this summer & will visit Nashville.

You can well imagine there are several of our friends who belong to an age which precedes yours who feel as yet a little tender. We have in our ranks four to 8 aspirants to the Presidency whose souls are bent upon the over loved object. I know nothing on your part which will have so great a tendency to cause a harmonious co-operation, with them all, as an intimation in your acceptance of the nomination that your course will be to serve but a single term. The turn of events may be such as to force you to deviate from such a course, but you must remember what small considerations often influence the greatest minds. I hope therefore you will take occasion if consistent with a proper sense of duty to intimate or express an opinion favorable to the one term principle. Wright, Benton, Calhoun, Buchanan, Woodbury, Cass & perhaps two or three others, think they are yet to be President before their day is spent. But a moment's reflection will convince you of all this. And the strength of your position is in your being disconnected with them all, friendly to all but particularly partial to none. Allow nothing to escape you even to friends which destroys the enviable position till the battle is fought & won.

I consider the known kindness of my feelings towards you of long standing justifies me in the liberty I take in these suggestions.

If convenient, write me.

J. THOMPSON

ALS. DLC–JKP. Addressed to Columbia.
1. Mississippi.

## FROM WILLIAM H. BABBIT[1]

Nassau Hall
Sir                          Princeton N.J. June 8th [18]44

I have to announce in the name of the Cliosophic Society[2] of the College of New Jersey, that you have been unanimously elected an honorary member of the same.

As the internal regulations of this Society are sealed exclusively to the initiated, it is impossible in this communication to give particulars. It is sufficient to say, however, that it is one of the oldest institutions of the kind in the country having been established in the year 1765.

I have only to say that we will be happy to introduce you to more particular acquaintance with our customs and regulations whenever you can make it convenient to attend; provided, however, that you have not received and accepted a similar offer of membership from the "American Whig Society" connected with this college; in which case this election is to be considered *null* as it is impossible to become connected with both.

WM. H. BABBIT

ALS. DLC–JKP. Addressed to Tennessee. Polk's AE on the cover states that he answered this letter on July 31, 1844.

1. A member of the class of 1846 at the College of New Jersey, later designated Princeton University, Babbit also attended Princeton Theological Seminary, 1850–53, and served his alma mater both as registrar, 1850–51, and as tutor, 1851–53.

2. Spirited competition for academic and debating honors characterized Princeton's two literary organizations, the Cliosophic Society and the American Whig Society; both were founded prior to the American Revolution.

## FROM JOHN CATRON

My dear sir            [Nashville, Tenn.] Saturday, June 8 [1844][1]

Mr. Van B.[2] was out of luck—we again have it. Had the Dem. Con. met a month sooner, we wd. have been ruined in the west, & South for ten years. Clay is out fully—many of the under-men, are out, on annexation, and we have the strength added of a *rejection* of Mr. V.B. on the precise ground, drawing in all the Calhoun strength—a vast, & controlling power, in the South. Among the leaders, you have many Jealousies to quiet; they feared to see you on any ticket as vice, for fear you would set up for chief, after the first success. My position has let me into the deepest recesses, of these things. I traversed the city night after night last winter encountering and *pleding* myself to the contrary of this opinion: But sir, I made no converts, as I then believed. Buchanan was for Johnson, Benton for King, the Van B. men for either, sooner than yourself; your truest and best friends were the Calhoun men—there, I found no tinge of Jealousy. Towards you, Tyler feels very kind; he is by no means so weak as represented. His conduct is good-tempered, his bearing highly respectable, and decidedly amiable. The course brutality of the Globe, was loathed last winter, by a large majority of our party.[3] It drove out Buchanan; as he believed in no such folly, and that the party was too weak, to elect any one presdt. He said to me, "All the chaft, & rotten part are fanned out—none but the *pure wheat* is to be left, but the naked floor, is plainly to be seen." Hence he quit & hence King, (B's shadow) went to France.[4] Wright's sentiments I did not know: I could not, for to the others I urged the folly of running Mr V.B., & the absurdity of Old Tecumseh,[5] being even named, for any thing. On this Mr V.B. had once rebuffed me, you remember. I view Benton as ruined—Buchanan & Wright, badly crippled. The latter ought to have gone on your ticket promptly; Still as author of that Sickly & ridiculous Sub-treasury plan,[6] he might have done worse than a new man. So Dallas is—nothing to assail him on but his letter avowing a corporate act can be repealed,[7] and as to Congress, it may, the constitution only providing *no state* shall pass any law &c., which the old Fedrl S.C. held applied to state *charters*.[8] Stick to the Fdrl Govt., when applying Mr. Dallas's doctrines, and all will work very well.

Your strength lies mainly as I think in this: you are of the present generation. The old leaders are thrown off; to do this has been an ardent wish by nineteen in twenty of our party in the House R. for two sessions, but they could not do it, as they believed, not as I believed. They are now gone. This idea operated on Pickens, to a goodly extent I think.

Genl. Jackson thinks Clay will now order his majority in the Senate to ratify the Texas treaty, to rid him of the question: I think not. Clay is exceedingly proud of his opinions, & all his friends are committed; they too have been treated as boys, and will not be willingly absurd, unless he recants first. They will reject the Treaty.

I am affraid of McDuffy's re[s]olution.[9] We must avoid extremes in every thing, & throw the other side on the extremes, such as cutting off the veto—an open, & avowed policy of Clay, as is the one term. I debated it with him last winter at Frankfort. The people will hear of no alterations in the Constitution—not one in ten will be willing to [do] it if put to the test.

A good-deal is said about the Native American question. I think it a very delicate one, not to be touched if to be avoided by you. Keep your paper free from it, if you think with me. The Catholics are with us, & the other side will keep them so, no fear of that.

Throw this in the fire.

As to Texas. I last winter at the instance of Mr Vanzant[10] got Genl. Jackson's letter to Houston to authorize Vanzant to make the annexation treaty. He wrote the day he got mine. It was forwarded by my direction to an agent at N.O.,[11] & from there by express (I believe,) sent to Houston. He gave the instruction. You may know how I felt on Mr V.B.'s letter coming out. I worked on the matter for Mr. Vanzant the whole winter, & saw every dispach f[rom][12] Texas, the day, or the hour, it arrived. I [had] regretted what I had done, until your [nom]ination occurred. Now, I am glad of it. I was [de]cieved as to the strength of the measure befor[e] the Senate, & decieved Genl J. & he decieved Houston, who refused to give the instruction, unless it was ascertained first, that the treaty could be ratified, as it would throw off both England & France, & without foreign aid the country could not get on.

This is too full of egotism to be seen by anyone but yourself.

J. CATRON

ALS. DLC–JKP. Addressed to Columbia.

1. Location taken from postal cancellation; date identified through content analysis.

2. Martin Van Buren.

3. Reference is to editorial attacks upon John Tyler in the Washington *Globe*.

4. Reference is to James Buchanan and William R. King, who was confirmed as U.S. minister to France on April 9, 1844.

5. Richard M. Johnson.

6. Silas Wright's Independent Treasury plan, which excluded the banking industry from having custody and management of U.S. Treasury funds, became law on July 4, 1840, and remained in force for one year. Although Whigs and conservative Democrats succeeded in repealing Wright's measure, the Independent Treasury system continued to function informally for want

of a national bank through which to conduct the general government's fiscal affairs.

7. In a letter of July 7, 1836, to the Democratic corresponding committee of East Smithfield, Bradford County, Penn., George M. Dallas maintained that the Bank of the United States' charter, recently granted by the Pennsylvania legislature, could and should be revoked by action of a state constitutional convention. The Washington *Globe* of September 17, 1836, printed the text of Dallas' letter.

8. In 1819 the U.S. Supreme Court ruled in *Trustees of Dartmouth College* v. *Woodward* that a corporation charter was a contract and as such was protected by the U.S. Constitution, Article I, Section 10, from alteration by state action.

9. Reference is to George McDuffie's joint resolution calling for the annexation of Texas.

10. Born in Franklin County, Tenn., Isaac Van Zandt migrated first to Mississippi and then to Texas, where he practiced law. He represented Harrison County in the Texas House, 1840–42, and served as chargé d'affaires to the United States, 1842–44.

11. In his letter to Andrew Jackson of January 12, 1844, Catron pressed the former president to write Sam Houston and urge him to authorize negotiations for the annexation of Texas. Catron suggested that Jackson route his letter through the Texas consul at New Orleans, who was William Bryan, a merchant in that city. ALS. Tx. Jackson, who wrote Houston at least two other times during January, 1844, again raised the annexation question on January 23 in a letter printed, in part, in Henderson K. Yoakum, *History of Texas,* Vol. II, pp. 424–25.

12. Sealing wax has obliterated the text here and below.

## FROM WILLIAM M. GWIN[1]

My dear Sir                                        Vicksburg June 8th 1844

I need not express to you the astonishment that seized us all this morning on the receipt of the news of your nomination for the Presidency, for I presume it was as unexpected to you as any man in the United States. After we became perfectly satisfied that the news could be relied on, the Democracy of this city & county were called to gether to ratify the nomination. General Foote one of our Electors addressed them. He was followed by N. D. Coleman[2] our post master who served with you in Congress as a member from Kentucky. At the opening of the meeting a salute of twenty six guns[3] was ordered to be fired but as we proceeded we warmed in the cause and Enthusiasm seized the Crowd. I was called on to review your political history, which I did altho at such short notice I could not do you or your character justice. What I said was recd. with enthusiasm. Instead of the Twenty Six guns one hundred were ordered to be fired & were with great spirit. The crowd instead of breaking up called up one after another of its members until at least a dozen speeches were made. When we finished firing one hundred guns, one hundred more were ordered & fired with encreased enthusiasm & for six hours was the celebration of the nomination kept up. I have never in my life seen such enthusiasm. So dark had been our prospects that there seemed to be no end to our mutual congratulations. Men who have been enemies for months met shook hands & pledged themselves to fight shoulder to shoulder through this contest. I acknowledge that this has been one of the happiest days of my life. Yesterday all was gloom, to-day all brightness. I fear not now since I see how your nomination has been recd. here by the members of our party, who are more split up than in any place in the Union. Magic could not more completely have quieted all old feuds. This state will give you a majority of at least six thousand and I have not the first doubt of your triumphant election.

As an old friend who dares not come to you now in your present lofty position, I most sincerely congratulate you. For years I have looked to you as one under whose banner we must fight the battles of the Democracy, but not so soon did I expect to realize these expectations. I am enlisted for the War until November and if all fight as resolutely I have no fears. It may be important for you to have correspondents in various parts of the Union to insure concert of action. If so & I can be of service to you write me fully & freely at all times or point me out to your confidential friends, as one to whom they can write freely. If any movement is at all necessary in this part of the country let me know it, and it shall be promptly attended to. Here nothing is needed for our success so this state is certain but it may be necessary for us to make movements here to produce effects in other parts of the country.

WM. M. GWIN

[P.S.] Can we rely certainly on Tennessee? I shall so say every where. I have just been invited to Jackson[4] to address the meeting of ratification on the evening of the 11th & on the 12th the Democratic association. In both I will vouch for Tennessee.[5]

ALS. DLC–JKP. Addressed to Columbia.
1. A native Tennessean, physician, and staunch supporter of Andrew Jackson, Gwin served as U.S. marshal for Mississippi, 1833–41, and sat in the U.S. House for one term, 1841–43. In 1849 he moved from Mississippi to California and represented that state for portions of two terms in the U.S. Senate, 1850–55 and 1857–61.
2. A Kentucky lawyer and member of the State house of representatives in 1824 and 1825, Nicholas D. Coleman won election as a Jackson Democrat to the U.S. House, 1829–31. He moved to Vicksburg, Miss., where he resumed

the practice of law and served as postmaster from 1841 until 1844.

3. The twenty-six guns represented the twenty-six states in the Union.

4. Reference is to Jackson, Miss.

5. Gwin wrote his postscript on the inside fold of his cover sheet.

## TO CHARLES J. INGERSOLL

My Dear Sir:　　　　　　　　　　　Columbia Tenn. June 8th 1844

Your very acceptable letter of the 30th ultimo,[1] came to hand to day. I thank you for the valuable suggestions which it contains & will endeavour to profit from them. I may expect to be interrogated upon many subjects, and shall probably feel myself constrained to answer. I shall do so frankly and with proper independence, but at the same time, prudently as I trust, and in such manner as may not injuriously affect our cause. I will be careful however not to respond unnecessarily, to idle or insidious inquiries which may be made.

I need scarcely say to you that the nomination for the Presidency was not anticipated by me. It was brought about by mutual concession on the part of the friends of other gentlemen who had been generally looked to for that high station. If it shall have the effect to restore harmony to the action of the Democratic party (without which all was lost), I shall be most happy in being the humble instrument in the hands of my friends, in effecting so great an object.

I shall be pleased My Dear Sir, to hear from you frequently, during the pendency of the contest, and to receive from you any further suggestions which you may deem to be useful.[2]

JAMES K. POLK

ALS. PHi. Addressed to Washington City and marked *"Private."*

1. Letter not found.

2. During the campaign Polk received two letters from Ingersoll, both dated June 18, 1844; on those two occasions Ingersoll focused attention on the tariff issue. ALsS. DLC–JKP.

## TO CAVE JOHNSON

[Dear Sir:]　　　　　　　　　　　Columbia, Tenn. June 8, 1844

Your letter of the 29th ultimo, with many others of the same date, conveyed to me the first reliable intelligence of my nomination at Baltimore. Rumors to the same effect had reached [me][1] the day before, but they were not of a kind to make it certain. The effect here and as far as I have heard has been to inspire a new spirit in our party. Many instances are reported of Whigs who say they will now act with us. I am under many personal obligations to my friends—and to yourself especially—for the agency which I know you had in bringing about the result.

I have as yet received no official announcement of my nomination by the committee of the Convention, and cannot of course answer until I do. By a letter from Philadelphia, I learn that *Mr. Dallas* has been notified of his nomination for the Vice Presidency and has accepted. In the *Globe* of the 30th ult. I see it stated that *"Mr. Hubbard* of New Hampshire, chairman of the committee to inform Messrs. Polk and Wright of their nomination, stated that they had forwarded communications to both these gentlemen."[2] If any was forwarded to me, it has not come to hand.

I shall desire to see you as soon after your return as possible. In the new position which has been assigned me, there are several weighty matters about which I wish to consult you. Our people here have resolved to have a *great public dinner* at this place on the 29th Instant, to which you will of course be invited. If you get home in time, you must not fail to attend. In the mean-time you will great oblige me, by giving me any suggestions before you leave Washington, which you may think will be useful. I may expect to be interrogated upon all the great questions of the day, and at the same time I shall answer frankly and independently. I shall desire to do so prudently. I am already advised that I will probably be called on soon upon the subject of the tariff. I see in the *Intelligencer* of the 1st,[3] which came today, a correspondence on that subject and in reference to my opinions between *Mr. James Irvin* of the House, and *Mr. John J. Hardin* of Illinois. Whether the latter be a member or not I do not know. His article was manifestly written by *Milton Brown* and signed by *Hardin.* It is a repetition of my controversy with *Brown* at Jackson[4] in the Spring of 1843, about which no one else but *Mr. Brown* had any information. This *Mr. Hardin* had merely lent his name to *Brown* and been used by him. *Brown* and *the trick* should be exposed. It contains a garbled and any thing but a fair account of my views.

If you have time before you leave cause *Brown* to be exposed in the *Globe.* Write me on receipt of this.

[JAMES K. POLK]

PL. Published in *THM,* I, p. 244. Addressed to Washington City and marked "Confidential."

1. Bracketed word supplied by *THM* editor.

2. The communication from Henry Hubbard and other members of the Democratic Committee was dated May 29, 1844.

3. The article appeared in the Washington *National Intelligencer* of May 31, 1844. See Henry A. P. Muhlenberg to Polk, June 3, 1844.

4. For Polk's debate with Milton Brown at Jackson, Tenn., in 1843, see Polk to Sarah C. Polk, April 4 and 7, 1843.

## TO JOHN K. KANE[1]

My Dear Sir:                              Columbia Tenn. June 8th 1844

Your kind letter of the 30th ult. came to hand to day.[2] If the nomination made at Baltimore shall have the effect of restoring harmony to our party, I shall be heartily rejoiced. I need scarcely say to you that the nomination for the Presidency was not anticipated by me. It was brought about by the mutual concession of the friends of other gentlemen, who had been generally looked to, for that high station. It has been well said that it was a station neither to be sought nor declined. I have certainly never sought it, but if voluntarily conferred I will not decline it. With yourself I have at all times been the ardent supporter of *Mr Van Buren,* and until the Texas question became one of paramount importance I did not doubt his nomination. I thank you for the suggestions which you make on the only question, on which as you state the Democracy are vulnerable in Pennsylvania, and will endeavour to profit from them. I may expect to be interrogated upon this and other subjects, and if I am, shall feel myself constrained to respond frankly and with independence, but at the same time prudently, and in a manner I trust which will not injuriously affect our cause.

I am happy to learn your opinion of the prospects of the Democracy in Pennsylvania. I shall be pleased to hear from you pending the contest, and to receive from you any further suggestions, which you may deem to be useful.

Make my kind regards to my friend *Mr Leiper,*[3] and be assured....

JAMES K. POLK

ALS. PPAmP. Addressed to Philadelphia and marked "Private."

1. A Philadelphia lawyer and an ardent Jackson Democrat, John K. Kane served from 1832 until 1836 as one of the spoliation claims commissioners appointed under the authority of the 1831 convention with France. He opposed rechartering the second Bank of the United States, an unpopular position to take in Philadelphia. Appointed attorney general of Pennsylvania in 1845, Kane resigned the following year to become U.S. district judge for the eastern district of Pennsylvania, a post that he held for twelve years.

2. In his letter of May 30, 1844, Kane predicted that Polk would unite Pennsylvania democrats and carry the state; he urged Polk to use "dignified reserve" in approaching the tariff question, the only issue on which Pennsylvania democrats were vulnerable. ALS. DLC–JKP.

3. William J. Leiper was the brother-in-law of John K. Kane.

## TO ROBERT J. WALKER

My Dear Sir:                                 Columbia Tenn. June 8th 1844

Your two letters of the 30th & 31st ultimo, have been received. I thank you for them, and especially for the valuable suggestions which they contain. In the new position which has been assigned me by my political friends I shall do nothing which I can avoid consistently with my principles, by which our cause may be injuriously affected. The views which you present are entitled to great consideration, and I do not at present see any thing incompatable in them, with those upon which I have heretofore acted. As you truly remark, my position is not now that of a Representative of a single state, but of the Democracy of the whole Union. Should it become necessary for me to speak upon the subject to which you refer,[1] or any other, I shall do so with frankness and independence, adhering strictly to all the great principles, upon which as a member of the Democratic party I have heretofore acted.

I am rejoiced that *Mr Dallas* received the nomination for the Vice-Presidency, and that he has accepted it. I have not received any official announcement of my nomination from the committee of the convention.[2] When I do I shall of course answer accepting it. It has been well observed that the high station for which I have been placed in nomination, was one which was neither to be sought nor declined. I have surely at no time sought it, but if it be conferred by the voluntary voice of my countrymen I will not decline it. I need scarcely say to you that the nomination was not anticipated or expected by me.

I shall be most happy to hear from you frequently pending the contest, and will thank you for any suggestions which you may think useful.

JAMES K. POLK

ALS. NHi. Addressed to Washington City and marked "*Private.*"
1. Reference is to the tariff question. See Walker to Polk, May 30, 1844.
2. See Henry Hubbard et al. to Polk, May 29, 1844.

## FROM ROBERT ARMSTRONG

Sunday night

Govnr,                            [Nashville, Tenn.] 9th June [1844][1]

I think you had better take a corner in the Stage on Tuesday or Wednesday. We have been arranging some new committees. One to correspond, to superintend all publications and prepare every thing for publication and one for *finance.* Both these I will have arranged by Monday night. The Old Central Committee to stand. This done we can go to work. All will be warm and devoted.

Let me tell you that Nicholson comes in, to all appearance in good faith and seems anxious to be placed in the *front.* Look at every thing and it is what he would do. He can be useful if he will and their is a *way* to make him.

I have never seen any nomination better recevd. No complaints, no faultering in the democratic papers. The Albany Argus, the City Pleabian,[2] and all the New York and Pennsyl. *Interior* presses are warm. The Evening Post I have not seen but understand he [....]³ Bennet[4] to night is shifting. Went off too quick.

Great meetings in Phil. Cincinnati Louisville &c. &c. We want a Convention here for Middle Tennessee. The 4th of July is appointed and is rather soon to suit other meetings. If we agree to about 10th July I think it will suit & be well attended. The Central Committee will issue a Card in the union[5] calling on all the Counties to send Delegates. This I will try and have in Tuesday Union.

I see a movement for a Grand *National* Convention of *all* the States to be held at Nashville. It does not come from the right quarter to be encouraged. Such a movement coming from the South would be recevd. perhaps in the *North* as a Southern move of "confederacy" &c &c.

I deem the Committees that I am arranging *Important.* The finance will be men that will take pleasure in doing the work. Humphreys, Nicholson, Ewing (who is warm), Jos. Horton, Mosely and Southall[6] &c will be the Committee to superintend *printing* and *selecting* and preparing for the *press,* distributing, &c &c. Conner, Stephenson, Sloan for money matters.[7] When all is arranged you will see it will work well.

The old Chief[8] is doing all he can by writing to his friends in every quarter. He is pleased and satisfied.

R. Armstrong

[P.S.] Take care of your *postage.* See the P.M. and understand from that postage on envelopes, News papers &c &c must be *deducted* (as one going to you to night rated $3.75). All annonimous letters returned *seald* by you as Refused &c &c.[9]

Catron has been over all this evening (Sunday) with me, and wants to be usefull. *We will make him so.* All the Indications are good. Meeting at Murfreesboro, Clarksville, Gallatin &c &c *15, 17, & 19th Inst.*

ALS. DLC–JKP. Probably addressed to Columbia.

1. Date identified through content analysis.

2. *Albany Argus* and New York *Daily Plebeian.*

3. Word illegible. Reference is to William Cullen Bryant. For the editorial position of the New York *Evening Post,* see Cave Johnson to Polk, June 1, 1844.

4. James Gordon Bennett, a southern sympathizer and member of New York's Tammany Hall, supported Martin Van Buren in 1836. Bennett enjoyed a successful career in journalism that included working for the *New York Enquirer,* 1827–28, and the *Morning Courier and New York Enquirer,* 1829–32; founding the *New York Globe* in 1832; editing the Philadelphia *Pennsylvanian,* 1832–33; and establishing the *New York Herald* in 1835. One of the first of the penny presses, the *Herald* opposed the renomination of Van Buren in 1840 and supported the election of Polk in 1844. Although considered non-partisan, the *Herald* generally sided with the Democratic party until the election of 1856.

5. *Nashville Union.*

6. West H. Humphreys, A. O. P. Nicholson, Andrew Ewing, Joseph W. Horton, Thomas D. Mosely, and Joseph B. Southall. Ewing, a Nashville Democrat, shared his legal practice with his Whig brother, Edwin. Andrew Ewing won election to a single term in the U.S. House, 1849–51. Sheriff of Davidson County from 1822 to 1829, Horton was cashier of the Bank of Tennessee's Nashville office.

7. Cornelius Connor, Vernon K. Stevenson, and Sloan. A native of Pennsylvania, Connor was a Nashville businessman and party operative. A Nashville merchant, Stevenson became president of the Nashville and Chattanooga Railway Company in 1848 and held that post until the close of the Civil War. Sloan is not further identified.

8. Andrew Jackson.

9. Syntax garbled. Armstrong's language seems to suggest that he wanted Polk to consult with the Columbia postmaster in anticipation of increased demands upon the candidate's postage account during the presidential campaign. Postage due on parcels and newspapers must be paid, but incoming letters from unidentified correspondents should be returned unopened to avoid unnecessary postal expense.

## FROM FRANCIS O. J. SMITH[1]

Dear Sir,                                    Washington, June 9th, [18]44

Since the result of the Baltimore Democratic Convention transpired, I have received from my old democratic friends in Maine, several earnest inquiries for such information as I may have, or such views as I entertain of the probable disposition of yourself and administration, should you be elected to the Presidency, towards those of the old Jackson & Republican party, who felt it to be not only their duty to withdraw from the support of Mr. Van Buren in 1840, but also to oppose his re-election by whatever honorable means & influence they could exert—openly, not stealthily, as democrats, not as Whigs, under their own Conservative banners, not as the subordinates of Whig organization.

As yet I have not felt assured in answering, except in general terms, founded upon my personal knowledge of your character, candor, and supposed sense of the forbearance due to honest differences of opinion among those who are by habit, association, principles, and circumstances in life, members of the same party, imbued, as by a second nature, with the same toned feelings.

But, this is not, and perhaps, ought not to be, satisfactory, when the matter of inquiry is one which may be so easily, and so very properly understood by all. And hence, although my engagements will be such, personally, as will forbid that I should contend for, or against any man, politically, in any contest which is likely soon to rise, with the same zeal and determination which I felt called upon to exert in opposing Mr Van Buren's continuance at the head of the democratic party, it will afford me great pleasure to assure those who stood with and by me in Maine, during the crisis of 1839 & '40, and helped to read to all classes of politicians an admonitory lesson against the proscriptive and intolerant spirit that cannot brook or suffer any difference of opinion from its own, without ascribing it to the worst of motives, and visiting upon it the most exterminating ostracism, although political brethren are to be the victims: to all such, I say, it would give me pleasure to feel authorised in saying, that, if elected to the Presidency, it will be your policy, and sense of right and justice, and unwavering determination, not to allow any of the dissensions, or prejudices, and denunciations, that seperated so decisively [a] large portion of the old Jackson republican party from Mr. Van Buren, to be *revived,* or remembered, to the injury of any man who shall feel himself justified *now,* in uniting with the republicans of the Union in the pending conflict for the restoration of their primitive party and principles to power, under your banner.

If I shall feel at liberty to say to the Conservatives of Maine, and of New England, as occasion shall offer, that I have your authority, or, if you so prefer, that I have, what to me are abundantly satisfactory and authentic reasons, for confiding in your determination *to sink in the future all remembrance of past dissensions in the republican brotherhood of the Union,* and to carry out the higher and juster policy I have indicated, and as you honorably may, I am sure, it will give me pleasure to do that much, for the advancement of your cause, and interests; and this, both from a desire to see a spirit of liberal republicanism, not ultraism, again pervade the land, and from the deep sense of respect I have, from my earliest personal acquaintance with you, cherished and expressed for what have ever seemed to me so much to resemble in your character, the qualities, habits, simplicities and unostentatious merits of a thorough New Englander, only engrafted upon a stock nurtured by the more virgin soil of *the Great West.*

I may remark, for your information, that while the anti-Van Buren democrats in Maine, say to the number of 2500 to 3500, and enough to turn the scale of elections in the State, *co-operated* with the Whigs in 1840, they have always refused to *amalgamate* with them, or enter into the organization at all of the Whig party. They have kept aloof, awaiting the return of more auspicious days and circumstances for the re-union and re-instatement of the old republican party, if *the republicanism* of Whig professions, when out of power, should not be blended with their proceedings and measures, when in power.

I will only add, that my residence is still in the vicinage of Portland, Me. to which place please address me. And in the mean time be assured of the sincere esteem with which I am ....

FRANCIS O. J. SMITH

ALS. DLC–JKP. Addressed to Columbia. Polk's AE on the cover states that he answered this letter on July 4, 1844.

1. A Portland lawyer, businessman, and politician, Smith served in the Maine House, 1831 and 1863–64; in the Maine Senate, 1833; and in the U.S. House, 1833–39. A partner of Samuel Morse, he assisted in the development of the telegraph; but the two men later became estranged. Smith ardently embraced the new Republican party of the 1850's, but his enthusiasm waned just prior to the election of 1860.

## FROM JOHN CATRON

Dr Sir                                    Nashville June 10 [1844][1]

I have no doubt the letters for your opinions on various matters by local bustling men will pour in upon you. Mr. Van Buren's letter formerly was to Sherrod Williams.[2] A leprous dog, unworthy in every sense, and an enemy at that. Then Pat Magenis wrote Gnl. Jackson a month ago from St. Louis, & shew the reply as a constant business.[3] A fellow so odious as to be likely to ruin Benton at home, and really mad with drunkeness, vanity, & impudence mixed. These are specimens only of thousands. Harrison was guarded against them most properly, because he wanted experience. You must be your own *committee,* & as such bear in mind, that a reply to such a would be great man, offends, or annoys, a dozen, or a hundred more worthy, and does harm one hundred times, where it does good once. Nay further: The old leaders will talk on stilts and the lower stratum of their underlings will forwith know of you, if you are with the old leader. As you have a soul to be saved keep clear of this perdicament. For two years have I stood by and heard it fulminated as a settled thing that all those Harrison turned out, must for the *honour* of the party be put back, Cabinet, & all! Not a place left open for the rank & file who put them back, who fought the battle with their money and talents. You who fought in the very van, and who the worthy old gentlemen thought last winter, had died in the *ditch,* have been brought out alive, not by their consent, nor help, but by those who look to chances for themselves. "Treason & traitor," "rotten to the core," have been the gentle epithets that have greeted every move tending to wrench the power as a party, from the old clique. Mr. Van Buren thought this public opinion; if Col. Benton let him think at all, which I doubt. To this state of things there were not ten friends in the House, the great presdt making power. Your nomination is a new element of party co-hesion, that will be likely to carry with it the democratic vote with something like unanimity; it has been too much broken into fragments for unanimity, entire; but if Mr. Tyler is *soothed,* & does not run, I think your election almost certain. You will rise every hour, & Clay sink, in all the slave holding states, & several of the others. The young are not with him even in Kentucky, but they cannot break his fetters there, I think.

As to the Sub Treasury plan, I said a word the other day.[4] I think it in fact, worthless as a weed, & ridiculed into utter contempt. Let it sleep in death. The money of the U.S. is now seperate from Banks; all is well enough for our purposes just now. It is not a thing for an issue in the pending contest. You have no use for any of the old guns of Mr V.B. They are all spiked; let Cambreling[5] keep them for history.

As to money at this point for the dissimination of printed matter, &c I think the[re][6] will be no difficulty whatever. I ordered [...]son & Armstrong yesterday to head the list for us with $500 & told Kiezer[7] this morning, that I wou[ld] double, any other man's subscription—to go for large sums. But be *prudent* yourself. We all expect and *desire,* you should. Your postages will be bad enough.

Burn this of course, for I would be ashamed for any one to see my views, & unguardedness, except James Walker,[8] & yourself, & except Mrs. Polk.

The Whig papers, especially Bell's Banner, are faining. This is a good sign. All enthusiasm is dead in regard to Clay; whether it can be revived as the [....]⁹

J. CATRON

ALS. DLC–JKP. Addressed to Columbia.
1. Date identified through content analysis.
2. A lawyer from Kentucky, Sherrod Williams served in the Kentucky House, 1829–34 and 1846, and sat in the U.S. House as a Whig, 1835–41. Martin Van Buren's letter to Williams, dated June 14, 1836, was in answer to Williams' letter of April 7, 1836. Williams had questioned Van Buren about the leading political issues of the day.
3. Arthur L. Magenis, a St. Louis lawyer, was an old friend of Thomas H. Benton. In his letter to Andrew Jackson of March 16, 1844, Magenis solicited the general's approval of recently adopted resolutions in St. Louis that praised Benton. Jackson replied to Magenis on March 28, 1844; his letter subsequently appeared in the Washington *Globe* on April 25, 1844. Jackson concurred with the tribute to Benton.
4. See John Catron to Polk, June 8, 1844.
5. Churchill C. Cambreleng.
6. Sealing wax has obliterated the manuscript here and below.
7. Timothy Kezer.
8. Walker, a prosperous Columbia businessman, married Polk's sister, Jane Maria Polk.
9. Word illegible.

## FROM CAVE JOHNSON

Dear Sir,                                    Washington Monday 10th June 1844
    The House has just adjourned on account of the death of Judge Read of Penn.¹ which gives me leisure to write you a line. I am entreated on all sides to beg you to be cautious in your answers to the thousand communications which you will receive. Fractions of our party in Penn. & N.Y. & Ohio will be strugling to extract something from you to aid their fractions at home. Southern democrats will be strugling to appear better friends than the Nothern democrats. I trust you will avoid answers wherever it can be done. Your public life for 20 years is guaranty enough. Great efforts will be made to convince you that you should look to the South for support rather than the North. You have nothing to fear *from the Nothern democracy.* Every indication shews a re-union of the old Jackson party on you & our triumph is certain unless we get a back set. I see but one difficulty now. The Treaty is rejected,² 15 demo. & one whig (Henderson)³ voting for it. Benton,

Allen, Tappan, Wright, Niles, voting agt. it.[4] Benton introduced a Bill
today for annexion upon *getting the assent of Mexico.*[5] The democrats
oppose except those alluded to. He made another speech today. I do
not see any good that can arise from it. I went to see Tappan & also
Wright, begged & entreated, that they might interpose & prevent a
wider breach than now existed. They did not like to approach him
on the subject, but think no evil will arise from it. I cannot but fear
otherwise. If the Whigs kill it in the Senate, all will be well; but if
they pass it & send it to the House, it will produce great confusion. It
is expected that Tyler will send it to the House & recommend annexation by Law. I cannot see how we are to get thro. without detrement.
It is intimated also that the *hot Texas* men will urge a postponement
of the adjournment & that the Whigs may join them. If that is done &
Texas got before the House there is no knowing the confusion which
may be produced in our ranks. All are now united except Dick Davis.
Hannegan is a good deal hurt but will go right. Howard I fear is
acting badly. He has accepted a nomination as Charge to Texas.

I have just seen Hallet[6] who says Bancroft will undertake your life.
I write to Bancroft today. The materials should all be prepared under
your own inspection and ready to forward under our franks. So far
as relates to your Congressional History, reference to the Register or
Globe[7] which can be had in Boston will be enough. He can do it
better than any body else. I recd a life this morning by Hickman in
Baltimore which I shall look over to day & so will Brown, before they
are circulated.[8]

Genl. Cass made a glorious speech for you in Detroit upon the reception of the nomination. Signs are better every where than I ever
knew them. Democrats seem to have caught inspiration from the whig
campaign. We out write, out speak & out sign them. We await the
news from Ten. & K—y with great anxiety tho we feel sure, it must
take well.

We shall leave here an Executive Committee of citizens as well as
an Executive Committee of members of Congress who will be here &
at the principal cities as circumstances may require.

Stand to your old position between the Nothern & Southern democrats and all will go well. I have suggested an immense mass meeting or barbacue at Nashville. Suspicion is excited at the North from
the declarations of some indiscreet Southern men, that there is to be
a *Southern convention,*[9] a sort of rally upon Southern principles agt
Nothern principles. Should such a meeting be gotten up *let every thing
like a convention* be *avoided carefully.*

You position is most delicate & will require the utmost prudence and caution—if you could avoid reading, writing or speaking from now until the election, our success would be certain. We shall leave here Sunday morning the 16th.

C. JOHNSON

[P.S.] M. Brown's Coffee Speech was re-published in the Intelligencer of the 6th.[10] It will be answered in a few days.

ALS. DLC–JKP. Addressed to Columbia.

1. Born in Vermont and educated in Massachusetts, Almon H. Read moved to Pennsylvania and began the practice of law in 1816. He sat in the Pennsylvania House, 1827–32; the state Senate, 1833–37; and as a Democrat in the U.S. House, 1842–44.

2. By a vote of 35 to 16, the U.S. Senate on June 8, 1844, rejected the Tyler administration's treaty for the annexation of Texas.

3. John Henderson, a lawyer, served in the Mississippi House prior to his election to one term in the U.S. Senate, 1839–45.

4. Thomas H. Benton, William Allen, Benjamin Tappan, Silas Wright, Jr., and John M. Niles. Prior to his lengthy political career, Niles established and edited the *Hartford Times*. A Democrat, he represented Connecticut in the U.S. Senate, 1835–39 and 1843–49; he also served as postmaster general in Martin Van Buren's cabinet from 1840 until 1841.

5. Benton's bill authorized and advised the president to open negotiations with Mexico and Texas for fixing by treaty a new international boundary west of the Nueces River and for annexing Texas to the United States. Benton's plan also outlined terms under which a portion of Texas, not to exceed the size of the largest existing state, would be admitted to the Union and the remainder would be accorded territorial status, provided that the new territory's northern half would be forever free of slaveholding.

6. A lawyer, editor, and Democratic party manager, Benjamin F. Hallett merged his *Boston Daily Advocate* with the *Boston Post* in 1838; during Franklin Pierce's administration he served as U.S. district attorney for Boston.

7. Until superseded in 1837 by the *Congressional Globe*, the *Register of Debates in Congress*, published by Joseph Gales, Jr., and William W. Seaton, provided daily coverage of congressional proceedings.

8. On June 8, 1844, George H. Hickman sent Polk twelve copies of a brief sketch of the nominee's life. ALS. DLC–JKP. A political operative and journalist in Baltimore, Hickman published three editions of his pamphlet biography of Polk in 1844.

9. In late May 1844, anticipating the Senate's rejection of the treaty for the annexation of Texas, public meetings in South Carolina began to agitate for a southern convention of the supporters of annexation. An assembly at Ashley on May 22 called for a convention to convene in Nashville; a public meeting at Barnwell on June 3 advocated August 5 as the appropriate time to assemble in Nashville. Talk of disunion was rife in both meetings; one orator succinctly demanded, "Texas or Disunion."

10. Reference is to a speech made by Milton Brown in a debate with Polk at Jackson, Tenn., on April 4, 1843; on that occasion Brown argued that Polk favored placing a tariff duty on coffee and other commodities of general consumption. See Polk to Sarah C. Polk, April 4 and 7, 1843.

## FROM JOHN I. MUMFORD[1]

Dear Sir.　　　　　　　　　　　　　　　Washington 10th June 1844

Though among the least I do not mean to be among the last, because I claim to be among the sincere of those who congratulate you on your nomination to the Presidency. Happy to be personally acquainted both with Mrs Polk & yourself, I beg to assure you that the choice of the convention has given great satisfaction to the friends of sound public principles and of distinguished private worth. In New York, I feel confident in predicting for you a majority exceeding that by which our present Governor was elected, for it is not to be denied that many of the friends of Mr Van Buren who opposed Govr Bouck, will rally on the nominees of the Baltimore Convention. The great body of our Western anti Masons, and the Hunters' Lodges[2] of the North, will vie in their efforts for a Democratic victory. I need not say to you that I presumed the choice would have fallen on one of those who had been addressed by the Indiana Convention,[3] and that considering the election of Mr Van Buren as utterly impossible, I zealously advocated the pretensions of Genl Cass, long honoring me with his friendship, and who from circumstances not here to be detailed, had won my warmest regards. Mr. Dallas and I were Classmates at Princeton, so that I am pleased to know personally those in whose behalf we are to endeavor to achieve a Democratic triumph. I have not the *least doubt* of victory, except in *Ohio,* and that state, for reasons which it would pain me to give, because they would reflect on men I would spare, I have *no hope* of. I speak of course of the large states more particularly, when expressing my great confidence. New York will be carried by her masses. The city is in the hands of the Native Americans[4] —the Custom House in Mr Tyler's—the State offices are generally filled, so that the mere office seeker will be compelled to follow the lead of the masses. It would not have been so had Mr V.B. been nominated, but the old office holders would have claimed the right to rule, and we should have been defeated. I say nothing in disparagement of Mr Van Buren. I think he erred in suffering his name to be used, and I think his friends at Baltimore fairly butchered him. So far as we have information here, the nominations are hailed with extraordinary enthusiasm every where. I shall return shortly, and hope to continue the Standard though the tax thus far has fallen upon two or three individuals, and the expense of a Daily and Country paper may be considered by them too onerous. No exertion shall be spared on my part to continue it, as I feel a renewal of the ardor with which I combatted for Jackson against the Bank, commencing in Sept 1830.

JOHN I. MUMFORD

ALS. DLC–JKP. Addressed to Columbia and franked by Lucius Lyon.

1. A Democratic partisan, John I. Mumford edited the *New York Standard*.

2. Organized in May 1838 in Vermont, the Hunter's Lodge became the largest and most important of the secret societies that proliferated along the northern border of the United States. A paramilitary force, the Hunters engaged British and Canadian authorities in military skirmishes, hoping to liberate Canada from British rule.

3. Convened in Indianapolis on January 8, 1843, the Indiana Democratic State Convention called upon leading presidential aspirants to reply to interrogatories on current issues. John C. Calhoun, James Buchanan, Richard M. Johnson, Lewis Cass, and Martin Van Buren responded to the inquiries.

4. See William Tyack to Polk, April 13, 1844.

## FROM SAMUEL H. LAUGHLIN

My dear sir, Washington City, June 11, 1844[1]

Do not deem me impertinent for troubling you with a few lines more on a subject mentioned in my letter of yesterday. I mean the tariff. As I have access to and free conversations with many of our leading friends here, from extreme south to extreme north, who are interested in, and *tied up* in the question, and who all earnestly desire your success, and desire to see as little weight thrown on you as possible on either side. From those who *hold* our doctrines in the north without deceipt or flinching, I (they in substance, but not in words)[2] put their position nearly in the following manner:

That all duties—any[3] the smallest duty by way of import is incidentally protection, *per se*, to the amount of the duty. That the low duties of 1789 in this manner, as perhaps they were intended to do, afforded incidental protection. That such duties ought to be imposed for revenue, incidentally affording this kind of protection, as would raise the means to support the goverment economically admnstered and no more—and that these duties should be so imposed as to afford equal protection to all the industrial pursuits of life, especially agriculture, manufactures, mechanics and commerce, and so as to equatize the burden of supporting the goverment among all the sections of [the] whole union, and among all the pursuits of life.

The ideas are here hastily and awkwardly expressed, but an opinion to approximate satisfaction to all, and in which there would be no *equivoque*, should as I sincerely believe, from close observation, and after hearing wise men talk while I listened, should present the *three* leading ideas of the foregoing, and all in one plain distinct sentence, which would do for continual reference, that all duties are protection, that all pursuits, especially enumerating agriculture, should be equally protected, that burdens imposed to support govemnt should be exactly equallized upon all sections and pursuits.

If what I write shall contain one single suggestion useful to you, I need not tell you that I shall be gratified. No one knows what I write, though I have told A. V. Brown that I had apprized you that you would be interogated. You know me however too well not to know, that I would permit no human being to know that I took the liberty of suggesting things either as to the matter or form of any public opinion you might be called on to avow.

From Indiana now, as well as Michigan, the glorious news of the glorious ratifications come in almost hourly.

I have had some conversation with Cost Johnson,[4] who expresses much pleasure on making my acquaintance, and I am well satisfied he will raise the flag for you in Frederick and his old district in Maryland. He has assured Williamson Smith and members of Congress of the same thing, and as I understand is only awaiting his time.

Col. Forrester[5] is here, stands better with the Mississippians than I expected he did, and he has again assured Linn Boyd and myself that he will take the stump for you whenever he goes home.

Last night, a Tyler meeting was drum'd up, by a band of music parading the Avenue first, which drew a crowd of boys, and at least 200 office hunters now at the Hotels, and after all, it was a poor affair, and the only speaker was Delazon Smith, a loafing editor of the Miamian from Dayton, Ohio,[6] who has been drum'd out of the party there by Medary & the democracy.

Tyler has, I am confident, communicated to Bayly,[7] Wise's successor, and possibly others that he will now, as of course, fall into the support of your nomination, as Calhoun does openly, as Wilkins does of course, Dallas being his brother in law. Nelson, the Atto Genl is understood to be warm and openly for the nominations.

The Whigs here are in a perfect calm, and fear is on every face. John White with all his [...][8] is down in the mouth. Gerret Davis,[9] a poor little pup, who is jealous of White as being Clays first pimp by assumption, still pretends to treat the nominations lightly.

Bennets Herald[10] started with treating it lightly. Within a week he has seen his error and is retracing his steps. He was admonished through his reporters here, for members dont write to him, that he must change, or they would withdraw every support. It has cured him.

We have men here who wish, even at this critical crisis, to openly throw off the Globe. It is folly to think of it. I have reasoned Cullom out of it, as Brown and Cave have done, but Jones is hopeless.[11] Alex. Anderson has ceased enlightening me with his advice. Cave long since set Mr. Wright &c. on their guard as to some persons. These are minor things, but I cant forget them.

A. V. Brown replied, in a personal explanation, which he previously carefully wrote out, and read it in his place to avoid possible misrepresentation to Col. Benton's invidious remarks on submitting his Texas Bill on Saturday.[12] It was due to himself and Gen. Jackson, and I hope no evil will grow out of it. He feels deeply his responsibility as your personal representative on the floor. You will see it.

Dromgoole and myself are now in active communication with our colleagues of the Sub committee of convention in regard to our address.[13] I regret the delay in getting home it has occasioned, but as a Tennessee delegate, and with my local and personal knowledge of you, the committee have required me to remain and see it done. I must, and will, submit it before published to Johnson and Brown. In the meantime my letters, and thousands of ratification speeches and resolutions will keep the Union & S.S. Banner full. I have at much trouble and expense collected all this history of 1824 to 1832—mostly Duff Greene,[14] &c.

[S. H. Laughlin]

N.B. I have not read over what I have written, as Blackwell has this moment come in from Fauquier, Va. where he has been for some days. All Virginia is glorified. The boy is waiting to carry this to the P.O.[15]
S. H. Laughlin

ALS. DLC–JKP. Addressed to Columbia, franked by Alvin Cullom, and marked "Confidential."

1. Content analysis indicates that Laughlin began his letter on June 11 and finished it the following day; the letter was postmarked June 13.

2. Parentheses supplied.

3. Laughlin probably intended to write the word "even."

4. A lawyer from Jefferson in Frederick County, Md., William Cost Johnson served as a Whig in the U.S. House, 1833–35, and 1837–43.

5. John B. Forester, a McMinnville lawyer, sat in the U.S. House, 1833–37, as a representative from Tennessee. Later he moved to Mississippi.

6. Born in New York, Delazon Smith settled in Ohio where he pursued careers in both law and journalism. John Tyler appointed him special commissioner to Quito, Ecuador, a post that he held prior to serving as editor of the Dayton *Miamian and Manual of American Principles*. After removing to Oregon, Smith briefly served that state as U.S. senator in 1859.

7. A lawyer and judge from Accomac County, Va., Thomas H. Bayly served several terms in the Virginia House of Delegates, 1835–40. Elected to the U.S. House as a States Rights Democrat in 1844, Bayly served in that body until 1856.

8. Several words in the manuscript have been obliterated.

9. Garrett Davis.

10. Reference is to James Gordon Bennett's *New York Herald*.

11. Aaron V. Brown, Cave Johnson, and George W. Jones.

12. Introducing his bill for the annexation of Texas on June 10, 1844, Thomas H. Benton censured those whom he felt had promoted annexation for political purposes. He singled out Aaron V. Brown, who in fact had arranged publication of a pro-annexation letter by Andrew Jackson; for Jackson's letter to Brown of February 12, 1843, see the Washington *Globe* of March 20, 1844. On June 12, 1844, Brown rose in the House and denied Benton's allegations of political intrigue.

13. See Laughlin to Polk, May 31, 1844.

14. Duff Green.

15. Laughlin wrote his note in the left margin of his first sheet.

## FROM JOHN E. TALIAFERRO[1]

Dear Sir                                        Oxford Miss June 11th 1844

Being but a very obscure member of the republican party, and one of the most humble of your friends, I feel much diffidence in addressing you, although by way of congratulation, on the subject of your nomination for the presidency, knowing that you are to be troubled with a very heavy correspondence until november. But as it is a matter of such deep interest to your friends, and feeling assured that you as a patriot and republican feel a corresponding interest about the matter, I have concluded to forego that diffidence, for the pleasure of informing you that the thing takes admirably well here: that the intelligence of your nomination has been received with pleasure and enthusiasm by the friends of democracy throughout this country. I have no doubt it takes better with the Southern democracy than the nomination of any other man could have done. It has inspired the friends of our principles with a zeal and ardour which they wouldnot have felt for any Northern or Northwestern man. I was at Pontotoc when the news was received, where I had been many days attending the District Court. A feeling of despondency seemed to prevail with the friends of the party generally, but when the news of the result of the Baltimore convention was received, this despondency & carelessness gave way for a different sort of feeling which was manifested in the *delighted* countenance, the hearty laugh, and the conversation of groups assembled to plan the mode of conducting the contest. The night before, Judge Gholson[2] made a speech, and believing that Mr Van Buren would be the nominee, he almost declared himself out of the ranks—and that he would have nothing to do in the canvass—but when he heard of your nomination he evinced more zeal than I have ever seen him do, and declared that he would take the field, and *"do battle"* until the election. Barton, Chalmers, and Mathews[3] are already out, and will fight valiantly until november. I understand that Foote and Howard[4] are actively engaged in the South, and I am convinced that there will be no lack of exertion on the part of any democrat, in this state. Your nomination has healed all dissentions here, and there will be a steady and constant *fight,* and in harmony too, until the day of election.

We learn here that Wright declines the nomination for the Vice presidency. If so, what are we to do for a candidate?

I should be pleased to hear from you.

J. E. TALIAFERRO

ALS. DLC–JKP. Addressed to Columbia.

1. An unsuccessful Democratic candidate for the Tennessee legislature in 1839, Taliaferro removed to Oxford, Miss., in 1840; he served multiple terms in both houses of the legislature in the period from 1850 to 1865.

2. A Mississippi lawyer, Samuel J. Gholson served several terms in the Mississippi House, 1835–39, and won election twice to the U.S. House, 1836–38. In 1839 he resigned his seat in Congress to become U.S. district judge for Mississippi; and he served in that post until Mississippi seceded from the Union in 1861.

3. Roger Barton, Joseph W. Chalmers, and Joseph W. Matthews.

4. Henry S. Foote and Volney E. Howard. Born in Maine, Howard represented Scott County in the Mississippi House in 1836, served as reporter of the High Court of Errors and Appeals, and edited the Jackson *Mississippian.* He served in the U.S. House as a Democrat from Texas, 1849–53, and later moved to California.

## FROM HENRY WELSH[1]

Dear Sir,                                    York Penna June 11 1844

I perform an agreeable duty (enjoined on me by the meeting) in transmitting you the annexed proceedings[2]; a duty peculiarly pleasant, as the meeting was the largest and most enthusiastic held here since the good old days of Jackson, when this County gave that great and good old man, *the magic majority of 1776!* The same glorious spirit now runs through our entire State. In all my political experience, I never knew so sudden a change from gloom, doubt, and despondency, to zeal, enthusiasm, and confidence as was brought about by the Baltimore nominations. Before those nominations, with the belief that Mr Van Buren would be the candidate, our party looked upon the contest as doubtful, if not entirely hopeless, particularly, after that gentleman's Texas letter and its ruinous consequences in the South & West; and you know how difficult it is to rally a party in a supposed forlorn hope. In 1840, the hard times and pressure in money matters; the military feeling in favor of Gen Harrison; the vile and infamous slanders of the federalists; and the constant desire of our people for change, drew thousands from our ranks. In this Co, hundreds who left us then, were willing to come back under a new man, but would not, under Mr Van Buren; though many of them were convinced that gross injustice had been done him; still they feard that going for him now, would subject them to the charge of inconsistency and the taunts of those who seduced them from their party. *These men are with us now, and are among the most zealous and active in the cause and several of them were officers of the meeting.* The result will be, that this Co, instead of giving a majority of 590 as it did in 1840, *will give us from 1250 to 1800!* No one regrets more than I do, that we could not triumph with Mr Van Buren in the coming contest. I have the kindest feelings for him, and voted for him, in preference to Gen Cass & Col Johnston,[3] in the 4th March Harrisbg Convention,[4] in the expectation that we could succeed with him; but his Texas letter destroyed all hope, and feeling that we owed a higher duty to our party and its principles than to men, I gave him up, and done every thing in my power to induce our delegates to give us a new man, & thereby save the party from defeat, and the Country from such a scene of misrule, violence & proscription as Clay's election would give us.

You may rest assured that we will elect Muhlenberg *with great ease and carry the State, at the Presidential Election, by an immense majority. Of this, there is not a shadow of doubt.*

HENRY WELSH

ALS. DLC–JKP. Addressed to Columbia.
1. A Pennsylvania journalist, Welsh was a political friend of James Buchanan and Henry A. P. Muhlenberg.
2. Welsh enclosed proceedings of a ratification meeting, which was held at York, Penn., on June 8, 1844; York County Democrats hailed "with unbounded gratification the glorious result of the deliberations of the recent

Convention at Baltimore."

3. Lewis Cass and Richard M. Johnson.

4. Reference is to the Pennsylvania State Democratic Convention that met in Harrisburg on March 4, 1844.

## FROM AUSTIN E. WING[1]

Sir,                                                    Monroe June 11th 1844

Supposing you to have but few personal acquaintances in our state, and presuming it would be gratifying to you to know something of public sentiment here in relation to the nominations at the recent Baltimore Convention, I take pleasure in saying to you, that this state, with the exception of 1840, when in common with most other states of the Union were prostrated with the heresies & calamities of that period, has always been essentially democratic, and at no time more so than for the last two years. Last winter there were but four whigs in both branches of our Legislature. The democracy of our state, previous to the late Baltimore convention were divided in their preferences for the presidency, between Mr. Van Buren & Genl. Cass, the greater number I think in favor of the latter. The nomination of yourself & Mr. Dallas however has been cheerfully & generally responded to by the democracy, and we shall give you & Mr. Dallas, if I do not greatly mistake, at the approaching contest, an overwhelming majority. Since I had the pleasure of seeing you in Congress, my business & pursuits have precluded me from being prominent in the active politics of the state. I am now however so far relieved from previous engagements as to breathe freely and under the present political aspect of our affairs shall feel it my duty to buckle on my political armour. One more Coonskin, Log Cabbin, hard cider triumph upon the heels of the former one, would I fear put an end to the hopes of the friends of civil liberty throughout the world; and if there ever was a time since the declaration of American independence when every democrat should put on his whole armor & fight manfully the fight of faith; *this is the time.* The Whigs have been in advance of us in their enthusiasm on account of their earlier nominations. But we are now ready for the rally; and shall be able very soon to create, *not* that frothy excitement produced by song singing & clamorous addresses to the cupidity and the worst passions of men; but that rational enthusiasm which breathes patriotically through the breasts of American citizens in behalf of the *extension* & perpetuation of rational liberty and equal rights, throughout this hemisphere & the world. Allow me to congratulate you & the country upon the harmonious results of the

Baltimore Convention. And accept my assurances of a cordial desire for your triumphant success.

A. E. WING

ALS. DLC–JKP. Addressed to Columbia. Polk's AE on the cover states that he answered this letter on July 4, 1844; Polk's reply has not been found.

1. Wing won election to three terms in the U.S. House, 1825–29 and 1831–33. He was a member of the Michigan House in 1842; sat on the board of regents of the University of Michigan, 1845–49; and served as U.S. marshal for the Michigan district from 1846 until his death in 1849.

## FROM AUGUSTE D'AVEZAC

Sir                  New-York Rockport[1] Monroe County June 12 1844

Since I had the Honor of writing to you after your nommination,[2] I have addressed at Baltimore the great Body of the Democracy before the Monument. On the following day a large meeting at Philadelphia.[3] On the 6th of June in this State, at Geneseo, Livingston County, a mass meeting of five counties, called by James S. Wadsworth[4] of Geneseo; on the eight an immense assembly at Rochester, Monroe County; on the 10th the largest meeting ever held at Buffalo, (not less than 8,000), and today I have spoken at Rockport (in the very heart of the infected District) to 3000 Democrats; and, to day, I am to speak at Lockport to a very numerous assembly. The following Itinary will show you, how earnestly *we go* the question here. I have accepted invitations to speak

At Albion     13
Canandaigua     21
Palmyra     22
Glensfall[5]     28
At Detroit—early the next month [and]
in Cleveland (Ohio) soon after I shall have been at Detroit.

James S. Wadsworth (of Geneseo) a gentleman of great popularity, and uncounted wealth, is one of your most determined friends. He has organized series of meetings in the southern counties of this State, in which I have promised to accompany him. I state this to you in order that you may be aware of his standing, influence, and zeal in the cause, before you answer the letter he intends to write you. General Baker,[6] the State Attorney is a person of weight and talent. He is devoted to the cause. Allow me to suggest that there ought to be formed a central Committee at Nashville (like that which so ably defended General Jackson during his first canvass) to correspond with the several Central State Committees. As for me Sir, I will serve your's, or rather the people's cause now incarnated in you, with the ardor I have displayed in behalf of my glorious old Chief.

I have been invited, by Judge Roane of Virginia, to address the Richmond State Convention,[7] and several gentlemen have requested my attendance at Halifax (N.C.) If you do me the honor to answer to my letter, please to direct (Barry Town, Duchess County, New-York).

AUGUSTE D'AVEZAC

P.S.: There is in New York, a Mr. Carr,[8] formerly Consul at Morocco, much attached to your cause. He is a good Speaker and an able worker.

ALS. DLC–JKP. Addressed to Columbia. Polk's AE on the cover states that he answered this letter on June 24, 1844; Polk's reply has not been found.

1. It is probable that D'Avezac wrote from Brockport, a post-village of Monroe County's Sweden township, located on the Erie Canal, twenty miles west of Rochester. Content analysis suggests that D'Avezac spoke in Brockport on June 11 and was appointed to speak in Lockport on June 12.

2. Letter not found.

3. See Gideon J. Pillow to Polk, June 2, 1844.

4. Wadsworth attended Harvard College, read law in the office of Daniel Webster, and studied at Yale Law School before being admitted to the New York bar in 1833. A Van Buren Democrat opposed to slavery, Wadsworth was a leader of the radicals or "barnburners" of the New York Democracy. When Wadsworth called the meeting at Geneseo for June 6, he believed that Van Buren would be nominated; he wrote Van Buren on June 1, 1844, "What shall we do with our great meeting called for the 6th, which would have been the next thing to the *Cattle show,* if all had gone well? I think we shall adjourn it, until we know where we stand." ALS. DLC–MVB.

5. Glenn's Falls, N.Y., is in Warren County on the Hudson River.

6. Baker is not identified further.

7. Reference probably is to an invitation to speak at the Virginia State Democratic Convention, which met at Charlottesville September 10–12, 1844, and ratified the Polk-Dallas ticket; William H. Roane served as first vice-president of that meeting. Although D'Avezac did not speak at Charlottesville, he did address a large crowd at Wheeling, Va., on September 12, 1844. Auguste D'Avezac to Polk, September 12, 1844. ALS. DLC–JKP.

8. Thomas N. Carr of New York was appointed U.S. consul for Morocco on May 15, 1838; he filled that post until March 1842.

## FROM JOHN C. EDWARDS[1]

Sir,                                                    Jefferson June 12, 1844

I have just reached home after a tour of two months through the southeast, south & southwest of Missouri.[2] The first news of your nomination I met at this place, and I assure you sir, I received it with heartfelt gratification, and so will the democracy of the state generally. We are divided here among ourselves in reference to our state elections, but in regard to yourself and Mr. Dallas there will be no division among democrats. I have been going for the admission of Texas since the commencement of our canvass, the opinion of Col. Benton to the contrary notwithstanding. The democracy here is with you on that question: and I am afraid that Col. Benton will suffer some from his course.[3] We shall have an uphill business in our state elections. We have a full independent ticket running against us.[4] Some of your relations about Springfield: Col. John P. Campbell[5] for example, is taking an active part against the nominees of our convention,[6] and will exercise a considerable influence: but I do not think his course will change a single vote against you. In short, I believe the democratic convention men, as well as the independents, will unite upon yourself and Dallas. I received a letter from Col. Laughlin some time ago in reference to your nomination for the vice presidency, with Mr. Van Buren. For that, in the event of Mr. Van Buren's nomination, we could not have gone in the convention. We were divided between Johnson and Van Buren for the Presidency. Our difficulties grew out of this. We should have been compelled in the convention to have supported Col. Johnson for the vice presidency in the event of nominating Mr. Van Buren for the Presidency. Our ticket is far better as it has been presented to us, and in Missouri we shall give Polk Dallas and Texas a cordial support.

I am very sure Col. Benton will present no obstacle to our course. I hope sincerely he may not. I hope we may be able to save him too.

JOHN C. EDWARDS

P.S. At some time you may have leisure to write to me. I shall be glad to hear from you.

ALS. DLC–JKP. Addressed to Columbia. Polk's AE on the cover states that he answered this letter on July 31, 1844; Polk's reply has not been found.

1. Edwards, whose early career in Missouri included service as secretary of state, state legislator, and Supreme Court justice, won election as a Democrat to one term in the U.S. House, 1841–43; he declined standing for reelection in order to run for the governorship in 1844. Edwards served as Missouri's governor from 1844 to 1848.

2. In the margin of his first page Edwards wrote, "I am the nominee for governor."

3. See Cave Johnson to Polk, June 10, 1844; and Samuel H. Laughlin to Polk, June 11, 1844.

4. Party organization in Missouri grew significantly after the 1839 Whig and 1840 Democratic national conventions, but partisan organization faced

continuing opposition from Missouri's independent-minded voters. In 1844 Missouri politicians divided between the "Hards" and the "Softs" on banking and currency questions. Charles H. Allen, a northwest Missouri lawyer and life-long Democrat, headed an Independent or "soft-money" ticket and received general support from Missouri Whigs.

5. John Polk Campbell was the son of John Campbell and Matilda Golden Polk, the sister of James K. Polk's father, Samuel Polk.

6. The Missouri State Democratic Convention of April 1844 nominated Edwards, who was a close friend and "hard-money" supporter of Thomas H. Benton. The convention renominated Benton for the U.S. Senate and endorsed David R. Atchison to complete Lewis F. Linn's U.S. Senate term.

## TO HENRY HUBBARD ET AL.[1]

Gentlemen:                                     Columbia Tennessee June 12th 1844

I have had the honour to receive your letter of the 29th ultimo, informing me that the Democratic National Convention then assembled at Baltimore, had designated me to be the candidate of the Democratic party for President of the United States, and that I had been unanimously nominated for that office.

It has been well observed that the office of President of the United States should neither be sought nor declined. I have never sought it, nor shall I feel at liberty to decline it, if conferred upon me by the voluntary suffrages of my Fellow Citizens. In accepting the nomination I am deeply impressed with the distinguished honor which has been unexpectedly[2] conferred upon me by my Republican friends. I am duly sensible of the great and weighty responsibi[li]ties which must ever devolve on any citizen who may be called to fill the high station, of President of the United States. I deem the present to be a proper occasion to declare that if the nomination made by the convention shall be confirmed by the people and result in my election, I shall enter upon the discharge of the high and solemn duties of the office, with the settled purpose of not being a candidate for re-election.[3] In the event of my election, it shall be my constant aim, by a strict adherence to the Old Republican land-marks, to maintain and preserve the public prosperity, and at the end of four years I am resolved to retire to private life. In assuming this position I feel that I not only impose on myself a salutary restraint, but that I take the most effective means in my power of enabling the Democratic party to make a free selection of a successor who may be best calculated to give effect to their will, and guard all the interests of our beloved country.

JAMES K. POLK

ALS, draft. DLC–JKP. Addressed to Robert Rantoul, Jr., at Boston and marked *"Copy."*

1. Polk's inside address includes the names of Henry Hubbard, William H. Roane, Benjamin H. Brewster, Romulus M. Saunders, and Robert Rantoul, Jr.

2. One copy of Polk's letter of acceptance, that sent to him by Cave Johnson, omits the word "unexpectedly." DLC–JKP. L, copy.

3. In the Cave Johnson copy of this letter, this sentence begins a new paragraph.

## FROM ALEXANDER WALKER[1]

Dear Sir                                          New Orleans June 12 1844

I take the liberty, not having the honor personally to know you, to state that your nomination has been received with the greatest cordiality, and unanimity, by the Citizens of New Orleans, by Whigs interested in the Texas question, as well as by the solid column of the Democracy, and will be supported with a vigor no where to be exceeded. You may have no doubt of Louisiana; her six votes may be relied on with perfect assurance.

If we succeed in adopting our *New Constitution* (to be framed in August), by November, by which suffrage will be extended beyond the property and other restrictions at present imposed on it Louisiana will be good for *six* thousand Democratic majority.[2] But a word from the Old Hero[3] would help us: a strong demonstration from the Hermitage would ensure our success in our approaching elections, (first monday in July).[4] It is, I think highly important, that in the first demonstration after the Presidential nominations, and the only one before the final decision, our party should be triumphant.[5] A Democratic victory, under the banner of *Polk & Dallas,* in the strong Whig City of New Orleans, would be a happy and cheering augury and inspire much confidence and enthusiasm. On our ticket for the *Convention* we have the name of Genl Plauché, the veteran and companion in arms of Genl Jackson. A letter from Genl J. to Genl P. might incidentally express the old Hero's sentiments in reference to the nomination of the National Convention & would operate powerfully on a class of voters we have, very difficult to arouse.[6] We intend to exert every nerve to carry the Election, for the moral effect it will have upon the great National Contest, as well as to secure the predominance of Democratic concepts in our State Govt.

With the best wishes for the success of our Cause I am . . . .

                                                      ALEX: WALKER

ALS. DLC–JKP. Addressed to Columbia.

1. A journalist, author, and party operative, Alexander Walker assisted in the management of the New Orleans *Jeffersonian Republican,* the Louisiana Democracy's leading newspaper; in 1856 Walker published his *Jackson and New Orleans,* a work that he subsequently revised and reissued as *The Life of Andrew Jackson* (1860).

2. By act of March 18, 1844, the Louisiana legislature called for a state constitutional convention to meet on August 5, 1844; the convention completed its work in May of 1845, well after the 1844 presidential election. The new constitution, ratified by voters in November 1845, did liberalize suffrage requirements, as forecast by Walker.

3. Andrew Jackson.

4. See John Slidell to Polk, June 1, 1844.

5. In order to fill a vacancy in the Louisiana Senate, one additional election in that state was held prior to the presidential vote on November 5, 1844; the legislature's senatorial vacancy was filled in September 1844.

6. In a letter to Jean Baptiste Plauché on June 14, 1844, Andrew Jackson predicted that the southwestern border of the United States would be endangered if Great Britain gained dominion or influence over Texas. Accordingly Jackson favored the immediate annexation of Texas to the United States and gave an enthusiastic endorsement to the Democratic presidential ticket, noting that Polk and Dallas, advocates of immediate annexation, were "the strongest and best selection that could have been made." Louisiana Democrats gave wide circulation to Jackson's letter through its publication in their party newspaper.

## FROM HENDRICK B. WRIGHT

My dear sir                                   Wilkes Barre Penna. June 12 1844

It was my design to have written you a letter of congratulation before I left Baltimore. The confusion and haste that is always inseperable from the disolution of so large a body & of such excitable materials, as the convention, alone prevented me. And now sir, although a stranger to you, still I feel as an old acquantance. Your fame and reputation have gone before you & you are now in a position which if attended with success or defeat, gives you a prominence that will render you familiar with every American citizen. I shall be satisfied with a *majority* of the votes of the good people of the United States (varying the rule we laid down in the convention as to the man who should be put in nomination) in November.[1] With Mr Van Buren we could not have carried Penna. Now I am satisfied, perfectly satisfied that Penna. will give her accustomed democratic majority, which will not, I think be less than ten thousand, more probably twenty! And had I not been fully impressed with the fact that Mr Van Buren was not the available man,[2] I should have thought twice before casting my vote for the 2/3 rule. But sir, the matter is over and the past should be forgotten.

There is but one difficulty in the way in Penna. and that has its origin in the tariff. The state has become in a great degree a protective principle state. Strange as it may seem it is nonetheless true. If you could make your views known, and they should recognize the rule of a tariff for revenue, under an economical administration of the Govermt. with incidental protection to the great staples of the country, then there would be no difficulty in Penna. Every obstacle would be removed. I throw out this intimation for your reflection and consideration. With the southern Gentlemen I met at Baltimore; an appeal on the above principles would be no objection. It would strengthen your course in the middle states.

Should you think proper to make your views public, you can of course select the channel of communication as may seem most advisable. I hd. thought of addressing you a letter, to be answered or not as you might choose, but concluded at this time to adopt the course in this letter. It is a matter in which I feel no interest, and am solely guided and influenced by the motive which will serve you most effectively, or serve the country in the restoration of the democratic standard, and the restablishment of our principles. The prospect of this, is now cheering and God grant that it may be speedily effected.

HENDRICK B. WRIGHT

ALS. DLC–JKP. Addressed to Tennessee. Polk's AE on the cover states that he answered this letter on July 6, 1844; Polk's reply has not been found.
1. Reference is to the nominating convention's two-thirds rule.
2. Archaic usage of the word "available," meaning "electable."

## TO SILAS WRIGHT, JR.

My Dear Sir:                    Columbia Tenn. June 12th 1844

It afforded me sincere pleasure I assure you to receive on yesterday your frank and friendly letter of the 2nd Instant. The reasons which you assign for declining the nomination for the Vice Presidency are entitled to great weight, and are such as I was prepared to anticipate. Had it been compatable with your views of propriety to accept either *that* or the nomination for the Presidency, both of which I have no doubt, were within your power, it would have been heartily responded to by the Democracy here. I need scarcely assure you, that my nomination for the Presidency was not only not anticipated, but was wholly unexpected by me. Until the Texas excitement arose I regarded it as certain that Mr Van Buren by the general view of the party, would be the nominee. After that excitement arose, though I saw that a powerful party was arrayed against him, I still believed he would be nominated. Certainly nothing was further from my thoughts, than that any state of circumstances could arise, by which the nomination would fall on me. You are perfectly correct therefore in the opinion which you express, that I "had no part in feeling or action," in any of the movements which led to his rejection by the convention. I was never consulted by any human being in regard to the 2/3 rule or any other movement which led to it. I need make no professions to you of my personal friendship for Mr Van Buren or of my admiration of him as a public man. This I have shown by my acts. From the hour that he was rejected by the Senate as minister to England, up to the present moment I have been his constant and ardent supporter and defender. For more than two years I have been engaged in a constant struggle, with his political opponents in this state, and that too at times when I was in imminent danger of being prostrated by the local popular excitement against him or rather in favour of another. One of these occasions you will remember was in the White excitement of 1836, by which every District in the state, two or three excepted (Cave Johnson's and mine among the number), were swept down. In the three state canvasses of 1839, 1841, & 1843, in the two last of which I was myself defeated, I was his unflinching friend and constant defender. When in 1840, my name had been used in some of the states in connection with the Vice Presidency, I voluntarily withdrew, rather than embarrass the party, & took the field in his defence & support, and because I did so (being at that time Governor) I encountered a volume of abuse from the Federal press which has seldom, if ever fallen to the lot of any man in this country. It was perhaps unnecessary for me to have referred to these facts, with which all here are familiar.[1]

My opinions on the Texas question of which you make mention have been long formed: and when on my return home from the state of Mississippi in April, after an absence of near a month, I received a communication from Cincinnati calling for them, they were honestly and promptly reviewed in the short letter which you have seen.[2] At that time Mr Van Buren's letter had not appeared. I had no knowledge of his opinions but believed they would accord with my own.[3] You say in your letter that you may write me again before you leave Washington. I hope you will do so. I shall be pleased to hear from you as often as your leizure may permit during the summer, and to receive from you any suggestions which you may think useful. Your letter as you desire it to be, shall be regarded as strictly confidential as I intend this to be.

JAMES K. POLK

ALS, draft. DLC–JKP. Addressed to Washington City and marked *"Copy"* and *"Confidential."*

1. Here Polk canceled the following sentence: "I will add that for months passed when my name has been mentioned in connection with the Vice Presidency, no other view was entertained by my friends here than that if I received the nomination, I would be placed on the ticket with Mr. Van Buren."

2. See Salmon P. Chase et al. to Polk, March 30, 1844; and Polk's reply, April 23, 1844.

3. Polk inserted this sentence as an interlineation.


## FROM JOHN T. ANDREWS[1]

Sir                    North Reading Steuben Co N.Y. June 13, 1844

Not doubting that you will be pleased at all times to hear from any of your democratic friends of this state who had the honor to hold s[eats][2] in the House of Representatives when you presided as Speaker, I take the liberty to write to you.

Permit me sir, to congratulate you on your unanimous nomination as a candidate for President and to assure you that no efforts on the p[ar]t of the Democracy of this state will be wanting to secure your election. It is true we felt anxious for the nomination of Mr Van Buren, he was a citizen of our own state, we knew that he was Democratic to the core, that his character was pure and unspotted, we admired his talents and unbending integrity and felt an ho[nes]t desire to see him again elevated to the Presidency, but our struggle is for principles. All that we would have done for him we will cheerfully do for you. Your nomination is well received, our Democratic clubs have all ratified it, and you will be supported with enthusiasm. Though the greatest and most unscrupulous exertions will be made in this state by our opponents to defeat us, we feel quite confident of success. Indeed were it not for the dearly purchased experience of 1840 we should not have a doubt as to the result.

As far as my own acquaintance extends I know of no one who would have voted for Mr Van Buren who will not vote for you. The Whigs are endeavouring to make some capital out of the Texas question, but it will avail them nothing. On that question very few except abolitionists appear to feel any interest and of those who do I am of opinion a large majority are in favor of annexation.

Should any publication be issued in your state, the circulation of which in this state would in your opinion tend to aid your election, you will confer a favor by forwarding a copy to me to republish here.

JOHN T. ANDREWS

ALS. DLC–JKP. Addressed to Columbia. Polk's AE on the cover states that he answered this letter on July 4, 1844; Polk's reply has not been found.

1. A school teacher and merchant, Andrews served as justice of the peace and sheriff of Steuben County, 1836–37, prior to his election as a Democrat to a single term in the U.S. House, 1837–39.

2. Manuscript faded here and below.

## FROM CLEMENT C. CLAY[1]

Dear sir,                                           Huntsville, June 13th 1844

In the discharge of a most agreeable duty, I have the honor to transmit, herewith, the proceedings[2] of a meeting of the "Democratic Association of Madison County," held in this place on the 10th inst., responsive to the nomination of candidates for the offices of President and Vice President of the United States, by the late Democratic National Convention.

The notice for the meeting was short, yet there was a large and respectable assemblage of our citizens from all parts of the county. It was never my good fortune to witness more unanimity and enthusiasm in the Democratic ranks, than were evinced on that occasion; and the sentiments and feelings of our meeting, I entertain no doubt, will meet the cordial and unanimous concurrence of the Democracy of Alabama. Indeed, I am gratified to perceive, through every medium of intelligence, from all quarters of the Union, the harmony with which the nominations have been received, and the cordiality with which they have been greeted by our friends. The spirit, with which the Democracy have enlisted for the present great national campaign, will bear down all opposition and ensure a decisive triumph of our principles, as impersonated in our nominees, over the factious mass of moral and political discordancies, arrayed under the Whig banner. That it may prove the final quietus of Federalism, in all its multiform phases and complexities, is my devout and ardent desire.

C. C. CLAY

ALS. DLC–JKP. Addressed to Columbia.

1. A lawyer and Alabama state legislator, Clement Comer Clay won three terms as a Democrat in the U.S. House, 1829–35; he also served as governor of Alabama, 1835–37, and as U.S. senator, 1837–41.

2. Enclosure not found.

## FROM CAVE JOHNSON

My dear Sir,                                    Washington 13 June 1844

I intimated in my last, that we had much difficulty still and as it seems to me matters are growing still worse & must soon come to a head. The struggle now is by a few Southern men to appropriate *you* & the nomination to their exclusive benefit whilst the nothern Democrats are determined to yield to no such thing. I had been induced to call a caucus to raise funds & to get an Executive Committee to frank &c. Last night was the time appointed. So soon as it was known, nothern Democrats became alarmed lest Mr R. of S.[C.] & Genl R.M.S. & Gov W. of N.H.[1] should have the control of it & the funds & power would be so wielded as to promote the *Spectator* & *immediate annexation* & of course the future aspirations of Mr C.[2] I was soon advised of the feelings of the north and had to set myself to work to avoid evils in the caucus. I could only do this by preventing any thing from being done, & I went to work & finally suceeded in getting nothing done & an adjournment last night without an explosion. This morning Benton made another speech on his Bill[3] denounced the *Admn.* &c the treaty & the nego[tia]tion &c as I learn. It will be in the Globe tomorrow. The Spectator will of course comment, as it does every day & abuse Benton and the war will go on between C—n & B—on,[4] to extermination. I have been to see S.W. Jr.[5] hoping to have it controlled in some way & ended. He is furious and I think determined to push C. & his clique to the wall or perish. In this battle, the object *of both* will be to make us take sides. The Nothern men know, that you have always been with them, whilst the South think that the question & the position of Genl. J.[6] will take you with them. How both are to be kept I cannot see. Already we have much secret talk of upsetting the Globe, turning Benton over board &c. I was disgusted today. Even Reuben Whitney[7] talked to me of turning Benton out of the Democratic Church. I am sick of this state of things & see no means of evading *the explosion,* & most anxious to leave here. We missed it in not adjourning the 27th. I shall leave here on Sunday morning 16th.

I shall write you tomorrow.

C. JOHNSON

ALS. DLC–JKP. Addressed to Columbia and marked *"private."*
1. Robert B. Rhett, Romulus M. Saunders, and Levi Woodbury.
2. John C. Calhoun.
3. On June 13, 1844, Benton spoke for about two hours on the question of annexing Texas. He focused particularly on John Tyler's message on that subject to the U.S. House of June 11, 1844, and excoriated the administration for carrying the Texas treaty to the lower house. Benton's address of June 13, 1844, was not carried in the Washington *Globe* until June 20 and 24, at which time Francis P. Blair published the speech in full, but misdated it as June 12, 1844. The earliest report of Benton's address was published in the Washington *National Intelligencer* on June 14, 1844. For Benton's bill on the annexation of Texas, see Cave Johnson to Polk, June 10, 1844; and Samuel H. Laughlin to Polk, June 11, 1844.
4. John C. Calhoun and Thomas H. Benton.
5. Silas Wright, Jr.
6. Andrew Jackson.
7. A Philadelphia businessman and former director of the Bank of the United States, Reuben M. Whitney was a trusted adviser to Andrew Jackson and to the Treasury Department. During 1833 he assisted Polk in an investigation of the Bank. Whitney was nominated as recorder of the General Land Office in December 1844 by John Tyler, but was not confirmed in that post.

## FROM ROBERT W. POWELL

Dear Sir                    Washington D.C. June 13th 1844[1]
I troubled you with a letter from N York,[2] in which I made a *suggestion* in relation to your Correspondence, and although it may have been presumption in me to do so, I do not upon reflection regard it the less worthy of consideration, and I again write you to be on your guard. "Be ware of your *friends,*"[3] I mean those who take to themselves, all the credit of having defeated Martin Van Burens nomination, and consequently promoting your's. I need not say to one of your discernment and experience that those who were most clamorous against Mr Van Buren, *were not* acting in reference to *your interests,* but it is from this class of your friends that you may expect to be most troubled with letters Interrogatories &c. &c. As your principles and views upon all the prominent questions of the day are too well understood by all who are heartily devoted to your interest as well as that of the great Democratic Party to make any further avowals or developments necessary, but as you must necessarily treat all your correspondents respectfully

I would *suggest* with due deference, that you write one general letter, setting forth in general terms your principles, and refer all your correspondents to that, always guarding against details. The Tariff is certainly a very delicate question [in] Pensylvania New Jersy and a portion of N York, but the platform upon which Mr Van Buren stood upon this question is the safe ground to occupy in relation to the tariff. Something stable and permanent is much desired by the North and especially the manufacturing interests.

Bentons Annexation Bill was laid on the table yesterday 25 to 20.[4] Duncans bill to bring on the Presidential election on the same day in every State was laid on the table today 26 to 25.[5] Both are therefore disposed of for this Session. I have spent several days in New Jersy Delaware and Maryland since I wrote you and I tell you without exaggeration that the confidence and enthusiasm that pervades the Democratic ranks at present reminds one of the old Jackson days. I have made arrangements with gentlemen of intelligence and standing to keep up an extensive correspondence during the contest. Encouraging letters are often powerful stimulants. They are also desirous to be able to procure such information as may be requisite at any time to head off Ogleisms.[6]

I was desirous to see for myself before returning home "what the signs of promise were"[7] and I go home satisfied that all will be well if we do our duty.

Benton certainly wants the virtue of patience, he doubtless regards his plans as disconcerted, and is behaving rather badly. His speech of today[8] is of a most mischievous character. The Whigs are sending out his speeches by the thousand to break the force of the Texas question, but fortunately the convention put forth a manifesto by which we must be judged. I fear Mr Bentons ambition is not bridled by patriotism. I would certainly be very unwilling to surrender him. He has fought well and fought long and I must there[fore] wait for further developments. But the Democracy can not be held responsible if he should perpetrate suicide, and however willing I might be to pardon errors of judgment, I can not look with the least allowance upon efforts to distract and there by endanger the success of the Democratic party.

R. W. POWELL

ALS. DLC–JKP. Addressed to Columbia, franked by Julius W. Blackwell, and marked "Private."

1. Content analysis suggests that Powell concluded his letter on June 14.

2. In his letter of June 5, 1844, Powell warned against making hasty pronouncements and urged the practice of waiting a week before mailing replies

to correspondents. ALS. DLC-JKP.

3. Possibly a paraphrase of the Portuguese proverb "Beware of the friend who was once your foe."

4. Thomas H. Benton's Senate bill for the annexation of Texas required the unlikely prior approval of Mexico.

5. Reference is to U.S. Senate action on a bill offered by Alexander Duncan of Ohio. Duncan's bill, a version of which had won approval in the U.S. House on May 15, 1844, provided that all subsequent polls for presidential electors be held on the Tuesday following the first Monday in November.

6. Allusion is to Charles Ogle's charges in 1840 that Martin Van Buren had spent extravagant sums of public monies on White House furnishings and that such aristocratic tastes belied Van Buren's professions of republican principles. A Pennsylvania Whig, Ogle won election to three terms in the U.S. House, where he served from 1837 until his death in 1841.

7. Paraphrase of a couplet in John Bowring's hymn text, "Watchman, Tell Us of the Night" (1825): "Watchman, tell us of the night, /What its signs of promise are."

8. Reference probably is to Benton's U.S. Senate speech of June 13; see Cave Johnson to Polk, June 13, 1844.

## FROM ANDREW J. DONELSON

My Dr Sir,                              [Nashville, Tenn.] 14th June 1844

I am here to day to transact some business with the central committee: and have not got through with the letters for the Genl.[1]

You cannot go amiss on the Tariff subject, if you will take care to keep within the revenue limit, making revenue the object, protection the incident and so discrimenated as to favor our own manufacturers when in fair competition with foreign manufactures.

I return home to night, and will write you the day after tomorrow, after the Genl. is done with his letters to Mr. Van Buren & others.

We are sending out the circulars for the mass meeting on the 24th July & our conclusion is to print them, and let them be signed by the central committee.[2]

I have written to Mr Wright of New York and informed him he need have no apprehension of the southern convention scheme, nor any other scheme that can detach you from the nothern Democracy.

Rely upon my doing all that is possible for one to do in giving the right complextion to the movements in your favor to the north.

A. J. DONELSON

ALS. DLC-JKP. Addressed to Columbia.
1. Andrew Jackson.

2. On June 11, 1844, the *Nashville Union* published a circular from the Nashville Democratic Central Committee announcing plans for a Democratic mass meeting on July 24, 1844; the committee called upon delegates from all the counties of Middle Tennessee to "give to our brethren in other States an evidence of our determination to merit the high honor conferred on our State, which will satisfy all that Tennessee is safe for Polk and Dallas." Two weeks later, on June 29, the *Union* published a notice from the committee postponing the meeting until August 15 so that appropriate preparations could be made; the committee believed that the Nashville rally would be "more numerously attended than any popular gathering of the kind ever assembled in this country." The committee expected delegations from all parts of the Union.

## FROM NATHANIEL W. FLETCHER[1]

Mobile, Ala. June 14, 1844

Fletcher congratulates Polk on his nomination and encloses a copy of the Mobile *Advertiser* of June 13, 1844,[2] which charged that Polk's grandfather was a Tory during the Revolutionary War,[3] a charge promptly denied by the Mobile *Register and Journal.*[4] Fletcher also encloses a copy of the *Register.*[5] Although he dismisses charges of Toryism against Polk's ancestor, he wishes to learn the truth "from a source that can be *relied upon.*"

ALS. DLC–JKP. Addressed to Nashville and forwarded to Columbia.

1. A native of North Carolina and a practicing physician, Fletcher took an active part in the Masonic Order of Alabama; he served as grand master of the state council in 1841.

2. Enclosure not found. A Whig newspaper, the Mobile *Advertiser* was edited by Charles C. Langdon.

3. Ezekiel Polk. See Edwin F. Polk to Polk, August 27, 1840.

4. The *Register and Journal,* a Democratic newspaper published in Mobile, was edited by Thaddeus Sanford and S. F. Wilson.

5. Enclosure not found.

## FROM SACKFIELD MACLIN

Little Rock, Ark. June 14, 1844

Maclin congratulates Polk on his nomination and indicates that the Democracy of Arkansas has responded enthusiastically to it. The Johnson family connection[1] has accepted the ticket "with hart and hand." If Van Buren had headed the ticket, the result in Arkansas would have been doubtful; Yell and the local Democratic newspaper[2] opposed Van Buren's nomination. Polk's margin of victory will equal and possibly exceed 4,000 votes. Benton is "an *egotistic, selfish, and tyranical man,*" and for a year and a half he and the Washington *Globe* have hurt the Democratic party. Benton would oppose Polk if he did not fear the loss of standing in the party.

ALS. DLC–JKP. Addressed to Columbia.
1. Reference is to Richard M. Johnson's relatives in Arkansas, including Robert W. Johnson of Little Rock.
2. Little Rock *Arkansas Democratic Banner.*

## FROM BROMFIELD RIDLEY[1]

Dr. Sir                                                        Ruthfd. 15th June [18]44
I must be allowed to express to you my congratulations at the result of the deliberations of the late Democratic Convention at Baltimore.

Although we are taken by surprise at your nomination for the Presidency seeing that there were *older* but not *better* soldiers in the field, we assure you (& I speak for the Rutherford democracy) that no nomination could have been made, so acceptable to us & in our estimation so available for the whole party throughout the Union. By it, heart burnings & jealousies amongst others are put down & the whole party bound together in chains of iron.

With Polk, Dallas & *Texas too* we'll carry Tennessee & the election in the Union by acclamation. All we lack in Tennessee my dear Sir is an efficient electoral ticket, which (it is needless to disguise) we have not got. I shall see Nicholson at our ratification meeting at Murfreesborough next week.[2] He must be induced to put on his armour to take the field until November. We need a soldier in E. Tennessee most especially. But I will not obtrude my crude notions of these matters upon you. I merely sat down to offer you what I sincerely feel, my cordial congratulations, & having done So I take the liberty to subscribe myself....

BROMFIELD RIDLEY

ALS. DLC–JKP. Addressed to Columbia.
1. A Tennessee lawyer, Ridley represented Warren County for one term in the Tennessee House, 1835–37. He moved to Rutherford County in 1840 and served as judge of the Chancery Court from 1840 until 1861.
2. Rutherford County Democrats held a large ratifying meeting at Murfreesboro on June 19, 1844. A. O. P. Nicholson was one of the speakers at the gathering of some five to ten thousand Democrats.

## FROM COLLIN S. TARPLEY[1]

My Dear Sir                               Stockdale Farm 15th June 1844

It has been just one week since we received intelligence of your nomination by the Baltimore convention and the enthusiasm of your friends has been so far above fever heat that we are just becoming sufficiently cool to look around and feel that it is time to send up our congratulations. Never have I seen more unanimity of feeling amongst the Democrats than prevails here at present. We were severed last year about Repudiation, Nullification State Banks Distribution &c and I had begun to fear that the party had become so divided about minor matters that we should fall this year under the sturdy and united blows of the "Universal Whig party." But bless my soul, (and ten thousand thanks to the Convention) your nomination comes with healing in its wings and every Democrat that I have seen or heard from be he bond payer or Nullifier, repudiator or Unionist, whether for Calhoun, Van Buren, Johnson, Cass or Buchanan has with one voice cried out "Hurrah for Polk." Without a single division in our ranks without murmur or word of complaint with the banner cry of "Polk & Democracy" we shall as surely march to victory in Missi next fall as that the harvest will be gathered. I have been appealed to a hundred times by members of both parties to say what Tennessee would do and my answer has ever been she will go for Polk. I think that I know the people of Tenn and particularly the *Leaders* of the whig party in that State. As between two of her own citizens she may possibly select another for chief magistrate for local reasons, but as between a citizen personally so popular, long known & confided in and Henry Clay personally unpopular and lately odious even to his own party in that State brave gallant old Tenn, the land of Soldiers and Statesmen and more than all the home of old Hickory[2] will go with a shout for her own Son. Am I right in this. I count for us Maine, New Hampshire, New York, Penn. Virginia So Carolina Georgia Tenn. Alabama Missi Arkansas Michigan Illinois & Missouri. I think that Ohio & North Carolina and possibly New York and Tenn may be put down as doubtful but the chances are more than equal that we shall get three out of the four. The late demonstration in old Virginia goes for nothing when we reflect that the contest was between the Tax & anti Tax party and not a question of national politics at all. The free trade principls of Virginia must and will defeat Mr Clay there aside from his Bank Distribution & internal improvment doctrines. But it is too early to enter into a cold formal calculation of events. The spirit is up, the Democracy aroused and in spite of coon skins, shuck collars, ribald songs aye even "sugar in the gourd" we will give them the D—l next fall.

As soon as the nomination reached Jackson we fired a salute of 100 guns and such shouts and huzzas, as then went up to the skies would have made any democrat's heart glad. It set the clouds in motion for it has been raining ever since and as we were suffering for the want of it, the good effects of the nomination is felt at once. The election should positively come off early in Sept. or the big guns and huzzas of the Democrats will keep it raining so steadily that we never shall gather in our crops. On Wednesday we had a large meeting which was addressed by Genl Felix Houston[3] of New Orleans, up to this time a leading Whig, but now a Polk man heart & soul. He intends to *travel and talk* until the election. We intend to keep the Ball rolling and from Tishomingo to Jackson from Kemper to Washington[4] at every Court House cross road & muster ground we will *stir up* the people to the good work. The Whigs are rather at fault. They had invented a large stock of stories and songs upon the expectation that Van Buren would be the nominee and now the labour ink & paper go for nothing. Of Cass they would have said that he had no politics, and leaned in favour of the North, but now what can they say. Why that Polk is too much under the influence of Genl Jackson. This is an objection that will not weigh very heavily against him I ween with the democratic party.

But I have said enough to show you the spirit with which your nomination has been hailed by the people here which was all that I intended and to assure you not only of my cordial approbation but of a pride and exultation which spring from personal considerations as much as political preference. Go ahead and nine cheers for the ticket. My cordial respects to Mrs P. Say to her that I hope to meet her in Washington on the 4th of March next and help to give a hundred cheers for the success of the good cause.

C. S. Tarpley

ALS. DLC–JKP. Addressed to Columbia.

1. Having read law in Pulaski under Aaron V. Brown, Tarpley moved to Florence in 1831 to practice law; five years later he moved from Tennessee to Hinds County, Miss.

2. Andrew Jackson.

3. Felix Huston. The Democratic meeting at Clinton, Miss., on June 12, 1844, is not further identified.

4. Reference is to counties located in the northern, southern, eastern, and western extremities of Mississippi.

## FROM ANDREW A. KINCANNON

Dear Sir,                                      Columbus Mi. 16th June 1844

Your letter covering the commission to take my deposition, was recd. some days ago,[1] when we were all in the midst of our gratulations and rejoicings at the result of the doings at Baltimore, and on that account was not answered as soon as it otherwise would have been.

I am fearful, that business out of the state will put it out of my power to give my deposition as you desire. If I should not leave home it will be done as you have directed.

Your nomination for the Presidency was unexpected to us here, as no doubt it was to yourself & friends everywhere; but whin it was announced, that you had recd. the unanimous vote of the convention, it was hailed by all branches of the democratic party here with enthusiastic joy & approbation. Van Buren men, Calhoun men, Cass men and Johnson men, all unite as one man, for Polk and Texas. You may well imagine what were my own individual feelings on the recpt. of such news. I was looking with sanguine hope for your nomination for the second office, but to be nominated with such unanimity for the first, was indeed a result almost too gratifying to be realized as true.

But so it is, and I for one, look upon it, as a certain presage, of a glorious victory for the cause of democracy in the battle now waging. If the north stands up, as I hope and believe she will, the majority will be overwhelming. If the Texas question does not injuriously affect you in that quarter, all is safe beyond a doubt. My own opinion is, that your position on that question will strengthen the ticket everywhere.

What is your own opinion of that, and the whole subject? You must write me *in confidence,* and all shall be "under the rose"[2] between us. You must pardon, my dear sir, the unreserved manner in which I am writing. You have not I know, forgotten, the deep anxiety I have felt in times gone by, when I saw you struggling against an organized and powerful opposition, and the pride and joy I felt, when you overcame it all. All, and more than I ever felt before, I feel now; and from my *Heart* do I believe, that the time has come, when you are to be rewarded for the many gallant deeds which you have done, in the cause of our democracy. And to know, as I do, with what grateful emotions, such a reward will be recd., is not amongst the least of the reasons, why I hope, and believe and trust in God, that such is in store for you.

You will, I know, be overwhelmed with letters from all quarters of the union, but you must not fail to let me hear from you soon.

Let me know how the signs are from all directions. I see Mr. Van Buren has come out like a man,[3] & I understand Calhoun & Benton has done the same. We will carry this state by 5 to 6000 votes *Sure.* No mistake in this. We will do it certain.

ANDREW A. KINCANNON

ALS. DLC–JKP. Addressed to Columbia. Polk's AE on the cover states that he answered this letter on June 27, 1844; Polk's reply has not been found.
1. Letter not found.
2. Quotation from Sir Thomas Browne, *Pseudodoxia Epidemica,* Fifth Book, Chapter XXII, meaning "kept in secret."
3. See Aaron Vanderpoel to Polk, June 3, 1844.


## FROM JOHN GALBRAITH[1]

Dear Sir,                            Erie, June 17. 1844
Allow me the pleasure of congratulating you upon the result of the national democrat Convention in Baltimore, and the manner in which it seems to be received by the democracy everywhere. It is so long since we met, that it is possible you have forgotten me, but I cannot avoid renewing an acquaintance which was cordial, friendly & confidential. You will therefore pardon the liberty I take in troubling you with a few lines, supposing it would not be entirely uninteresting to you, (troubled as I have no doubt you are with numerous communications) to hear from an old friend & learn something of the feelings entertained in relation to the approaching election here.

I am pleased to have it to say, that in this quarter the party are perfectly united. We had some warm for "Tecumsey,"[2] some warm for Cass & some decidedly for Mr. Van Buren, among whom I was, mainly, that we could have the chance for a fair trial, & that the nomination of either of the other gentlemen would be construed into an abandonment of our former principles. I am well satisfied, now however that we can do better than if he had been nominated. I have been through the counties in which I practice, Crawford, Venango & Warren as well as this county (Erie) since the close of the Convention & am delighted to find our friends as entirely harmonious & united. I think we shall harmonize equally upon the "Young Hickory" as upon the "Old."[3] I send you a paper[4] containing the proceedings of a meeting called here on very short notice, one of the most spirited & enthusiastic we have had here for some time, at least since 1840. This county (Erie) gave a majority for Harrison of 1575. I feel confident they cannot get for Clay over 1000, notwithstanding the cry of Protective Tariff, with which they try to humbug our people. The Tariff, it must be confessed is rather a favorite in Pa, we have so many iron and other factories. We put the Compromise act brought forward by Clay[5] at them & his resignation of his seat in 1842 before the vote was taken on the Tariff. In the other counties in which I practice, we shall have decided majorities, as large as usual.

Please present my kindest respects to Mrs. P.

JOHN GALBRAITH

ALS. DLC–JKP. Addressed to Columbia. Polk's AE on the cover states that he answered this letter on July 4, 1844; Polk's reply has not been found.

1. A Pennsylvania lawyer, John Galbraith won election as a Democrat to the U.S. House, where he served three terms, 1833–37 and 1839–41. Subsequently, he was elected presiding judge of Pennsylvania's Sixth Judicial District in 1851 and served until his death in 1860.

2. Richard M. Johnson.

3. Andrew Jackson.

4. Enclosure not found.

5. Reference is to the Tariff Act of 1833.

## FROM HENRY HUBBARD

Dear Sir,                              Charlestown N.H. June 17, 1844

I need not say to you that next to our mutual friend, Mr Van Buren I preferred your nomination as our Candidate for the Presidency to that of any other man in our country. And I am truly happy to add that the nomination has been recieved by the Democratic party in this section of the Republic with the same approbation and enthusiasm with which it was made. I am very sure that no nomination could have been made which could have given more satisfaction or produced greater union and harmony. Since the close of the convention I have visited Boston and much of my own State. I have met with large assemblies of the people in different parts who have given the most hearty response to our proceedings. I have the highest confidence of success and I feel assured that no nomination could have been made giving more discomfiture to the Whig Party. They feel alarmed.

I may and probably will write you again soon. Make my kind remembrances to Mrs. Polk in which Mrs. Hubbard & Sarah[1] join with me, and accept for yourself My Dear Sir, the assurance of my unfeigned respect.

HENRY HUBBARD

ALS. DLC–JKP. Addressed to Columbia.

1. Sarah C. Polk, Sally Walker Hubbard, and Sarah Dean Hubbard Gilchrist. Henry Hubbard married Sally Walker, daughter of Aaron and Phyla Dean Walker of Charlestown, N.H. The Hubbards had one daughter, Sarah; she married John J. Gilchrist, chief justice of New Hampshire and law partner of Henry Hubbard.

## FROM CHARLES J. INGERSOLL

Dear Sir          Washington June [18, 18]44[1]
I recd. this morning your favor of the 8. inst.[2] Since then Mr. Walker of Mississippi & I have been conferring on the subject, and the result is our united opinion that I shall address you the letter herewith,[3] in order to draw your answer which we both think may be all important. I hope you will think so too. It need not be long, but explicit and *national.*

         C. J. Ingersoll

[P.S.] Mr. Walker will also write to you by this mail.[4]

ALS. DLC–JKP. Addressed to Columbia and marked "Confidential."
1. Ingersoll dated his letter "June 8"; correct date identified through content analysis.
2. Letter not found.
3. Ingersoll's letter to Polk, dated June 18, 1844, and enclosed under cover of this letter, solicited Polk's position on the tariff question.
4. Ingersoll wrote his note in the left margin of the page. See Robert J. Walker to Polk, June 18, 1844.

## FROM CHARLES J. INGERSOLL

Dear Sir          Washington June 18. [18]44
You are aware how violent are the seeming, but as I think reconcileable, differences, respecting the Tariff, between North and South, East and West. In my humble opinion all these are little more than seeming differences. At any rate the real is much less than the ostensible. We *must* have impost *enough* to support government in its various branches, civil and military. It is arithmetically demonstrable that about twenty eight per cent on the now dutiable imports is *indispensable.* Impost to that amount paid in cash is all the *protection* wanted; some more, some less, whatever it may be called. What then is there to dispute about? Simply whether this *incidental* protection shall be *called* protection; that's all, is it not? I must say I think so.

There is indeed a corollary to the problem involving the minor vexed question of discrimination. But is it practicable to dispense with that? I think not. What do you think?

On the eve of leaving Washington for home I venture to trouble you with these notions imperfectly put in a familiar way, and I confess that it will be very agreable if you favor me with your view of the matter, so that I may make it known in Pennsylvania, where I expect to find anxiety, to know precisely your doctrine on this subject.

Excuse therefore rather an abrupt and quite a hasty letter about it from ....

C. J. INGERSOLL

ALS. DLC–JKP. Addressed to Columbia. Written for publication, this letter was enclosed in Ingersoll's cover letter to Polk of the same date.

## FROM JULIUS P. B. MacCABE[1]

Hon Sir,                    Southport, Wisconsin Territory June 18th 1844
With heart-felt pleasure, I beg leave to congratulate you upon your nomination as the Democratic candidate for the highest office, in the gift, of a free and mighty people. I consider your nomination a source of congratulation to the whole of that party to which I have the honor to belong and I mistake, very much, the feelings of the great mass of the Citizens of the United States, if the result of the election next fall will not humble the friends of *Clay* with the *dust.*

Our prospects are every day becoming more bright, and we here in the Territory are continually in receipt of communications from our democratic friends in the Eastern States, filled with expressions of joy at the happy result of the Convention and with the strongest assurances of a glorious victory at the Polls next fall. I have just now read a long and ably written communication from a gentleman in New York State, in which he states with perfect confidence that several of the heretofore Whig counties in that State, including Wyoming, will go for Polk and Dallas with a large majority.

The Democrats of this Territory regret that they cannot vote at the Presidential election. We have an overwhelming majority here, including about 3,600 Irish families. For my part, I assure you my heart pants with a desire to take an active part in the contest, and as I can not vote at the election (owing to my being a citizen of the Territory) I am determined God willing to make an electioneering tour through the States of Illinois, Indiana, Michigan & Ohio, at my own expense for the purpose of exhibiting the frauds, the bigotry, the intolerance and general corruption of the leaders of the Clay party.

I deem it my duty to exert my influence amongst my countrymen (the Irish) and others in the states above named as I have reason to believe that the Abolition party is determined to use the most inveigling artifices to gain support at the coming contest.

As you may not recolect me, by name, I will here state that I am the Irishman who intended to get up a Directory of Nashville in 1841 and that I had the honor of having your name at the head of my subscription list.[2] Anxiety for my family, then in Michigan, & from whom I had not heard for several mo[n]ths (as I stated to Genl. Jackson) induced me to hurry home & of course abandon the idea of publishing the work.

I would take the liberty, Hon Sir, of asking the favor of your presenting my compliments to Genl. Jackson and intimating to him my ardent wish that he would furnish me per mail with a copy of any one of his Presidential messages or other public document, having his autograph, that I may keep the same as a memorial of that great and good man, of whom every Irishman feels justly proud as a descendant of that race which at one time gave poets warriors, statesmen and divines to the whole civilized world. That my countrymen still claim him will be seen from a toast given at the celebration of the Anniversary of Irelands patron Saint, at this place in March last, and of which the following is a copy. *"Major Genl Andrew Jackson, a fine scion of Shellelagh Oak, engrafted by propitious fortune on the American Hickory. He at New Orleans paid the British a portion of the debt due to them by Ireland, may the countrymen of his father soon pay them the balance with interest."*

I would have written to the Genl long ago but I understood [...]³ health was feeble and I would not for any consideration [...] him with a communication; but you Honl. Sir, [...] are his intimate friend will I trust have an opportunity, of remembering me to him. I spent a night at the Hermitage in February 1841, and had the pleasure of enjoying the edifying & instructing conversation of the Hero of New Orleans & never can I forget the impression made upon my mind on that occasion.

I have become a citizen of Wisconsin for which Territory I am now engaged in publishing a Gazetteer, having already traveled all over it. I have been nearly 15 years a resident and eight years a citizen of the U States. At present I hold two offices here, which occupy but very little of my time, namely Notary Public for Racine County and Commissioner for the State of Ohio in the Territory of Wisconsin.

Wishing you every success earthly & eternal, I remain....

JULIUS P. B. MACCABE

ALS. DLC–JKP. Addressed to Nashville and forwarded to Columbia.

1. Julius P. Bolivar MacCabe prepared and marketed city directories for numerous towns in the Wisconsin Territory, including publications for Madison in 1842, for Southport in 1843, and for Beloit, Janesville, and Racine in 1843–44. He published Milwaukee's first city directory in 1847.

2. In 1841 Polk served as governor of Tennessee and thus resided in Nashville at the time of MacCabe's subscription solicitation.

3. Word or words obliterated here and below by sealing wax oil.

## FROM JOSEPH C. POTTS[1]

Sir                                        Trenton June 18th 1844

The Democrats of Mercer County New Jersey propose celebrating the anniversary of our Country's Independence at Camp Washington, near this place, and have imposed upon me the agreeable duty of inviting you to be present.

Selected, as you have recently been by the great National Council of Republicans at Baltimore, to lead the Republican forces, and bear the Standard of their principles in the coming contest you may well imagine that the Democratic phalanx of other states, and none more so than this, would thrill with pride and pleasure, in sharing some portion of your presence with the tried cohorts of Tennessee. An army takes fresh courage from seeing the General's face and hearing his voice, and in civic affairs, the presence of the popular champion invariably stimulates his adherents. I trust therefore you may find it convenient, as well as consistent with your feelings, to make a visit to New Jersey.

Before closing this letter, allow me to call your attention to a question of some importance to the people of this state. To some extent we are a manufacturing community, and regard the tariff as an important feature in the political contests of the day. The Democracy of this state are in favor of a tariff for revenue, sufficient to supply the wants of the government, economica[lly][2] administered, discriminating agains[t] the luxuries and in favor of the necessaries of life, and incidentally protecting the home manufactures. They regard the doctrine of free trade, which would withdraw incidental protection, break up imposts, and make a resort to direct taxation necessary, as visionary in the present state of commercial regulations throughout the world. These we understand as the doctrines of General Jackson and his administration, and before the vote in the Baltimore Convention was taken, which happily resulted in your unanimous nomination, I enquired of the Hon. Cave Johnson whether your sentiments on the subject of the tariff agreed with those of that great man, such being my impression. He answered that they did, an answer which I have every confidence you will confirm.

Repeating the assurance of the pleasure it would give us could you assent to [ma]ke us a visit ....

Jos. C. Potts

ALS. DLC–JKP. Addressed to Tennessee.

1. A leader of Mercer County Democrats, Potts served as a member of New Jersey's delegation to the Democratic National Convention at Baltimore in 1844.

2. Word or words obliterated here and below by sealing wax oil.

## FROM ROBERT J. WALKER

Dear Sir,                 Washington City June 18th 1844

I have been shown a letter from Mr. Smith[1] of Maine, written to induce you to open the door to the return of the conservative democrats of 1840. This would be of great importance in Maine, Connecticut, New York, & New Jersey, & it would be of some service in several other states. The prodigal son, particularly if repentant for past errors, should be welcomed home with joy, & if the conservatives would vote for you, a sub-treasury man, it is good evidence in their favor. Your letter to Mr. Smith will be very important, as I learn by an interview this day with Senator, now Gov. Talmadge.[2] Could you not then talk kindly to these gentlemen, & say that the return to the party of all the Jackson democrats of '28, '32, & '36, would be hailed with joy by every true friend of the republican cause, & by none more cordially than by yourself, who had cooperated with them in those great contests? If you think proper, in addition to your letter to Mr. Smith, to write to me on this subject, not for publication, but to use discreetly, it might be of great service. One thing is certain, unless many of the wanderers of 1840 return to our party, we are again beaten. But very few would have returned to Mr. Van Buren against whom they voted, but, with a little encouragement from you, they would nearly all come back to us.

And now as to the great difficulty, the tariff. From your letter to me of June 8th, your determination on this subject is wise & patriotic. From peculiar circumstances, the tariff is much stronger now throughout the Union, than it ever was before, & in Pennsylvania, New York, Connecticut & New Jersey, it is irresistible. In Pennsylvania, the last

legislature, nearly two thirds of whom were democrats, passed resolutions of instruction *unanimously* in favor of the tariff, & the entire
democratic press of the state has assumed the same ground. Many
new manufactories are springing up throughout the state, & the old
establishments are all again in successful operation. No man now attempts in that state to oppose the tariff policy. And this is the ground
upon which the friends of Mr. Clay are so very sanguine of success in
Pennsylvania. In view of all these facts, could you not say that every
patriot & true friend of the Union, should desire to harmonize, as far
as possible, all conflicting interests on this dangerous & difficult question. That a permanent system, & one adopted as far as practicable,
by general consent, was most desirable. That to that end you would
propose:

1st A Revenue tariff, not to exceed the wants of the government, administered in a spirit of republican simplicity & economy.

2d That, within the range above indicated, all should delight to see
every branch of domestic industry deriving such incidental aid, as
would enable it to realize fair & reasonable profits, & maintaining
such wholesome competition, as would prevent the monopoly of our
markets by foreign products & manufactures.

This is the doctrine of the Philadelphia free trade address of 1831[3]
& not so strong for the tariff as Col. Benton's late speech,[4] or most of
Gen. Jackson's messages. It is drawn with great deliberation, & after
consultation with many of your warm friends, tariff & anti-tariff. We
all think *"aid"* a better word than *"protection,"* and that your opinions
had better be expressed in the shape of a *desire for a result,* than in
any other form. If you should give an opinion similar to the above,
& should subsequently be asked your views as to the tariff of '42, it
might be justly said, that you would desire to see such modifications
only, as experience would prove to be most wise & salutary, & most
conformable to the above principles. Many would like to see you go
much further for the tariff, & the very few would not like to see you go
so far, & certain it is that you cannot remain silent without defeating
the ticket. Your own sound judgement will suggest better language
than this, with which to clothe your ideas, but these views are the
result of a careful comparison of opinions derived from every quarter
of the Union.

I remain here for some time to write the address of the Democratic
Convention,[5] & perform some other duties, in aid of the good cause,
& will be glad to hear from you.

                                                    R. WALKER

ALS. DLC–JKP. Probably addressed to Columbia.

1. A lawyer, Albert Smith served as U.S. marshal for Maine, 1830–38, and won election as a Democrat to one term in the U.S. House, 1839–41.

2. Nathaniel P. Tallmadge.

3. Reference probably is to the Philadelphia Free-trade Convention of 1832. Called together by H. D. Sedgwick of Massachusetts, delegates from fifteen states met in Philadelphia on September 30, 1832. Presided over by Philip P. Barbour of Virginia, the convention declared that the existing tariff laws of Congress, in so far as they were designed to protect manufactures, were both unconstitutional and inexpedient. The delegates further resolved that the people should be urged to unite in obtaining such changes as would accommodate the interests of all sections of the union.

4. See Robert J. Walker to Polk, May 30, 1844.

5. See Samuel H. Laughlin to Polk, May 31, 1844.


## TO JOHN K. KANE

My Dear Sir:                                Columbia Tenn. June 19th 1844

I enclose to you herewith a statement of my views briefly expressed upon the subject of the tariff.[1] The letters which I have received upon the subject have all been from political friends.[2] None of them, except from Pittsburg in your state, have asked me to make a declaration of my views. I desire to avoid appearing before the public as far as I can do so with propriety. If however it be deemed important that I should re-declare my opinions upon this or any other public subject, I will not shrink from the responsibility. Still I think my friends should not press it upon me, unless it be deemed absolutely necessary.

I address to you the enclosed letter & request that you will shew it to *Mr Dallas,* and my friend *Mr Henry Horn,* and consult with them *confidentially* as to the necessity or propriety of its publication. I have not the slightest objection to its publication if my friends in Pennsylvania think it necessary or proper. I submit it intirely to *Mr Dallas, Mr Horn & yourself* to publish it or not as you may think proper. I think it probable that I will be called upon soon, by our political opponents and in that event I *must* answer.

I will add that by reference to the Bill reported by Mr Verplanck in December 1832,[3] and which you can procure from the Clerk of the House of Representatives at Washington,[4] and to my speech[5] made in its support, my views in reference to revenue, discriminating duties and protection will be seen. I believe the iron-interest was fully satisfied with that Bill. The Bill is House Bill No. 641, 2nd Session 22nd Congress; and my speech will be found in Gales & Seaton's Register of Congressional Debates Vol    , Part    , page    .[6]

If you conclude not to publish my letter, it may be proper for you to correspond with my friends at Pittsburg, or some of them, who have addressed me, on the subject. I would address this letter to them, but I have no personal acquaintance with them. They are *Messrs Philips and Smith* Editors of the Pittsburg Post, *Mr John B. Butler, Wm McEllroy, John Bigler, W. L. Moorehead, Charles Barnett, John M. Irwin & James E. Newhouse.*[7]

I have intended for several days to write to *Mr Dallas,* but my time has been so much occupied that I have not done so. I will write to him in a day or two.

I thank you for your kind letter of the 5th Instant. Before it was received a friend at Nashville had undertaken to collect the material which you desired, and with the same object which you had in view.[8]

JAMES K. POLK

ALS. PPAmP. Addressed to Philadelphia and marked *"Confidential."*

1. See below, Polk to John K. Kane, June 19, 1844.

2. Polk received numerous letters from political allies, each giving him advice or seeking his position on the tariff. For examples, see above, Robert J. Walker to Polk, May 30, 1844; Andrew J. Donelson to Polk, May 31, 1844; and Samuel H. Laughlin to Polk, June 10, 1844. Also see calendar entries for Thomas Phillips and William H. Smith to Polk, June 7, 1844; and John B. Butler to Polk, June 9, 1844.

3. On December 27, 1832, the House Committee on Ways and Means, chaired by Gulian C. Verplanck, introduced a bill to reduce and otherwise to alter the duties on imports. See the *Register of Debates in Congress,* 22nd Congress, 2nd Session, Appendix, Vol. IX, pt. 1, p. 39. Verplanck, a New York lawyer, sat in the U.S. House as a Democrat, 1825–33, and in the New York Senate, 1838–41.

4. Caleb J. McNulty of Ohio served as clerk of the U.S. House from December 6, 1843, until January 18, 1845.

5. On January 21, 1833, Polk spoke in favor of Verplanck's tariff bill. His speech was printed in the *Register of Debates in Congress,* Vol. IX, pt. 1, pp. 1162–75.

6. Polk left blank spaces for completing his citation to his speech printed in the *Register;* presumably he did not have that information at hand.

7. Thomas Phillips, William H. Smith, John B. Butler, William McElroy, John Bigler, W. L. Moorhead, Charles Barnett, John M. Erwin, and James E. Newhard. In copying Polk's letter, Kane corrected the spellings of "Phillips," "McElroy," "Moorhead," and "Newhard." L, copy, in the hand of John K. Kane. DLC–JKP. On September 1, 1842, William H. Smith, editor of the weekly *Pittsburgh Mercury and Democrat,* and Thomas Phillips, editor of the Pittsburgh *American Manufacturer,* merged their newspapers and formed the *Pittsburgh Daily Morning Post,* which in 1847 became the first local newspaper to utilize telegraphic dispatches on a regular basis.

8. See calendar entry for John K. Kane to Polk, June 5, 1844. Reference probably is to Samuel H. Laughlin, who undertook the labors of gathering data for a campaign biography of Polk.

## TO JOHN K. KANE

Dear Sir:                                        Columbia Tennessee June 19th 1844

I have received recently several letters in reference to my opinions on the subject of the tariff, and among others yours of the 30th ultimo. My opinions have been often given to the public. They are to be found in my public acts, and in the public discussions in which I have participated.

I am in favour of a tariff for revenue, such an one as will yield a sufficient amount to the Treasury to defray the expenses of the Government economically administered. In adjusting the details of a revenue tariff, I have heretofore sanctioned such moderate discriminating duties as would produce the amount of revenue needed, and at the same time afford reasonable incidental protection to our home industry. I am opposed to a tariff for protection *merely,* and not for revenue. Acting upon these general principles it is well known, that I gave my support to the policy of Genl. Jackson's administration on this subject. I voted against the tariff act of 1828. I voted for the act of 1832, which contained modifications of some of the objectionable provisions of the act of 1828. As a member of the committee of Ways and Means of the House of Representatives I gave my assent to a Bill reported by that committee in December 1832,[1] making further modifications of the act of 1828, and making also discriminations in the imposition of the duties which it proposed. That Bill did not pass, but was superseded by the Bill commonly called the compromise Bill, for which I voted.

In my judgment it is the duty of the Government, to extend as far as it may be practicable to do so, by its revenue laws, and all other means within its power, fair and just protection to all the great interests of the whole Union, embracing agriculture, manufactures, the mechanic arts, commerce and navigation. I heartily approve the resolutions[2] upon this subject passed by the Democratic National Convention lately assembled at Baltimore.

JAMES K. POLK

ALS. PPAmP. Addressed to Philadelphia and enclosed in Polk's cover letter of this same date. Written with a view toward probable publication, this letter soon appeared in newspapers published throughout the Union.

1. Reference is to Gulian C. Verplanck's tariff bill. See above, Polk to John K. Kane, June 19, 1844.

2. Here Polk inserted an asterisk in the text of his letter and attached after the close of the letter a fragment of a newspaper clipping of the fourth resolution of the Democratic National Convention of May 1844, which read in part, "That justice and sound policy forbid the federal government to foster one branch of industry to the detriment of another ...."

## FROM WILLIAM HENDRICKS[1]

Sir                                                     Madison Indiana June 20. 1844

Allow me to congratulate you in relation to the recent nomination at Baltimore and to say that no one more cordially wishes you success than myself, and I now give it as my decided opinion that the ticket will be a stronger one than could have been formed with either of the other individuals spoken of at its head. This state I consider one of the doubtful ones but there are here a class of men who though Democrats in principle and in practice too except in 1840 who wd not now vote for Mr. V.B.[2] but who will sustain the present nomination. We shall have strong hopes of carrying this state but shall not be much disappointed if we are defeated; but of the General result we are now quite sanguine and the feeling is growing into enthusiasm. We had an excellent political meeting 12 days ago at this place and the task was devolved on me to make a speech and prepare and offer the resolutions. A paper containing them I send you.[3]  I never saw a meeting of more cordiality and accounts from various quarters show the same state of things elsewhere.  Genl. Milroy[4] of this state passed home from the Baltimore convention 4 days ago and returned through northern Pennsylvania his native country.  He says that the nominations are taking well in that state and that there is but one subject that you will be distrusted upon. That is the tariff. He said how ever that the principles of the resolution contained in the paper I send you on that subject wd entirely satisfy the Democracy of that state: that is tariff for revenue with incidental protection and said that your friends were placing you on that ground there. That is the doctrine of the Demos here and it is presumed to be the doctrine of Democracy very generally.

Yesterday evening our Lieut. Gov. Bright[5] of this state returned home from the convention. He has been to Phila. to Richmond & elsewhere in Va. He says the noms. are recd with enthusiasm wherever he has been, & that the Whigs have generally given up Va.

WILLIAM HENDRICKS

ALS. DLC–JKP. Addressed to Columbia. Polk's AE on the cover states that he answered this letter on July 4, 1844.

1. Born and educated in Pennsylvania, Hendricks migrated first to Ohio, where he taught school and read law, and then to Indiana, where he enjoyed a lengthy political career. He served as a member of the U.S. House, 1816–22; as governor of Indiana, 1822–25; and as U.S. senator, 1825–37.

2. Martin Van Buren.

3. Enclosure not found.

4. Born in Pennsylvania, Samuel Milroy moved to Indiana and settled in Washington County, which he represented in the state legislature for eight sessions. After removing to Carroll County, he again won election to the state legislature and served from 1836 to 1839.

5. A lawyer from Madison, Jesse D. Bright served as lieutenant governor of Indiana, 1843–45, before being elected as a Democrat to the U.S. Senate, in which body he served from 1845 to 1862.

## FROM JESSE MILLER

My Dear Sir                                         Harrisburg Pa June 20 1844

I know you are over run with Correspondence. I will therefore try to be brief. Nothing has transpired to change the opinion I expressed as to this State giving its vote for the nominees of the National Convention but ever thing to confirm it. From every indication, it is my opinion, we shall carry the State by a decided majority. The tariff is almost the only hobby the Whigs have, and they are constantly harping on it.

The democrats with us take ground decidedly against distribution of the proceeds of the Lands and go for a revenue tariff with discrimination in favor of the manufactures & productions of our own Country, which we call incidental protection. We say we mean by this that we are in favor of laying higher duties on those articles of importation that come in competition with our own productions than on those that do not and that we are in favor of lower duties on the necessaries of life which enter into general consumption of all classes & Conditions of Society which we do not manufacture or grow in our own Country. These are the doctrines we go on here.

I should be pleased to hear from you if you can find a moment of leisure from the other numerous calls on your time.

I feel great confidence of success.

J. MILLER

ALS. DLC–JKP. Addressed to Columbia. Polk's AE on the cover states that he answered this letter on July 3, 1844.

## FROM CAVE JOHNSON

Dear Sir,                                     Louisville Friday 21st June [1844][1]

I take a moment before we leave to say that from every part of the country, the united voice of the democracy proclaims to the Baltimore Convention "well done." I have heard of no democrat who will not sustain the nomination thoroughly. G. C. Verplank, Jas Garland, Tazwell, Cramer,[2] with hundreds of others will now join us. The only difficulty I fear arises from the course of T. H. Benton, when connected with the movements of S.C. The latter uses *immediate annexation* for the purpose of uniting the South and killing T.H.B.[3] & will if practicable *identify you & Genl. J.*[4] with all their future movements. Fears are entertained in the North, that this *may be so,* & if any incident takes place to confirm the suspicion, our cause is jeoparded. I have given every assurance to S.W. Jr.[5] & a few others that you could not be induced to separate yourself from the Northern democracy, instanced your former course, in the case of White &c &c and also thought it impossible that Genl. J. should lend himself to any such purpose. The only danger of the latter taking any step to favor the Southern movement they think will arise, from some letter to be extracted from him, that will seem to favor the movement without his sufficiently weighing the consequences.

Can not you see him & have a free conversation as to the Southern movement & put him on his guard? A *Southern Convention* will be proposed, probably at Nashville, to excite the South in behalf of immediate annexation. A call session will be held in September. Our cause will be in great danger. S.W. Jr. will sink or swim with T.H.B. So will A. & T. of Ohio,[6] Niles of Con. If we can avoid a Southern Convention, have a mass meeting or barbacue at Nashville S.W. Jr. will attend & many from the North as well as the South & good will come of it.

I have the most serious apprehension from this Southern movement not only to our cause but the country. Mason & Dickson's line now divides the Methodist church & will soon divide the other churches.[7] This movement will tend to divide political parties by it. The Texas question brings into the contest the fanaticism of the North with increased fervor. Our only safety for the country & our cause depends upon the southern democracy maintaining the position we have heretofore occupied, firm & consistent friends of the Northern democracy, yeilding much for conciliation & harmony.

We have not yet heard a word from you since the nomination. Think of these things maturely & in my judgment you should see Genl J. as soon as possible.

We are in very good health.

C. JOHNSON

[P.S.] We left W. the 16th & will be at home the 25th.[8]

ALS. DLC–JKP. Addressed to Columbia and marked *"Private."*
1. Date identified through content analysis.
2. Gulian C. Verplanck, James Garland, Littleton W. Tazewell, and William E. Cramer. A Virginia Democrat, Garland served in the U.S. House from 1835 until 1841. Tazewell served in the U.S. House, 1800–1801, and in the U.S. Senate, 1824–32, prior to serving as governor of Virginia, 1834–36.
3. Thomas H. Benton.
4. Andrew Jackson.
5. Silas Wright, Jr.
6. William Allen and Benjamin Tappan.
7. Convened in New York City in May 1844, the General Conference of the Methodist Episcopal Church became embroiled in the issue of slavery. A plan of separation, adopted by the conference, led to the organization of the Methodist Episcopal Church, South, at a conference held in Louisville, Ky., in May 1845. The northern and western conferences of the church continued as the Methodist Episcopal Church, while the southern conferences formed the new denomination.
8. Johnson was en route from Washington City to Clarksville, Tenn.

## FROM ARCHIBALD YELL

My Dear Sir                                        Little Rock 21st June [18]44

Allow me in the sincearity of my heart to congratulate you and the Democratic party in your Nomination for the Presidency!

I need not say to you that I am more than gratified at the position you occupy before the Nation, and I am full of hope and sanguine of your success. In Ark. you are only second to *"Old Hickory"*[1] and we shall carry you through most triumphantly and no mistake!

Your Nomination has saved us in this state from defeat at least so far as my election to Congress is concerned. When I learned that Van Buren had taken ground against the Annexation of Texas, I took the ground on the stump that I would vote for no man who was opposed to the emediate Annexation. If Van.[2] had been Nominated I should have been compiled to dicline or had the state thrown for Clay, for my position was approved by the Demcts Generally. From that dilema your Nomination has relieved me and our party in this state. I played a bold & hazardous game but Luck favered me, and now alls safe. The

Democracy was never more firm & united in this state than at this time so I expect to be elected by a hansom majority, enough to make things cirtain for you. Since I reached this place from the south where I have been for the last 30 days, I found many of our old Tennessee friends such as Col McKisick, Maclin[3] & others all the true great & devoted friends of yours. McK[4] will get up a Polk county meeting when he returns to Washington Co. Maclin is a fine fellow & a true friend. Dr Borland[5] the Editor of our Organ the "Banner" is warmly your friend & will do good service this summer. But so far as this state is concerned you may have no fears. The *Johnson* men[6] will go hartily for you, tho. they once had their supicions of me about your Nomination here for Vice President but now alls right!

I wish our friends would get up a Polk & Texas Meeting at *Memphis* this summer say about the 1st Sept. We would attend from Ark by hundreds. I would go & if an oppertunity offered make a speech. I now feel all the solicitude for *"Young Hickery"* that I ever did for the old turk[7] and I will stop short of nothing honorable in my power to advance your cause.

Against my will I have been induced to become a candidate for Congress. If you are *President* I shall be pleased to be in the Ho of Reprs to lend my feble aid to your Admst.

My respects to Madame. Col McK & Genl Maclin send their kind respects & best feelings to you.

YELL

ALS. DLC–JKP. Addressed to Columbia.

1. Andrew Jackson.

2. Martin Van Buren.

3. James McKisick and Sackfield Maclin. A good friend both to Yell and Polk, McKisick served as court clerk of Bedford County, Tenn., before moving to Arkansas about 1836.

4. James McKisick.

5. Solon Borland, a physician, had published the *Western World and Memphis Banner of the Constitution* prior to becoming editor of the Little Rock *Arkansas Democratic Banner* in 1843. During the Mexican War he served as a major in Yell's Arkansas Volunteer Cavalry. In 1848 the Arkansas legislature sent Borland to the U.S. Senate; in 1853 he resigned to become U.S. minister to Nicaragua. During the Civil War he rose to the rank of brigadier general in the Confederate service.

6. Reference is to Richard M. Johnson's family connection in Arkansas, which included Benjamin Johnson, Robert W. Johnson, and Ambrose H. Sevier. A native of Kentucky and a brother of Richard M. Johnson, Benjamin Johnson was a judge of the Superior Court in the Arkansas territory from 1819 until 1836. When Arkansas became a state in 1836, Benjamin

Johnson was appointed to a federal judgeship, a position that he held until 1849. Benjamin's son, Robert W. Johnson, was a lawyer in Little Rock prior to his election as a Democrat to the U.S. House, where he served from 1847 until 1853. Appointed to the U.S. Senate to fill the vacancy occasioned by the resignation of Solon Borland, Robert W. Johnson served in that body from 1853 until 1861. Sevier married Juliette E. Johnson, the daughter of Benjamin Johnson, in 1827.

7. Andrew Jackson.

## FROM LEONARD P. CHEATHAM

On the road to Illinois, at a Country tavern
Dr. Sir: near *Princeton.* June 22nd 1844
I am compelled to sell some stock, & the prospects are so dull I may go on to Illinois; if so, I may not be at home until after the Democratic *Mass* Meeting at Hopkinsville, which will be on the 11th of July.[1] Several of our speakers will be invited from Tennessee, among them Wm. Polk. *He must come* & bring with him any document & particularly, Benton's & Wrights speeches on the Tariff[2] & Your Inaugural.[3] And *you must* send by him a private letter to me (which shall be sacred,) stating to me precisely the attack of Wise on you,[4] the substance of Genl. Jacksons letter to you[5] & the reason he wrote it. You may ask what is the matter? At the *Whig Convention* held at Hopkinsville on thursday last, you were the worst abused man living, partly by the Kentucky speakers, but principally by N. S. Brown from Pulaski & Jones Rivers[6] from Clarksville. The Democrats were so enraged some 200 or more called a meeting at the Court-house, appointed a deputation to wait on me & request me to defend *you* & *our principals* at the court house next day at 1 o'clock. I assented, the Court house was full, & when I commenced runing a parallel between *P. & C.*[7] & also on the Texas question, I never *saw* more attention & *when* I got to that part when I admited *P* was never *Secretary* of *State, with a change of voice,* there was a general burst of applause for 5 minutes; the enthusiasm was great when I touched on annexation, it had never been argued here. To cut things short, Colo. Butler[8] took my hand as we walked out, complimenting, said it was the best speech he had heard in the campaign, *(excuse me for this).* The crowd said the same. One leading Whig was asked what he thought of the speech, the best I ever heard in that *House,* but *dam him* he is paid by *Polk* to ride & speak for him. It is said *four* or *five* have come over to us on the Texas subject, & *one* expressly on the Tariff argument, when I showed that the exports of to-bacco were less under the *high Tariff* & greater under the *lower one*; this is a to-bacco region you know. Any

document of this sort will help. William's appearance here will gain votes if he does not say a word, but he must speak, not touching *Clay* nor *P.* Write to *Nicholson to come.*

*Colo* Butler thinks his chance a fair one. This is enough at present. It is night & bad pen & ink. I send this by a friend in the morning to Nashville.

The main object you will see is to get Wm. Polk & other speakers from Tennessee & the above documents. C. Johnson will be invited & Dick Johnson & Marshall.[9]

L. P. CHEATHAM

*P.S.* Wm., Nicholson & others will be invited from Tennessee. Aris Brown[10] is with me. He was busy in town yesterday & to day stamping part of the Whig speeches with falsehood, & he says there are more changes than I had said above. This letter is only for you & William.

ALS. DLC–JKP. Written near Princeton, Ky.; addressed to Columbia; and posted in Nashville.

1. A large crowd of Democrats, including some 1,500 women, gathered at Hopkinsville, Ky., on July 11, 1844. Among the principal speakers at the meeting were A. O. P. Nicholson, Linn Boyd, Barkly Martin, and Leonard P. Cheatham.

2. For the positions of Thomas H. Benton and Silas Wright, Jr., on the tariff bill of 1842, see Cave Johnson to Polk, August 19 and 28, 1842; William M. Gwin to Polk, August 27, 1842; Hopkins L. Turney to Polk, September 4, 1842; and Alexander O. Anderson to Polk, September 14, 1842.

3. Reference is to Polk's Inaugural Address as governor of Tennessee, delivered in Nashville on October 14, 1839.

4. See Polk to Samuel H. Laughlin, January 17, 22, and 30, 1836.

5. See Andrew Jackson to Polk, May 3, 1835.

6. Neill S. Brown and Jones Rivers. A Pulaski lawyer, Brown represented Giles County in the Tennessee House, 1837–39; ran an unsuccessful race for Congress against Aaron V. Brown in 1843; and won election as a presidential elector on the Whig ticket in 1844. Brown served one term as governor of Tennessee, 1847–49, and went to Russia as U.S. minister from 1850 to 1853. Joining the Know-Nothing party, he served one term as Speaker of the Tennessee House, 1855–57. A Stewart County lawyer, Rivers was a Whig candidate for the Tennessee legislature in 1843.

7. Reference is to Polk and Henry Clay.

8. In 1844 William O. Butler ran as the Democratic candidate for governor of Kentucky; he lost his race to the Whig candidate, William Owsley.

9. Cave Johnson, Richard M. Johnson, and Thomas F. Marshall. A Kentucky lawyer, Marshall served in the U.S. House from 1841 until 1843.

10. A Nashville Democrat, Aris Brown filled the several offices of constable, deputy sheriff, and deputy U.S. marshal in Davidson County. He assisted

in the direction of the Bank of Tennessee, the Nashville and Chattanooga Railroad, and the state prison board.

## FROM JOHN K. KANE

My dear Sir,                                            Philada., 22 June, 1844

Since I did myself the honour of writing to you, the sentiment of our State has been fully expressed, and I can now congratulate you on the perfect consolidation of our party in support of the Baltimore nominations. In fact, we have got back into our ranks very many who have been astray for years, and are at this moment stronger than we have been since the second election of Gen. Jackson. We are cordial and enthusiastic, and our opponents altogether out of heart.

All that we have to apprehend now, not in Pennsylvania but elsewhere, is the introduction of the squabbles of individual politicians into the party arena. If Col. Benton and Mr. Rhett will consent to keep the peace, the election will go by default. The people have made up the right issue; but now, as in 1824 and 28 even, some of their representatives are less happy. I have been much struck by the difference between the tone of some of our returning congressmen and that of the masses. There is an elasticity and vital force about the popular atmosphere, which is wanting at the seat of government.

Our news from New York and New Jersey is much better than I hoped for. It really looks as if we were going to carry both of those States. Mr. V. Buren's friends in N.Y. seem to make your election a point of honour. In our own State, I am told Mr. Buchanan is about to be equally strenuous.

J. K. KANE

ALS. DLC–JKP. Addressed to Columbia.

## TO CAVE JOHNSON

[Dear Sir,]                                       Columbia [June 24, 1844][1]

I received on yesterday your letter of the 21st from Louisville. I wrote to *Genl. Jackson* to day—putting him on his guard against any attempt which may be made to get up a *sectional* or *Southern* convention.[2] No countenance must be given to any attempt should it be made.

A great mass-meeting has been appointed for the 24th July at Nashville. I think the time too short to enable our distant public men to attend. I have written to *Genl.* Armstrong[3] to call the State Committee[4] together immediately to consider of the propriety of postponing the day until about the middle of August. I think it should be so postponed and that invitations should be sent to every Democratic member of Congress and other leading men from the North, the South, the East and the West to attend. Call upon the whole Democracy to attend the *great mass-meeting,* and thousands would seize the occasion to make a pilgrimage to the Hermitage. The meeting would be, what it ought to be, an immense assemblage. The moral and political effect too, of bringing together the great men of the nation, would be incalculable. If such a thing is resolved on the State Committee should make an appeal to the whole Democracy, beginning with *Maine,* then the *granite State,* and ending with Louisiana, calling upon all to come up to the great gathering in the vicinity of the Hermitage. What do you think of these suggestions?

I wrote you to Washington[5] in time as I thought to reach you before the adjournment.

In my letter of *acceptance,* which was addressed as requested to *Robert Rantoul, Jr., Esqr.* of Boston,[6] I took occasion to express my determination in the event of my election to retire at the end of four years. I said nothing to commit the party upon the *one-term* principle, but expressed simply my own determination.

I have received many letters, and especially from Pennsylvania on the subject of the tariff, some of them pressing me for a re-declaration of my opinions. I have addressed a letter upon that subject to *Hon. John K. Kane* of Philadelphia, with a request that he would show it to *Mr. Dallas* and *Mr. Horn,*[7] and if in their judgment, it was absolutely necessary, they were at liberty to publish it, but not otherwise. It is but a re-declaration of the opinions upon which I have acted on that subject; it was carefully prepared and upon its doctrines I am ready to stand. It is very short. In the course of a few days I will know whether they deem it necessary to publish or not.[8]

I desire very much to see you, and must do so as soon as I can. We will have a *mass-meeting* at this place on the 13th July (a Dinner given to the Delegates to Baltimore, electors, and members of Congress) at which you must not fail to attend.[9] On next Saturday the 29th *Turney* and *Bell* have a meeting here. When can I meet you at Nashville? If you will name a day I will write you whether I can be there.

My letters from all parts of the Union continue to give the most flattering prospects. The Union of our party seems to be perfect, and the greatest enthusiasm is every where prevailing. My correspondence is immense. I am overwhelmed with letters. I endeavor to give very short answers to most of them.

[JAMES K. POLK]

P.S. I wish you to send to Genl. Armstrong at Nashville immediately a *Congressional Directory* of the present Congress if you have [one], with a mark or note designating who are *Whigs* and who are *Democrats.* The object is to enable the Committee to send invitations to the Democratic members.

PL. Published in *THM,* I, pp. 245–46. Addressed to Clarksville.
1. Incorrectly dated June 21; date of June 24 identified through content analysis.
2. Letter not found.
3. Polk's letter of June 24, 1844, not found; for Armstrong's reply, see Armstrong to Polk, June 25, 1844.
4. Nashville Democratic Central Committee.
5. See Polk to Johnson, June 8, 1844.
6. See Polk to Henry Hubbard et al., June 12, 1844.
7. See both of Polk's letters to Kane, June 19, 1844.
8. Known as the Kane letter, Polk's terse statement of his views on the tariff was quickly embraced and published by Pennsylvania Democrats.
9. Johnson attended the Columbia meeting and addressed a crowd reportedly numbering in the thousands. Others who spoke included Gideon J. Pillow, David M. Currin, Barkly Martin, A. O. P. Nicholson, and Aaron V. Brown. Polk received well-wishers at his home, but did not attend the public festivities.

## FROM J. G. M. RAMSEY

My Dear Sir                 Mecklenburg June 24, 1844
Mr Eastman informs me that there is a renewal of the defamatory articles about one of your ancestors in a late Jonesboro paper[1] & that he supposes it may be republished elsewhere. He has requested me to furnish a reply to that accusation when it becomes tangible by being endorsed in a reputable paper. This may become necessary. I hope it will not. But it is best to be prepared with all the counteracting testimony should the necessity for it arise. The vindication[2] I once prepared of the character of your ancestors would save me the trouble of re-examining several authorities in my possession. It was forwarded in 1841 to Edwin Polk Esq.[3] of Bolivar for your inspection & is perhaps still in his possession. It is desirable that a copy of it should be sent

to me as soon as practicable, & instead of writing to E.P. for it I have chosen to bring the subject to his attention through you, that nothing may be done in reference to that base charge[4] without your concurrence.

It occurs to me that if the charge appears in any respectable print it should be promptly met by a biographical notice of your paternal & maternal ancestors, embracing, as such a memoir should do, the principal & leading transactions of the *times* in which they lived, & incorporating in it necessarily those of other members of your family Genl. Thos. Polk Col. William Polk &c. &c.[5] The charge would by this means not only be made harmless but the reply to it be subservient to your advancement. If you concur in this will you please request E.P. to send to me at once either the original or a copy of the piece I sent him in 1841, & can you furnish me further information about your grand-father Knox,[6] the battles he fought & the campaigns he served? &c. &c. &c. I shall fortify the whole matter with the best testimony, carefully arranged & set forth in the proper temper.[7]

I see you are invited to a great barbacue at Charlotte the 24th proximo. If you attend a single entertainment out of Tennessee it ought to be that.[8] I have received myself a very pressing invitation to attend. If I should not I will write a reply that the occasion calls for. Some Tennessean that can make a good table speech should be there & answer for you.

We are going into the fight here with the best spirit. Rowles demolished John Crozier at Knoxville & his sub-elector Swan has not ventured before the people since.[9] We organised a Dem. Association in this Civil District last Saturday. It went off well. A. R. Crozier, Mr. Cummings & a new convert *Lindsay* addressed the meeting.[10] No Whig replied. They are evidently afraid of the Texas question. Have you seen Barrows speech against the Treaty & his argument against cheap lands?[11] His position is very vulnerable any where out of Louisiana.

Our Cent. Comtee.[12] has called two Mass Meetings at Greeneville the 8th & Athens the 1st August. Turney or Nicholson or Coe should attend. We want Rowles to meet Bell somewhere. We notice a call in S.C. of a great Texas Rally of the whole Union at Nashville.[13] It ought to take place *after* the Ky. elections.[14]

J. G. M. RAMSEY

P.S. Please have the *"vindication"* forwarded the earliest opportunity. I have a copy of E.P.s commission.[15]

ALS. DLC–JKP. Addressed to Columbia.

1. On June 12, 1844, the *Jonesborough Whig and Independent Journal,* published by William G. Brownlow, ran an article intimating that Polk was a coward. The piece suggested that Polk's cowardliness was inherited from an unnamed ancestor who had allegedly surrendered troops under his command to the British during the Revolutionary War.

2. Ramsey's treatise has not been found.

3. A Hardeman County lawyer and farmer, Edwin F. Polk was the youngest child of Ezekiel Polk and was twenty-two years younger than his nephew, James K. Polk.

4. Reference is to the accusation that Ezekiel Polk was a Tory during the Revolutionary War.

5. Thomas Polk was an older brother of Ezekiel Polk. On May 1, 1775, Thomas Polk, commanding officer of the Mecklenburg County regiment of North Carolina militia, called for the election of two representatives from each of the county's nine militia districts to assemble and consider the troubled state of the country and adopt measures to safeguard liberties. Delegates convened at Charlotte on May 19 and on the following day declared their constituents' independence in what came to be known as the Mecklenburg Declaration of Independence. A son of Thomas Polk, William Polk of Raleigh, N.C., served as a colonel in the Revolutionary War and later became a successful businessman and a member of the North Carolina House, 1785–87, and 1790.

6. A militia captain, James Knox of Mecklenburg County, N.C., enjoyed local distinction for his bravery during the Revolutionary War. After the war he prospered as a farmer and blacksmith. His daughter, Jane, married Samuel Polk in 1794 and gave birth to James K. Polk the following year.

7. Ramsey played a key role in efforts mounted by Polk and his friends to refute Whig charges that Ezekiel Polk had been a Tory in the Revolutionary War. Ramsey supplied William H. Haywood, Jr., material with which to answer the allegations. Commissioned by the North Carolina Democratic Central Committee, Haywood prepared a *Vindication* that appeared in the Washington *Globe* of September 2, 1844. Haywood's essay was reprinted in Democratic newspapers throughout the Union. Another *Vindication,* this one published by the Nashville Democratic Central Committee, appeared about the same time as Haywood's pamphlet; Samuel H. Laughlin headed the Tennessee effort. For the text of the Nashville *Vindication,* see Mary Winder Garrett, "Pedigree of the Pollok or Polk Family, from Fulbert, the Saxon, (A.D., 1075) to the Present Time," *American Historical Magazine,* III (April 1898), pp. 157–90.

8. On June 22, 1844, William J. Alexander invited Polk to attend a mass meeting in Charlotte, N.C., on July 23. ALS. DLC–JKP. Ramsey's expression of preference for the Charlotte invitation alludes to the fact that Polk was born near Charlotte.

9. George W. Rowles, John H. Crozier, and William G. Swan. A Bradley County lawyer and Democrat, Rowles won election to two terms in the Tennessee House, 1841–43 and 1857–59. In the presidential campaign of 1844, Rowles ran on the Democratic slate for elector from the Third Congressional

District, which included Knox, Roane, Bledsoe, Rhea, Meigs, McMinn, Polk, Bradley, Hamilton, and Marion counties. Son of John Crozier, longtime Knoxville postmaster, John H. Crozier had numerous business, civic, and political interests in addition to his Knoxville legal practice. A Whig, he represented Knox County in the Tennessee House, 1837–39, and served in the U.S. House, 1845–49. A lawyer, Swan owned extensive real estate in Knoxville and served as district attorney general, 1851–54; as mayor, 1855–56; and as a representative in the Confederate Congress, 1861–65.

10. Arthur R. Crozier, David H. Cummings, and William A. Lindsay. Cummings was a Knoxville lawyer and Democratic party worker. An organizational meeting, held at Athens on June 9, 1844, appointed Crozier and Cummings "assistant speakers" for the election campaign in Knox County. A farmer and Knoxville businessman, Lindsay won election to one term in the Tennessee House, 1827–29. At the Knox County Democratic Association's meeting of June 15, 1844, Lindsay disavowed publicly his former connection to and support of the Whig party.

11. A Louisiana planter, Alexander Barrow served in the state legislature prior to his election as a Whig to the U.S. Senate, 1841–46. In a public letter to his constituents, dated May 24, 1844, Barrow explained his opposition to the Texas annexation treaty. He maintained that annexation would "involve the nation in an unjust war," that sugar and cotton prices would decline drastically, and that land in Louisiana would be significantly devalued.

12. Reference is to the Knoxville Democratic Central Committee.

13. See Cave Johnson to Polk, June 10, 1844.

14. State elections in Kentucky were scheduled for August 5 and 6, 1844.

15. Ramsey wrote his postscript on the inside fold of his cover sheet. His concluding reference is to Ezekiel Polk's commission as an officer in the Revolutionary War.


## FROM ROBERT ARMSTRONG

                                                              at night
Dear Sir                                          Nashville June 25 [1844][1]

I collected the Committee[2] to night and with the aid of A. V. Brown postponed our *mass* meeting untill Thursday 15 August.[3] After to night it could not have been well Controled. It is rather a troublesome affair now, but it must be done and *properly* done. The only reason I was in favour of the 24th July was that it was a short time before the Kentucky Elections and perhaps could have been made to do some good in that quarter.

Brown & Jones came on to night with Foster & Peyton.[4] All the accounts are first rate. It is impossible that their is any mistake.

Gadson[5] has come on from Charleston and gives a very good report. We must expect the *whole* south and *Cultivate* the north a *"little."* *Write* Harris to attend to the Union. Laughlin is still absent.

R. ARMSTRONG

ALS. DLC–JKP. Addressed to Columbia.
1. Date identified through content analysis.
2. Reference is to the Nashville Democratic Central Committee; the other two "central" committees for the Tennessee Democracy operated from Jackson and Knoxville.
3. See Andrew J. Donelson to Polk, June 14, 1844; and Polk to Cave Johnson, June 24, 1844.
4. Four members of Tennessee's congressional delegation, Aaron V. Brown, George W. Jones, Ephraim H. Foster, and Joseph H. Peyton, were en route from Washington City to their residences in middle Tennessee.
5. James Gadsden, a Charleston businessman, served in the War of 1812 and the Seminole War; he removed to Florida in 1821, served as a commissioner for the removal of the Seminole Indians, and gained a seat on Florida Territory's first Legislative Council. He returned to Charleston in 1839 and the succeeding year became president of the Louisville, Cincinnati, and Charleston Railroad Company. Appointed U.S. minister to Mexico in 1853, Gadsden arranged the purchase of a small strip of border lands south of the Gila River; the "Gadsden Purchase" would facilitate a more direct southern route to California, should such be the course chosen by Congress for the proposed transcontinental railroad.

## FROM J. GEORGE HARRIS

My Dear Sir,                                    Nashville June 25, 1844
I have this moment made up all my packages for Mr Bancroft,[1] and committed them to the mail. I have also sent to Columbia by Mr. J. Knox Walker[2] the nos. of Gales & Seaton's Reg. Deb.[3] of which you gave me a list, with *one* exception, which I cannot find. There are none of them in the Secretary of State's office—they have the Executive Journals, but not the Debates; nor could I find them in the late Mr. Grundy's library. The nos. sent are from the broken set with which you furnished me five or six years ago.

On Saturday night on my arrival here, I went immediately out home eleven miles distant. On Monday morning I came in and took my bundles up to Gen. Jackson who seemed to be in excellent spirits. I immediately made my business known to him when he said he would frank them with pleasure; and taking my arm walked into his private room where he requested me to sit down and write such a letter as I wished him to send to Mr. Bancroft. I did so, but with some reluctance and delicacy, as it was *my* notes of which he was to speak. He however promptly approved the draft by giving it his signature. As soon as it was done, after taking "a bite and a glass of wine" as the Old Hero called it, I returned, stopping at Donnelson's[4] a few moments, whose family I had not seen for more than a year. Donnelson inquired of me if you had written the Tariff letter[5] you had been thinking of writing. I told him I believed you had, and that it was of the old Jackson stamp. He said he was daily at work for you, but had not attended to something about which you and himself had had some conversation. I thought it would not be amiss, since Donnelson seemed to enjoy your confidence to request him to write a letter to Bancroft also urging him to prepare the history forthwith. He readily consented to do so by the next mail.

On arriving at Nashville that night I mailed all the bundles that Gen. Jackson had franked, writing a letter to Bancroft by same mail explanatory of the matter. Some-what fatigued by thirty-five miles horseback riding, and it being after ten o'clock, I put off attending to your letter by last night's mail[6] until this morning. The first thing I did to-day was to prepare the additional enclosures to Bancroft and to write him a more full and lengthy explanatory letter. I faithfully copied the memorandum enclosed in your last,[7] carefully noting all the additional references, and again referring to the main *points* of my previous notes. I also enclosed to him *both* of your messages to the Legislature[8] and invited him to the *Executive method* as exhibiting an Executive mind; together with the proceedings of the State Convention, &c. &c.

I believe now that everything is *square up* in this matter, and I expect to hear from Bancroft in a few days, of which I will advise you. Meantime if there be anything that I can do here of a special character I will thank you for your commands.

I have been away from my family so much for a week or two that I must go out to them to-night. I shall be in again day after to-morrow and stay a day or two, previous to which time please write.

J. GEO. HARRIS

P.S. Gen. Jackson was a good deal excited at Benton's course, said "he shall hear from *me* soon"; and insists that ever since the explosion of the big gun[9] Benton has not been in his right mind. I think so too.

Please present my compliments to Mrs. Polk; and if convenient excuse me to Gen. Pillow for not calling on him, and to Mr. Walker for not paying a parting call, in return for his attention. J. Geo. H.

ALS. DLC–JKP. Addressed to Columbia.

1. Harris hoped to persuade George Bancroft to write a campaign biography of Polk. See Aaron V. Brown to Polk, May 30, 1844; and Cave Johnson to Polk, June 10, 1844.

2. Joseph Knox Walker, third son of James and Jane Maria Polk Walker, served as private secretary to Polk during his presidency. Walker later practiced law in Memphis and represented Shelby and Fayette counties as a Democrat in the Tennessee Senate from 1857 until 1859.

3. Reference is to Joseph Gales, Jr., and William W. Seaton's serial publication, *Register of Debates in Congress.* 14 vols. Washington D.C., 1825–37.

4. Andrew J. Donelson.

5. See Polk to John K. Kane, June 19, 1844.

6. Letter not found.

7. Memorandum not found.

8. Polk's two "State of the Government" messages to the Tennessee General Assembly were dated and communicated October 22, 1839, and October 7, 1841.

9. Reference is to the explosion of the gun "Peacemaker" aboard the U.S.S. *Princeton* on February 28, 1844, by which Benton was badly shaken and several others were wounded or killed. See Aaron V. Brown to Polk, February 28, 1844.

## FROM RICHARD M. WOODS[1]

Greeneville, Tenn. June 25, 1844

Woods states that Democrats in Greene County will meet on July 1 to make plans for an East Tennessee convention scheduled for August 8 in Greeneville. He notes that local Democrats thank the Whigs for the name "Young Hickory" and adopt it with pleasure. Although he would be much gratified to have Polk's company on August 8, he thinks that "prudence forbids the invitation being given."

ALS. DLC–JKP. Addressed to Columbia.

1. Appointed U.S. marshal for East Tennessee in 1838, Woods held that post at least until 1843; he also served as sheriff of Greene County and as a trustee of Tusculum Academy.

## FROM GEORGE M. DALLAS

My Dear Sir,                                    [Philadelphia] 26 June 1844

We have recently been placed in a public relation towards each other that no doubt surprized us both. Fortunately the Convention, tho' acting without consulting their candidates, have not jostled on the same ticket men who can entertain any personal disrelish to their being associated. For my part, annexed as a bobtail to the great kite, I feel myself exceedingly flattered, as well by being connected with one whom I hold in most cordial esteem and respect, as by the prospect of being dragged upwards by his buoyancy. I had broken out for Polk clamorously during the twenty-four hours in which we had his name and that of Wright before us in this City; the next morning introduced another Vice, and deprived me thenceforth of the appearance of disinterestedness in maintaining the nomination, but could not silence me entirely. You may rest assured that, independently of my fate as a candidate being inseparably and subordinately tied to your's, no one in the Country more ardently wishes you success than I do. Indeed, if at any time, and owing to any cause, just or unjust, you find my companionship a drag upon your flight, pray cut me loose instantly and resolutely. Personally, I have not the slightest wish to quit the pursuits of private life; but politically, I should almost regard myself as criminal if I desired to be kept in the field, without having the impression that I was, in some manner and in some sections of the Country and of the party, helping on the chief and great object.

I have postponed writing to you in order to be able to speak with some confidence as to the condition of things here, and in the adjoining states. My office table had been daily crowded with letters and newspapers, from all parts of Pennsylvania, during the last three weeks; and I am quite sure that your nomination has been welcomed with an enthusiastic hurrah! from the entire democracy of the Keystone.[1] A more unanimous, firm, and resolved state of the republican party I do not remember ever to have witnessed. If you do not carry Pennsylvania by a majority considerably exceeding 20,000, it will be, because, unknown to any politician within her bounds, she has ceased to be a democratic and has become a federal state, or because the ultra Tariff is stronger than I conceive it to be and had deprived you of some 5 or 6000 votes. Nothing else can prevent your realizing in November an old-fashioned Jackson victory. As to pipe-laying, it will not dare to shew itself in the presence of Judge Lynch.[2]

I was going to tell you something about N. Jersey and Delaware; but take it for granted, on reflection, that I should only repeat what you will have heard from active and warm friends in both states. The description I have given of Pennsylvania applies equally to N. Jersey, where it seems almost conceded that our cause must triumph.

Of New York, I have admirable accounts from the *very best* sources. If the party be not greatly disturbed by the nomination of their Governor, the result is not doubted. As it was here, the candidates may fret and fume, and seem irreconcileable before the nomination is made, but once made, it heals all disorders.

There are several questions about which you will no doubt be interrogated, in every form and from various quarters. I explained to Genl.
Pillow those which might be made important by our adversaries in this
quarter. I know your natural disposition to pour out your sentiments
frankly and fully; and do not desire to intimate an opposite course. I
think your doctrine as to the Tariff[3] will impair your strength here
very little, if at all; and perhaps it is the matter on which brevity
would be the soul of wit.[4] The Bank, the Public Lands, Assumption
of State Debts, Texas, & Abolition are all matters as to which the
northern will chime with the southern democracy. From what I notice
at some of the southern meetings of our friends, it strikes me that
there is an unnecessary readiness to introduce another point; I mean
the controversy between Nativism and Naturalization. In our cities,
as you may have seen, this has worked itself into indiscriminating
ferocity.[5] Prudence would suggest that this controversy is as yet too
young and undefined to warrant a judgment on its merits.

I am myself, of course, averse to entering, at the call of any in-
quisitive correspondent, upon matters not perfectly and universally
settled. I have no idea of running the risk of doing harm to the only
really important matter, the Presidential ticket, in any quarter, by
dealing out my individual opinions.

It will give me great pleasure to hear from you, and whenever I have
something worth communicating, you must pardon me if I intrude a
few lines upon you. I beg you, when the opportunity occurs, to give
my devoted respects to Genl. Jackson, and to remember me kindly to
Maj. Donelson & Genl. Pillow.

G. M. DALLAS

ALS. DLC–JKP. Addressed to Columbia.
1. Reference is to Pennsylvania, the geographic "keystone" that for four
decades had locked together the political alliance of the Union's three largest
democracies, Virginia, Pennsylvania, and New York.
2. A few weeks before the presidential election of 1840, a Whig operative
named "Glentworth" was arrested and charged with voting frauds alledged to
have been committed in the 1838 New York gubernatorial election. According to Thurlow Weed in his *Autobiography*, Glentworth had received the office
of tobacco inspector as compensation for having recruited gangs of Pennsylvania laborers to lay water pipes between Lake Croton and New York City;
Glentworth's out-of-state pipe layers only worked on election days and in such
places as their illegal votes could be counted with safety. Dallas' second allusion refers to Charles Lynch, a Virginia justice of the peace celebrated for his
summary suppression of Tories during the Revolutionary War.
3. See Polk to John K. Kane, June 19, 1844.
4. Paraphrase of the quotation "Brevity is the soul of wit." William

Shakespeare, *Hamlet,* act 2, scene 2, line 90.

5. Armed conflict in Philadelphia between Protestant nativists and Irish Catholic immigrants in early May of 1844 produced several deaths and substantial property damage. In the wake of those riots, citizens of Philadelphia sent numerous memorials to Congress requesting that residency requirements for U.S. citizenship be extended from five to twenty-one years; Congress did not alter the naturalization laws during that session.

## TO ANDREW J. DONELSON

My Dear Sir:                                          Columbia June 26th 1844

I call your attention to an article on the first page of the Semi-Weekly Globe of the 17th Instant, headed *"South Carolina Mode of Annexing Texas."*[1] The extracts which are given from the South Carolina meeting, and newspapers, I think it was unnecessary if not of mischevous tendency to re-publish. They are only the opinions of a few persons, and do not embody the Southern sentiment on the subject of annexation.

My object in writing to you, is to suggest the importance, of preparing with care a proper article for the Union.[2] The idea of a Southern Convention or sectional meeting to be held at Nashville or elsewhere *must not for a moment be entertained.* In the article which I hope you will prepare for the Union, it will not be necessary to allude specifically either to the article in the Globe, or to the proceedings in South Carolina which it quotes. It strikes me that the object can be as well or better attained, in a rallying article, addressed to the Democracy of the whole Union, & calling upon, the North and the South, the East and the West, to attend the proposed mass meeting at Nashville in August. Let the article strongly enforce the leading idea, that a meeting of the masses from all sections of the Union, is what is intended, and let any thing giving it the appearance of a sectional or Southern affair, be expressly negatived. This would have the effect of allaying the fears of the North, by satisfying them that we in Tennessee gave no countenance to the suggestion for a Southern Convention, upon the Texas or any other subject.

I suggested to Armstrong in a letter on yesterday,[3] that the State committee of whom I believe you are one, should in a publication over their names, announce that the mass-meeting proposed embraced the whole Union, and invite our Northern friends to attend it. A paper of this kind would be published in the Democratic papers of the North, and would at once quiet all apprehensions. This would be better than an Editorial.

I think the mass meeting at Nashville in August, properly gotten up and conducted will do great good. I have no doubt *Wright, Cass* and others would attend it. Will you go to Nashville on receipt of this letter, see my letter to Armstrong & prepare the proper paper for the committee to sign, or the proper article for the Union, or both as you may think best. It is important I think that it should be attended to without delay. Let me hear from you.

JAMES K. POLK

ALS. DLC–AJD. Addressed to Nashville and marked *"Confidential."* Published in St. George L. Sioussat, ed., "Letters of James K. Polk to Andrew J. Donelson, 1843–48," *THM,* III (March, 1917), pp. 56–57.

1. Published in the daily Washington *Globe* of June 15, 1844, the article reviewed pro-annexation resolutions adopted at meetings held in Barnwell, Sumter, and Edgefield counties of South Carolina. The *Globe* noted that in reprinting the resolutions from the *Charleston Mercury,* the *Richmond Enquirer* had deleted all references to disunion. The *Globe* article chided John C. Calhoun and his supporters for thinking that threats such as "Texas annexation or disunion" would unite the Northern Democracy with that of the South in favor of Texas' annexation or Polk's election.

2. On July 2, 1844, the *Nashville Union* published an address issued by the Nashville Democratic Central Committee; the address stated that the mass meeting, scheduled to gather in Nashville on August 15, 1844, was being organized for the purpose of bringing together "democratic brethren, professing the same faith, having an identity of interests, living in every section of the Union ...." On July 4, 1844, an article in the *Union* repeated the theme that the August 15 convention was not sectional "in its objects, purposes and design, but *national in the broadest sense of the term."*

3. Polk's letter of June 25, 1844, has not been found; for Armstrong's reply, see Armstrong to Polk, June 28, 1844.

## FROM J. GEORGE HARRIS

My Dear Sir                    Near Nashville Thursday June 27. 1844

A few moments before I left Nashville, on the evening of the day before yesterday, I had a short interview with the Hon. A. V. Brown who had just returned from Washington, and whom you have no doubt since seen. Among other things he hinted at a call that was made on him the day before he left W., by the *real* John Jones of the Madisonian,[1] the object of which call was to suggest *something,* tho' rather indefinitely it seems, about my becoming an associate of his in conducting the Madisonian through the present campaign. He spoke of making such a proposition to me. You and I know very well that if such a proposition is to be made, it is by special advice from Head

Quarters, the advice of "the captain" himself,[2] who by-the-bye is, of course, not to be known or acknowledged in it.

The "captain's" *object* in all this is clearly seen. He wants to be handsomely wheeled into the democratic ranks, to co-operate with us on the Texan Question, and to return to his first love. Holding himself to be one of the Old Jackson men who went off for White, and who has uniformly declared that he never intended to go over to Clay and the federalists, he wants to make a *show of consistency* in rallying with all his "guard" for "Polk Texas & Democracy." He knows John Jones cannot wheel him in *decently.* He thinks, probably, that I could do it better. He knows that if he could be fairly and squarely and honorably *wheeled in* at this time, it would improve his political history and the history of his administration in the opinion of posterity. Of this there is no doubt. And I really believe "the captain" is disposed (since he cannot get the nomination himself) to give you a cordial support, if he can only see a straight path to travel.

But the idea of my being associated *publicly* and *in name* with the questionable identity of John Jones! It is amusing. He lacks judgment and energy, while he possesses neither editorial tact or talent. He is entirely unfit for the editorial chair of an official gazette. He neither knows, *when* to speak, *what* to say, or *how* to express it. He would ruin everything by ignorance and imprudence in management. He either knows nothing of our elementary principles, or knows not how to advocate and defend them. He is the last man who I should desire to be publicly associated with in a capacity so highly responsible. Nevertheless, if it were thought essential to the cause I would not shrink from even *that* post of duty in this great campaign.

How would such an arrangement affect the cause? It would wheel in "the captain's" forces *after a fashion,* but further than that it would not be productive of any very great benefit. The Madisonian is an *old hack* that has boxed the compass two or three times, and is now groaning under insupportable loads of heinous political sins; of *itself* it can have but little general influence in the country. John Jones is worse.

But Mr. Brown's suggestion has prompted in me a train of reflection, that I will here communicate.

Is it not essential that you should have a paper at Washington? Blair will give you all the support he can; *and that is not much* for *his heart* is with Benton. Like Benton he will give a *square* shoulder but it will be a *cold* one after all. Jones is Tyler's; the Spectator is Calhoun's. Now, suppose it could be arranged so that on the 20th of Aug. a new democratic paper should be started in Washington under a popular and imposing title, into which the Madisonian and Spectator should immediately fall with their subscription lists; and that this new paper should be devoted from that time to the election day almost *exclusively* to republishing the voices of press from every State of the Union, reflecting off to the people in a condensed form the national sentiment, thus expressed; or in other words to be the *heart* of the democratic press of the country receiving and sending out to the farthest extremities the life-blood of the party. I think the Spectator would agree to it. I think the Madisonian would agree to it on the ground that it should be conducted by those who would give the captain a fair chance, and defend his administration from the assults of the whigs, the common enemy.

A new, fresh, vigorous paper of this character, free from old broils and from all prejudice, would if properly conducted have all the effect that the captain would produce by uniting me in the management of the Madisonian; and what is of more importance than this, it would unite and strengthen all hitherto disaffected friends. It should start and continue upon the broad platform of our principles, avoiding detail and sectional issues, mainly devoted to a *reflection* of the national sentiment respecting our candidates and our cause.

When there was a sort of half way division among political friends in Massachusetts in 1838, and all attempts at *perfect* reconciliation had failed, I started the Bay State Democrat at Boston for *three months* before the Governor's election (the first *campaign paper* printed in the Union) and the *consequence was* (said Gov. Morton[3]) we made an increase of 17000 votes, and harmony & energy was completely restored. And *it strikes me* that some similar movement on a broader scale, would be of signal advantage at this moment, *under all the circumstances.*

The policy of it would be to *war with no one;* but to reinforce the enthusiasm throughout the country by cheering intelligence from all the States at every issue, not even war with enemy, unless in a few *main* points. And as for the Globe, &c., why strive to *outstrip them* in the good work. Would not a national paper of this character for three months before the election (if no longer) be at least *useful?*

How it could be gotten up, how sustained, or by whom it should be conducted, are matters that could no doubt be arranged satisfactorily. I have merely noted down some of the reflections produced by my short conversation with Mr. Brown.

My ideas may be crude and unimportant. I do not place a very high estimate on them myself. But I thought it would do no harm to note them down; and if you should think this long letter worth reading, they might be of some service to you when thinking of the subject to which they relate.

J. GEO. HARRIS

ALS. DLC–JKP. Addressed to Columbia.

1. "John Jones" was the editorial pseudonym used by Thomas Allen, publisher and editor of the Washington *Madisonian.*

2. John Tyler.

3. Marcus Morton, a Democrat, stood for governor of Massachusetts sixteen times between 1828 and 1843; he defeated Edward Everett in 1839 and John Davis in 1842.

## FROM ROBERT ARMSTRONG

12 O'clock

Dr Sir                           [Nashville, Tenn. June 28, 1844][1]

The Meeting for 15 Augt is arranged and the necessary preparations in progress &c.

The next Union will contain the address of the Committee &c.[2]

In all my little experience I have never seen things political brighten so fast. See the meeting at Castle Garden & Brooklyn.[3] See them every where. If we carry Kentucky in August, if Butler is Elected, Clay will not be the Candidate of the Whigs. Bell and Foster both at Franklin to day. I could get none of our men to go. Try and send Barkley Martin[4] in. I wrote him & he has not answered. We have meetings every night. Have 300 volunteers, a fine Band of Music, and in *Mass* Prominade the Streets. We have got them and they know it. We ought to have some strong man at Hopkinsville Ky on 10th July.[5]

R. ARMSTRONG

ALS. DLC–JKP. Addressed to Columbia. Polk's AE on the cover reads, "J. Geo. Harris Esqr and Genl. R. Armstrong." Harris' letter to Polk of June 28, 1844, was enclosed in Armstrong's letter of the same date.

1. Date identified through content analysis.

2. See Andrew J. Donelson to Polk, June 14, 1844.

3. On June 19 at Castle Garden in New York City, approximately eight thousand persons attended a Democratic mass meeting in support of the Democratic presidential ticket. A similar meeting in Brooklyn the following night drew about six thousand people. At both rallies Silas Wright, Jr., addressed the crowds; while praising the convention's choice of Polk and Dallas, Wright linked his own refusal of the vice-presidential nomination to his loyalty to Martin Van Buren.

4. A Columbia lawyer and politician, Barkly Martin served as a Democrat for three terms in the Tennessee House, 1839–1841, 1847–49, and 1851–53,

and sat for one term in the Tennessee Senate, 1841–43. He subsequently won election to the U.S. House and served from 1845 until 1847.

5. See Leonard P. Cheatham to Polk, June 22, 1844.

## FROM JOHN H. COOK[1]

Pendleton, Ind. June 28, 1844

Cook writes that Polk's prospects are excellent in Indiana, Illinois, and Michigan. He reports that Democrats in Ohio are hopeful that the abolitionists will abandon Clay and thus give Polk the win. Cook expresses doubts about such prospects, as most of the abolitionists are Quakers and Whigs.

ALS. DLC–JKP. Addressed to Columbia.

1. A former resident of Tennessee and a practicing physician, John H. Cook represented Madison County voters in the Indiana House in 1836; he ran unsuccessfully in 1850 for a seat in the Indiana Senate.

## FROM J. GEORGE HARRIS

Dear Sir,                                                    Nashville, Te. June 28. 1844

The idea given in your two letters[1] and which was referred to in your letters to Gen. Armstrong,[2] I plied my attention to immediately upon arriving in town this morning. In to-morrow's Union an *official* notice of the postponement[3] will appear, which I think is in proper *form,* assigning as a reason something that *every* mind will understand. In the *next* Union will appear the same notice accompanied by an address[4] embodying all your suggestions, and cordially inviting friends from every section of the Union. The Whigs are sick of the idea of making a *flare up* about the imprudent resolution at Beaufort S.C. and have postponed their meeting[5] to the latter part of next week. It will end in smoke. I have made a rough draft of the address that you suggested. I hope to see Donnelson[6] to-morrow; and have it preparred for Tuesday. Gen. Pillow's *guide*[7] is a good one; but I have enlarged upon it a little, embracing as I think some *strong* points. Every thing looks remarkably well. Kentucky is calling on us for aid at Hopkinsville July 11.[8] Cannot Maury send them a speaker? I enclose one of our badges.

J. GEO. HARRIS

ALS. DLC–JKP. Addressed to Columbia and enclosed in Robert Armstrong to Polk, June 28, 1844.

1. Letters not found.
2. Letters not found.
3. See Andrew J. Donelson to Polk, June 14, 1844.

4. See Polk to Andrew J. Donelson, June 26, 1844.

5. On July 6, 1844, Davidson County Whigs held an "Anti-Disunion Meeting... to enter their solemn protest against the desecration of the soil of Tennessee, by any set of men who are disposed to sever our glorious Confederacy, and, who propose to hold a Mass Convention in this city for that purpose." The Whigs denounced the Texas and Disunion resolutions of the South Carolina county meetings.

6. Andrew J. Donelson.

7. Reference probably is to an outline of Polk's campaign biography; Pillow's "Guide" is not further identified.

8. See Leonard P. Cheatham to Polk, June 22, 1844.

## FROM CAVE JOHNSON

Dear Sir,                                          Clarksville 28 June 1844

I recd. yours to day.[1] My directory is in my box of books that has not yet arrived.[2] I have written to Armstrong, suggesting, that the invitations[3] should be general; to the North, South, East & West, & that we might address private letters to distinguished speakers urging their attendance. Mr Brown could write to the South, I to the North & both of us to the West. There is danger if particular invitations should be resorted to that some of our friends may feel themselves neglected. This idea was suggested by S. W. Jr.[4] I also suggested a caution to the Genl.[5] as to the propriety of being cautious in the use of language as to the objects of the Convention. Nothing should be put in it, that by possibility could be construed into an adoption of the ideas of the South Carolina Conventions, that annexation or a dissolution of the Union must be the alternatives.[6] I also suggested to him that *propositions* might be made from Washington to place J. G. Harris at the head of the Madisonian &c &c because the relation he formerly bore to you, designed to create a rival establishment of the Globe, & urged him to permit no such move to take place.[7]

It is my intention at present to be at Columbia on the 13th July (the Barbacue given the delegates).[8] I suppose that you will not be present & if it suits your engagements I should like to meet you at Genl Jacksons two or three nights before. What he says & writes, is of vast importance & he should be made acquainted with all the facts. We are certainly safe, if we make no false move.

I think you should not undertake to answer all the letters you receive. You will have a load thrown upon you that will bear down any man.

Write me if you can go to the Genls at the time I suggest. If it be not entirely convenient I will of course see you before I leave Columbia.

I hope you will have the materials for your life soon ready. (Brown sd. he had urged it.) Bancroft will do it better than any other.

C. JOHNSON

ALS. DLC–JKP. Addressed to Columbia and marked *"private."* Polk's AE on the cover states that he answered this letter on July 1, 1844.

1. See Polk to Cave Johnson, June 24, 1844.
2. See Polk's postscript to his letter to Cave Johnson, June 24, 1844.
3. Reference is to invitations to the mass meeting of Democrats in Nashville held on August 15, 1844.
4. Silas Wright, Jr.
5. Robert Armstrong.
6. See Cave Johnson to Polk, June 10, 1844.
7. See J. George Harris to Polk, June 27, 1844.
8. See Polk to Cave Johnson, June 24, 1844.


## FROM SAMUEL H. LAUGHLIN

My dear Sir,                                   Nashville, June 28, 1844

My crippled arm rendering it very inconvenient to ride in the stage, I concluded after returning to Washington from Philadelphia, and seeing the body of the address[1] made to my satisfaction, to take the nearest and quickest route home. I came by the Mountains and river to Louisville, and then the stage by Bollingreen, Ky., &c. I left Washington last Friday, and would have made the trip in six days but for a fog that stopt the boat last Sunday night.

Nothing new had transpired at Washington when I left. I came with Sevier, Fulton, Labranch,[2] &c. They are most earnest and hearty in the cause. Fulton you know is, and I am glad to find Sevier equally warm. I was also pleased to learn from Fulton, that immediately after the nominations, Sevier took decided and warm ground, and had a principal hand in cooling down the momentary discontent of Hannegan. The fact is, Hannegan, Henley of In. and one or two others, who were much stronger for Cass than any of the Michigan men were, hoped, that if Cass succeded they would all be Secretaries and foreign ministers. This discontent is all dead now.

There is no appearance of excitement, zeal, or clamor for Clay, neither on the water nor on the land from here to Philadelphia. I speak comparatively and in reference to 1840. The Clay leaders are warm and noisy, but it produces no effect. There is no Clay flags hung out at towns, cities and boat-landings. I saw none between here and Philadelphia. At Elkton in Maryland and Brownsville Pa. long poles, true young hickory trees were planted, with green tops, and surmounted by green poke stalks of large size. At Wilmington, at a democratic association, I made one short speech and at Elkton, being at the close of a meeting, I said a few words, more as an apology for not speaking, and for the purpose of making grateful acknowledgements for my state, than the purpose of speaking.

Our friends at Cincinnati, some of whom I saw during a delay of a couple of hours, are in the highest spirits. Brough of the Enquirer[3] is perfectly confident of the result in Buckeyeland, as is Dawson, the latter not being now an editor.

At Louisville, where Our friends are bad off for a newspaper just now, the right spirit is up.

In my absence, I have made at least fifty important correspondents, that is men who will give information when asked, will write for it when they want it, and be active in circulating. A good number of these are in Missouri, Indiana, and Illinois. They will write to Dr. Robertson, chairman &c.[4]

Mr. Brown has gone on home, and left this county before I arrived yesterday evening. I brought on some things for him, which he had directed persons at Washington to send by me.

You will see Gen. Houston[5] as he goes through Columbia. I spent my last evening at Washington 'til a late hour with Mr. Chapman and Mr. Shields[6] of Alabama, the latter having been in the last Congress, and being an active man in this Canvass. He and Turner were the men that did most in getting Alabama to the right mark in Convention. Shields has gone to Philadelphia; and will return by Pittsburgh and Nashville, wishing to see the Old Chief,[7] and yourself as he goes home. I have promised, if things here permit, to go to Columbia with him when he arrives. Chapman will remain at Washington and in Virginia with his wife[8] til August. If a called session takes place he will remain til its end. He is useful; and prudently talks to Blair as he ought to do.

I suppose you have the few letters I troubled you with. I say troubled, because I know the press of letters you are compelled to read.

I left H. C. Williams[9] provided for by Mason, with a $1000 office, all he desired, and ready to serve us here in all things. In fact he is the *safest* man we have at Washington who lives there, whom we know and can trust.

I believe I wrote you that Blair had pledged his sacred word and honor to Boyd and others, to lay down all Benton & Calhouns jealousies, and go in like a man for the party, with his course. I think Blair will do it. We have great and pressing need for a Committee at Washington. I suppose Mr. Brown has told you *how* and *why* none was appointed formally in caucus. Chapman and Shields told me the particulars. If it had been pressed, there would have been an explosion. Rhett stays at Washington, and is keeping House, and supporting the Spectator.[10] We must not have a too certain, or a too open connexion with him, and that concern, nor any connexion or association but as men of the same party in a common cause, and for the causes and not for any thing future.

If I come down with Shields, before I return here, I shall have several things to consult you about. In the meantime, I hope the book[11] is in progress. Will Brown return to Washington and go East. In connextion with that matter, distinctly unwilling to have the slightest authorship except as a clerk in copying, and as stationary in connexion with any members of Congress or others who may be a corresponding Committee at Washington, I am willing, hard as travelling and the work will be, and little as I am able to bear the expense, yet if I can be spared from here for the whole or any portion of the summer and fall, I will be found ready and willing to make the sacrifice, if it is a sacrifice to do good at any expense, and go at any thing you may approve, or that Brown and Johnson may approve. Write to me immediately.[12]

S. H. LAUGHLIN

ALS. DLC–JKP. Addressed to Columbia and marked "Private." Polk's AE on the cover states that he answered this letter on July 1, 1844; Polk's reply has not been found.

1. Reference is to the drafting of the address or platform of the 1844 Democratic National Convention. See Laughlin to Polk, May 31, 1844.

2. Ambrose H. Sevier, William S. Fulton, and Alcée Louis La Branche. A planter and member of the Louisiana House, 1831–33, La Branche served as chargé d'affaires to Texas, 1837–40; won election as a Democrat to one term in the U.S. House, 1843–45; and received an appointment as naval officer at the port of New Orleans in 1847.

3. A locofoco Democrat, John Brough edited the Marietta *Western Republican* and the Lancaster *Ohio Eagle,* 1833–41, before becoming editor of the *Cincinnati Enquirer.* A leading Democratic newspaper, the *Cincinnati Advertiser* was purchased from Moses Dawson in 1841 and renamed the *Cincinnati Enquirer.* Brough served as state auditor of Ohio from 1839 until 1845; he subsequently left the Democratic party and won election as a Republican to the governorship of Ohio in 1864.

4. Felix Robertson, a physician, was the son of Nashville's founder, James Robertson. Elected mayor of Nashville in 1818, 1827, and 1828, Felix Robert-

son headed the Nashville Democratic Central Committee in 1844.

5. George Smith Houston of Athens, Ala., served in the U.S. House, 1841–49 and 1851–61; he later served as governor of Alabama, 1874–78, and as U.S. senator in 1879, the year of his death.

6. Reuben Chapman and Benjamin G. Shields. An Alabama planter, Shields served four terms in the Alabama legislature as a Democrat, 1835–38, before winning election to a single term in the U.S. House in 1841. He was appointed U.S. minister to Venezuela by Polk and served from 1845 until 1850; he was defeated in his bid for the Alabama governorship in 1851. Shields moved to Texas in 1854 and engaged in planting.

7. Andrew Jackson.

8. In 1838 Chapman married Felicia Pickett, daughter of Steptoe and Sarah Orrick Chilton Pickett of Limestone County, Ala.

9. A former resident of Franklin County, Tenn., an active party worker, and a clerk in the Fourth Auditor's Office, Hampton C. Williams was confirmed justice of the peace in the District of Columbia on June 11, 1844.

10. The Washington *Spectator*.

11. Reference is to preparation of a Polk campaign biography.

12. The last three lines of the letter and Laughlin's signature are written in the right margin of the letter's fourth and final page.


### FROM WILLIAM L. MARCY

My dear Sir:                                         Albany June 28. [18]44

Though you are undoubtedly burdened with letters I have thought you would be desirous of knowing the aspect of things in this state[1] and have taken the liberty to address you. No one could have anticipated the favorable reception the dem. nominations made at Baltimore have met with. Though there are many democrats in this state who differ from you in some degree on one or two subjects they all so far as I know not only profess but feel disposed to give the ticket a cordial support. I have not yet seen a single individual of our party who hesitates in his course. There is now as there always has been a diversity of opinion among us on the subject of the tariff. There are many branches of manufactures established in this state and those interested in them are in favor of high duties on foreign articles coming in competition with those made by themselves. Yet there are very few ultra tariff men among democrats. The whigs consider the tariff their best card and hope to make by it some division in our ranks but it will be much less than they expect. In regard to annexation there is a shade of difference between your views and the great body of the Dem. party. They generally concur in the sentiments of Mr. Van Buren on this subject, but this is viewed rather as a speculative question among us except with abolitionists. With the utmost efforts which the whig press can make our ranks will, as appearances now indicate, be very little disturbed by it. Indeed there is among all except only those who may have a tincture of abolition feeling a desire to have Texas become a part of our country but they would not have this desire gratified at the expense of national good faith or an act which should look like an aggression upon a feeble power, & they fear that immediate annexation would involve these consequences. Suffice it to say that the annexation question cannot be made a prominent issue in this state.

I have great hopes of success in this state and were we rid of domestic difficulties I should be very confident. We have a very upright Gov. who is serving out his first term and a large majority of the party are willing to give him a renomination but there are individuals in several counties of the state who have become dissatisfied with him without, as I conceive, any good cause and they are intent upon getting up another candidate. Their success I fear would be fatal to our prospects in the coming election, and if Gov. Bouck should as I think he will be nominated they may be unwise enough to oppose him & might thereby defeat his election. There is no sufficient cause for this state of things. This scism[2] does not & will not extend beyond the local tickets but in its consequences it may have an injurious effect upon the national nominations.

It is now quite certain that the whigs can not get up an excitement any thing like that of 1840. The gloss is worn off of Clay. The attempt to get up something like the log cabin *fooleries* has thus far failed; bankrupts are not now as they did in '40 paying the money which belonged to their creditors over to committees to be expended in bribery & corruption. It is true we shall have to contend with the money-power but that has always been the case.

There is another element to be taken into account in calculating upon the result in this state. That is the abolition feeling. For the two last years the abolitionists have had a distinct organization. Of the 400.000 votes in this state they cast nearly twenty thousand. It is now represented to them that the annexation question is a movement purely for the cause of slavery and Mr. Calhoun's mode of treating the subject gives plausibility to this pretence. Upon this consideration they may be induced to abandon their own distinct organization and cast their votes for the whig[s].[3] This ticket as to the Vice President[4] is very acceptable to [....] In this event our chances of success will be somewhat lessened. After all, my misgivings so far as I have any, as to New York arise from our local disentions. I have done & shall

continue to do what I can to allay them. Unless they assume a bad
shape our state will in my judgment give its electoral votes for the
democratic candidates.

Should the appearances essentially change for the worse or better
I will again trouble you. We shall certainly do our duty and I flatter
myself the result will be what the honor & interest of the country
require.

W. L. MARCY

ALS. DLC–JKP. Addressed to Columbia. Polk's AE on the cover states that
he answered this letter on July 9, 1844.
1. New York.
2. Misspelling of the word "schism."
3. Sealing wax oil has obscured portions of the text here and below.
4. Theodore Frelinghuysen served as Clay's running mate in 1844. A
lawyer from New Jersey, Frelinghuysen was state attorney general, 1817–
29; U.S. senator, 1829–35; and mayor of Newark, 1837–38. From 1839 until
1850 he was chancellor of New York University, prior to becoming president
of Rutgers College, a post he held from 1850 to 1862. Active in many organizations, he served as vice-president of the American Colonization Society and
as vice-president of the American Sunday School Union.

## FROM J. GEORGE HARRIS

*My Dear Sir.*                              Nashville June 29. 1844
I have a *new* subject to-day. Enclosed are *two* papers which will
explain all.[1] The first a mere *scrap of reflections* on the intimation
given me by Hon. A. V. Brown that a proposition similar to that of
the second would be made to me. The *scrap* was written *before* the
proposition was received; *before* I knew exactly what it would be. The
*proposition itself* does not *materially* change those opinions. It con-
vinces me *the more* of the importance of your having a *prudent* and
*reliable* organ at Washington, if possible. If the *name* of the press[2]
can be *changed,* as he[3] says it can; and he is disposed to make "any
editorial arrangement" with me for the campaign, the project is feasible, and with your approbation might be carried into effect. By a
glance at the *blue-book* you may have some idea of its *probable effect*
if judiciously managed. Its effect in other respects would in my judgment be still greater. Think of it *deeply* for an hour or two and write
me *frankly* and *freely* if you please. Do you intend to come down here,
or to Mr. Childress's in Williamson next week? If so, when? If not,
and this matter is of *any great importance* when can I see you? If any

thing is to be done it should be done without delay. Pardon brevity and Believe me ....

J. GEO. HARRIS

[P.S.] I have prepared the best address for the Come.[4] that I was capable making, profiting from all your suggestions. Donnelson[5] has taken it home to criticise it and cool it off a little at my request on tomorrow. It will appear in the next Union. Please return Jones's letter to me. I shall want to refer to it, in my reply.[6] I have made this known to *no soul* excepting our mutual friend Gen. Armstrong; nor shall I.[7]

ALS. DLC–JKP. Probably addressed to Columbia.
1. Enclosures not found. However, it is probable that one enclosure was Harris' letter to Polk of June 27, 1844, in which he notes his recollections of an interview with Aaron V. Brown on the subject of the Washington *Madisonian*. A second enclosure was a letter from Thomas Allen, who edited the *Madisonian* under the pen name of "John Jones." The exact date of Allen's letter is unknown. See below, Harris' postscript to Polk; see also Robert Armstrong to Polk, June 30, 1844.
2. Reference is to the Washington *Madisonian*.
3. Thomas Allen.
4. See Polk to Andrew J. Donelson, June 26, 1844.
5. Andrew J. Donelson.
6. The two preceding sentences were written in the right margin.
7. The last sentence of the postscript was written on the left margin of the letter.


## FROM ANDREW JACKSON

My dear Sir,                                    Hermitage June 29th 1844
I have this moment received your letter of the 24th instant[1] with Col. C. Johnsons of the 21st enclosed; and tho I am truly very unwell I hasten to answer & return Col. Johnsons letter herewith enclosed.

Whilst I thank you for the perusal of C.J. letter, I assure you it was not necessary to put me upon my guard. In my reply to Col Bentons first letter to me,[2] in which he adverted to my tost, "The Federal Union must be preserved," amonghst other things, I said to him, *"The Federal Union must be preserved"* and to do this effectually & permanently, Texas must be reannexed to the United States, the laws of the Union extended forthwith over the Oregon, which would place this Federal Union on as permanent bassis as the Rockey Mountains, and preserve our Glorious Union, & our Republican System as long as time lasted.

I found from his letter, that his hatred to Calhoun & his Jealousy of the growing popularity of Tyler had deranged him. I undeceived him in all, had a sincere desire to preserve him if I could politically, but I am now convinced that it was him & some others that led Van Buren into his unfortunate Texas position. More when I see you. Nothing but a Mass meeting should be held. You will perceive I have estoped Benton or any others from believing that you or I could countenance nullification or disunion. Every letter I get gives us Joyfull news. You will get 20 states at least & your one term principles I think will get you 22. The Texan question must be kept up with energy and firmness. In haste ....

ANDREW JACKSON

P.S. Every democrat must put his face against any meeting of *Disunion,* or nullification. We must & will have Texas, with & in our *glorious Union.* The Federal Union must be preserved. A.J.

ALS. DLC–JKP. Addressed to Columbia. Published in Bassett, ed., *Correspondence of Andrew Jackson,* VI, pp. 298–99.
1. Letter not found.
2. For Jackson's letter to Benton of May 14, 1844, in reply to Benton's letter of May 3, 1844, see Bassett, ed., *Correspondence of Andrew Jackson,* VI, pp. 291–93.

## FROM JOHN K. KANE

My dear sir,                                        Philada. 29 June 1844

I received yesterday your two letters,[1] and have shown them to our friends Dallas and Horn. They unite with me in thinking that the one which gives your views of the tariff question will do much good, and we propose therefore to publish it early in the week. Mr. Clay's Raleigh Speech[2] has just reached us: the coincidence of his language with yours on this topic is such as to leave his party without excuse for assailing you.

I do not myself think that we are to lose any thing in Pennsylvania in consequence of any difference about minor questions. We have rallied as a party, and the men who have come back to us are too happy in their deliverance from whiggery to fly off again for trifles.

J. K. KANE

ALS. DLC–JKP. Addressed to Columbia.

1. See both of Polk's letters to Kane of June 19, 1844.

2. Touring the state of North Carolina, Henry Clay delivered on April 13, 1844, a major political address in Raleigh on the fundamental differences between the Whig and Democratic parties; the Washington *National Intelligencer* of June 29, 1844, printed Clay's post-delivery revision of the speech.

## FROM ROBERT ARMSTRONG

Dear Sir,                                           Nashville 30th June [18]44

Harris writes you by the mail of to night and encloses a letter from Jones of the Madisonian.[1] Mr. Tyler wishes to draw off as easily as posible and Jones is not the *man* to cover his retreat and bring him & *friends* safely in. Therefore Jones makes the proposition to Harris for *your official* paper[2] in case of your Election (of which there is no doubt). They see it. I expected from information received by Genl. Jackson that Mr. Tyler was paving the way back & to decline. I have no faith in a backing and filling politician, but their is *much* in this proposition and I deem it very Important for you if properly persued and carried out in the right *hands*.

Blair is in very bad health and if the *three* papers could be consolidated it would be a great move before the Election, and secure every thing to go on safely afterwards. If a friend of yours from Nashville was to take the Madisonian and merge the Spectator, the Globe and its friends perhaps would complain. We wish nothing to divide us now, every thing depends on Harmony.

Do you expect to be in shortly? Harris ought not to take any course in this matter without a full understanding.

I expect their was something like *an* engagement for some such kind or arrangement as Harris came on[3] but of this I know nothing. The arrangement as *now* proposed is Important. You ought to think of it.

We are in a blaze here and have the Whigs down and will keep them so. What is most mortifying to them is that we beat them at *every* thing.

Depend on it Butler will be Elected in Kentucky, unless Clay turns a new Trump. Tuesdays Union will contain the arrangements of the Committee for 15 August.[4]

R. ARMSTRONG

[P.S.] Harris wants to see you on Tuesday. He can go out.

ALS. DLC–JKP. Addressed to Columbia. Polk's AE on the cover states that he answered this letter on July 1, 1844; Polk's reply has not been found.

1. No letter dated June 30, 1844, from J. George Harris to Polk has been found; but see Harris to Polk, June 29, 1844.

2. Thomas Allen, who edited the Washington *Madisonian* under the pen name of "John Jones," had urged J. George Harris to become his co-editor and thereby link Polk informally to the newspaper and in turn to its principal patron, John Tyler. See J. George Harris to Polk, June 27 and 29, 1844.

3. For the terms of Harris' employment as editor of the *Nashville Union* in early 1839, see Polk to Harris, December 27, 1838.

4. See Polk to Andrew J. Donelson, June 26, 1844.

# July

## FROM ANDREW J. DONELSON

Dr Col.                     [Hermitage, Tenn.] Monday July 1st 1844

You will get the circular embodying your suggestions respecting the project for a Southern convention in the Union of this evening.

I was disposed to treat the tariff as one of the pretexts of the Federal party for assailing you as a sectional man, thinking that the occasion would be a good one for some general remarks in relation to your views. But this part of the circular has not been retained. A majority of the committee doubted the propriety of saying any thing on the subject.

I did not send you my ideas about a tariff, because I could not have prepared them soon enough for your purpose; and on reflection I did not doubt that you could better hit off what was proper than any one else. I have written many letters for the General,[1] omitting only up to this time the hint to Mason.[2] That will be attended to tomorrow.

Every thing goes on smoothly. The Whigs are frightened, your friends bold and confident.

Col Williams of Mississippi[3] says that he will take up the cudgels for you warmly in that state.

Genl Jackson has health enough to help you materially by letters to his old friends in Penna. He does it cordially. The only fear is that zeal on his part may produce too much in the shape of correspondence.

With my kind regards to Mrs. Polk I remain....

A. J. Donelson

*303*

ALS. DLC–JKP. Addressed to Columbia.

1. Andrew Jackson.

2. Reference probably is to Andrew Jackson's subsequent suggestion to John Y. Mason that John Tyler withdraw from the presidential contest; Jackson and Mason later served as spokesmen for Polk and Tyler respectively in arranging the Tyler connection's return to the Democratic party.

3. A planter in Pontotoc County, Thomas H. Williams sat for a brief period in the U.S. Senate as a Democrat, 1838–39; later he served as secretary and treasurer of the University of Mississippi, 1845–51.


## FROM BENJAMIN B. FRENCH

Dear Sir,                                    Office H. Reps. U.S. July 1. 1844

Yours of the 20th June[1] was recd. this morning, and it gives me pleasure to comply, as far as possible, with your request.

I cannot obtain a Directory of the 3d Session of the 27th Cong. I enclose those of the 1st & 2d Sessions, together with one of the 1st Sess. 28th Cong.

All our information here, from all parts of the Union, is most cheering. The nominations at Baltimore are responded to with a unanimity which, to me, is a sure harbinger of success.

No man in this country is *naturally* a Federalist; all Americans *are born* Democrats, and it is only by some temporary diversion of public opinion from its natural channel, that the democracy of the Union can be beaten. A peculiar operation of certain political events upon the public mind, caused such a diversion in 1840, and, connected with the most unblushing frauds, at the ballot box, enabled the whig party to get up a hurra and obtain a short lived triumph. The political stream has now settled back into its natural channel, and men wonder how they were so imposed upon 4 years ago. They now see clearly the true democratic course, and, by it, they are determined to move on to victory.

As a very slight evidence of the difference of feeling here, I will state, that in the summer of 1840, the whigs determined to build a log cabin, and it rose on Pa Avenue, almost like the fabled palace of Aladdin, amid the firing of cannon and the shouts of the multitude.

Two or three weeks since the Clay Club here resolved to build a Club House. It was commenced, day after day passed, & there stood the bare frame with, perhaps a dozen boys & two or three men at work upon it as if they were enged[2] by days works for the summer. The steam of 1840 could not be got up, the inspiration of hard cider was wanting, and for two weeks the chances were at least even against the completion of the building. But, by degrees, it rose in *all the grandeur* of unplaned scantling and rough boards to the height of some ten feet, was roofed in, and there it stands, a disgrace to the City and to those who built it.

This is one example of the difference between the whig enthusiasm of 1840, & at this time.

God defend the right, as he will, & we shall conquer.

*Any* commands from you will be most cheerfully attended to.

B. B. FRENCH

ALS. DLC–JKP.
1. Letter not found.
2. French probably intended to write the word "engaged."

## TO CAVE JOHNSON

[Dear Sir,]                                        Columbia, July 1, 1844

I received your letter of the 28th to day. All your suggestions are sound and accord with my own opinions. I write now to say that it is important you should be here on the 13th Instant, at the dinner to be given to the Delegates, electors, and members of Congress. *Coe* has been written to and I have no doubt will come.[1] Our friends desire to make it the occasion of holding a consultation and laying down the plan of the campaign in the State, and of coming to an understanding of the part each is to act. There is another reason why you should come and bring as many as possible with you. It is this. The Whigs are making extensive preparations to have a *grand rally* here (at my door) with a view to effect abroad.[2] Our friends desire very much that ours shall be a great meeting, otherwise the Whigs will give it out that it was a failure and that there is no enthusiasm at home. There is still another reason why you should not fail to come. You have been several times invited here and have never attended. Our whole democracy are exceedingly desirous to see you. You must come to my house the night before the meeting. It will be impossible for me to meet you at Nashville or the Hermitage at the time you suggest. I have said to our friends that they could make it public, that you would *certainly* be here. I suggest that you answer their letter immediately, that it may be published some days in advance of the dinner.

[JAMES K. POLK]

PL. Published in *THM*, I, p. 246. Addressed to Clarksville and marked *"Confidential."*
1. Letter not found.

2. Reference is to a mass rally held by the Whigs in Columbia on August 27, 1844.

## FROM JOHN K. KANE

My dear sir,                                                    Phila. 2 July, 1844

I send you two of our Whig papers of today,[1] that you may see how your letter on the tariff[2] affects your opponents. With your friends here, its influence is altogether happy. I have a letter this morning from Mr. Buchanan, in which he says: "I have this moment seen the Pennsylvanian, and I congratulate you upon your agency in bringing Col. Polk out on the question of the Tariff. His letter removes all difficulties from his way in Pennsylvania, and ensures him the State by a large majority. I had thought of writing to him myself on the subject. The Whigs are busy in every quarter of the State on the Tariff question; but this letter will cast a damper on their efforts."[3] Mr. B. then passes to another subject, but adds at the close of his letter: "But I sat down merely to express the pleasure which I feel, that Mr. Polk has gone as far as he has done on the question of the Tariff. I do not see how it can injure him even in the South." Another letter, which Mr. Dallas received at the close of last week from Mr. Muhlenberg, after declaring that under all circumstances Penna. is safe, went on to say that the only thing, which could mend our prospects, would be a letter from you, admitting the policy of "discriminating in favour of home industry by provisions in a tariff for revenue."

I have no doubt from all that I see and hear, (and my correspondence is extensive in our State,) that your majority will go beyond 15,000. Our friends say, much more; but I am content with our *full* party majority, and that is little beyond what I have named.

I have appointments for the stump for the next five or six weeks, which will enable me to observe personally the party feeling on this side the Susquehanna; but I am sure it is wholesome.

I forwarded a copy of your letter to Pittsburg in time for the celebrations of the 4th.

                                                             J. K. KANE

ALS. DLC–JKP. Addressed to Columbia.
1. Enclosure not found.
2. See Polk to John K. Kane, June 19, 1844.
3. James Buchanan's reference is to his having seen the text of Polk's tariff letter to Kane as printed in the Philadelphia *Pennsylvanian*, the leading Democratic newspaper in the state.

## FROM GIDEON J. PILLOW

Govr.                                    [Maury County, Tenn. July 2, 1844][1]
    I hand you by Mr. Estes,[2] a letter upon the subject suggested
tonight.[3] Dispose of it as you deem best. I do not think any prejudice could be done by the publication of *the* Letter, but still I would
Somewhat prefer it should not be published.
    I will write to Gill[4] tomorrow & to Some other Gentlemen at a
distance when I come in next day.

                                            GID. J. PILLOW

P.S. The more I have thought about *that* matter referred to in the
Communications from W—n,[5] the more thoroughly I am convinced
that your views are right. But as the *door* is now *opened* it is of
the *first importance to enter* & *occupy.* H.[6] ought therefore *at once by
all means* to go forthwith to W. and never leave till *all's fixed.* The
necessity of the entire arrangement being *Confidential,* is to apparent
to need any suggestions upon that subject. The great thing to be
affected is to get T.[7] to give *ground* & come to us which *can* be done
I presume. Make H. come out *here immediately.* G.J.P.

    ALS. DLC–JKP. Addressed locally.
    1. Date identified through content analysis; see note three below.
    2. Not identified further.
    3. Pillow's reference is to his letter to Henry Horn and John K. Kane of
July 2, 1844. ALS. PPAmP. In this letter Pillow states that Polk wishes to
withhold publication of his tariff letter to Kane of June 19, 1844, if same has
not already been published.
    4. Not identified further.
    5. Reference is to a suggestion by Thomas Allen of Washington City that
J. George Harris become associated with the Washington *Madisonian;* Harris
interpreted Allen's proposal, first made through A. V. Brown, as an effort to
facilitate John Tyler's withdrawal from the presidential race.
    6. J. George Harris.
    7. John Tyler.

## FROM WILLIAM KENNON, JR., ET AL.[1]

                                St. Clairsville, Ohio. July 3, 1844
    A committee appointed by a Democratic meeting held on June 22 at St.
Clairsville, Ohio, invites Polk and George M. Dallas to appear with David
Tod[2] at St. Clairsville on September 2 or on such date as may be convenient.
The committee reaffirms its opposition to a national bank, tariff protection,

assumption of state debts, and distribution of land-sale revenues. The committee states its support for "a revenue tariff, a frugal administration, the veto power, a strict construction of the constitution ... and the reannexation of texas to this Union." A postscript signed by Kennon requests that Polk reply by August 1.

LS. DLC–JKP. Addressed to Columbia. Polk's AE on the cover states that he answered this letter on July 17, 1844, and that he replied to Kennon in a separate letter. Polk's reply to Kennon was dated July 10, 1844.
1. Signed by William Kennon, Jr., and four others. A St. Clairsville lawyer, Kennon served one term in the U.S. House, 1847–49; he was a cousin of William Kennon, Sr., also a resident of St. Clairsville and a three-term member of the U.S. House, 1829–33 and 1835–37.
2. David Tod, a Democrat, ran unsuccessfully for the Ohio governorship in 1844 and 1846, served as U.S. minister to Brazil from 1847 to 1851, and in 1862 won his third race for the governorship of Ohio.

## TO JESSE MILLER

My Dear Sir:                              Columbia Ten. July 3. 1844
I have received your two letters of the 1st and 20th ultimo and should have answered the former earlier but for other engagements which have occupied my whole time.[1] I thank you for the valuable sugestions which they contain. I am gratified to hear that the prospects of the Democracy in the Key-stone state are so flattering. In the whole south and south-west as far as I have learned our party are perfectly united, and I have no doubt we are now stronger than we have been at any time since Genl. Jackson's second election. Our Democracy in this state are confident of success: they are roused to the most energetic action and I have never known so fine a spirit prevail.

I have transmitted by to day's mail my answer to an invitation of a committee of my democratic friends at Harrisburg to visit Pennsylvania, which I hope may be satisfactory.[2] Since my nomination I have received numerous invitations of a like character, from various parts of the union, all of which I have declined, to accept. Indeed they have been so numerous that if all other objections had been removed, it would have been physically impossible to have attended to all of them. To all of them I have placed my *declination* upon the same ground that I have done to your committee. I think my democratic friend[s] will see the propriety of my course, and will duly appreciate the motives which produced it. And moreover my observation has been, that a traveling candidate for the Presidency is more likely to injure than to bennefit his party. I shall remain quietly at home and leave the decission to the people.

I shall be pleased my Dear Sir, to hear from you often during the canvass, and to receive from you any sugestions which you may deem useful.

JAMES K. POLK

L, copy. CSt-V. Addressed to Harrisburg, Penn., and marked *"Private."*
1. Miller's first letter was dated May 31, not June 1, as Polk indicated.
2. Polk's reply was addressed to John B. Bratton et al. L, copy. DLC–JKP.

## FROM DUTEE J. PEARCE [1]

Newport, R.I. July 4, 1844
Pearce reports that although Rhode Island Democrats are organized, Clay is certain to win the state. He expects that Clay will win Massachusetts and Vermont only "by the intervention of their respective legislatures." Polk will carry Maine, New Hampshire, and possibly Connecticut.

ALS. DLC–JKP. Addressed to Columbia. Polk's AE on the cover states that he answered this letter on July 18, 1844; Polk's reply has not been found.
1. Dutee J. Pearce, a Democrat and lawyer from Newport, R.I., won election to six terms in the U.S. House, 1825–37.

## TO FRANCIS O. J. SMITH

Dear Sir: Columbia Tenn. July 4th 1844
I received some days ago your letter of the 9th ultimo, and should have answered earlier but for the pressure of other indispensible engagements which have occupied my whole time.

It will be a source of sincere gratification to me, if the unsought and unexpected position in which my Republican friends have placed me, shall have a tendency to heal our dissentions, and restore harmony and union to the action of the Democratic party. None would hail with more joy than I would the re-union of all the old Jackson Democrats of '28 & '32, with whom I co-operated for so many years in maintaining our common cause. If my political friends shall succeed in electing me to the Presidency, I shall assume the high trust, with the firm purpose of maintaining my principles, and certainly with no prejudices or unkind feelings towards any portion of the party. My great desire would be to see Democratic principles [1] prevail in the policy of the Government, and with that object in view to witness an harmonious re-union of the whole party. I have thus frankly expressed to you my feelings and desires upon the points refered to in your letter. [2]

I do not wish to appear unnecessarily before the public, and therefore I have marked this letter *private,* intending it for your own individual satisfaction.

JAMES K. POLK

ALS, draft. DLC–JKP. Addressed to Portland, Me.; marked *"Copy"* and *"Private."*

1. Here Polk cancelled the words "firmly re-established in" and interlined the words "prevail in the policy of"; Polk's original word choice implies that under John Tyler's administration Democratic principles had lapsed.

2. Here Polk concluded his paragraph and began a new one, the first eight lines of which were cancelled; this extended cancellation reads as follows: "You state that your friends in Maine who have 'kept aloof' from us in late contests 'have always refused to amalgamate' with our political adversaries or to make any sacrifice of principles, and trust that in the event of our success in the present contest, the 'more auspicious days and circumstances' to which you refer will have returned."

## FROM SUTHERLAND S. SOUTHWORTH[1]

New York City. July 4, 1844

Southworth states that Polk's prospects in New York are encouraging. Polk's letter to Kane[2] has been republished in New York, giving "unusual satisfaction." Southworth also promises to keep the *Nashville Union* advised of New York events, but he asks that his name be kept secret, as he holds office in the New York Custom House.

ALS. DLC–JKP. Addressed to Columbia.

1. Formerly a newspaper correspondent in Washington City, Southworth also wrote for newspapers in Baltimore, Philadelphia, and Boston; during the 1844 campaign he wrote for the *New York Aurora;* Southworth's post in the customs service is not identified further.

2. See Polk to John K. Kane, June 19, 1844.

## FROM ROBERT ARMSTRONG

Dear Sir                                                      Nashville July 5. [18]44

We had a night of it last night, a grand display. The Whigs are Confounded and give it up. I told Harris to write you and give you a description.[1] Our *own* friends had no thought of our preparations, of Transparencies[2] &c. &c. All was done in fine order. The city in a blaze, and all life with fine speeches from Nicholson and Ewing. I am arranging to send 200 Texan volunteers Equipt  & the Company of *Hickory Dragoons* with the Bands of musicians, and all the Transparencies out on the 13th.[3]

Nicholson agrees to go to Kentucky 11th.[4] I would be glad you would send me all the Evidences &c. of the service of your grand father[5] in the Revolution. This Question is stirred in Kentucky and you will recollect that Genl Jackson was assailed in every way. I hope you will feel no delacacy about giving the Statements, Certificates of Service &c &c. Nicholson will take it over with him and prepare and article on his return and put it to *rest.*

We are gaining here every day. The Whigs know it and feel themselves *whiped.*

The arrangement of the Madisonian (for Harris)[6] I fear would do injury at *present,* if agreed upon at all. Great care should be taken that the *North* are Satisfied.

Secure the *Globe* first and then merge the Madisonian & Spectator. Their is great danger in Jones[7] proposition tho. it is very Important to Our Party that something of the kind takes place.

It is 12 Oclk. In haste....

R. ARMSTRONG

ALS. DLC–JKP. Addressed to Columbia.

1. Arnold S. Harris, a resident of Arkansas, was Armstrong's son-in-law; see Harris to Polk, July 5, 1844.

2. Transparencies were boxed display signs illuminated from within. In this instance, a Democratic militia company carried the transparencies as it paraded in formation before the assembled crowd.

3. Reference is to preparations for the Democratic mass meeting in Columbia on July 13.

4. Reference is to a Democratic mass meeting at Hopkinsville, Ky.

5. Ezekiel Polk.

6. J. George Harris.

7. Reference is to Thomas Allen, who wrote under the pseudonym of "John Jones."

## FROM ARNOLD S. HARRIS

Dr Sir                                   Nashville July 5th 1844

We had a glorious night on the anniversary of our natl. independence. The democratic boys of Nashville are engaging in the contest with a zeal and hearty good will that must achieve a glorious victory in Tenn. I never saw such determined fellows in my life. I wish the people of the whole union could but see them and hear them. I think the enthusiasm would be contagious and the torrent irresistable.

About 8 o'clock in the evening a procession of 5 or 600 (without ex-aggeration) formed on Broad street and marched up to the square with brilliant transparences borne aloft—*twenty six stars,* each on a sepa-rate standard, strung along for several hundred yards. In the rear came the lone star larger and more brilliant than any in the galaxy. On one side was "Polk, Dallas & the Constitution." On the other, "Extend the Area of Liberty." The procession marched around the square, increasing as it went and tried to get into the Court house but it would not hold half of them. They then formed out side and Mr. Nicholson opened with the best Texas speech I have yet heard. He laid the question so plain before them & took the proper grounds—Clay dead against it, Polk for it and that it was now U.S. and Texas vs. Great Britain and Mexico and for the hardest send off, his hits were happy and all in all the most effective and argumentative speech I have heard. Mr. Ewing came next and scored the whigs dreadfully on their cry of *disunion.*[1] I think the *disunion effort* will recoil terribly on the whigs. Gov Jones[2] disclaims all participation in starting it—so does Jennings[3] —they will all do so soon, but they cannot escape the consequences. Ewing was terrible on them and really was eloquent. He charged home on them, their Adamses, Giddings[4] &c. and the Mas-sachusetts resolutions.[5] The shouting was long, loud, and in earnest. A few more such meetings and the courage of the Whigs is crushed even here in their strong hold. If the other parts of the country and throughout the union will do but half as well as your Tennessee boys, victory is sure.

I leave tomorrow for the east, passing through Ohio, to Buffalo and so on. I will take pleasure in writing to you from all points and will give you the true state of the case, as far as I can ascertain and my humble judgement goes. I have a very extensive acquaintance in NY, and can *pick up much item,* to use an Ark phrase.

A. HARRIS

ALS. DLC–JKP. Addressed to Columbia.

1. Beginning on June 26, 1844, the Nashville *Republican Banner* ran a se-ries of editorials insinuating that Polk and the Democratic party of Tennessee advocated Texas annexation or disunion, an extremist position first espoused in public meetings by South Carolina Democrats.

2. James C. Jones, a Wilson County farmer and one-term member of the Tennessee House, 1839–41, served as a Whig presidential elector in 1840. He defeated Polk in the Tennessee gubernatorial elections of 1841 and 1843. In 1850 Jones moved to Shelby County and became president of the Memphis and Charleston Railroad. He was elected as a Whig to one term in the U.S. Senate, 1851–57, but supported James Buchanan for the presidency in 1856.

3. Thomas R. Jennings, a Nashville physician and member of the medical department of the University of Nashville, served as a Whig member of the Tennessee Senate from 1839 until 1845. In 1844 he served as a Whig presidential elector for Tennessee's Eighth Congressional District.

4. Reference is to John Adams, John Q. Adams, and Joshua R. Giddings. A lawyer and abolitionist from Ohio, Giddings served in the U.S. House from 1838 until 1859; during his lengthy congressional career he changed his party affiliation from that of Whig, to Free Soil, and finally to Republican. Giddings resigned his seat on March 22, 1842, following a 125 to 69 vote of censure against him for his resolutions defending the British ministry's refusal to return the American brig *Creole* and its mutinous slaves. Giddings won re-election that same year and returned to Congress on December 5.

5. See Cave Johnson to Polk, January 13, 1844.

## FROM SAMUEL H. LAUGHLIN

My dear Sir,                                    Nashville, Tenn. July 5, 1844

I received your favor of the 1st instant[1] on the next day after it was written, and have been complying with its intimations as far as opportunity has permitted. There are two old men in Warren, who knew your Grandfather, and, I believe, all your ancestors in N. Carolina. Some time since, I caused an editorial statement to be published at McMinnville according to the substance of their statements.[2] I had intended to have gone home this week to spend a day and night with my father and children, but when I learned from your letter that you had forwarded to Dr. Ramsey the proofs in regard to your Grandfather's course in the Revolutionary war, which I supposed he would forthwith publish in the Argus, I concluded to postpone my intended visit until I should see the publication.[3] As I intend, it being one purpose of my visit, to take the depositions of Smith[4] and others when I go home on the subject, I had better have the other testimony before me. These statements then can be made perfectly corroborative, and all discrepancy avoided. In some instances, where all the witnesses speak the perfect truth in substance, a small seeming contradiction, amounting to nothing of itself, impairs the weight and clearness of the whole. The moment I receive the paper in which Ramsey may publish, I will proceed to take the other proof, and publish it also. But for fear Ramsey may not publish soon, please send me a genealogical list of your ancesters (paternal) back to your great grandfather, and note particularly any incidents you may have collected of your grandfather who is falsely implicated. Say where he lived, who he married, when and where he died &c. Upon that I can take the proof plainly and strongly without Ramsey's publication. I have not the paper in which

Ford published the facts, written by myself, as stated by the witnesses. The witnesses are both men of the first respectability. Their credit I will also prove by Gen. Smartt, Gen. Shields &c.[5]

Letters of invitation, many of them accompanied by private letters, to our 15th of August Convention, have gone out in all directions, most of them filled up by Capt Harris, Gen. Armstrong's son-in-law. I procured a Congressional Register of the present Congress and brought it home with me for such use as the State Committee[6] and myself might have for it. I found, however, that Judge Catron had furnished one already, and that A. V. Brown or G. W. Jones, had marked the names of all democratic members of Congress &c.

I have sent some blank invitations to H. C. Williams, for the heads of the democratic Association at Washington, Hoban[7] &c. and to Old Henry Horn of Philadelphia in whom you have a most sincere and zealous friend. I have had invitations sent to Judge Sheffer,[8] with whose son in law, Gen. Bittinger[9] of Preble Co Ohio, I formed a good acquaintance coming down the Ohio. I think I exchanged cards with about fifty gentlemen of different states, for purposes of correspondence, during my absence. I have had letters addressed to these.

I have seen no conversion to our ranks that has pleased me more than that of Gen. Geo. W. Crabb of Tuscaloosa.[10] It is true, we could have done without him in that state, but he brings many with him, and it shows the strength of our cause.

I have commenced upon Foster and Jarnagin for their vote against the Zoll Verein Treaty.[11] I hope to make something out of it in the two articles I have written, one of which, in nearly two columns, is in type.

The fourth of July came off gloriously with us. We are daily making converts here.

I have an article written, though possibly it may be postponed in tomorrow's paper, in favor of foreign emigrants, their right to naturalization without delay of 21 years, and showing the opposing policy of both parties in regard to Aliens and foreigners since 1798. The oppression of foreign emigrants, settled among us bona fide, had more influence in producing the civil revolution of 1800 than is generally supposed. It is a good subject,and we have made votes by it here. I made it the principle matter of a speech the other night.

Williams writes that the fire burns stronger and stronger at Washington, and Col. Davenport of Lawrenceburg,[12] has written an order, and sent by a wagon to buy on his own account, and send out by the wagon, a six pound cannon for the use of the democracy of his county. In Cannon, a ratification meeting has been held. They are waiting in

Warren for me to appoint a time when I can go up. In Coffee I will have the thing done, and in DeKalb. I must try to be at them.

The subscriptions to the Star Spangled Banner are coming in at the average rate of 100 pr. day.

Write me the information asked in former part of this letter forthwith. I am charged with Hon. Henry Horn, and Hon. D. D. Wagener's respects[13] to Madam Polk, which you will please communicate with those of your friend.

S. H. Laughlin

P.S. I think Donelson made the Committees publication of their invitation, and vindication of the call of the Mass meeting, a very good article.[14] The Southern statesmen, McDuffie, Colquit, Pickens &c will all come. We must bend our efforts to get the northern men here to help us to hatch treason.[15] Is there any baseness of falsehood too low and mean for whiggery to stoop to.

The Texas Volunteers here now amount to enough for *four* companies. Their uniform is handsome. We will be down at Maury,[16] *en potence* as Gen. Harrison said of a movement of his army at the Thames.[17] Make my respects to W. H. Polk and Gen. Pillow. I had no knowledge of Pillow's worth, his moral worth, feelings, and energy, and whole-soul'd devotion to his friends, 'til I travelled and served with him. S.H.L.

N.B. Old Mr. Fain writes me that Orville Bradley[18] is for you. When will wonders cease!

ALS. DLC–JKP. Addressed to Columbia; franked by Andrew Johnson; and marked "Private."

1. Letter not found.

2. Reference is to affidavits by John Smith and Thomas Gribble affirming that Ezekiel Polk was a loyal supporter of the American revolutionary cause; Laughlin's editorial statement, probably placed in John W. Ford's McMinnville *Central Gazette,* is not identified further.

3. Laughlin's father, John Laughlin, removed from Virginia to Warren County, Tenn., in 1829; Laughlin's children residing in Warren County in 1844 were Samuel Houston Laughlin, John James Laughlin, Andrew Jackson Laughlin, Sarah Louise Laughlin Smartt (Mrs. Thomas Calhoun Smartt), and Mary Laughlin Argo (Mrs. T. P. Argo). Publication of J. G. M. Ramsey's vindication evidence in the Knoxville *Argus* is not identified further.

4. John Smith of Warren County, Tenn.

5. George R. Smartt and Alexander Shields. A farmer in Warren County, Smartt was one of the founders and owners of a summer resort at Beersheba Springs, Tenn.; he served as a Democrat in the Tennessee House, 1843–45. Shields, a McMinnville merchant, is not identified further. A statement tes-

tifying to the good character of John Smith and Thomas Gribble was included in the *Vindication* pamphlet published by the Nashville Democratic Central Committee in 1844; Smartt and Shields, along with Jesse Locke, L. D. Mercer, Thomas H. Hopkins, and William L. S. Dearing, signed the testimonial.

6. Nashville Democratic Central Committee.

7. James Hoban received a recess appointment from Polk in 1845 to be U.S. attorney for the District of Columbia; Hoban died before the U.S. Senate acted on his nomination.

8. Daniel Sheffer served as associate judge of Adams County, Penn., from 1813 until 1837; a Democrat, he served one term in the U.S. House, 1837–39.

9. Not identified further.

10. Having won election to the Alabama House, 1836–37, and Senate, 1837–38, George W. Crabb served as a Whig in the U.S. House from 1838 until 1841. His deceased brother, Henry Crabb, had been a member of the Nashville bar and a justice of the Tennessee Supreme Court. George W. Crabb renounced the Whig party and Henry Clay at a mass meeting in Tuscaloosa, Ala., on June 22, 1844.

11. Reference is to a commercial treaty signed in April of 1844 by the United States and the Zollverein, or German Customs Union, which had been formed in 1834.

12. An early Giles County settler, Thomas D. Davenport moved in 1821 to Lawrenceburg in Lawrence County, where he engaged in farming. An unsuccessful Democratic candidate for Congress in 1833, Davenport subsequently served two terms in the Tennessee House, 1835–37 and 1843–45.

13. A businessman and banker in Pennsylvania, David D. Wagener served in the U.S. House as a Democrat from 1833 until 1841.

14. Reference is to an invitation to a mass meeting in Nashville called for August 15 by the Nashville Democratic Central Committee.

15. Reference is to Whig charges that Democrats in the South planned to secede from the Union should Texas annexation efforts fail. The appearance of George McDuffie, Walter T. Colquitt, and Francis W. Pickens at the Nashville mass meeting, without the presence of equally prominent leaders of the Northern Democracy, would lend credence to the notion that the Nashville rally was a Southern convention, not a genuinely national gathering.

16. Laughlin's reference is to a Democratic mass meeting scheduled to convene in Columbia on July 13, 1844.

17. At the Battle of the Thames, October 5, 1813, William Henry Harrison attacked the British and Indian forces "en potence," a French phrase describing a military formation in which the flank is formed at an angle to the main column of horse.

18. Nicholas Fain and Orville T. Bradley. A Rogersville merchant and postmaster, 1823–39, Fain won election to the Tennessee House for two terms, 1839–43. He was the father-in-law of George R. Powel. Reared in Hawkins County during its early settlement, Bradley inherited large tracts of land from his family; he studied law under Hugh L. White and supported his mentor for the presidency in 1836. Bradley served as a Democrat in the Tennessee

House, 1833–35, and in the Tennessee Senate, 1835–37, but after 1836 joined the Whig party and backed William H. Harrison for the presidency in 1840.

## FROM WILLIAM TYACK

New York City. July 5, 1844

Tyack reports on his campaigning in New England and tells Polk that "the People were not well acquainted with your Merits," but assures him that Eastern Democrats are united behind him. He predicts that Democrats who voted for the American party in the New York City spring elections will return to regularity and give Polk a "powerfull Majority in the fall." Tyack disclaims the story that the Tyler men in the New York City Customs House have been promised job retention in return for supporting Polk.

ALS. DLC–JKP. Addressed to Columbia.

## FROM GEORGE BANCROFT

My dear Sir,                                                    Boston, July 6 1844

The last time I had the pleasure of conversing with you was the fine frosty morning when, after our long interview,[1] we took a quiet walk, just before you were leaving the scene of your fourteen years' service for the arduous and to you most glorious campaign of 1839. I watched your progress with intensest interest, made the more near & personal by the zeal of our friend Harris; & I shared in the exultation that followed your unexampled success.

My eye was immediately turned towards you for the service of the nation, & our Massachusetts Democracy which at any rate has to rely on firm opinions & men to meet the immense opposition of the proudest & wealthiest aristocracy in our country, & which at all times has the hearty sympathy of its friends in New England, very readily received & acted upon the suggestion of rallying around you on the ticket with Van Buren. The convention of 1840 most unwisely did not make the nomination & by that neglect greatly weakened the ticket.

This year before the assembling of the national convention of which body I was delegate for the state, I did not fail to put myself in correspondence with friends of New Hampshire & New York and other states; and while some friends of Mr V.B. seemed to think that R. M. Johnson should be nominated V.P., I took every occasion to express the opinion, in which I found afterwards, that Gen Jackson coincided, that the choice should fall on none other than yourself. Mr. Wright of New York[2] encouraged me in concentrating opinion on you.

At the convention I immediately exchanged a few words with our friend Gen. Pillow, of your neighborhood, who conducted himself throughout with the modesty and firmness, which deserved highest commendation; & I renewed my old acquaintance with Gen. Donelson. I was able to assure them that on the first ballot for V.P. Massachusetts would certainly throw ten, probably twelve votes for Yourself.

You know the events of Monday & Tuesday. On Tuesday many of my friends gave way to despair. Cass was gaining. The R. M. Johnson & all doubtful ones,[3] were ready to join him; this would have swelled his vote to 157, and then it would have seemed factious to have held out. It flashed in my mind, that it would be alone safe to rally on you. This I mentioned to my friend Mr Carrol of Concord New Hampshire,[4] who fell in to it heartily. We spoke with Gov. Hubbard; he agreed; & the N.H. delegation were fixed. I then opened the matter to our excellent friend Gov. Morton of our delegation & he coincided & his coinciding was very important, and then went to your faithful friends Gen. Pillow & Donelson. They informed me that if we of N.E. would lead off, they would follow with Mississippi & Alabama & some others. Mississippi hesitated.

Certain of this I repaired with Gen Donelson & Pillow to the house where were the delegations of Ohio & New York. & I spent the time till midnight in arguing with them. Mr Medary saw the bearings of the matter & before I left the hotel assured me his delegation would go for Polk rather than for Cass. With many of the New York delegation I spoke; but opened the matter most fully to our friend *Gouverneur Kemble*,[5] who I think was in Congress with you. You may suppose that the N.Y. delegation was in a great state of agitation. Kemble was calm and decided. After hearing me at length, he[6] gave in his adhesion decidedly to my view of the Duty of V.B.'s supporters; & such were his statements, that I returned to my lodgings.

I returned to my lodgings before midnight tranquil & happy. I enjoyed as quiet sleep as you did on the night before your journey to Warrensburg.[7] In the morning I saw my friend Frick, state delegate of Maryland, who heartily came in to the scheme, & Pillow I believe and I certainly spoke with the principal delegate from Louisiana, who was at once hearty on the course.[8]

It came to voting. You should have heard the cheers as Hubbard for N.H. & I for Mass announced, he the whole vote of NH, I the majority of Mass. But the thing that pleased me most was, to see the Virginia delegation, all vehement for Cass, taken aback, and I had a feeling of triumph as I saw Roane lead out his Virginia train to consult, & return to announce a change of the vote from Cass to yourself.[9]

On reaching home, I met my constituents in Faneuil Hall, the largest Democratic meeting I ever saw there[10]; they listened to my tale for an hour & a half, and broke the silence only by bursts of delight at the nomination.

By the special invitation of our N.H. friends I went to their great ratification meeting,[11] where I found your hearty & ardent friend Franklin Pierce, a man of true metal, a fine fellow, when in Congress with you; but improved in talent & power by assiduous culture. Here was the same enthusiasm.

Day before yesterday I was at Worcester; a great gathering; & but one heart.

You will be pleased I am sure to know that Mr Van Buren most heartily in conversation & with his pen zealously advocates your election. Yesterday I received from him a long letter, from which I quote confidentially the following words.

"The success of the nominees is of vital importance to the country. That they will succeed I have not the slightest doubt. In this state, unless we get into a distracted snarl about our Governor (which I do not anticipate) our success will be very great. It is not possible that our friends could be more zealous."

I have just received a manuscript sketch of your life by J. G. Harris. He proposes to me that I should revise it, should make an elaborated biography of three hundred pages & print the volume as my own. Now on the score of explaining & supporting your democratic opinions & canon & your public & private character, I have not the least hesitation, doing it constantly before very large audiences. But several reasons prevent my writing a volume at this time.

1. I have been interrupted in my pursuits by *the Baltimore convention & ratification* meetings, so that I am in arrears. I am at this moment publishing a volume of the History of the American Revolution,[12] & am sure you would frown on me, if I should assert I could [...][13] if I would, put it aside. My engagements with the printers, publishers & the public will not permit it. My time is so filled up, that I am obliged to use every minute of it, being at the head of our State organization, and constantly pressed into service as a public speaker. To write your life as I think it ought to be written would require at least two months close & undivided study.

2. You are on the point of being elected President. To say of you less than should be said, would be an injustice. To say all that you deserve, if written by me at this moment, would be set down as mere worship.

3. The Democracy of the country will take care of this election and

as one of them I have done & will do my part; but as a writer, I can aid your reputation best only by some work of a permanent character, and addressed to the forum of Humanity.[14]

You can have little leisure to write; were you to find a moment's time, I should be charmed to receive a letter from you. But at any rate, you may rely on the enthusiastic & determined support of the Democracy of New England.

G.B.

ALI, draft. MHi. Probably addressed to Columbia. Extract published in M. A. DeWolfe Howe, *The Life and Letters of George Bancroft* (2 vols.; New York: Charles Scribner's Sons, 1908), I, pp. 251–55.

1. Here Bancroft cancelled the words "in Mr Grundy office."

2. Here Bancroft cancelled the words "was clearly of the opinion that if R.M.J. could be avoided, the convention should concentrate" and interlined the words "encouraged me in concentrating opinion."

3. Here Bancroft cancelled the words "some of the Pen[nsylvania]."

4. Henry H. Carroll, formerly a law student under Franklin Pierce, edited the Concord *New Hampshire Patriot and State Gazette;* he served as one of the secretaries of the 1844 Democratic National Convention.

5. A New York cannon manufacturer, Gouverneur Kemble sat in the U.S. House from 1837 to 1841. He was a delegate to the state constitutional convention of 1846 and to the Democratic National conventions of 1844 and 1860.

6. Here Bancroft cancelled the words "said to me he was in favor of a decided move not an uncertain one; told me frankly he adopted my views, and informed me the next day, that he had been compelled in the consultations of their delegation to take the lead and give the decision."

7. Reference is to an anecdote in Polk's campaign biography, the authorship of which Bancroft attributes to J. George Harris. At the close of his 1839 gubernatorial campaign Polk made a quick and arduous journey from Nashville to East Tennessee to contest the efforts of his opponent, Newton Cannon. On the night prior to his Warrensburg debate with his rival, Polk is said to have "enjoyed the first night of undisturbed and quiet rest" of his journey. A portion of the Polk campaign biography, including the "Warrensburg anecdote," was published in the *Nashville Union* on September 4, 1844.

8. William Frick, a delegate representing the Western Shore of Maryland, was a vice-president of the 1844 convention. Collector of customs at Baltimore from 1837 until his removal by Tyler in 1841, Frick later served in the Maryland legislature and on the bench of the Court of Appeals for Baltimore County. Bancroft's reference to the "principal delegate from Louisiana" may have been to Gilbert Leonard, a delegate from the state at large. Mentioned as a possible U.S. senatorial candidate in 1844, Leonard was killed in a duel later in the year. On the convention's eighth ballot, which was the first ballot on Wednesday, Maryland gave Polk one vote, while Louisiana gave him all six of its votes.

9. On the eighth ballot Polk received all six of New Hampshire's votes and seven of Massachusett's twelve. Virginia gave her seventeen votes to Cass. Following the balloting, the Virginia delegation "asked leave to retire for consultation." After speeches, the ninth ballot proceeded with most of the larger delegations being passed over until the Virginia delegation had returned and announced its vote for Polk. When New York switched, Polk's nomination was certain.

10. The Democratic ratification meeting in Faneuil Hall was held on June 4, 1844.

11. Bancroft was a principal speaker at the New Hampshire ratification meeting, which was held in the State House yard at Concord on June 6, 1844.

12. The first two volumes of Bancroft's *History of the American Revolution* were published in 1852.

13. One or two words are illegible.

14. Here Bancroft cancelled the following words: "4. On the eve of an election I would not make an authoritative statement of your opinions, but after it."

## FROM GEORGE M. DALLAS

No. 2

My Dear Sir                                    [Philadelphia] July 6, 1844

Your letters of the 20 & 27 June[1] have been duly received, the latter yesterday morning. As I intend writing to you with the utmost freedom, whenever I have any thing to say, I will not also inflict upon you mere bulletins of courtesy to acknowledge the receipt of yours. Bye-the-bye, as it occurs to me just now, let me suggest the expediency of our taking a simple and practical method of being sure that we receive each others' letters without fail and in their proper series. I am very little given to suspicion; and yet, in bad times, some security may not be superfluous. By merely numbering each letter, as this is, the objects are obtained.

I think, as all our friends here think, that you have been eminently happy in your two published letters, of acceptance and on the Tariff.[2] As to the one term resolution, in the first, nobody would have liked to suggest it, and it has come from yourself most gracefully. I certainly could not have counselled it, because I disapprove its principle; but I agree that there are occasions when in order to attain numerous and paramount objects, expediency alone must be consulted for a guide on a single and subordinate one, especially in deciding as you have done.

I spent the 4th of July at Reading, expecting, as it turned out, not merely to meet my friend Mr. Muhlenberg and his neighbors, but to meet many others from the northern and middle counties of our State at the celebration of the anniversary. A better feeling never prevailed. The whole State Democracy is united and cordial. Their meetings are all thronged and all enthusiastic. The tide of song and shout and zeal had suddenly turned against the Whigs. Your young hickories shoot up almost spontaneously in every direction. Converts are hourly declaring themselves; many of them I personally know; all of them have a certain local importance. Mr. Muhlenberg is obviously beyond all danger.

Your Tariff letter, which proved to be exactly what I had predicted from my recollection of your speeches on Verplanck's bill in 1832, has given entire satisfaction. All the gentlemen at Reading were content. One of its paragraphs has taken so much that it will be engraved on the reverse-side of a medal in process of manufacture representing our two heads in profile. It was the only point on which solicitude was felt. Mr. Kane was peculiarly fortunate in placing it in direct association with an extract from Mr. Clays Raleigh Speech. The two things are identical, and greatly annoy your assailants. However, a story once begun is never retracted by party and politics, and we shall have to keep up an endless battle on this topic. The letter of Genl. Pillow to Mr. Horn[3] I was apprehensive might weaken the simple force of your short creed, and therefore advised that it should not be used just now, and when used, that it should be converted into an editorial.

The German Society in New York addressed me also. I have not replied and, unless you desire it, I will not. We certainly cannot avoid agreeing, in condemning a party[4] founded on religious intolerance and civil proscription; but, as I urged upon Dr. Horner,[5] one of our most eminent physicians and surgeons, who is a Roman Catholic, and who called on me to enquire my sentiments, if the whole course of the Democrats, from the foundation of the Government down to the present moment, is not a sufficient guaranty as to the liberal spirit and principle of the party on this very subject, I could not imagine that any individual assurance would be effective. You might as well be called upon to subscribe afresh to the Declaration of Independence, or to give a written repudiation of the union of Church and State. I told Dr. Horner that he should not have, except that argumentatively, my personal opinions, as I was really a secondary candidate, and would not incur the risk of affecting the Presidential Ticket by a single vote. He said there were in this district, 5000 Catholic voters prepared on this ground, to move, for or against, as one man; and he had doubted whether they ought to exercize the right of suffrage at the next election, and until the two great parties shewed their hands decidedly. I convinced him very promptly, of the extreme folly of such abstinence, but concluded by telling him that if his own intelligence did not convince him that there was but one truly liberal and generous party in its principles and measures, and that that was the party entitled to the votes he referred to, he would certainly not be persuaded by any views or arguments from me. He said that he appreciated and approved the motives upon which I refused to let him have my sentiments, explicitly and for communication to others; and he supposed it would be necessary to write to you. This is the most formal and urgent call I have had upon the subject. I remain still of the opinion expressed in my former letter, that we owe it to our friends in New York and here not to be too prompt in answering the catachism on this topic.[6] In a little time, the matter will be better developed and the fever cooled. Even now, the prevailing opinion of the day is that the steam is subsiding in this City; the procession of the 4th of July having exhibited much less numerical and infinitely less moral force than was looked for.

You will find, my Dear Sir, that, without adverting to them in detail, I shall carefully and cheerfully conform to your several suggestions in practice.

Genl. Jacksons letter to Genl. Plauché reached here today; and like every blow he strikes, it has produced a strong impression here.

I am strongly persuaded and as strongly dissuaded, on the score of paying visits to various parts of the country. My impression is that the Party would, on the whole, be better pleased at our remaining tranquil.

G. M. DALLAS

ALS. DLC–JKP. Addressed to Columbia.

1. Letters not found; for an extract from the June 20 letter, see *The Collector,* LXII, p. 237.

2. See Polk to Henry Hubbard et al., June 12, 1844; and Polk to John K. Kane, June 19, 1844.

3. Gideon J. Pillow's letter to Henry Horn is not identified further.

4. Native American party.

5. A member of the University of Pennsylvania's medical faculty from 1816 to 1853, William E. Horner left the Episcopal Church and converted to Catholicism in 1839.

6. Dallas expressed his view on the nativist issue in his letter to Polk of June 26, 1844.

## TO CAVE JOHNSON

[Dear Sir,]                         [Columbia, Tenn.] July 6, 1844

I write mainly to urge upon you that it is on many accounts very important that our *mass-meeting* here on the 13th Inst. should be well attended from a distance. This is the place of my residence: —the Whigs here are making great efforts to have a *grand rally* of their part[y]¹ at this place (at my door) shortly after ours is over. If our meeting on the 13th should not be well attended it will be given out that it was a *failure* and was evidence of want of enthusiasm in Tennessee. There will be a great disappointment if you do not. Come prepared to make one of the main speeches. It will be expected. Bring Garland, Chase² and as many others with you as you can prevail on to come. There is no other point in the State so far as effect abroad is concerned, that is half so important as this. You must impress this on your friends. You must yourself be at my house on Friday the 12th. There will be speaking on Friday night and Saturday and Saturday night, and at Spring Hill on the way to Nashville on Monday. The Nashville and Gallatin military companies have promised to attend. You will of course say nothing to any one about my having written to you on the subject.

[JAMES K. POLK]

P.S. We fear we may be scarce of speakers and on that account *Garland* and *Chase* must come with you. *Nicholson* and *Bartly Martin*³ will be at Hopkinsville Ky. on the 11th and they will go from Tennessee.

PL. Published in *THM*, I, pp. 246–47. Addressed to Clarksville and marked *"Private."*
1. Bracketed word-completion supplied.
2. Hudson S. Garland and Lucien B. Chase. A native of Virginia, Garland studied law at the University of Virginia prior to establishing a law practice in Clarksville, Tenn., where he took an active part in local politics; he was a son of James Garland. Chase practiced law in Charlotte, Tenn., until 1843, when he removed to Clarksville and formed a law partnership with Willie B. Johnson; Chase won election as a Democrat to two terms in the U.S. House, 1845–49. At the end of his second term he moved to New York City.
3. A. O. P. Nicholson and Barkly Martin.

## FROM LEVIN H. COE

Somerville, Tenn. July 7, 1844

Coe regrets that his speaking schedule will not permit him to attend the Democratic mass meeting at Columbia on July 13. He reports with optimism about Democratic prospects in Mississippi and in Tennessee's Western District. He expects the Texas question to hurt the Whigs in Shelby County. Coe discusses his campaign itinerary, including plans to debate Gustavus A.

Henry; notes in passing that Stanton and Topp[1] are beginning a debate tour; and describes a Democratic meeting held in Somerville on the previous day.

ALS. DLC–JKP. Addressed to Columbia. Polk's AE on the cover states that he answered this letter on July 16, 1844; Polk's reply has not been found.

1. Frederick P. Stanton and Robertson Topp. A lawyer, landowner, and railroad promoter, Robertson Topp represented Shelby County in the Tennessee House from 1835 through 1839; in the 1844 election he was the Whig presidential elector for the Tenth Congressional District of Tennessee.

## FROM JACOB M. McCORMICK[1]

Tompkins County
Dear Sir        Post Office Ithaca July 7th 1844
I mail with this Letter a Speech Delivd. by Senator Miller of New Jersey and a Speech Delivd. in Congress by the Hon Mr Stephens of Georgia.[2] These Speeches as well as Other Documents are Distributed Extensively in this State Under the Frank of Mr. Jarnagin U.S. Senator from Tennessee. I forward them that You & Your Friends May be apprizd. of the Course Your Honorable Senator is pursuing in Distant States from the One he Represents. It would Seem To Me that this Hon Senator Does Not Truly Represt the good people of His State, *Even the Whig portion.* While writing I would Remark that the Nominations at Baltimore are Extremely well Recd. in the Empire State. More particularly in Western New York where I am Most acquainted. If I am Not Very Much Mistaken in the Signs of the Times New York will give One of her Old Democratic Majorities. There is Most perfect Unanimity and the Best of feeling. Not So with the whigs or Federals. Changes are Constantly going On from the Whig to Democratic party. The Election in Your State Takes place Early in August.[3] We feel great Solicitude for the Result. Will You Yourself or will You cause Some One to give me Such Information as Can Reasonably be given of the Probable Result from Time to Time and the Most Early Result?

Your Letter On the Tariff[4] has Just Reach Us through the papers. This Letter Relieves Us of Much Labour in Defending You from the free Trade Notions Charged on You by the Whigs. This and the Texas question are the Main Hobbies of Our Opponents. On the Tariff Your Letter is a Damper and the Texas question is gaining Strength. Many of Our Friends have hesitated Coming Out in Vindication of the Annexation. Where Ever it has Been Done we gain Strength and I have No Doubt it will be the Strong side of the question, Even at the North & East.

What is The Prospect of Kentucky? Will Our Friends Sustain their Present Position in that State in Congress?

J. M. McCormick

ALS. DLC–JKP. Addressed to Columbia.

1. McCormick served as deputy postmaster of Ithaca, N.Y.; named to his post by John Tyler in 1843, he was reappointed in March 1847.

2. Jacob W. Miller and Alexander H. Stephens. An attorney in Morristown, N.J., Miller served as a Whig in the U.S. Senate from 1841 until 1853. Stephens, an attorney from Crawfordville, served both in the Georgia House, 1836–41, and in the Georgia Senate, 1842; from 1843 until 1859 he held a seat in the U.S. House, initially as a Whig and later as a Democrat. During the Civil War, he served as vice-president of the Confederate States of America. He was elected to the U.S. Senate in 1866, but was denied his seat. In 1872 he returned to the U.S. House and served in that body until 1882, when he was elected governor. Stephens served but a few months in that capacity and died in 1883. McCormick's enclosures have not been found or identified further.

3. Tennesseans elected their governor, legislature, and congressmen on the first Thursday of August every odd-numbered year; in 1844 they selected their presidential electors on November 5.

4. See Polk to John K. Kane, June 19, 1844.

## FROM ALFRED BALCH[1]

At Genl Rogers[2]
My Dear Sir,                    near New Castle Delaware 9th July [18]44

I reached Guyandotte more than a month ago, travelled on to Richmond, and all the way made anxious enquiries about the state of public feeling with reference to the pending Presidential contest. Virginia will most certainly cast her electoral vote for you. Colquitt, Belser, Weller, Chapman[3] all of Congress and myself addressed a very large and enthusiastic audience at Richd.[4] Ritchie has not the remotest doubt of the result in the old Dominion. Private business took me to Fredricksburg and on arriving there the Democratic association invited me to speak which invitation I accepted. The crowd was large and profoundly attentive & respectful. The subjects of discussion were The annexation of Texas & the Tariff. And by the way this latter question engrosses much of the public attention in Va and the people are willing to hear you upon it for hours. After detaining my audience at Fred. upon it for an hour and twenty minutes, I said I feared I should weary them when they cried out go on we will hear you about this Law all night if you can hold out.

This week I am to speak in Wilmington in reply to Jno. M. Claytons lying infamous speech made to a mass meeting & published ten days ago in the Intelligencer.[5] I found my presence both in Richd. & Fredricksburg valuable from the fact that I could speak from personal knowledge of you and the details which I gave were listened to with the most intense interest and were recd with thunder gusts of applause.

The greatest and most important of all secrets in a great political contest is to know the real strength of the enemy. First I will state what our strength in the north and middle states really is. Beyond all possible question we shall carry Maine, New Hampshire, and Pennsylvania. The other N. England states will go for Clay. In N. York the contest is furious and doubtful. Neither party can hope to succeed by a majority of more than 10 or 12 thousand and the number of votes cast will not be far short of half *a million*. From what I saw & heard in Cincinnati & other towns of Ohio I count her vote to be doubtful and that of Ky. not at all so. Michigan will give her vote to you, by a sweeping majority. Your chance in Little Del. is good and improving. In the lower part of the state there are very many who bear your name, who say they are of the same stock and who are respectable as well as active. In Maryland my native state, there are large nos of John Adams Federalists. The Whigs are sly & active in that quarter and are pouring out their money like water. But your friends are meeting them every where with courage and high hopes.

I travelled in a steam boat as I came on with a large no of whigs. They were boasting that they would even carry Ten and were sure of her. To stop their mouths I stepped up to the crowd and said I will bet you gentlemen 5000 dollars that Ten will give her vote for Polk. They all declined & said not another word. Those sedate thinking men whom I have seen from N. Carolina say, that the result there is doubtful for which I feel the deepest regret because her general election comes off the first of the coming month.[6] The loss of Saunders in 40 was a fatal blow struck at Van Buren. Still we shall think it strange if every man in Mecklenburg County does not support you except some 50 or 100 black mouthed Clayites. The Whig majority in the old North State is not large and therefore may be overcome. In N. Jersey both parties are sanguine and exceedingly active.

After a calm review of the whole ground over which I have travelled within the last six weeks, with free access all the time to our leading & most efficient *enlightened* friends, I believe that a triumphant victory is within our grasp and that our success will depend mainly upon a *bold untiring unceasing activity for the next one hundred days.* It gives me pleasure to say that every where that I have been, this activity sustained by the most buyant hopes prevails. We are greatly relieved by the fact that we have no *defences* to make which would have been necessary in Van Burens case, and that we are left free to charge upon our adversaries without stint. In Pen and particularly at Phila I did not see a single Whig who did not admit that Muhlenburg will be elected Govr, nor a single Democrat who did not boldly claim for him a majority varying from 15 to 25,000.

It is deeply to be regretted that North Carolina could not be brought out decisively for you but there prevails there a quiescence which amounts almost to apathy on the part of the Democracy. If she were earnestly for us it would do us good even in Georgia and encourage our folks every where south of Masons & Dicksons line. If any plan can be devised to secure us additional strength in that quarter, the moral effect would be decisively salutary.

In this quarter I find that the Whigs universally believe that Clays opinions in his speech at Raleigh are to be taken by the *protectionists* as "mere Leather and Prunella," [7] and that he will if elected "keep this promise to the ear and break it to the sense." [8] Of this I have never entertained a single doubt for I sincerely believe Harry of the West [9] to be one of the worst men [in] [10] the Nation. It is understood here that Benton will go [...] his power for you which gives me great pleasure. Wright has written me a letter. He regrets the defeat of our friend Van but his spirits are better and he is cordial in his support. He is certainly one of the best men in the world.

I hope to reach Nashville by the 20th August when I shall mount my poney and do a soldiers duty. May God in his mercy send us a speedy deliverance from such a political dynasty as that of Jim Jones, Eph Foster, Spence Jarnigan [11] &c &c &c.

ALFRED BALCH

P.S. The people at Wilmington request that I will give your Biography in full in my speech which I have promised to do.

ALS. DLC–JKP. Addressed to Columbia.

1. Balch, a Nashville lawyer and an influential political strategist, was named to a four-year term as judge of the U.S. Middle District of Florida in 1840; he resigned his judgeship before the end of his term and declined all subsequent overtures to run for public office.

2. Not identified further.

3. Walter T. Colquitt, James E. Belser, John B. Weller, and Augustus A. Chapman. An attorney from Union, Va., Chapman served two terms in the U.S. House as a Democrat, 1843–47.

4. Reference is to a meeting of Democrats in Richmond held on June 18, 1844.

5. John M. Clayton, a lawyer, won election to a seat in the Delaware House

in 1824; served as Delaware's secretary of state, 1826–28; sat in the U.S. Senate as a National Republican, 1829–36, and as a Whig, 1845–49 and 1853–56; presided as chief justice of the Delaware Supreme Court, 1837–39; and negotiated the Clayton-Bulwer Treaty with Great Britain during his tenure as U.S. secretary of state, 1849–50. Reference here is to a speech that Clayton delivered to a mass meeting of Whigs in Wilmington on June 15, 1844; his speech appeared in the Washington *National Intelligencer* on July 4, 1844.

6. North Carolina held its state elections on August 1, 1844; the Whigs elected their gubernatorial candidate and majorities in both houses of the legislature.

7. Paraphrase of a quotation from Alexander Pope, *Essay on Man,* Epistle IV, part 1, line 204.

8. Paraphrase of a quotation from William Shakespeare, *Macbeth,* act 5, scene 8.

9. Henry Clay.

10. Manuscript obliterated here and below.

11. James C. Jones, Ephraim H. Foster, and Spencer Jarnagin.

## TO WILLIAM L. MARCY

My Dear Sir: Columbia, Tenn. July 9th 1844

I had the pleasure to receive on yesterday your frank and very acceptable letter of the 28th ultimo. You give me more distinct and satisfactory information of the existing state of the parties in New York, and of their respective prospects in the pending political contest than I had received from any other source.

I can truly say that nothing was further from my thoughts than that *any state of circumstances* could arise, which would result in placing me in my present position before the country. I am much gratified to learn from you, that unsought and unexpected as my nomination was, it is likely to have the cordial and hearty support of the whole Democracy of the Empire State. I hope that the domestic difficulties to which you allude, in the approaching nomination of your Gubernatorial candidate, may be so far overcome as to prevent injury to the party. I know from some experience in this state, the bad effects which such difficulties produce. We felt their effects in our last contest, in the collisions which unfortunately arose between different aspirants of the Democratic party for places in Congresss and in the General Assembly, and to that cause, and the consequent want of harmonious and united action of the Democratic party, is mainly to be attributed, as I verily believe the defeat which we suffered. All such collisions are happily at an end, in the pending contest in this state. Perfect union of the Democracy exists. I have never known so fine a spirit prevail in the state. Our whole Democracy are roused to energetic action, and have the greatest confidence that they will carry the state. All the indications of the public sentiment in the South and South-West as far as they have reached me, show a like unanimity and enthusiasm.

You are kind enough to say, that should appearances in New York essentially change for the worse or the better, you will advise me of it. I shall be *pleased* My Dear Sir, to hear *from* you *often* during the contest, and hope you will not fail to write, giving me any information and making (as I hope you will do freely) any suggestions which you may deem to be important or useful.

JAMES K. POLK

ALS. DLC–WLM. Addressed to Albany, N.Y., and marked *"Private."* Marcy's AE on the cover, dated July 9, 1844, reads as follows: "Did not 'Suppose' any State of circumstances could arise 'to place him in his present position before the country.' Gratified to hear of the cordial Support of the 'whole Democracy' of N.Y."

## FROM ROBERT ARMSTRONG

D Sir                                                    Nashville July 10th 1844

The news from City of New Orleans recd. by the Whigs is not confirmed. Our dates are only up to 1st Inst. I think perhaps that it may be true that the Whigs have carried the City by a small majority, *or that* they have Elected their Congressman. But we will then carry the Legislature by 5 or 6 if the high Water does not keep our friends from the polls.[1]

Laughlin says he is going out to see you. *Say to him* that he must take the *stump* and follow Barrow[2] in his appointments and that he must *also ask Harris* to attend to the *Union.* The truth is the Union wants *Fire, Metal, Tact* &c &c and we Must have quick work. Harris can do it & will. I understand him and can make him strike the right note. You can effect this and do it. Norvell[3] is at *Home* & the Banner has to day rather the advantage of Laughlin.[4] He is too slow and wants *Tact* & *fire.* He will Make a good *soldier* on the stump. This must be done or we suffer in the Newspaper way.

Turner goes Out with 150 Volunteers. Two hundred including Cavalry &c with regular Baggage Train &c.[5] Every Speaker must be in the field. Give the Whigs a partner to every appointment they Make.

You did not say how you Disposed of the Madisonian[6] proposition.

I have prevailed on Humphreys to attend to Barrow at Gallatin on Saturday. Craighead[7] goes to Wilson on that day. Nicholson & Martin will be at Columbia by *12* Saturday.

Attend to what I say of the Union. It will not do in this way. Here we Must Send Out the fire to the State & and the Union.

R. ARMSTRONG

ALS. DLC–JKP. Addressed to Columbia.

1. Reference is to the results of state elections held in Louisiana on July 1, 1844. Whigs in the parish of Orleans, which included New Orleans, elected six delegates to the state constitutional convention and seven representatives to the legislature; Democrats won four seats in the convention and three in the legislature. Portions of New Orleans were included in two of the state's four congressional districts. John Slidell won reelection without opposition in one of these, while in the other Alcée Louis La Branche, the Democratic incumbent, lost his seat to Bannon G. Thibodeaux, a Whig. For the entire state, the Democrats won nine seats and the Whigs claimed eight places in the Louisiana Senate; in the Louisiana House, the Democrats won twenty-nine seats, while the Whigs won thirty-one places. In joint balloting the Whigs would hold a majority of one vote.

2. A lawyer from Tennessee and briefly a resident of Mississippi, Washington Barrow served as U.S. chargé d'affaires to Portugal, 1841–44; edited the Nashville *Republican Banner*, 1845–47; and won election to one term in the U.S. House as a Whig, 1847–49. In July and August, 1844, Barrow toured Middle Tennessee and spoke in behalf of Whig principles and in support of Henry Clay for president. Barrow had scheduled his first appearance at Gallatin on Saturday, July 13.

3. Caleb C. Norvell, editor of the *Nashville Whig*, had been absent from Nashville for several months.

4. In July 1844, Laughlin and Donald Macleod, the editor of the Nashville *Republican Banner*, swapped insults in the columns of their respective newspapers in a conflict fueled by the presidential contest. In a lengthy article on July 10, Macleod defended Whig principles and his own editorial standards, while vilifying Laughlin and his journalistic practices.

5. Reference is to the journey of Nashville's volunteer militia companies, commanded by Robert B. Turner, to the Democratic mass meeting in Columbia. Turner was a lawyer in Nashville and principal organizer of the party's militia companies in Davidson County.

6. Washington *Madisonian*.

7. David Craighead, a wealthy Nashville lawyer, served one term as a Democrat in the Tennessee Senate, 1835–37.

FROM GEORGE M. DALLAS

*No. 3*

Dear Sir,                                          [Philadelphia] 10 July 1844

At the anxious request of the Engraver, who is preparing a Medal, I am bound to beg you to send me, if you can, a daguerrotype of your *side face.* Should such a thing be out of your power, then any correct profile. The former would be much preferred by the artist, as giving him a perfect notion of his subject. The engravings we have of you altho excellent in their way, do not enable us to define the side-face with precision.

What *does* the Globe mean? Surely Col. Benton cannot cherish a lurking hostility to your nomination. He writes to his correspondents here that he is entering upon the canvass with ardor: and he is not one to profess what he dont feel and think. Yet certainly Mr. Blair's columns are exceedingly cold, and now and then seize upon a topic the only tendency of which seems towards disaffecting the party. I have, by-the-bye, received a long letter from one of our best and most reliable friends who was a member of the Baltimore Convention from Maryland, and am extremely anxious to send it to you; but it is quite a large package, and is of a character that I am unwilling to confide to the risks of the mail. He complains of the tone of the Globe with great warmth; and adverts particularly to the unceasing laudation of the disinterested course of Mr. Van Buren and of Mr. Wright; as to the former of which, he enters upon a long and minute analysis of the votes and action of the Convention to prove its utter untruth. He wants me to make use of his letter, and even requests me to send it to Mr. Blair; but I am averse to do any thing which would seem to plant the seed of quarrel or to call upon the Globe for defense and explanation. Is there any mode by which I can be sure that you will safely get this letter? If I could get a proper private opportunity, I would send it confidentially to Mr. Ritchie, knowing that his experience and whole-souled devotion would make the best use of it.

It would seem to me that the Republican party has every reason to be satisfied with the conduct of Mr. V. Buren since the nominations. I cannot say the same as to Col. Benton or Mr. Wright, or Col. Johnson. Genl. Cass early and promptly acted well. Mr. Buchanan, tho' tardy and perhaps reluctant, has at last done himself justice in an ardent letter to the Harrisburg Celebration of the 4th of July.[1] I can discern the effect of Mr. Col. Benton's and Mr. Wright's tone upon a few of our active men here; they do not, in the slightest degree, resist or thwart the nomination; but they maintain Col. Benton's theory that the whole was a conspiracy against their favorite and that the result was a successful treason upon the principles and practices of the party; and they indicate a settled and understood purpose hereafter to vindicate their opinions. Mr. Wright was generally regarded here as having, by the use of a few phrases in his N. York and Brooklyn speeches, betrayed the same discontent. It may be well for you to reflect seriously upon the probable future consequences of this feeling, and I should like to have your suggestions as to the manner in which it had best be treated in the event of your election. Of your success, even without the electoral votes of N. York and Ohio, I can entertain no misgiving; but your administration of the government may be embarrassed by any thing which even neutralized the Congressional representations from those states. To be sure, in proportion to our loss of strength in those representations will be our increase of energy and numbers in the representations from Pennsylvania and Virginia; and perhaps this indicates the points from which we can best fortify ourselves against any injurious effects of the N. York disappointment. These, however, are speculative forebodings, thrown out as if I were talking to you, and may, perhaps, be esteemed premature or idle.

The course of President Tyler in perversely maintaining a substantive position, is the result of bad advice. Can you devise no mode of ind[ucing][2] him to give fair play to his intelligence and integrity, and to be cont[ent] with contributing his aid to the attainment of the main object? Not that his aid or his opposition can possibly be of much consequence; but any apparent division of the great republican body does some harm.

We are kept in considerable agitation, in this city, by the menacing attitude of a mob in Southwark, who have collected as many as twenty cannon, have fortified themselves in a market-house, and have defied the military forces, now numerous & headed by Gov. Porter. The popular feeling is unaccountably and extensively on the side of the mob, and against the soldiery. A company of U.S. light artillery reached here, under Capt. Ringgold,[3] this morning. The Governor had I am told, resolved on effectually putting down the opposition to the laws, and meditates an assault. We are in momentary expectation of hearing the discharge of ordonnance. You are aware that this springs directly out of the controversy in relation to the Naturalization Laws.[4]

G. M. DALLAS

P.S. I thought it best, before sending this, to ascertain positively the facts about our rioters, as rumor has a thousand tongues. I find there are no U.S. troops here yet, that there is no fortified market-house, that the lawless are not believed to possess these pieces of artillery, & that no very great apprehension is felt by the public officers, altho much excitement prevails.

ALS. DLC–JKP. Addressed to Columbia. Polk's AE on the cover states that he answered this letter on July 24, 1844; Polk's reply has not been found.

1. In his letter, dated July 1, 1844, to members of a Democratic committee

in Harrisburg, Penn., Buchanan predicted that Polk and Dallas would carry Pennsylvania and that they would have a prosperous administration.

2. Manuscript obliterated here and below.

3. Probably Samuel Ringgold, a captain in the 3rd regiment of artillery.

4. The Philadelphia riots of 1844 gave rise to the rumors that Dallas repeats here and retracts in his postscript.


### FROM J. G. M. RAMSEY

My Dear Sir                              Mecklenburg July 10, 1844

Before I received yours of June 29, inclosing the article forwarded to you at Bolivar in 1841,[1] I had noticed the revival of the calumnies against your ancestors, & I called our friends together to confer about the proper course to be pursued in counteracting them. It appeared to be the general conviction that they could do you no harm. I mentioned the testimony that could be adduced & amongst the rest the statement of George Alexander & Wm. Polk (copies of which I have had in my possession since 1841).[2] The most considerate of our friends believed that if a statement went forth from us admitting that E.P.[3] had taken protection from the British it would be trumpeted forth that we had admitted all that was charged, —& that all the explanations we could make would not correct the public or rather *vulgar* opinion on that subject. Here in E.T.[4] where such disparity exists in the number of Whig & Democratic papers it might have been more difficult to present the truth understandingly than elsewhere. I was waiting to hear from you when yours of the 29th came to hand. I immediately set to & revised & corrected the original vindication, observing particularly your suggestions about the claims of Wm. P.[5] & altered it so as to give him the prominence at Eutaw &c. Still a reader of *Johnsons life of Greene* would not know that E.P. was not the Col. P. there mentioned.[6] I also went at considerable length into the *Protection* such patriots and soldiers as Hayne took from the enemy[7] & I think have explained it fully to the satisfaction of all honest & candid minds (others would not withdraw their slanderous charges tho one rose from the dead & denied them). I made it as perfect as I could. A. V. Brown was right in advising its appearance in your native state & I accordingly inclosed it to Genl. R.M.S. & Hon. W. H. Haywood[8] at Raleigh, leaving it to their discretion how to bring it before the public but advising that it should be done *soon* & allowing them after surveying the whole ground to add to or amend it, which they are very capable of doing. Should I hear from them before its publication I will immediately write you. In the mean time I hope Brown has written to them, as I have not the pleasure of their acquaintance.

To days mail brought me yours of July 3d with the Charlotte correspondence inclosed.[9] I wish I could feel authorised to comment on the Comtees letter before it is published in the Jeffersonian, but that would be improper, & this weeks Argus is already under press.[10] An article now on that subject would have to deal only in *generalities* to avoid running into the same channel with the vindication forth coming in N.C. I will prepare something of that kind for next weeks paper. But Eastman & no body else notices Brownlow.[11] The other day at a public meeting an active Whig denounced the slander as unworthy of their party. Here it is thread bare & I believe harmless. Still it shall be noticed.

This Comtee[12] has already invited Col. Nicholson & Dr. Robertson informs me he will attend in E.T. An invitation accompanies this to Bartly Martin Esq.[13] (addressed to Columbia—have it forwarded to him if that is not his address). We hope he will come to Athens & Greeneville & go elsewhere also. Let him report himself to us. Could he or some one else attend at Charlotte & respond for Tennessee?[14]

I hope I am not deceived myself, & I know I would not deceive you one iota, when I state that things are favorable as I hear all over E.T. & here in Knox County. Many say they will not go for Clay; others that they will go for you, who have heretofore been against you, and for Harrison & Jones. I know several such personally & hear of many others. The Whigs are certainly alarmed, and are making extra exertions to get up the excitement of 1840. But I have not seen our friends even in 1839 so enthusiastic. Our electors & sub-electors (except in the 2nd Dist.) are exceedingly active & reports reach us daily of the best results. Accounts from the Gubernatorial race in N.C. promise no certainty of Hokes election,[15] while those from Ky. are very cheering & satisfactory.

Allow me before I close to say one word through your letter to Mr. Walker or Major Wm. Polk[16] or others more suitable. Certificates will be hunted up, perhaps fabricated to counteract any & every vindication that may be made of your ancestors conduct, & even if they should contradict history & the records of the country they will be published as irrefragable proofs against his character. I know this will be done. These can be best counteracted by procuring the written statements of the old people in Middle & West Tennessee establishing his character. I have no doubt many such can be found in Maury Rutherford & other counties. Only a few weeks since two young men from Bedford returning this way from N.C. told my sons (I was absent from home or I would have got their names) that they had heard their grandparents still living often speak of E.P. as a genuine whig &c &c. (They had a Buggy & two small negroes with them.) I doubt not there are many such; their certificates ought to be got & published. None are near me or I would procure them.

J. G. M. Ramsey

ALS. NcU.

1. Neither Polk's letter of June 29, 1844, nor its enclosure, written in 1841 by Ramsey in defense of Polk's ancestors, has been found.

2. George Alexander was a resident of Mecklenburg County, N.C., during the Revolutionary War; he subsequently moved to Mississippi, where his statement was taken by Edwin F. Polk in March 1841. William Wilson Polk, fourth son of Ezekiel Polk, received a captain's commission in the Maury County militia in 1808; he subsequently moved to Middleburg in Hardeman County. By 1840 he had removed to Phillips County, Ark., where he owned a large plantation. Copies of the statements by Alexander and Polk can be found in a pamphlet published by the Nashville Democratic Central Committee under the title, *Vindication.*

3. Ezekiel Polk.

4. East Tennessee.

5. William Polk of Raleigh, N.C.

6. William Johnson, in his *Sketches of the Life and Correspondence of Nathanael Greene, Major General of the Armies of the United States, in the War of the Revolution* (2 vols.; Charleston, S.C.: A. E. Miller, 1822), wrote of a Colonel Polk who commanded state troops at the Battle of Eutaw Springs, S.C., September 8, 1781.

7. Isaac Hayne was a militia colonel who came under British authority with the surrender of Charleston in 1780. He took protection to remain with his sick wife and children. When he subsequently took arms again in the patriot cause, he was captured and executed as a traitor by the British.

8. Romulus M. Saunders and William H. Haywood, Jr. A lawyer, Haywood served several terms in the North Carolina House of Commons; elected as a Democrat to the U.S. Senate in 1843, he served until 1846, when he resigned in protest to his having been instructed by the state legislature.

9. Polk's letter and its enclosure have not been found.

10. Charlotte *Mecklenburg Jeffersonian* and Knoxville *Argus.* The committee's letter is not identified further.

11. A minister, editor, and politician, William G. Brownlow became editor of the Elizabethton *Tennessee Whig* in 1839. The following year he moved the paper to Jonesboro, where it was known as the *Jonesborough Whig and Independent Journal.* Ten years later Brownlow again changed his residence and moved to Knoxville, where he published his *Brownlow's Knoxville Whig.* A Whig congressional candidate in 1843, he was defeated by Andrew Johnson; but later he twice won election as governor and served from 1865 to 1869. He also served in the U.S. Senate from 1869 to 1875.

12. Knoxville Democratic Central Committee.

13. Barkly Martin.

14. References are to Democratic rallies scheduled for Athens on August 1, Greeneville on August 8, and Charlotte, N.C., on July 23, 1844.

15. Michael Hoke, a lawyer and member of the North Carolina House of Commons from 1834 to 1842, was the Democratic candidate for governor of North Carolina in 1844. He died in September 1844, shortly after his defeat by the Whig candidate, William A. Graham.

16. J. Knox Walker and William H. Polk.

## FROM ROBERT J. WALKER

Dear Sir                                          Washington City July 10, 1844

On the 4th of July last two important meetings were held by the friends of Mr. Tyler in different parts of the city of Philada. at which it was resolved to run separate Tyler electoral tickets & for congress & state & county offices, & this course it seems was to be adopted throughout the Union. Our friends in Philada. & also in N. Jersey & N. York, have written to me in great alarm. Yesterday, altho it was a most disagreable duty, I called upon Mr. Tyler, resolved if possible to ascertain his ultimate views. I had a conversation with him of several hours in which he disclosed to me confidentially all his views. He said he knew that he was to retire to private life in any event on the 4th March, & that he would *at once* withdraw, but that were he to do so *now,* it would not aid the democratic cause, for that his friends were so exasperated by the assaults of the Globe & other presses, that if he withdrew, they would either remain neutral, or many of them join Mr. Clay, that they considered themselves proscribed & invited not to join our party. He stated his deep regret at this state of things, & his great anxiety that Polk & Dallas should be elected. After some remarks from me as to the unjustice of holding you & Mr. D responsible for the course of two or three papers, he remarked that his friends numbered about 150,000, that they were chiefly republicans who voted for the whigs in 1840, & that if a different course were pursued towards them, that if they could be assured on reliable authority that they would be received with pleasure & confidence by you & your friends generally into the ranks of the democratic party, & treated as Brethren & equals, that he would *at once withdraw,* & that his friends with all their influence & presses would then he had no doubt come in, & uniting every where zealously & efficiently with us, render our victory certain. Of Genl. Jackson he spoke in terms of deep affection. Mr. Van Buren also he said would be disposed to do him justice, if left to his own impulses, but that he was or at least had been misled by others. I returned him my thanks for the confidence he reposed in me, by this disclosure of his views, & which as a political opponent I had no right to ask at his hands, and concluded by assuring him, that no honourable effort would be omitted on my part, to produce an honourable & cordial union between the democratic party & himself & his friends.

Now I think that the importance of this union & cooperation *cannot be overated.* In my judgment it would be *decisive* in our favour, & is right in itself. Now it is a delicate matter for you to act, but could you not write a private letter to a friend, which could be shown in confidence to Mr. Tyler, expressing such views as you entertain of his services to the democratic party, & welcoming his friends as brethren & equals back into our ranks. Could not Genl Jackson write a letter to some friend, (which might be published) expressing his views of Mr Tylers services to the party, & expressing the opinion that his friends, upon his withdrawal, would be welcomed back with cordiality & joy by the democratic party, & be placed on the same platform of equal rights & consideration, with any other portion of the democracy. I deem this matter of such high importance, that, if it corresponded with your own views, it would seem to me to justify an interview at your earliest convenience, with Genl. Jackson, to whom you can show this letter. If any thing is to be done, the sooner the better, as it will prevent commitments to Mr Clay, & rally the confidence of our friends.

Your two letters, the one to the committee, & the other to Mr Kane, have done us very great service.[1] They could not be bettered in any way. I finished a few days since sending 14,000 copies of my Texas letter & Texas speech to N. Carolina & Indiana, & still the demand is unabated.[2] Such is the interest taken in those states in the Texas question. I shall be here until the 12th of August doing what I can for the good cause, & where, if there is any thing requiring my attention, you can write to me.

R. J. WALKER

P.S. Since writing the above I have received further news from Pennsylvania. Mr. Muhlenberg, our candidate for Governor, thinks the greatest distraction & distrust in our ranks would be produced by the running Tyler tickets in Pennsylvania. In addition to a letter which might be published, could not Genl. Jackson write a private letter to Mr Blair assuring him of the importance of bringing about Mr. Tyler's withdrawal & the invitation of his friends into our ranks. Already I think Mr Blair is becoming more inclined to this course. R.J.W.

ALS. DLC–JKP. Published in Tyler, ed., *Letters and Times of the Tylers,* III, pp. 139–41.

1. See Polk to Henry Hubbard et al., June 12, 1844; and Polk to John K. Kane, June 19, 1844.

2. Walker's letter, dated January 8, 1844, was published in pamphlet form under the title, *Letter of Mr. Walker of Mississippi in Reply to the Call of the People of Carroll County, Kentucky* (Philadelphia: Mifflin and Parry, 1844). Walker's speech was published as a separate under the title, *Speech of Mr. Walker of Mississippi Delivered in the United States Senate May 20 and 21* (Washington: Globe Office, 1844). A staunch advocate of Texas annexation, Walker argued that Texas was a part of the Louisiana Purchase and should not have been relinquished in the Adams-Onís Treaty of 1819; that the sovereign people of Texas had established their freedom and had indicated their desire to enter the union of American states; and that such an annexation could be accomplished legally by treaty, by an act of Congress, or by the power of any one of the states to extend its boundaries, provided Congress so consented to the annexation. Walker rejected contrary arguments that Texas annexation would despoil Mexico of her territory and provide her government with a just cause for war. According to Walker, Texas annexation would remove British influence in Texas, provide fertile lands and home markets for the American people, and open an escape zone into and through which slavery might recede until it disappeared entirely into northern Mexico.

## FROM ALEXANDER O. ANDERSON

My Dear Sir,                                    Washington City July 11th 1844

I have been detained by business in Washington, but hope to leave here in ten days or two weeks. I should have written you within the last three weeks, but I have had my right hand injured by the bite of a spider, or something of that kind, & have had it in a sling for three weeks. This is the third day since I began to use my pen freely.

Events are transpiring here which make it proper I should communicate to you immediately, and also the information which I obtain from a confidential source fully to be relied upon. I do not stop now to comment upon the outrage which has been perpetrated upon our Party by Mr Benton, nor his Union of action with Mr Clay in regard to the Texas question,[1] which we feel sensibly in Virginia, in the pending contest. The Whigs have franked one hundred thousand of his speeches, & they are now making the false issue in Virginia upon his plan, & dont venture to resist the question of annexation, but after having resisted the Treaty, now say they go for annexation, & that Mr Clay will go for it. The true issue is the *immediate* annexation, & my information in regard to the posture of things in Mexico & Texas makes it necessary, that the most efficient efforts should be made by

Genl Jackson to induce President Houston to resist the designs which
are now in the course of maturity.

The facts are these. The British Govt. have been advised by their
minister here[2] (of which there is no doubt) to press at this moment
upon Texas an arrangement with herself & France—and as little doubt
can be entertained, from all the circumstances, that there have been
advisers, east of this, who have urged this moment as the most favorable in order to put an end forever to our views upon Texas. The
French are determined to Press Mexico upon the subject of the retail
trade to the utmost extremity. France will unite with England to insist
upon Mexico acknowledging the Independence of Texas. Her inducement is our Tariff. England had the same, & the hope of greater power
over Texas than she now holds. The subjects of Great Britain have a
Debt of 80 millions against Mexico, and the terms she will propose
to Texas are, *first, That England will guarantee the acknowledgement
of her Independence by Mexico* & guarantee against the world that
Independence—& will *relieve Texas, if that be necessary, in the payment of the interest of her Debt,* and for this she will *propose that Texas
shall forthwith* make a formal withdrawal of all propositions from this
Govt. whatever, as to annexation, & shall form a commercial Treaty
with England & France, giving them peculiar advantages in the rate
of duties over other nations. This is aimed at us. In addition to the
reasons which will influence France to unite in this English project
against the prosperity of our Country, Louis Philip[3] is now more than
ever anxious to secure the friendship of England, so that his Dynasty
may pass on, to the Crown undisturbed at his death. My information
may be relied upon. It is confidential, but there is no question now
that this whole project is in the course of being brought to bear. Genl.
Henderson, has left here, & will exert his utmost power with *Houston
against it,* & will urge him to await the result of the Presidential election. In this attitude of affairs it is certain that the annexation of
Texas depends on your election. It that fails no human power can induce Texas to trust us. She will not confide in either Mr Clay or Mr
Benton. But the alarming difficulty before us is the powerful pressure
which is to be made, & probably is now making upon Genl Houston
to induce him *to withdraw forthwith all propositions* from before this
Govenmt.

England proposes that she will make a Treaty forthwith with Texas,
& pledge herself that *within so many days Mexico* shall acknowledge
her Independence, but a provision of that Treaty, & promptly to be
done, is to be the withdrawal of the Texan propositions to this Government. This result would be disastrous to us, and would fall heavily

& irretrievably upon our Party & our Country. The thing to be done, therefore, in this emergency, is for you to see Genl. Jackson, without a moments delay. You are at liberty to shew him this letter, & urge him to press upon Gen Houston, the justice, patriotism, and importance of awaiting the Presidential Election, & that it is due to the vast future of this great Country & the rising fortunes of Texas, the pledged zeal, & faith, & efforts of hundreds of thousands of friends, that at a moment like this he should stand by us, & not abandon us, & our Country, & his adopted Country, to the nefarious & factious spirit that seeks to rule or ruin. *Every effort is making from this quarter to save us in Texas,* & you may rely upon it the struggle will be intense, & Elliot's[4] movements *now in the United States* are *connected with all these things.* But all that can be done by others will not be equal to the efforts of that great & immortal patriot of the Hermitage, whose last act, in this earnest conflict between British cupidity & arrogance on the one side, & American rights & interests on the other, is destined, as I firmly believe, under Providence, to be the crowning mercy of his glorious life. See him, by all means—no matter if he has written to Houston, let him write again. You may rely on it *the Crisis is at hand.* I *speak advisedly,* and if there is any man going directly to Texas let the letter go by him. No time is to be lost, & let the friends of Houston, if there are such about Nashville write also. If this daring, & cunning project of the British can be prevented now, & Houston will await the election, I firmly believe, if every man will do his duty, that we shall elect you by a triumphant majority. But this cannot be done by half-way measures. Benton must be met boldy by every Republican, & he & his speeches thrown over-board, & Clay with him, branded with the Anti-American spirit of what they have published in the recklessness of their individual ambition. Let them both be scathed with words of lightening! We are in no danger except we fail to fight as we ought, gallantly, generously, & fiercely, or except Houston shall be overreached by the British, & now is the moment to continue our efforts to prevent that.

The other subject upon which I intended to write you was as to the movements of Mr Tylers friends, & the course to be pursued by yourself & friends, but I have not time now, as this mail will close in a very short time, & it is important this letter should go tonight. As to that subject, however, I have conferred fully to day with Mr Walker of Misspi. who is here, & exerting himself with great energy for you. I have only time to say he is to write you to night as to the important moves now making here by some of us to clear the tracks. The Cabinet will stand by you & insist, & Mr Tyler will be disposed to act rightly.

He has so expressed himself in a full conversation with Mr Walker. This course has been made necessary (I mean the interview with him) by the state of things in Penn & Virginia. But all will be right, & with friendly consideration he will withdraw, & says he desires to see your election, but his friends have been pushing things to extremities in Penn. & now if the spirit to receive them kindly into our ranks is manifested he will *take position*. In this affair Walker has acted with great judgement, firmness, & skill, & he will write you to night in details. I will write you more fully to morrow. I must now end this letter to get it into the mail. The contents are of the most confidential character, known here only to one or two persons, & I prefer that no one should see this letter but Genl. Jackson.

The reply of the Mexican Govt. was in substance expressive of their determination to hold on to Texas. In about the spirit of Bocanegra,[5] bating its offensive character. This was not, however, the tone until Almonte's despatch reached Santa Anna[6] declaring that the Senate would reject. Previous to that the Tone was decidedly that Mexico would have acquiesced if the Treaty had passed.

Altho I have been detained here on business, my pen has not been idle. When I could not write I employed an amanuensis. I have continually kept the blows falling for the great cause. I hope to leave in Ten Days, or two weeks, & whenever I have an opportunity I shall address the people, & when I reach Old East Tennessee I will stir the fires.

Present my kind regards to your Lady, & tell her we shall make her Mistress Presidentess certainly. The last hope of our opponents is the British effort. Look now to that promptly, and all will be right. I assure you great anxiety prevails here upon this point. Very great, and it is the turning point of the Contest. Let the Press open uncompromisingly upon Clay & Benton. You may depend upon it that it is necessary in relation to this Texas question. Present me most kindly to Genl. Jackson.

A. ANDERSON

ALS. DLC–JKP. Adressed to Columbia and marked *"Private & Confidential."*

1. Reference is to Benton's Texas annexation bill.
2. Sir Richard Pakenham.
3. Louis Philippe, King of the French, 1830–48.
4. Charles Elliot served as British chargé d'affaires in the Republic of Texas, 1842–45; he urged the Texas government to adopt policies embracing abolition, free trade, and peace with Mexico; and he worked actively against Texas' annexation to the United States.

5. José María Bocanegra, who had briefly been interim president of Mexico in 1829, served as Mexican minister of foreign affairs from November 18, 1841, until July 22, 1844. He complained of United States policy toward Texas and indicated that the Mexican government would consider annexation the equivalent of a declaration of war.

6. A general in the Mexican army, Antonio López de Santa Anna often headed the central government during the period from 1833 to 1855; he commanded Mexican armies in the Texas rebellion and in the Mexican War with the United States.

## FROM AUGUSTE D'AVEZAC

Barrytown, N.Y. July 11, 1844

D'Avezac explains that his many speaking engagements have delayed receipt of Polk's letter.[1] Anticipating that the opposition will concentrate their efforts on winning the state of New York, he must first use his talents where they are most influential; accordingly, he declines an invitation from the Nashville Democratic Central Committee.[2] On his late speaking tour he has found indications of new unity and energy among New York Democrats. He reports that support for Texas annexation has drawn cheers wherever he has spoken. D'Avezac also describes a July 4th meeting of more than 8,000 Democrats in Albion, N.Y.; he notes that about seven hundred women attended the rally. On that occasion he urged "the propriety of American women manifesting their sentiments on subjects of such deep interest to the society of which they were, not (as in Times when female education was comparatively neglected) the mere ornament, but of which they in fact, lay the solid foundation, by imbuing the infant mind with the principles of eternal religious and political Truths."

ALS. DLC–JKP. Addressed to Columbia.
1. Reference probably is to Polk's letter of June 24, 1844, which has not been found.
2. Reference probably is to an invitation to attend a Democratic mass meeting in Nashville scheduled for July 24 but subsequently postponed until August 15, 1844.

## TO ANDREW J. DONELSON

My Dear Sir: Columbia July 11th 1844

Your letter of the 8th is at hand.[1] I scarcely know how to advise about inviting Mr Tyler & his cabinet. If letters were carefully *written* (not the *printed* copy), they could scarcely take exceptions to the civilities extended to them.

*Genl. Jackson's* letter to *Genl. Plauché* of New Orleans, which appeared in the Banner of yesterday, was manifestly not written for publication.[2] It was imprudent in *Genl. Plauché* to publish it. I think the suggestion should be made to *Genl. J.* to mark his letters not intended for publication *private.* You see the *Banner* is disposed to revive the wolf cry of *Dictation.* Care should be taken to prevent this. The *General's* wishes are now fully known to the country, and can acquire no additional force by the frequent re-declaration of them. I make this suggestion for yourself alone, & think it important.

JAMES K. POLK

ALS. DLC–AJD. Addressed to Nashville and marked *"Private."* Published in *THM,* III, p. 57.

1. Donelson's letter of July 8 expressed hesitation about inviting John Tyler and his cabinet to the August 15th Democratic meeting in Nashville. He feared that "If Mr Tyler should be obstinate Genl Jacksons suggestions might be turned against you, by the revival of the old charge of dictation." ALS. DLC–JKP.

2. The July 10, 1844, Nashville *Republican Banner* reprinted an excerpt from Jackson's letter of June 14. The newspaper used the letter, which urged support for Texas annexation and the election of Polk and Dallas, as occasion for a denunciation of Jackson's "partisan" attempts at dictation.

## FROM ROBERT J. WALKER

Dear Sir                                             Washington City July 11, 1844

Since writing to you yesterday I have seen a private letter of Genl Jackson to one of his friends in this city. The letter is most kind & respectful to Mr. Tyler & says all that could be desired, expressing also a deep anxiety for his withdrawal. It speaks however of Benton as *crazy,* & therefore will not do to be published or even shown to Mr. Tyler. Besides it is strictly a private letter & ought not to be & will not be used in any way. Now I say in confidence for your eye alone, & cannot doubt but you will unite with me on opinion that any letter Genl. Jackson may write for publication on this subject, should contain no allusion to Benton nor any attack upon any portion of our party. Mr Tyler can be praised as to the Bank, Texas &c without assailing any member of our party.

R. J. WALKER

ALS. DLC–JKP. Addressed to Columbia and marked "Private." Published in Tyler, ed., *Letters and Times of the Tylers,* III, p. 141.

## FROM J. GEORGE HARRIS

Nashville, Tenn. July 12, 1844

Harris relates that he will not attend the mass meeting of Democrats at Columbia on July 13. He expresses gratification at Polk's approval of his "course touching the Washington office."[1] He advises delay in replying to "the German Committee,"[2] since the immigrants are "already *well enough* disposed"; he notes that he has forwarded two copies of the *Nashville Union* to the Committee as requested.[3] Harris encloses Bancroft's letter of declination with respect to writing Polk's campaign biography; Harris requests that Polk return Bancroft's letter under cover to Armstrong.[4] Four volumes of the *Register of Debates in Congress,* part of an earlier shipment of books to Polk in Columbia, are missing; Harris speculates that the missing volumes may have become separated from William H. Polk's luggage and may have been left at the Columbia stage office. He asks that William H. Polk inquire of the stage driver as to the missing volumes.

ALS. DLC–JKP. Addressed to Columbia and marked "Private."

1. Thomas Allen had proposed that Harris become associated with the Washington *Madisonian;* Harris interpreted the proposal as an effort to facilitate John Tyler's withdrawal from the presidential race. On July 9, 1844, Harris wrote Polk that he had determined "to make a careful and full reply" to the proposal and had written "to Washington, Boston, &c., in a spirit calculated to put the wheels in motion if not to bring about the result." Polk's reply of July 10 has not been found.

2. See Elijah F. Purdy to Polk, July 16, 1844.

3. On July 6, 1844, the *Nashville Union* published an article entitled "Naturalization Laws—Foreign Emigrants—Whig Injustice," which stated that it had "ever been the settled policy and practice of the democratic republican party by legislation, to encourage and protect foreigners, and to render the means of naturalization cheap, simple, and within the reach of all." The article charged that the Whig party intended to institute a twenty-one-year waiting period for naturalization.

4. Enclosure not found.

## FROM ANDREW T. JUDSON[1]

Dear Sir:                                       Canterbury, Ct. July 12, 1844

Prior to the late Baltimore Convention, it was very generally believed in this quarter, that Mr. Van Buren would have received the nomination of that body for the Presidency; and yet very few saw or even hoped for success. I confess, that to me, defeat appeared certain as reality, and equally, if more disasterous than in 1840. Why it was so, I will not stop at this time to speculate. But we not only saw but felt it in all our movements. Our friends faltered and the people themselves could not be brought up to the work. In this State we have very much cause to perceive its effects upon the democratic ranks. At our election in April we were defeated on the question of Mr. Van Buren alone.[2] Our State administration was without fault. Our Govr. was popular,[3] but all State questions were lost sight of and the great contest lay between the two Candidates for the Presidency. Our State Convention had instructed the Delegates, so that we could not deny that Mr. Van Buren was our candidate and that the party had adopted, and desired to carry out all his principles.[4] This defeated us then and surely would in November.

Since the Convention[5] a new spirit has risen up, and our friends are not only animated but united and zealous.

It will now be a fair contest and we anticipate a successfull result over the union. Under existing circumstances, better nominations could not have been made. The feeling in New England is right and the end will be glorious. Such are our present impressions.

Allow me to say that the nominations are peculiarly gratifying to me. I speak of my personal feelings; they are strong and ardent for your success. I do not however take part in any public political meetings or discussions. All I do is go to the polls in a quiet way & deposit my vote, and in this instance I can do it most cheerfully. Remember me kindly to Mrs. Polk, and say to her that we hope to meet her on the 4th of March.

ANDREW T. JUDSON

ALS. DLC–JKP. Addressed to Columbia. Polk's AE on the cover states that he answered this letter on July 27, 1844; Polk's reply has not been found.

1. A native of Windham County, Conn., and a practicing attorney, Judson served in the Connecticut House, 1822–25, before his election as a Democrat to Congress in 1835; he resigned his seat the following year to accept an appointment as U.S. district judge for Connecticut, in which position he served until his death in 1853.

2. In the Connecticut elections of April 1, 1844, Roger S. Baldwin, the Whig candidate for governor, garnered 30,093 votes while Chauncey F. Cleveland, the Democratic incumbent, received 28,846. The Whigs also elected majorities in both houses of the state legislature.

3. A lawyer, Chauncey F. Cleveland was elected to the Connecticut House twelve times between 1826 and 1866, serving as speaker in 1835, 1836, and 1863. Governor of Connecticut in 1842 and 1843, he served two terms as a Democrat in the U.S. House, 1849–53; he later switched parties and served as a delegate to the Republican National conventions of 1856 and 1860.

4. The Connecticut Democratic State Convention met in Middletown on

October 25, 1843, and endorsed the candidacy of Martin Van Buren.

5. Reference is to the Democratic National Convention in Baltimore.


## FROM SAMUEL H. LAUGHLIN

Nashville, Tenn. July 14, 1844

Laughlin encloses a letter[1] for publication in the Columbia *Tennessee Democrat.* In a postscript he explains that inquiries from a dozen newspapers and many letters from Massachusetts and Mississippi have occasioned his answering the "charge of tory slander."[2] In a second postscript Laughlin informs Polk that "In adding matter to your Life in pamphlet, publishing from Hickmans,[3] and the matter in the Union,[4] I have added about the same on tory charge, and made a page on your course towards occupants,[5] and page on the charge of your conduct to poor,[6] as answered in C. Democrat."[7]

ALS. DLC–JKP. Addressed to Columbia and marked "Private." Polk's AE on the cover states that he answered this letter on July 26, 1844.

1. Laughlin's letter to M. G. Lewis, J. Knox Walker and others, dated July 12, 1844, expressed regret that he would not be able to attend the Columbia meeting on July 13. He described Polk's nomination as "an important preliminary step ... towards a great work of reform" that would "restore the government to its original simplicity, accountability, and economy." He also reported that while en route home from the Baltimore Convention he had found no signs of Whig enthusiasm and many indications of Democratic unity. ALS. DLC–JKP.

2. Reference is to an article, "Gov. Polk's Ancestors—Refutation of a Vile Slander," in the *Nashville Union* of July 13, 1844.

3. George H. Hickman, *The Life and Public Services of the Hon. James Knox Polk, with a Compendium of His Speeches on Various Public Measures* (Baltimore: N. Hickman, 1844).

4. Reference is to an article, "Biographical Sketch of the Life and Character of James K. Polk," in the *Nashville Union* of June 8 and 13, 1844.

5. During Polk's 1839 gubernatorial campaign, rumors circulated that Polk had opposed the Tennessee Land Bill, which was favorable to the interests of squatters on public lands. Polk vigorously denied the charge.

6. On January 17, 1831, the U.S. House considered a resolution to distribute forty cords of surplus wood among the "suffering poor" of the District of Columbia. Polk moved to lay the resolution on the table and later voted against the measure, which passed. On February 1, 1831, Polk spoke against a similar resolution, which authorized the distribution of thirty cords of wood to the poor of Georgetown. Conceding that it was an "ungracious task" to oppose aid to the poor, he argued that "the precedent of appropriating the public funds for such purposes was a bad one." The duty of the House was "to legislate on the great concerns of the Union, and not to give away the

public property." Polk supported an amendment to allow House members to contribute one day's salary to purchase fuel to aid the poor. Whig orators in 1844 used this incident to charge that Polk thought it "undignified" for Congress to aid the poor.

7. The Columbia *Tennessee Democrat* article has not been found.

## FROM JOHN W. DAVIS

My Dear Sir                                      Carlisle Ind July 15 [18]44

Your kind favor of June 10th reached me a few days ago[1] and I was glad to hear of your good health, and of your readiness to become the standard bearer of the democracy of this great nation. We have a glorious prospect in this state. The old Jackson men that were swayed of[f] from their party by falshood in '40, are every one so far as I have heard returning to your standard, and you will recollect how Old Hickory swept over our state. You must not forget that Henry Clay never did receive the vote of Indiana and I am well satisfied he never will.

To show you something of the enthusiasm that pervades our friends in this state I can say to you that I have now before me no less than eight invitations to mass meetings in this state all to come of[f] within the next month.

I have a suggestion to make to you; it is this—do not permit your friends in the south (if posible to avoid it) to rest the annexation question upon a sectional or southron basis, nor to carry the excitement to[o] far. I say this as a southron and immediate annexation man, but I say it also as your devoted friend. There is no necessity for it and it may excite some jealousy in the north. I should greatly deprecate any convention of the southron states upon this question at present.

JNO. W. DAVIS

P.S. Please give my respects to Mrs. P.

ALS. DLC–JKP. Addressed to Columbia.
1. Polk's letter has not been found.

## FROM J. G. M. RAMSEY

My Dear Sir                                      Mecklenburg July 15, 1844

Yours of July 8th came to me by yesterdays mail.[1] I beg you never to consider that your correspondence can be troublesome to me. I have looked into the whole subject, slept upon it & taken time to come to a deliberate conclusion, have tried every expedient to see if I could go to Charlotte, but find it to be for a variety of reasons which need not be detailed entirely impracticable. This gives me no other trouble than that which arises from the fear that you may think that *one means* has been neglected that could counteract the base aspersions upon the memory of E.P.[2] & for that reason if it were at all practicable I would go. But I assure you that anything I could do by being there in person shall be as effectually done in that behalf, perhaps better than I cou[ld][3] do [wer]e I on the gr[ound]. I had e[arl]y seen that counter certificates must be had & published, & so I informed you in one or more of my late letters, to be procured from old men & citizens of N.C. & Tennessee. I wrote twice to S. & H.[4] at Raleigh to the same purport & told them *they* must have them prepared to come in at the close of the *vindication* to sustain it & have also written to a special friend at Charlotte on the same subject & it was for this reason that I said in my last[5] that Edwin P.[6] or whoever attended from Tennessee *must see me* as he went on. I will still expect him, & if not this week, some early day afterwards. But moreover Tennessee ought to have a *speaker* there on the 23rd. I write to day to Blair & Powell, one of whom I will urge to go, & by the mail of to morrow I will write again to Wm. J. A.[7] & others to have certificates procured over there & published, & renew my former suggestions to the same effect to S. & H. who will probably be there. I will prompt the enquiry how & when E.P.[8] became Col., keep up the known distinction between *toryism* & *protection* & go as minutely in my suggestions on the whole subject as I could possibly do were I on the spot.

Nothing shall be omitted that I could do by going. Still I wish I could go. I have been trying ever since I first saw the barbacue was to be given, to get there, but early found it would be impossible. If I hear or see anything of interest about the matter you shall immediately hear from me.

J. G. M. RAMSEY

ALS. DLC–JKP. Addressed to Columbia.

1. Polk's letter has not been found.
2. Ezekiel Polk.
3. Parts of this word and several words following have been obliterated by the letter's seal.
4. Romulus M. Saunders and William H. Haywood, Jr.
5. Ramsey's letter to Polk of July 12, 1844, has not been found.
6. Edwin F. Polk.
7. William J. Alexander, a Charlotte lawyer, served seven terms in the

North Carolina House, 1826–34; he presided as Speaker during the 1829, 1833, and 1834 sessions; and in 1844 he ran as the Democratic candidate for presidential elector for the Ninth Congressional District of North Carolina. Alexander and Polk were related through the line of William Polk, father of Ezekiel Polk and of Susan Polk, who married Benjamin Alexander.

8. Ezekiel Polk.

## FROM ROBERT ARMSTRONG

Dr Sir                                               [Nashville July 16, 1844][1]
Laughlin leaves for McMinnville in the mornings stage. I do not know his business. Craighead says he cannot go to Spring Hill[2] so you must send some person also.

Foster leaves in the morning or in a few days for a flying trip to East Tennessee to oversee Bell & rouse up and Enlist for the Whig convention.[3] All our men speaking should be Instructed to urge our friends in the different counties to *come* and bring force. Much depends on this convention[4] being the largest ever held in the state. I have it seems the whole management. The Committee[5] have never met—done nothing. It should be done on a great scale—military & civil and shall astonish the Whigs. The news is fine and all we want is to keep up the fire. The Union won't do. It is by no means a strong paper—blundering on without a plan of opperations—or any thing that aids our speakers going out on duty. I was out of patience with his long article on Disunion.[6] It has killed itself. You must make a change or call in aid to Laughlin.

We are all in high spirits. The Whigs down. Fosters day (*Saturday*) with Jones to aid him proved a failure in numbers and speaking.[7] In haste ....

R. ARMSTRONG

ALS. DLC–JKP. Addressed to Columbia.

1. Date identified through content analysis.

2. David Craighead had been requested to observe the Whig meeting held at Spring Hill in Maury County on July 19, 1844.

3. On August 21 and 22, 1844, the Whigs held a mass convention at Nashville. Distinguished politicians from Tennessee and other states attended the gathering along with approximately thirty-five thousand militiamen from Tennessee and neighboring states.

4. Reference is to the Democratic mass meeting in Nashville that convened on August 15, 1844.

5. Reference is to the arrangements committee for the Nashville Democratic mass meeting.

6. In a lengthy article in the *Nashville Union* on July 16, 1844, Samuel H.

Laughlin denied Whig charges that dissolution of the union was an objective of the forthcoming Nashville Democratic mass meeting. See Arnold S. Harris to Polk, July 5, 1844.

7. Whig militia companies paraded through the streets of Nashville on July 13, 1844; afterwards Ephraim H. Foster and James C. Jones addressed a crowd assembled at the courthouse.

## FROM ANDREW J. DONELSON

Dr Sir,                                                      Nashville July 16, 1844

I wrote to you on Saturday stating that Craighead & myself had a little Wilson meeting to attend to.[1] It went off well, and we are to follow it up.

You refer to the Plauché letter.[2] I did not know of the existence of such a letter. As soon as I saw it I called on the Genl, and made the suggestion and much more, that you have. He took it kindly. I have written many letters for him. Wherever there has been a doubt of the propriety of their publication, I have generally sent a private note calling attention to the fact.

Every thing goes on well. Your letter to Kane will kill Clay.[3] It would have done this without the last paragraph.

If Louisiana is against us, I shall take the ground at once that she is seduced by the sugar duty; and that if the people of this country want sugar on good terms they must go for Texas.

It is horrible that the people there should be so blind to their true interests.

A. J. Donelson

ALS. DLC–JKP. Addressed to Columbia and marked *"Private."*
1. Donelson's letter of July 13 has not been found. For information on the Wilson meeting, see Robert Armstrong to Polk, July 10, 1844.
2. See Polk to Donelson, July 11, 1844.
3. See Polk to John K. Kane, June 19, 1844.

## TO CAVE JOHNSON

Columbia, Tenn. July 16, 1844

Polk requests that Johnson urge "our leading Northern and North-Western friends" to attend the mass meeting in Nashville on August 15. He also encloses a note left by a servant who wishes to live with Johnson.[1]

PL. Published in *THM,* I, p. 247. Addressed to Clarksville and marked "Private."
1. Enclosure not found.

## FROM ELIJAH F. PURDY[1]

Esteemed Sir                                    New York July 16, 1844

Respect entertained and friendship formed in days gone by, emboldens me to address you in a spirit of freedom and candor. Ere this reaches you, you will have received a letter from a Committee of our German citizens[2] asking your opinion on certain questions contained therein. This Committee represent many voters of undoubted Democratic faith, who feel a deep & lively interest in the success of our Candidates at the approaching Contest. A new party was formed in our City last spring called "Native Americans" who succeeded and have now the possession of the City Government.[3] They are as proscriptive against Democrats, as I think they will be short lived. It is partially so in our sister city Phil. They are organizing there as well as here, and intend I think to unite with the Feds. In our City many, very many heretofore voted with us and will do so again as they openly avow themselves the friends of Polk & Dallas. While I detest this new party and their proscription and illiberal doctrine and oppose without reserve their selfish acts, yet, we fight the battle for principle and *victory too*. Union, harmony and consert of action must be our rallying cry. We must get all the votes we can, without any abandonment of our principles. We shall act in consert here. We mean to succeed, if prudent and conciliatory measures will effect an object so desirable. Many Republicans who left us are returning to their first love, and many more will follow. To be explicit, may I as a personal & political friend respectfully suggest that you delay answering the letter for a short time. God knows that in suggesting this, I am sincerely of the opinion that good may come from it. I intend to prompt the same committee that addressed you to address a letter to Clay. Let us have his views. We may profit by it. I am told that the "Natives" intend writing to each candidate on the subject of an alteration of the Naturalization Laws, asking their opinions thereon. If you have confidence in my friendship write me before sending an answer. I am here, I know something of the public feeling & most assuredly will truly state all to you. No man will go further to see you president than he who pens this letter.

You well know my friend my first choice was our own Van Buren for President & Jas. K. Polk for Vice-President. That preference was freely expressed to you, two years since.

You are known to be the personal as well as political friend of Van Buren which fact does much good in our state. I think you may safely depend upon the Electoral Vote of N.Y. What I write to you I trust will be confidential. I assure you as a friend & a Democrat that yours shall be strictly so for all time to come.

ELIJAH F. PURDY

ALS. DLC–JKP. Addressed to Columbia and marked *"Private."*

1. First elected an alderman in 1838, Purdy became a powerful figure in Tammany Hall and municipal politics. A wealthy banker, he served as acting mayor of New York in 1841 and later sat for three terms as president of the Board of Supervisors. In 1845 Polk appointed him surveyor and inspector of revenue for the port of New York.

2. Letter not found.

3. See William Tyack to Polk, April 13, 1844.

## FROM J. G. M. RAMSEY

Mecklenburg, Tenn. July 16, 1844

Ramsey informs Polk that he has written to Bussey of Maryland.[1] He reports on the progress of his investigations of Polk's ancestors and on his efforts to organize the North Carolina vindication of Ezekiel Polk. He stresses the distinction between "protection" and toryism, arguing that Ezekiel Polk's need to take protection from tory cruelties showed him to be a true patriot. Ramsey expresses regret that he cannot go to Charlotte as Polk has requested,[2] but offers assurance that his attendance will be unnecessary. He also expresses approval of the selection of George Bancroft to write a campaign biography of Polk and promises to supply Bancroft with information about Polk's ancestors.

ALS. DLC–JKP. Addressed to Columbia. Polk's AE on the cover states that he answered this letter on July 23, 1844; Polk's reply has not been found.

1. On June 13, 1844, B. F. Bussey wrote Polk to inquire whether or not the Polk who commanded a company of North Carolina militiamen in the Revolution was one of Polk's relations. L, copy. DLC–JKP. Bussey is not identified further.

2. Reference is to the Democratic meeting of July 23, 1844, at Charlotte, N.C.

## FROM JOHN H. WHEELER[1]

My esteemed Sir                      Raleigh NC. 16th July [18]44

If not too late, allow me to congratulate you on your nomination as the Democratic candidate of our party for the Presidency. I took occasion to be present at Baltimore, & no one more heartily rejoiced that I did at the harmonious action of that talented & patriotic Convention.

For the first time in the history of our Republic does "the old North State" present one of her native sons for the highest office on earth, and my firm belief (and I have a good opportunity of knowing since I am here at the seat of Goverment the only Democrat in the Goverment holding in her executive the responsible post of Public Treasurer) that the state will be ranked among the earliest and most ardent of your supporters.

Our canvass for Governor and the Legislature waxes with unusual warmth; Every democrat is infused with resistless ardour and contends as if the eventful crisis depended on his vote & exertions. Our enemies are dispirited and downcast. They are torpid and occasionally vent their spleen by a slur on the illustrious dead. You are aware to what I allude. We have a publication for this or the next Standard which places this matter in its true and faithful light.[2] The testimony of Captain Jack[3] who bore the Mecklenburg Declaration to Phila. mentions the name of Ezekiel Polk as one of the foremost friends of liberty in the Revolution. I procured when at Charlotte (for I resided there six years, five as Superintendent of the US Branch Mint and one as a practising Lawyer) an original copy of the Declaration which now hangs in the US Mint there, and *Ezekiel Polk* is one of the signers. That a name might be *omitted* is probable; but that one should be *inserted* is too poor a forgery to be done, without any motive whatever. I pledge myself to set this matter beyond all cavil or dispute. The testimony of poor old Thomas Alexander[4] given (1841) in a heated canvass, to unscrupulous politicians of that day does not prove the fact, but the contrary for he expressly swears that Ezekiel Polk was a captain, and "proceeded with his company on his Expedition against the Tories not far from 96."[5]

I recollect your urbanity to me with much gratitude, and the portrait of yourself that you gave me I have had framed and hangs in the Capitol in my office, and is daily shown as one who is to be our next President. I gave the others to whom you sent them Eunice (who I regret to learn has died) and to Marshall.[6]

I sent to you the Standard last week, and I send you one this week. It is a bold & talented Sheet, and spreads dismay among the Fedral ranks.

I start tomorrow to the great mass meeting at Charlotte (on the 23d). Genl Saunders, Genl Drumgoole[7] will certainly accompany me, or start the next stage. Genl McDuffie & other of the South Carolina delegation will be there.

Allow me to hear from you as your·leisure may be permit, and with my respectful complements to Mrs Polk ....

JNO. H. WHEELER

ALS. DLC–JKP. Addressed to Columbia. Published in Elizabeth Gregory McPherson, ed., "Unpublished Letters from North Carolinians to Polk," *NCHR,* XVI (July 1939), pp. 338–40.

1. A lawyer, diplomat, and historian, John H. Wheeler served five terms in the North Carolina House, 1827–30 and 1852. He also served as superintendent of the Charlotte branch of the U.S. Mint, 1837–41; North Carolina state treasurer, 1842–44; and U.S. minister to Nicaragua, 1854–56.

2. The Raleigh *North Carolina Standard,* a Democratic weekly edited by William W. Holden, printed an article on "Col. Polk's Ancestry" in its issue of July 17, 1844.

3. The testimony of James Jack, given December 7, 1819, was printed in both the North Carolina and the Tennessee vindications of Ezekiel Polk.

4. Thomas Alexander's statement of June 19, 1841, was widely published in Whig papers as evidence that Ezekiel Polk was a Tory. Alexander, who had served under Ezekiel Polk in the militia, asserted that after two early campaigns, he "did nothing to favor the Whigs during the war." He also noted that Ezekiel Polk had taken protection from the British. The Democratic vindications countered with a statement dated August 5, 1844, in which Alexander testified that Ezekiel Polk "never took sides in any shape, manner or form against his country."

5. Ninety Six was a community in Greenwood County, S.C.

6. Roxana Eunice Ophelia Polk and Marshall Tate Polk, Jr., were the children of Polk's deceased brother Marshall Tate Polk and Laura Wilson Polk. Eunice Polk had died in October of 1842.

7. Romulus M. Saunders and George C. Dromgoole.

## FROM JOHN CATRON

Dr Sir. [Nashville] Wednesday, 17 July [1844][1]

Some one said in my hearing that they thought you ought to come here during the Dem. meeting.[2] So I think. Not to go on the ground where speeches are made of which you are the staple, but to see all those worth seeing from abroad, and from this state. And I think Mrs. Polk ought to come with you. She ought to be seen also by those from abroad. The *wife* of a man aspiring to the White house is no minor circumstance. Few have passed muster there. The thing should be very quiet; Mrs. P.'s and your abiding place not at a Hotel, & I think my House would suit as well as any could be found. It would afford the excuse to have it open to all suitable visitors; and I very much desire this. I desire that Mrs. Polk should be visited by Whigs and democrats, of her own sex—& so she will, as the ladies of the other side uniformly speak well, and generally highly of her, as I am informed. I learn this through Mrs. MacKenzie and Mrs. Benson, & others.[3]

This may look like a small matter. I think otherwise. The matter was mentioned to Mrs. Catron by Doctr Eselman,[4] & she consulted me. On the subject I have no doubt, nor has Mrs. Catron, to whom I stated no reasons. Her's extends to gentlemen from abroad, principally. The Whitewashing Committee,[5] (of which Mr. Chief Justice Catron had the honour to be a member,) had more trouble in the first and 2d. Jackson campaigns, *on the wife head,* than with all else that came before them. More public men have received potent help from the wife in this country than any in the world, not excepting France. The working, axious, and troubled husband, has no time or tact, to concilliate and please the women, the young men, nor the vain old ones. This is the very business of the wife; and one not fit for it, is a dead weight. That she is fit in high places, should be well known to friends and opponents.

You want the Horse.[6] He could travel well enough, but I doubt whether he is fit for use yet. He cripples a good deal, has been exclusively on grass, & before he travels must be fed on cut oatts some three days. He will be very little injured in the end. Write me exactly when you'l send, & I will have him shod & fed three days before.

J. CATRON

P.S. Write me precisely, & in a day or two, in regard to Mrs. Polk and yourself coming in. Your carriage is not done, & may not be. I have just got a new one for Mrs. Catron, & can furnish every facility in this way. Still, I hope Mrs. P.'s may be ready, & only offer Mrs. C.'s on the contingency.

Mr. Sloan is my builder,[7] & I can push him if you will instruct me.

I have all necessary conveniences to keep carriages & horses, & dont think of anything else than bringing yours here, when you come. J.C.

ALS. DLC–JKP. Addressed to Columbia. Polk's AE on the cover states that he answered this letter on July 22, 1844; Polk's reply has not been found.

1. Year identified through content analysis.

2. Reference is to the Democratic mass meeting scheduled for Nashville on August 15, 1844.

3. Catron's sources are not identified further.

4. Matilda Childress Catron and John N. Esselman.

5. An 1827 public meeting in Nashville appointed a committee of eighteen prominent Tennesseans to "detect and arrest falsehood and calumny, by the publication of truth, and by furnishing ... full and correct information upon any matter or subject within their knowledge ... properly connected with the

fitness or qualification of Andrew Jackson to fill the office of President of the United States." James Parton, *Life of Andrew Jackson* (3 vols.; New York: Mason Brothers, 1860), III, p. 142.

6. On July 2, Polk's slave Elias had left a sick horse with Catron. Catron to Polk, July 2, 1844, ALS. DLC–JKP.

7. G. L. & F. Sloan manufactured carriages on Lower Market Street in Nashville.


## FROM J. GEORGE HARRIS

My Dear Sir,                                    Nashville July 17. 1844

You will perceive that Bancroft declines making the biographical sketch, for several substantial reasons. This is what I feared. I send you his letter.[1] You see he is something sensitive on the point of *authorship,* and well he may be for in that is his pride. I have replied to him *right.* I have acknowledged that the blunder was *altogether mine,* stating that I had mistaken the opinions of friends for his "consent." It will satisfy him fully. He is a good fellow—truly a great man—and he is at work for the Cause like a Trojan.

You say you would like to see the Nash. Union what it was in 1839. With all due modesty, I may perhaps be permitted to say "So would I." You know the duty of an editor is (as we say) to *get up a paper for effect.* To write an article or two is but a small part of the task. When Mr. L.[2] is here—he being the editor—he "gets up the paper." All the aid that I could ascertain would be acceptable to him I have rendered him, and that is not much. He left on a visit to the mountains this morning, asking Nicholson to make him a paper for Saturday. I have written two articles for to-morrow. The balance is of his own architecture. To conduct a paper like the Union it is necessary that one's whole time should be devoted to it; that he should be at his post every hour of the day and late at night until the contest is over. He is like a sentinel on guard and should not be a moment absent.

I would not say a word to offend Mr. Laughlin, but one thing is certain, that if he *pretends* to be the editor and continues to be so much absent, the paper must necessarily suffer more or less for want of *system* in management. Albeit, you know I will throw in my arm whenever and wherever I can have a fair chance.

Maj. Donnelson[3] will be here to-night. I have conferred with Gen. Armstrong as you suggested about sending the manuscript of the *biog. sketch* to Mr. Kane at Philadelphia. He inclined to favor the proposition; and if Maj. Donnelson is of the same opinion they will be sent on by him.

Please say to your brother Wm[4] (if you think of it) that such have been my constant engagements it has been utterly impossible for me to attend to that little affair which he named to me at Columbia.

J. Geo. Harris

I am of the opinion that the biography should as well be used at once in the Union. Time will not wait. Its republication will be immediate. The people want the facts. Pride of authorship should be lost sight of, or if insisted on, let it go to the real author. A.J. Donelson[5]

I think it just as well be published here. R. Armstrong.[6]

Unless you disapprove of this decision the first part of it will appear in the Union on Tuesday. [J.G.H.][7]

ALS. DLC–JKP. Addressed to Columbia. Polk's AE on the cover states that he answered this letter on July 18, 1844; Polk's reply has not been found.
1. Enclosure not found.
2. Samuel H. Laughlin.
3. Andrew J. Donelson.
4. William H. Polk.
5. Donelson wrote his endorsement in the left margin of the second page.
6. Armstrong wrote his endorsement at the bottom of the second page.
7. Harris penned his unsigned addendum in the right margin of the second page. Beginning on August 1, 1844, the *Nashville Union* ran Polk's sketch in installments.

## FROM MINER K. KELLOGG[1]

Dear Sir:                                              Florence Italy, July 17th 1844

In remembrance of your kind efforts in forwarding my designs of coming abroad some 4 years since, I am desirous of letting you know something of the results which have attended my stay in Italy, for it cannot but be satisfactory to those who interest themselves for a young man's success, to know that their efforts have not been made in vain, and that he is not forgetful of their endeavors to promote his welfare at one of the most critical periods of life.

Friend Harris will, no doubt, have told you something about me. My studies have been mostly directed to gaining such knowledges as lay at the foundation of Art. Hence few *pictures* have been painted, as yet: still I may say that those few have received such notice here, as gives me much encouragement for the future. My health has been good, and I have lived in a secluded and economical manner. After having seen most of the best works which Italy has produced—in Rome, Naples, Venice and other places, I went to the *East,* for such information as a painter requires, who intends to devote himself to the illustration of Scripture History. The tour was extensive, including Egypt, Syria, The Holy Land and parts of Asia Minor and Turkey. I have but just returned, and brought home drawings and notes of the most interesting places on the journey. So that now I feel much more capable of undertaking works of an Eastern character than when I left Italy. I have as much employment as I wish, and thus far have not been under the necessity of asking assistance from friends. It is not possible to say how long I will remain abroad.

It gives me real pleasure to hear of your nomination for the Presidency. Mr. Van Buren was my choice, but I consider that under all circumstances, there was great danger of our defeat had he been chosen at the Baltimore convention. I think your chances of election are greater than Mr. Clay's and shall look forward to the expressions of public opinion with the liveliest interest.

The question of *Annexation* is of such importance, that I am sure the *whole* American people will be excited enough to come forth *to a man* at the next election. I think if they could read *daily* the English papers upon this subject they would not be long in deciding what course to pursue in relation to it. It seems quite certain that England has her eyes directed towards Texas, and she never looks long and seriously at *anything* for the sole purpose of benefitting her neighbors. This nobody doubts on this side of the channel, and I dont see what reason *Americans* have to do so. There is no place where she is so anxious to plant her cannon, as in that part of the western Hemisphere, not even excepting Egypt, where she has been laboring arduously for so many years to obtain a foothold.

The loss of Texas to us would prove a public calamity. I thank you therefore with all my soul, for coming out *boldly* as the Champion of *American* interests. God grant that you may be elected, for our Country's sake.

Please make my best regards acceptable to Mrs. Polk. Her cheerful countenance is often present, when I joyfully call to mind, the time spent under your hospitable roof.

If I do not ask too much, I wish you to remember me to my friends in Nashville. To name them is not necessary, as you are aware to whom I refer. Also to General Jackson. How much I regret the distance which separates me from the council of so great a man.

With the warmest wishes for your health & prosperity ....

MINER K. KELLOGG

ALS. DLC–JKP. Addressed to Columbia.
1. A nineteenth-century American author, traveler, and artist, Kellogg

painted portraits of Andrew Jackson, Polk, and Martin Van Buren in 1840. In 1848, he painted another portrait of Polk and one of Sarah C. Polk.

## FROM GOUVERNEUR KEMBLE

My dear Sir,                                    Cold Spring N.Y. 17th July 1844

I have abstained from congratulating you on your nomination at Baltimore until I could form some opinion of the manner in which it would be supported by the Democracy in this State. At first they appeared much disappointed, for the great mass of our farming interest in all the older counties are sincerely attached to Mr. Van Buren, and it took some time to explain the reasons why his friends in the convention should have withdrawn his name after he had received a majority of votes, and have given the vote of the State to you for the presidency, instead of the vice presidency, as first intended.[1] This could not be done in a day, because the publication of our reasons in a formal manner might have acted injuriously to the cause in other parts of the union, and they could therefore only be communicated privately or in conversation with the leading men in the different Counties.

But, now, I am happy to tell you that a glorious spirit is rising in all directions, and to forward it we have in this County called a mass meeting of the Democracy,[2] the second only in our political history. The grounds which I have taken are briefly, that you were from the first our second choice; that you had been intirely free from all the intrigues of the convention whereby the nomination of Mr. Van Buren had been defeated; and that throughout your political life you had always been a firm and consistent supporter of the principles of the party, and particularly in an undeviating opposition to the Bank, that by supporting your nomination in a manner to secure the election, they would not only prevent that of Mr. Clay, with the restoration of the Bank, and all the train of evils which such an event would entail, but at the same time triumph over all those disorganizing and faithless men of our own party, whose combination had prevented the restoration of Mr. Van B. to the presidency, and indeed nothing satisfied me so fully of the propriety of the course which the delegates from new york pursued in the convention, as the consternation and dismay displayed by the friends of Mr Calhoun on the announcement of our change of vote. It was a finale which they little dreamt of.

But to return, the feeling which here exists against Calhoun; and the virginia faction; will do more to rouse the people and bring them to the polls than any thing else. You must therefore be cautious in no way to identify yourself with them. For the rest, you know them and their thirst for power, as well and probably better than I do, for you fought them longer, and from a position more conspicuous than my own. I do not spare them in conversation, for I believe that a more unholy fraternity of grasping and ambitious men were never collected together, not even under Cataline[3] himself, and that they would not hesitate to involve the country in a civil war, if by so doing their ambition might be gratified.

It is the misfortune of every party long in power, that it draws within its vortex, not alone the straws and lighter materials that float upon the body politic, but every species of corruption whether below or above the surface, and so with us at this moment. God grant that we may be able to rid ourselves of them.

I write as I think, but I do not ask you to agree with me always, nor to answer my denunciations.

Continual inquiries are made of me about you—your personal appearance, character &c. My answer is that you are made of bone & muscle, no fat, 6 ft high, that you are as tough as the old General,[4] and can not be better described than as Young Hickory.

With my best respects to Mrs. P. believe me ....

GOUV. KEMBLE

ALS. DLC–JKP. Addressed to Nashville and forwarded to Columbia. Polk's AE on the cover states that he answered this letter on July 31, 1844; Polk's reply has not been found.

1. Throughout the first eight ballots for the presidential nomination, the New York delegation consistently cast all thirty-six of its votes for Van Buren. During the ninth and final ballot, the New Yorkers retired from the convention hall to caucus. When they returned, Benjamin F. Butler reluctantly announced the withdrawal of Van Buren's nomination; New York then gave thirty-five votes, later corrected to thirty-six votes, for Polk.

2. The Democratic meeting in Putnam County is not identified further.

3. Defeated in his effort to win election as consul, Lucius Sergius Catiline led a conspiracy against the Roman republic in 63 B.C. In a fierce battle the following year, loyalist forces defeated the rebels, and Catiline died in the action.

4. Andrew Jackson.

## FROM ARNOLD S. HARRIS

Dear Sir                                          Buffalo July 18th 1844[1]

I will inflict upon you a brief history of my trip and the observations made on the way and at this place.

My route was through Ohio to Lake Erie and down the Lake to this place where I have been for several days and shall probably be a week longer. I might tell you in a ten words what the impression on my mind is but I will be more particular and give my reasons.

Ohio is a *doubtful* state at present and is in great danger of being lost to the cause. Such is my conviction though the party pretend to be sanguine. The reason why I think so is that I fear a coalition will to a great extent be effected between whigs and abolitionists. I passed through Giddings district. He is trying to throw the abolition votes of his district in for Clay, and says that Clay will *do what is right for the party.* I was astonished to find so many abolitionists in Ohio—they are over 1000 in Giddings dist.

One thing will save the state and the democrats are doing their utmost to bring it about—induce the *Liberty party* to maintain their separate organization. If they do not amalgamate with the whigs the state will go democratic by a handsome vote.

They have all been mistaken in Nashville about the strength of the Liberty party in Ohio. Mr. Craighead thought they could not number 500 in the state. Trumbull County alone will poll over 500, and they say they have 15 or 20,000 in the state and I do not doubt it. If the abolitionists reject the overtures of the whigs and remain firm to their man, the democratic majority will be 10, or 15,000. Clay is far from being as strong as Harrison was, and the fact of a bargain being proffered to the abolitionists will alienate many strong whigs from their party. I therefore call Ohio doubtful—all depending on the course of the abolitionists—the chances however in favor of democracy.

Pennsylvania is certain or I am wofully decieved. An intelligent whig from Pittsburg acknowledged to me that Muhlenburg[2] would be elected, but he thought Clay would get the vote of the state by from 3 to 5,000. I think this was an admission of weakness and that if they can hope for nothing better they feel themselves beat. So far as I can learn all their hopes on the tariff question have been crushed since your letter to Mr. Kane.[3]

And now for the main spoke in the wheel—the old empire state with her cartload of votes—the all important state, for as goes N.Y. so I think will the general result be.

I have been as busy as a bee, have read every little paper printed in the state, had access to all the reading rooms, printing offices, and conversed with dozens from all sections of the state and I am happy and proud in saying that the democracy of New York are doing the work manfully—zealous and united on the main question and sanguine of success. Only one thing is wanting to make success certain and make the victory the most brilliant ever achieved in the state. You are aware that the party is split on the question of their candidate for Gov. A strong fragment of the party is opposed to Bouck and would not go into the contest with any good will if he is nominated. The object is to get a man to unite these factions and Silas Wright is the one if he will only consent. It is hoped that he will. Primary meetings are being held all over the state and his name is taken up by acclamation. Delegates will be appointed here to night instructed to go for him as first choice and Geo. P. Barker (atty Gen) 2nd choice.[4] Barker is a powerful man—unobjectionable in all points but Wright is an older soldier better known and on account of his having been before the national convention under the peculiar circumstances of the case, his name would have an influence in other states, particularly Ohio. Silas Wright, the friend of Van Buren, as standard bearer in New York and the effect would be beyond calculation. Can you not with propriety write to him and urge him to accept. The nomn will be made first week in Sepr. If this can be effected I verily believe N.Y. will give not less than 25,000 perhaps as high 35,000.

This city of Buffalo is a busy place. Erie county gave Harrison 3100 maj. The whigs now refuse to bet on 1500. The talent and zeal in the city is with us. Many of my old friends and associates live here. They are good & true and labor with a will and not without effect. I shall visit other parts of the state & if I can give the same good acct, the state is sure. Our party here bet freely on this state and on the general result.

I will write you again after passing through more of the state. I shall leave here in a few days but return again here by 5th next month and try to be in Nashville on the 18th.

A. S. HARRIS

ALS. DLC–JKP. Addressed to Columbia.
1. Harris first sent this letter under separate cover to Robert Armstrong in Nashville; Armstrong subsequently franked the letter's cover sheet and sent the item to Polk in Columbia. See Armstrong to Polk, July 27, 1844.
2. Henry A. P. Muhlenberg.
3. See Polk to John K. Kane, June 19, 1844.
4. George P. Barker is not identified further.

## FROM ROBERT ARMSTRONG

Dear Sir                                Nashville July 19th [18]44
Nicholson did not arrive in time for last Union. His appointments and Martin's could not go in, and strange to tell in looking over the Union to night they are not in. Nicholson & myself made them out from the map and he told me they would be in the paper tonight. He

has gone to attend the meeting at Charlotte[1] and Hisse[2] cannot be found. I will have them in or in an Extra if they are in Heiss' hands. Nicholson may have neglected to hand them in.

Will Williams lost his Wife[3] last evening. Doctor Robertson & Williams have both been absent. We will arrange the movements of the Speakers &c. Donelson is hard to move, but the letters have been written and sent off. The News from Louisa. is *Settled* and *Confirmed.* The Democrats have three members to Congress. The Senate by 2 and the House by 3 or 4 and a large Majority for Convention.[4] The Flag to the Volunteers will be presented 27th Inst.[5] On that day we will Celebrate the Louisiana Victory and so I have engaged a Hickory Pole 184 feet. We will raise that also, have all the Volunteer Companies of the County, fire 100 Guns and Kill off Whiggery. They are nearly gone now, if we keep up the fire as we are doing. The *fun* will be over too soon. All Our Companies meet tomorrow (Saturday below Nashville 12 miles).

On Monday in the *Hermitage* District, go to both places in a boat, will take the *transparencies* and light up the Old Chief's grounds, give him round or two and come home.

Laughlin took up Nicholson's & Martin's appointments on Wednesday. Others he enclosed to Eastman.

R. Armstrong

[P.S.] I regret that Ramsey could not go to N. Carolina. He ought to have done so. Write to him to send Bradley over & to publish his appointments for *Middle Ten.* in the Argus.[6]

ALS. DLC–JKP. Addressed to Columbia.
1. Reference is to a Democratic barbecue scheduled to meet at Charlotte, N.C., on July 23, 1844.
2. John P. Heiss.
3. Nancy D. Nichols Williams, wife of Willoughby Williams, is not identified further.
4. Reference is to Louisiana's convention for revising the state constitution.
5. After a one-week postponement, a group of Democratic ladies presented a banner to the Nashville Texas Volunteers on August 3, 1844.
6. Knoxville *Argus.*

## FROM GRANVILLE S. CROCKETT

Dear Sir                                           Frankfort July 19th 1844
After the Convention adjourned, I spent some ten days in Washington, and returned to the neighborhood of this place, where I have

remained ever since, attending the numerous meetings of the Sterling democracy of this state; among whom there is a complete spirit of enthusiasm prevailing. I never have seen or heard any thing to equal it, and such numerous changes have taken place that the friends of Butler & Pilcher[1] have thrown aside all doubt and are now certain of success. They show their confidence by throwing defiance in the face of their opponents who exhibit all the signs of fear, anger and dismay, in their looks.

The Democrats have real cause to know they will succeed. This enlists[2] in the numerous changes that are daily going on, wherever I have been. I am told of scores that have come over and their names are given and they come out themselves and boast that they are evermore free. I could name hundreds but the most of them are not known abroad. I can name such as R. Wickliffe Sr., Hon Tho. F. Marshall, Hon. Jas. C. Sprigg, Hon. John Pope,[3] the three last members of the 27th Congress. Such is the revolution now going on in this state that the most intiligent of the Whigs acknowledge that Col. Butler will be elected. Should this be so, the contest for Prest. will be considered as settled. Of one thing I am certain Kentucky never has been in such commotion since 1828. We have a majority of public speakers and a decided advantage in point of tallents, with all the zeal that confidence inspires. I have been with our friends at Sligo, Connersville, Bridge-Port, Harrodsburg and many other places, where the numbers of the people who turned out astonished every body. In Louisville business has almost given way and nothing is thought of but politics. Guthrie[4] defies them openly and I am told there is more than five hundred changes in that city. At Harrodsburg every thing went off finely. Old *Poin* was there denouncing the great embodiment openly.[5] I was told of many who came over and done the same. I also see it stated in the Penna. papers that Cost Johnson is doing the same thing.

Except Crittenden, B. Hardin and Leslie Combs[6] I hear but little from the whig orators, whilst on the other hand I could name such as Butler, Pilcher, Wickliffe, Guthrie, Willis, McCalla,[7] all the Congressmen and fifty others who are riding and speaking continually. On Saturday the 20th a great meeting is anticipated at Lexington. It will be a grand affair. Ashland[8] will be made to trimble to its centre. Mr. Wickliffe promised me at Harrodsburg to be at Nashville on the 15th of next month *certain,*[9] and if the old man is at himself, he will afford Ten. a fine treat. You may look out for a goodly number from this state as well as others.

Accounts from Inda. are equally favourable and that state is counted for us as certain as Alabama. In Ohio, Tods majority for Governor is given up by the whigs to be over fifteen thousand. Pennsylvania is also given up, and all admit that Muhlenberg will be elected by over twenty thousand. The Maryland papers declare it to be no race between Carroll and his competitor,[10] and since Johnsons somerset that the state will go in the same way next fall. You may be well assured that the friends of equal rights, and of Texas are doing their duty here, and such a fight never has come off in this state as will take place in August.[11] The result cannot fail to be disastrous to Mr. Clay *for I know* that Butler will be elected or else beaten by a very lean majority. In either case Mr. Clays prospects are blighted and they all see and feel it now.

Tomorrow I will go up to Lexington, and see the Lyon bearded in his den. Several hundred intend to go up from this Co and if the weather is favourable we will alarm the Mill Boy.[12] I wish you could hear Wickliffe & Sprigg & Marshall & Pope. It seems to do them good, and they talk as tho' a new song was put in their mouths, all declaring they have severed the bonds which bound them to a *man* and that they can now go for their Country and the Constitution.

I think I will be able to get off for home in a few days.

G. S. CROCKETT

ALS. DLC–JKP. Addressed to Columbia.

1. William O. Butler and W. S. Pilcher. Pilcher was the Democratic nominee for lieutenant governor of Kentucky.

2. Faulty word choice.

3. Robert Wickliffe, Thomas F. Marshall, James C. Sprigg, and John Pope. Wickliffe, one of Kentucky's most successful real estate lawyers, represented Fayette County in the Kentucky Senate from 1825 until 1833; he was one of the key leaders of the anti-relief party in the General Assembly. A lawyer in Shelbyville, Sprigg served several terms in the Kentucky House prior to winning election to the U.S. House, where he served one term, 1841–43. Pope, a lawyer, served several terms in the Kentucky House before being elected to one term in the U.S. Senate in 1807. He later won election to two terms in the Kentucky Senate, 1825–29; went to Arkansas as territorial governor, 1829–35; and served three terms in the U.S. House, 1837–43.

4. A lawyer in Louisville, James Guthrie served in the Kentucky House, 1827–29, and Senate, 1831–40; from 1853 until 1857 he was secretary of the Treasury in the cabinet of Franklin Pierce; in 1865 he won election to the U.S. Senate and served until 1868.

5. George Poindexter, a former congressman, senator, and governor of Mississippi, practiced law in Lexington. The sobriquet, "Great Embodiment" of Whig principles, referred to Henry Clay.

6. John J. Crittenden, Benjamin Hardin, and Leslie Combs. A Bardstown lawyer, Hardin served several terms in the Kentucky House and Senate and

was secretary of state of Kentucky from 1844 until 1847; he served five terms in the U.S. House between 1815 and 1837. Combs, a Kentucky lawyer, fought with the Kentucky volunteers during the War of 1812; between 1827 and 1859 he served several terms in the Kentucky legislature; an ardent Whig, he was a Clay elector in the election of 1844.

7. William O. Butler, W. S. Pilcher, Robert Wickliffe, James Guthrie, possibly William T. Willis, and John M. McCalla. Willis is not identified further. McCalla served as U.S. marshal for Kentucky during the Jackson and Van Buren administrations; in 1844 he was an electoral candidate on the Democratic ticket in Kentucky; and in 1845 Polk appointed him second auditor of the U.S. Treasury.

8. Reference is to Henry Clay's estate, which was located just outside Lexington.

9. Reference is to the Democratic mass meeting in Nashville, August 15, 1844.

10. James Carroll and Thomas G. Pratt. A Baltimore judge and businessman, Carroll won election as a Democrat to one term in the U.S. House, 1839–41. Pratt, a lawyer, held seats in both the Maryland House, 1832–35, and Senate, 1838–43, prior to his election to the governship of Maryland in 1845; he subsequently served in the U.S. Senate from 1850 until 1857.

11. Kentucky state elections were scheduled for August 5, 1844.

12. Admirers of Henry Clay had dubbed him "the Mill Boy of the Slashes," a person of humble origins; Clay's family resided in Hanover County, Va.


## FROM J. GEORGE HARRIS

My Dear Sir,                                        Nashville July 19, 1844

Yrs. of the 17th & 19th are at hand.[1] Although the miscarriage of those books[2] was but a small matter, comparatively, I had much anxiety about them and am rejoiced that they are not lost. I shall tomorrow go out to my library (now at Hu: W. McG.,)[3] and make search for the additional vols. which you name. If they are not there, I may find it difficult to procure them, for the Exec. Dept. of State, you know, contains files of Exec. Journals but *no* Reg. of Deb. Nor does the work seem to be in Mr. Grundy's Library. Nevertheless, I hope to get them, and if I do I will send them out on Monday.

I am glad Bancroft has written to you *direct.*[4] He is every way *reliable.* I *know* his reasons are sincere for declining. I have traced your letter through again and again on the subject of the biog. sketch and am clearly of the opinion that the mode which you suggest of disposing of it, is *the best.* There is *no necessity* for a *formal biography*—it were better "served up" as *leading editorials* for the Union; and there is manifest propriety in devoting the *leaders* of our paper at this capital to that subject at this time. There is another reason why in their present form the manuscripts should not be sent to Kane or any one else. Bancroft, relying on my caution has made several suggestions and amendments in his own hand writing on the margin, which it would be imprudent to expose, perhaps. I am clearly of the opinion that it should be converted into articles for the Union, and I will endeavor to do it in a proper manner profiting from Bancroft's suggestions and any others that you may please to make.

As for the editorship of the Union, and my taking the "laboring oar" there, you know that I would do it at a "word" if deemed important, occupying the position as a private one (according to your suggestion) and producing no *scene* by a change of editors. Your thoughts in this connexion, as in reference to the biog. sketch, perfectly accord with mine.

Well: we have *"got em"* in Louisiana, sure enough.[5] The returns to night place it beyond all doubt. A bright dawn indeed! God grant it may be the precursor of "the sun of Austerlitz."[6]

J. Geo. HARRIS

[P.S.] You will see by the papers that Mexico has appealed to the monarchies of Europe for aid in preventing the annexation of Texas to the U.S.

ALS. DLC–JKP. Addressed to Columbia.
1. Letters not found.
2. Reference is to a shipment of several volumes of the *Register of Debates in Congress.*
3. Abbreviation probably stands for Hugh W. McGavock, who is not identified further.
4. See George Bancroft to Polk, July 6, 1844.
5. Reference is to the outcome of state elections in Louisiana held on July 1, 1844.
6. At dawn on September 7, 1812, as he prepared to fight the Battle of Borodino, Napoleon Bonaparte exclaimed to his officers that "It is the sun of Austerlitz." Napoleon had won a major victory over the Russo-Austrian army at the Battle of Austerlitz on December 2, 1805.

## FROM J. G. M. RAMSEY

My Dear Sir                                    Mecklenburg T. July 19, 1844
The day I wrote you last I received the "Jeffersonian"[1] making a very bold denial of all the aspersions upon E.P.[2] I am now sincerely

glad that I did not publish here as I once thought of doing one of the statements in my possession which admitted that he had taken protection. In my answer to the letter of Dr. Bussey of Md,[3] I said, "It had been charged that E.P. took protection &c. &c. & then I went on to run the parallel between Haynes & this case.[4] But being unwilling that even that admission should be made I wrote to him again yesterday giving the Jeffersonians refutation of even the protection charge—so that if B. publishes my letter the whole will now appear clear & fair as it should do. I also wrote again yesterday to W.J.A.[5] that where the Jeffersonian article says E.P. *resigned* his commission it might have said that, after the enemy was repulsed at Sullivans Island, & quiet restored in the interior (as it was for years after) the Regiment of Rangers was disbanded, but that the commission was retained & is yet in the possession of his family. I moreover gave him the names of your mat. & pat. Grandmothers,[6] & asked him to ascertain their position in the Rev. war, & to examine whether *Robert Gillespie* were not brother to Capt. afterwards Col. John Gillespie[7] whose prowess is mentioned in the Regulation war & afterwards in the Revolution, & refered him to page 211 of Caruthers life of Rev. Dr. D. Caldwell of Guilford for instances of his conduct & courage.[8] (Have you seen it?) And also suggested the necessary inquiries about the Wilson family in Hopewell.[9] I know them to be very respectable & I think were whigs.

So soon as the entire facts are published & the vindication is complete I will have their substance forwarded to Bancroft.

All shall be carefully attended to. Next weeks Argus[10] will contain something further, but I think your pol. opponents are becoming ashamed of it, & have despaired of injuring you with it & will urge it no further. It has not lost you a single vote but I know how annoying it must be to your feelings. My wife is quite sick this morning, (tho the children are better) & I write in haste & with frequent interruptions. I shall watch carefully the different phases & complexion the whole matter may put on & act accordingly. You take the Jeffersonian I suppose or I would extract the article for you. My own paper I sent yesterday to the Argus.

A. R. Crozier our sub-elector is every day on the stump, & is one of our very best & most effective speakers in E.T.[11] *Lea* the ex-Secretary of State is blackguarding you every day almost on the stump & Crozier & Lyon are answering him—R. B. Reynolds & Cummins being often on their circuit.[12] I like the complexion of things decidedly better than two or three weeks ago. We are certainly gaining.

J. G. M. RAMSEY

ALS. DLC–JKP. Addressed to Columbia. Polk's AE on the cover states that he answered this letter on July 23, 1844; Polk's reply has not been found.

1. Charlotte *Mecklenburg Jeffersonian.*
2. Ezekiel Polk.
3. See Ramsey to Polk, July 16, 1844.
4. See Ramsey to Polk, July 10, 1844.
5. William J. Alexander.
6. Lydia Gillespie Knox and Mary Wilson Polk.
7. Not further identified.
8. Eli Washington Caruthers, *A Sketch of the Life and Character of the Rev. David Caldwell, D.D.* (Greensborough: Swaim and Sherwood, 1842).
9. Reference is to the family of Mary Wilson Polk.
10. Knoxville *Argus.*
11. East Tennessee.
12. Luke Lea, Arthur R. Crozier, either William or Thomas C. Lyon, Robert B. Reynolds, and David H. Cummings. Lea won election as a Democrat to two terms in the U.S. House, 1833–37, and served a partial term as Tennessee's secretary of state, 1837–39. An early advocate of Hugh L. White's presidential candidacy in 1836, Lea became a leading supporter of the Whig party in Tennessee. Thomas C. Lyon, a son of William Lyon, was appointed U.S. attorney for the eastern district of Tennessee in 1844.


## FROM RICHARD RUSH[1]

Sydenham,
My dear Sir:                near Philadelphia July 19, 1844

Yesterday's mail brought me your letter of the 9th instant,[2] which is very gratifying to me.

It will be a great pleasure to me to write to you under its invitation, though I should abuse such a privilege to use it too often, or to count upon returns, situated as you are; but I shall be most happy to drop you a letter whenever there may seem any thing on hand to me worth your hearing from this quarter of the union, during the pendency of the great contest before us; and I shall always venture to feel sure of its reception in a friendly spirit, after your valued letter of the 9th. I made our common friend Mr Muhlenberg a visit lately, staying a few days at his house in Reading. Observing the number of letters which every mail brought him, I remarked, "but you don't answer all?" He replied, "most of the writers seem to expect it"; to which I could not help rejoining, "the game would surely be a hard one on your side—something like 100 to one, perhaps; one letter apiece for each of your correspondents to write, but one hundred for you, if all are answered." The game might fall still harder upon you, by the larger scale on which it is most probably played against you.

My stay with Mr. Muhlenberg, took in the 4th of July, and its celebration in Berks county. The occasion drew together many of our
staunchest friends, from populous, neighboring, counties; and we had
Mr. Dallas there also, to add to the interest of the whole scene. Nothing could be more heartcheering than the accounts all gave of our
solid prospects of a great triumph in the fall on both tickets, national
and state. Tangible evidences were referred to, too numerous to detail
to you, in the coming over of Harrison-men to our ranks. The whigs
have doubtless some offsets to this; but full information justifies the
belief that our gain overwhelms theirs entirely. We lose individuals,
now and then, from personal pique; but we gain in *masses,* on the
broad ground of principle throughout the union. Your letter to our
Mr Kane[3] was very well-timed and judicious for this division of the
union! It is a jewel. It gives all we want on a subject on which it does
not do to be silent, and where to speak (for the whole nation) requires
the nicest adjustment of thought and words. To *write* about a tariff,
seems as difficult as to make one.

The deplorable tumults in Philadelphia, are likely to work in our
favor, in political results. Their main root has been in this new party
of 'native Americanism,' the first movements of which, hereabouts
at least, were being turned by whig address to their own account at
the polls; but the horrible excesses already flowing from this new
political organization which, under a popular but delusive name, seeks
to create, for the first time in our country, a distinction of races, is
recoiling upon its authors. It is getting into bad odor fast; our honest
democrats will no longer be seduced by it, and the whigs are rather in
danger of being caught in a snare they had themselves set. It takes
no hold, Mr Muhlenberg tells me, in the interior of our state [or none
deserving notice].

The fatal riots are suppressed for the present by our patriotic citizen
soldiery, and we all fervently hope, and are now disposed to believe,
that we shall have no more of them.

I rejoice to hear through such a channel as your letter, such good
accounts of the south and south west. I shall of course make no use
whatever of them or any thing else you honor me with, in connexion
with your name; and beg you to believe me dear Sir with the most ....
                                                                          RICHARD RUSH

P.S. When the opportunity may at any time conveniently occur, may
I ask the favor of tendering, through you, my thanks to the venerable patriot and sage of the hermitage for his kind transmission of my
letter.[4] O, for a single hour of *his* decision in the Philadelphia mag-

istracy when the church-burnings, and house-burnings, and murders occurred in May! If we had *had* it then, there would have been no recurrence of the still more deplorable scenes which this month of July has witnessed, as you will have known by the papers. R.R.

ALS. DLC–JKP. Addressed to Columbia.

1. A lawyer, diplomat, and writer, Richard Rush served as U.S. attorney general, 1814–17; as acting secretary of state, 1817; as minister to Great Britain, 1817–25; as secretary of the Treasury, 1825–29; and as minister to France, 1847–49. An unsuccessful vice-presidential candidate on John Q. Adams' ticket in 1828, Rush moved into the Democratic ranks during the fight over rechartering the Second Bank of the United States.

2. Polk's letter has not been found.

3. See Polk to John K. Kane, June 19, 1844.

4. Rush's letter to Polk of June 7, 1844, was enclosed in a letter sent to Andrew Jackson.

## TO GEORGE BANCROFT

My Dear Sir:                              Columbia Ten. July 20th 1844

I was much gratified to receive your kind letter of the 6th Inst., and thank you for the information which you give me, of political prospects in New England. It will be a source of sincere gratification to me, if the unsought & unexpected position in which my political friends have placed me before the country, shall have the effect, to heal our dissentions, or tend in any degree to promote the success of our cause. My friends *Mjr. Donelson, Genl. Pillow* and others early apprised me of your active and successful labours in bringing about the nomination. Since it was made, I have not failed to observe, with feelings of sincere gratitude, the part which you have borne in sustaining it. Towards *Mr Van-Buren* (from whose letter you give me an extract) both personally & politically my feelings have always been of the most friendly character; & there is no man to whom I was prepared to give a more cordial support, if he had been the candidate of the party. His magnanimous and zealous support of the nominations which *were* made, is characteristic of the man, and places me under lasting obligations to him.

I am sorry that my friends have troubled you about the biographical sketch, without having first consulted you on the subject. Your reasons for declining the task are conclusive & perfectly satisfactory. I had myself but little, I may say no agency in the matter. Immediately after the nominations at Baltimore, several of my friends, at Washington, addressed letters to myself and my friends in Tennessee, urging the importance of having such a sketch prepared, and mentioning your name as the author. Shortly afterwards, my friends here, became anxious that it should be done, and my friend *Harris*, was desirous to prepare as he did, the manuscript notes which he forwarded to you. During all this time I rested under the impression that you had been consulted, upon the subject by my friends at Washington. In this I find I was mistaken. I need scarcely assure you, that if such a sketch was to be prepared, I preferred that you should do it. In what has been done I only yielded to the importunity of friends, who thought it important, for the pending canvass. I am now satisfied that it is not necessary and that its publication, in the heat of the battle, unless prepared with great care and caution, might do mischief rather than good. Under this impression, I have written to *Mr Harris*, from whom I have received a letter since the manuscript was returned to him, giving it as my decided opinion that nothing of the kind should be now done. As you remark "The Democracy of the country will take care of this election," and enough is probably known of their candidates to supercede, the necessity, which was at first supposed to exist, for such a work.

I shall be pleased My Dear Sir, to hear from you often during the pendency of the contest, & to receive from you any information or suggestions which you may deem to be useful.

JAMES K. POLK

ALS. MHi. Addressed to Boston and marked *"Private."*

## FROM RANSOM H. GILLET

My Dear Sir,                                     Ogdensburgh July 20. 1844

Your favor of the 4th inst[1] came to me a day or two since, from which I am happy to learn, that you & Mrs. Polk are in good health & spirits. The action of the democratic party throughout the union, upon the proceedings at Baltimore, ought to make you selfsatisfied & happy. Never have the party responded to a nomination with more enthusiasm & sincerity. The tokens of success are legible in every countenance. While your competitor has laboured for a quarter of a century to make himself the head of the nation for four years, the nation itself is accomplishing that object for you, without your personal exertions. I have long looked to the period when you would be our candidate, but in point of time, the event is in advance of my expectations. It will afford you pleasure, I presume, to learn the progress of events in our state. You will learn much from our papers. Some things, however, do not get into print. We have serious dissentions on the subject of Governor. If not healed, you must carry our local ticket (or it will fail) instead of the local ticket buoying you up. We also have our difficulties with the Texas question. Some of our good & true men are hostile to the admission of Texas in any form. The leaders on this subject will, however, support you & Mr. Dallas most cheerfully, but they wish to elect anti Texas men to congress, & to our legislature so as to fill Mr. Talmadges[2] vacancy with one who will be opposed to annexation. How far we shall be able to controul these things, I cannot say. In our local convention, I tried to make a Tixion platform on which we could all stand. So far as our county is concerned, the effort was successful. Beyond here, things are uncertain. Though there is some special pleading in my resolutions, I think they will stand the test. The spirit is the same as the one adopted at Baltimore, which was suggested by me to Mr Butler in New York just before the convention. The plan of readopting my Baltimore resolutions of 1840,[3] was the invention of some other person, to which of course, I cannot object. I have full confidence that these questions, which are mostly those of expediency, will not do us essential injury, so as to defeat us. I was most happy to see your Tariff letter.[4] You are on the ground that the northern democracy occupy. The terms, "tariff," "free trade," "protection" &c are quite technical, & are made to mean different things in different parts of the country. The use of plain intelligible terms, will show that our party at the North & South, East & West, all occupy the same ground on this subject. The technicalities & quibling of Mr. Clay on this, & other subjects, are unworthy of a statesman. Success, under such auspices, would be worse than defeat to an honest highminded man. A clear & frank development of a candidates opinions will, if he succeeds, give him a fair field for usefulness, with a consciousness, that a majority are with him, without which no man should desire office.

Last Wednesday Mr Wright, Mr King[5] & I addressed the people at Gouverneur in this county. Yesterday, Mr W. & Mr K. did the same at Potsdam & to day at Massena. Next Tuesday, they will be at Malone, Franklin Co. Professional matters prevented my going the whole round. In a short time, I have promised to go with Mr. W. to Watertown & Syracuse (Wardwell & Taylors districts).[6] No man goes into the canvass with more spirit & zeal, than Mr Wright. He had been at home but three days before he took the field. I do not think he will have two weeks quiet this summer & fall. He vouches for you & Mr Dallas, in a way that might touch your *bump of vanity,* if you had one. He will *not* be a candidate for Governor. If you are elected, you will have the aid of his talents & experience in the senate, where, of all places, I think, he prefers to be. Until the democratic party, *with a common voice,* call him to be a national standard bearer, I hope to see him remain where he is. I mention this, so that his motives may not be misconstrued in certain contingencies which are not unlikely to occur.

I like the call to your Mass Meeting.[7] It is death to certain disunion schemes which are afloat, being the last issues of a distempered brain. I should like most dearly to be there & take some friends by the hand. But I am tied to Blackstone & Kent[8] by the chain of poverty, & must content myself with breathing a prayer for them, & doing what I can for the good old cause in my native state.

I saw friend Wardwell last week. He is a happy man about these days. He says he was never so elated at a nomination in his life as at yours. He resides at Pulaski, Oswego Co. He promise[d ...][9] himself to a vigrous action & to continue until the vot[ing is] over. This is the course of all your old acquaintances in this state. They are at work because it is a pleasure to do so.

As we cannot all go to see you, we shall expect next year that you will visit the north, where we will give you a hearty welcome. You must see the noble St. Lawrence, on the banks of which you will find your old friend's *cabin, with the latch string hanging out.*

Make my best respects to Mrs. Polk. Mrs. G.[10] is sitting by me & desires to be remembered to you both. Hoping to hear from you, as your leisure shall permit, I remain....

R. H. GILLET

ALS. DLC–JKP. Addressed to Columbia. Polk's AE on the cover states that he answered this letter on August 7, 1844; Polk's reply has not been found.

1. Letter not found.

2. Nathaniel P. Tallmadge resigned from the U.S. Senate on June 17, 1844, to accept an appointment as governor of the Wisconsin Territory.

3. Gillet served as chairman of the Resolutions Committee of the Democratic National Convention of 1840. His committee prepared a set of nine resolutions setting forth the party's basic principles.

4. See Polk to John K. Kane, June 19, 1844.

5. Silas Wright, Jr., and Preston King. A lawyer in Ogdensburg, King sat in the New York Assembly, 1835–38; won four terms in the U.S. House, 1843–47 and 1849–53; and served one term as a Republican in the U.S. Senate, 1857–63.

6. Daniel Wardwell and William Taylor. A lawyer in Rome, Wardwell served both in the New York Assembly, 1825–28, and in the U.S. House, 1831–37. Taylor, a physician in Onondaga County, N.Y., won three terms in the U.S. House, 1833–39, and sat in the New York Assembly in 1841 and

1842.

7. Reference is to the Democratic mass meeting in Nashville scheduled for August 15, 1844.

8. Gillet's allusion is to the practice of law and to the works of William Blackstone and James Kent, noted English and American legal scholars.

9. Manuscript obliterated here and below.

10. Gillet's wife is not identified further.


## FROM WILLIAM E. CRAMER

                                                               Argus Office
Respected Sir,                                          Albany, July 21st 1844

The contest is becoming exceedingly animated. I might say bitter. The result in Louisiana is regarded by the Whigs as decidedly favorable to their prospects. They already begin to term Texas annexation, a humbug! Our friends do not feel discouraged but they certainly were disappointed. We are now most anxiously looking to Tennessee and North Carolina and Kentucky. The Whigs now anticipate a victory in all those States. The Democrats Count upon Tennessee but not upon Carolina or Kentucky.

Matters look well in Pennsylvania. Though they are all Tariff men there. Your last letter to Mr Kane[1] seems to give satisfaction. But It is manifest that the great battle is to be fought in this State. You at a distance can scarcely appreciate the fury of the Contest. The Whigs are trying very hard particularly in the Western Part of the State to make it a direct issue on Slavery. The extension and perpetuity of Slavery is industriously circulated upon all their Hand bills, to be the *great principle* of the supporters of Gov Polk. This in a Free State is a sharp sword. To add to our embarrassment, John C. Calhouns followers boldly come out for Disunion and Nullification. Their past cry is Texas and Disunion.

To Counteract this most dangerous Current last week we published in the Argus an article from the Nashville Union, accompanying which I penned a strong endorsement. We democrats here feel no great pleasure in being sunk "five fathoms deep" by the chivalry of the Imperial Kingdom of South Carolina.

Our friends are working manfully and from all sections send us cheering accounts.

Your great Mass Convention is approaching. Has *Gansevoort Melville* of New-York been invited?[2] He would feel the Compliment and he is deserving of it, As he is one of the ablest Stump Orators we have in the Northern States. His voice is so powerful that he can easily be heard by thousands. Perhaps he may come. If so, our South Western friends will not be disappointed. I anticipate one of the mightiest gatherings ever held in this Country. It is understood that McDuffie is to be one of the Speakers, but he should strive to be somewhat moderate as his late remarks at Richmond (wherein he denounced the Tariff States as Pirates and robbers) are stabbing us under the fifth rib.[3]

Wm E. CRAMER

ALS. DLC–JKP. Addressed to Columbia. Polk's AE on the cover states that he answered this letter on August 3, 1844; Polk's reply has not been found.
1. See Polk to John K. Kane, June 19, 1844.
2. Melville spoke at the Democratic mass meeting in Nashville, August 15, 1844.
3. George McDuffie addressed a Democratic meeting in Richmond, Va., on June 25, 1844. Cramer's phrase "under the fifth rib" is an archaic expression meaning "close to the heart."

## FROM ROBERT ARMSTRONG

Dear Sir                                        Nashville July 22 [18]44
Genl. Jackson has anticipated you in addressing Houston. His letter leaves to night.[1] It is one that Houston will give ear to. The Genl. says every thing you could wish. Takes hold of the strong points in The Texas Question and ends by giving him the best Kind of advice. It will do. The *work* was prepared by Donelson, and I retain a copy.
I have prepared a notice of Our Mass Meeting comeing from the Committee for the Union to night.[2] It will *cover* any *neglect* of Invitations &c &c &c and bring out our friends. The Whigs will Disband their forces and go to *work privately*. They published in the Banner an Order that they should attend in the Hermitage district *to day*.[3] Not one *Marched*. Not a drum heard. Our Volunteers 200 plus went up on a boat and the last heard from they were paying their respects to The old Chief.[4] *Guild* killed off *Jennings* to day.[5] The Whigs were astonished, and Dispirited. All looks well. I wish you could come in.
Henry Horne & Kane,[6] say by to nigts mail that they will be here 15 Augt.
I intend to have Genl Jackson here, and you and him ride in the *Constitution Carriage*,[7] to Our Camp, & then with draw if you think proper.
I have written Mathews.[8] I hear our Troops, Music &c coming from the boat. It has been a great day in the old Man's District. In haste.

R. ARMSTRONG

[P.S.] (*See the Union.*) To What office shall I address *Casey* of *Ill?*[9]

ALS. DLC–JKP. Addressed to Columbia.

1. In his letter to Sam Houston of July 19, 1844, Andrew Jackson anticipated victory for Polk and the friends of annexation; and he urged the Texan president to avoid any action or alliance that would make annexation difficult. LS. Tx.

2. On July 23, 1844, the *Nashville Union* carried a notice from the Nashville Democratic Central Committee inviting all Democrats to attend the mass meeting in Nashville on August 15, 1844.

3. An order published July 22, 1844, in the Nashville *Republican Banner* summoned the U.S. Clay Dragoons to a meeting of the company on that day.

4. Reference is to the excursion made by Democratic militia units to visit Andrew Jackson.

5. Josephus C. Guild and Thomas R. Jennings. A Gallatin lawyer, Guild served three terms in the Tennessee House, 1833–36, 1845–47, and 1851–53, and sat for one term in the Senate, 1837–39. He was a Democratic candidate for presidential elector in 1844. Armstrong's reference is to the outcome of a debate in Davidson County between the two men.

6. Henry Horn and John K. Kane.

7. Citizens of New York presented the carriage to Andrew Jackson at the White House on February 22, 1837. Constructed of wood removed from the U.S. frigate *Constitution,* the carriage was one of Jackson's most cherished possessions. Armstrong's reference is to his plans for the Democratic mass meeting in Nashville.

8. Robert Mathews was an Irish-born Shelbyville merchant and Democrat.

9. Zadoc Casey, lieutenant governor of Illinois in 1830, served five terms as a Democrat in the U.S. House, 1833–43. Armstrong penned this second sentence of his postscript in the fold of his cover sheet.


## TO ANDREW J. DONELSON

My Dear Sir:                                    Columbia July 22d, 1844

Since the nominations at Baltimore, none can fail to have observed the *coldness or indifference* of the Globe. After *Blair's* professions made confidentially to you, I had expected that he would come zealously into support of the nominations, and not throw cold water upon them. To show you that I am not singular, in the conclusions to which I have come in regard to the course of the *Globe,* I venture to give you the following extract from a *highly confidential* letter received from *Mr Dallas* of date 10th Instant, vis— "What does the Globe mean? Surely *Col. Benton* cannot cherish a lurking hostility to your nomination. He writes to his correspondents here that he is entering upon the canvass with ardour, and he is not one to profess, what he dont feel and think: yet certainly *Mr Blair's* columns are exceedingly *cold,* and now and then seize upon a topic, the only tendency of which seems towards dissaffecting the party."

He adds much more, & says, he can "discern the effect upon a few of our active men here. They do not in the slightest degree resist or thwart the nomination, but they maintain Col. Benton's theory, that the whole was a conspiracy against their favourite &c." Mr *D.* asks if there is any way, to remedy this, and induce the *Globe* to enter more zealously and decidedly into the contest. I know of none unless your intimacy with *Blair* would authorize you to write him, a *plain,* but at the same time friendly and conciliatory letter, urging him as a matter of duty to the party to take, stronger ground than he has yet done. If the *Genl.*[1] is able to write him one of his strong letters in his own hand-writing, and you could write one yourself it would effect the object. The truth is, that for several weeks past the *Globe* has scarcely alluded to the election in an editorial article. If he continues this course, the conclusion with many democrats, will be that to say the least of it he is indifferent as to the result. Think of it, and if you think it proper, write yourself & get *Genl. Jackson* to write to *Blair.* When you write, beg him to cease the war upon *Mr C.*[2] and his Southern friends, and upon the Texas question, until the pending election is over at all events. The only effect of keeping up that *war* is to weaken us. It can by no possibility do good.

I enclose to the General by to day's mail a very important letter in relation to *Texian affairs* and the movements of Mexico, England & France.[3] I have no great confidence in the writer; still he is at Washington & his letter comes to me under the frank of Mr *Senator Walker* of Mississippi. It may be of vast importance, not only as regards, the ultimate annexation of Texas, but as affecting the pending political contest, that the General should write the letter to *H.*[4] suggested. If he and you think so, you must assist him in its preparation, and the sooner the better. You will of course see my letter to the *General* & the one enclosed.

Have you written the letters to our distinguished friends at a distance, urging them to attend our mass meeting on the 15th?[5] To which of them have you written? Did you include Senator Allen & Dr. Duncan of Ohio, in the number? If not will you yet write to them. In haste.

JAMES K. POLK

P.S. If the *General* writes to *Houston,* as I hope he will, let his letter be addressed in a different hand-writing from his own & go *without his frank.* There is a danger if it bears his frank that it would be arrested in passing through the mail. It might be enclosed to some reliable friend at New Orleans with a request that he would give it a speedy conveyance. J.K.P.

ALS. DLC–AJD. Addressed to Nashville and marked *"Strictly Confidential."* Published in *THM,* III, pp. 57–58.
1. Andrew Jackson.
2. John C. Calhoun.
3. A letter from Alexander O. Anderson to Polk, July 11, 1844, was enclosed in Polk's letter to Andrew Jackson of July 22, 1844.
4. Sam Houston.
5. Reference is to the Nashville Democratic mass meeting of August 15, 1844.

TO ANDREW JACKSON

My dear Sir,                                    Columbia July 22. 1844

I send you the enclosed letter from Genl. Anderson,[1] formerly a Senator in Congress from this State, who has been at Washington for some time past. You know the man & can place the proper estimate on his opinions, and views. I confess I have no great confidence in his judgement; still the information which he gives, if true, is important, and there is reason to believe it is true. If Houston should unfortunately yield to the British scheme, it would not only be fatal to our future hopes for the annexation of Texas, but would, I apprehend, operate most prejudicially upon the pending Presidential election in the U.S. I concur therefore in the opinion that a letter from you to Houston, presenting to him the reasons which should induce him to decline making any negotiation, such as Genl. Anderson mentions, with England, or France, may be important, *very important.* Induce him if possible to hold on to his present position until after the meeting of our Congress.

I differ widely with Anderson in that part of his letter in which he advises that Mr. Benton should be denounced. I disapprove Mr. B's course on the Texas question, and regret it as much as any man, I think it unfortunate for himself as well as for the Country, but still he and his friends have not broken off from our party and are yielding their support to the national nominations, and it would be worse than madness to make war upon them. Genl. A's feelings are very violent towards Mr. Benton, and his advice, in regard to him is to be rejected.

I wish the tone of the *Globe* was more cordial. Its apparent coldness and indifference is attracting some attention in Pennsylvania and elsewhere. I have written to Maj. Donelson upon that point today. He will show you my letter.[2]

James K. Polk

P.S. General A's letter came to me under the frank of Senator Walker, of Mississippi.

L, copy. T–Misc. File. Addressed to the Hermitage. Copy contains corrections in an unknown hand.
1. See Alexander O. Anderson to Polk, July 11, 1844.
2. See Polk to Andrew J. Donelson, July 22, 1844.

## FROM J. G. M. RAMSEY

My Dear Sir                         Mecklenburg July 22. 1844
You will see from the date of this that as I informed you in my two last letters I am still at home. Your two last of the 12 & 13[1] & Bishop Polks[2] of the 4th reached me by yesterdays (the 21st) mail, a very unaccountable delay. Do you receive all mine? I have written to you by nearly every mail Westward for two weeks, viz the 10, 12, 15, 17, 19.[3] Please inform me whether they have all come to hand. I fear some P.M. has delayed or detained them. Be that as it may I have kept you informed from time to time of all I have done & have also written to Haywood & Saunders & W. J. Alexander & prompted them to every thing within my reach beside the long vindication[4] I made out & sent to them at Raleigh. Even of that I have received no acknowledgment from Raleigh but suppose from an article I have seen in the Jeffersonian[5] that it went safely, but do not know it certainly.

The Bishop makes some good suggestions & I will reexamine my authorities & furnish other instances of the taking *protection* by others than Hayne & E.P.[6] My present impression is that Col. Pickens[7] himself & many others did so. I will send what I find to Charlotte or Raleigh.

I consider myself peculiarly unfortunate in not being able by any effort to go to Charlotte.[8] About the time I should have started two of my children took sick & the very day I would have done so, tho they had got better, my wife[9] was taken with a very violent hemorrhage of the most dangerous character & which brought her in a few hours to the point of death. Doctor Paxton[10] one of our most experienced physicians has been with her ever since. She is not yet out of danger but we hope is better. In the mean time if my letters have been received at Raleigh & Charlotte I have no doubt the whole *vindication* will be perfect & complete & is before this time in press.[11] When it is out if there is a single hiatus in the narrative or an anachronism in the dates, or an omission of any essential circumstance it can be supplied or corrected in an appendix or through the news-papers. Nothing shall be omitted that either friendship to you or respect for the honored dead can dictate.

After your second request to go to Charlotte I would certainly have gone but for the illness of my wife & family. I hope however nothing *essential* has been lost by my not going tho I could wish that the necessity which prevented it had not existed.

I have to reply to the Bishop this morning, go over Drayton, Ramsay, Simms, Johnsons life of Greene &c,[12] in time for tomorrows mail, & have therefore time only to say things are brightening here. I find new evidence every day that Clay cannot get Jones vote by a large number. The Argus will have another article this week on the slanders of E.P.[13]

J. G. M. RAMSEY

ALS. DLC–JKP. Addressed to Columbia. Polk's AE on the cover states that he answered this letter on July 29, 1844; Polk's reply has not been found.

1. Letters not found.

2. A son of William Polk of Raleigh, N.C., and a graduate of the U.S. Military Academy at West Point, Leonidas Polk resigned his army commission to enter the ministry in the Protestant Episcopal Church. In 1838, he was elected missionary bishop of the Southwest; three years later he was chosen bishop of Louisiana. During the Civil War he served as a general officer in the Confederate army.

3. Letters of July 12 and 17 have not been found; Ramsey also wrote to Polk on July 16.

4. Reference is to a refutation of Whig charges that Ezekiel Polk had been a tory during the Revolutionary War.

5. The article in the Charlotte *Mecklenburg Jeffersonian* is not identified further.

6. Isaac Hayne and Ezekiel Polk.

7. A native of Pennsylvania, Andrew Pickens removed to South Carolina with his parents. During the Revolutionary War, he served as an officer in the state militia; he rose through the ranks from captain to brigadier general. After the fall of Charleston in 1780, Pickens took protection from the British until tory forces raided his home; that violation of his property led him to resume his fight against the British. Pickens served several terms in the South Carolina House and one term in the U.S. House, 1793–95.

8. Reference is to the Democratic barbecue in Charlotte, N.C., on July 23, 1844.

9. Ramsey's children and his wife, Peggy Barton Crozier Ramsey, are not identified further.

10. Joseph W. Paxton, who is not identified further.

11. Reference is to the *Vindication* of Ezekiel Polk, a publication prepared by William H. Haywood, Jr.

12. Reference is to historical works by John Drayton, David Ramsay, William G. Simms, and William Johnson, whose biography of Nathanael Greene is mentioned here.

13. The article in the Knoxville *Argus* concerning Ezekiel Polk is not identified further.

## FROM JOHN CATRON

My dear sir:                                    [Nashville, Tenn.] July 23d, 1844

In answer to yours of yesterday,[1] it is enough to say for myself that the opinion expressed in mine of the 18th,[2] is not only unchanged, but confirmed by the concurrence of every man who I have consulted. This morning I conversed with Mr. Nicholson, whose caution, and knowledge are far superior to mine, on subjects having a political aspect. He says there is not a single dissent; on the contrary a strong and decided concurrence, that you ought by all means to be here on the 15th of August.[3] That the matter was the subject of conversation last eving in the Committee[4]; thought of well; & the conclusion unanimous, to this effect.

And as to *Mrs. Polk:* The opinion is as decided. My compliments to her—& say on the score of *"inconvenience,"* of which your letter speaks, it is no great matter in an empty house, with a fair larder, and a *full* cellar—& where none are so green, as to trouble themselves by oppressing visitors with useless attention. That she shall have the easy comfort of shifting for herself, on one side of the House—you and your frds on the other, in the library; but especially, in the office, having two rooms, very neat, but too small somewhat, with a gate and door off on the cross street. For especial occasions, the library up stairs will answer all the higher purposes. *Individuals,* must be seen alone. I'll make it work like the old clock, & with less noise.

Don't believe that I have any squeamishness on the Judgeship score. One of my brethern is openly seeking the Presidency,[5] & founds himself on this ground as a Judge, and is praised for his patriotism. Ewing,[6] the now Chief Justice of Ky, was here at the Whig Convention of 1840, & is lauded for his patriotism. Judge Reed[7] was for years the W. Dstrct chairman of the Whig Comtee. The entertaining [of] friends, will be nothing amiss.

I am perfectly idle—not a letter to write; & if I can be of any service to you, *personally,* it will be afforded with hearty good will.

J. CATRON

P.S. The Horse is shod, feeding on oates &c. My people ride him in & out to the farm, and I think he is better recovered than any horse so badly foundered I have ever known. Send for him any time three days hence. This, especially for Elias's comfort. J.C.

ALS. DLC–JKP. Addressed to Columbia.
1. Polk's letter to Catron of July 22, 1844, has not been found.
2. Reference is probably to Catron's letter to Polk of July 17, 1844.
3. Reference is to the Democratic mass meeting in Nashville, August 15, 1844.
4. Reference is probably to the Committee of Arrangements for the Nashville Democratic mass meeting.
5. John McLean. McLean served as a member of the U.S. House, 1813–1816; Ohio Supreme Court judge, 1816–22; U.S. postmaster general, 1823–29; and as an associate justice of the U.S. Supreme Court, 1829–61. A group of Ohio congressmen attempted to promote McLean as a Whig presidential candidate in 1843; and McLean, who had also been mentioned as a presidential candidate in the 1830s, did nothing to discourage the movement.
6. Ephraim M. Ewing, a lawyer from Russellville, Ky., represented Logan County in the Kentucky House, 1830–32; became associate justice of the Kentucky Court of Appeals in 1835; and served as chief justice of that court from 1843 to 1847.
7. Reference probably is to John Read, who served as judge of the Circuit Court for the Tenth District of Tennessee from 1836 until the Civil War.

## TO ANDREW J. DONELSON

My Dear Sir:            Columbia July 23d, 1844

I send by *Genl. Pillow* a letter to *Genl. Jackson*,[1] inclosing one to me from *Mr Senator Walker of Miss.* of the 10th Inst. It relates to *Mr Tyler's* position, and the means by which he may be induced to withdraw. It is of great importance that he should do so. *Mr Dallas* concurs in this opinion. I have given the *Genl.* an extract from a letter received from *Mr D.* of the 10th Instant. I believe *Genl. Jackson* is the only man in the country, who can effect it. I desire *Genl. Armstrong, Genl. Pillow,* and *yourself* to confer together freely, in regard to what is proper to be done. I believe *Gen. Jackson* is the only man in the country whose advice Mr Tyler would take. I doubt the propriety of *Genl. Jackson's* writing a letter for the public, as suggested by *Walker,* but of this you will judge. *Pillow* knows the contents of my letter to *Genl. Jackson* and of course Genl. *Armstrong* and *yourself* will see it. I have handed to *Pillow* a letter received from *Walker*[2] one day later than the one enclosed to the General. From it you will see that a letter written by Genl. J. to some one at Washington is in the proper tone and would answer a most valuable purpose, but for an allusion in it to *Mr Benton,* which prevents it from being used or even shown to Tyler. Another might be written leaving out that allusion, which might reach the President's ego. The Genl. can certainly induce *Blair* of the Globe to change his course. To continue his attacks on Tyler can do no good, but must result in harm. Confer fully and freely with *Pillow, Armstrong* & the *General,* and do what is thought best.

There is another matter to which I wish to call your attention. It is that mentioned in the enclosed letter of *Jonas E. Thomas Esqr* (former Speaker of the Ho. Repts. of our Legislature) to *Genl. Jackson.*[3] A. V. Brown replied to *Mr Henry's* charge, & stated that it had been denied by *Genl. Jackson* and was untrue. He further stated that when *Mr Adams* first made the statement, some years ago, and *Genl. Jackson* denied it through the *Globe,* that it was ascertained by reference to dates that on the day *Mr Adams* stated he handed the Treaty to *Genl. Jackson* for his examination, being according to Mr Adam's statement the day before it was signed, that he *Genl. Jackson* was taking a public dinner at New York. This accords with my recollection of the facts as they occurred at the time. To this statement of *Mr Brown, Mr Henry* replied that by an examination of the tavern-keepers books at Washington, it appeared that *Genl. Jackson* was not in New York, but in Washington, on the day *Mr Adams* said he had submitted the Treaty to him for his examination. Here as I learn the discussion ended. *Mr Thomas* deemed it to be unnecessary to go into these details in his letter to the General. Can you or the General turn to the Globe of that period and see what the statements and proofs were. If they are full it may be sufficient to re-publish, without calling a fresh letter from the General to the public. *Mr Thomas* does not desire the Genl. to answer unless he deems it proper to do so. *Henry's* statement is calculated to do harm, if uncontradicted, & it is proper to meet it, either by a direct letter from the Genl. in reply to *Mr Thomas,* or by the publication of the old proofs. Confer with *Pillow* & *Armstrong* about this also, and let me know what will be done. *Pillow* is a friend, is an honourable man & you may safely confide in him.

JAMES K. POLK

ALS. DLC–AJD. Addressed to Nashville and marked *"Confidential."* Published in *THM,* III, pp. 58–59.

1. See Polk to Andrew Jackson, July 23, 1844.

2. See Robert J. Walker to Polk, July 11, 1844.

3. Thomas' letter to Jackson has not been found. The matter at hand was whether Jackson in advance of the signing had approved of giving up the United States' claims to Texas, as provided in the Adams-Onís Treaty of 1819.

John Q. Adams stated in a speech to the U.S. House on May 7, 1836, that he had shown the proposed treaty to Jackson and received his approval. On May 10, the Washington *Globe* reported that Jackson denied Adams' assertions. Adams reiterated his statements in the House on May 10, and on May 13 the *Globe* published a detailed refutation using newspaper reports to show that Jackson had been absent from Washington from February 11 to March 1, 1819, the period in question.

## FROM J. GEORGE HARRIS

My Dear Sir, Nashville. July 23. 1844
I enclose Jones's reply.[1] You will perceive that "all things work together for good."[2] The President is on his bridal tour to his Va. plantation—hence the necessary delay.[3] I wrote him the most pressing (yet prudent) letter I could form—appealing to *such* considerations as I thought would *move* him. I am *now* well satisfied that "it will work."

I send you *two* of the five vols. of G. & S. Reg. Deb.[4] *These* I have found in my own library. The other *three* are not in the Exec. office, not in Mr. Grundy's library. I shall make further inquiry, and send them at earliest moment.

Every thing works well here; and if *all* the newspapers from abroad do not belie the times, there has never been so much *substantial* and *reliable* movement of the people *upon principle,* since the formation of the government as there is at this moment.

It must be exceedingly gratifying to you as it is to your friends.

Some of our friends think it possible that since Mexico has appealed to England France, Russia, Prussia, & through their ministers resident at her court, Houston will be *bribed* in one way or another to refuse *annexation,* or[5] I do not think so. Gen. Jackson has written him a most powerful & beseeching letter to await the result of the present contest. He will do it. Nor will the appeal to the Allied powers of Europe avail any thing. Whatever may be the inclination of French ministers *Frenchmen themselves* are opposed to any movement which has a tendency to prevent the "extension of the area of freedom,"[6] and it would cost Louis Phillippe[7] his crown to enterfere. It would be at once transferred to the head of the Bourbon heir (Duke of Bordeaux)[8] who is young and ambitious, and whose head is aching to receive it. Russia has as much as she can do, in Siberia, Circassia, on her eastern border, and in maintaining her claims on the Black Sea & the Baltic. Austria can scarcely take care of herself and keep Bohemians & Hungarians, and her Italian provinces in subjection. Prussia might possibly sympathize with but she could give but little aid to

England. *England* herself will do all she can to aid Mexico, to bribe Sam Houston, or do any thing else for the sake of gaining the same power at the mouth of the Mississippi that she has at the mouth of the Mediterranean. Their peaceable mode is to *rush* their countrymen into Texas and seize it under the Texan constitution by *popular vote.* God grant they may not be successful.

J. Geo. Harris

[P.S.] In my reply to *J*,[9] think I have made some valuable suggestions to him, though I have carefully guarded every period.[10]

In addition to the President's absence, the absence of his Private Sec. *John* jr.[11] who went south to shoot at Pleasants, ed. Rich Whig,[12] "and found him too drunk to fight" —is probably another reason why there may be a week or two of delay.[13]

Give yourself not a moment of uneasiness about this Madisonian matter. I shall, I trust, manage it *prudently,* for in that reposes certain success. In the enclosed letter I recognize a good deal of the *feeler—* and, upon reflection, I will *merely acknowledge it* in a cordial manner, awaiting further developments.

ALS. DLC–JKP. Addressed to Columbia. Polk's AE on the cover states that he answered this letter on July 26, 1844; Polk's reply has not been found.

1. Harris corresponded with "John Jones" (Thomas Allen) regarding the editorship of the Washington *Madisonian* or a successor paper; Allen's letter to Harris has not been found. Polk's AE on the cover indicates that he returned Allen's letter to Harris on July 26, 1844.

2. Partial quotation of the scriptural verse, "all things work together for good to them that love God." Romans 8:28.

3. John Tyler and Julia Gardiner Tyler left Washington City for Virginia during the first week of July and did not return until August 12, 1844.

4. Reference is to the *Register of Debates in Congress,* published by the firm of Gales & Seaton.

5. Archaic use of the conjunction "or" for the conjunction "but."

6. Quotation is not identified further.

7. Louis Philippe.

8. Henri Charles Ferdinand Marie Dieudonné d'Artois, Comte de Chambord and Duc de Bordeaux, had been proclaimed King Henri V of France by the Legitimist faction in 1836.

9. Reference is to "John Jones," the pseudonym of Thomas Allen.

10. Harris wrote this sentence in the left margin of the first page of his letter; the remaining paragraphs were written on the inside folds of his cover sheet.

11. John Tyler, Jr.

12. John H. Pleasants founded the Richmond *Constitutional Whig* in 1824, renamed it the *Richmond Whig and Public Advertiser* in 1833, and edited it

until his death in 1846.

13. Quotation is not identified further.

## TO ANDREW JACKSON

My Dear Sir:                                    Columbia July 23rd, 1844

I received on yesterday the enclosed letter from *Mr Senator Walker* of Mississippi.[1] I have communicated its contents *confidentially* to my friend *Genl. Pillow* who will hand you this letter, & who will confer with you in regard to the steps proper to be taken, if any thing should be done in reference to its suggestions. *Genl. Pillow* is my friend, and an honorable and reliable man, with whom you may safely communicate freely. The object which *Mr Walker* desires to attain, is an important one, and yet occupying the position which I do, it is one of so much delicacy, that I do not see how I could write on the subject to any one. I submit it to your better judgment, what you may deem it proper to do. The main object in the way of *Mr. T's*[2] withdrawal seems to be the course of the *Globe* towards himself and his friends. There is certainly no necessity for the *Globe* to continue its attacks upon him or his administration. A seperate *Tyler* ticket, might put in jeopardy the vote of several closely contested States, and *perhaps* affect the final result. Surely Mr *Blair* of the Globe can be induced to cease his war upon the administration during the pendency of the contest at least. I have desired *Genl. Pillow* to have a few conferences with yourself, *Genl. Armstrong* and *Majr. Donelson,* upon the subject as also in relation to the letter of *Genl. Anderson,* which I enclosed to you on yesterday.[3] These two measures are at this moment of greater importance, than any that have arisen or likely to arise. *Mr Dallas* from whom I received a letter of the 10th Inst. says, "The course of President Tyler in perversely maintaining a substantive position, is the result of bad advice. Can you devise no mode of inducing him to give fair play, to his intelligence and integrity, and to be content with contributing his aid to the attainment of the main object?" I believe you are the only man in the country whose advice would be likely to influence him. How far you would deem it proper to give advice, I leave to your own good judgment. I ought not to write to him or his friends, or to make any pledges to anyone, except as it regards my political principles, in advance of the election. To *you* however I can say that in the event of my election, I shall assume the high trust, with the firm purpose of maintaining my principles, and certainly with no prejudices or unkind feelings towards any portion of the party. My great desire would be to see Democratic principles prevail in the policy of the Government, and with that object in view to witness a harmonious re-union of all the old Jackson Democrats of '28 & '32, with whom I co-operated for so many years, in maintaining our common cause.

My information from all quarters contin[ues][4] to be of the most cheering character, and if Mr T. would withdraw, and the Texian Government, shall enter into no negotiations with Great Britain, or France, I should regard the result as almost certain.

JAMES K. POLK

P.S. When you are done with *Mr Walker's* letter, be pleased to return it to me. J.K.P.

ALS. DLC–AJ. Addressed to the Hermitage and marked *"Confidential."*
1. See Robert J. Walker to Polk, July 10, 1844.
2. John Tyler.
3. See Alexander O. Anderson to Polk, July 11, 1844.
4. Manuscript obliterated here by oil from sealing wax.

## FROM ANDREW JACKSON

My dear Sir,                                Hermitage July 23d 1844

I have recd yours of the 22d *confidential* with Genl Alex. O. Anderson enclosed.[1] I have written to Genl Saml Houston some days past as strong a letter as I could dictate.[2] The information communicated by the Genl I have been some time in possession of & it may be, he has derived his information from a confidential letter I wrote some time since to my friend in Washington. Be this as it may, it is certainly true, that the combined influence of both France and England are now employed to induce Genl Houston to withdraw the proposition of reannexation to the U. [States][3] and to yield to their propositions such as the [one] stated by the Genl and to be candid with you, necessity may compell Texas to yield herself to the propositions of England & France. If the threatening invasion by Santa Anna is real, and he can raise the means to carry it into effect, Texas has not the fiscal, nor the phisical means, to resist the invasion successfully without aid. But this movement of Mexico may be under British influence to alarm Texas & induce her to adopt the measure proposed. But the speeches of some of our Senators in Congress was well calculated to arouse Santa Anna to make the flourish of an effort at invasion and knowing that if he could drive the Texans east of the Sabine that he could sell Texas to Great Britain in ten days for at least sixty millions, and by the transfer, clear Mexico of the British debt. Texas is in danger. If our president would now take the ground, that Texas by the cession of

1803,[4] became part of the United States, that no treaty with Spain,[5] or other power, could free us from our obligations to the citizens of Louisiana, now Texas, that treaty being the supreme law of the land and could not be abrogated unless by the consent of France and the inhabitants of Texas, and Texas having demanded our protection &c &c and the present Government of Mexico never having any just right to Texas, that the United States are bound by treaty stipulations to protect her, that her national honor is bound to do so, & that Texas will be *protected* agreable to the obligations of the Treaty of 1803, it would make St Anna pause and upon this basis call congress, and lay the subject before it. Congress could not refuse to pass a law for this purpose, based upon the precise terms of the Treaty of 1803. These things I have suggested to Col Gadsden,[6] & it is probable he will suggest them to Calhoun. Let the raising of Texean Corps be adopted throughout the south & west & it will carry Terror into Mexico, & may arrest any attempt at invasion. The Idea of attacking Benton with Clay shows a weakness in the Genl[7] not to be adopted. Lash Clay on his rejecting Texas for the abolition votes severely, but let others lash Benton if the[y] choose, but not Tennessee. Let us have all the strength we have or can acquire. I am exhausted and must close. The fatigue of yesterday has prostrated me.[8] With Kind regards to your lady by us all adieu.

ANDREW JACKSON

P.S. Genl Andersons letter is herein returned. A.J. I have not time or vision to read over & correct this hasty scrall. Let me hear from you. A.J. Mr. Tyler will withdraw in due time. The Texas question must be urged strongly & alls well.[9]

ALS. DLC–JKP. Addressed to Columbia and marked "private."

1. See Alexander O. Anderson to Polk, July 11, 1844.

2. Reference is to Jackson's letter to Houston of July 19, 1844.

3. Manuscript obliterated here and below.

4. Reference is to the acquisition of the Louisiana Territory by the Louisiana Purchase Treaty of 1803.

5. Reference is to the Adams-Onís Treaty, signed in 1819.

6. Businessman, politician, and U.S. minister to Mexico, 1853-56, James Gadsden of Charleston, S.C., promoted plans for constructing a transcontinental railroad linking the South to the Pacific Ocean; to facilitate selection of a southern route he negotiated the general government's purchase of a narrow strip of land on Mexico's northeastern border, known subsequently as the "Gadsden Purchase."

7. Alexander O. Anderson.

8. Democratic militia units honored Jackson with a visit to the Hermitage

on July 22, 1844.

9. Jackson wrote the last two sentences of his postscript in the left margin of his last sheet.

## FROM ANDREW J. DONELSON

Dr. Govr. Nashville July 24, 1844

I have just recd. your letter of the 22d. The letter to which you refer as proper to be sent by the Genl.[1] to Houston was sent 4 or 5 days ago.

It was made as strong as I could write, urging Houston to hold on to the policy of annexation and putting him on his guard against British influence. Some weeks ago I had also written to Blair. I will write again to the latter by tonights mail, urging him to take more decided steps to arouse the Democracy in your behalf.

I fear that the big men of our party may not come to our mass meeting[2] in sufficient numbers. I wrote special letters to

| | | |
|---|---|---|
| Butler[3] | Van Buren | Morton |
| Nevis[4] | Wright | Bancroft |
| Cambrelleng[5] | Cass | Hubbard |
| Benton | Buchanan | |
| Dick Johnson | Woodbury | |
| Medary [of] Ohio | Williams of Mississippi | |
| & all the members | McDuffie | |
| of the convention | Allen [of] Ohio | |
| with him | Johnson[6] | |
| | Thompson [of] Va[7] | |

I shall also write to Dr. Duncan of Cincinnatti and Mr Roane of Va by tonights mail.

Genl Jacksons letter to the mass meeting at Harrodsburgh is published in the Kentucky papers.[8] They say there it will do good. McAffee[9] says to Genl Jackson that Butler[10] is gaining daily, and has a chance for success.

I omitted to say to you in the above list that I had written specially to Ficklin[11] at Lexington requesting him to see Mr Wickliffe, Mr Bullock,[12] & other speakers there and get them to visit us on the 15 of August. I have also written specially to Butler the candidate for Govr.

Your cause in my opinion is progressing rapidly, and if we do our duty in Tennessee it is obliged to succeed. You had better cause the proper letters to be sent to Alabama, to bring out the crowd from that state to our meeting.

A. J. DONELSON

ALS. DLC–JKP. Addressed to Columbia.
1. Andrew Jackson.
2. Reference is to the Democratic mass meeting at Nashville on August 15, 1844.
3. Benjamin F. Butler.
4. Not identified further.
5. Churchill C. Cambreleng.
6. A farmer and lawyer in Bridgeport, Va., Joseph Johnson served several years in the Virginia House and in the U.S. House for seven full terms and a partial term, 1823–27, 1833, 1835–41, and 1845–47. From 1852 until 1856 he was governor of Virginia.
7. Reference probably is to George W. Thompson, a lawyer and deputy postmaster at Wheeling. In 1848 Polk appointed Thompson U.S. attorney for the western district of Virginia; in 1851 he won election to the U.S. House and served one term.
8. Andrew Jackson's letter to Thomas P. Moore et al., dated June 25, 1844, was also published in *Niles' National Register* on August 31, 1844. Jackson declined an invitation to attend a meeting of the Democratic party in Harrodsburg, Ky., on July 12, 1844. He also took the occasion to reiterate his opinion that Texas should be annexed to the United States.
9. A soldier and lawyer from Mercer County, Ky., Robert B. McAfee served as a member of the state legislature and as lieutenant governor of Kentucky, 1824–1828. From 1833 until 1837 he was chargé d'affaires to Colombia.
10. William O. Butler.
11. Joseph Ficklin was postmaster at Russellville, Ky., for ten years, 1802–12, and served continuously in the same capacity at Lexington from 1822 until 1850, except for the two year period, 1841–43. At one time he had published the Lexington *Kentucky Gazette*.
12. Robert Wickliffe and possibly E. I. Bullock. A native of Virginia, Bullock served as circuit judge of Kentucky's First Judicial District and as U.S. attorney during the administration of James Buchanan.

## FROM E. S. DAVIS[1]

My Dear Sir,                                      Washington City July 25. 1844

Mr. Donoho[2] will leave here in time to reach Nashville a day, or two, before the Great mass meeting,[3] and will be able to communicate to our friends the most cheering intelligence.

Mr. D. is a worthy merchant here and deserves great credit for his untiring exertions in the cause of democracy. He will carry with him several boxes of documents for the use of our friends. I need not ask your kind attention to him, as I am sure it will be extended to him. I believe I mentioned to you in a former letter,[4] that Col. Thompson[5] who was sent to Mexico as a special agent from this government, found out, while at the City of Mexico, that Gales and Seaton[6] had recd. ten thousand dollars from the Mexican Minister[7] here as a quid pro quo, for services rendered the Mexican government in opposing the Texan Treaty &c.

I sent this statement to Coe, at Somerville and to Judge Dunlap[8] at Memphis with a request to cause it to be published.

Should this not be attended to in time by them for the mass meeting I wish you would furnish a friend with the information with authority to use it before the people on that day.

Thompson is prepared with the proof and it has been held back here in order that it might appear first in the papers at a distance. I furnished Maclin, at Little Rock, and Mathews of Miss. with the information.[9] The latter will use it in his speeches before the people, in his canvass for Elector of Pres & V. Pres. This venal and corrupt press ought to be Exposed. It has always been foreign in its feelings, and sentiments and as the organ of Mr. Clay, it advocates all the anti-republican measures of that man.

E. S. DAVIS

ALS. DLC–JKP. Addressed to Columbia.

1. Apparently a physician, Davis had been a railroad promoter in Tennessee's Western District prior to his removal to Washington City.

2. John A. Donohoo is not identified further.

3. Reference is to the Democratic mass meeting in Nashville, August 15, 1844.

4. Davis probably refers to his letter of July 20, 1844, although the letter does not mention Thompson's disclosures.

5. Gilbert L. Thompson was sent as a special messenger to Mexico, bearing news of the Texas annexation treaty. He arrived in Mexico City May 22, 1844, and returned to Washington on June 17, 1844.

6. Joseph Gales, Jr., and William W. Seaton had formed an editorial partnership in 1812. Among the publications of Gales and Seaton were the Washington *Daily National Intelligencer,* the *Register of Debates in Congress,* the *Annals of Congress,* and the *American State Papers.* Both editors were politically active: Gales served as mayor of Washington City, 1827–30, and Seaton served as an alderman, 1819–31, and mayor, 1840–50.

7. Juan N. Almonte.

8. A lawyer from Bolivar, Tenn., William C. Dunlap served as a Democratic congressman, 1833–37, prior to his election as a state judge in 1840.

9. Sackfield Maclin and Joseph W. Matthews.

## FROM ANDREW J. DONELSON

My Dr Sir                                     Nashville July [25] 1844[1]

After writing to you last night I received a letter from Mr. Butler of New York dated the 15th of this month. It is in reply to one in which I referred him to your letter of acceptance[2] and made him such assurances, as the address of our committee contained, repelling the idea that the mass meeting at Nashville savored at all of disunion.[3] Speaking of your position he says "It is honorable to his *head,* as well as to his heart, for it requires real greatness of mind to exhibit greatness of soul. We were doing well in this state before that letter appeared but there was some misgiving, and some heartburning which the noble stand taken by him will entirely remove." There are also letters from Cambrelleng & Vanderpoel[4] in reply to the invitations to the mass meeting which show that the friends of Mr V[5] are feeling right, and that what we see in the papers is not mere formal support of your nomination. The only doubt I entertained of your success was the result of a fear that Mr V's friends might not take the interest in it necessary to secure the vote of New York, but I entertain now no such doubt.

I have written by last nights mail to Mr Butler urging him to send us some speakers to the meeting of the 15 of August. Among the replies yet received all decline but Horn and Kane & Boyd. It is remarkable, however, that they all breathe the same confident sentiment in respect to the future and seem to be inspired by the same feeling.

Genl Jacksons letter to Houston is dated July 19th 1844, and was sent under his frank to the Texas consul at New Orleans by mail.

The letters adverted to in my note preceding this as for the mail of last night were dispatched in due time.

A. J. DONELSON

ALS. DLC–JKP. Addressed to Columbia.

1. Donelson dated this letter July 24, but content analysis indicates that he wrote on July 25.

2. See Polk to Henry Hubbard et al., June 12, 1844.

3. Reference is to a statement by the Nashville Democratic Central Committee inviting Democrats from every part of the Union to attend the mass meeting in Nashville on August 15, 1844. The invitation appeared in the *Nashville Union* on July 2, 1844.

4. Churchill C. Cambreleng and Aaron Vanderpoel.

5. Martin Van Buren.

## FROM J. GEORGE HARRIS

My Dear Sir, Nashville July 25. 1844

The New Orleans Bulletin of the 17th, received to-day by steamer, states that the first act of the Mexican Congress at its late extra session, was to pass a law for raising *four millions of dollars* for the opening campaign against Texas. The army is to consist of 30,000 men. Munitions of war are arriving at Vera Cruz from this country and England, and as soon as distributed it is expected that the troops will be put under marching orders. Provision is also made to raise *more money* if it be necessary to reconquer the revolted province.

What is to be the result? Is a war to be forthwith brought on between Texas & Mexico; and all our best men to be drawn off to that point? Or will Mexico, now that Texas is weakened by a protracted suspense, be run over and *reconquered*,[1] thus placing annexation out of the question, or at least upon any terms short of the consent of Mexico or an open war with her?

If Mexico, as is expected, should invade Texas before our next election I should not be surprised if our people, despite of existing Treaty stipulations, should make common cause with the Texans.

Albeit, this excitement has but one tendency and effect with reference to the presidential election. It will continue to give an increasing interest to the Texas question of annexation, and will continue to strengthen the hands & hearts of our political friends, bringing new recruits to our ranks.

It is now settled that we have a decided victory in Louisiana.[2]

Gen. Pillow was here to-day; and made some suggestions about the Tariff discussion. You know how *very* delicate a question it is, under all the circumstances, and how carefully it should be treated at this moment. After sleeping on the subject I condensed into a short leader for the Union to-morrow the *differences* between your position and the position of Mr. Clay, throwing him upon his *old* ground, or making his friends admit that he has *changed* or come over to you, if they rely on his Raleigh speech.[3] Depend upon it, your letter to Kane[4] makes you President, by securing the North, especially New York & Pa.; the object of the Banner[5] in declaring that you are *for* Free Trade out and out, is to invite *denial*, so that free trade men may be made dissatisfied here at the South. The Kane Letter is gall and wormwood to them as it stands. They would be delighted to get you to say something *any thing* more. They are over anxious to get a *late* declaration from you that you are opposed to the Tariff of '42—they would use it industriously in the North. Their newspaper articles on that point are not believed in N.Y. & Pa. In a word every thing seems to be going on swimmingly. We are off before the wind—they are beating up against both wind and tide.

J. Geo. Harris

ALS. DLC–JKP. Addressed to Columbia.
1. Harris probably intends here to refer to the possibility of Mexico reconquering Texas.
2. Reference is to the results of the state elections held in Louisiana on July 1, 1844.
3. Reference is to Clay's speech delivered at Raleigh, N.C., on April 13, 1844.
4. See Polk to John K. Kane, June 19, 1844.
5. Nashville *Republican Banner*.

## FROM EDWIN F. POLK

Mecklenburg, Tenn. July 25, 1844

Writing from the residence of J. G. M. Ramsey, Edwin F. Polk observes that the local debate between John Bell and Hopkins L. Turney[1] aroused "less excitement than in any political meeting I have seen"; he reports Turney's opinion that "there certainly was a gain of *two thousand* in this end of the state." He also discusses the vindication of Ezekiel Polk and suggests that J. Knox Walker write "a full history of the character" of Ezekiel Polk "from the evidence of those who knew him in Tennessee."

ALS. DLC–JKP. Addressed to Columbia.
1. Bell and Turney spoke at Knoxville, July 24, 1844.

## FROM RICHARD RUSH

Sydenham,

Dear Sir:                              near Philadelphia, July 25, 1844

I have just conversed with a person from Lancaster county in this state, who is of our party but not active in it, and a calm-minded, intelligent man. He tells me it is true that the old antimasons of that county, are coming over to us in whole squads. I had seen this stated in the newspapers, but feared at first it was too good to be true, and rejoice to have had it so confirmed. It is a good sign of what may be hoped from our late antimasons in other counties of the state. Lancaster was their stronghold in this state—their very head quarters in fact. They voted for Harrison in solid column, in '40, and swelled his majority in that county, to some four thousand or thereabouts.

Mr Clay's avowal about a national bank in his North Carolina speech,[1] has startled persons in this state hitherto inclined to support him. On Pennsylvania, as the chief theatre of the late banks enormities, fell the heaviest of all the losses (including loss of character) incident to its crash; and they are still bitterly remembered. Never was truth better condensed or expressed than that which declared during the last bank war, that it had become a question with us whether to have "A Republic without a bank, or a bank without a Republic"[2]; and I am satisfied that there are many whigs in this state, not of the violent or deluded kind, whom no party drill can induce, after the experience of the past, to vote for a candidate with the certainty of a new bank of the U.S. staring them in the face, should he succeed. I observe by the last foreign advices, that Sir Robert Peel in renewing the charter of the bank of England,[3] has rigorously provided that henceforward every one of its notes must be, not the nominal or *promissory,* but the *real* representative of money; a vital improvement this to be sure, if acted upon, but impossible ever to be introduced into a bank of the U.S. had we not other and decisive objections to such an engine of consolidated power and wide-spread corruption in our country after all that has happened to us in those ways already.

May I be allowed to suggest that if, at the great democratic assemblage at Nashville, fixed for the 15th of August, any of the exercises might fitly admit of the foregoing idea in reference to Pennsylvania, being alluded to, viz, that that state, as having grievously suffered from the late bank, could little be expected in reason to go for a candidate who had at length openly declared we must have another, I think good would flow from it. Such a sentiment coming from a source to which all will now be looking, would be immediately transferred to our papers, and circulate with advantage all over Pennsylvania.

I intend forthwith to recommend to our committee of publication, the wide dissemination in this state of General Jackson's letter of the 24th of June,[4] taken from the Indiana State Sentinel, as embracing multum in parvo,[5] from a source no where more habitually looked up to with reverence than in Pennsylvania. It will serve as an excellent and impressive little manual. After all, the great difficulty is in the press reaching the great bulk of the people; so that, when we have a good thing, especially if not too long, it seems true wisdom to keep pushing it into every nook and corner until finally every body is made to see it. Scarcely can the rightful influence of the press be otherwise felt.

I had not intended to break in upon you so soon with another letter, overwhelmed with such intrusions as you most probably are; but have been moved to this by the agreeable impulse and anticipations created by reading the account of the great meeting at Nashville in such near prospect to us all, which I had not happened to know of until today; and which I hail, as frought with good results to our cause, to be felt, I trust, all over the union; remaining again ....

RICHARD RUSH

ALS. DLC–JKP. Addressed to Columbia.
1. In a speech delivered at Raleigh, N.C., on April 13, 1844, Clay claimed that the country needed a "national currency" and suggested that much of the opposition to the establishment of a national bank came from "a foreign influence" that hoped to retard the growth of the United States.
2. Quotation is not identified further.
3. Sir Robert Peel, in his second term as prime minister of Great Britain, expounded his financial program and hard money views in a speech of May 6, 1844, which was widely reported in the American press.
4. Although Andrew Jackson's letter to the citizens of Indiana praised Polk and Dallas and attacked Clay on a variety of issues, it focused primarily on Texas annexation, arguing "that the question is soon to be, if it be not already, whether Texas and Oregon are to be considered as auxiliaries to American or British Interests." Jackson's letter was also published in *Niles' National Register,* August 3, 1844.
5. Latin phrase meaning "much in little."

## TO ROBERT ARMSTRONG

My Dear Sir:                                        Columbia July 26th 1844
I wrote you in haste on yesterday morning, but as I learned in the afternoon my letter reached the P.O. too late to go by yesterday's mail.[1] I am satisfied *Mr Dallas* ought to come in the way I suggested, and I am satisfied further that, *he* and *Buchanan* & *Walker* of Miss. will all come if pressed to do so.[2] There is still time for letters to reach them. A letter from *Judge Catron* to *Dallas* and *Buchanan* will bring them. I begin to be concerned for fear our distinguished men from a distance will not attend. You should write a strong letter to *Moses Dawson* of Cincinnatti & *Thos. P. Moore* of *Harrodsburg* urging them to come and bring over their ablest debaters. It is particularly desireable that *Allen* of Ohio should attend. His residence is at *Chillicothe. Mr Henley* of Indiana is said to be a fine debater. His residence is at *"New Washington Indiana." Laughlin* knows him.
Levin H. Coe reached here on yesterday, on his way to join *Henry.* He will overtake him at *Lynchburg* or *Shelbyville. Brown* will be with him to *Fayetteville* or *Lynchburg.* He will not leave him until

*Coe* reaches him. Coe says that *Roger Barton Esqr.* of Holly-Springs, who is one of the best popular orators in America, was at Jackson on the 18th and says, there is no use for him in Mississippi, & he is ready to spend the summer in Tennessee. He is a native of East Tennessee; read law at Knoxville. He resides at *Holly-Springs.* Has he been invited to the meeting of the 15th. Will you write to him to come. Write to him to bring *Totten, Judge Chalmers, & Matthews* with him.[3] If *Barton* will go to East Tennessee, he can take care of our *Luke Lea jr* who is also of Mississippi. Have letters written to *Gov. Clay* of Huntsville, *Nat Terry, Houston* & others of Alabama.[4] It will never do for our great meeting not to be attended by our distinguished men from a distance. No pains should be spared to get them here. If *Dallas* comes it will raise the wind, as he comes down the Ohio, & bring a vast crowd from that quarter after him.

Why did not the Union publish *Brown & Boling Gordon's*[5] appointments, which I sent to you in yesterday's paper. Have them in the paper of tomorrow. They were published in last saturday's Democrat,[6] but it has but little circulation in the West.

Has *Laughlin* returned? I am distressed at the tameness and inefficiency of the Union. Will *Harris* take hold? *Laughlin* if he has some one with him can be of service on the stump.

*Coe* will remain here to day. He and others are suggesting the plan of the campaign, so as to gain system and efficiency to it. It is, that after attending the proposed mass-meetings immediately around Nashville after the 15th, that *four sets of debaters,* going two together start out from Nashville—two sets going East & two sets going West— so as to take the whole state abreast. *Cave Johnson* can head one set: *A. V. Brown* another: & the other two must be arranged hereafter. I merely suggest this now. If approved it can be consummated hereafter. The enthusiasm must be kept up and all is safe.

The Shelbyville meeting for the 27th August must be made a great affair. Have you heard from Matthews.[7] We are anxious to learn that they are moving in it. In haste ....

JAMES K. POLK

P.S. Have the committee invited *Jos. Watkins Esqr* formerly of Virginia to attend.[8] His address is "Birch Pond P.O. Fayette County." J.K.P.

ALS. IaU. Addressed to Nashville and marked *"Private."*
1. Polk's letter to Armstrong of July 25, 1844, has not been found.
2. Reference is to invitations to the Nashville Democratic mass meeting on August 15, 1844.

3. James L. Totten, Joseph W. Chalmers, and Joseph W. Matthews.

4. Clement C. Clay, Nathaniel Terry, and George S. Houston. Terry, a Limestone county planter, served in the Alabama Senate from 1836 through 1844; he was president of that body for four years. In 1845, he ran unsuccessfully as the Democratic candidate for governor.

5. Aaron V. Brown and Boling Gordon. Gordon, a Hickman County planter, served three terms in the Tennessee House, 1829–35, and two terms in the Senate, 1835–37 and 1843–45.

6. Reference is to the Columbia *Tennessee Democrat*.

7. Robert Mathews.

8. Reference probably is to Joseph S. Watkins, formerly a member of the Virginia legislature and leader of Martin Van Buren's friends in the Virginia Democracy.

## TO ANDREW BEAUMONT[1]

My Dear Sir:                                    Columbia Tenn. July 26th 1844

I was much gratified to receive your kind letter of the 7th Instant. There is no one of my old Congressional friends for whom I entertain a higher regard or from whom I would have been more pleased to hear than yourself. Our intercourse in Congress was an intimate one, and I believe we seldom, if ever differed in regard to the public policy.

If the unsought and unexpected position in which I have been placed by my political friends, shall have a tendency to promote the success of our cause, I shall be most happy to have been the instrument in their hands of affecting so great a good. I am gratified to learn from yourself and others that the prospects of the Democracy are so flattering in Pennsylvania. All the indications in the South and South-West, as far as they have reached me show that there is perfect union in the action of the party, and a zeal and enthusiasm which has been rarely witnessed. In this State our whole Democracy are roused to the most energetic action, and they have the greatest confidence that they will carry the State.

I shall be pleased my Dear Sir, to hear from you again during the summer, and receive from you any information or suggestions which you may deem useful.

JAMES K. POLK

ALS. DLC–AB. Addressed to Wilkes-Barre, Penn., and marked *"Private."*

1. Andrew Beaumont served several terms in the Pennsylvania House, 1821, 1822, 1826, 1849, and in the U.S. House, 1833–37. Polk nominated him as commissioner of public buildings for the District of Columbia in December 1846, but the Senate rejected the nomination in March of the following year.

## FROM ANDREW JACKSON

My dear Sir,                                    Hermitage July 26, 1844
I have been surrounded with company since Genl Pillow was here
that until this night I had not a moment to write you. I read Mr. R.
J. Walker's letter[1] with great attention, and altho I have full confidence in him & in his high order of talents, still I could not help being
surprised in his display of the great want of common sense in his suggestion that I should write a letter for publication to shew that all
the Tyler men on Mr. Tylers withdrawal from the canvass should be
received & be upon the same level with all other Democrats in the selection for office, merit & fitness being the only enquiry. Why my dear
friend such a letter from me or any other of your conspicuous friends
would be seized upon as a bargain & intrigue for the presidency—Just
as Adams & Clays bargain. Let me say to you that such a letter from
any of your friends would damn you & destroy your election. I have
suggested to Major Lewis, that Mr. Tyler now withdrawing from the
canvass would give great popularity, and as he can have no hope of
being elected, that his own sagacity with his fondness for popularity
will enduce him to withdraw—no letter from you or any of your friends
must be written or published upon any such subject.
I am now writing scarcely able to wield my pen, or to see what I
write—with all our kind salutations to you & your amiable lady, I
remain your friend.

ANDREW JACKSON

P.S. Tylers friends are a mere drop in the buckett, & they nor nothing but such imprudent letter as suggested can prevent your election;
therefore all you have to do is be silent—answer only such letters that
may call upon you for your political principles.

ALS. DLC–JKP. Addressed to Columbia and marked *"Confidential."* Polk's
AE on the cover states that he answered this letter on August 3, 1844. Published in Tyler, ed., *Letters and Times of the Tylers,* III, pp. 142–43.
1. Reference is to Walker's letter to Polk of July 10, 1844.

## TO SAMUEL H. LAUGHLIN

My Dear Sir:                                    Columbia July 26th 1844
I am mortified that your letter to our festival here on the 13th has
not been published.[1] The cause is that the paper has been crowded
with matter—*Pillow's* speech[2] &c—and I learn that they cannot put it

in the next paper. I sincerely desired its publication but fear now, that it would appear *out-of-time*. The events of your journey home which you relate had transpired three weeks before it was written, and it has now been two weeks since. Several other letters which were received, have not been published, for the same reasons, which have excluded yours. It is all wrong, but you know the troubles of printers, and those who have to deal with them, sufficiently well to make "many grains of allowance,"[3] for their short-comings.

You will pardon me I know, and will receive in the kind spirit in which it is meant, when I say, that it is of the greatest importance that the *Union* should be a *great paper*, during the pending contest. It is looked to from all parts of the Union & is expected to be so. It is perhaps more than any one man can do, to make it such. The understanding was, that *Nicholson* & *Humphreys* were to contribute their aid. *Nicholson* has now gone to East Tennessee, & *Humphreys* I presume is engaged in his law-business. *Harris* I have no doubt would willingly aid if requested, without appearing as being known—viz connected in any-way with the Editorial Department. Mr *Ritchie* & the *Globe* and indeed all the leading organs have numerous contributors in this way. *Harris* has a remarkable talent in infusing spirit and enthusiasm into any paper with which he is connected. The whole party who can write or speak, every-where else, contribute, and should do so here. *Harris* I am sure will assist, but may feel some delicacy in tendering his services, unless you invite him to furnish an article occasionally. We want the aid of our whole talent & force, & if you see no objection to it (and I see none) I hope you will see him on the subject. I hope you will not put what I say down to a spirit of complaining. I repeat it is not so intended. *Majr Heiss* should give more space for Editorial, and more spirit should be thrown into the paper. The ascendancy of political parties not only now, but for years to come, depends on the events of the next 100 days, and nothing can have so much influence in controlling these events as the public press. If we can keep up the present enthusiasm al[l][4] will be well. If we suffer it to ab[ate], it may be otherwise. I hope you will concur with me in these suggestions & that you will see *Harris* as soon as practicable and invite him to give his aid.

James K. Polk

ALS. Forbes Magazine Collection, New York. Addressed to Nashville and marked "*Confidential.*"

1. Reference is to Laughlin's letter of July 12, 1844, to M. G. Lewis, J. Knox Walker, and others, which was enclosed in his letter to Polk of July 14, 1844.

2. Speaking to a Democratic mass meeting held in Columbia on July 13, 1844, Gideon J. Pillow stressed the necessity of Texas' immediate annexation to the Union.

3. Quotation's source is not identified.

4. Parts of words here and below have been obliterated by the letter's seal.


## FROM ELY MOORE[1]

My dear Col,                                        New York, July 26, 1844

You would have heard from me ere this, had it not been for the incessant labor that has been imposed upon me. From the time of your nomination, until the present moment, I have been travelling and speaking in this state, as well as in New Jersey and Pa. and I have now upwards of thirty engagements on hand. So you perceive that I have very little time to devote to epistolary correspondence.

All things look well in this section of the Union, and especially in this state, and unless some deep defection in our ranks shall take place, you may rely on New York. It is true, that a conspiracy has just been detected, which has greatly alarmed some of our friends, but I think that we shall be able to render the efforts of the traitors comparatively harmless. You will perceive by the papers of the day the nature and character of the treason in question. It is true that some of our prominent men are concerned in it. G. P. Barker, the present atty Gen. of the state, Wm. C. Bryant, Ed. of the Ev. Post, Isaac Townscend, J. W. Edmonds, Theo. Sedgwick, Thos. W. Tucker, D. D. Field, and some others whose names are not attached to the secret circular.[2] Samuel J. Tilden,[3] late Corporation Atty, is also one of the conspirators, and one of the most active of the traitor band, but his name is not on the private circular. They will accomplish some mischief, but not to the extent they anticipate. Their own political destruction they have already accomplished. The true hearted democrats of the state will work with greater energy, and, I doubt not, will carry our ticket triumphantly, in despite of the clandestine and treasonable efforts of the conspirators in question.

You may calculate, I repeat, on this state as well as on N.J. and Pa. I have travelled in all three and therefore, I speak understandingly.

Have the goodness to inform me, by return of mail, of the prospects in Tenn. and in such other southwestern states as you may be able to speak of advisedly.

Mrs. Moore[4] desires to be affectionately remembered to Mrs. Polk.

ELY MOORE

ALS. DLC–JKP. Addressed to Columbia and marked *"Confidential."* Polk's AE on the cover states that he answered this letter on August 6, 1844; Polk's reply has not been found.

1. A journalist and trade union leader in New York City, Moore served two terms in the U.S. House, 1835–39. From 1839 until 1845, he was president of the board of trade and surveyor of the port of New York, and in 1845 Polk appointed him marshal of the southern district of New York.

2. George P. Barker, William Cullen Bryant, Isaac Townsend, J. W. Edmonds, Theodore Sedgwick, Thomas W. Tucker, and David D. Field were signers of a confidential circular letter that surfaced in New York in late July 1844. The circular supported Polk and Dallas but rejected the immediate annexation of Texas.

3. Tilden, a prominent attorney and leader of the Democratic party of New York, won election as governor in 1875, but lost his bid for the presidency in 1876.

4. Not identified further.

## FROM ROBERT ARMSTRONG

Dr Sir　　　　　　　　　　　　　　　　　Nashville July 27, [18]44

I send out by the mail today 200 printed notices of Browns appointments. They will appear in the Union Monday night. Their is nothing that is received by the evenings mail that can be got into it. You can find no one at the office and their is no person belonging to it who [...]¹ to attend the Post office for any thing *new* or *late*. I have been sick three or four days.

Guild has taken sick at Woodward in his appointments with Jennings. Mosely will take his place. Cheatham will go to Marshall (Lewisburg) and I suppose will go on with Brown, tho he has an appointment in Robertson at which he can do some good. Still send him on and I will see that Humphreys & Craighead attend at Springfield. The whigs have their hopes on East Tenss. and an *effort to be made* in the District. Our friends both in the East and West must be greatly mistaken if our ranks are not rapidly filling up.

In Middle Tenss. our majority will reach that of '39. If all things go well, (go as now going) in Davidson & Nashville I know we shall increase (have increased). We have nine *newly* raised companies in city & county, with an average of ten whigs in each. Their is many men both in the city and county belonging to the whig party who have declared off and their is many that say "they are whigs but cannot support *Clay.*" The news from the whole state is highly satisfactory and cheers up our friends nightly as it is received.

I would be glad to see you for a day. Now is the time to secure the state. It is the time for the work to be done. It is Impossible for me to Leave here. I have not been absent a moment.

Their is not *care* taken in geting up the Docmt. for Publication.[2] Nicholson done it hastily as Heiss thinks only for the profit.

Now that Harris[3] can be employed I will have out 10 thousand of a pamphlet that will tell after Humphreys Bargain is out.[4] I send you a line from Harris.[5] He gives me a good report from his line of march—indeed all looks bright North East South & West. In haste....

R. Armstrong

[P.S.] Tell William Polk to Send a man with the money to Lewisburg. They will be a head of the Union & the mail.

ALS. DLC–JKP. Addressed to Columbia. Polk's AE on the cover states that he answered this letter on July 30, 1844; Polk's reply has not been found.

1. Word illegible.

2. Reference probably is to one of several pamphlets offered for sale in the pages of the *Nashville Union.* Titles included "Clay against the Occupant Settlers," "Chancellor Bibb on Annexation," "Biography of James K. Polk," and "The Tariff Acts of 1828 and 1842 Compared." The price was two dollars per 100 copies.

3. Reference is to J. George Harris' writing for the *Nashville Union* and its campaign pamphlets.

4. Reference probably is to "The Bargain and Intrigue of Clay and Adams," a pamphlet offered for sale by the *Nashville Union* in August.

5. See Arnold S. Harris to Polk, July 18, 1844.


## FROM JEREMIAH Y. DASHIELL[1]

Hon: James K. Polk.          Lake Providence La July 27th 1844

Will you permit me to obtrude upon your recollection and give to you, alike for the cause of Democracy and your own gratification a succinct statement of facts connected with our recent election in this State.[2]

You will bear in mind, the fact that the Democrats have not had a majority in the legislature since 1838. That at the last apportionment, the Congressional districts were arranged according to the suggestions of the Central Clay Club at Washington City addressed to several members of the Legislature under the frank and over the signature of the Hon. John Moore[3] then a representative in Congress, the successor of Rice Garland.[4] The gerrymandering was so palpable as to produce a tremendous reaction, and in this state where we could never return previously but one member of Congress, disgust gave us the whole delegation. Yet at the regular election (1842) the Whigs returned a majority of nine on joint ballot. Our Constitution unequal and oppressive in its operations, the Democrats had repeatedly urged the call of a Convention, to democratize its features, in accordance with the progress of the Age, but our Adversaries having the control of the legislature, as frequently rejected it. Thus stood parties at the close of our last election in 1842 (biennial). The Democrats rallied with renewed energies, in fact with the extreme energy of desperation, in behalf of the call for a convention, and with it they went to the people, determined as a party to rise or fall with it. The Whigs alarmed—temporized, but on finding the people were becoming indignant, they consented to submit the question to them. It was submitted at the special election held for Representatives to Congress in July 1843. As the Constitution required a majority of all the qualified voters in the state to cast their sufferages expressly for it, our opponents endeavoured to defeat it insidiously by numbers of them leaving the state to avoid voting against it expressly. While their absence would have all the effect of a negative vote. Fortunately the people had become restive under the incubus, and determined to rid themselves of it.

These circumstances were operating silently it is true, but very certainly in our favour, which was amply tested, by filling the several vacancies in the legislature with democrats, until we reduced the majority on joint ballot to two. Thus stood parties at the opening of the canvass last spring. Our determination was, at every hazard to carry the Convention, and if practicable the legislature, but certainly the *Convention.* We deemed the legislature of secondary importance, because we have no senator to elect. The Texas question was not a party measure in this state. It would prove a Texas legislature, and one in favour of instructions, whichever party obtained the ascendancy. Further, it was very uncertain whether the legislature to be elected, would ever convene, and should it even meet, the session would be very brief, merely to put in force the requisitions of the new constitution which will be submitted to the people for ratification at the November elections. Under these circumstances many of our most popular men concluded not to offer for the legislature, most of them desired a seat in the convention, and when not taken up for that body declined running for any. Other causes incidental and temporary in their influences, though not the less fatal in their result, operated against the cause of democracy. In New Orleans, the Elliott votes, then rejection.[5] However our latest advices from thence, assures us of the adjustment of that question before the fall Election. Again, the unprecedented flood, which has swept over this portion of Louisiana devastating to a fearful extent, the two senatorial districts lying contiguous, and embracing the parishes of Carroll, Concordia, Tensas, and Madison, together with Ouachita, Union, Caldwell, Morehouse & Franklin, which have with the two senators a representation of six in the legislature, in the[...][6] stood five democrats to one whig. Now it is reversed, solely attributable to the flood, as our strength, lies on the Bayous, which being lower than the banks of the river (Mississippi) the water accumulates upon them. It was utterly out of the question, to get to the polls. I speak from personal inspection. Just on the eve of the election, the flood approaching in all directions, witnessing not only the destruction total of their crops, but in many instances, having to make strenuos exertions for the preservation of their families and stock. The result of the Election when summed up is as follows

|              | Dem. | Whig |
|--------------|------|------|
| Congress     | 3    | 1    |
| Convention   | 47   | 30   |
| Legislature  | 38   | 39   |

It is but fair to state in reference to the legislature, that the Whigs claim one of the members from Assumption, and the member from Sabine, both decidedly democratic parishes. If they are correct parties will stand Demo 36, Whig 41. Senator Morse (dem) having been elected to fill the vacancy of Genl. Bossier,[7] there will be a vacancy in the senate. As it is a strong Whig district, such may be the character of its representative. In relation to the Convention, the Whig press have laid great stress upon a division in our ranks, which does not exist. There is an entire agreement in all essentials—1st Suffrage freed from its present incumbrance property qualification, 2nd Equal representation & Equal Taxation, Election of all parish officers by the people, limited tenure of all offices. The Inhibition of pledging faith of the state save in War or Insurrection. There is but one debateable point—Whether the Judiciary shall be elected directly by the people or by a joint ballot of the Legislature.

I trust that I have not trespassed too far on your courtesy in inflicting on you the above details. Yet as we have obtained the popular vote for Congress, Convention & Legislature, and as the Whig presses have systematized their efforts to deceive, I could not resist the impulse, to narrate to you simply the facts. Likewise to tender you the assurance that the vote of this state you may depen upon. With my sincere congratulations to Mrs Polk & yourself....

J. Y. Dashiell

ALS. DLC–JKP. Addressed to Columbia and forwarded to Nashville. Polk's AE on the cover states that he answered this letter on August 16, 1844; Polk's reply has not been found.

1. A physician from Maryland, Dashiell helped to establish the Louisville Medical College. He practiced medicine in Mississippi and Louisiana before removing to Texas in 1849; there he served for a time as editor of the *San Antonio Herald*.

2. Reference is to state elections held on July 1, 1844.

3. Moore, a Whig, served in the Louisiana House, 1825–34, and in the U.S. House, 1840–43 and 1851–53.

4. Garland, a Whig, was a member of the U.S. House from 1834 until 1840, when he resigned his seat to become judge of the Supreme Court of Louisiana, a position he held until 1846.

5. Reference is to action taken by Whig poll officials in New Orleans in denying the vote to many naturalized citizens. These immigrants had been naturalized by B. C. Elliot, judge of the city court of LaFayette, prior to his impeachment and removal from office in April 1844 for issuing fraudulent certificates of citizenship.

6. Manuscript obliterated.

7. Isaac E. Morse and Pierre E. Bossier. A lawyer in New Orleans and St. Martinsville, Morse served one term in the Louisiana Senate, 1842–44, prior to winning election as a Democrat to the U.S. House, where he completed Bossier's term and won election to three terms of his own, 1844–51. Bossier, a sugar and cotton planter, sat in the Louisiana Senate from 1833 to 1843; elected to the U.S. House in 1843, he served in that body until his death in April 1844.

## FROM JOHN H. BILLS[1]

Bolivar, Tenn. July 29, 1844

Bills describes a Democratic mass meeting held July 25–26 at Davis' Mills on the Tennessee-Mississippi border. A crowd of some four to eight thousand people heard "at least a dozen speeches" by prominent men from the two states. He also reports having received "cheering" accounts from Pennsylvania, Virginia, Ohio, and other states.

ALS. DLC–JKP. Addressed to Columbia.

1. Bills, postmaster and merchant at Bolivar, was married to Polk's first cousin, Prudence Tate McNeal.

## FROM ANDREW J. DONELSON

Dr Sir,                                      Nashville July 29, 1844

Enclosed you will receive the reply of the Genl to Mr Thomas,[1] which is in substance the same he has made to others.

Since Genl Pillow was here, I have seen a letter from Mr Blair to Genl Jackson, also one from Mr Lewis, the latter adverting particularly to the views of Mr. Tyler.

The Genl has answered Mr Blair, and has suggested the points in the course of that paper, which are necessary to give effect to the will of the Democratic party. There is no reason to doubt Mr. Blairs sincerity, and I think we will see hereafter his columns free from all objectionable matter.

Lewis account of Tylers feelings does not correspond with Mr Walkers. My judgement is that your friends as well as yourself should say or do nothing capable of being construed into an understanding, respecting the patronage of your administration in the event of your success. You are the *nominee* of the Democratic party, and if Mr Tyler decides to oppose this nomination it cannot be helped. He cannot get a state in the Union, and he must be aware if he continues in the field, he must be regarded as an ally of the whigs. His support of us can do no good unless he bases it upon the approval of our leading measures and this to be effective ought to be done in such a manner as to leave no doubt of its being disinterested and patriotic.

You may rely on us here to do all that is practicable to secure the union and harmony so necessary to your success and the just vindication of the measures of the party. In my judgement this is already done if no new issues are created.

I send you letters from Mr Buchanan & Mr Wright (which are private).[2] There are many others of the same tone to the committee,[3] all of them full of confidence in your success, and entirely satisfied that nothing is now wanting but the time to declare the votes in November.

Some of our friends are quite uneasy at the situation of Texas. Some think Houston will be bribed, others that no matter how pure he will be obliged to yield to the Mexican force which will shortly appear on the field. Some fear that British & French influence will guarantee the independence of Texas on terms so favorable that Houston must accede to them in order to preserve his popularity. I think the latter suggestion quite probable; and that we are really in danger of losing that important territory for the present at least.

If Genl Jacksons letter to Houston[4] has the proper effect on him, he may make battle until he knows the judgement of the American people on the question of annexation: but to do this he must have help from our people, that sort of help that he received at *St. Jacinto*.

An extremity of this kind, in respect to Texas we cannot provide for. Enough for the day is the evil thereof. It will not do for us to say beforehand that Texas ought to be occupied by our troops and held with arms. A case may arise to justify it but the responsibility belongs to the present administration. I am not in favor of asking as much for the Democratic party without having the control of the whole subject, and hence I say let us have no new issue on the question. Let us do all we honorably can to gain the territory consistent with the resolutions at Baltimore,[5] and with your commitment in favor of immediate annexation, but let us not be responsible for war without the consent of the people and of congress. Let us be responsible for no act of Mr Tyler which may make war necessary.

Genl Pillow saw the Genls. letter to Houston. It will be communicated to Mr Calhoun through Col Gadsden; and so will the Genls. view of Mr Tyler's position, if he wishes to preserve his popularity with the Democratic party. Tyler is obliged to withdraw, unless he is determined to do what he can to elect Mr Clay. If he has friends who want to be assured beforehand of the protection of the democratic party, they ought to be told at once that measures and not men are the guides of democracy. If there be nothing in our measures to justify support & preference we can do without them.

Please return me Wright's & Buchanan's letters.

Remember me kindly to Mrs Polk and believe me....

A. J. DONELSON

ALS. DLC–JKP. Addressed to Columbia and marked *"for your own eyes."* Polk's AE on the cover states that he answered this letter on July 31, 1844; Polk's reply has not been found.

1. Andrew Jackson's letter to Jonas E. Thomas has not been found.

2. Reference probably is to Buchanan's letter to Donelson of July 17, 1844. See Polk to Donelson, August 3, 1844. Wright's letter is not identified.

3. Nashville Democratic Central Committee.

4. Reference is to Jackson's letter to Sam Houston of July 19, 1844.

5. Reference is to the plank in the Democratic party platform of 1844 calling for the immediate annexation of Texas.

## FROM JOHN P. HEISS

Dear Sir                                    Union Office July 29 1844

Our friends are complaining sadly about the manner in which the "Union" is conducted and I am at a loss to know what course to pursue in regard to this matter. I am compelled to hear these complaints, yet cannot remedy them. You, yourself, must percieve, how tamely the Union submits to everything coming from our opponents; and I assure you, it is not without much regret on my part, that it is the case. Col: Laughlin, I have no doubt, feels that he is doing our cause good service, but I believe that his talents on the "stump" would result more to the success of our principles, and in the mean time the "Union" could be made more spirited under the control of other of our friends. Will you my dear sir advise me as soon as possible, if it will not be expedient to make some other arrangement?

J. P. HEISS

ALS. DLC–JKP. Addressed to Columbia and marked *"Private."* Polk's AE on the cover states that he answered this letter on August 1, 1844.

## FROM SAMUEL H. LAUGHLIN

My dear Sir,                     Nashville, Tenn. July 29, 1844
    I am duly in the receipt of your favor of the 26th instant, and was only prevented from replying to it on yesterday by the press of other letters requiring immediate answers, and papers to accompany them which required to be copied. I did not care a straw whether my letter to your committee were published,[1] and possibly it ought not to have been published, situated as I am here, because it presents the question of *reform* in a point of view in which I have considered it myself, but which, perhaps, ought not now to be published by the *Editor of the Union,* whatever I may think of the matter in my *personal capacity.* This was one leading reason why I sent it through you, to be witheld if it contained a sentiment which ought not to be promulgated.
    I spent two days in Warren last week, being however only one night and a few hours at home after an absence of nearly five months. My chief purpose in going up was to obtain the statements of old John Smith and old Thomas Gribble in regard to your Grandfather.[2] I did obtain them. They are full, clear, positive and explicit. They are highly respectable men. I obtained also the statement of half a dozen of the best men in the County—public men including the present and former members of Assembly—testifying to the full faith and credit due to any statement made by Smith and Gribble. I have forwarded the statements and attestations to Gen. R. M. Saunders and Hon. Lewis D. Henry at Raleigh, N.C.[3] I will send you copies as soon as I can find time to make them in a fair hand. Perhaps I had better not publish them here until they first appear in Carolina.
    You will see that the Great Columbus, Mississippi Festival has been postponed to give Mr. Walker and others an opportunity to come here on the 15th prox.[4] I wrote four weeks ago pressingly to A. A. Kincannon and Col. Weir to have it done, also to Barkesdale,[5] and they have accomplished our wishes.

The news is good from every point of the compass.

I have again and again pressed Harris to write just such articles as you suggest, but although he talks and talks, he has done nothing as yet. Tyler and the Zoll Verein Treaty[6] are too much uppermost. I wrote myself one No. on the latter and have another ready as a hit at Foster and Jarnagin, but not in praise of Tyler. Mr. Harris promised me to-day that he would write some articles to rouse up people to the meeting. Tomorows Union has a renewed call to all to come by myself.

Fletchers *Mero,*[7] to prove that Grundy was *first* and Clay *second* greatest man in the war, which Heiss had in type when I got home, was *out of place greatly.* It was praised next day in the Banner.[8] His next piece—much better but too long—about Gen. Jackson, Dictation and a history of the last war, took up too much room, and though good, will not be read.[9] The last paragraph or two, is worth all the rest of it.

I make the paper as good as I can, with not space enough to say half I want to say. As to spirit—the kind of appeals which Harris can make—that have no sober reason in them, I acknowledge I have no proficiency in such though they are the very things now most needed. I cannot address a thing as a reason to another man's mind which could have no influence as such on my own. I wish to make the next several succeeding papers up very much of extracts, short and pointed, of letters from all of the state which are lying before me.

I think we shall have a glorious meeting. I have written to men at a distance, and especially to the western Virginians, that I do not expect you will be here to mingle in the festivities, but that you will be near enough I hope to receive the congratulations of all your visiting friends.

The account I wrote here, from Heiss notes, of what was done at your Maury festival,[10] contained the best account I could give. In it, I said, "not being present, and writing from notes, there were doubt-less omissions." That apologetic part, after I left for Warren, Heiss, for some cause—perhaps having promised that *he* would report, and wishing it to pass so, he struck out. As his wife[11] is complimented for her account of Voorhies' speech and which in truth had to be corrected, I would have supposed he would have, of all things, most desired *not* to be thought to have written the report. I mention these things, because the report may not have been accurate, and to show the liberties Heiss assumes when I am not looking on. All these little things of course in confidence—for with you I can have no secrets—but with others, I must have many.

                                                S. H. LAUGHLIN

ALS. DLC–JKP. Addressed to Columbia and marked "Private." Polk's AE on the cover states that he answered this letter on August 1, 1844; Polk's reply has not been found.

1. Laughlin enclosed his letter of July 12, 1844, to M. G. Lewis, J. Knox Walker and others, in his letter to Polk of July 14, 1844.

2. The statements of John Smith and Thomas Gribble denying that Ezekiel Polk had ever been a Tory were published in the *Nashville Union,* August 3, 1844.

3. Romulus M. Saunders and Louis D. Henry. Henry was chairman of the North Carolina Democratic State Central Committee. A Fayetteville lawyer, he won election to five terms in the North Carolina House, 1821–22 and 1830–32, and served as Speaker in 1832. He ran unsuccessfully as the Democratic candidate for governor in 1842.

4. The Democratic Association of Lowndes County, Miss., had planned to host a dinner in honor of Robert J. Walker at Columbus on August 15, 1844. On July 30, the *Nashville Union* published a notice from the committee of invitation postponing the dinner until September 12 in deference to the Nashville Democratic mass meeting also scheduled for August 15, 1844.

5. Andrew A. Kincannon, probably Adolphus G. Weir, and William Barksdale. Weir served as U.S. marshal for the northern district of Mississippi from 1838 to 1841. He attended the Mississippi Democratic state conventions in 1844 and 1845. Barksdale, born in Tennessee, was a Columbus lawyer and a delegate to the 1844 Mississippi Democratic state convention. He edited the Columbus *Democrat* in the 1840's and served on the committee of invitation for the 1844 Columbus dinner. Later he fought in the Mexican War and represented Mississippi in Congress from 1853 until his resignation in 1861. A Confederate general, he was killed at Gettysburg.

6. See Laughlin to Polk, July 5, 1844.

7. On July 25, 1844, the *Nashville Union* printed an article on "Mr. Grundy and the War of 1812," signed by "Mero." The author was probably Thomas H. Fletcher, a veteran of the War of 1812. A Nashville lawyer, he represented Franklin county in the Tennessee House, 1825–27, and served as secretary of state, 1830–32.

8. Reference is to the Nashville *Republican Banner.*

9. On July 27, 1844, the *Nashville Union* contained an article on "General Jackson and Dictation," signed by "Robertson."

10. Reference is to the Democratic mass meeting held at Columbia, Tenn., on July 13, 1844.

11. Clarissa Richmond Heiss.


## FROM JOHN McKEON[1]

My Dear Sir,                                           New York July 29. 1844

I have delayed writing until I had learned something of the interest of our state. I have been absent at the Saratoga Springs for some days and there met with a number of our political men. From present indications there is no doubt of our carrying the state. We have had within a few days past a circular published signed by a few of our leading men in this city protesting against the Texas question being part of our creed.[2] They profess to support the Baltimore nomination but wish to get up candidates for Congress against the annexation of Texas. Fears were entertained that the movement would affect the Presidential ticket but I am satisfied that it will not injure us in the least. I have no doubt myself of the triumph of our ticket in the state. The leading democrats in this city all regret & repudiate the circular to which I allude. The Albany Argus has also rebuked it. The Texas question is popular even in this state—at the public meetings before which I have spoken any allusion made to Texas was always well received. I have never known more enthusiasm. I have never received so many invitations to address meetings & this is a sign to me that meetings are held in every direction. In the taverns in the country I find that they have your likeness pretty well plastered on the walls.

I have seen a letter from Dallas in which he says Pennsylvania is safe for our ticket. Cass' friends write me from Michigan that the West is safe. I saw a letter from Mr Disney[3] the Chairman of the Finance committee of the Ohio senate in which letter he says there never was a better spirit in Ohio. Mr D. expresses great hope of that state. New Jersey is perfectly on fire. I have seen many from that state & they say it will go for us. Slidell of Louisiana is here & asserts that Louisiana will be with us in the Fall.

I cannot but congratulate you in the two letters which have appeared from you on the Tariff & the one term.[4] I have no doubt they will do infinite service to the cause.

JOHN McKEON

ALS. DLC–JKP. Addressed to Columbia and marked "Private."

1. A New York City lawyer, John McKeon served three terms in the New York Assembly, 1832–34, and two terms in the U.S. House, 1835–37 and 1841–43.

2. See Ely Moore to Polk, July 26, 1844.

3. A Cincinnati lawyer, David T. Disney served three terms in the Ohio House, 1829 and 1831–32, and two terms in the Ohio Senate, 1833–34 and 1843–44. A delegate to the Democratic National Convention of 1848, he represented Ohio in the U.S. House from 1849 to 1855.

4. See Polk to John K. Kane, June 19, 1844, and Polk to Henry Hubbard et al., June 12, 1844.

## FROM HENDRICK B. WRIGHT

My dear Sir                                    Wilkes Barre Pa. July 30th 1844

I returned yesterday from the great mass meeting at Northumberland in the 13th district. It was a most grand & imposing affair, there being not less than 5,000 of the democracy of this state. More enthusiasm I never saw & a more determined disposition to conquer was never written on the brows of men. A vote taken on *the tariff as it is* and carried without a dissenting voice. It was in this district that Snyder[1] was defeated in 1842 & 3 & especially on the ground of the tariff. I allude to this fact to apprise you of the true condition of things in Penna and if the doctrine be adhered to contained in your letter to Mr Kane[2] then our friends may safely count upon 20,000 in the state, unless some unforseen accident should occur. The right feeling is abroad and there seems to be no abatement. On the 6th of Aug. we hold a mass meeting for the northern counties. We are making arrangements on a large scale, and the matter is in such hands as will turn it to the best advantage. You were good enough to request me to inform you of any thing I might deem important in this state touching the canvass. I know of nothing at this time that may be important, as the only question about which there was any necessity of interference on your part has been done in the correspondence with Mr. Kane. Our democracy on the questions of the Bank, distribution, Oregon, Texas, state rights &c is united and firm. The tariff is the only one of any diference of opinion & this is now at rest.

I speak to you frankly and with candor as you may very readily conceive I feel as much interest in your Election as *you* possibly can. It does not require the prediction of prophecy to point out the fate of the 12 2/3's rule men in Penna in the Baltimore Convention[3] if you are defeated. With your success the act is sealed & approved, nay ratified & confirmed. Secret opposition to us is now at work, and I presume we are on the proscribed lists, probably our doors are checked. Under this view I feel a most lively intest[4] in your success, and my time from this out will be spent in the cause. It goes gloriously now and the signs of the times are ominous for our success. The battle is already fought in Penna and victory is written upon our banner.

Yours was received in due time.[5]

HENDRICK B. WRIGHT

ALS. DLC–JKP. Addressed to Columbia and franked by Benjamin A. Bidlack.

1. A businessman in Pennsylvania, John Snyder served one term in the U.S. House as a Democrat, 1841–43.

2. See Polk to John K. Kane, June 19, 1844.

3. At the Democratic National Convention in Baltimore, the delegation from Pennsylvania split over the question of requiring a two-thirds majority for the presidential nomination. Twelve delegates voted for the rule, and thirteen voted against.

4. Wright probably meant to write the word "interest" here.

5. Letter not found.

## FROM J. GEORGE HARRIS

My Dear Sir,                          Nashville July 31, 1844

I shall not, *cannot* fail of success in the Washington undertaking[1] unless the efforts of some of our friends shall have a tendency to prevent the desirable consummation. I never disclosed my purpose or correspondence to a soul with the exception of yourself and Gen. Armstrong. It seems that Gen. Pillow broached it to Gen. Jackson and Maj. Donnelson,[2] and I am afraid that *their* letters to Billy Lewis, who should *not* be a confident in this case, may lead to unfortunate results. Perhaps not, but Donnelson has just informed me that he has written to Lewis on the subject intimating in his letter that if Tyler comes in he must do so without any reciprocal feeling on the part of your friends. Thus *it should be* to all appearances, and *thus it would be* under the circumstances of my own private correspondence, *but there was no necessity for saying it*—indeed it was a voluntary and uncalled-for sentiment, which can do no good and may do much harm. But I live in the belief that his letter will be too late. Billy Lewis is playing *his own game.* If Walker's letter[3] to you was dated between the 11th and 16th of July *that* is another link in the chain. Greene, of Boston writes me that Jones[4] was in New York on the 17th making "preparation." Meantime, I perceive that some of our imprudent friends in Virginia and Gen. Dix[5] of New York, are making assaults upon Tyler and his administration, while Donelson throws in a stumbling block which may do injury.

How utterly unnecessary this gratuitous letter of Donnelson's, for I have no where uttered a solitary word about *agreement,* or any other sort of *stipulation,* nor have I pretended in any way whatever to speak by any other man's authority, or by advice of friends even. Nothing has been said by me of *reciprocal benefits*—these if contemplated by them, may be *inferred.* There was no *necessity* for it. I have never so much as said that it was for your sake that I wanted to see Tyler in a right position. I carefully and powerfully urged it as a point of interest for Mr. Tyler himself on the score of *consistency* and *fame.* I have been *prudent,* rely on it; and there was no *necessity* for Donelson's unadvised and gratuitous letter. There was no necessity for offering Mr. Tyler any thing more than *a welcome.* The door had been slammed in his face by Benton & Blair; and although he wanted to enter, he dare not attempt it again unless the door should be thrown open to him. Like Texas, having been refused admittance, and being unable to maintain his own sovereignty, he wanted to come in, and would as soon as he could see the door open. If let alone now, and not influenced by the causes adverted to he will come in speedily and heartily without any price whatever.

The moment I heard of Donelson's letter to Lewis, I wrote privately to Jones to pay no regard to any thing he should hear from any other source than my own letters, on this subject; and I *yet* think it will all work out right. If it should not, I shall feel justified in a knowledge that it was no fault of mine.

Tyler does not expect to *trade* with the Polk Party. The Polk Party did not originate by trading, nor will it be maintained by trading. It is the People's Party against the Trading Politicians. Tyler knows this; he does not propose nor expect to trade. It is idle to think so, and it is hazardous to predict a letter either *pro* or *con* on such a supposition, especially if written to Billy Lewis. It were better not mentioned— better let alone entirely.

On the preceding pages I have disclosed all my thoughts on the present position of this question, without the slightest reservation. Perhaps I place too much confidence in what I have been able to do, and misapprehend or cannot appreciate the efforts of others. You will pardon, therefore, the freedom of expression.

I shall do all in my power to aid Col. Laughlin in discharging his duties as editor of the Union; in every paper a few of my contributions appear—he still *gets up* the paper according to his own judgment, inserting such articles as he thinks best; but I understand that it is his determination to go off *speaking* after the August Convention.[6] Whenever it is possible for me to *take hold* I do so cheerfully. I am sorry to hear that Coe's health is too imperfect to follow Henry; but Bright[7] will match him any where.

You will of course be here at our Convention on the 15th, ready to shake the hands of your friends who may call to see you. The Inn[8] would, perhaps, be the most convenient place for the thousands of sovereigns to approach, while, if your choice, it would perhaps be more agreeable to some of your friends to see you at morning and evening at the private residence of some one of your friends in the city. You may prepare for a hard day's work, to shake hands with more men than you ever shook hands with in one day before.

The Committee of Reception, to which I seem to belong, would be glad to know what day and at what hour you will be *coming in,* that we may make the necessary arrangements to do the honors handsomely. Suppose you were to come in about nine o'clock a.m. on the 15th? Of this, however you are the better judge.

I never saw anything like the enthusiasm which seems to prevail throughout the country at this moment. We must certainly triumph.

J. GEORGE HARRIS

ALS. DLC–JKP. Addressed to Columbia. Polk's AE on the cover states that he answered this letter on August 3, 1844; Polk's reply has not been found.

1. Reference is to a proposal by Thomas Allen that J. George Harris become associated with the Washington *Madisonian;* Harris interpreted the overture as an effort to facilitate John Tyler's withdrawal from the presidential race.

2. Gideon J. Pillow, Andrew Jackson, and Andrew J. Donelson.

3. Reference probably is to Walker's letter to Polk of July 10, 1844.

4. Reference is to "John Jones," the pseudonym used by Thomas Allen as editor of the Washington *Madisonian.*

5. Soldier, lawyer, and railroad president, John A. Dix served as adjutant general of New York, 1831–33, and a member of the New York House, 1842. He won election as a Democrat to the U.S. Senate seat vacated by Silas Wright in 1845 and served until 1849. In 1848 Dix ran an unsuccessful race for governor at the head of the Free Soil ticket. After service as a general officer in the Civil War, he won election as governor on the Republican ticket and served from 1873 to 1875.

6. Reference is to the Democratic mass meeting in Nashville scheduled for August 15, 1844.

7. Levin H. Coe, Gustavus A. Henry, and John M. Bright. A Fayetteville lawyer, Bright was a Democratic presidential elector in 1844 and 1848. He served in the Tennessee House, 1847–49, and in the U.S. House, 1871–81.

8. Reference is to the Nashville Inn, a landmark hotel located on the north side of the public square.

## TO JOHN P. HEISS

My Dear Sir:                                    Columbia July 31st, 1844
*R. P. Flenniken Esqr.*[1] of Union Town Pennsylvania, requests me to forward to him some Democratic paper published in this state, during the pendency of the present contest. Will you send him the *"Tri-weekly Union & the Star-Spangled Banner."*[2] Mr *Flenniken,* is a distinguished lawyer of Union Town, and is the President of the

Democratic association of Fayette County. He gives me a most flattering account of the Democratic prospects in that part of Pennsylvania.

I hope the arrangement can be made to have the aid of our friend *Harris's* talents in the Union. The Union should be made in Tennessee, what *Medary's* Statesman[3] is in Ohio, and what the Union itself was in 1839. It is looked to from all parts of the Union & must be a *great paper* during this canvass. It would do well enough as it is, *in ordinary-times,* but we are now in a *storm,* and it wants more spirit & fire. Let *Harris* & *Laughlin* both labour for it. *Harris* is willing at a word. I have written to Laughlin & feel sure he will consent & take no offense. Much depends on the next 90-days, and there is not a paper in the Union, whose location makes it so important as the *Union* during that period. Harris is willing. Let him lay hold immediately. There is not a day to be lost. All *Laughlin* can desire, is the good of the common cause, and he cannot and must not take offense, at having *Harris's* aid, in the great work. If the present enthusiasm & confidence of our party can be kept up for the next 90-days all will be well in the state, and in the Union. I have written to *Armstrong* on the subject.[4] Consult him. This letter is for your own eye alone. In haste ....

JAMES K. POLK

ALS. T–JKP. Addressed to Nashville and marked "Private." Published in *THM,* II, p. 143.

1. Robert P. Flenniken represented Fayette County in the Pennsylvania House in 1838 and 1840–41. Polk appointed him chargé d'affaires for Denmark in January 1847.

2. Two publications are mentioned here: the triweekly edition of the *Nashville Union* and the Nashville *Star Spangled Banner.*

3. Reference is to the Columbus *Ohio Statesman.*

4. Polk wrote to Armstrong on July 30 and July 31, 1844; those letters have not been found.

## FROM JOHN W. P. McGIMSEY[1]

Baton Rouge, La. July 31, 1844

McGimsey congratulates Polk on his nomination for the presidency. He recalls that Polk's first election contest was that of assistant clerk of the Tennessee Senate. After the first round of balloting, which produced no winner, William Edmiston[2] suggested that Polk withdraw from the race and stand for the office of principal clerk of the Senate. McGimsey remembers having heard Polk say that his election to the Senate clerkship was his first step toward political preferment. McGimsey solicits an appointment as army surgeon in Baton Rouge.

ALS. DLC–JKP. Addressed to Columbia and forwarded to Nashville.

1. McGimsey had been a physician in Columbia before moving to Mississippi in 1834; he settled in Baton Rouge in December 1840.

2. William Edmiston of Lincoln County served both in the Tennessee House, 1815–17, and in the Tennessee Senate, 1819–21.

# AUGUST

## TO JOHN P. HEISS

My Dear Sir:                                        Columbia Augt. 1st 1844

Your letter of the 29th ulto. is at hand. I had anticipated your views in my letter to you of yesterday, which I sent under cover to *Genl. Armstrong,* lest it might fall into the hands of some one else in your office. I had also written to *Laughlin* and received his answer on yesterday.[1] He says he is desirous to have *Mr Harris's* aid. I think he prefers to remain, but will be entirely willing, that *Harris* should lay hold with him, and make the Union, such a paper as the crisis demands. *Harris* is ready at a moments notice. Let it therefore be done. The two can & will make the Union the *great paper* of the country for the next 90 days, and this is what it ought to be. Both *Laughlin* & *Harris* can be well employed their whole time in making it a powerful organ. Let it be done. You cannot imagine the importance I attach to it. It is indeed indispensible, that fire & spirit & power should be thrown into it. The Nashville Whig press, must be boldly & promptly met at every point & driven back, by exposing their falsehoods & misrepresentations. Can you not in the emergency and for the next 90 days spare more space in the Union for political matter. This is important if you can possibly do it, as I hope you can. In haste.

JAMES K. POLK

ALS. T–JKP. Addressed to Nashville and marked *"Confidential."* Published in *THM,* II, p. 143.

1. See Polk to Samuel H. Laughlin, July 26, 1844, and Laughlin to Polk, July 29, 1844.

## FROM JULIUS W. BLACKWELL

Dear Sir,                                   Athens Ten. Aug. 2nd, 1844

At the particular request of Mr. B. Martin of your Co. & feeling that way inclined myself, I undertake to write you and give you some account of what is going on in this section of E. Ten. In the first place Messrs Nicholson and Martin are very much fatigued and worn dow[n] in boddy; but in the very best sperits and sound of mind. They give glowing acounts of our prospects where ever they have travelled, and I heard Nicholson and Crozier in Decatur on wednesday, and never was a coon more completely cornered (or tree'd) than was the latter. Martin and Luke Lea (former Secretary of state) addressed a large crowd the day before, at Washington, Rhea Co. and Mr. Martin was very successfull. At the old Cumberland stand near Athens, there was near three thousand persons assembled at our mass meeting on yesterday. Crozier proposed to have the time divided, and our committee proposed to give them half the time here, provided Mr. Crozier would promise that the Democrats should have a like division of time at the Knoxville mass meeting on the 14th this month. This offer was declined on the part of the whigs, alias Coons, and Nicholson & Martin occupied the day to the entire satisfaction of the Democracy. At nigt Messrs Lyon, Reynolds, Mullay and Washington Ballew[1] addressed the people at the stand. I am not capable of writing glowing discriptions of anything; or I could do so on the present occasion; but I can only tell you a plain tale. I can say to you that the Democrats never did, in this section of the State, seem to be in finer spirits, or more actively engaged. They fight as men determined to conquer; and in evry county numerous changes are said to have taken place, and hundreds of Whigs say they will not vote at all—that they cannot, and will not vote for Clay. The Coon leaders are evidently alarmed, and are using evry exertion to hold their own, for they know they can gain nothing. They struggle hard to get, and keep up an excitement, thinking thereby to urge on the whigs to vote for Clay; they may get nine out of ten whigs to vote for Clay, who say they will not go it; this will do. If one out of ten whigs will hold off, who say they will, it will give us a large majority in the State, when we take into consideration the actual gaines we have made. Nicholson and Martin left Athens for Madisonville this evening, to attend the mass meeting there tomorrow. I expect to follow on in the morning, and will go on as far as Knoxville.

J. W. BLACKWELL

ALS. DLC–JKP. Addressed to Columbia.

1. Thomas C. or William Lyon, Robert B. Reynolds, John C. Mullay, and David Washington Ballew. Mullay, a former editor of the Jonesboro *Tennessee Sentinel* and a Democratic operative in McMinn County, moved to Washington City in 1845 and held a number of minor federal posts during the Polk administration. Ballew, a lawyer from McMinn County, served as a Democrat in the Tennessee House, 1847–49, and the Tennessee Senate, 1855–57.

## FROM LEVIN H. COE

Dear Sir                                      Beersheba Springs Augt 2 1844

You have heard the result of the Bedford meeting.[1] Bright sustained himself well. Nothing saved Henry but the last speech. I met him at an interpolated appointment at Davis Mills on Wednesday. I was weaker than I supposed & able only to speak to the Texas question. Yesterday we met at Manchester. I led off. I held him all the time to the Texas question except that in his last replication he spoke 15 minutes on the Tariff. He had (or his friends) thrown out upon one days notice a meeting for today at Pelham. I notified him I should not attend & am here. He closed at Lewisburg, Pulaski, Fayetteville, Shelby. & Manchester & would have closed tomorrow at Winchester[2] but if he has others pitched ahead now he has to abandon them or I take the county seats.

Since I met him his remarks of you are respectful. At Shelby. they were as before most abusive. He has heard I expect that I did not intend to permit it. Yesterday he remarked to me privately that he hoped we would have a pleasant race upon gentlemanly principles. I told him I preferred it but it could be as rough as he thought proper to make it. I dont feel that he is making any thing off of me. I think I can check mate when I go first, gain when I follow, but these d—d spinning Jennies, hemp patchs & water falls through this country are troublesome.

Permit me to say that there is a very soft malitia fight going on in Middle Tennessee so far as I have been. We have no organization, no concert, no documents circulating, no neighbour who feels it his duty to appeal all the time to his neighbours. My breast is very sore. I will have to be relieved at Sparta[3] & had better go West. Henry I think it probable will go East after the 21st. Roger Barton must be fastened upon him.

Barton will suit E. Ten. better than any man in America. My mode of debate is better suited to the West.

I will still hold Henry to Texas alone until we separate. I make so many points he has to do so or give them up.

L. H. COE

[P.S.] There is some gain where I have been but not much.

ALS. DLC–JKP. Addressed to Columbia.
1. Reference is to the public debate held at Shelbyville, July 30, 1844. John M. Bright spoke in place of Coe, who was present but ill.
2. References are to speaking engagements at which Whig elector Gustavus A. Henry met such Democrats as Bright, Coe, and Aaron V. Brown in debate. The meetings were held July 22 at Lewisburg, July 25 at Pulaski, July 27 at Fayetteville, July 30 at Shelbyville, August 1 at Manchester, and August 3 at Winchester.
3. Reference is to a debate to be held at Sparta, August 8, 1844.

## FROM JOSEPH B. GILMAN[1]

Dear Sir                           Fall Branch Te August 2nd 1844
I have ret'd from my trip to Mo a few days since and I do assure you the sign is right in Mo. from one End of the State to the other—and from travelers from all quarters of the Union. I find we are ganing strength daley in my neighbourhood altho but very few Whigs have been for several years. Thare are changes in the Countys of Sullivan Washington Green & Hawkins. Many very many have changed to my knowledge. Your friends are very active & in better spirits, than I Ever saw them. I saw 9 returning from the Brittish Barbacue at Greenville.[2] Thare faces ware long & thare countennances sad. A shocking dinner was given on 29 & 30, at which time thay left the ground and many complained that they did not get Enough to Eat. On the whole it was a very badly managed. We will set an example on the 8th at that place that will go off better or we will quit the hunt.[3] I believe that from the voice of the people we will have from 8 to 10 thousand and 4 to 5 hundred waggons and all the carts in the district. We are taking great paines to accomodate the crowd on that day. I am willing to take all my Bacon. I tell you we will carry East Te in Novr next. Business is very dull here. The Election appears the order of the day. My wife sends her love to your lady. She will recolect Sarah Gammon her school mate at Salem NC in 1816.

JOSEPH B. GILMAN

[P.S.] I will write you again in a few weeks.

ALS. DLC–JKP. Addressed to Columbia.
1. Gilman was postmaster at Fall Branch in Washington County.

2. Reference is to a Whig convention held at Greeneville, Tenn., July 29–31, 1844. A barbecue was held the second day of the convention.

3. Reference is to a Democratic meeting scheduled for Greeneville, August 8, 1844.

## FROM J. GEORGE HARRIS

My Dear Sir                                                     Nashville Aug 2, 1844

Detained with my family in the country—12 miles from town—on yesterday, I did not get your letters[1] until to-day at noon; and I shall not be able to send the *Journals* until next stage. Rely on it, I shall do all in my power to make the Union all that you desire. I obtained some of Laughlin's correspondence with papers to-day and shall condense the substance for a rally on Tuesday. Do not forget however that Laughlin is the "chief cook" and is responsible for the dish. No pains however shall be spared on my part.

I am more than delighted with the progress of my northern arrangement. It is working well and prudently. Greene and Jones[2] have taken my hints, and the thing is *doing* fast enough for safety.

Old Ritchie put the ball in motion, and it rolled northward, our friends of Connecticut and Rh. Island kicking it along; when Greene receives it in Boston and bends it back in the right spirit to the Madisonian, which modestly receives it with a *kind spirit*—nothing more—scoring Clay and talking of a "reunion of what the party was before 1841." So it goes, swimmingly. Billy Lewis, nor any of the hangers-on & watchers can prevent it.

I shall transfer Old Ritchie's article to the Union on Tuesday,[3] and let such other scraps drop in incidently as must do good and can do no harm.

A good deal of my time is necessarily occupied in having an eye to my dwelling house now building within a mile of town.

J Geo. Harris

ALS. DLC–JKP. Addressed to Columbia.

1. Polk's letters have not been found.

2. Reference is to Charles G. Greene and Thomas Allen. Allen wrote under the pseudonym "John Jones."

3. On August 6, 1844, the *Nashville Union* printed an article from the *Richmond Enquirer* with endorsements from the *Boston Post and Statesman* and the Washington *Madisonian*. The article praised the policies of John Tyler and continued, "we invite Mr. Tyler and his friends to a re-union with the democratic party; we invite them as brethren and as equals, to the support of Polk and Dallas; we say to them, welcome—thrice welcome in their return to the democratic party."

## FROM J. G. M. RAMSEY

My dear Sir                                                        Mecklenburg Aug. 2, 1844

Yours of July 23 was duly received.[1] The certificate it contained of Mr. Potts[2] was immediately forwarded to Haywood (Saunders as I see being in the Western counties of N.C. till yesterday, & I hope now that election being over I may meet him if I go to Greeneville on the 8th) with a request to use it as he deems best. I am finding & forwarding to him the strongest of the innumerable cases in the Carolinas of Protection. We will make the clearest case immaginable of that whole matter. I believe I wrote to you that H. & S. would make a *joint* publication as the latter informs me by letter.[3] You will see in the Jeffersonian the proceedings at Charlotte.[4] They will certainly send you a number. I would send mine containing them but that I have sent it with an editorial to Eastman & as they are long it cannot be spared for a few days.

The meeting was the very thing, time & place. Nothing could be better. Droomgoole[5] of Va. spoke first, next Saunders. He vindicated E.P.[6] first by asserting all we have proved of his participation at that place of the Declaration of Independence in 1775[7] & in the whole of the Revolutionary War & in support read all the documents we have furnished him, & then appealed to my old friend Genl. McLeary[8] 80 years old & a compatriot & fellow soldier of E.P. who was by his side & has always lived there, ever since. The vindication is most ample & the foul slanders of your political enemies will react in your favor. Protection then is admitted & I am ready & so are H. & S. with the proofs on that subject to show that the truest Whigs of 1776 were reduced to the same necessity. If you dont see the Charlotte proceedings earlier you will in next weeks Argus.[9]

I will forward to Bancroft all the *characteristics* I know of yourself. They will be of service again.

I went to town Wednesday & fortunately found *all three* of the letters written to you from Sevier Knox & Blount in 1841.[10] They are ready for use the moment Jones gets on the stump & I will direct Nicholsons & Martins & others attention to them next Monday at the speaking.

Our friends all like the notion of swaping Johnson to you a while for Martin or some one else for a month or two & it will be so arranged at Greeneville. Of all which we will apprise the central Comtees at Nashville & Jackson.

Some of us will go to Maryville tomorrow & take the Anti-Polk letters above alluded to to be used if we hear that Jones is really stumping it. We will guard every point but are much obliged by any suggestions that reach us from you or others West of the Mountains.

We are in excellent spirits. We are certainly gaining even in Whig counties, & very much in Democratic places & our opponents have no enthusiasm among the rank & file. Their leaders are busy & active but the people apathetic. The Whig Mass meeting at Greeneville had as Lowry[11] writes us not 800 all told.

The first news from Charlotte you shall hear again. Mrs. R.[12] is still quite weak but we hope better.

J. G. M. RAMSEY

ALS. DLC–JKP. Addressed to Columbia.

1. Letter not found.

2. John Potts' laudatory statement about the character and service of Ezekiel Polk in the Revolutionary War was included in the *Vindication* of Ezekiel Polk published by the Nashville Democratic Central Committee.

3. In his letter to Polk of July 29, 1844, Ramsey reported that William H. Haywood, Jr., and Romulus M. Saunders would jointly publish a vindication of Ezekiel Polk. ALS. DLC–JKP. The authorship of the *Vindication* published in North Carolina was solely attributed to Haywood.

4. Reference is to the Charlotte *Mecklenburg Jeffersonian* and the Democratic barbecue held in Charlotte, N.C., on July 23, 1844.

5. George C. Dromgoole.

6. Ezekiel Polk.

7. Reference is to the Mecklenburg Declaration of Independence.

8. A resident of Mecklenburg County, Michael McLeary served several terms in the North Carolina Senate, 1819–24 and 1826. As part of his speech at the Charlotte barbecue, Saunders stood beside McLeary and spoke for him, saying that Ezekiel Polk had been a patriotic Whig of the Revolution and respected member of the Mecklenburg community.

9. Knoxville *Argus*.

10. Reference probably is to published letters addressed to Polk during his gubernatorial contest with James C. Jones; these letters have not been identified.

11. A business, personal, and political friend of Andrew Johnson, Lowry served as postmaster of Greeneville, 1843–50, and as U.S. marshal for the Eastern District of Tennessee during the years before the Civil War.

12. Peggy Barton Crozier Ramsey.

## FROM AUSTIN E. WING

Dear Sir,                                              Monroe [Mich.] Aug. 2nd 1844

Yours of July 4th was duly received.[1] I discover nothing as yet in this section of the Union which indicates any thing but the most prosperous condition of the democracy; of the state, I have attended several mass meetings, numbering from three to ten thousand in which the utmost harmony, and an unusual degree of enthusiasm have prevailed. We feel confident that we shall carry this state by a majority of from five to seven thousand. I am not a little pleased to see our old friend Genl. Cass taking a more active part in politics than I have ever known him to take before. He is in great demand as a speaker all over the state and has responded to every call with great cheerfulness and with great effect. I understand he has accepted an invitation to address a mass meeting at Indianapolis (Indiana) to be held about the 18th of this month. He will have influence in that state & I hope he may avail himself of opportunities to address meetings in Ohio. Those two states will be strongly contested, yet if we can rely upon the judgments of our friends we may expect a triumph in both. I have more fears of New York growing out of the warm contest among our democratic brethren in relation to their nomination for Governor. There is too much acrimony of feeling on that subject. If they should at their convention, as at the Baltimore convention, harmonize in their nomination, there will be no fear of the result. If otherwise it cannot but be doubtful. It is said, I know not with how much truth, that the manufacturers of Boston are raising large sums of money to be distributed throughout the states for electioneering purposes. I trust they will get a rebuke which will last them for many years. The question of annexation is pretty fairly sustained by the democracy of the north, but it is not so much as at the south the all absorbing subject. There is during the harvest with us a slight suspension of public demonstrations, but our mass meetings will soon commence again. On the 10th of September we shall have at Marshall near the centre of the state, a state Mass meeting at which I presume there will not be less than fifteen or twenty thousand democrats.

                                                          A. E. WING

ALS. DLC–JKP. Addressed to Columbia.
1. Polk's letter has not been found.


## TO ANDREW J. DONELSON

My Dear Sir:                                Columbia Augt. 3rd 1844
    I will be at Nashville on friday next, on my way to Murfreesborough with my wife. I will be at *Wm. G. Childress's* on thursday night, when I would be glad to meet *Armstrong* and *yourself* that we may have a full conference before the meeting of the 15th.[1] If it does not put you to, too much inconvenience meet me at *Childress's* on thursday night.

I hope you can have the *Resolutions* for the 15th prepared by that time. I have written to *Harris* to aid you in their *preparation.* Every paragraph of them must be well considered, as great importance will be attached to them throughout the Union. *Mr Buchanan* is right in the caution which he gave to you.[2]

I fear there is not entire harmony in the party in New York. I see *Bryant* of the Post[3] & six others have issued a *private circular* about Texas,[4] which has fallen into the hands of the Editor of the Pleabian,[5] who publishes it, and denounces the authors & reads them out of the party. This however being confined to a few, may not do much harm. The chief trouble of our party however grows out of their divisions, in the selection of a candidate for Governor. The *Hon. Mr Gillet* formerly of the Ho. Repts. writes to me[6] that *Mr Wright* will decline the nomination—absolutely—& he fears the party will be weakened. Their convention to nominate, meets 1st of September. *Gov. Marcy* too has written me[7] expressing apprehensions, concerning the nomination to be made. I have not written a word in reply, to either.[8] You will however see that it is of the greatest importance that harmony and union, should be preserved, in their state politics. I suppose *Butler* and others will do all they can, to preserve, the strength of the party. I cannot with propriety write to him or any one else in N.Y. on the subject. A letter from you to *Butler,* urging harmony & union, in making their state nominations, might draw his attention more earnestly to the subject and do good.

JAMES K. POLK

ALS. DLC–AJD. Addressed to Nashville and marked *"Confidential."* Published in *THM,* III, pp. 59–60.

1. Reference is to the Democratic mass meeting in Nashville, August 15, 1844.

2. In his letter to Donelson of July 17, 1844, Buchanan warned that the Nashville proceedings must avoid "every appearance of the slightest tendency towards nullification or disunion." He also expressed the wish that "nothing may be done at Nashville to impair the effect" of Polk's June 19, 1844, letter to Kane. St. George L. Sioussat, ed., "Selected Letters, 1844–45, from the Donelson Papers," *THM,* III (June, 1917), pp. 136–37.

3. New York *Evening Post.*

4. See Ely Moore to Polk, July 26, 1844.

5. New York *Daily Plebeian.*

6. See Ransom H. Gillet to Polk, July 20, 1844.

7. See William L. Marcy to Polk, June 28, 1844.

8. Polk replied to Marcy's letter of June 28 on July 9, 1844; he replied to Gillet's letter of July 20 on August 7, 1844. Polk's reply to Gillet has not been found.

## FROM JOHN P. HEISS

Union Office
Dear Sir                                    [Nashville, Tenn.] Aug 3d [18]44

Yours of the 1st is at hand; and if the arrangement can be made as you intimate between Laughlin and Harris, I feel confident the Union will be conducted more energetically in future than it is at present. I will converse with Harris the first opportunity, and no doubt some settled arrangement will be made.

It will be impossible for us to put more matter in the "Weekly Union" than it contains in the weekly publications at present. The Tri-Weekly might contain *one* or *two colums* more at each publication, yet it could not get circulation in the Star Spangled Banner, or Weekly unless the weekly was much enlarged.

JOHN P. HEISS

P.S. We will have a glorious time in Nashville to-day.[1]

ALS. DLC–JKP. Addressed to Columbia.
1. Reference is to a parade of Democratic militia companies, which featured the presentation of a banner from the Democratic ladies of Nashville to the partisan Texas Volunteer companies.

## TO ANDREW JACKSON

My Dear Sir:                              Columbia August 3rd, 1844

I received some days ago, your letter of the 26th ult., returning Mr Walker's letter.[1] I concur fully with you in the view which you have taken in regard to Mr W's suggestions. I have not written a line to a human being on the subject and will not. I have not even answered Mr Walker's letter, because I could not do so, without saying something on the subject. When I enclosed it to you for your advice,[2] I had not reflected, so fully as I should have done upon the use which might have been made of any letter from yourself or any other of my friends upon the subject.

I am gratified to see that the two or three last numbers of the Globe, are giving a fair support to the nomination, and have now no doubt that such will be its future course. I regret to learn from my friends in New York, that some division exists in the party in reference, to the nomination of the Democratic candidate for Governor, which it is feared will have a tendency to weaken the ticket in that state. *Mr*

*Gillet* writes to me[3] that *Mr Wright* will positively refuse the nomination. *Gov Marcy* wrote to me[4] some time ago that he apprehended difficulty in making a satisfactory nomination. It will be most unfortunate, if the domestic difficulties in the state shall have the effect to weaken our cause, as I think there is some reason to fear they may. It is a matter however in which neither I, nor my friends, *out of the State,* can interfere. You have no doubt seen the *confidential circular*[5] of *Bryant* of the Post[6] and a few others, on the Texas question, which has lately been published in the Plebian.[7] It shows a dissatisfied & disorganizing spirit on the part of its authors, but I hope, may do no great harm. These are the only unfavourable signs which I see from any quarter. My information from all other parts of the union, is of the most cheering character.

My friends at Nashville think that I ought to be there on the 15th but that I ought not to attend the discussions or take any part in the proceedings.[8] I have concluded to do so, and will visit you before I return home.

JAMES K. POLK

ALS. DLC–AJ. Addressed to the Hermitage and marked *"Private."*
1. Reference is to Robert J. Walker's letter to Polk, July 10, 1844, in which Walker suggests that Jackson write a letter to conciliate John Tyler and his supporters.
2. See Polk to Jackson, July 23, 1844.
3. See Ransom H. Gillet to Polk, July 20, 1844.
4. See William L. Marcy to Polk, June 28, 1844.
5. See Ely Moore to Polk, July 26, 1844.
6. New York *Evening Post.*
7. New York *Daily Plebeian.*
8. Reference is to the Democratic mass meeting to be held at Nashville, August 15, 1844.

## FROM SAMUEL H. LAUGHLIN

My dear sir,                                    Nashville, Tenn. Aug. 3, 1844
    The Tennessee Whig papers, especially in the Western District were attempting continually to make such a handle of the charge against your deceased Grandfather that I considered it false delicacy, and an acquescence by silence, any longer to withhold the proofs, and to-day's paper contains a continuation of the notices of yourself and ancesters which was commenced on Thursday.[1] Another No. will contain more proofs, after which Harris promises to follow up the subject with a

number of notices and reminiscences of yourself, with a number of which I can supply him.

The original of one of the statements I obtained, and a copy of the other,[2] it being blotted and interlined, together with the statement of Smartt, Mercer, Shields, &c.[3] as you will see them, I forwarded with a letter to Hon. Lewis D. Henry[4] on 24th or 25th of July. The copy in the Union, as I send it to you, is perfect—the one mailed yesterday evening for you having a typographical error in it, of no consequence however.[5]

I will make you a perfect copy, verify it by my affidavit if you wish it, and by the original statement of Smartt, Locke &c.[6] and send it to you.

God forbid that I should have any pride of editorship, or any thing else, that would make me dislike aid. I refused to agree to be Editor, during the responsibilities of the contest, without Nicholson and others, for then *he* was in the humor of first professing great zeal for the cause, would write and help me. Harris was not then here, or I would have asked him to write. Some things he can write better than any one we have. He can throw a sudden dash of cold or of hot water from his engine, though its effects may soon dry up afterwards, better than any of us. You do me but justice on this subject. The more help I have the better for the cause. The cause is everything—me nothing.

I have continually been desiring more room. I cannot have more than half the room I could fill myself with matter that I think profitable. I shall do all I can.

One reason why I am the more ready to have help, is the large press of correspondence I have brought on myself, and that I seek by writing to men at every point of the compass. In this correspondence I remit documents to places they would not otherwise reach, in the state and out of it, at the rate of from one to two hundred weekly.

I have an excellent correspondent, or rather two, at Uniontown, Pennsylvania, Fayette Co. One in the person of Maj. R. P. Flinnken[7] a lawyer at the head of the Bar there, and the Rev. John T. A. Henderson[8] a Cumberland Presbyterian of great popularity there. Flinniken is, I believe, of the same church. They both write me under date of 23 July, that Pennsylvania is perfectly safe—majority by no possibility less than 12 or 15 thousand—possibly 20. I send them documents for use under cover to Dr. Sturgeon the Senator who lives there.

I have been sending facts, documents and statements, one procured from a fellow named Potter by Thos. Martin in Giles, to Massachusetts and other states.[9] I have set in for a nine months hard work from the day I begun, and nothing but providence or an act of God shall hinder me from performing it. I have Register of the present Congress, and I write and send documents by it *ad lib.* I was lucky in getting introduced, and pretty well acquainted with many of them in May.

My Thursday article on foreign citizens[10] was finally to secure some dutch and irish here, and because I am advised from Ohio, Indiana, Illinois and Missouri, that the ground I take is proper.

Yours of the 1st inst. is before me,[11] though I have not acknowledged its receipt.

To-day, in the delivery of the Flag by Miss Cheatham[12] (Len's girl) and raising the poles, and they are higher than 3 of Hamans Gallows[13] would have been one on top of another, and in the speaking this afternoon we have had a glorious parade. It outdid the Foster and Jones Mass meeting here at the time of your Festival, as two to one.[14] Maj. Childress, Jas. C. Moore and E. A. Keeble have been with us to-day.[15]

On 14th, the Treat at Buchanans of a Free Barbacue to the people and Delegations coming here on the 14th,[16] when some of our military will those coming in,[17] will, of itself, be a grand affair. Old Burrell Perry[18] is here to-day. He says he has five hands at work at Buchanans, and will send over a wagon load of "bread and meat" on night of the 13th. He lives you know, five miles from Buchanan's on Stones river.

In addition to our Brigade in Davidson, Ralph Martin[19] and others will have a new company in five days over the river. The Whites Creek and Ridge boys were in to-day in a fine uniformed full company of Cavalry. They brought in besides their colors, about 20 of the largest poke stalks I ever saw, some with ripe berries on them. In coming from the ridge to-day, Joel Smith[20] says the gates and draw-bars on the way, and fronts of Houses and cabins were adorned with fresh green poke stalks.

I have heard five or six Whigs to-day, Hagan[21] one of them and some from the country, admit that we will carry Tennessee, but that it will do us no good. Jennings is here to-day, and looks like a run-down hound. Smith Brien[22] I think is to address the Whig Club to-night. It will be no go.

S. H. LAUGHLIN

N.B. You will see that John Lea[23] has resigned as district Atto to take the field. I am surprized at this. Though a young lawyer of promise, he has no *stump powers.* Calf Bilbo[24] is in East Tennessee speaking. *They are hard run.*[25]

ALS. DLC–JKP. Addressed to Columbia and marked *"Private."*

1. Two articles discussing Polk's ancestry, "James K. Polk" and "James K. Polk—Col. Ezekiel Polk," appeared in the *Nashville Union,* August 1 and August 3, 1844.

2. References are to the statements of John Smith and Thomas Gribble denying that Ezekiel Polk had been a Tory.

3. Reference is to a statement testifying to the character of Smith and Gribble. The statement was signed by George R. Smartt, L. D. Mercer, Alexander Shields, Jesse Locke, Thomas H. Hopkins, and William L. S. Dearing. Mercer, a McMinnville merchant, served as a clerk of the circuit court for Warren County.

4. Louis D. Henry.

5. Neither copy has been found.

6. Reference is to the statement testifying to the character of Smith and Gribble. Jesse Locke had been a clerk of the circuit court for Warren County and a delegate to the Tennessee Democratic State Convention in November 1843.

7. Robert P. Flenniken.

8. Henderson is not identified further.

9. Potter is not identified further; Thomas Martin, a businessman who later became president of the Louisville and Nashville Railroad, staunchly supported both Jackson and Polk; he declined appointment as secretary of the Treasury in the Polk administration.

10. Reference probably is to an article that appeared in the *Nashville Union* on Saturday, August 3, 1844. The article argued that "the true policy of our government" was to give "full protection and encouragement" to immigrants and to extend citizenship "at the earliest convenient time"; it charged that the Whigs wished to extend the waiting period for citizenship from five years to twenty-one years.

11. Polk's letter has not been found.

12. Sarah Cheatham, daughter of Leonard P. Cheatham, presented "on behalf of the democratic ladies of Nashville" a banner to the Texas Volunteer militia companies during ceremonies on Capitol Hill, August 3, 1844.

13. According to the Book of Esther, Haman was hanged on a gallows "50 cubits high," which he had prepared for the execution of the Jew, Mordecai.

14. On July 13, 1844, the Democrats held a large mass meeting at Columbia while the Whigs held a parade of the "Whig military and other Volunteer Associations" in Nashville. The Whigs were addressed by Ephraim H. Foster and James C. Jones.

15. John W. Childress, James C. Moore, and Edwin A. Keeble. Moore was a Murfreesboro grocer; Keeble, a lawyer and editor of the Murfreesboro *Monitor,* served as mayor of Murfreesboro in 1828 and 1855, campaigned successfully as a Democratic presidential elector in 1856, and represented Tennessee in the Confederate Congress in 1864 and 1865.

16. The *Nashville Union* reported that 7,000 people attended the barbecue given August 14, 1844, at Buchanansville, in Rutherford County, fifteen miles from Nashville along the Murfreesboro turnpike. The barbecue was given in

honor of delegates to the Democratic mass meeting in Nashville, August 15, 1844.

17. Laughlin's syntax is garbled here.

18. Burrell Perry is not identified further.

19. Ralph Martin, a Nashville merchant, was scheduled to serve as a marshal for the Nashville Democratic mass meeting, August 15, 1844.

20. Joel M. Smith had been part owner of the *Nashville Union* in the 1830's. He had also served as a Nashville alderman, 1827–28 and 1837–38.

21. Hagan is not identified further.

22. John Smith Brien addressed a meeting of Nashville Whigs at the Court House on the evening of August 3, 1844. Brien, a lawyer, served in the Tennessee House, 1837–39 and 1866–67; he was a Whig presidential elector in 1848.

23. John M. Lea, a Nashville lawyer and a son of Luke Lea, was appointed U.S. attorney for the middle district of Tennessee in 1842. On August 3, 1844, the *Nashville Whig* announced that he was resigning his office to campaign in place of John D. Tyler, the Whig elector for the Ninth Congressional District. Lea later won election as mayor of Nashville in 1849, and he served in the Tennessee House, 1875–77.

24. William N. Bilbo was a Nashville lawyer; he became associated with the *Nashville Gazette* in 1856.

25. Laughlin wrote his note in the left margin of the final page of the letter.


## FROM ROMULUS M. SAUNDERS

My dear Sir,                                            Raleigh Augt. 3, [18]44

I have delayed writing in order to give you the result of our elections,[1] so that you might be able to know to some certainty how things stand with us. The elections have gone against us, that of the Legislature much worse than I had any idea of. In several Counties we lost for the want of proper candidates. But I doubt not the course of our party at the last session, when we had 24 majority, operated much against us. The whigs now claim 36 majority on joint ballot. As to Gov, full returns are not yet in, but Graham's[2] majority will be between 4 & 5000. We shall renew the battle for Nov. but I cannot flatter myself with any reasonable prospect of success. There are some half dozen or more of our Western Counties, which give such large majorities against us, that I cant well devise any means for overcoming them, tho we shall try. I have my fears of New York & Ohio, through the coalition of the abolitionists & Whigs, tho our friends in both seem to think otherwise, but I have not much confidence in them.

You will see what was done at Charlotte as to the charge agt. your Grandfather.[3] That in the end is to operate in our favour.

R. M. SAUNDERS

ALS. DLC–JKP. Probably addressed to Columbia. Published in *NCHR*, XVI, pp. 340–41.

1. Reference is to state elections held in North Carolina on August 1, 1844.

2. William A. Graham, a lawyer, served as a Whig in the U.S. Senate, 1840–43, and as governor of North Carolina, 1845–49.

3. Reference is to a Democratic barbecue in Charlotte, N.C., on July 23, 1844; on that occasion Saunders defended Ezekiel Polk against Whig allegations that he had been a Tory during the Revolutionary War.

## FROM ROBERT ARMSTRONG

Dear Sir,                                      Nashville Augt 4th [18]44

Govr Cass, Woodberry, Kain, Horn, McDuffy (I think Allen) Tom Marshall, Wickliffe, Gutherie &c &c will be here.[1] Will be announced on Tuesday.[2]

We had a great day on Saturday. Large meeting; the presentation of the colours and the aray of Military &c &c was splendid and went off well.[3] We failed in raising the *great* pole but will never give it up.[4] I have order[ed] all navy sailors &c to meet at 9 o'clock in the morning. Joe Miller[5] is here and I will make him take charge of it. It must be raised and shall be.

I have again written Mathews urging him to the meeting on 27 at Shelbyville.

Genl Jackson has a letter from Jn. Y. Mason on the subject of Tylers withdrawal. It all works well and will work great good to us. A little time and the old Chief will have it done up in proper style. No pains. I will go to Childress' if I can, but the truth is I am so engaged that I have not a moment. I am determined to have this pole up & *well* up. The Whigs have had some little exultation at the failure and our friends somewhat mortified. I want to turn the *tables* and have a great day here *before* our convention.

We have triumphed over them. We done so on *Saturday*. Never was their party so *cut down,* and *whiped* in Nashville.

We must keep it up. I have got Andrew Ewing to go today to Springfield. Craighead goes to Castalian Springs on *friday* & *Saturday* to Hendersonville. In haste.

R. ARMSTRONG

ALS. DLC–JKP. Addressed to Columbia.

1. Lewis Cass, Levi Woodbury, John K. Kane, Henry Horn, George McDuffie, William Allen, Thomas F. Marshall, Robert Wickliffe, and James Guthrie. Reference is to the Democratic mass meeting in Nashville on August 15, 1844.

2. The *Nashville Union* of Tuesday, August 6, 1844, carried a list of dignitaries who planned to attend the Democratic mass meeting in Nashville.

3. Reference is to the festivities of August 3 during which the Democratic ladies of Nashville presented a flag to the Texas Volunteer militia companies of Davidson County.

4. Reference is to the largest of several hickory poles that together formed the substructure for an elevated platform.

5. Joseph Miller was the captain of the steamboat *Nashville*.


## FROM AUGUSTE D'AVEZAC

Barrytown, N.Y. August 4, 1844

States that an "imprudent circular" opposing Texas annexation[1] was written to correct a misapprehension in several rural counties that assent to annexation "was required as a Test of sound Democracy." It was feared that the Texas issue would prevent some one hundred abolitionists in the "infected District" from returning to the ranks of the New York Democracy. Urges that although the signers of the circular are "somewhat unlikely, on the Texas question," they do not support abolitionism either. Details his schedule of speaking engagements for September. Suggests that Polk communicate his opposition to nativist attempts to alter the naturalization laws or to abridge "the constitutional guarantee of religious freedom," by which protection all citizens "are placed on a footing of perfect equality."

ALS. DLC–JKP. Probably addressed to Columbia.
1. See Ely Moore to Polk, July 26, 1844.


## FROM ROBERT ARMSTRONG

Dear Sir                                    Nashville Augt 5, [18]44

I send you enclosed the Invitation for Mr Sykes.[1] The others for Alabama have been sent. Brown and Johnston[2] should be here and every County in Middle Tennessee should press out their Thousand for this Convention.

The Whigs are making every effort in their power to have a large meeting[3] and our men should take pains to get our friends out. This can be done *best* by Cave Johnston, Brown, Jones,[4] and the leading men in the different sections.

I have written every day, and every spare moment to effect a large turn out. If posible I will go to Childress's with Donelson. I will have the *pole* up and well up with an addition of 20 feet with a round top 12 feet large & space *60 feet* up where We can have a Band of music & a small peace of artillery.[5] In haste.

R. ARMSTRONG

ALS. DLC–JKP. Addressed to Columbia. Polk's AE on the cover states that he answered this letter on August 7, 1844; Polk's reply has not been found.

1. Probably Francis W. Sykes, a planter and physician who practiced first at Decatur and later at Courtland, Ala. He attended the University of Nashville prior to his enrollment in medical school. A Democrat, Sykes served several terms in the Alabama legislature beginning in 1855. Sykes' invitation to the Democratic mass meeting at Nashville on August 15, 1844, has not been found.

2. Aaron V. Brown and Cave Johnson.

3. Reference is to the Whig mass convention held in Nashville on August 21 and 22, 1844.

4. Cave Johnson, Aaron V. Brown, and George W. Jones.

5. See Robert Armstrong to Polk, August 4, 1844.

## FROM ANDREW J. DONELSON

Dear Sir,                       Nashville August 5, 1844

I have recd. your letters returning Wrights & Buchanans'.[1] Will meet you on Thursday at Mr C's.[2]

Your several requests have been attended to. Terry has accepted and says *if he is alive* he will be here.[3]

Since I wrote you an occasion has offered for a declaration of the Genl's views in regard to Mr Tyler's position. Mason has asked his advice as a friend. The General in reply runs over all the points in the case, and offers his opinion in such language and terms as cannot fail to have the desired effect.[4]

Marshal[5] of Kentucky has written me a private note stating that he would certainly come. So has Genl. Cass and several others. I have also a private letter from Mughlenberg[6] of Penna. He says you will get that state by a large majority.

All ahead looks bright. The Bryant affair[7] will take a good turn, and increase the democratic vote.

A. J. DONELSON

ALS. DLC–JKP. Addressed to Columbia and marked *"Private."*

1. In a letter to Polk of July 29, 1844, Donelson had enclosed letters from James Buchanan and Silas Wright; Polk's endorsement of Donelson's letter indicates that he answered on July 31, 1844; Polk's reply has not been found. Polk also wrote Donelson on August 3, 1844.

2. William G. Childress.

3. Reference is to the Democratic mass meeting at Nashville, August 15, 1844.

4. Andrew Jackson's letter to John Y. Mason, dated August 1, 1844, suggested that John Tyler ought to withdraw from the presidential race. ALS. DLC–AJ.

5. Thomas F. Marshall.

6. Henry A. P. Muhlenberg.

7. Reference is to a circular letter among New York Democrats opposing the annexation of Texas. See Ely Moore to Polk, July 26, 1844.

## FROM WILLIAM M. LOWRY

My Dear Sir                                    Greeneville, Ten Aug 5 1844

Presuming that you would be pleased to hear occasionally from this part of the State is the only reason I shall offer for addressing you this hasty note. It seems that E Tennessee and more particularly Old Greene is the Battle Ground of this Divission of the State. The Whigs have just closed a mass meeting at this place which was in my humble opinion an entire failure.[1] Senator Jarnigan[2] has been with us some 2 weeks and seems to have taken up his residence here. Senator Foster was here also & made us one of his Jim Crow[3] addresses. The truth is the Whigs now are not the Whigs of 1840. They seem out of hart & disperited and defeat is verry ledgeably written on their countanances, & we will most certainly beat them this time handsomely. The parade of the Whigs here last week was truly disgusting with their flags, mottos, gourds, coon skins &c. It lost them a number of votes. On the 1st day of the Whig meeting that night Senator Jarnigan announced that he would speak on the next day and that he would attend to the case of one Andrew Johnson.

Which caused some excitement amongst the Democrats who were out early the next day to hear the Senator give Johnson a skinning. He spoke some 2 1/2 hours. After he concluded the Democrats contended as Johnson had been publicly assailed that in all fairness he ought & must have a chance to defend himself. Which they Whigs refused at the time but stated that Col Johnson should occupy their stand on the next day in reply to Jarnigan.

Johnson was to have 2 hours, Jarnigan 1/2 hour reply. Then Johnson was to conclude with a 15 muinets reply. I presume a set of fellows never got such a lashing as Johnson gave them at their own Barbecue. They Whigs fear & hate Johnson awfully. So soon as Jarnigan finnished his 1/2 hour that infamous Scamp, Brownlow, mounted the stand and call'd for Bell. Mr Bell then came forwd but refused to speak untill Justice was done Col Johnson, & he was allowd his 15 muinets to reply. Col Johnson then rejoined 15 muinets, and I presume 15 muinets were never used to grater advantage. They Whigs done their best to interupt Col Johnson but he heeded them not, and triumphed most nobly upon the enemys ground for the Whigs (the more candid of them) admit that Jarnigan cannot compete with Johnson even if his side of the question was correct. We will certainly increase the Democratic vote largely in this 1st Destrict. We need a good deal of canvassing in the 2nd Destrict. We can make much capital in that Destrict. If It can be canvassed rightly. I think we will try and press Martin into that Destrict. Upon the whole our prospects in this Divission of the State were never more flattering. I cannot concede the Whigs any majority in E Tenn. I think we will make a drawn Battle so far as E Ten is concerned. They Whigs are making a Desperate Onset in this Hawkins Washington & Sulivan Co. Report says to day that Nave[4] the representative from Carter & Johnson has renounced Clay, and I have no doubt of the truth of the report which will make grate *inroads* into Whiggery in those counties. The truth is We are gaining largely in those counties anyhow. Present my kind regards to Mrs Polk ....

WM. M. LOWRY

ALS. DLC–JKP. Addressed to Columbia.

1. Reference is to the Whig convention held in Greeneville, Greene County, Tenn., on July 29–31, 1844.

2. Spencer Jarnagin.

3. Thomas D. Rice introduced his popular song, "Jim Crow," in an 1830 minstrel show; Lowry's point of reference is that of a comedian performing in blackface make-up.

4. Godfrey C. Nave served three terms in the Tennessee House, 1837–41 and 1843–45, and one term in the Senate, 1853–55.

## FROM J. G. M. RAMSEY

Mecklenburg, Tenn. August 5, 1844

Ramsey acknowledges receipt of Polk's letter of July 29.[1] He discusses additional sources of testimony for the vindication of Ezekiel Polk and reviews possible publication strategies for the same. He reports that Johnson "obtained a complete victory" in a debate with Jarnagin at Greeneville,[2] mentions that Nicholson will speak in Knoxville this date and that efforts will be made to exchange his remaining appointments with those made for Johnson in East Tennessee, and indicates that Anderson will substitute for "Genl. Wallis" as an elector.[3] He states that prospects appear to be good for carrying the large states, although success in New York is yet uncertain. North Carolina, he fears, is lost.

ALS. DLC–JKP. Addressed to Columbia. Polk's AE on the cover states that he answered this letter on August 19, 1844; Polk's reply has not been found.
1. Polk's letter has not been found.
2. At a large Whig convention held in Greeneville on July 29–31, 1844, Andrew Johnson replied to a campaign speech by Spencer Jarnagin.
3. Thomas Von Albade Anderson and William Wallace. An East Tennessee physician, Anderson was a son of Joseph Anderson and brother of Alexander O., Pierce B., and Addison A. Anderson. An active railroad promoter, Wallace served as sheriff of Blount County, 1820–42, and sat in the Tennessee House, 1853–55. Nominated as Democratic elector for the Second Congressional District of Tennessee in 1844, he declined for reasons of health.

## FROM THOMAS O. BLACK[1]

Dr Sir                                  Hawesville, Kentucky, 6th August 1844
After an absence of 35 years I have no doubt you have entirely forgotten me. I have heard from you frequently & am proud to see you occupy the station in life you do. I have no news. I live here in Hancock County Kentucky & have made a good living & am doing very well. How you will succeed in your coming race, I cannot at this time tell, but I am proud to see my old schoolmates flourishing. Do you remember the many sports & amusements we had together at Ben Weathers, at old field, when we went to school to John Sale?[2] After a man has lived out nearly all his time, he naturally looks back, & when he does, nothing is more gratifying than to think of his old schoolmates & the many scenes that occured at that time & to hear that they are all doing well. I write this letter because I have nothing else to do & hope you will answer it without fail as nothing could be more gratifying to hear from you. Direct your letter Lewisport Hancock County Ky. God bless you.

THOMAS O. BLACK

NB. Write me what has become of your Uncle Wm Polke[3] & tell me where your sisters Mariah & Eliza[4] are & all the news concerning my old school mates. THOS. O. BLACK

ALS. DLC–JKP. Addressed to Nashville.
1. Not identified further.
2. Weathers and Sale are not identified further.
3. William Wilson Polk.
4. Jane Maria Polk married James Walker, and Lydia Eliza Polk married Silas M. Caldwell, a physician and planter in Haywood County.

## FROM GEORGE M. DALLAS

No. 5

Dear Sir,                                              [Philadelphia] 7 Aug. 1844

Your two last letters, of the 24th & 25th of July,[1] I found waiting my short absence from home. Had I in fact been able to leave this place for three weeks, it would now be too late to arrange so as to reach you by the 15 instant.[2] I have cases in our courts of too serious a character to permit me to risk their being disposed of without my presence. Under other circumstances, I should derive much gratification from an approach to the Hermitage, and would have ventured, under the persuasive force of your invitation, to the South, for the first time in my life. I know and feel that nothing would give me more pleasure than to mingle for a few days with just such an assemblage as you will have at Nashville.

I received this evening a fresh letter from a Committee of Naturalized Citizens in N. York, invoking an expression of my sentiments. It is accompanied by a sort of compilation of the opinions of others, in print; and I am told that a similar communication had been addressed to other candidates—of course, yourself among the rest. As my views are known to you, I will do exactly what you may think most expedient. I certainly have a misgiving suspicion that this call upon us is not intended as a friendly proceeding; but emanates from such of the naturalized foreigners who are whigs (a class in our cities by no means small) and who want to deprive us of the votes of the democratic native Americans, while, come what may, they are secretly resolved not to give us their own. The democrats among these "Natives" distinctly disclaim the introduction of their principles into the Presidential question; and I am not aware that they have put us to answer; but, if we come out, they may think themselves obliged to oppose.

You will have noticed that I somewhat prophetically, as well as over-jealously, "scented treason on the tainted gale"[3]; and that the singular speeches and toasts, to which I have before called your attention, were condensed and exploded in the N. York "Secret—or Confidential—Circular."[4] The sudden disclosure of this undermining and insinuating document has created considerable excitement; but I am assured that the effect is rather beneficial to the general cause than otherwise. The article in the Albany Argus was admirable in it's promptness, it's coolness, and it's directness; while no one accustomed to the manner in which Mr. Van Buren habitually handles political movements could avoid the impression that it either flowed from his pen, or was caught up and forwarded from his lips by his son John or Smith, both of whom are actively canvassing the democratic ticket in Albany.[5] Mr. V.B.[6] is very different in spirit and purpose from many who are esteemed his nearest friends and advisers.

The N. Carolina election is much as we expected; and now our turn comes for a manifestation or two.

I am told that Mr. Gallatin[7] stated to a gentlemen his opinion that if the democratic ticket got *either* New York *or* Pennsylvania, it's success was inevitable. I warrant Penna for you, out and out.

GEO. M. DALLAS

ALS. DLC–JKP. Addressed to Columbia. Polk's AE on the cover states that he answered this letter on August 29, 1844.

1. Polk's letters have not been found.
2. Reference is to the Democratic mass meeting at Nashville, August 15, 1844.
3. Quotation is not identified further.
4. See Ely Moore to Polk, July 26, 1844.
5. Martin Van Buren, John Van Buren, and Smith T. Van Buren. The fifth son of Martin Van Buren, Smith T. Van Buren, served his father as a political operative and was himself associated with the "Barnburner" faction in Albany.
6. Martin Van Buren.
7. Albert Gallatin, a major figure in the early Jeffersonian party, served as a member of the U.S. House, 1795–1801; as secretary of the Treasury, 1802–14; and as minister to France, 1816–23, and to Great Britain, 1826–27.

## FROM J. G. HIGH[1]

Oakland County
Dr Sir          Pontiac Michigan Augst 7 [18]44

You will I think excuse the liberty I take in addressing you when you see it is for the good of the country & the *Party* that I now do so.

The whigs have raised a hue & cry about your having abandon'd the doctrin of Free trade and the anexation of Texas, in order to make capital, at the report—injures your popularity here, for we cant get them to vote for a man that is disposed to shuffle in the rank. Now the only way we can successfully contradict the *Lie* the whigs have started, is to obtain an expression from under your own hand and therby show them you are now as ever, in favor of the immediate annexation of Texas therby relieving that opressed & slanderd nation from the yoke of Mexico, & the Grasp of Great Britton, and the repeal of that Black Tarriff of 1842. As this is a new state and compell'd to purchase from other states all we consume, consequently free trade is a popular measure here.

And another statement the whigs have made here is that you have disposed of your slaves lately in order to procur the abolition vote of some of the free states. This as you well know is a free state but still after your nomination you owned slaves. We prefer you to continue to own them and use them as you had done, thereby showing the people, you did not seek any low groveling device to obtain votes. So you will also state (if it is not enquiring into your private matters too much) how many slaves you owned on the 1st of June 1844 & how many you now own.

J. G. HIGH

P.S. Recollect I want the letter for Publication.

ALS. DLC–JKP. Addressed to Columbia.
1. Not identified further.

## FROM JOHN McKEON

Dear Sir,                                      New York [Aug. 7, 1844][1]

This morning appeared in the Herald a letter which purports to come from the adopted citizens of New York & addressed to the candidates for the Presidency, on the subject of Native Americanism the new party organized in this section of the country.[2] I have taken the trouble to make inquiries as to the origin of the paper & its object. I have reason to believe it is at bottom a Tyler movement. The letter is addressed to John Tyler as one of the candidates! Is signed by several of Mr. Tylers office holders—was circulated by Mr Tyler's friends. The internal evidence shews that it is the production of Philadelphia the residence of Mr Robert Tyler[3] & of New York City where some of his devoted office hunting friends reside. There are some few worthy & highly respectable mens names subscribed but I am sure they could not have suspected the object of the movers of the paper or they never would have signed it. The object is to give Tyler an opportunity of making a great parade previous to his final departure from the stage or perhaps to distract us by rallying the entire force of the adopted citizens around him. There never was any public or private meeting held authorising signers to speak on behalf of the adopted citizens of New York.

I have heard that a letter has been addressed to you to the care of Genl Jackson.[4] This I heard from a Tyler office holder. I have conferred with several of the leading democratic adopted citizens &

they have desired me to write you. My advice is for you to let the matter rest where it is. Not to answer them. Publication only tends to keep alive a feeling already highly excited in this section of the country. Even in the democratic party this Native American prejudice has broken out and we find that the letter I allude to has already excited a feeling.

I have no doubt of your opinions. They are unquestionably those of Mr. Jefferson in his message of 1801.[5] You agree with the Baltimore Convention which renominated Mr Van Buren in 1840, & passed resolutions against the Native American doctrine. If you choose you may write me a letter (which I can use if necessary authorising me to declare your opinions on this question).

You must excuse my presumption in writing to you in this frank manner but the anxiety I feel for our success must be my apology. I have no doubt some action will be had by the adopted citizens in this section & in the meantime *quieta non movere*[6] is the safe doctrine.

JOHN MCKEON

ALS. DLC–JKP. Addressed to Columbia and marked *"Confidential."*

1. McKeon dated his letter August 6, but content analysis indicates that he actually wrote on August 7.

2. The letter in the *New York Herald,* which bore the names of twenty-eight signatories, also solicited responses regarding the naturalization laws.

3. Robert Tyler, eldest son of John Tyler, served in the Land Office at Washington during his father's tenure as president. Later he practiced law in Philadelphia, served as register of the Confederate Treasury, and was editor of the Montgomery *Daily Advertiser.*

4. Not identified further.

5. Reference is to Thomas Jefferson's message to Congress dated December 8, 1801.

6. Latin phrase meaning "Do not arouse the sleeping."

## FROM JOHN K. KANE

My dear Sir,                                         Philada. Aug. 9, 1844

I have just returned from a tour of some five hundred miles through our Northern and Eastern counties, in most of which I met large assemblages of our party, and in all of them conferred with the leading men. If I could have doubted before of the result of the canvas, this visit would have made me certain. It is the Tariff region of the State, the great coal field, studded with furnaces and forges, and our principal wool growing district, and where of course, if anywhere, Mr. Clay's friends might hope to make an impression. But up to the present moment they have failed utterly. Our party was never so united, and it is not possible to imagine a higher degree of enthusiasm than that which pervades them.

On my return I passed through Harrisburg, and learnt the general aspect in the West middle counties from gentlemen who had just left there. The entire State is alike. At the Governor's election our majority will scarcely fall short of 25000.

From my brother-in-law, Mr. Taylor of Caroline,[1] who is now in Philadelphia, I get the best accounts of Virginia. He goes as high as 5000 in his estimate of our majority.

I had intended visiting Nashville this month, to attend the mass meeting there,[2] and take another farewell of our venerable friend Gen. Jackson, but I am obliged to forego the pleasure, or break appointments of more urgency.

J. K. KANE

ALS. DLC–JKP. Addressed to Columbia.
1. Taylor of Caroline County, Va., is not identified further.
2. Reference is to the Democratic mass meeting scheduled for August 15, 1844.

## FROM JAMES BLACK[1]

Newport, Penn., August 10, 1844

Black advises Polk not to reply to a letter about Texas and the tariff from the representatives of "a meeting purporting to be a democratic meeting" in Carlisle, Penn.[2] He warns that "they do not belong to the democratic party but want to have some pretext to come out in the papers in favour of Clay believing that those at a distance will take them for members of our party and it may have its effect abroad."

ALS. DLC–JKP. Addressed to Columbia.
1. A merchant, James Black served in the Pennsylvania House, 1830–31; on the bench of the district court of Perry County, Penn., 1842–43; and in the U.S. House, 1836–37 and 1843–47.
2. Reference is to the letter from Thomas C. Miller et al. to Polk, July 24, 1844.

## FROM J. GEORGE HARRIS

Saturday Morn

My Dear Sir                    Nashville [August 10, 1844][1]

I have just been conversing with your brother-in-law Childress of Rutherford, (and it has been mentioned to me by several of our friends), concerning the *rumor* here that you propose to receive your friends at Catron's on the 15th or rather that you have consented or will consent to occupy his house for the day on that occasion. I have uniformly said that I did not believe it was your intention.—that you would probably stop there, breakfast dine & sup there, but would have public rooms at the Nashville Inn[2] where the sovereigns could have access to you without scraping feet or looking like "poor men at a frolic."[3] I give you an idea of the *tone* of feeling so far as I can know it; because I know it will not be unacceptable. Several have spoken about it, or I would not have referred to it; perhaps, after all, it is of no consequence. You know I write with perfect freedom, and without reserve.

I send by *Elias* the Journals.

J. GEO. HARRIS

ALS. DLC–JKP. Addressed to Columbia and marked "Confidential"; Harris' notation on the cover indicates that he sent his letter by Elias.

1. Date identified through content analysis.
2. Polk stayed at the Nashville Inn during the mass convention.
3. Quotation not identified.

## FROM GEORGE M. DALLAS

*No. 6.*

Dear Sir,                    [Philadelphia] Sunday 11 August 1844

My only purpose at present is to tell you that, by the steam cars of this morning, I received a letter from a friend communicating the exceedingly painful intelligence that Mr. Muhlenberg was, last night, at about 11 o'clock, in Reading at his own house, struck with apoplexy, and that he was not expected to live beyond an hour or two. This afflicts all who Knew and were able to appreciate his worth, deeply and sincerely.

Politically, it will not produce much, if any, embarrassment. I have taken measures to have the Convention of the 4th of March last reassembled in about a fortnight; and I do not doubt that the gentleman who was Mr. Muhlenberg's competitor for the nomination, Mr. Francis R. Shunk,[1] will now be almost unanimously selected. He is in all respects, an unexceptional democrat, enjoys great popularity in the west of our state, and has conciliated universal Kindness and respect by the frankness with which he submitted to his defeat before the Convention and espoused the cause of his rival. His only snag is in the dislike of Gov. Porter; but I hardly think that will shew itself.

G. M. DALLAS

ALS. DLC–JKP. Addressed to Columbia. Polk's AE on the cover states that he answered this letter on August 29, 1844.

1. A Democratic convention held at Harrisburg on September 2, 1844, nominated Shunk, a lawyer from Pittsburgh, for governor. Shunk had served as clerk of the Pennsylvania House and as secretary of the commonwealth, 1839–42. Elected governor in 1844 and reelected in 1847, Shunk served from 1845 until 1848, when ill health forced him to resign.

## FROM ALFRED BALCH

Dear Sir,                                        Cincinnati 12th Augt. [18]44

It almost seems to me that I have seen and conversed with hundreds of intelligent and active politicians from every state in the Union on both sides of the pending contest. I have kept notes and reviewed them coolly and circumspectly. I give you my deductions which will be taken by you for what they are worth.

1st. I believe that you are *certain* of Maine. N. Hamp. Penn. Michigan. Va S.C. Missisi. Arkansas, Missouri Illinois. Ala. equal to 105 exclusive of Ten.

2d. I believe that Clay is certain to receive Massa. R.Isd. Connecticut Vermont Del. *Maryland,* N.C. Kentucky *N. Jersey.* equal to 70. From this statement you will perceive that I consider N. Yk Ohio Indiana La Georgia doubtful. Our friends in Indiana will fight hard and the contest there will be close *very* close but the whigs are the richest men every where and I am credibly informed have poured out their money in this last named state like water. Our friends therefore must not *rely* on Indiana. Whitcomb[1] was elected Gov. by only 2000 votes out of 120 thousand. In former contests for the Presidency much— almost every thing, has depended on N. Yk Pen. & Ohio. So now. My own humble opinon is (after free access obtained to many leading politicians of the North) that our prospects are brighter in New York than in Ohio & that in the former our march is onward continually. In this state nothing can exceed the courage and energy of our friends but here men many *very many* of the tillers of the soil are decieved and cheated by the cry of Protection! Protecti[on]![2] Direct and outright. There is no doubt that Clay wrote his let[ters] declaring himself opposed *utterly* to the repeal of the infamous act of the 30th Augt 42,[3] on very full and pressing advisement from Pennsylvania & New York as well as this state. Gentlemen from La who are your friends say to me, that you may & most probably will get that State, but there are only in fact a few hundreds of difference in the strength of the opposing parties, *all being mustered.* No human being can certainly tell or perhaps even *guess* how Georgia will go. Our friends hope for the best but say that either party will have nothing to brag of & the whigs admitted to me that the affair will not be any thing like that of 40 tho they think they may succeed. All Penna. is in a blaze and hickory poles are seen in every town and village. In some places as many as a *dozen.*

In this state the whigs say they will have a majority of from 5 to 10 thousand. Our friends that they will have a majority of 10,000 if the abolitionists hold off. Some of the most distracted of these abolitionists may refuse to vote for Clay, but I *believe* that an intrigue is *now* going on between the whigs and abolitionists to secure their votes to the Mill Boy.[4]

Tyler has *some few* friends in each county of this state probably may they equal altogether 6000. I have had two interviews with Miller one of the Editors of the Tyler paper at Columbus.[5] You know that Miller is the Brother in Law of Tyler. I think it probable that Tyler will withdraw in a few weeks & that his interests every where will be identified with yours. More of this *when I see you.* Ritchie is earnest in urging & desiring this identification. I was in Accomack part of Wises District [and] saw a large no of your leading friends as well as many of the opposition. Matters are straight in that quarter as well as in most other parts of Virginia.

You will perceive that I have said nothing in this letter of Tennessee because you know one hundred times as much as I do about the state of our party at home. If there are changes in each county we must best the enemy. But, remember that the whigs from every state of the north are pouring in documents upon our people and that your competiter is writing letters about Texas the Tariff &c &c &c every day to suit every latitude. I have told our friends every where to have no fears about Ten. She will wheel at last into the Republican ranks and go "straight out," for Polk & Dallas.

If there are any errors in the foregoing views I have promulgated them to you unwittingly for these views have been carefully compared with those of our warmest coolest and *most enlightened* friends from Maine to Geo & from the Atlantic to the Missouri. I did not see Woodbury but I recd a letter from him when at the East. He writes in high spirits and as if he was all on fire.

We have not the aggregate vote from Indiana but you will have perceived before you read this, that the Whigs have a majority on joint ballot in the Legislature a matter of some consequence as a senator is to be elected in the place of White.[6] The small majority of Owsley[7] compared to that which the whigs expected, has disheartened them. The Democrats of Ohio and Ky have won largely on the majority which the whigs gave him.

I shall probably write you again in ten or 15 days.

ALFRED BALCH

ALS. DLC–JKP. Addressed to Nashville.

1. A lawyer from Terre Haute, Ind., James Whitcomb served as a member of the Indiana Senate, 1830–36, and as governor, 1843–49. From 1849 until his death in 1852, Whitcomb sat in the U.S. Senate as a Democrat.

2. Manuscript obliterated here and below.

3. Tariff Act of 1842.

4. Shortened form of Henry Clay's nickname, "Mill Boy of the Slashes."

5. N. M. Miller, a physician and journalist, became the proprietor of the Columbus *Old School Republican and Ohio State Gazette* in 1841. In 1844 he became second assistant postmaster general, a post he held for about a year. Polk demoted him to third assistant in 1845 and eventually removed him from office.

6. Albert S. White, a lawyer and businessman from Lafayette, Ind., served two terms in the U.S. House, 1837–39 and 1861–63, and one term in the Senate, 1839–45. White began his public career as a Whig and later joined the Republican party.

7. A farmer and lawyer, William Owsley served as a Whig in the Kentucky legislature, as an associate justice of the state supreme court, and two terms as governor, 1844–48.

## TO ANDREW J. DONELSON

Tuesday Morning

My Dear Sir:                                   Nashville Augt 13th [18]44

I was much disappointed in not meeting you here last night. Tomorrow, the crowd will be coming in & there will be so much confusion that nothing can be done with deliberation. It is very important, that you be here to night, that we may look over what you have written carefully. Come down without fail, to night. I have a private room at the Nashville Inn. Your presence is indispensible not only in reference to the paper which you are preparing, but to other matters also. In haste.

JAMES K. POLK

ALS. DLC–AJD. Addressed to Nashville. Published in *THM*, III, p. 60.

## FROM ALBERT GALLUP[1]

Dear Sir                                        Albany August 14. 1844

I regret to see in the Nashville Union an article in relation to the candidates for Gov. in this State.[2] No man can entertain a higher opinion of Mr. Wright than I do. His present position is all he now desires & his, & the true friends of the Democracy in this state believe that the time has not yet come when it will be safe to take him from the U.S. Senate.

He is there the giant of the party. His feelings are adverse to a nomination for Gov. The presentation of his name was without his consent & against his will. It was got up by the same class of politicians who wrote the *Secret Circular*[3] —men who having failed to, in some instances, obtain office for themselves or friends, now oppose the nomination of Gov. Bouck (than whom a purer democrat does not exist) only for the purpose of carrying out a contemptibly revengeful feeling. Gov B. is right upon all the great questions now agitating the country. He deserves as he has the confidence of all the democrats in the state whose good opinion is worth having. He will if nominated receive a large majority of the votes in this state & is now only opposed here by men who when the result of the Baltimore convention was heard, said, "The party is all blown to hell—we will not wear a black Texas collar." This language I heard uttered—by men who now come into the traces in favor of the nomination of Polk & Dallas. I am sorry to say that these men were those who claimed to be *par excellence* the friends of Mr. V.B.[4] One of his sons[5] said a few days since when asked to address a political meeting, "I can't do it. I shall hereafter eschew politics." The Editors of the Atlas[6] here & their coadjutors are disposed to make all the mischief they can. The nomination of Gov. etc will, unless, I much misunderstand the signs of the times, rebuke them. I write thus plainly, because, I desire you to know who are & have been from the first your real friends & also others who like whipped curs now come on the tracks, & claim the game, because they howl the loudest.

The course of Mr. Wright in this matter, has been, such as all who know him, must have expected him to pursue. Had he left the Senate two vacancies would have to be filled by the next Legislature Tallmadge being about to leave for Wisconsin. Suppose (not a supposable case) that the Whigs should carry the state! I mean a majority of the Legislature. Into whose hands would the two senators go? I do not say this because I have any fears. I have none. We shall carry the State by a large majority. Our differences are more in appearance than reality. The Whigs in this State are a doomed party. They will be defeated.

ALBERT GALLUP

ALS. DLC–JKP. Addressed to Columbia and marked "Confidential."
1. A lawyer, Gallup served one term in Congress, 1837–39; Polk appointed

him collector of customs for Albany.

2. On August 3, 1844, the *Nashville Union* published an article expressing the hope that Silas Wright would agree to run for the governorship of New York.

3. See Ely Moore to Polk, July 26, 1844.

4. Martin Van Buren.

5. Reference is not identified further.

6. The *Albany Atlas* started publication in 1841. By 1843 the paper had come under the management of William Cassidy and James M. French, and it served as the organ of the radical Democratic faction led by Azariah C. Flagg.

## FROM STEPHEN D. ADAMS

Dear Sir                 Aberdeen Ms. 16th August 1844

I have hesitated for some time about writing to you on account of our limited acquaintance, not haveing seen you since the fall of '33. I then saw you at Nashville on your way to Washington and formed some acquaintance with you but suppose you have forgotten me. I am apprised that many of your friends have written to you upon the subject of your prospects in this State. But hope you will not think it an intrusion upon your patience to give you my opinion of the prospects of the good cause in Miss. We had a Democratic Mass meeting in this place on the 13 & 14th Inst. We invited the Whigs to participate in the discussion, which they did, although they had refused us a similar favor a few days before. I will not trouble you with the details of the discussion; suffice it to say that our side was sustained triumphantly; the Whigs failed in securing their champions that made battle, though their resistance was verry feeble; Genrl. Footes disposition of Mr. Clays Raleigh speech was the finest thing I ever listened to. You would be pleased If I could give you an Idea of it, but I cannot. The laughing part of the speech was made to show off Mr Clay in the most ridiculous manner and the most humerous style.

The Democratic party in this State, stands as one man in support of the nominees of the Baltimore Convention. In fact the news of the nominations acted as magic upon the troubled waters, and many who have acted with the Whigs will support you. The changes however are not from the Whigs proper, but Democrats in principle, who were carried away by fraud in '40 and are now returning to their first *love*. We will carry this State by about 5000, perhaps something over that estimate. I think I have as correct an Idea of the vote of the State as any other man. I preside in the strongest Democratic judicial District in the State, and mingle freely with the people. I have favorable opportunities to learn publick sentiment throughout the State, and set down the estimate of 5000 as the lowest.

I have recently visited my old friends in Franklin & Lincoln, and think you may safely calculate on an increased majority in Franklin of 175 and in Lincoln of 100. I was much pleased with the prospects in Tenn. From what I learn from my Brother in law G. W. Fisher[1] & others in the W. Dist. I have no fears in that State. If I could hear from Dick Moore[2] of your Town I would be satisfied. Your position upon the Tariff, is satisfactory to the people of the south. In fact the Democrats seem perfectly amazed that the entire Whig party in the south cannot see their best interest and unite with them in this great contest for principle.

I hesitatingly venture this epistle and fear the opinions expressed and suggestions made will not be worth your time in reading.

STEPHEN ADAMS

ALS. DLC–JKP. Addressed to Columbia.
1. A farmer and merchant, George W. Fisher represented Fayette County for two terms in the Tennessee House, 1843–47, and served one term in the Senate, 1849–51, for Fayette, Hardeman, and Shelby counties.
2. Probably Richard B. Moore.

## FROM THOMAS PHILLIPS AND WILLIAM H. SMITH

Dear Sir: Pittsburgh, Aug. 16, 1844

Your kind favor[1] came duly to hand. The letter to Mr. Kane,[2] was as you anticipated, perfectly satisfactory to your friends here, and they agree in the opinion that the Democratic candidate for the Presidency, need not again appear before the public on the Tariff, or, indeed any other subject.

You may be anxious to hear something of the effect of Mr. *Muhlenberg's* death on the prospects of the Democracy of Pennsylvania. There is but one voice among our party in the expression of regret for Mr. M's decease. He was eminently a good, a kind, and an able man, as you no doubt have had opportunity to discover when he sat in Congress with you. But, owing to the unhappy schism in the party in '35, when he and Mr. Wolf[3] were rival democratic candidates, and owing to alleged unfairness by his friends in the procurement of his late nomination, *he could not have concentrated the vote of the party.* In this part of the State, where the federal candidate resides,[4] a heavy loss was feared. It was the deliberate opinion of many who would have gone for him heartily, that he would not have received the party vote in the State, by 1000. And this was our opinion.

The choice of the party will now fall, with most gratifying unanimity, on *Francis R. Shunk,* Esq. He lives in this county, and Whigs and Democrats agree that he will poll 300 votes more here than Mr. M. could have done.

In saying this, we have no intention of speaking with the slightest disrespect of the distinguished dead. It is the *consequences* of his demise of which we speak. On this subject, we may say, in conclusion, that if there *could* have been a doubt about Pennsylvania, it is now removed. Mr. Shunk will carry the State by from 20 to 25,000 and this, you will readily see, would render it useless for the Whigs to contest the Presidency in Pennsylvania .

With us, throughout this region, the work, to use a common phrase, "goes bravely on." There is no comparison between the unanimity and spirit which now prevail and that of 1840. Now, all is hope. Then, all was doubt. We shall do nobly. In the confidence that the campaign will result in a glorious triumph for Democracy ....

PHILLIPS & SMITH

LS. DLC–JKP. Addressed to Columbia.
1 Letter not found.
2. See Polk to John K. Kane, June 19, 1844.
3. George Wolf served two full terms and one session of another in the U.S. House, 1824–29. He was governor of Pennsylvania, 1829–35; first comptroller of the Treasury, 1836–38; and collector of customs at Philadelphia, 1838–40.
4. Joseph Markle, a Westmoreland County farmer, was the gubernatorial candidate of the Whig party in 1844; in previous political contests, he had run unsuccessfully for seats in the Pennsylvania House and the U.S. House.

## FROM AMASA J. PARKER[1]

My Dr Sir,                                              Albany N.Y. August 17. 1844
I have been intending to write you ever since the Baltimore convention to congratulate you on your nomination & to express to you how much I was gratified at the result. Even as a New Yorker, with a candidate of our own, I would not change it if I could. You are perhaps aware that I have recently removed to this place, having accepted a Judicial station which requires my presence here most of the year. How long I shall continue to hold it is uncertain. I only regret, at this time, that my position renders it improper for me to take the stump in this State in your behalf & I have expressed this regret to many of my friends in the State who are I think making up much more than my absence from the stump by their own active exertions. Rest assured

I feel none the less interest in the result & shall do all that I can do with propriety to ensure a favorable result here.

I think we shall carry this State. We have some difficulties to encounter here in our own ranks on the subject of nominating a candidate for Governor, but we are entirely united as to the Presidential nomination. An unfortunate nomination for Governor would no doubt detract some from the rest of our ticket.

You have doubtless seen something in the papers of the "confidential circular" issued in this State by a few individuals opposed to the immediate annexation of Texas.[2] You need apprehend no difficulty from that quarter. The men whose names are appended to the circular are among our tried democrats & leading & influential men & will do all they can for your success. I think it was ill advised to issue such a circular & still more so to publish it, for it is very important to keep out of view just now every question on which our friends differ. I think nothing however need be apprehended & that we shall go into the field not only united but zealous & ready for the fight. That portion of the party here, honestly opposed to annexation, (& there are many such), will I think make no objection on that score to our ticket.

Our opponents in this State are united & active. They will no doubt run Fillmore for Governor. You will no doubt recollect he was with us in 25 Congress. He [is a][3] popular man & will call out all their strength.

We are fast getting into your southern fashion of "stump speeches." On both sides, there are mass meetings every week in some part of the State & many able men are addressing the people.

I shall be happy to hear from you & to advance your interests in any way in my power.

AMASA J. PARKER

ALS. DLC–JKP. Addressed to Columbia. Polk's AE on the cover states that he answered this letter on October 3, 1844; Polk's reply has not been found.

1. A lawyer from Delhi, N.Y., Parker served in the New York legislature, 1833–34, and in the U.S. House for one term, 1837–39. He was vice-chancellor and circuit judge, 1844–47, and a justice on the state supreme court, 1847–55. In 1856 and 1858, he lost bids to become governor of New York.

2. See Ely Moore to Polk, July 26, 1844.

3. Manuscript obliterated.

## TO CAVE JOHNSON

[Dear Sir,]          [Columbia] August 20, 1844

I saw the *Hon. George Houston* of Al. after you left Nashville. The appointments for you and himself have been made—commencing at

Pulaski on the 29th Inst., and thence through *Lawrence, Wayne, Etc.,* crossing the Tennessee River at *Carrollville.* Hand bills have been struck and circulated for the appointments East of Tennessee River. The appointments West of the River will be circulated by *Hon. Austin Miller* and *Mr. Williamson*[1] of Somerville, both of whom I saw after you left. I will send you a full list of all the appointments to-morrow. I have not now time to make a copy before the mail leaves. The printed notices or hand bills are in your name alone. As Houston was a non-resident it was thought best that his name should not appear in the hand-bills. He will fall in, and authorized me to assure you that he would *certainly accompany you.* Miller says he will see to it that you will be met by some leading friend, probably himself as soon as you cross Tennessee River, who will accompany you through the route. The whole of the notices will be given forthwith by hand-bills, though they will not appear in the Union. I regard this tour of immense importance. Your name will draw great crowds to hear you and much good will be done. Nothing I hope will occur by which you will by possibility disappoint them. I told *Houston* I had advised you to travel in a *buggy.* He approves it, and says he will be on a fine riding horse, so that you may interchange to suit your convenience.

*Judge Douglas* of Ill. and *Judge Brice*[2] of Louisiana made speeches at Spring Hill on yesterday. Tomorrow they will speak at Mt. Pleasant. *Melville* will probably be at *Mt. Pleasant.* They will then attend their appointments in Giles and Marshall, and be at the great mass-meeting at Shelbyville on the 27th Inst. *Pickens* of South Carolina I learn reached Nashville on Monday, and [will] be at Shelbyville Probably. He will be here on to day or to-morrow or next day. I would like very much for you to be at Shelbyville on the 27th. It is a fine turn-pike road from Nashville to Shelbyville. From Shelbyville to Pulaski—where you would have to be on the 29th—is about 40 miles over a good road. Write to me whether you will be at Shelbyville. I would like for you to meet *Pickens* there and have a conversation with him before he speaks.

JAMES K. POLK

PL. Published in *THM,* I, p. 247. Addressed to Clarksville and marked *"Private."*

1. Austin Miller and James M. Williamson. Williamson, formerly a resident of North Carolina and a member of that state's House of Commons, 1834–36, moved in 1838 to Somerville in Tennessee's Fayette County and took up the practice of law. He served in the Tennessee Senate from 1845 until 1847.

2. Stephen A. Douglas and James G. Bryce. Bryce is not identified further.

## FROM C. T. H. WILLGOHS AND ERNEST MOFFETT[1]

Marshallville P.O.

Dr Sir.                    Wayne Co. O. August 20th [18]44

We the undersigned have been instructed & appointed a committee by the Marshallville democratic Club to request you of your opinion in relation to the following great national questions at issue: On the naturalization of foreigners, Tariff, Texas, national bank, distribution of the proceed of the public lands, & the redemption of the debts of the States. By you favoring us with your opinions you would oblige a great body of the democracy of northern Ohio. It is charged upon us by the opposition that your opinions are but little known on these subjects & to meet [them][2] the most effectually the democracy unanimously adopted this course. We wish to use your answers for publication. If convenient, please let us have your answers as soon as possible under the address of Marshallville P.O. Wayne Co. O.

C. T. H. WILLGOHS
ERNEST MOFFETT

[P.S.] We have mentioned in our questions Naturalization first, because it is one that has created immense excitement in Ohio. Foreigners are very numerous in our State & more about here in Wayne, Stark, Ashland than elsewhere. The Germans can give at least 20,000 votes in Ohio. Of course their support to either party must decide the matter, as far as we are concerned at least. Mr. Tod, our candidate for Governor, told me that in his opinion foreigners might even be sooner naturalized than they are at present. Mr. Tod will run a stronger ticket than any we could have taken at present. A neighbouring Clay Club has wrote allready several times (I understand six times) to Mr. H. Clay, particulary on naturalization to influence many, but received no answer. I believe we will have a tied contest, and a favorable opinion of yours on the subject would give us a great advantage after the Philadelphia occurrences[3] in this very strongest democratic part of Ohio. The democracy is much more alert than the whigs throughout Ohio, many of the latter intending to vote the negro ticket. The tariff seems to have the next, if not an equal influenze. The bank is hated by all the true friends of freedom, but is but little urged about by our opponents. I think it to be off all the federal measures the most deadly hostile to our institutions. Our Congressional district[4] is the strongest in the state, but unhappily we are but little united. A soft sort of democrats sprung up (bankers) with an aspirant for Congress at their head (Mr. S. Lahm).[5] Last winter we were most flagrantly abused by that individual, when through his influenze he representing us in legislature, an anti democratic bank law, by aid of the whigs, was passed. We will have a great mass meeting here on the 7th of September, and if your letter could be here till then it would be very convenient. It is expected, because allready 3 weeks ago we were instructed to write, but were prevented by desease. C. Willgohs [and] Ernest Moffett

LS. DLC–JKP. Addressed to Nashville.
1. C. T. H. Willgohs and Ernest Moffett are not identified further.
2. Word supplied.
3. Reference is to nativist rioting in Philadelphia in May and July of 1844.
4. Ohio's Eighteenth Congressional District included Wayne and Stark counties in northeastern Ohio.
5. A native of Maryland and lawyer from Canton in Stark County, Ohio, Samuel Lahm served one term in the Ohio Senate, 1842–43; he failed in his 1844 race for Congress but won election to a single term two years later.

## FROM ALEXANDER O. ANDERSON

My Dear Sir,                                    Washington City Augt. 22d 1844
I enclose you by this mail Mr. Tylers address to his friends.[1] The affair is handsomely done, and will do us great good. Your friends who are here have acted in the progress of this matter with great prudence, perseverance, & faith, and I trust that our Democratic journals will respond most cordially in Tennessee. I also enclose you the Madisonian of to-day. You will find your name at the head of the leading editorial there. Tennessee ought to send some subscribers to the Madisonian forthwith, & such a compliment would be well-timed from Old Maury.

Mr. Walker & myself have been busy in getting up documents &c &c & next week we shall start a fresh supply for Tennessee. He has franked upwards of 170 thousand papers, pamphlets &c. The Spectator has kept up a good fire. The Enquirer has done, & is doing & will do manfully, & nobly. You need not doubt Virginia—Nor Pennsylvania. We have good private news from New York, & the federalists throughout are thoroughly alarmed. I sent, under Mr. Walkers frank, a great many of his abridged speeches to Tennessee, as he did also. At Richmond they ordered 80 thousand of them from this place. The Texas question grows by discussion, & every effort is made here to keep it strong before the people.

There is not the shadow of doubt of our success. I shall not leave here for 10 or 12 days yet. In the meantime, every leisure moment I have, & many that are not leisure moments, I direct to our noble cause. I shall join my friends in Tennessee shortly. They shall have additional ammunition in less than 10 days, making out the strongest & clearest case of interference by Great Britain, that has ever been seen, between Nations standing in the relations in which we do. Mr. Walker, & *others,* think that the evidence, as amassed, will be conclusive. The Pamphlet is now in the Press.[2] I shall have the first proof sheets to-day. I am just from Walkers quarters, he had returned within the last hour from the Printers, & told me he had promised him to hasten as fast as possible. Walker loaded a hack, literally, with Polk ammunition, while I was at his end of the City, jumped into it, & carried it to the Office of the Secretary of the Senate.

We are in high spirits here, and rest assured there has never been such enthusiasm since the days of Jackson. Calhoun thinks it will equal the defeat of 1828.

The present inclination of the Administration is rather against a call session—that is against an earlier meeting of Congress than usual. Mr. Walker & myself have conferred freely with our friends here & the Texian Minister,[3] & I have expressed the opinion, that if it can be avoided without risking the safety of Texas, it ought to be. The Texian Minister is full of all the anxious emotions that you might suppose would inspire a devoted patriot. Unless some great extremity shall appear to be coming, within the next 10 days, Congress will not be called to meet earlier than usual.

Say to our friends they may be of good heart; that there is not a drooping democratic spirit in all the land; that we are certainly advancing with a triumphant banner.

We should have carried North Carolina, but for the course and speeches of that arch Traitor Benton. So say our letters from North Carolina. The Whig committee have flooded that State *with 70 thousand of his speeches,* & they still send them.

Walker will leave here as soon as we can get thro' the arrangements of the print pamphlets &c &c. Say by the 1st of Sept? This will be a serious loss.

Present my kind regards to your lady.

A. ANDERSON

P.S. I expect to leave about the 1st of Sept. *Have you answered Walkers Letter to you?*[4]

ALS. DLC–JKP. Addressed to Columbia.
1. Anderson enclosed copies of John Tyler's reply of August 22, 1844, to four appreciative resolutions, which had been adopted at a meeting of Democrats, held at New York City's Charlton House on August 6, 1844, and which had been communicated in a letter of the same date under the signatures of Abra-

ham Hatfield and seven other members of the corresponding committee. The President had announced his withdrawal from the presidential contest in a notice published in the Washington *Madisonian* on August 21, 1844. Tyler stated in his letter to the New York City Democrats that their resolutions had contributed to his decision to retire from the race. The Charlton House resolutions praised Tyler's record and urged his supporters to join with Polk's friends in defeating "the Federal candidate Henry Clay."

2. Pamphlet not identified further.

3. Isaac Van Zandt.

4. Probably a reference to Walker's letter of July 10 or July 11, to which correspondence no Polk reply has been found.

## FROM WILLIAM H. HAYWOOD, JR.

My dear Sir                                                   Raleigh 22nd Aug 1844

I have just completed a formal vindication of your G. Father and the Central Com will order it published tomorrow.[1] To facilitate its appearance & hasten its circulation it will be sent forthwith to our friend Blair to put in *Dollar Globe*[2] &c as its first appearance in our paper here[3] (a weekly one) would delay it 10 days. I regret that there is not time to send you the MS. and more that I have not had time for the essay to lay on the table to be revised. To my own mind the calumny is refuted entirely.

The delay to make the publication has proceeded from the delay of our friends in Mecklenburg to send me the proofs. Even now it goes out without a copy of Record showing that he was *Sheriff* of Mecklenburg.

The Elections in N.C. are known to you. The body of talent & wealth in Fedl party is too strong to vanquish in *one* contest. Besides we had no organization when I got here from W. City. None at all. I enclose you a copy of *Confidential* circular that explains the *past* & the *present*.[4]

I have not associated Mr Saunders in making the defense. I regretted that the Docts. from Tenn were sent to our *joint* address as he insisted upon using a part before we had got all the proofs & in fact he is not a person in whose discretion I have confidence. I more than doubt if his effort to gain *eclat* by speech-making did not hurt us. And I am not alone in that opinion. As we say here he goes off "half cocked" always.

I cannot flatter you with any strong expectations of carrying N.C. in Nov. But it shall be tried. My whole time has been given up to organizing and stimulating our friends in the *general election* and I *hope* we may play the same game on the Feds we did in 1836. The Fedl.

majority in our Legislature cannot embarrass me at all by instructions. If they should attempt it my friends need not fear for my conduct.

I shall direct the Globe to send you the *Defense* of course & you can order Extra copies if you wish it or your friends in Tennessee.

I am *worked down* myself and hardly feel able to write a letter. That I have not written to you oftener is because I have been compelled to devote all my time in writing to others *for* you & *about* you & yours.

I don't like our majority in Indiana being so small! Mr Tyler I see has at last got out of the way. In N.Y. & Penn. & Virga. this will aid your ticket. Now that Benton is thro his conflict in Missouri[5] I hope to see the Globe more & more violent for Texas. The rumour of a called session of Cong. in October is unfounded I *hope.* If Mr Tyler will let us alone I think the People will elect you Prest. His officious aid will do more hurt than his past efforts to run himself.

My very highest respects to Mrs. P. God bless you & yours.

WM. H. HAYWOOD

ALS. DLC–JKP. Addressed to Columbia. Published in *NCHR*, XVI, pp. 343–44.

1. Reference is to Haywood's *Vindication* of Ezekiel Polk, a pamphlet commissioned by the Central Democratic Committee of North Carolina.

2. The Washington *Dollar Globe* was a Democratic newspaper published during the campaign of 1844 by the proprietors of the Washington *Globe*.

3. Raleigh *North Carolina Standard.*

4. This printed circular, which bore the name of Louis D. Henry as chairman of the Central Committee of the Democratic party, asked one man in each county of North Carolina to report weekly on local political activity. C. DLC–JKP.

5. Sharp opposition to Benton had been a significant feature of the Missouri state elections held on August 5, 1844.


## TO CAVE JOHNSON

[Dear Sir,] [Columbia] August 22, 1844

I send you two hand-bills containing your appointments as far West as Hardiman.[1] As *Houston* was a non-resident it was thought best not to insert his name. He will however *certainly* be with you. *Judge Douglas* of *Ill.* and *Judge Brice*[2] of Louisiana are here and will speak at Mt. Pleasant to day. *Melville* of *N.Y.* and *Pickens* of S.C. will be here to day, and will speak at Lynnville in Giles tomorrow, and return to a *Hickory pole* raising here on Saturday. They will all be *Shelbyville* on the 27th, where I hope you can meet them on your way to Giles.

Your appointments in the District after Whiteville in Hardiman on the 11th Sept. will be made by your friends there. They will have some two or three large mass-meetings at which yourself, *Craighead* and others are desired to be.

[JAMES K. POLK]

PL. Published in *THM*, I., p. 248. Probably addressed to Clarksville; marked *"Private."*

1. Enclosures not found; incorrect spelling of Hardeman County.
2. Stephen A. Douglas and James G. Bryce.


## FROM JOHN O. BRADFORD[1]

Respected Sir                                              Philad August 23rd 1844

When I wrote you a few weeks since,[2] giving you an account of the position and prospects of the Democratic party in this state, I little dreamed that Mr Muhlenberg would so soon be taken from us. The remark I then made respecting the nomination of Mr M. did not originate in any feeling of hostility towards that excellent man; but from the fact that as he had some years since allowed himself to be seen in opposition to the late Gov: Wolf, thereby causing his defeat and the election of the Whig candidate,[3] I was apprehensive that the old friends of Gov: Wolf would not cordially support him. And therefore while I sincerely deplore the loss of Mr Muhlenberg, you may rest assured that the democratic strength will not suffer thereby. Mr Shunk who will undoubtedly be the nominee is a much stronger man; he has even greater personal popularity than Mr Muhlenberg, and is wholly free from those old prejudices which operated so strongly against him. I told you we would elect Muhlenberg by 10,000 majority, we will carry Shunk by 20,000, the majority of Polk & Dallas will be about the same.

You will remember what I stated respecting the peculiar position of the friends of Mr Tyler and the hope I expressed that something ought and could be done to secure to the Dem: party their influence and cooperation in the pending contest; before this reaches you, you will perhaps have seen the formal withdrawal of Mr Tyler and the manner leaves no doubt as to who will receive his countenance and aid. I am highly gratified myself with this course of Mr Tyler, and I most sincerely trust that his advances will be met in a conciliatory and proper manner. At the present time when the Whigs are using such extraordinary means to carry their candidate, it behooves the Democratic party to be united, and to conciliate as much as possible all who are opposed to Whig policy; the time, the circumstance, sound policy, and patriotism require that it should be done.

The contest in this state will be severe, tho the result will not be doubtful. Within the last eight weeks I have visited sixteen counties and have attended as many meetings; the old Jackson spirit is up and you can rely upon me when I say that the Key Stone will give Polk & Dallas full 20,000 majority; as goes Penn, so goes the Union. In New York I am sorry to see that Bryant, Sedgewick[4] and a few other abolitionists are endeavoring to produce discord in our ranks; they cannot harm us unless they can attach to Mr Clay the full abolition vote which is impossible. In Jersey all is right; the New constitution a democratic measure has just been submitted to the people, and confirmed with a most singular unanimity; it will greatly increase our strength. All eyes here are turned upon Tennessee. I can scarcely fear that she will be found wanting, although I am aware of the desperate efforts making by Bell, Foster and others to carry the state. It is their death struggle; they die hard, but die they must, their numerous galvani[c] appliances cannot save them. I would mention further as a fact that the Democracy of Tennessee may know how to marshall themselves for the conflict, that they have not alone to contend with the Whig party of Tennessee, but also with the money of the New England manufacturer, and the Aristocratic Capitalists of this and neighboring cities. I have myself heard them boast that they would at *all* hazzards carry Tenn. If they had not votes enough, they had the means to *make votes*. And I have no doubt if necessary but what some $100,000 to $200,000 will be furnished from the east for such purposes. Let Tennesseans be on their guard, and by their firmness and integrity, give the lie to those who slander their fair fame by insinuating that they can be bought like sheep in the shambles.

We do not need the vote of Tennessee to assure your election; granting that you receive all the votes given to Mr V.B. we have with the following undisputed and undoubted States enough and to spare—Viz Maine, Penn, Louisiana, Miss, Indiana, Michigan.

Our friends here are all delighted with the result of the recent elections; and for my own part, I believe were the election six months farther off, the Whigs would scarcely make a respectable fight. There is a great change going on among the farmers, upon the subject of the present Tariff; they now begin to feel its oppressions, and witness its injustice. They begin to enquire why it is or how it is that in 1841 they got $1.30 per bu: for wheat, while now they get but 80 cents, but at the same time have to pay more for everything they buy. They begin to understand that the real "modus operandi" of the present Tariff, is not so much to prevent foreign goods from coming into the country, as it is to prevent our own growth from going out—facts prove this;

in the year 1841 we exported $106,302,232. In 1842, $92,969,997. In 1843, $77,793,783. This heavy falling off, in the face of greatly increased production is enough to awaken anxious inquiry. The truth is we have so exorbitantly taxed the productions of some of our best customers that they can no longer trade with us. Our exports of flour, cornmeal, beef, pork etc to the West Indies & South America have fallen off within the past two years nearly one half. Our policy has reduced them to procure these things nearly all from Germany and other agricultural countries of Europe, that will admit their produce. on more liberal terms. The extra demand for cotton for the East India market prevents for the present a decline in that staple, but so sure as cause follows effect you will in time feel it to your full content. Is it right, is it just, that while the capitalist who employs his money in manufactures should realize 30, 40, 50 and even 70 per cent the Agriculturist should only realize 3 to 4. Their great protection to American labor is being understood in its true character as protection to *manufacturing capital* alone. The thousands of the rich capitalists are enormously increased; while the sweat and the toil of the laborer are unrequited. I write "canuti calami"[5] you will please excuse all errors. I wrote an Article for the "Union" respecting the course of Mr Tyler. I however will not send it. I think that ought to be fairly met. Will you excuse me for suggesting that it would make a good impression if the article from the Rich. Enquirer should be published in the "Union" and Democrat, with suitable remarks.[6] I am Cast about living here; if I could become situated in some good Democratic Journal, I would happily change my location. I send this per favor of Col Jos Armstrong,[7] and if worth nothing it will cost nothing; you know how I feel towards you and your family. I owe you much, I am always at your service, and will ever remain....

JOHN O. BRADFORD

[P.S.] If you deem anything I have written worth printing it can be done with very little alteration. I would be pleased to take the Democrat; will you please ask them to send it to me direct to Philad.

ALS. DLC–JKP. Addressed to Columbia.

1. Bradford served briefly in 1837 as editor of the *Nashville Union;* the following year he went to Puerto Rico as U.S. consul at St. Johns; and in March 1845 Polk appointed him to the post of purser in the navy.

2. Letter not found.

3. Incumbent Governor George Wolf lost his 1835 bid for reelection to the Whig candidate, Joseph Ritner; for details of the factional split between the "wolves" and the "mules" of the Pennsylvania Democracy, see Andrew Beaumont to Polk, September 5, 1835.

4. William Cullen Bryant and Theodore Sedgwick. Nephew of the popular novelist, Catharine Maria Sedgwick, and namesake of his father, a Massachusetts reformer, Theodore Sedgwick developed an extensive law practice in New York City and published numerous works on legal, judicial, and political problems of the antebellum period.

5. Latin phrase for "aged reed."

6. References are to the *Richmond Enquirer,* the *Nashville Union,* and the Columbia *Tennessee Democrat.*

7. Reference probably is to Joseph Armstrong, son of Nashville's postmaster, Robert Armstrong.

## TO CAVE JOHNSON

[Dear Sir,]                                                    [Columbia] August 23, 1844

*Mr. Williamson* of Somerville (who was the Democratic candidate for the Senate in 1843), left here on yesterday, and took with him the *hand-bills* giving notice of your appointments in the District.[1] You will have large crowds and you must on no account fail to fill them. *Houston* of Al. promised me *positively* that he would meet you and go the route with you. He would not however go alone. *Leonard P. Cheatham* was here to day. He says if you will meet him at *Shelbyville* on the 27th and desire it, that he will go with you also, so that in that event, you would have three speakers in company, and would be under no necessity of speaking, except when you felt perfectly able to do so. He will go or not as you may desire. He will not of course go unless you meet him at *Shelbyville* and request it. It is no flattery when I say to you that your fame will draw out large crowds and you must not disappoint them; you must be present and if on any occasion you do not feel like speaking, you can make the proper apology and let *Houston* or *Cheatham* (if he is along) speak.

I hope *Garland* has given extensive notice of *Coe's* appointments in your District.[2] Will you see him on the subject? I still hope *A. V. Brown* will agree to go to *East Tennessee.* I think it important. If you meet him at *Shelbyville* urge it upon him. If he will go *Bright* of Fayetteville will accompany him.

We had a glorious meeting of between 3,000 and 4,000 people at Mount Pleasant in this County to day. *Judge Brice* of Louisiana, *Cheatham* and Judge *Frierson*[3] of Ala. made speeches. There will be a still larger meeting at *Lynnville* on the line between *Giles* and *Maury* on tomorrow. The speakers who were at *Mt. Pleasant* to day, with *Judge Douglas* of Illinois who is here will be there. They will all be at *Shelbyville. Melville* of N.Y., *Pickens* of S.C., *Gov. Clay, Col.*

*Terry, Col. McClung* of Alabama.[4]

[JAMES K. POLK]

P.S. I advise you to travel in a *Buggy*. It will give you much less fatigue than on horseback. The road from Nashville to Shelbyville is a fine Turnpike; and at this season you will find the roads all good, and especially West of Tennessee River, where there is no rock.

PL. Published in *THM*, I, pp. 248–49. Probably addressed to Clarksville; marked "*Private.*"

1. Reference is to the Western District of Tennessee.

2. Johnson represented Tennessee's Ninth Congressional District, which included Robertson, Montgomery, Stewart, Dickson, Humphreys, Benton, and Henry counties.

3. James G. Bryce, Leonard P. Cheatham, and Gideon B. Frierson. A native of Tennessee, Frierson removed to Alabama where he served as assistant clerk and then clerk of the Alabama House; solicitor of Alabama's Seventh Judicial Circuit; and judge of the Sumter County Court.

4. Gansevoort Melville, Francis W. Pickens, Clement C. Clay, Nathaniel Terry, and James W. McClung. McClung, born in Knoxville, Tenn., was the nephew of Hugh L. White. McClung removed to Alabama where he practiced law in Huntsville. He served several years in the Alabama House, presiding as Speaker in 1835, 1837, and 1838. An unsuccessful candidate for governor in 1841 as an independent, McClung won election in 1845 to the Alabama Senate, where he served until his death in 1848.

## FROM JOHN LAW[1]

My Dear Sir                                      Vincennes August 23d 1844

Yours was duly received.[2] You no doubt have learnt ere this that the Whigs have succeeded in gaining a small majority in the Legislature, which gives them on joint ballot the election of Senator. The Senate is tied with the casting vote to the Lt. Gov. who is a democrat.[3] In the House the Whigs have seven majority. You may judge of the closeness of the vote when I inform you, that an aggregate of 86 votes majority in twelve counties lost us 14 Senators and Reps, and making a difference of 28 in joint ballot. In the popular vote we have largely increased since last year when we elected our Gov by nearly two thousand votes.[4] The abolitionists who at the August election 1843 polled nearly 1700 votes for their Candidate for Governor,[5] all voted the Whig ticket this year for Senators and Representatives, having no ticket of their own. They have at the Novr. election, Birney for president, Morris—Vice.[6] They have run electoral tickets and will poll I think [not] quite 3000 votes which may be considered as a deduction from Mr. Clay's total amount, they being nearly to a man Whigs. Our friends in Tennessee must not be discouraged at all by the result here at the late election, for while the Whigs have by a Series of accidents been enabled to get a bare majority in the joint ballot of the two Houses, the popular vote as compared with that of 1843, shows a very large gain to the democrats. The only evil is, the election of a Whig Senator. I would be willing to pledge my all on the result of the election in November. *We shall carry the State* not *less than 5000 votes* for the *democratic nomination* and such is the opinion of every intelligent and well informed democrat in the State. Local causes not easily explainable to those out of the State, produced the results mentioned. In November no such causes can effect the election, and we have a clear democratic majority in the State from 5 to *10,000.* I speak advisedly. The democracy are up and doing every where. The late success of the Whigs has only tended to make them more active and vigilant, and from this untill November, we shall constantly be in the field. But for a Series of appointments in the Southern portion of the State which I have just returned from fulfilling, with Owen,[7] I should have been at the great gathering at Nashville, where I was exceedingly desirous of being. We have another such Mass Meeting and Barbacue here in October.

A highly respectable and influential democrat in Pike County, Judge Sawyer,[8] informed me while there the other day that he had written you in reference to your views upon the subject of preemption laws. There are a large number of preemptioners in his County, and it had been represented that you were unfriendly to the preemption laws, that he had received no answer &c &c. I replied by saying, that of course you could not reply to all the communications you were daily receiving from all parts of the Union, especially from individuals with whom you were unacquainted, and whose motives might not be the best in making the enquiries, that I intended shortly to write you, and would mention the subject. He seemed perfectly satisfied, and requested me so to do.

Thus if you have no objections, all though well enough acquainted with your opinions, and acts in the matter referred to, myself, yet as it is a Subject of a good deal Importance in our State, and the opinions of Mr. Clay having been expressed in Strong terms against this highly meritorious and valuable class of Western Settlers, it would gratify your friends here, if you would reply to the question, "What are your views in reference to the preemption laws now in force, and the propriety and policy of continuing them?" I need not say, that the answer is with your consent intended for publication.

I received a letter last night from I believe a mutual friend, and former college classmate of mine, John K. Kane, of Philadelphia. He has been making a tour through Pennsylvania, and expresses his belief *unhesitatingly* that we shall carry that state by 20,000 votes. He is fearful however of New York, and writes me that the vote of Indiana is looked to with great interest. I have written him to put us down as good for 5000. I forwarded you a day since the proceedings of our Mass Meeting, and Resolutions adopted by acclamation.[9] They contain the whole democratic creed.

My best regards to friend Brown, and say to him he must write me. I want also a paper containing the proceedings of the Nashville meeting. Mr Van Buren wrote me this week, that he had sent an answer to the invitation to be present there, in which he had expressed his views in reference to the nominations made at Baltimore. I have not seen it.

JOHN LAW

ALS. DLC–JKP. Addressed to Columbia and marked "Private."

1. An Indiana lawyer and legislator, Law served as a delegate to the 1844 Democratic National Convention, as a judge for the Seventh Circuit Court of Indiana, and as a two-term member of the U.S. House, 1861–65.

2. Letter not found.

3. Jesse D. Bright.

4. James Whitcomb.

5. A physician from Lafayette, Ind., Elizur Deming lost both his 1843 gubernatorial race and his 1845 congressional contest.

6. James G. Birney and Thomas Morris. Birney, a native of Kentucky and a graduate of Princeton University, practiced law in Alabama and Kentucky prior to his founding the *Philanthropist* in 1836; he moved his anti-slavery operations from Ohio to New York in 1837 and headed the anti-slavery presidential tickets in 1840 and 1844. Elected as a Democrat to the U.S. Senate in 1833, Morris ended his influence among Ohio Democrats by publicly defending the abolitionist cause in an 1839 Senate debate with Henry Clay; Morris' political sacrifice earned him second place on the Liberty Party ticket in 1844.

7. Son of Robert Owen, British industrialist and social reformer, Robert Dale Owen assisted in the founding of the New Harmony community in Indiana in 1826; he served three terms in the state legislature, 1836–38, and two terms in the U.S. House, 1843–47.

8. Not identified further.

9. Resolutions not found.

## FROM DANIEL GRAHAM[1]

Dear Sir,                                        Nashville, Tenn, 25 Augt 1844

The Whig affair came on the day before the meeting[2] in pretty much of a flourish, & departed on to day & the day after the meeting in very questionable spirits. Bell presided & opened with too long a speech, at least so say some of Fosters friends. He introduced Prentiss[3] first who addressed the women for more than half his speech in Moffit[4] style and fell short of every bodys expectation. Clingman then ranted for a while and the labours of the day were closed by cousin Rayner who made a respectable & respectful talk next day.[5] Hunt of New Orleans, Jimmy Jones & other minor lights occupied the stand.[6] After night Graves of Ky ranted a while against Genl McCalla & against the Ezekiel branch of the Polk family.[7] Last night the speaking dwindled down to Humphrey Marshall of Ky, who married Doct McAlisters daughter in Franklin.[8] On friday it was proposed by the Captains to their companies that they should adjourn the convention to Columbia, but the men refused unanimously to go. There was a manifest dissatisfaction in the camp on the ever fruitful source of militia disquiet. Rations was the inciter. Camp meat was deficient in quantity & quality, & there was much grumbling. A portion of straightouts have been induced to attend your Columbia meeting this week & they set off yesterday with musick and with the Big Bell which Mrs. Bell presented to a Williamson Company at the Convention.[9] Today three wagons went off loaded with men and tis said that Prentiss & Graves have gone out to beard the young lion in his den. I would prefer that you may have gone up to the Shelbyville meeting. These fellows & their adjuncts will make a point of annoying you if you be at home. The last caucus resolutions here on friday were to carry their purposes by violence if they cannot succeed otherwise. Neither money nor harsh measures are to be spared.

Maxey who was beaten by the Whites Creek ruffians was carried out home yesterday evening by his brother the doct.[10] One eye is torn out, the condition of the other not known & his mouth smashed in, several of his teeth were picked up on the floor. The fellows continued to parade about the public square and were bullying James & Wm Irvine when Maj Turner stept up to suppress the quarrel.[11] One of them Sims Casey[12] advanced quickly on Turner, cursing him & drawing a pistol. Turner drew & fired promptly but his pistol was struck up by one of Caseys party. Casey fired & struck Turner in the left breast with two small balls (which have been extracted). Turner then closed with him and was immediately shot in the back, near the shoulder blade, by another of the party. They then fell together & Casey soon turned on top & beat Turner on the head with his pistol. They were pulled apart and as they rose some one handed Turner a pistol with which he shot Casey just above the navel, of which he died in some 36 hours. The ball which struck Turner in the back has not been extracted. He has had no bad symptoms except a little vomiting of blood & some sickness of stomach. The doctors are to redress the wounds today & will make a more satisfactory opinion. At first the case was worse than doubtful. Afterwards it is thought to be quite hopeful. It has excited much feeling with us & I have been thus minute.[13]

Melville has gone off today for Shelbyville. Marshall[14] addresses the demos tomorrow night by request of the working classes. He goes next day to speak at Gallatan on his way home. The death of Muhlenberg will bring out Shunck who will be the stronger stake in Pennsy. The Whigs here are giving up the Keystone but are still claiming N York against all our evidences. The Empire state is of great importance. The issue may hang upon it. I start in a few days for the Mountain dist.

D. GRAHAM

ALS. DLC-JKP. Addressed to Columbia.

1. Graham, formerly a resident of Murfreesboro, served as Tennessee's secretary of state, 1818–30, and as state comptroller, 1836–43.

2. Reference is to a two-day Whig meeting in Nashville, the official proceedings of which began on August 21, 1844.

3. Sergeant S. Prentiss, a native of Maine and graduate of Bowdoin College, moved to Mississippi in 1828 and subsequently practiced law in Vicksburg. In the summer of 1837 he ran for a seat in the U.S. House in a special election occasioned by a called session of Congress; his Democratic opponent, John F. H. Claiborne, claimed victory and was seated for the full term. Whig members of the House bitterly asserted that the Democratic majority in the called session had stolen Prentiss' seat. When the House met in December for its first regular session, Prentiss contested Claiborne's seating; the House reversed its previous decision and called for a new election. Prentiss defeated Claiborne and served a partial term; he did not seek relection in 1839.

4. Misspelling of "mofette."

5. Thomas L. Clingman and Kenneth Rayner. Clingman, a lawyer from Asheville, N.C., won election as a Whig to one term in the U.S. House, 1843–45, and as a Democrat to five terms, 1847–58; he served two partial terms in the U.S. Senate, 1858–61. Kenneth Rayner, a lawyer from Hertford County, N.C., served two terms in the North Carolina House of Commons before his election as a Whig to the U.S. House, where he served from 1839 to 1845.

6. Randell Hunt and James C. Jones. Whig orator, lawyer, and civic leader from New Orleans, Hunt supported John Bell's presidential bid in 1860; in 1865 Hunt won election to the U.S. Senate but was denied admission on grounds that Louisiana had not yet been readmitted to the Union.

7. William J. Graves, John M. McCalla, and Ezekiel Polk. Elected twice to the lower house of the Kentucky General Assembly, 1834 and 1843, Graves served three terms as a Whig member of the U.S. House, 1835–41; he killed Jonathan Cilley, a Democratic congressman from Maine, in a duel in 1838.

8. Humphrey Marshall, nephew of James G. Birney and graduate of the U.S. Military Academy, practiced law in Louisville, Ky., prior to his election as a Whig to his first term in Congress in 1849; he went to China as U.S. minister in 1852; in 1855 he won election on the American Party ticket to the first of two terms in the U.S. House; and during the Civil War he held the rank of brigadier general and served in the Confederate Congress. He married Frances McAllister, daughter of Charles McAllister of Franklin, Tenn.

9. The Nashville Straightouts of 1840, a Whig militia company headed by W. F. Tannehill, and the Cumberland Straightouts, captained by F. N. McNairy, attended the Whig mass meeting in Columbia on August 27, 1844. Jane Erwin Yeatman Bell, daughter of Andrew Erwin of Bedford County and widow of Thomas Yeatman of Nashville, married John Bell of Davidson County in 1835. A "mammoth" bell was presented to the Bell highlanders militia company of Williamson County in recognition of that unit's drill performance at the Whig mass meeting in Nashville on August 21, 1844.

10. William and John Maxey. William Maxey, an early settler of the Haysboro community of Davidson County, was the father of Powhatan W. Maxey, the Whig mayor of Nashville in 1844; John Maxey, a Nashville physician, was a leader in the Democratic party organization of Davidson County.

11. James Irvine, William Irvine, and Robert B. Turner. James and William Irvine are not identified further.

12. Charles Simms Casey is not identified further. On November 11, 1844, the Davidson County grand jury indicted Samuel Casey and Reuben Chick, Jr., for the assault and battery, with intent to murder, of William Maxey; first heard in the County Criminal Court's 1845 October term, the prosecution's case failed in a hung jury; tried a second time, but on reduced charges, Casey won acquittal and Chick received a three-year jail sentence. Davidson County Criminal Court Archives, Minute Book B, pp. 88–89, 137, 163, 230, 358, 361–63, 376, 379, 394, 431–33, 442, and 483.

13. In a brief notice of the Casey-Turner fight of Wednesday afternoon, August 21, The *Nashville Whig* of August 24 assured readers that the fatal affray was "disconnected from politics." On August 27 the *Nashville Union* explained that it had withheld reporting "the unhappy fracas" in order to avoid "adding anything to the excitement of the times." The *Union* article also mentioned that on Friday evening, August 23, S. C. Manning, a member of one of the local Texas Volunteer militia companies, had been killed near his home in the Capitol Hill area of Nashville. On January 16, 1845, the *Union* carried notes on the Criminal Court trial of William W. Merchant for Manning's murder; the jury found that Merchant had acted in self-defense and acquitted him. The *Union* account of the trial testimony revealed that Manning had sought revenge upon Merchant for the recent beating of a Democrat, had recruited the assistance of several Texas Volunteer militiamen in "rocking" Merchant's store on the evening of August 22, and had returned to Merchant's store the next night armed with a hickory stick and determined to do Merchant injury. Merchant had answered Manning's call with a single pistol shot fired at point blank range. Graham's concern for Polk's safety

during the forthcoming Whig mass meeting in Columbia must be read in the context of the late killings in Nashville, where measures to prevent such violence, during the two-week period of Nashville's Democratic and Whig mass meetings, had been attempted. On August 9 representatives of both political parties had agreed upon a set of regulations designed "to prevent collisions between the volunteer companies attached to the respective Parties and for the general preservation of peace and order in the City during the present canvass for the Presidency." Regulation number five had provided that if any difficulty arose, it was to be referred to a joint committee of militia officers of the two parties. The full text of those regulations was published in the *Nashville Whig* of August 10, 1844. Over thirty thousand armed and highly partisan militiamen from Tennessee and neighboring states attended each of the political/military encampments in Nashville. Although warned that the Whig militiamen marching from Nashville to Columbia were spoiling for a fight, Polk remained in Columbia during the Whig rally of August 27-28.

14. Thomas F. Marshall.

## FROM JOSEPH HALL[1]

Boston, Mass. August 25, 1844

Hall recalls his former congressional service with Polk and reports enthusiasm among Democrats in Massachusetts, Maine, and New Hampshire. He expects Polk to carry the states of Maine, New Hampshire, New York, Pennsylvania, Virginia, South Carolina, Alabama, Mississippi, Louisiana, Arkansas, Missouri, Illinois, Tennessee, Indiana, and Michigan. He calculates that New Jersey, Georgia, and Ohio are "uncertain."

ALS. DLC–JKP. Addressed to Columbia.

1. Hall served in the U.S. House for two terms as a representative from Maine, 1833–37. From 1838 until 1846 he held the post of measurer in the Boston customhouse. In 1849 he ran unsuccessfully for the mayorship of Boston.

## TO CAVE JOHNSON

[Dear Sir,]                                    [Columbia] August 26, 1844

The *Hon. Geo. S. Houston* writes me under date of the 22nd that he has made all his arrangements to meet you at the appointment at Pulaski on the 29th and to accompany you through the whole list. He says however that he cannot go without you, and fears as he has not heard from you since he made the agreement with you, that possibly you might disappoint him. He will be at Pulaski at all events on the 29th. I have written to him[1] that if you did not meet him at Pulaski on the 29th that you certainly would at Lawrenceburg on Saturday the 31st, if life and health permitted. Your whole list of appointments have been forwarded in Hand-Bills along the whole line. Col Jones and Mr. Williamson[2] of Somerville passed here on Thursday and would give extensive notice of them as they went down. It is a very important route. Great good will be done if you attend the appointments, and great harm if the people are disappointed. Not having heard from you since you left Nashville, I write thus urgently, to say that I hope nothing has, or can occur to induce you to fail to fill the appointments. You will have immense crowds, such as no other man in the State could draw out. If you desire it, *L. P. Cheatham* of Nashville will go with *Houston* and yourself, and so make your personal labors still the lighter. *Pickens* of S.C. was here on yesterday, and has gone to Shelbyville. Judge *Douglas* of *Illinois* and Mr. *Brice*[3] of *Louisiana* spoke at [a] very numerously attended meeting in this County and Giles last week, and will be at Chapel Hill in Marshall to day. We have now decidedly the advantage of our opponents in the State, and if the present enthusiasm and activity can be kept up, the State is perfectly safe. Within the next three weeks, the whole people will have settled down in their opinions and but few changes will take place in the State after that time. Your appointments are of more importance than any others, and I should regard it as most unfortunate if any accident should prevent them from being filled. I repeat if any accident has prevented you from being at *Pulaski* on the 29th, you must if possible join *Houston* at Lawrenceburg on the 31st. If you do not *Houston* will turn back and go home, and the people will be disappointed at all the other places. *A. V. Brown's* engagements are such that he cannot go with *Houston*.

[JAMES K. POLK]

PL. Published in *THM*, I, pp. 249–50. Addressed to Clarksville and marked "*Private*."

1. Letter not found.
2. William A. Jones and James M. Williamson. A farmer and businessman in Fayette County, Jones served one term in the Tennessee House, 1847–49.
3. Stephen A. Douglas and James G. Bryce.


## FROM ROBERT ARMSTRONG

Dr Sir                           Nashville Augt 27 [18]44
"What of to day."[1] I expect the Whigs have given themselves *great* Trouble to try and give you a little. It matters not. They are desperate and are using Desperate Men and Means to Keep up their rank and file. The Convention here[2] has done them serious injury & with

Marshalls speech last Night following we see evident signs of depression and want of Spirits. They are whip[p]ed, if we only keep up the fight. I have not heard a word from Johnson. A. V. Brown came in the Stage to night, goes back in the morning and will take up the appointments. Our Commt.[3] or I will myself write Keeble and Bright one of them to go Immediately on. Coe, Doughlass, Brice, & Cheatham[4] all got in this evening.

We will do all we can to keep them *at it.* Guild writes me and Duffy,[5] that all is in readiness for Craighead & Barton &c. I wish you could come in. Tyler's Letter of *withdrawal* is *published.* I have not been able to see the old Genl.[6] Their is something in the wind. All I fear is that it is too *soon* by a few weeks. Nothing Ought to be done *now* to Interfere with the work or to Change the force of things. *If the Old Genl's last letter reached Tyler in time nothing will be done.* I think that was in time, and has brought out the Letter of withdrawal *first.* In haste.

R. Armstrong

ALS. DLC–JKP. Addressed to Columbia and marked *"Private."*

1. Armstrong's quotation is not identified, but his reference is to the Whig mass meeting held in Columbia on August 27, 1844.

2. Reference is to the Whig mass meeting in Nashville that convened on August 21, 1844.

3. Nashville Democratic Central Committee.

4. Levin H. Coe, Stephen A. Douglas, James G. Bryce, and Leonard P. Cheatham.

5. Josephus C. Guild and probably Francis Duffy, postmaster at Hartsville in Sumner County.

6. Andrew Jackson.


## TO ANDREW J. DONELSON

My Dear Sir:                                    Columbia Augt. 27th 1844

I fear *Mr Tyler* may call Congress together. If he does, it will in my judgment do mischief. The present Congress, will do nothing on the Texas question, however urgent the necessity for prompt action may be. It would be useless to call Congress with any such hope. The only effect of convening Congress would be, to bring together the leaders of Federalism, who would do nothing but *agitate* upon the Presidential question. They would undoubtedly devote their whole time to laying plans and schemes to carry that election, and would think little and care less about Texas. I hope there will be no extra Session. No good, but much harm I fear would result from it. *Mr Tyler* will listen to *Genl. Jackson* and I hope if the General has not, that he will promptly advise him against such a step. I have not time to give you all the reasons for the conclusion to which I have come. I have a strong conviction that nothing could so much jeopardize the result of the pending Presidential election as the call of an extra Session of Congress. I fear from what I learn that it may be now too late for a successful interposition to prevent it. Will you see the General, and if he and yourself concur with me in opinion, write immediately to *Tyler* advising against such a step. In haste.

JAMES K. POLK

ALS. DLC–AJD. Addressed to Nashville and marked *"Private."* Published in *THM,* III, pp. 60–61.

## FROM DANIEL SHEFFER

York Springs, Penn. August 27, 1844[1]
Sheffer reports that the Democratic party will carry Pennsylvania, although the Whigs have been active. Acknowledging that the Whigs have more money than the Democrats, Sheffer says the Whigs' "chief hope and reliance is in corrupting the people." Shunk will be nominated without dissent in the place of Muhlenberg and will have a majority of at least 20,000 votes. Since Tyler has withdrawn from the election, Sheffer thinks the Democratic party "will cease molesting him."

ALS. DLC–JKP. Addressed to Columbia.

## FROM HOPKINS L. TURNEY

Winchester, Tenn. August 27, 1844
Turney predicts that Polk will carry Tennessee by 5,000 votes; he regrets fatigue and legal business prevent his attending the Shelbyville meeting; and he attributes to Nicholson the party's decision to assign Coe the task of tracking Bell.

ALS. DLC–JKP. Addressed to Columbia. Polk's AE on the cover states that he answered this letter on August 31, 1844; Polk's reply has not been found.

## FROM ROBERT ARMSTRONG

Dr Sir                                          [Nashville August 28, 1844][1]
You have seen A. V. Brown who left here this morning. He will take Johnsons *place* untill Cheatham releaves him.

Coe passed on to day to Cross Plains. Craighead leaves in the morning at daylight to meet Barton & Cullum.[2] When he closes at Macon he will join Coe at Paris. Ewell is *yet* here & is of no force. See the Banner[3] of to day for Fosters appointments &c &c. Coe has addressed him to devide *time,* &c. All seems to go on well. I will try and prevail on Doughlass[4] to go to Springfield on *Monday.* Conrad[5] has written me for him.

You must have treated the poor whiggys badly in Columbia. They are the worst looking coons that ever came this way. The Nashville and Columbia Whig Conventions will be long remembered.[6] Great suffering and privations. No provisions. Mutiny and Desertion. Defeat must follow.

R. ARMSTRONG

[P.S.] Tyler will do *nothing now. The Genl.*[7] writes by Doctr. Curry[8] who goes out in the morning to Columbia. The Old Man is well pleased and in health & spirits. Is *sure* of 19 states and *likely 20.*

ALS. DLC–JKP. Addressed to Columbia.
1. Provenance and date identified through content analysis.
2. Roger Barton and Alvin Cullom.
3. Nashville *Republican Banner.*
4. Stephen A. Douglas.
5. George C. Conrad was a Springfield merchant and Democrat.
6. Reference is to the Whig convention in Nashville on August 21 and the Whig mass meeting at Columbia on August 27, 1844.
7. Andrew Jackson.
8. A Nashville physician, Richard O. Currey received his medical degree from the University of Pennsylvania. From 1846 until 1850, he taught chemistry at East Tennessee University in Knoxville; he later taught the same subject at Shelby Medical College in Nashville.

## FROM J. GEORGE HARRIS

Nashville, Tenn. August 28, 1844

Harris states that he is writing most of the columns for the *Nashville Union* and that he hopes the newspaper will improve. He has heard cheering reports from New York City and has received word of Bancroft's entry into the gubernatorial race in Massachusetts. Armstrong has mentioned Polk's plans to prepare a public statement on the naturalization question; Harris suggests Madison and Franklin as good sources for writing that subject.

ALS. DLC–JKP. Addressed to Columbia and marked *"Private."*

## TO CAVE JOHNSON

[Dear Sir,]                                    [Columbia] August 28, 1844

I received your letter of the [25th]¹ on yesterday. I most deeply regret your state of health, and the disappointment which the people will feel at your inability to meet your appointments. I still hope that when you received my last letter you may be able to come to Lawrenceburg. I have written to Armstrong² this morning that *L. P. Cheatham* should come to *Lawrenceburg*. I will send a messenger to *Boling Gordon's* today to see if he cannot go. *Gordon however* is an uncertain man and will probably not be ready upon such short notice. The appointments will call out great crowds and are vastly more important than *Caruther's* appointments in your District. Every effort will be made to induce *Houston* to go on; but I have fears he may be inclined to return home, unless he has assurance that he will be joined by you. I have written to Pulaski explaining to him why you will not be there.³ What adds to the embarrassment is, that *A. V. Brown* passed here on yesterday, as I hear, in the stage to Nashville, and will not of course be at home. If he was there, he could go with him. As it is we will do the best we can. I hope you will strike your line of appointments at the earliest possible day; at Lawrenceburg if you feel able.

[JAMES K. POLK]

PL. Published in *THM,* I, p. 250. Addressed to Clarksville and marked *"Private."*

1. Transcribed as the 22nd by Sioussat, but content analysis suggests that the 25th is the correct date.
2. Letter not found.
3. Letter not found.

## TO GEORGE M. DALLAS

My Dear Sir:                          Columbia Tenn. Augt. 29th, 1844

I was absent from home when your two letters of the 7th & 11th Inst. reached here. Since my return my time has been so constantly occupied, that I have been unable to answer earlier. I have received a letter, from adopted citizens of New York,¹ accompanied by, a printed compilation of opinions of others, similar to the one which has been addressed to you. I have no personal knowledge of the persons who address me. I have been advised by some friends in New York, that there is no necessity to answer. I have not as yet answered, and will not, unless the necessity to do so becomes imperative. I am inclined to think that your suspicion of the object of those who address the letter, is correct. Mr *Clay* has not yet answered & probably will not. If a necessity shall arise to answer it strikes me that the Resolution adopted by the Baltimore convention covers the whole ground. I refer to the 9th of the Series of Resolutions adopted by that body.[2] That Resolution is very strong, in its terms, and cannot fail to be satisfactory to all adopted citizens. In accepting the nominations, we have adopted it as a part of the Democratic policy. Will it not be sufficient simply to avow our approval of it? Indeed if the Democratic newspapers would present it prominently as a part of the Democratic creed, it would go far to supersede the necessity of any answer from us on the subject. If you concur with me in opinion, might it not be well to call the attention of the *Pennsylvanian*[3] and other leading Democratic papers in the East to it?

I deeply regret the death of Mr Muhlenberg. I had the pleasure to know him as a personal as well as a political friend. I am greatly gratified to see the party so well united in the choice of his successor as the Democratic candidate for Governor. I hope the domestic difficulties in New York may all be over and the party harmoniously united, as soon as their Gubernatorial nomination is made. My friends in that state write me confidently that such will be the result.

I see Mr *Webster* and leading Whigs every-where are making powerful appeals to the abolitionists to induce them to abandon their distinctive organization. Will they be able to succeed? *Genl. Cass* & Ex-Senator *Norvell*[4] of Michigan, whom I saw at the mass-meeting at Nashville,[5] are of opinion that they cannot succeed in the North-West. They assure me that *Mr Birney* will not abandon his present position. *Mr Clay's* late letter to the South, on Texas, may have the effect to confirm this determination. *Mr Norvell* told me that he heard *Mr Birney* address a meeting of abolitionists, at Detroit a few weeks ago, in which he announced in strong terms, his determination not to amalgamate with the Whig party. Still the pressure upon them by the Whig leaders will be very great, and I have my fears that a large portion of them may yet yield. What is your opinion of their probable course?

*Mr Tyler's* letter of withdrawal reached here last evening. It is a well written paper. What will be its effect upon his friends? Will it not strengthen the Democratic ticket, and especially in New Jersey and Connecticut, where we need the aid of his friends?

Our great mass-meeting at Nashville passed off admirably. It was the largest assembly of the people ever convened in this part of the union. A degree of enthusiasm and confidence of success, pervaded the immense mass, such as I have never witnessed before. The Whig's held their mass-meeting on the 21st,[6] and again convened at this place on the 27th. Both were failures except as to *numbers*. Their leading and most distinguished speakers, were *Graves* of Ky. (the murderer of *Cilly*),[7] *Prentiss* of Miss. and three or four others of no reputation in the country. The effect has been decidedly to the prejudice of the Whig cause. On the same day they held their meeting at this place (27th Inst.) the Democracy held a mass-meeting, of not less than 12,000 present at Shelbyville, 40 miles from this place. *Pickens* of S.C. Mr *Melville* of N.Y. and several able speakers from Mississippi & Alabama attended and addressed them. I learn that the greatest enthusiasm prevailed, large accessions to our ranks were reported, and all went off well. The whole state is in a blaze: every man of both parties, who can debate, is on the stump. The Whig leaders—*Foster, Bell Jarnigan*[8] &c. —are becoming desperate, and making desperate efforts, to stay the current of popular sentiment which[9]

[JAMES K. POLK]

AL, fragment. PHi. Probably addressed to Philadelphia; marked *"Private."*
1. Letter not found.
2. The ninth resolution of the Democratic National Convention of 1844 committed the party to resist vigorously any efforts to restrict the naturalization laws.
3. Philadelphia *Pennsylvanian*.
4. Lewis Cass and John Norvell. Norvell was postmaster at Detroit, 1831–36, prior to his service in the U.S. Senate, 1837–41. From 1846 until 1849, he was U.S. district attorney of Michigan.
5. Reference is to the Democratic mass meeting in Nashville on August 15, 1844.
6. Reference is to the Whig convention that met in Nashville.
7. Jonathan Cilley.
8. Ephraim H. Foster, John Bell, and Spencer Jarnagin.
9. Extant text ends here with the conclusion of Polk's fourth page.

## TO HERSCHEL V. JOHNSON[1]

Dear Sir:                    Columbia, Ten. Augt. 29th 1844
I should have acknowledged the receipt of your kind letter of the 29th ult. earlier, but for the pressure of a very heavy correspondence and other indispensible engagements which have occupied my whole time. I was moreover absent from home for several days after it reached here.

My determination not to participate personally in the pending political contest, was formed after full reflection, and I do not see how I can with propriety, yield to your pressing solicitation to depart from it, by visiting the State of Georgia. It would certainly have given me sincere pleasure to have met, the people of Georgia, at Macon on the 22nd, if I could have done so consistently with the determination which I had announced to the public, not to accept any invitation of the kind. I regret that I shall be denied the pleasure of accepting your invitation to visit your house. You state that Mrs. J. is the daughter of the late Judge Polk of Maryland and that she is related to me.[2] I have no doubt that we are descended from the same stock. My ancestors first settled on the Eastern Shore of Maryland. From thence the branch of the family from which I sprang emigrated to Pennsylvania, then to N. Carolina & then to this state. I have often heard my relative the late Col. Wm. Polk of Raleigh N.C. say, that Mrs. Genl. Winder[3] and the family of our name residing in Maryland and Delaware were related, but I am unable to trace the degree of relationship. I am gratified to learn that Mrs. J. takes so lively an interest in my success, in the pending contest, and especially that she feels indignant as we all do, at the base calumny, which has been recently incubated upon the memory of my Grandfather, the late Col. Ezekiel Polk. The charge of toryism is unqualifiedly and basely false. I learn from a friend in N. Carolina, that a *vindication* of his memory, accompanied by the most incontrovertible proof, will shortly appear, which ought to put the slanderers of the dead to shame. Though personally unacquainted with you I thank you for your kind letter, and hope that the day may come when I may have it in my power to make the personal acquaintance of yourself and Mrs. J. to whom I beg you to make my respectful regards.

JAMES K. POLK

ALS. NcD. Addressed to Milledgeville, Ga., and marked *"Private."*

1. A lawyer in Milledgeville, Johnson was a Democratic presidential elector in 1844. He served as U.S. senator, 1848–49, as judge of the superior court, 1849–53, as governor of Georgia for two terms, 1853–57, and as senator in the Confederate Congress, 1863–65. In 1860, he ran unsuccessfully for vice-president on the Democratic ticket with Stephen A. Douglas.

2. Ann Polk Johnson and William Polk. Ann Polk, who was born in 1809 in Somerset County, Md., married Johnson in 1833. William Polk served as a judge on the Maryland Court of Appeals from 1806 until 1812.

3. Esther Polk Winder, the wife of William H. Winder, was the daughter of William Polk of Maryland and the half sister of Ann Polk Johnson.

## FROM AUGUSTE D'AVEZAC

Baltimore, Md. August 31, 1844

D'Avezac reports on his speaking engagement at Winchester, Va., on August 29th; he estimates that some 1,400 of the 10,000 participants were women. His speech scheduled for September 5th at Trenton, N.J., will be followed by appointments at Baltimore, Md., on September 6th and at Wheeling, Va., on September 12th.

ALS. DLC–JKP. Addressed to Columbia.

# CALENDAR

N.B. Items entered in *italic* type have been published or briefed in the Correspondence Series.

1844

| | |
|---|---|
| 1 Jan | From Silas M. Caldwell. ALS. DLC–JKP. Reports that he has collected $88 due the estate of Samuel W. Polk. |
| *1 Jan* | *From Samuel H. Laughlin.* |
| 1 Jan | From Wilie Ledbetter. ALS. DLC–JKP. Writes from Jacinto, Miss., and urges prompt action on his legal suit. |
| *1 Jan* | *From William H. Polk.* |
| *1 Jan* | *From William H. Polk.* |
| *2 Jan* | *From Daniel Kenney.* |
| *4 Jan* | *From J. G. M. Ramsey.* |
| 6 Jan | From Thomas H. Williams. ALS. DLC–JKP. Requests Polk's assistance in providing evidence of the claim of Sampson Williams, deceased; encloses copy of his deposition to be laid before Congress by Robert W. Roberts of Mississippi. |
| *7 Jan* | *From Robert Armstrong.* |
| *7 Jan* | *From Levin H. Coe.* |
| *7 Jan* | *From Cave Johnson.* |
| 8 Jan | From J. Percy Brown. ALS. DLC–JKP. Informs Polk that the Mississippi State Democratic Convention has just nominated Martin Van Buren for the presidency and Polk for the vice-presidency. |
| *9 Jan* | *From Leonard P. Cheatham.* |
| 9 Jan | From Nicholas Hobson. ALS. DLC–JKP. States that he has renewed Polk's note at the Planter's Bank of Nashville. |
| *9 Jan* | *To Samuel H. Laughlin.* |
| 10 Jan | From John Barham. ALS. DLC–JKP. Introduces William I. Hamlett, his brother-in-law. |

| | |
|---|---|
| 10 Jan | From Levin H. Coe. ALS. DLC–JKP. Discusses charges of political corruption leveled against Polk by the Whigs. |
| *10 Jan* | *From J. G. M. Ramsey.* |
| *10 Jan* | *From Archibald Yell.* |
| 10 Jan | From Henderson K. Yoakum. ALS. DLC–JKP. Seeks Polk's assistance in obtaining a position as naval purser for William F. Leiper of Murfreesboro. |
| *11 Jan* | *From Samuel H. Laughlin.* |
| 12 Jan | From James Cone. ALS. DLC–JKP. States that he went to Jackson, Tenn., on December 30 last and paid the first note on his debt to Polk. |
| *13 Jan* | *From Cave Johnson.* |
| 14 Jan | From J. C. Brassfield. ALS. DLC–JKP. Seeks Polk's assistance in procuring subscribers to the Shelbyville *Free Press.* |
| *14 Jan* | *From John W. Childress.* |
| 15 Jan | From John C. Blackburn. ALS. DLC–JKP. Acknowledges receipt of Polk's letter of December 18, 1843; states that he has no further information on the sale of Polk's Wayne County lands to Samuel Cade. |
| *15 Jan* | *From Adam Huntsman.* |
| *17 Jan* | *From James M. Howry.* |
| 17 Jan | From Ezekiel P. McNeal. ALS. DLC–JKP. Encloses a statement of Polk's account for managing his lands in the Western District from February 1842 to January 17, 1844; states that he will sell Polk's lands near Bolivar should the opportunity arise. |
| 18 Jan | From John McKeon et al. C, copy. DLC–JKP. Invite Polk to a meeting in New York City on February 6; expect the convention will nominate Lewis Cass for the presidency. |
| 18 Jan | From Thomas J. Winston. ALS. DLC–JKP. Requests that Polk send copies of all decrees issued in the suit of W. K. Hill, Gideon J. Pillow, Thomas J. Winston, and B. M. Jones in the Chancery Court of Maury County. |
| 19 Jan | From Samuel J. Hays. ALS. DLC–JKP. Introduces Jeremiah Y. Dashiell, a physician from Lake Providence, La. |
| 19 Jan | From Robert B. Reynolds. ALS. DLC–JKP. Replies to Polk's letter of December 19, 1843, and states that he has been unable to locate a deed of gift from James King, deceased, to Sally King Dempsey in the Knox County records. |
| *20 Jan* | *To Samuel H. Laughlin.* |
| *20 Jan* | *To William H. Polk.* |
| *21 Jan* | *To Thomas W. Hogan and John P. Heiss.* |
| *21 Jan* | *From Cave Johnson.* |
| *21 Jan* | *To Cave Johnson.* |
| *22 Jan* | *From Aaron V. Brown.* |

22 Jan     From Albert T. McNeal. ALS. DLC–JKP. Discusses affairs at Polk's Mississippi plantation and relates state political news.

24 Jan     From William Bobbitt. ALS. DLC–JKP. Discusses legal matters and Mississippi politics.

27 Jan     From Levin H. Coe. ALS. DLC–JKP. Reviews politics of the vice-presidential question and the position of the Arkansas State Democratic convention.

*28 Jan*     *From Robert Armstrong.*

*31 Jan*     *From Cave Johnson.*

1 Feb     To Thomas Ewell. ALS. DLC–AJD. Responds to Ewell's request of January 24 for a letter of introduction to Archibald Yell of Little Rock; urges Ewell to remain in Jackson rather than migrate to Arkansas.

1 Feb     From John W. Ford. ALS. DLC–JKP. Mentions his letter to Polk of November 3, 1843, and again solicits payment of Polk's account with the McMinnville *Central Gazette.*

*2 Feb*     *From Aaron V. Brown.*

6 Feb     From Levin H. Coe. ALS. DLC–JKP. Discusses Whig attacks upon Polk and denounces Richard M. Johnson.

*6 Feb*     *From Cave Johnson.*

*6 Feb*     *From Samuel H. Laughlin.*

6 Feb     From Williamson Smith. ALS. DLC–JKP. Informs Polk of details regarding the Madison County Democratic Convention and the Mississippi State Democratic Convention.

8 Feb     From Thomas Ewell. ALS. DLC–JKP. Acknowledges receipt of Polk's letter of February 1 and explains his reasons for wishing to remove to Arkansas.

8 Feb     From Ezekiel P. McNeal. ALS. DLC–JKP. Acknowledges receipt of Polk's letter of February 1; forwards a check in the amount of $210 for rents received; states the terms of a proposed sale of Polk's land near Bolivar to Samuel and William McNeal; and requests approval of said terms.

*9 Feb*     *To Silas Wright, Jr.*

10 Feb     From Cave Johnson. ALS. DLC–JKP. Acknowledges receipt of two letters from Polk and of one letter by Polk to Aaron V. Brown; states that four hundred copies of Hopkins L. Turney's "A Tennessean" have been ordered; and sends brief account of recent activities in Congress.

11 Feb     From John P. Pryor. ALS. DLC–JKP. Wishes letters of introduction from Polk to William T. Brown and Frederick P. Stanton.

11 Feb     From Felix Robertson. ALS. DLC–JKP. Advises Polk that the Tennessee Democratic Central Committee was directed immediately after the Baltimore Convention to select the state's at-large electors.

*14 Feb*     *From John P. Heiss.*

| | |
|---|---|
| *18 Feb* | *To Thomas W. Hogan and John P. Heiss.* |
| 18 Feb | From Adam Huntsman. ALS. DLC–JKP. Discusses Whig and Democratic nominations in the Western District and the Democratic vice-presidential question. |
| 19 Feb | From Julius W. Blackwell. ALS. DLC–JKP. Encloses a letter from a young man in Rhea County; advises that Martin Van Buren will be run against Henry Clay; believes that only Richard M. Johnson stands in the way of Polk's vice-presidential nomination; and thinks that a majority of Democrats in the Congress oppose Johnson's running with Van Buren. (Enclosure not found.) |
| *19 Feb* | *From William Tyack.* |
| 20 Feb | From William B. Allen. ALS. DLC–JKP. Invites Polk to address the Agatheridan and Erosophian societies of the University of Nashville on October 1 next. |
| 20 Feb | From John W. Ford. ALS. DLC–JKP. Acknowledges receipt of $10 enclosed in Polk's letter of February 1; explains that at the time of billing Polk for a subscription to the McMinnville *Central Gazette* he did not know that Polk had been among those Democratic friends who had advanced funds to sustain the newspaper in the fall of 1839. |
| 21 Feb | From William C. Hazen. ALS. DLC–JKP. Acknowledges receipt of Polk's letter and states that Benjamin Adams will pay two notes due by April. |
| *22 Feb* | *To John P. Heiss.* |
| 22 Feb | To Andrew Jackson. ALS. DLC–AJ. Encloses a letter from William Kennon and urges Jackson to write Antonio López de Santa Anna requesting the release of a friend of Kennon's. |
| *22 Feb* | *To Samuel H. Laughlin.* |
| 23 Feb | From Aaron V. Brown. ALS. DLC–JKP. Addressed to Polk and his brother, William H. Polk. States that he has sent two hundred franked documents to Polk, William H. Polk, and Jonas E. Thomas for distribution throughout Maury County. |
| 24 Feb | From B. M. G. Blackwell. ALS. DLC–JKP. Discusses Arkansas politics and asks Polk to send him documents for use in his own campaign for a seat in the Arkansas House. |
| *25 Feb* | *From Aaron V. Brown.* |
| *25 Feb* | *From Cave Johnson.* |
| 27 Feb | From "Yankee" Hill. ALS. DLC–JKP. Invites Polk to an evening lecture and entertainment at Masonic Hall in Nashville. |
| *27 Feb* | *From Silas Wright, Jr.* |
| *28 Feb* | *From Aaron V. Brown.* |

28 Feb  From John M. Daniel. ALS. DLC–JKP. Seeks legal counsel from Polk.

*1 March*  *From Adam Huntsman.*

1 March  From Samuel H. Laughlin. ALS. DLC–JKP. Urges Polk to come to Nashville no later than Sunday evening, March 3; expresses concern about the choice of Democratic at-large electors; and reports that Leonidas N. Ford has raised Martin Van Buren's name with that of Polk's to the masthead of the McMinnville *Central Gazette.*

3 March  From Hopkins L. Turney. ALS. DLC–JKP. States that a severe attack of rheumatism may prevent his being a candidate for Democratic elector at-large; urges Polk to launch an early campaign in Tennessee against Henry Clay's presidential bid.

*4 March*  *From Robert Armstrong.*

4 March  From John B. Fowler. ALS. DLC–JKP. Requests that Polk prove a deed and forward the certification to Cornersville.

5 March  From John Sommerville. ALS. DLC–JKP. Encloses Polk's cancelled note for $500 drawn on the Union Bank of Tennessee. (Enclosure not found.)

*6 March*  *From Cave Johnson.*

6 March  From William H. Polk. ALS. DLC–JKP. Reports news of the explosion aboard the U.S.S. *Princeton.*

*7 March*  *To Samuel H. Laughlin.*

7 March  From Henderson K. Yoakum. ALS. DLC–JKP. Discusses political affairs in Rutherford County.

*9 March*  *From Theophilus Fisk.*

*10 March*  *From Aaron V. Brown.*

*10 March*  *From Cave Johnson.*

12 March  From West H. Humphreys. ALS. DLC–JKP. Relates that Democrats in the Western District are proposing to publish a pamphlet on the "corrupt bargain" made by Henry Clay in 1825.

*12 March*  *From Samuel H. Laughlin.*

12 March  From Robert Mathews et al. LS. DLC–JKP. Addressed to Polk and A. O. P. Nicholson. Requests aid in securing the release of James T. Peacock, who is held captive at Perote Prison in Mexico.

*13 March*  *From Theophilus Fisk.*

14 March  From Aaron V. Brown. ALS. DLC–JKP. Discusses the nominations of John Y. Mason to head the Navy Department and Reuben H. Walworth to sit on the Supreme Court.

14 March  From John W. Childress. ALS. DLC–JKP. Offers to accompany Polk to Mississippi; reports on a meeting of the Democratic Association of Murfreesboro.

15 March  To Andrew Jackson. ALS. DLC–AJ. Introduces Mr. Pea-

cock of Bedford County, who seeks the release of his brother, James T. Peacock, from Perote Prison in Mexico.

15 March    From J. G. M. Ramsey. ALS. DLC–JKP. Relates that members of the Democratic Central Committee at Knoxville are divided over the approval of candidates to run as at-large electors in the presidential campaign.

16 March    From G. T. Orr et al. LS. DLC–JKP. Invite Polk to membership in the Few Society of Emory College at Oxford, Ga.

*18 March*    *To Cave Johnson.*

20 March    From Robert Armstrong. ALS. DLC–JKP. Reports that Ex-governor William Carroll is near death.

*20 March*    *To Theophilus Fisk.*

*21 March*    *From Robert Armstrong.*

21 March    From John W. Childress. ALS. DLC–JKP. States that if his expected child arrives in time, he will accompany Polk to Mississippi.

*21 March*    *To Cave Johnson.*

*21 March*    *To Cave Johnson.*

*22 March*    *From Robert Armstrong.*

25 March    From Henry Simpson et al. C, copy. DLC–JKP. Solicit Polk's assistance in establishing Democratic Associations across the country; enclose printed copy of the Philadelphia Association's constitution.

26 March    From West H. Humphreys. ALS. DLC–JKP. Wishes Polk to accompany him from Columbia to Jackson on Thursday evening next.

*26 March*    *From William H. Polk.*

28 March    From Julius W. Blackwell. ALS. DLC–JKP. Discusses possible Democratic nominees for the presidency and vice-presidency.

28 March    From A. Cathey. ALS. DLC–JKP. Writes from Mississippi and requests Polk's assistance with debt collections in Maury County.

*29 March*    *From Cave Johnson.*

*30 March*    *From Salmon P. Chase et al.*

30 March    To William Harrison. ALS. Pvt. Ms. of Mrs. Floyd C. Moore, Nashville, Tenn. Arranges payment of $85 for a horse sold by Harrison, a resident of Williamson County.

8 April    From Hopkins L. Turney. ALS. DLC–JKP. States that he will make the best that he can of a "hard bargain" in being selected one of the two Democratic electors at-large for the presidential canvass.

*10 April*    *From Cave Johnson.*

*13 April*    *From William Tyack.*

*15 April*    *From Cave Johnson.*

| | |
|---|---|
| 15 April | From George N. Sanders et al. LS. DLC–JKP. Solicit Polk's views with respect to the proposed "reunion" of Texas and the United States. |
| 16 April | From W. S. Pickett. ALS. DLC–JKP. Replies to Polk's letter of March 30 requesting information on the payment of Thomas Gregory's bills drawn on Frierson, Dale & Co. from 1839 to date. |
| 16 April | From Archibald Wright. ALS. DLC–JKP. Wishes to know if the case of Caruthers, Harris & Co. will be tried at the spring term of the Maury County Circuit Court; requests that Polk agree to lay over John B. Hays' suit against James Black. |
| 20 April | From John Windt et al. CS. DLC–JKP. Solicit Polk's views on a proposal to end the sale of public land, a tenet of the New York Central Committee of the National Reform Association. |
| 22 April | From J. M. Alexander. ALS. DLC–JKP. Wishes advice in preparing speeches for his legislative race in Arkansas. |
| *23 April* | *To Salmon P. Chase et al.* |
| [23 April 1844] | From Joseph B. Gilman. ALS. DLC–JKP. Requests letters of recommendation to prominent men in St. Louis whose aid will be required in securing his share of Jeremiah Conner's estate. |
| *24 April* | *From Samuel H. Laughlin.* |
| 25 April | From Aaron V. Brown. ALS. DLC–JKP. Invites Polk to ride with him to Nashville. |
| 25 April | To George N. Sanders et al. ALS, draft. DLC–JKP. Answers their inquiry regarding his views on the Texas question by referring them to his letter of April 23, 1844, to Salmon P. Chase et al., a copy of which he encloses. |
| *26 April* | *From Samuel H. Laughlin.* |
| 26 April | From E. W. Polk. ALS. DLC–JKP. Requests financial assistance to pay for prospective medical expenses. |
| 27 April | From William J. Freeman. ALS. DLC–JKP. Seeks financial advice and assistance for removing from Wilson to Maury County. |
| *28 April* | *From Cave Johnson.* |
| 28 April | From William Kennon. ALS. DLC–JKP. Requests assistance in securing the release of Thomas S. Smith from Perote Prison in Mexico. |
| 29 April | From F. G. Smith. AN. DLC–JKP. Extends invitation to attend a May Day reception at the Columbia Institute. |
| *29 April* | *From Williamson Smith.* |
| 30 April | From Aaron V. Brown. ALS. DLC–JKP. States that his wife's illness has detained his departure for Baltimore. |
| *30 April* | *From Cave Johnson.* |
| [1 May 1844] | From J. George Harris. ALS. DLC–JKP. Regrets that he |

|  | cannot attend the meeting in Nashville on Saturday next. |
| 2 May | From Aaron V. Brown. ALS. DLC–JKP. Remains at home to attend his critically ill wife; reports that the Giles County campaign will begin on Monday, the day William H. Polk and Barkly Martin are expected to be present in Pulaski. |
| *3 May* | *From Cave Johnson.* |
| 4 May | From Levin H. Coe. ALS. DLC–JKP. States that he wrote to friends in Alabama as suggested, that he met with Richard Sneed of Granville County, N.C., and that Sneed expects his delegation will support Richard M. Johnson for vice-president. |
| *4 May* | *To Cave Johnson.* |
| 5 May | From Robert Armstrong. ALS. DLC–JKP. Writes that the meeting of May 4 was successful, although subdued by news of Martin Van Buren's public statement on Texas annexation; fears that the "South is gone" and that the Baltimore Convention will "do nothing," thus aiding Henry Clay's election. |
| *5 May* | *From Cave Johnson.* |
| 6 May | From Benjamin Adams. ALS. DLC–JKP. Discusses payment of his note, previously held by Polk. |
| 6 May | From William G. Childress. ALS. DLC–JKP. Indicates that many Democrats in Nashville are dismayed by Martin Van Buren's stance on the proposed annexation of Texas. |
| *6 May* | *From J. G. M. Ramsey.* |
| *7 May* | *From Robert Armstrong.* |
| 7 May | From Samuel P. Caldwell. ALS. DLC–JKP. Encloses legal documents and discusses sentiments in Memphis with regard to the proposed annexation of Texas, including reactions to Clay's Texas letter and to rumors of Martin Van Buren's opposition to annexation. |
| *7 May* | *From Leonard P. Cheatham.* |
| 7 May | From William L. D. Ewing. ALS. DLC–JKP. Reports that many Democrats in and around Springfield, Ill., want Polk nominated for vice-president or president. |
| 8 May | From Nicholas Hobson. ALS. DLC–JKP. Encloses Polk's note to the Planter's Bank of Nashville for $900. |
| *8 May* | *From Cave Johnson.* |
| *8 May* | *From Samuel H. Laughlin.* |
| 8 May | From William C. Tate. ALS. DLC–JKP. States that Marshall T. Polk, Jr., is eager to live with Polk and that Marshall's mother, Laura Wilson Polk Tate, is agreeable to the arrangment; adds that the boy will be ready to go to Tennessee as soon as Polk may send for him. |
| *9 May* | *To Samuel H. Laughlin.* |

| | |
|---|---|
| *10 May* | *From Robert Armstrong.* |
| 10 May | From John N. Charter. ALS. DLC–JKP. Discusses the proposed annexation of Texas and urges Polk to publish his views on the question. |
| *10 May* | *From Andrew J. Donelson.* |
| 10 May | From Samuel H. Laughlin. ALS. DLC–JKP. Reports that he will travel to Baltimore with Andrew J. Donelson, Gideon J. Pillow, and William G. Childress; urges Polk to come to Nashville. |
| 11 May | From Edwin F. Polk. ALS. DLC–JKP. Reports from the Western District that Martin Van Buren's Texas letter has provoked great opposition to his nomination; seeks Polk's counsel regarding an appropriate response. |
| 12 May | From John H. Bills. ALS. DLC–JKP. Discusses Martin Van Buren's Texas annexation letter and his subsequent decline in popularity in the Western District. |
| *12 May* | *From Cave Johnson.* |
| *13 May* | *To Cave Johnson.* |
| 13 May | From Henderson K. Yoakum. ALS. DLC–JKP. Expects that Martin Van Buren will receive little support in Rutherford County because of his stand against Texas annexation. |
| *14 May* | *To Cave Johnson.* |
| *14 May* | *From Hopkins L. Turney.* |
| 15 May | From Julius W. Blackwell. ALS. DLC–JKP. Relates that Martin Van Buren's support in East Tennessee has plummeted since the publication of his letter opposing the annexation of Texas. |
| *15 May* | *To Cave Johnson.* |
| 16 May | From John Blair. ALS. JKP–JKP. Thinks that Martin Van Buren's Texas letter will render his presidential bid unsuccessful. |
| *16 May* | *From Cave Johnson.* |
| 16 May | From A. O. P. Pickens. ALS. DLC–JKP. Solicits a loan to finance his education at Berea Academy. |
| *16 May* | *From Gideon J. Pillow.* |
| 16 May | From Samuel G. Smith. LS. DLC–JKP. Requests support for Emory and Henry College's Hermesian Society, which plans to establish a library independent of the College. |
| 20 May | From George A. Chapman et al. C, copy. DLC–JKP. Invite Polk to a Democratic meeting in Indianapolis, Ind., on June 17, 1844. |
| 20 May | From H. W. Conner et al. C, copy. DLC–JKP. Report proceedings of a pro-annexation meeting recently held in Charleston, S.C. |
| 20 May | From J. G. M. Ramsey. ALS. DLC–JKP. Believes that Martin Van Buren is "gone forever" and that Polk and |

|  | Cass will form the Democratic ticket. |
| [21 May 1844] | From B. M. G. Blackwell. ALS. DLC–JKP. Solicits Polk's assistance in securing anti-Whig documents for use in the coming campaign. |
| *22 May* | *From Gideon J. Pillow.* |
| 23 May | From William T. Brown. ALS. DLC–JKP. Requests documents for use in his forthcoming debate with Leroy Pope on the currency question. |
| *23 May* | *From Samuel H. Laughlin.* |
| 24 May | From J. George Harris. ALS. DLC–JKP. Encloses a letter from Charles G. Greene and predicts that they will see "the effect of his efforts in the National Convention." |
| *24 May* | *From Cave Johnson.* |
| *24 May* | *From Gideon J. Pillow.* |
| 25 May | From Julius W. Blackwell. ALS. DLC–JKP. Relates that he has met with Gideon Pillow and other members of the Tennessee delegation to the Baltimore Convention; expects that Martin Van Buren will be nominated and that John Tyler will be run as a Texas candidate, thus assuring Henry Clay of victory. |
| *25 May* | *From William G. Childress.* |
| 25 May | From John M. Daniel. ALS. DLC–JKP. Seeks Polk's legal assistance. |
| 25 May | From E. G. Eastman. ALS. DLC–JKP. Wishes to consult with Polk on the course of the Democratic Party; writes that William Wallace has been chosen Democratic elector for Tennessee's second congressional district. |
| *25 May* | *From Cave Johnson.* |
| *25 May* | *From Gideon J. Pillow.* |
| 26 May | From James H. Campbell. ALS. DLC–JKP. Wishes Polk to verify the "Go Home, God Damn You!" remark attributed to Henry Clay in a House debate in February 1819 and repeated by Clay, with reference to Polk, on February 6, 1838. |
| *27 May* | *From Cave Johnson.* |
| 28 May | From Julius W. Blackwell. ALS. DLC–JKP. Reports on the first seven presidential ballots taken at the Democratic National Convention; describes "a most disgracefull scene" ignited by the Ohio delegation. |
| 28 May | From William G. Childress. ALS. DLC–JKP. Discusses the balloting at the Democratic National Convention. |
| 28 May | From William Neil. ALS. DLC–JKP. Addressed to Polk and James H. Thomas. Wishes Polk to review the claims of William Aldridge against the heirs of Charles R. Neil. |
| *28 May* | *From Gideon J. Pillow.* |
| 29 May | From Julius W. Blackwell. ALS. DLC–JKP. Informs Polk of his nomination for the presidency. |

| | |
|---|---|
| 29 May | From William G. Childress. ALS. DLC–JKP. Tells of events leading to Polk's nomination. |
| [29 May 1844] | From Granville S. Crockett. ALS. DLC–JKP. States that Polk has been unanimously nominated for the presidency. |
| 29 May | From John W. Davis. ALS. DLC–JKP. Congratulates Polk on his nomination by the Baltimore Convention. |
| *29 May* | *From Benjamin B. French.* |
| 29 May | From E. B. Gaither. ALS. DLC–JKP. Offers Polk congratulations on his presidential nomination. |
| 29 May | From Daniel Gold. ALS. DLC–JKP. Extends congratulations to Polk on his nomination and offers to assist in the coming compaign. |
| 29 May | From William H. Haywood, Jr. ALS. DLC–JKP. Promises to assist Polk in carrying his native state of North Carolina. |
| *29 May* | *From Henry Hubbard et al.* |
| *29 May* | *From Cave Johnson.* |
| *29 May* | *From Gideon J. Pillow.* |
| *29 May* | *From Gideon J. Pillow.* |
| 29 May | From Robert W. Powell. ALS. DLC–JKP. Informs Polk of his victory at Baltimore. |
| 29 May | From Robert Rantoul, Jr. ALS. DLC–JKP. Encloses official notification of Polk's selection as the presidential nominee of the National Democratic Convention meeting in Baltimore. |
| *29 May* | *From Williamson Smith.* |
| 30 May | From Anonymous. L. DLC–JKP. Congratulates Polk on his nomination and pledges the support of Lewis Cass and the people of Michigan for Polk's election. |
| 30 May | From William A. Benjamin. ALS. DLC–JKP. Congratulates Polk on his unanimous nomination. |
| 30 May | From Benjamin A. Bidlack. ALS. DLC–JKP. Pledges support to Polk and "our cause." |
| *30 May* | *From Aaron V. Brown.* |
| 30 May | From Alvin Cullom. ALS. DLC–JKP. Expresses delight with the convention's choice and urges Polk to pledge himself to but a single term. |
| 30 May | From E. S. Davis. ALS. DLC–JKP. Congratulates Polk on his nomination and suggests that a speech by Francis W. Pickens influenced the delegates' choice. |
| 30 May | From Henry Horn. ALS. DLC–JKP. Extends congratulations and predicts that Henry A. P. Muhlenberg, Democratic candidate for governor, and Polk will both carry Pennsylvania in the fall. |
| 30 May | From John K. Kane. ALS. DLC–JKP. Expresses great satisfaction with the convention's choice and urges Polk to assume "a dignified reserve" on the tariff question, |

|              | thus helping the Democratic ticket in Pennsylvania. |
|--------------|-----------------------------------------------------|
| 30 May       | From William Kennedy. ALS. DLC–JKP. Offers congratulations and anticipates Polk's winning Delaware. |
| 30 May       | From John M. Read. ALS. DLC–JKP. Congratulates Polk and praises his nomination, which will help Democrats carry state elections in Pennsylvania. |
| 30 May       | From Peter D. Vroom et al. LS. DLC–JKP. Extend congratulations of the Democratic members of the New Jersey Constitutional Convention. |
| *30 May*     | *From Robert J. Walker.* |
| [31 May 1844] | From Anonymous. L. DLC–JKP. Urges Polk to decline the nomination of the Baltimore Convention. |
| 31 May       | From Samuel P. Caldwell. ALS. DLC–JKP. Wishes Polk to sign a contract for the purchase of a cotton gin from Jacob F. Farrington of Memphis; relates details of a Whig meeting in Memphis on May 29 and 30. |
| *31 May*     | *From Andrew J. Donelson.* |
| *31 May*     | *From Theophilus Fisk.* |
| 31 May       | From Albert Gallup. ALS. DLC–JKP. Congratulates Polk on his nomination and assures him of success in New York. |
| 31 May       | From John Hibler. ALS. DLC–JKP. Seeks information with regard to Tennessee's liability in the fraudulent sale of Morgan County land to Hibler by Charles W. Parks during Polk's governorship. |
| *31 May*     | *From Cave Johnson.* |
| *31 May*     | *From Samuel H. Laughlin.* |
| 31 May       | From Allen McLane. ALS. DLC–JKP. Extends congratulations and declares Delaware's enthusiastic support; inquires if Polk has relatives in Sussex County, Del. |
| 31 May       | From Jesse Miller. ALS. DLC–JKP. Offers congratulations and urges a tenable position on the tariff question, which is essential if the Democrats are to carry Pennsylvania. |
| 31 May       | From Thomas Phillips and William H. Smith. LS. DLC–JKP. Advise Polk that his nomination is well received and volunteer their services as editors of the *Pittsburgh Daily Morning Post*. |
| 31 May       | From Henry Simpson. ALS. DLC–JKP. States that a portrait will be needed and asks if an artist should be sent from Philadelphia. |
| 31 May       | From Robert J. Walker. ALS. DLC–JKP. Advises that George M. Dallas has accepted the Baltimore Convention's vice-presidential nomination. |
| 1 June       | From John Adams. ALS. DLC–JKP. Recalls Polk's friendship while serving as a member of Congress (from New York) and pledges his support in the coming election. |

1 June      From Aaron V. Brown. ALS. DLC–JKP. Urges Polk to send an "elegant" daguerreotype of himself for use in the campaign.

1 June      From Aaron V. Brown. ALS. DLC–JKP. Suggests that Polk support "a Tariff for revenue with incidental protection."

1 June      From John Cole. ALS. DLC–JKP. Requests that Polk sit for a full-length portrait and reports that after holding an "enthusiastic" meeting in front of Independence Hall, a crowd of 6,000 had marched to (George M.) Dallas' residence to hear his response to their Polk-Dallas endorsement.

1 June      From William Huffington. ALS. DLC–JKP. Asks if Polk were born in Delaware and expresses hope for carrying that state.

*1 June*      *From Cave Johnson.*

1 June      From Zadock Pratt. ALS. DLC–JKP. Congratulates Polk upon his nomination and assures him of New York's support.

*1 June*      *From John Slidell.*

1 June      From John Windt et al. CS. DLC–JKP. Repeat their prior request for Polk's views on a proposal to end the sale of public land, a tenet of the New York Central Committee of the National Reform Association.

*1 June*      *From Fernando Wood.*

2 June      From John Fairfield. ALS. DLC–JKP. Expresses pleasure that Polk's nomination will unite the party and assure victory for the ticket in all parts of the country, including the state of Maine.

*2 June*      *From Cave Johnson.*

2 June      From Kenedy Lonergan. ALS. DLC–JKP. Relates positive reactions in Cincinnati to Polk's nomination and states that the great majority of voters are in favor of annexing Texas.

*2 June*      *From Gideon J. Pillow.*

*2 June*      *From Silas Wright, Jr.*

3 June      From Mark Alexander. ALS. DLC–JKP. Observes that Polk's nomination has unified the party in the southern states, including Virginia, where (John) Tyler has no real party support.

*3 June*      *From Robert Armstrong.*

3 June      From William C. Bouck. ALS. DLC–JKP. Congratulates Polk on receiving the nomination and assures him that New York will give "cordial support" to the ticket.

3 June      From James Graham Clinton. ALS. DLC–JKP. Reports positive response to Polk's nomination from different parts of New York, where the ticket "is *not only safe* there

|  | but will cause a greater majority than any other named." |
| *3 June* | *From Granville S. Crockett.* |
| [3 June 1844] | From West H. Humphreys. ALS. DLC–JKP. Urges Polk to come to Nashville and advise party leaders how to respond to convention results when they are known. |
| 3 June | From Wilie Ledbetter. ALS. DLC–JKP. Requests information concerning his suit in the Maury County Court. |
| *3 June* | *From Isaac G. McKinley.* |
| *3 June* | *From Henry A. P. Muhlenberg.* |
| 3 June | From Daniel Sheffer. ALS. DLC–JKP. Extends congratulations and assurances of support among Democrats in the locality of York Springs, Penn. |
| *3 June* | *From Aaron Vanderpoel.* |
| *4 June* | *From Robert Armstrong.* |
| 4 June | From C. H. Brackette. ALS. DLC–JKP. Assures Polk of Democratic support in Louisville, Ky. |
| *4 June* | *From William E. Cramer.* |
| 4 June | From Sutherland S. Southworth. ALS. DLC–JKP. Offers to assist with editorial labors at the *Nashville Union.* |
| 4 June | From Peter D. Vroom, S. G. Potts, and Joseph E. Edsall. LS. DLC–JKP. Request Polk's views on tariffs, a question of great concern in New Jersey. |
| 4 June | From George White. ALS. DLC–JKP. Assures Polk of support in Pennsylvania and requests copies of Polk's speeches on the tariff question. |
| *5 June* | *From Robert Armstrong.* |
| 5 June | From Julius W. Blackwell. ALS. DLC–JKP. Reports favorable reactions in Washington City to Polk's nomination. |
| *5 June* | *From J. George Harris.* |
| 5 June | From Cave Johnson. ALS. DLC–JKP. Encloses letter to Polk from William E. Cramer, June 4, 1844, and relates that Cramer's father, John, expects Polk to carry New York by a larger margin than Martin Van Buren might have received. |
| 5 June | From John K. Kane. ALS. DLC–JKP. Solicits biographical sketch from Polk for publication in pamphlet form. |
| 5 June | From John McKeon. ALS. DLC–JKP. Congratulates Polk on the reception of his nomination by the citizens of New York City; relates that "the monster meeting" was the largest ever assembled in that city. |
| 5 June | From Thomas Maxwell. ALS. DLC–JKP. Predicts that Polk will carry New York and inquires how the Tennessee vote will go. |
| *5 June* | *From Thomas P. Moore.* |
| *5 June* | *From James M. Porter.* |
| 5 June | From Robert W. Powell. ALS. DLC–JKP. Reports that during his travels home to Tennessee he has spoken at a |

Democratic meeting in Philadelphia and has attended one in New York City, the size of which gathering is thought to be the largest in recent years.

5 June From Romulus M. Saunders. ALS. DLC–JKP. Observes that fellow members of Congress from Pennsylvania and Virginia are supportive of Polk's nomination; promises that he will arrange a mass meeting in July for friends in Charlotte, N.C.

5 June From Henry Slicer. ALS. DLC–JKP. States that his personal acquaintance with Polk has evoked numerous inquiries by fellow delegates presently attending the Methodist General Conference, which has been in session in New York City for the past month.

5 June From John R. Thomson and Richard P. Thompson. LS. DLC–JKP. Believe that New Jersey Democrats will rally to Polk's support; forward letter of May 30, 1844, from Peter D. Vroom to Polk.

5 June From Fernando Wood. ALS. DLC–JKP. Discusses plans for dividing New York into districts and promises to canvass the western counties in September.

5 June From A. M. Young. ALS. DLC–JKP. Expects to leave Young's Point, La., for a visit to Washington City and New York City; solicits letters of introduction to some of Polk's friends in the East.

[6 June 1844] From Robert Armstrong. ALS. DLC–JKP. Suggests that Polk come to Nashville on Saturday for private meetings and that he come for a more public occasion at a later date.

6 June From Aaron V. Brown. ALS. DLC–JKP. Observes that Francis W. Pickens and others from South Carolina are "wheeling into line" behind Polk's candidacy; regrets that he, Cave Johnson, and Andrew Johnson were unable to participate in the House debate on the appropriations bill.

6 June From Reuben Chapman. ALS. DLC–JKP. Anticipates that Polk will carry Alabama by a large majority and notes that the Whig congressmen from Tennessee are so alarmed that "they back out today from bets they would have jumped at last week."

*6 June* *From Edwin Croswell.*

6 June From Thomas L. Halbach. ALS. DLC–JKP. Requests money from Polk and reports strong support in Berks County, Penn.

6 June From William Holdridge. ALS. DLC–JKP. Solicits high position in the New York City customs house.

6 June From Leonard Jarvis. ALS. DLC–JKP. States that in Maine the Whigs are slandering Polk's name with the

charge of his being a duelist; thinks that Polk's nomination has unified the party to such extent as to render Maine "secure" for the national ticket.

6 June  From John Ledyard et al. LS. DLC–JKP. Report that a "large and enthusiastic" meeting held in Newburgh, N.Y., has endorsed the national ticket.

6 June  From R. B. Longaker et al. C, copy. DLC–JKP. Invite Polk to attend a Montgomery County celebration scheduled for July 4th in Crooked Hill, Penn.

6 June  From Leonard Maison. ALS. DLC–JKP. Predicts that the Democratic ticket will carry New York by 15,000 votes unless "the abolitionists abandon their candidate and unite upon Mr. Clay"; reports that Poughkeepsie Democrats held their largest meeting ever and endorsed Polk's nomination.

6 June  From Thomas K. Price. ALS. DLC–JKP. Pledges his vote and influence among fellow businessmen of New Orleans, La.

6 June  From E. Worrell. ALS. DLC–JKP. Communicates endorsement of the Democratic Association of Wilmington, Del.; asserts that party unity in Delaware has not been so complete since the presidency of Andrew Jackson.

7 June  From Samuel P. Caldwell. ALS. DLC–JKP. States that Whigs in Memphis are "astounded" at Polk's nomination and are afraid of losing Tennessee.

7 June  From Robert J. Chester. ALS. DLC–JKP. Reports much "shouting for Polk" in Jackson, Tenn.

7 June  From William G. Childress. ALS. DLC–JKP. States that northern political friends request a sketch of Polk's life and urge the nominee to make a tour through their section of the country.

*7 June*  *From Philemon Dickerson.*

7 June  From William C. Dunlap. ALS. DLC–JKP. States that Polk's nomination was received "with joy & *enthusiasm*" in Raleigh, Tenn.

7 June  From John Hamm. ALS. DLC–JKP. Expects Ohio to support Texas annexation and the Democratic national ticket.

7 June  From Littleton Kirkpatrick. ALS. DLC–JKP. Extends congratulations and encloses letter of June 5, 1844, from John R. Thomson and Richard P. Thompson to Polk.

*7 June*  *From Samuel H. Laughlin.*

7 June  From Medicus A. Long. ALS. DLC–JKP. Extends congratulations and decries the corrupt and "wretched set of officers" governing the Territory of Florida.

*7 June*  *From Lucius Lyon.*

7 June  From Stephen C. Pavatt. ALS. DLC–JKP. Recounts the excitement that Polk's nomination has generated among

Democrats of Huntingdon, Tenn.

7 June　　From Thomas Phillips and William H. Smith. LS. DLC–JKP. Report great anxiety among Pennsylvania Demo crats over Polk's tariff views; request a statement on the question of tariffs; and promise to send copies of their newspaper, the *Pittsburgh Daily Morning Post.*

7 June　　From Richard Rush. ALS. DLC–JKP. Offers congratulations and predicts success in Pennsylvania.

7 June　　From Williamson Smith. ALS. DLC–JKP. Reports from Washington City that Democrats of all persuasions are eager to claim Polk as one of their own; believes that some of Martin Van Buren's closest friends are "very much dissatisfied," including Thomas Hart Benton and Silas Wright, Jr.; and warns that it would be "dangerous" to discard the old Democratic Party of the North in favor of John C. Calhoun's friends in the South.

*7 June　　From Jacob Thompson.*

*8 June　　From William H. Babbit.*

*8 June　　From John Catron.*

*8 June　　From William M. Gwin.*

8 June　　From George H. Hickman.　ALS. DLC–JKP. Encloses twelve copies of a brief sketch of Polk's life, the preparation of which publication was arranged by Baltimore Democrats.

8 June　　From Elijah Hise. ALS. DLC–JKP. Urges that the Tennessee Whig leadership be coaxed into switching parties; suggests that many of the Whig newspapers could be won over for a price; and states that he will "battle gallantly for the cause" in Kentucky.

*8 June　　To Charles J. Ingersoll.*

8 June　　From Abijah Ingraham.　ALS. DLC–JKP. Encloses two tracts on the tariff question and solicits any printed document containing Polk's views on that important issue.

8 June　　From Joseph W. Jackson. ALS. DLC–JKP. Encloses a recent issue of the *Savannah Georgian,* which contains proceedings of a Chatham County meeting at which Polk's nomination was ratified. (Enclosure not found.)

*8 June　　To Cave Johnson.*

*8 June　　To John K. Kane.*

8 June　　From William M. Smyth. ALS. DLC–JKP. Relates that his newspaper, the Jackson *Southern Reformer,* has endorsed Polk's candidacy and that Mississippi will give him a larger vote than the state has ever given in a presidential contest.

*8 June　　To Robert J. Walker.*

8 June　　From Aaron Ward. ALS. DLC–JKP. Extends congratulations and assurances that Polk will carry Westchester

|  | County, N.Y., as well as the state at large. |
|---|---|
| *9 June* | *From Robert Armstrong.* |
| 9 June | From John B. Butler. ALS. DLC–JKP. States that the tariff question requires "caution" in Pennsylvania and relates that Polk's nomination received "enthusiastic" support at a recent Democratic meeting in Pittsburgh. |
| 9 June | From John F. H. Claiborne. ALS. DLC–JKP. Promises to write favorable editorials for the Natchez *Mississippi Free Trader* and *Vicksburg Sentinel* during the campaign. |
| 9 June | From William L. D. Ewing. ALS. DLC–JKP. Encloses congratulatory letter from Thomas Ford, governor of Illinois, and from leading Democratic friends in Springfield. |
| 9 June | From James Robinson. ALS. DLC–JKP. Doubts that Tennessee Democrats could have carried the state for Martin Van Buren and predicts that Tipton County will support Polk. |
| *9 June* | *From Francis O. J. Smith.* |
| 10 June | From Anonymous. L. DLC–JKP. Predicts victory for Polk in the election; suggests that Polk nominate Cave Johnson to be his secretary of the navy. |
| 10 June | From J. Barnard. ALS. DLC–JKP. Details arrangements with Washington B. Cooper of Nashville to paint a full-length portrait of Polk. |
| *10 June* | *From John Catron.* |
| 10 June | From Thomas Ford et al. LS. DLC–JKP. Extend congratulations and give assurances of a victory in Illinois. |
| 10 June | From J. George Harris. ALS. DLC–JKP. Expresses pleasure on learning from Robert Armstrong that Polk plans to visit his Nashville friends "in a quiet way" on Wednesday or Thursday. |
| *10 June* | *From Cave Johnson.* |
| 10 June | From Samuel H. Laughlin. ALS. DLC–JKP. Urges Polk to be guarded in his comments on internal improvements and protection; discusses personnel matters relating to the *Nashville Union;* and argues against the idea of running a joint Tyler-Polk ticket in each state, leaving the voter to make his preference. |
| 10 June | From Rufus McIntyre. ALS. DLC–JKP. Offers his personal support; commends Polk's straightforward stand on the Texas question; and gives assurances that Maine Democrats are unified in support of the ticket. |
| *10 June* | *From John I. Mumford.* |
| 10 June | From Robert Orr et al. LS. DLC–JKP. Invite Polk to attend a public July 4th celebration in Steubenville, Ohio. |
| 10 June | From Henry Simpson. ALS. DLC–JKP. Forwards Polk a copy of plans for organizing Democratic associations in every county in Pennsylvania. |

| | |
|---|---|
| 10 June | From D. Solomon. ALS. DLC–JKP. Encloses a Mobile newspaper reporting Polk's endorsement by Mobile County Democrats. (Enclosure not found.) |
| 11 June | From Thomas B. Claiborne. ALS. DLC–JKP. Extends congratulations; reports positive reactions in Trenton, Tenn.; and inquires about prospects in the North. |
| 11 June | From David T. Disney. ALS. DLC–JKP. Relates that Polk's prospects in Ohio are promising and encloses a copy of the *Cincinnati Enquirer* containing "the proceedings of the ratification meeting in this place." (Enclosure not found.) |
| [11 June 1844] | From William Fitzgerald. ALS. DLC–JKP. States that Polk's nomination "has infused new life & vigor into our party" in Paris, Tenn.; urges that the *Nashville Union* stress the Texas annexation issue. |
| 11 June | From William C. Hazen. ALS. DLC–JKP. Reports favorable response throughout Tipton County, Tenn., to Polk's nomination. |
| 11 June | From Adam Huntsman. ALS. DLC–JKP. Anticipates a close electoral contest in Tennessee's Western District; details plans to put Thomas Ewell and Levin H. Coe to work on the campaign trail. |
| *11 June* | *From Samuel H. Laughlin.* |
| 11 June | From William M. Lowry. ALS. DLC–JKP. Rejoices that Polk's nomination and the Texas question will lead Democrats to victory in Greene County, in Tennessee, and in the Union. |
| 11 June | From H. B. Mathews. ALS. DLC–JKP. Predicts that Fulton and Hamilton counties in New York will give Polk a 150 vote majority in the fall. |
| *11 June* | *From John E. Taliaferro.* |
| *11 June* | *From Henry Welsh.* |
| 11 June | From John A. Wilcox. ALS. DLC–JKP. Relates that Democrats in Aberdeen, Miss., are pleased with Polk's nomination and requests that copies of Polk's congressional speeches be sent. |
| *11 June* | *From Austin E. Wing.* |
| 12 June | From F. Bosworth. ALS. DLC–JKP. Assures Polk of victory in Carroll Parish, La. |
| 12 June | From Zadoc Casey. ALS. DLC–JKP. States that on his trip from Illinois to New York City he did not meet a single Democrat who was not enthusiastic about Polk's nomination; predicts that Polk will carry Illinois. |
| *12 June* | *From Auguste D'Avezac.* |
| *12 June* | *From John C. Edwards.* |
| 12 June | From Thomas Fletcher. ALS. DLC–JKP. Forecasts that Polk will carry Mississippi and solicits Polk's views on |

state banking.

12 June    From Josephus C. Guild. ALS. DLC–JKP. Urges that the Texas annexation question be stressed in the forthcoming campaign; regrets that he may be unable to attend the next district convention, which will meet in Clarksville, Tenn., on June 16.

*12 June*    *To Henry Hubbard et al.*

12 June    From William L. May. ALS. DLC–JKP. Assures Polk of strong support in Peoria and throughout Illinois; requests biographical information for campaign purposes.

12 June    From Henry W. Phillips. ALS. DLC–JKP. Urges Polk, with whom he has no personal acquaintance, to support a national rather than sectional tariff policy; believes that if Polk takes a protectionist stand, the Whigs can win only eight states: Massachusetts, Vermont, Rhode Island, Connecticut, Delaware, Maryland, Ohio, and Kentucky.

12 June    From John Tomlin. ALS. DLC–JKP. States that news of Polk's nomination has given new spirit to the Democrats of Jackson, Tenn.

12 June    From G. Vogelsung. ALS. DLC–JKP. Encloses copies of his essays advocating an international system of measures, weights, and coins. (Enclosure not found.)

*12 June*    *From Alexander Walker.*

*12 June*    *From Hendrick B. Wright.*

*12 June*    *To Silas Wright, Jr.*

*13 June*    *From John T. Andrews.*

13 June    From B. F. Bussey. L, copy. DLC–JKP. Inquires about the revolutionary war service of Polk's grandfather, Ezekiel Polk. Polk's AES states that he sent the original copy of Bussey's letter to J. G. M. Ramsey on July 4, 1844, with a request that Ramsey supply the information requested.

*13 June*    *From Clement C. Clay.*

13 June    From W. R. Frink. ALS. DLC–JKP. Requests that during Polk's present stay in Nashville he sit for a *"Daguerrotype* likeness" to be made at the writer's rooms on Union Street.

13 June    From Ransom H. Gillet. ALS. DLC–JKP. Encloses copy of his speech to the Democratic Association of Ogdensburgh, N.Y.; pledges his strong support; and rejoices at the prospect of Polk's election.

13 June    From Eli Harris. ALS. DLC–JKP. States that Democrats in Carroll Parish, La., hail Polk's nomination as "a sure sign of success."

*13 June*    *From Cave Johnson.*

13 June    From Sidney C. Posey. ALS. DLC–JKP. Reports great enthusiasm for Polk in Florence, Ala.

*13 June*    *From Robert W. Powell.*

14 June    From J. D. Blair et al. LS. DLC–JKP. Advise Polk on behalf of the Democratic Association of Boonville, Mo., that "a state convention of ratification will be held at this place on the 17th of next month."

*14 June*    *From Andrew J. Donelson.*

14 June    From William L. D. Ewing. ALS. DLC–JKP. Predicts large majority for Polk in Illinois; encloses an address on Texas issued by a public meeting held recently in Springfield. (Enclosure not found.)

*14 June*    *From Nathaniel W. Fletcher.*

14 June    From Landon C. Haynes. ALS. DLC–JKP. Reports strong support for Polk in Jonesboro and Greeneville, Tenn.; notes numerous defections from Whig ranks in East Tennessee.

*14 June*    *From Sackfield Maclin.*

14 June    From J. G. M. Ramsey. ALS. DLC–JKP. Writes from Mecklenburg, Tenn., that Polk's nomination has brought new life to Democrats in East Tennessee; discusses initiatives to be taken in launching the canvass in his part of the state as well as in the western part of North Carolina.

14 June    From Charles S. Wallach. ALS. DLC–JKP. Informs Polk that a group of young Democrats in Washington City have formed an association called the "Young Hickory Club" and that members of same have endorsed Polk's candidacy even though as residents of the District of Columbia they will not be able to vote in the election.

15 June    From William J. Alexander et al. LS. DLC–JKP. Solicit Polk's presence at a public barbecue to be held in honor of his nomination and to be met in Charlotte, N.C., on July 23.

15 June    From B. F. Bosworth. ALS. DLC–JKP. Requests that Polk send information on Henry Clay's early stand against preemption; advises that energetic Democrats can carry Carroll Parish, La.

15 June    From G. W. Graham et al. C. DLC–JKP. Invite Polk to attend a military encampment in Union County, Penn., on August 27.

15 June    From John W. Nesbitt et al. LS. DLC–JKP. Extend Polk an invitation to attend a July 4th celebration to be held in Philadelphia by Democrats of Pennsylvania's First Congressional District.

15 June    From John Norvell. ALS. DLC–JKP. Relates that the Democratic Association of Detroit, Mich., met yesterday and endorsed Polk's nomination; states that Lewis Cass attended the "immense gathering" and pledged his support for the ticket.

*15 June*    *From Bromfield Ridley.*

| | |
|---|---|
| 15 June | From Romulus M. Saunders. ALS. DLC–JKP. Encloses endorsement resolution passed by a Convention of North Carolina Democrats. (Enclosure not found.) |
| *15 June* | *From Collin S. Tarpley.* |
| 15 June | From Collin S. Tarpley. ALS. DLC–JKP. Introduces A. M. Foote of Mississippi. |
| 15 June | From Thomas H. Williams. ALS. DLC–JKP. Assures Polk that Mississippi will vote Democratic in the fall and pledges his active participation in the canvass. |
| 16 June | From R. M. Boyers. ALS. DLC–JKP. Offers services of his factorage firm, Boyers, Breedlove & Co. of New Orleans. |
| [16 June 1844] | From David Craighead. ALS, fragment. DLC–JKP. Outlines his views on the tariff question and urges Polk's caution on this and other public issues. |
| 16 June | From William Hawk. ALS. DLC–JKP. Invites Polk to attend a barbecue to be held in his honor at Houston in Wayne County, Tenn., in July or August. |
| *16 June* | *From Andrew A. Kincannon.* |
| 17 June | From James Davis et al. LS. DLC–JKP. Invite Polk to attend a mass meeting at Lafayette, Ind., on July 27. (In private note written on separate sheet, Davis predicts that Polk's presence would attract a crowd of twenty or thirty thousand citizens.) |
| 17 June | From Gideon B. Frierson. ALS. DLC–JKP. Introduces Willis Crenshaw, a neighbor from Livingston, Ala. |
| *17 June* | *From John Galbraith.* |
| *17 June* | *From Henry Hubbard.* |
| 17 June | From E. P. Palmer et al. LS. DLC–JKP. Inform Polk of his election to honorary membership in the Phi Kappa Society of Franklin College, located in Athens, Ga. |
| 17 June | From John W. Ritenour. ALS. DLC–JKP. States that his fellow citizens of Fayette County, Penn., favor "a judicious tariff"; solicits Polk's views on the subject. |
| 17 June | From Henry Schects et al. LS. DLC–JKP. Invite Polk to attend a "Harvest Home" celebration in Montgomery County, Penn., on July 27. |
| 17 June | From James H. Stark et al. LS. DLC–JKP. Invite Polk to attend a mass meeting of Georgia citizens at Indian Springs in Butts County on July 25. |
| 18 June | From William Bobbitt. ALS. DLC–JKP. Assures Polk that his nomination "was cheering to the Democracy of Mississippi." |
| 18 June | From John B. Bratton et al. LS. DLC–JKP. Tell of Polk's endorsement by "an immense and enthusiastic assemblage" of Democrats who met in Harrisburg, Penn., on June 4; invite Polk to visit their state capital at his convenience. |

| | |
|---|---|
| 18 June | From Granville H. Frazer. ALS. DLC–JKP. Offers the use of his collection of documents relating to American diplomatic history; states that he resides in Bedford County, Tenn. |
| 18 June | From David C. Glenn. ALS. DLC–JKP. Reports that in Holly Springs, Miss., Polk's nomination has "cured all divisions" among Democrats and assures prostration of the opposition party. |
| *18 June* | *From Charles J. Ingersoll.* |
| *18 June* | *From Charles J. Ingersoll.* |
| *18 June* | *From Julius P. B. MacCabe.* |
| 18 June | From James McKisick. ALS. DLC–JKP. Reports from Little Rock that the northwestern part of Arkansas, which is largely settled by former Tennesseans, will give Polk large majorities in the fall election; expects that Archibald Yell will win his race for a seat in the U.S. House. |
| 18 June | From William H. Noble. ALS. DLC–JKP. Recounts serving with Polk in Congress and reports strong support for the ticket in Cayuga County, N.Y. |
| *18 June* | *From Joseph C. Potts.* |
| 18 June | From James L. Totten. ALS. DLC–JKP. Reports strong support for Polk in Holly Springs and the northern counties of Mississippi. |
| *18 June* | *From Robert J. Walker.* |
| *19 June* | *To John K. Kane.* |
| *19 June* | *To John K. Kane.* |
| 19 June | From John C. Weber. ALS. DLC–JKP. Writes in behalf of the German Democratic Hickory Club of Columbus, Ohio, and conveys the membership's strong endorsement in the coming election. |
| 20 June | From Anonymous. LS. DLC–JKP. Predicts Polk's defeat in the presidential contest and signs letter, "A Young Whig." |
| 20 June | From Miles N. Carpenter et al. L. DLC–JKP. Invite Polk to attend an Independence Day celebration sponsored by the Democratic citizens of Philadelphia and scheduled to begin at nine o'clock in Independence Square. |
| 20 June | From Thomas Ewell. ALS. DLC–JKP. Reports that the young Democrats of Jackson, Tenn., have formed an association and have endorsed Polk's nomination with great enthusiasm. |
| *20 June* | *From William Hendricks.* |
| 20 June | From M. P. Jarnagin. ALS. DLC–JKP. Extends Polk an honorary membership in the Beth-Hacma Ve-Bereth Society of Maryville College. |
| 20 June | From Lucius Lyon. ALS. DLC–JKP. Writes from Washington City that recent accounts from Michigan indicate |

|  | that the "Peninsula State" is safe for Polk and Dallas. |
| *20 June* | *From Jesse Miller.* |
| 20 June | From David B. Molloy. ALS. DLC–JKP. Encloses an account of a June 17 meeting of Democrats in Holly Springs, Miss.; reports that party spirit has not been so high since 1828. (Enclosure not found.) |
| 20 June | From Thomas P. Moore et al. L. DLC–JKP. Invite Polk to attend a mass meeting of the Kentucky Democracy, which will gather in Harrodsburg on July 12 and 13. |
| 21 June | To William C. Bouck. ALS. MB. Acknowledges with thanks Bouck's congratulatory letter of June 3rd. |
| *21 June* | *From Cave Johnson.* |
| *21 June* | *From Archibald Yell.* |
| 22 June | From William J. Alexander. ALS. DLC–JKP. Urges Polk to attend a mass meeting to be held on July 23 in Charlotte, N.C. |
| 22 June | From Montgomery Chambers. ALS. DLC–JKP. States that the register of Cannon County, Tenn., cannot find the records of his land purchase; requests that Polk certify whether or not as governor he executed a deed on the disputed 5,000 acres. |
| *22 June* | *From Leonard P. Cheatham.* |
| 22 June | From John Horn et al. C, copy. DLC–JKP. Invite Polk to attend a public dinner to be held on July 4 in Philadelphia. |
| *22 June* | *From John K. Kane.* |
| 22 June | From John J. Nicholson. ALS. DLC–JKP. Encloses copy of the *Southern Quarterly Review* for October, 1843; singles out the article on "The Maritime Interests of the South and West" for Polk's special consideration. (Enclosure not found.) |
| 23 June | From Amos David. ALS. DLC–JKP. Urges Polk to decline the presidential nomination; argues that only Lewis Cass can defeat Henry Clay. |
| 24 June | From A. Cathey. ALS. DLC–JKP. Requests Polk's assistance with debt collections in Maury County. |
| *24 June* | *To Cave Johnson.* |
| 24 June | From Wilson McCandless et al. C, copy. DLC–JKP. Invite Polk to attend a July 4th celebration sponsored by the Democracy of Allegheny County, Penn. |
| 24 June | From Thomas S. Matthews. ALS. DLC–JKP. Relates that the Whig press in Cincinnati has misled the public with regard to Polk's stand on the tariff question; solicits such documents or explanations as may be helpful in countering opposition claims. |
| *24 June* | *From J. G. M. Ramsey.* |
| 24 June | From Joseph Strong. ALS. DLC–JKP. Offers his support |

in Rochester, N.Y., for the coming campaign; explains his past ties with the Tyler administration.

25 *June*    *From Robert Armstrong.*

25 June    From William P. Bradburn. ALS. DLC–JKP. Takes great satisfaction in learning of Polk's nomination and recounts his personal history since resigning from the navy in 1836.

25 June    From John C. Brodhead. ALS. DLC–JKP. Relates political news of Ulster County, N.Y.

25 June    From Lewis Carr et al. LS. DLC–JKP. Extend invitation to a public dinner to be held on July 4 in the Kensington district of Philadelphia.

25 June    From John W. Cook. ALS. DLC–JKP. Discusses Whig convention held on June 20 in Hopkinsville, Ky.; thinks that Clay's letter opposing the immediate annexation of Texas "was written with an eye to the abolition vote."

25 *June*    *From J. George Harris.*

25 June    From John Stites et al. LS. DLC–JKP. Invite Polk to attend a Democratic meeting on July 11 in Hopkinsville, Ky.

25 *June*    *From Richard M. Woods.*

26 June    From Benjamin E. Carpenter et al. LS. DLC–JKP. Invite Polk to attend a July 4th festival to be held by the Democracy of Philadelphia.

26 *June*    *From George M. Dallas.*

26 *June*    *To Andrew J. Donelson.*

26 June    From John W. Fokney et al. LS. DLC–JKP. Invite Polk to attend a July 4th gathering of Democrats in Lancaster, Penn.

26 June    From J. B. Lamb. ALS. DLC–JKP. Reports allegations by Whigs in Randolph, Tenn., that Polk had opposed congressional relief to the poor residing in Georgetown, D.C., in the winter of 1831.

27 June    From Joel Branham. ALS. DLC–JKP. Solicits appointment as superintendent of the branch mint at Dahlonega, Ga.

27 *June*    *From J. George Harris.*

27 June    From Lucius C. Lamar et al. LS. DLC–JKP. Inform Polk that he has been elected to honorary membership in the Phi Gamma Society of Emory College in Oxford, Ga.

27 June    From William D. Moseley. ALS. DLC–JKP. Writes from Monticello, Fla., of his fear that Henry Clay's election would lead to the disunion of the states.

27 June    From Levi D. Slamm. ALS. DLC–JKP. States that Polk's prospects in New York City are promising.

28 *June*    *From Robert Armstrong.*

28 *June*    *From John H. Cook.*

| | |
|---|---|
| *28 June* | *From J. George Harris.* |
| 28 June | From William H. Haywood, Jr.  ALS. DLC–JKP. Reports George E. Badger's charges that Polk's grandfather, Ezekiel Polk, had taken protection from the British during the revolution. |
| *28 June* | *From Cave Johnson.* |
| 28 June | From Milton S. Kidd. ALS. DLC–JKP. Solicits account of Polk's services as governor of Tennessee for use in answering the Whigs of Cecil County, Md. |
| *28 June* | *From Samuel H. Laughlin.* |
| *28 June* | *From William L. Marcy.* |
| 28 June | From William A. Simmons et al. LS. DLC–JKP. Inform Polk that he has been elected to honorary membership in the Phi Gamma Society of Emory College in Oxford, Ga. |
| [28 June 1844] | From William Tyack. ALS. DLC–JKP. Pledges his campaign efforts in New York and requests biographical information. |
| *29 June* | *From J. George Harris.* |
| 29 June | From Abner Holliday. ALS. DLC–JKP. Extends congratulations and recalls hearing Polk argue a case in Columbia some twenty-four years earlier. |
| *29 June* | *From Andrew Jackson.* |
| *29 June* | *From John K. Kane.* |
| *30 June* | *From Robert Armstrong.* |
| 30 June | From Samuel Martin. ALS. DLC–JKP. Reviews political issues past and current. |
| [July 1844] | From E. Campbell et al. LS. DLC–JKP. Invite Polk to attend a Texas annexation dinner on July 31 at Cochran's Spring in Marshall County, Tenn. |
| 1 July | From John Anderson. ALS. DLC–JKP. Expects victory in Maine and warns against misrepresentation of Polk's tariff views. |
| *1 July* | *From Andrew J. Donelson.* |
| 1 July | From Bernard Fauth. ALS. DLC–JKP. Writes from Portsmouth, Va., that party dissensions "will soon be healed" and that Polk's victory appears certain if not "frustrated by the friends of the Present incumbent." |
| *1 July* | *From Benjamin B. French.* |
| 1 July | From Turley Hopper. ALS. DLC–JKP. Requests extension on the repayment of his note. |
| *1 July* | *To Cave Johnson.* |
| 1 July | From Edward Jones. ALS. DLC–JKP. Writes from Shropshire, England, and solicits Polk's assistance in contacting a former acquaintance, Thomas Gross, with whom he had sailed on the American brig, *Mary*. |
| 2 July | To William J. Alexander et al. L, copy. DLC–JKP. Declines committee's invitation of June 15, 1844, to attend |

a public dinner to be given on July 23 at Charlotte, N.C.

2 July    From Julius W. Blackwell. ALS. DLC–JKP. Reports that on his return from the late session of Congress, he learned from Democrats in Virginia and North Carolina that "the signs were right" for victory in November; thinks that Polk will carry Tennessee's Third Congressional District.

2 July    From William C. Bouck. ALS. DLC–JKP. Urges Polk to visit New York in July or August and to treat the tariff and Texas questions with caution.

[2 July 1844]    From John Catron. ALS. DLC–JKP. Details treatment administered to Elias' sick horse; observes among Nashville Whigs a lack of warmth for Henry Clay's candidacy.

2 July    From John P. Chester. ALS. DLC–JKP. Reports plans for a mass meeting of Democrats scheduled for July 4 in Jonesboro, Tenn.

2 July    To James Davis et al. L, copy. DLC–JKP. Declines invitation to attend on July 27 a meeting of Democratic citizens at Lafayette, Ind.

2 July    From Cave Johnson. ALS. DLC–JKP. Sends copy of a speech by Ransom H. Gillet of New York; mentions Democratic meeting of July 1 in Montgomery County, Tenn.; and expresses satisfaction with Democratic efforts in Tennessee's Ninth Congressional District. (Enclosure not found.)

*2 July*    *From John K. Kane.*
*2 July*    *From Gideon J. Pillow.*
3 July    From Alvin W. Bills. ALS. DLC–JKP. Offers congratulations to his boyhood friend and discusses political affairs in Bourbon County, Ky.

3 July    To John B. Bratton et al. L, copy. DLC–JKP. Declines invitation to visit Harrisburg, Penn., during the presidential campaign.

[3 July 1844]    From Aaron V. Brown. ALS. DLC–JKP. Tells of his verbal exchange with John Bell over the Texas question, which was debated by Bell and Hopkins L. Turney at a recent public meeting in Pulaski, Tenn.

3 July    From James Garland. ALS. DLC–JKP. Predicts Polk's victory in Virginia and requests literature with which to repel Whig allegations against Polk.

*3 July*    *From William Kennon, Jr., et al.*
*3 July*    *To Jesse Miller.*
3 July    To Henry Schects et al. ALS, copy. DLC–JKP. Declines invitation to attend a "Harvest Home" celebration to be held on July 27 for citizens of Montgomery County, Penn.

3 July    From James Ross Snowden. ALS. DLC–JKP. States that he has addressed enthusiastic meetings in Venango, Mercer, and Crawford counties, Penn.

| | |
|---|---|
| 3 July | From John Addison Thomas. ALS. DLC–JKP. Reports that James T. Armstrong has failed in his studies at the United States Military Academy at West Point. |
| 4 July | From Peter Adams et al. LS. DLC–JKP. Endorse Polk's position on Texas annexation, provided that this course be followed with "strict Neutrality towards contending foreign powers" and that the abolition of slavery be included in the terms of admission. (Enclosed in Peter Adams to Polk, August 22, 1844.) |
| 4 July | To Zadok Casey. ALS. In private hands. Acknowledges receipt of Casey's letter of June 12. |
| 4 July | From John A. Donohoo. ALS. DLC–JKP. Sends Polk a sample lapel pin, some two thousand of which he has distributed to Democrats in Washington City. |
| 4 July | From John P. Heiss. ALS. DLC–JKP. Presents to Polk a miniature likeness on satin, "of our next President." |
| 4 July | To William Hendricks. ALS. InHi. Acknowledges receipt of Hendricks' letter of June 20 with its enclosed proceedings of a recent public meeting in Madison, Ind. |
| 4 July | From James Henry. ALS. DLC–JKP. Communicates extended proposal for a new national banking scheme based on retrenchment of government expenditures; requests that Polk's response be directed to Maryville, Tenn. |
| *4 July* | *From Dutee J. Pearce.* |
| *4 July* | *To Francis O. J. Smith.* |
| *4 July* | *From Sutherland S. Southworth.* |
| 4 July | To Aaron Ward. ALS. MB. Acknowledges with thanks Ward's congratulatory letter of June 8. |
| *5 July* | *From Robert Armstrong.* |
| 5 July | From John M. Bass. ALS. DLC–JKP. Acknowledges payment of Polk's note for $400 held by the Union Bank of Tennessee. |
| *5 July* | *From Arnold S. Harris.* |
| *5 July* | *From Samuel H. Laughlin.* |
| 5 July | From William Nichol. ALS. DLC–JKP. Returns cancelled notes previously held by the Bank of Tennessee. (Enclosures not identified; endorsement reads, "Bk. Tennessee/ $1000 note renewed/Due 6th Novr. 1844.") |
| *5 July* | *From William Tyack.* |
| *6 July* | *From George Bancroft.* |
| *6 July* | *From George M. Dallas.* |
| 6 July | From Albert Gallup. ALS. DLC–JKP. Reports enthusiastic support of the ticket in western New York, as well as elsewhere in the state. |
| 6 July | From J. B. B. Hale. ALS. DLC–JKP. Writes from Wheeling, Va., that prospects are good for carrying the ticket in Pennsylvania, Ohio, New York, and Virginia. |

6 *July*       *To Cave Johnson.*

7 July       From Andrew Beaumont. ALS. DLC–JKP. Recalls Polk's long-standing loyalty to Martin Van Buren and his "heroic struggles in Tennessee"; expects that the Pennsylvania counties of Luzerne and Wyoming will vote Democratic in the presidential canvass.

7 July       From Hezekiah Burhans. ALS. DLC–JKP. Maintains that "the labouring class will not be duped nor gulled by the Coon party" in the presidential election; thinks that his native state of New York, along with New Jersey and Pennsylvania, will support the Democratic ticket.

7 *July*       *From Levin H. Coe.*

7 *July*       *From Jacob M. McCormick.*

8 July       From John Adams. ALS. DLC–JKP. Writes from Catskill, N.Y., that the Whigs use tariff protection as their principal argument, but that as he is himself in manufacturing, he is "fully able to place that question in its true light."

8 July       From Michael D. Black. ALS. DLC–JKP. Writes from Louisville, Ky., an incoherent statement of his personal feelings; Polk's AE on cover reads, "Anonymous— Insane."

8 July       From Michael D. Black. ALS. DLC–JKP. Writes incoherently of his present confinement; Polk's AE on cover reads, "Michael D. Black—Deranged or worse."

8 July       From Andrew J. Donelson. ALS. DLC–JKP. Regrets that he cannot attend the Democratic meeting in Columbia on July 13; fears that the Whigs will carry New Orleans.

8 July       From James A. Garland. ALS. DLC–JKP. Solicits money with which to buy votes in Virginia; asserts that he formerly represented the Albemarle district in the U.S. House; Polk's AE on cover reads, "A forgery and written by a scoundrel."

8 July       From Lucius Lyon. ALS. CSmH. Introduces John S. Bagg, who owns "the leading Democratic Journal" in Michigan and will attend "the great Democratic meeting at Nashville."

8 July       From Y. S. Pickard. ALS. DLC–JKP. Recalls his Maury County background and predicts a Democratic victory in Savannah, Ga., where he currently resides.

9 *July*       *From Alfred Balch.*

9 July       From Thomas Claiborne, Jr. ALS. DLC–JKP. Relates that Democrats in Gibson County, Tenn., have formed in every civil district a committee to identify the names of each Democrat and "to discover the wavering Whigs."

9 July       From Thomas L. Hallack. ALS. DLC–JKP. Solicits loan of $10 cash to be forwarded to his residence in Kutztown, Penn.

| | |
|---|---|
| 9 July | From J. George Harris. ALS. DLC–JKP. States that he has written letters to Washington City and Boston about implementing the "John Jones" proposal; regrets that he cannot attend the mass meeting in Columbia. |
| 9 July | From Allen McLane, Jr. ALS. DLC–JKP. Requests sketch of Polk's political career for use locally in Platte City, Mo. |
| *9 July* | *To William L. Marcy.* |
| 9 July | To James H. Stark et al. L, copy. DLC–JKP. Declines invitation of June 17 to attend a Texas meeting to be held in Indian Springs, Ga., on July 25. |
| *10 July* | *From Robert Armstrong.* |
| 10 July | From Lewis Cass. ALS. CSmH. Introduces bearer of this letter, John S. Bagg; states that Bagg is editor of a Democratic newspaper in Michigan. |
| 10 July | From Greenville Cook. ALS. DLC–JKP. States that many of the leading Whigs in Copiah and Claiborne counties, Miss., have left their party over the Texas annexation question. |
| *10 July* | *From George M. Dallas.* |
| 10 July | To William Kennon, Jr. ALS, draft. DLC–JKP. Declines invitation of July 3 to attend a Democratic meeting appointed for September 2 at St. Clairsville, Ohio. |
| 10 July | From Thomas H. King et al. LS. DLC–JKP. Extend Polk an honorary membership in the Phi Delta Society of Oglethorpe University in Milledgeville, Ga. |
| *10 July* | *From J. G. M. Ramsey.* |
| 10 July | To Peter D. Vroom. ALS. DLC–JKP. Refers inquiries relating to his tariff views to the published text of his letter to John K. Kane of June 19, 1844, and to his 1833 congressional speech, which has been published in the *Register of Debates.* |
| *10 July* | *From Robert J. Walker.* |
| 10 July | From Erwin Wilson. ALS. DLC–JKP. Assures Polk that the Democracy in Pulaski County, Mo., supports his views on the Texas annexation question. |
| *11 July* | *From Alexander O. Anderson.* |
| *11 July* | *From Auguste D'Avezac.* |
| *11 July* | *To Andrew J. Donelson.* |
| 11 July | From William M. Gwin. ALS. DLC–JKP. Introduces William M. Smyth, editor of the *Southern Reformer,* which is published in Jackson, Miss. |
| 11 July | From Samuel H. Laughlin. ALS. DLC–JKP. Expects to go by stage to Columbia for the mass meeting there on Saturday; reports having written "pressing letters" to Sam Houston and to northern friends concerned about southern threats of "Disunion" should Texas annexation fail. |
| *11 July* | *From Robert J. Walker.* |

| | |
|---|---|
| 11 July | From Fernando Wood. ALS. DLC–JKP. Writes from New York City that although Democrats in his state are divided over their choice of gubernatorial candidates, they are firmly behind the national ticket; reports warm support in western New York, from which part of the state he has recently returned. |
| 12 July | From W. M. Grimes et al. LS. DLC–JKP. Invite Polk to honorary membership in the Philosophical Literary Society of Franklin College in New Athens, Ohio. |
| *12 July* | *From J. George Harris.* |
| *12 July* | *From Andrew T. Judson.* |
| 12 July | From John Law. ALS. DLC–JKP. Writes from Vincennes that Indiana favors Polk's election and Texas' annexation. |
| 12 July | From George N. Sanders. ALS. DLC–JKP. Reports that in recent travels to Sault Ste. Marie, Mich., he has observed strong support for "Polk & Texas" and much opposition to Benton and Blair's anti-Texas views; warns that New York and Ohio may be lost to the Whigs on the protection and slavery questions; suggests that Polk have Ritchie "assume editorial management" of the Washington *Globe*. |
| 13 July | From Thomas Irwin. ALS. DLC–JKP. Writes from Pittsburgh, Penn., and introduces Robert P. Flenniken, a lawyer and legislator from Uniontown; explains that Flenniken tried to secure for Polk the legislature's endorsement in 1840 contest for the vice-presidential nomination. |
| 13 July | From Abram Welch. ALS. DLC–JKP. Requests a "Polk and Dallas" banner to display in Split Rock, N.Y. |
| 14 July | From Thomas H. H. Cocke. ALS. DLC–JKP. Complains of inadequate coverage by the *Chronicle and Old Dominion*, a newspaper published in Portsmouth, Va., by Theophilus Fisk. |
| *14 July* | *From Samuel H. Laughlin.* |
| 14 July | From A. M. M. Upshaw. ALS. DLC–JKP. Congratulates Polk on his nomination. |
| 15 July | From Julius W. Blackwell. ALS. DLC–JKP. Expects that Polk will carry the Third Congressional District of Tennessee; inquires if Hugh Lawson White voted against giving firewood to the poor of Georgetown, Md., in 1831. |
| 15 July | From John C. Calhoun. ALS. DLC–JKP. Introduces Isaac S. Ketcham of Michigan, who will work zealously for the ticket in the approaching election. |
| 15 July | From Levin H. Coe. ALS. DLC–JKP. Reports that nearly 2,000 citizens attended a rally in Germantown, Tenn., on Saturday last and that he and William N. Porter will speak in Memphis for the Democrats at a night meeting this date. |

| | |
|---|---|
| 15 July | From John Costigan. ALS. DLC–JKP. Introduces himself as a son of Ireland, a railroad supervisor in Albany, N.Y., and an opponent of the conservative wing of the Democratic party; states that William C. Bouck's bid to win renomination will retard Polk's chances of carrying the state. |
| *15 July* | *From John W. Davis.* |
| 15 July | From W. Dunbar et al. C, copy. DLC–JKP. Invite Polk to attend a mass meeting of Stark County Democrats scheduled to gather at Massillon, Ohio, on August 22. |
| 15 July | From Joseph Hall. ALS. DLC–JKP. Recalls with pleasure their service together in the U.S. House; expects Polk to lose Massachusetts, but to carry Maine, New Hampshire, and possibly Connecticut and Vermont. |
| 15 July | From Robert R. Laurimore. ALS. DLC–JKP. States that Polk will carry Centre County, Penn., by a majority of 900 votes. |
| *15 July* | *From J. G. M. Ramsey.* |
| 15 July | From John C. P. Tolleson. ALS. DLC–JKP. Solicits tariff statement to be published in the Helena *Arkansas Journal,* a Democratic newspaper under his editorship. |
| *16 July* | *From Robert Armstrong.* |
| 16 July | From Henry L. Claiborne et al. CS. DLC–JKP. Invite Polk to honorary membership in Nashville's Hickory Cavalry. |
| *16 July* | *From Andrew J. Donelson.* |
| 16 July | From Simeon B. Jewett. ALS. DLC–JKP. Writes from Clarkson of Democratic prospects in New York; observes that "Polk & Texas are the watch words." |
| *16 July* | *To Cave Johnson.* |
| 16 July | From James H. Otey. ALS. DLC–JKP. Reports that Marshall T. Polk, Jr., is deficient in his Latin studies. |
| *16 July* | *From Elijah F. Purdy.* |
| *16 July* | *From J. G. M. Ramsey.* |
| 16 July | From Edward G. Roddy. ALS. DLC–JKP. Notes plans for holding a meeting in Polk's behalf on August 15 in Petersburg, Penn. |
| *16 July* | *From John H. Wheeler.* |
| 17 July | From Cyrus Beers. ALS. DLC–JKP. States that in Ithaca, N.Y., there is as much excitement for Polk's candidacy as there was for Andrew Jackson's in 1828; predicts that Tompkins County will give Democrats a majority of 400 votes. |
| 17 July | From Aaron V. Brown. ALS. DLC–JKP. Relates that he will come to Columbia on Friday or early Saturday to answer Gustavus A. Henry; encloses letter from Henry D. Foster of Pennsylvania. |
| 17 July | From G. Carpenter. ALS. DLC–JKP. Solicits in behalf of |

Democrats of Blissfield, Mich., Polk's responses to three interrogatories on the Texas annexation issue.

17 July      *From John Catron.*

17 July      From Francis Duffy. ALS. DLC–JKP. Requests that he be named to the honor guard accompanying Polk to Washington City; explains that he is a member of the Polk Guards, a militia company recently formed at Hartsville, Tenn.

17 July      From Robert P. Flenniken. ALS. DLC–JKP. Encloses letter of introduction from Thomas Irwin to Polk; asserts that Uniontown, Penn., will support Polk's candidacy; urges caution on the tariff question.

17 July      *From J. George Harris.*

17 July      *From Miner K. Kellogg.*

17 July      *From Gouverneur Kemble.*

17 July      To William Kennon, Jr., et al. ALS, draft. DLC–JKP. Declines invitation to speak at St. Clairsville, Ohio.

17 July      From Peleg B. Phelps. ALS. DLC–JKP. Reports that in Louisiana's recent canvass Democrats have won three of four congressional races and gained a twelve-delegate majority in the forthcoming state constitutional convention; predicts that Polk will carry Louisiana by a thousand-vote majority.

18 July      From Levin H. Coe. ALS. DLC–JKP. Writes from Somerville, Tenn., that he will depart from his speaking schedule in order to attend a meeting in the southern part of Fayette County on Saturday; specifies documents that Gideon Pillow should forward to Fayetteville, where the debate with Gustavus A. Henry will resume.

18 July      From Philip B. Glenn. ALS. DLC–JKP. Urges that the Democratic presses publish more speeches in favor of Texas annexation; complains that the Whig newspapers are exploiting Thomas Hart Benton's opposition to annexation.

18 July      *From Arnold S. Harris.*

18 July      From James W. Jeffreys. ALS. DLC–JKP. Encloses a newspaper clipping and predicts Polk's victory in Caswell County, N.C.

18 July      From Amos Lane. ALS. DLC–JKP. Recalls their former association in the U.S. House; reports strong support for the ticket in Indiana; and praises Lewis Cass for his efforts in Michigan and Indiana.

18 July      From Edwin F. Polk. ALS. DLC–JKP. Writes from Nashville that he will leave tomorrow for Charlotte, N.C., and stop en route for consultation with J. G. M. Ramsey.

19 July      *From Robert Armstrong.*

19 July      From Levin H. Coe. ALS. DLC–JKP. Encloses state-

ments concerning the loyalty of Ezekiel Polk; reports that Ephraim H. Foster will attend the Whig rally in Somerville, Tenn., on August 14.

| | |
|---|---|
| *19 July* | *From Granville S. Crockett.* |
| 19 July | From Ulysses F. Doubleday. ALS. DLC–JKP. Writes from Auburn, N.Y., and expresses gratification at Polk's nomination; predicts victory in New York, Ohio, and Pennsylvania; and indicates that the tariff issue helps the Democrats. |
| *19 July* | *From J. George Harris.* |
| 19 July | From Leonard Jones. ALS. DLC–JKP. Recalls meeting Polk in Louisville, Ky., in 1842; urges Polk to maintain a religious and moral position in the campaign. |
| *19 July* | *From J. G. M. Ramsey.* |
| *19 July* | *From Richard Rush.* |
| 19 July | From J. D. Swan. ALS. DLC–JKP. Promises to campaign for the ticket, provided that Polk send $200 to him at Shepherdtown, Va., to support his family while he is away from home. |
| 19 July | From Fernando Wood. ALS. DLC–JKP. Encloses proceedings of a meeting of New York City Democrats; explains that he will not be a candidate for Congress; and reports encouraging prospects for Polk's election. |
| 20 July | From Anonymous. L. DLC–JKP. Writes from Sumter County, Ala., and complains that Polk conceals his positions on the issues; predicts that Clay will win the election. |
| *20 July* | *To George Bancroft.* |
| 20 July | From James S. Clark. ALS. DLC–JKP. Encloses a Whig newspaper containing a speech by William H. Seward; asserts that Seward's speech demonstrates Whig efforts to forge an alliance with New York abolitionists. |
| 20 July | From E. S. Davis. ALS. DLC–JKP. Reports from Washington City on Democratic election prospects; describes his personal efforts for the cause; urges Polk to "reply promptly to every call made on you, whether by friend, or foe." |
| 20 July | From Charles G. Eastman. ALS. DLC–JKP. Proposes to send the Woodstock *Age,* a Vermont newspaper of which he is the editor. |
| 20 July | From Horace Foote. ALS. DLC–JKP. Claims to be a prophet of the Lord and requests Polk's acknowledgment of this communication. |
| *20 July* | *From Ransom H. Gillet.* |
| 20 July | From Henry Hand. ALS. DLC–JKP. Writes from Newbern, Va., and gives assurances that Virginia is safe for the Democrats, despite the local distribution of Whig pam- |

phlets printed by William F. Bang & Co. of Nashville.

20 July From William E. Ward. ALS. DLC–JKP. Requests that Polk send him money to be used to promote the Democratic cause in Pennsylvania.

*21 July* *From William E. Cramer.*

21 July From William C. Hazen. ALS. DLC–JKP. Forwards $100 received from Benjamin Adams as partial payment of a note held by Polk; reports on Whig and Democratic activities in Tipton, Fayette, Lauderdale, and Haywood counties, Tenn.

*22 July* *From Robert Armstrong.*

*22 July* *To Andrew J. Donelson.*

*22 July* *To Andrew Jackson.*

22 July From Cave Johnson. ALS. DLC–JKP. States that he has invited those leading men whom Polk wishes to attend the Nashville meeting of August 15; encloses a letter from John L. O'Sullivan, who asks for information with which to refute Whig charges against Ezekiel Polk and who solicits funds with which to sustain a campaign newspaper in New York; advises against sending money to O'Sullivan.

*22 July* *From J. G. M. Ramsey.*

*23 July* *From John Catron.*

*23 July* *To Andrew J. Donelson.*

23 July From James K. Dudley. ALS. DLC–JKP. Writes from New York City and reports that Democrats have "stolen into" the Whig camp "under the disguise of co-operation" and discovered Whig plans to blacken Polk's political and personal reputation; advises Polk to ignore personal slanders.

*23 July* *From J. George Harris.*

*23 July* *To Andrew Jackson.*

*23 July* *From Andrew Jackson.*

*24 July* *From Andrew J. Donelson.*

24 July From Thomas C. Miller et al. LS. DLC–JKP. Write on behalf of a Democratic meeting held in Cumberland County, Penn.; inquire regarding Polk's position on tariffs.

25 July From Anonymous. L. DLC–JKP. Writes from Carlisle, Penn., and warns Polk that local Whigs purporting to be Democrats will request his views on the tariff; states that Cumberland County Democrats oppose repeal of the present tariff.

25 July From Edwin Croswell. ALS. DLC–JKP. Introduces Gansevoort Melville of New York.

[25 July 1844] From David M. Currin. ALS. DLC–JKP. Requests information with which to explain Polk's "action, while in Congress, upon the different Pension Laws" and to defend Polk's record at forthcoming campaign appointments in Williamson County, Tenn.

| | |
|---|---|
| *25 July* | *From E. S. Davis.* |
| *25 July* | *From Andrew J. Donelson.* |
| 25 July | From Theophilus Fisk. ALS. DLC–JKP. Introduces F. W. Byrdsall of New York. |
| *25 July* | *From J. George Harris.* |
| *25 July* | *From Edwin F. Polk.* |
| *25 July* | *From Richard Rush.* |
| *26 July* | *To Robert Armstrong.* |
| *26 July* | *To Andrew Beaumont.* |
| 26 July | From William C. Bouck. ALS. DLC–JKP. Introduces Gansevoort Melville of New York. |
| *26 July* | *From Andrew Jackson.* |
| *26 July* | *To Samuel H. Laughlin.* |
| 26 July | From A. C. Moore. ALS. DLC–JKP. Reports that Democrats of Otsego County, N.Y., are very enthusiastic about Polk's candidacy; asks Polk to write his views on the tariff and Texas annexation issues in order to counter Whig arguments. |
| *26 July* | *From Ely Moore.* |
| 26 July | From Aaron Vanderpoel. ALS. DLC–JKP. Encloses a copy of the New York *Daily Plebeian* containing a confidential circular of some New York Democrats and an account of a Tyler meeting; praises Martin Van Buren's letter to the Democrats of Columbiana County, Ohio, and Polk's position on the tariff; predicts that Polk will carry New York by a large majority. |
| *27 July* | *From Robert Armstrong.* |
| 27 July | From John B. Butler. ALS. DLC–JKP. Reports that Polk's letter to John K. Kane gives satisfaction in Pennsylvania; predicts a Democratic victory in the state. |
| *27 July* | *From Jeremiah Y. Dashiell.* |
| 27 July | From James Parker. ALS. DLC–JKP. Writes from Frewsburg, N.Y., and requests Polk's autograph; asks whether Polk has ever engaged in a duel. |
| 28 July | From Robert Armstrong. ALS. DLC–JKP. Reports on the progress of arrangements for the Nashville meeting of August 15; suggests locations and speakers for other meetings in Tennessee. |
| 28 July | From P. S. Loughborough. ALS. DLC–JKP. Congratulates Polk on favorable Democratic prospects throughout the Union; reports that "the Democrats of Kentucky will make a gallant fight." |
| 29 July | From Robert Armstrong. ALS. DLC–JKP. Encloses letter from Robert Mathews regarding a Democratic meeting proposed for Shelbyville on August 27; complains about the management of the *Nashville Union*. |
| *29 July* | *From John H. Bills.* |

[29 July 1844]     From Aaron V. Brown. ALS. DLC–JKP. Describes his de-
                   bate with Gustavus A. Henry in Fayetteville, Tenn.; sug-
                   gests that Polk send an explanation of his votes against
                   revolutionary pension bills to friends in Fayetteville;
                   praises John M. Bright as "one of the best debaters now
                   in the field."

29 July            From John Cramer. ALS. DLC–JKP. Introduces Ganse-
                   voort Melville of New York.

*29 July*          *From Andrew J. Donelson.*

*29 July*          *From John P. Heiss.*

29 July            From Herschel V. Johnson. ALS. DLC–JKP. Requests
                   that Polk attend a Democratic mass meeting at Macon,
                   Ga., on August 22; mentions that his wife, Ann Polk John-
                   son, is related to Polk.

*29 July*          *From Samuel H. Laughlin.*

*29 July*          *From John McKeon.*

29 July            From Leonidas Polk. ALS. DLC–JKP. Encloses a letter
                   from J. G. M. Ramsey regarding the vindication of Ezekiel
                   Polk.

29 July            From J. G. M. Ramsey. ALS. DLC–JKP. Describes his
                   efforts toward the vindication of Ezekiel Polk; reports
                   on Democratic electoral prospects in North Carolina and
                   East Tennessee.

29 July            From James S. Wadsworth. ALS. DLC–JKP. Urges Polk
                   to "send a confidential and discreet friend" to New York
                   to encourage the withdrawal of William C. Bouck from
                   the contest for the Democratic gubernatorial nomination.

30 July            From James D. Allen. ALS. DLC–JKP. Writes that he
                   may be related to Polk.

30 July            From H. Croswell. ALS. DLC–JKP. Asks whether Polk's
                   views on Texas annexation coincide with those of Thomas
                   Hart Benton.

30 July            From William M. Gwin. ALS. DLC–JKP. Introduces G. S.
                   Cook of Mississippi, who will attend the Nashville meet-
                   ing of August 15; reports making great efforts to arrange
                   his affairs so as to permit his attendance as well.

*30 July*          *From Hendrick B. Wright.*

31 July            To William H. Babbit. ALS, copy. DLC–JKP. Acknowl-
                   edges with thanks his election to honorary membership
                   in the Cliosophic Society of the College of New Jersey.

*31 July*          *From J. George Harris.*

*31 July*          *To John P. Heiss.*

*31 July*          *From John W. P. McGimsey.*

31 July            To E. P. Palmer et al. ALS. GU. Acknowledges with
                   thanks his election to honorary membership in the Phi
                   Kappa Society of Franklin College in Athens, Ga.

31 July            From William Riley. ALS. DLC–JKP. Writes from Car-

|          | lisle, Penn., and warns that the Cumberland County Democrats who met on July 21 and appointed a committee to address Polk on the tariff serve Whig interests. |
|----------|---|
| *1 Aug*  | *To John P. Heiss.* |
| 1 Aug    | From Jesse P. Smith. ALS. DLC–JKP. Solicits contribution to aid in building a new hall for the Dialectic Society of the University of North Carolina. |
| *2 Aug*  | *From Julius W. Blackwell.* |
| 2 Aug    | From Jesse B. Clements. ALS. DLC–JKP. Reports encouraging prospects for Democratic victories in Mississippi and Tennessee; urges that Polk resist any temptation to add to the tariff position stated in his "Pennsylvania letter." |
| *2 Aug*  | *From Levin H. Coe.* |
| 2 Aug    | From Benjamin Cowell et al. CS. DLC–JKP. Extend invitation to a Democratic mass meeting, called in support of the election of Polk and Dallas and the "liberation" of Thomas W. Dorr, to be held in Providence, R.I., on September 4, 1844. |
| 2 Aug    | From Arthur R. Crozier. ALS. DLC–JKP. Reports writing to Andrew Johnson "relative to appointments for speaking in the West." |
| 2 Aug    | From Robert A. Dabney. ALS. DLC–JKP. Requests information with which to refute Whig charges that Polk had opposed pensions for Revolutionary War soldiers. |
| *2 Aug*  | *From Joseph B. Gilman.* |
| *2 Aug*  | *From J. George Harris.* |
| 2 Aug    | From Isaac Hugus. ALS. DLC–JKP. Writes from Somerset, Penn., and inquires whether or not Polk has ever been a Mason. |
| 2 Aug    | From I. F. Maguire. ALS. DLC–JKP. Writes from Randolph, Mass., and inquires about Polk's tariff views. |
| 2 Aug    | From Joshua L. Martin. ALS. DLC–JKP. Introduces John W. Womack of Eutaw, Ala., who will pass through Columbia on his way to the Democratic mass meeting at Nashville on August 15. |
| *2 Aug*  | *From J. G. M. Ramsey.* |
| *2 Aug*  | *From Austin E. Wing.* |
| *3 Aug*  | *To Andrew J. Donelson.* |
| *3 Aug*  | *From John P. Heiss.* |
| *3 Aug*  | *To Andrew Jackson.* |
| *3 Aug*  | *From Samuel H. Laughlin.* |
| *3 Aug*  | *From Romulus M. Saunders.* |
| 4 Aug    | From Robert Allen. ALS. DLC–JKP. Writes from Springfield, Ill., and introduces D. B. Campbell. |
| *4 Aug*  | *From Robert Armstrong.* |
| 4 Aug    | From William A. Bowles. ALS. DLC–JKP. Reports "flat- |

|                  |                                                                                                                                                                                                                                                      |
| ---------------- | ---------------------------------------------------------------------------------------------------------------------------------------------------------------------------------------------------------------------------------------------------- |
|                  | tering" prospects for Democratic success in Indiana's First Congressional District; requests information regarding Polk's votes on pension bills and his defeat in the 1843 Tennessee gubernatorial election.                                          |
| *4 Aug*          | *From Auguste D'Avezac.*                                                                                                                                                                                                                              |
| 4 Aug            | From John C. Edwards. ALS. DLC–JKP. Assures Polk that "local divisions" in Missouri "will make no difference in our presidential elections"; predicts victory for the regular Democrats in the state election.                                          |
| *5 Aug*          | *From Robert Armstrong.*                                                                                                                                                                                                                              |
| 5 Aug            | From Seth Clover. ALS. DLC–JKP. Writes from Clarion, Penn., and requests that Polk send documents to show the kind of tariff principles that Henry Clay advocates in the southern states.                                                               |
| *5 Aug*          | *From Andrew J. Donelson.*                                                                                                                                                                                                                            |
| 5 Aug            | From Abraham Hatfield and Isaac V. Fowler. LS. DLC–JKP. Introduce William A. Walker, a secretary of the Democratic Republican General Committee of the City of New York.                                                                                |
| 5 Aug            | From Lee Roy Kramer. ALS. DLC–JKP. Writes from Morgantown, Va., and inquires about Polk's tariff views.                                                                                                                                                |
| *5 Aug*          | *From William M. Lowry.*                                                                                                                                                                                                                              |
| *5 Aug*          | *From J. G. M. Ramsey.*                                                                                                                                                                                                                               |
| 5 Aug            | From James Robinson. ALS. DLC–JKP. Predicts that the Democrats will gain fifteen hundred votes west of the Tennessee River.                                                                                                                            |
| 5 Aug            | From J. Marion Ross. ALS. DLC–JKP. Writes from Arkansas and requests that Polk appoint him to a clerkship in Washington City after the election.                                                                                                       |
| 5 Aug            | From George W. Somarindyck. ALS. DLC–JKP. Writes from Syracuse, N.Y., and inquires regarding Polk's tariff views.                                                                                                                                      |
| 5 Aug            | From Robert C. Wickliffe. ALS. DLC–JKP. Relates that Whig speakers in Kentucky have attacked Polk's position on the tariff and his vote against giving firewood to the poor of Washington City; requests copies of Polk's speeches for use in the campaign. |
| 5 Aug            | From I. C. Woodburn. ALS. DLC–JKP. States that his wife's maternal grandfather, who moved from Pennsylvania to the Carolinas in the 1780's, bore the surname of "Pollock"; thinks that his wife and Polk may be descended from the same family.         |
| [6 Aug 1844]     | From Robert Armstrong. ALS. DLC–JKP. States that John C. McLemore, who journeys to Pulaski, will stop at Columbia and provide Polk with political intelligence.                                                                                         |
| *6 Aug*          | *From Thomas O. Black.*                                                                                                                                                                                                                               |
| 6 Aug            | From John W. Cook. ALS. DLC–JKP. Reports that Polk's                                                                                                                                                                                                  |

"own cousin one *Mr. Alexander*" of Cadiz, Ky., has charged him with secretly purchasing lands in his own name with moneys belonging to his father and intended for other purposes; states that he has refuted the slander and that Alexander now attributes the allegation to hearsay sources.

6 Aug    From Andrew A. Kincannon. ALS. DLC–JKP. Introduces A. B. Moore of Columbus, Miss., who will attend the Democratic mass meeting in Nashville.

6 Aug    From William M. Lowry. ALS. DLC–JKP. Encloses a statement of the vote in five North Carolina counties; indicates that Democratic gains allow some hope for the gubernatorial race. (Enclosure not found.)

6 Aug    From Aaron Ward. ALS. MB. Assures Polk that the circular in opposition to Texas annexation signed by prominent New York Democrats will not prevent the state's voters from giving Polk a large majority in the coming election.

7 Aug    From Pierce B. Anderson. ALS. DLC–JKP. Reports enthusiastic activity among Democrats of East Tennessee.

7 Aug    From William C. Beattie. ALS. DLC–JKP. Writes from Orange County, N.Y., and inquires about Polk's religious beliefs.

7 Aug    *From George M. Dallas.*

7 Aug    *From J. G. High.*

7 Aug    From Andrew A. Kincannon. ALS. DLC–JKP. Introduces Ewing F. Calhoun of Columbus, Miss.

7 Aug    *From John McKeon.*

7 Aug    From Clinton Roosevelt. ALS. DLC–JKP. Encloses a copy of the *New York Democrat,* of which he is an editor; solicits aid in obtaining southern subscriptions; and offers to speak for the Democrats if his expenses might be paid. (Enclosure not found.)

8 Aug    From F. Adams. ALS. DLC–JKP. Writes from Akron, Ohio, and inquires about the number of slaves owned by Polk.

8 Aug    From John Marshall Booker. ALS. DLC–JKP. Writes from Georgia and requests that Polk contribute to the payment of his medical expenses.

8 Aug    From Philip Clover. ALS. DLC–JKP. Writes from Clarion County, Penn.; states that some Democratic newspapers say that Polk is opposed to the present tariff; and inquires about the basis of that opposition.

8 Aug    From Levin H. Coe. ALS. DLC–JKP. Reports success in his recent debates with one of the Whig electors, Gustavus A. Henry.

8 Aug    From H. M. Leedes. ALS. DLC–JKP. Requests that Polk write a letter in answer to the Whig charges contained in

|        |                                                                                      |
|--------|--------------------------------------------------------------------------------------|
|        | the enclosed newspaper. (Enclosure not found.)                                       |
| 8 Aug  | From George S. Mann. ALS. DLC–JKP. Warns that John Tyler's friends in New York are not to be trusted; asserts that they control but few votes. |
| 8 Aug  | From Ely Moore. ALS. DLC–JKP. Introduces William A. Walker of New York City; suggests that Democrats in Tennessee and other southwestern states urge Silas Wright to accept the New York gubernatorial nomination. |
| 8 Aug  | From Henry E. Riell. ALS. DLC–JKP. Warns that a New York City circular on the subject of naturalization laws originates with political enemies who may suppress Polk's reply unless it is sent to a reliable Democrat; requests a lock of Polk's hair. |
| 8 Aug  | From William J. Whitthorne. ALS. DLC–JKP. Reports favorable Democratic prospects in Bedford County; requests that Polk "intimate to me who would be best to send invitations to" for the Democratic barbecue at Shelbyville on August 27. |
| 9 Aug  | From Henry K. Hardy. ALS. DLC–JKP. Asks whether he may safely recoup losses from the 1840 election by betting on Democratic success in Virginia and in the general election; reports political intelligence from Arkansas and Louisiana. |
| *9 Aug*  | *From John K. Kane.*                                                                |
| 9 Aug  | From Jesse Miller. ALS. DLC–JKP. Reports that the death of Henry A. P. Muhlenberg will not impede Democratic success in Pennsylvania since the party is united behind Francis R. Shunk, the new nominee for governor. |
| 9 Aug  | From J. G. M. Ramsey. ALS. DLC–JKP. Reports on progress of efforts to vindicate Ezekiel Polk; asks that Roger Barton be sent to East Tennessee to campaign; describes news of the North Carolina state elections as "thus far very favorable." |
| 9 Aug  | From William S. Walker. ALS. DLC–JKP. Claims that "a large number" of Methodists in the neighborhood of Marcus Hook, Penn., are prepared to vote for Polk "if *satisfied from good authority*" that he is a Methodist. |
| 10 Aug | From Anonymous. LS. DLC–JKP. Writes from St. Louis and reports that the Whigs are "propagating" stories that Polk's father and grandfather were tories; signs the letter "Veritas & Texas." |
| *10 Aug*  | *From James Black.*                                                              |
| 10 Aug | From Julius W. Blackwell. ALS. DLC–JKP. Mentions several Democratic meetings in East Tennessee; states that Democrats have successfully answered the charge that Ezekiel Polk was a tory. |
| 10 Aug | From F. W. Byrdsall. ALS. DLC–JKP. Suggests that                                     |

although Polk's nomination has unified the New York Democracy, the ticket faces "a hard struggle"; adds postscript, dated August 26, and reports John Tyler's withdrawal from the presidential contest; relates plans to make Tyler a member of the Tammany Society; appends another postscript, dated September 6, and notes the nominations of Silas Wright for governor and Addison Gardiner, "a Calhoun man," for lieutenant governor.

| | |
|---|---|
| *10 Aug* | *From J. George Harris.* |
| 10 Aug | From Joseph Hart. ALS. DLC–JKP. Writes from Indiana; requests that Polk state his views on major issues and reply to Whig charges of toryism and the misuse of state funds. |
| [10 Aug 1844] | From James S. Headen. ALS. DLC–JKP. Writes from Missouri and inquires of Polk's views on the currency and the tariff. |
| 10 Aug | From Cave Johnson. ALS. DLC–JKP. Encloses letter from Henry Simpson of Pennsylvania requesting extracts for publication from Polk's tariff speeches; reports optimistic intelligence regarding elections in Kentucky. |
| [10 Aug 1844] | From Barkly Martin. ALS. DLC–JKP. Discusses Whig vote changes in East Tennessee. |
| 10 Aug | From Shadrach Penn, Jr. ALS. DLC–JKP. Introduces Samuel Treat of Missouri. |
| [10 Aug 1844] | From John Woody. LS. DLC–JKP. Writes from Pennsylvania and inquires about Polk's views on the tariff. |
| *11 Aug* | *From George M. Dallas.* |
| 11 Aug | From John K. Kane. ALS. DLC–JKP. Reports the death of Henry A. P. Muhlenberg; states that Francis R. Shunk, who will be nominated for governor in Muhlenberg's place, will undoubtedly carry Pennsylvania. |
| 11 Aug | From Wilson McCandless. ALS. DLC–JKP. Expresses optimism about Polk's prospects in western Pennsylvania; states that Polk's letter to John K. Kane gives satisfaction on the tariff question; suggests that Polk might win votes by sending a letter, not for publication, to satisfy the Anti-Masons of Pennsylvania. |
| 11 Aug | From James W. McClung. ALS. DLC–JKP. Introduces George Reese of Chambers County, Ala., who will stop at Columbia on his way to attend the Nashville Democratic mass meeting. |
| 12 Aug | From Anonymous. LS. DLC–JKP. Writes from Brunswick, Me.; addresses "Honorable, Pokestalk Esq. son of a British Tory" and celebrates Polk's inevitable defeat; signs the letter "Jeremiah." |
| *12 Aug* | *From Alfred Balch.* |
| 12 Aug | From Henry Horn. ALS. DLC–JKP. Reports the death of |

Henry A. P. Muhlenberg; predicts that Francis R. Shunk will be nominated for governor.

[12 Aug 1844]   From Edward B. Hubley. ALS. DLC–JKP. Requests that Polk write him at Orwigsburg, Penn.

12 Aug   From John K. Kane. ALS. DLC–JKP. Confirms news of the death of Henry A. P. Muhlenberg; expects that Francis R. Shunk will not obtain "that large majority which would have been Mr. Muhlenberg's."

12 Aug   From J. H. Kilpatrick. ALS. DLC–JKP. Requests policy statement for use in his newspaper at Holly Springs, Miss.

12 Aug   From James Lavely. ALS. DLC–JKP. Announces Polk's election to membership in the Democratic Institute of the City of Pittsburgh.

13 Aug   From E. Kennady Crawford. ALS. DLC–JKP. Informs Polk that the Tariff Act of 1842 has been helpful to shoe-makers and inquires whether Whig claims that Polk opposes all protective duties are correct.

*13 Aug*   *To Andrew J. Donelson.*

13 Aug   From Amos Kirkpatrick. ALS. DLC–JKP. Reports that Democrats are gaining support in Jackson County.

13 Aug   From John K. Shab. ALS. DLC–JKP. Writes from Hamilton, Ohio, and inquires whether Polk is in favor of John Tyler's Texas annexation treaty.

*14 Aug*   *From Albert Gallup.*

14 Aug   From Edwin Stearns et al. LS. DLC–JKP. Write as members of the Connecticut Democratic State Central Committee to solicit a statement of Polk's opinion on the tariff.

15 Aug   From Joab H. Banton. ALS. DLC–JKP. Claims that the Tennessee counties that furnished the officers who "mutinised and desearted ther Cuntry's flag" during the Creek War in 1813 also cast the largest Whig votes in the two preceding elections; reports Whig slander of Ezekiel Polk in Mississippi.

15 Aug   From James R. Clayton et al. LS. DLC–JKP. Write from Ohio and ask whether Polk would have voted to ratify the Texas annexation treaty submitted by John Tyler.

15 Aug   From Richard Rush. ALS. DLC–JKP. Predicts that Francis R. Shunk will receive a larger vote as the Democratic candidate for governor in Pennsylvania than Henry A. P. Muhlenberg would have received.

15 Aug   From Jesse Speight. ALS. DLC–JKP. Reports success in public debate with the Whigs at Aberdeen, Miss.; queries Polk about Democratic prospects in Tennessee.

15 Aug   From David D. Wagener. ALS. DLC–JKP. Expresses regret at the death of Henry A. P. Muhlenberg and satisfaction at the likely nomination of Francis R. Shunk; states

|          | that Pennsylvania "is safe for Polk & Dallas." |
|----------|------------------------------------------------|
| 15 Aug   | From Robert Williams. ALS. DLC–JKP. States that Democrats in Huntingdon County, Penn., "have gone in strongly for the Tariff of 1842"; solicits Polk's opinion on the subject to combat Whig claims that Polk is "an *out & out Free trade man.*" |
| *16 Aug* | *From Stephen D. Adams.* |
| 16 Aug   | From Walter F. Leak. ALS. DLC–JKP. Congratulates Polk on his nomination; recalls their college friendship. |
| 16 Aug   | From L. D. Mercer. ALS. DLC–JKP. Requests aid in locating a report that shows the fees received by Henry Clay from the Bank of the United States. |
| 16 Aug   | From G. P. Nunn. ALS. DLC–JKP. Asks whether or not Polk was once a citizen of Rutherford County, Tenn. |
| *16 Aug* | *From Thomas Phillips and William H. Smith.* |
| 16 Aug   | From J. G. M. Ramsey. ALS. DLC–JKP. Insists that he "must not be given as authority for saying" that Ezekiel Polk fought at the Battle of Eutaw Springs. |
| 16 Aug   | From Henry H. Sylvester. ALS. DLC–JKP. Congratulates Polk on favorable Democratic prospects for the November election. |
| 17 Aug   | From Edward Hughes. ALS. DLC–JKP. Writes from Kentucky and requests a statement of Polk's principles in regard to the tariff. |
| 17 Aug   | From Isaac G. McKinley. ALS. DLC–JKP. Warns that the letter addressed to Polk from Thomas C. Miller and others is a "Whig scheme to obtain an expression from you against the tariff act of 42"; expresses satisfaction with Polk's letter to John K. Kane; states that the death of Henry A. P. Muhlenberg will not damage the Democratic campaign in Pennsylvania. |
| *17 Aug* | *From Amasa J. Parker.* |
| 19 Aug   | From Paul R. Baldy. ALS. DLC–JKP. Writes from Pennsylvania and solicits a statement of Polk's views on the tariff and other important questions; states that the Whigs claim that Polk's previous letters "are all forgeries and lies." |
| [19 Aug 1844] | From Aaron V. Brown. ALS. DLC–JKP. Discusses his speaking engagements and correspondence. |
| 19 Aug   | From William L. S. Dearing. ALS. DLC–JKP. Reinforces L. D. Mercer's request for documents. |
| 19 Aug   | From W. M. Naudain. ALS. DLC–JKP. Propounds interrogatories on a national bank, distribution of land-sale revenues, tariffs, and abolitionism. |
| 19 Aug   | From Arnold Plumer. ALS. DLC–JKP. Reports that Pennsylvania Whigs "have abandoned all the other issues & are devoting themselves to the tariff of 1842 alone"; pre- |

dicts Democratic victory in the state.

20 Aug        From John P. Chester. ALS. DLC–JKP. Praises speech delivered by Barkly Martin at Jonesboro; expects Democratic progress in East Tennessee.

20 Aug        From Thomas R. Cocke. ALS. DLC–JKP. Requests that Polk help negotiate the settlement of debts charged to the estate of Thomas J. Winston.

*20 Aug*       *To Cave Johnson.*

20 Aug        From James G. McKinney. ALS. DLC–JKP. Appeals to Tennessee Democrats through Polk, asking that money be raised for the presidential campaign in Kentucky.

20 Aug        From Henry Simpson. ALS. DLC–JKP. Mourns the loss of his close friend, Henry A. P. Muhlenberg; urges great vigilance in guarding against Whig voting frauds; and reports promising prospects in both Pennsylvania and New York.

*20 Aug*       *From C. T. H. Willgohs and Ernest Moffett.*

21 Aug        From George W. Key. ALS. DLC–JKP. Announces the death of Wilie Ledbetter and inquires about the progress of Ledbetter's suit.

22 Aug        From Peter Adams. ALS. DLC–JKP. Propounds three interrogatories concerning the abolition of slavery.

*22 Aug*       *From Alexander O. Anderson.*

22 Aug        From Alfred Flournoy. ALS. DLC–JKP. Recalls Polk's first election to Congress; judges that the Louisiana election may depend on Democratic efforts in New Orleans.

*22 Aug*       *From William H. Haywood, Jr.*

22 Aug        From George S. Houston. ALS. DLC–JKP. Desires additional information about his speaking engagements.

*22 Aug*       *To Cave Johnson.*

22 Aug        From J. G. M. Ramsey. ALS. DLC–JKP. Declines because of illness Polk's request of August 20 for campaign assistance; relates news concerning South Carolina politics.

23 Aug        From William Anderson. ALS. DLC–JKP. Expresses concern regarding Whig efforts to revive Polk's former difficulties with Henry A. Wise of Virginia.

*23 Aug*       *From John O. Bradford.*

*23 Aug*       *To Cave Johnson.*

23 Aug        From Presley Carr Lane and S. T. Glover. LS. DLC–JKP. Pose interrogatories on Polk's possible responses as president to acts of nullification or secession.

*23 Aug*       *From John Law.*

23 Aug        From Christian M. Straub et al. LS. DLC–JKP. Write as members of the Hickory Club of Pottsville, Penn., and assure Polk of a large Democratic majority in Schuylkill County.

23 Aug        From Henderson K. Yoakum. ALS. DLC–JKP. Reports on

|  | the Democratic mass meeting at McMinnville, August 22, and on preparations for the Democratic mass meeting at Shelbyville, August 27. |
|---|---|
| 24 Aug | From William B. Osburn. ALS. DLC–JKP. Asks if the Ezekiel Polk listed in "Gaines New York Pocket Almanack for the year 1792" was Polk's grandfather. |
| 24 Aug | From John F. Russ et al. LS. DLC–JKP. Write on behalf of the Democrats of Salem, Me., and inquire if Polk owns any slaves. |
| [24 Aug 1844] | From John Scott. ALS. DLC–JKP. Recalls serving with Polk in Congress; encloses a poem that he has written. |
| [25 Aug 1844] | From Robert Armstrong. ALS. DLC–JKP. Expresses concern that John Tyler "may make too *Strong* a move in support of Texas"; asks that Polk come to Nashville to discuss the editing of the *Nashville Union*. |
| *25 Aug* | *From Daniel Graham.* |
| *25 Aug* | *From Joseph Hall.* |
| 25 Aug | From John P. Heiss. ALS. DLC–JKP. Suggests that A. O. P. Nicholson be sent to the Northeast to campaign for the ticket. |
| [25 Aug 1844] | From Cave Johnson. ALS. DLC–JKP. Reports that he is too ill to fulfill his speaking engagements; states that he will try to meet his appointment at Pleasant Exchange, Tenn. |
| 26 Aug | From Anonymous. LS. DLC–JKP. Urges Polk to withdraw from the presidential contest; signs the letter "Edwin Coonberry." |
| 26 Aug | From Benjamin H. Brewster. ALS. DLC–JKP. Reports from travels in the rural counties of Pennsylvania that Polk's prospects are good and that Henry A. P. Muhlenberg's death will not divide or defeat the party in November. |
| 26 Aug | From Thomas H. Clarke. ALS. DLC–JKP. Writes from Indiana and requests Polk's views about the completion of the Cumberland Road. |
| *26 Aug* | *To Cave Johnson.* |
| 26 Aug | From James L. Jones and James M. Furgeson. LS. DLC–JKP. Inquire about Polk's views on the Tariff Act of 1842 and the distribution of the revenues from public land sales. |
| 26 Aug | From Jonathan Longstaff. ALS. DLC–JKP. Notifies Polk of his election to honorary membership in the Franklin Literary Society of Pittsburgh. |
| 26 Aug | From Enos Page. ALS. DLC–JKP. Asks Polk to answer questions about banking and slavery. |
| 26 Aug | From V. M. Swayze. ALS. DLC–JKP. Questions Polk about his tariff views. |

| | |
|---|---|
| 26 Aug | From W. H. Ward. ALS. DLC–JKP. Relates evidence of growing enthusiasm for the Democratic presidential ticket in Washington City. |
| 27 Aug | From Young D. Allen. ALS. DLC–JKP. Asks whether or not Polk would veto legislation providing for a new national bank. |
| *27 Aug* | *From Robert Armstrong.* |
| *27 Aug* | *To Andrew J. Donelson.* |
| 27 Aug | From Ransom H. Gillet. ALS. DLC–JKP. Discusses his political activities in association with Silas Wright, Jr.; predicts a Democratic victory in New York. |
| *27 Aug* | *From Daniel Sheffer.* |
| *27 Aug* | *From Hopkins L. Turney.* |
| 27 Aug | From Aaron Vanderpoel. ALS. DLC–JKP. Indicates that the Democratic party in New York is united and will carry the state in the November election. |
| 28 Aug | From Anonymous. LS. DLC–JKP. Solicits loan of two or three hundred dollars; signs the letter "Philip Strubbs." |
| 28 Aug | From Anonymous. L. DLC–JKP. Urges Polk to withdraw from the presidential contest. |
| *28 Aug* | *From Robert Armstrong.* |
| 28 Aug | From James Callin and M. F. Miller. LS. DLC–JKP. Solicit Polk's position on reviving the Sub-Treasury system. |
| *28 Aug* | *From J. George Harris.* |
| *28 Aug* | *To Cave Johnson.* |
| 28 Aug | From Lucius C. Lamar et al. LS. DLC–JKP. Advise Polk of his election to honorary membership in the Phi Gamma Society of Emory College at Oxford, Ga. |
| 28 Aug | From J. G. M. Ramsey. ALS. DLC–JKP. Discusses the vindication of Ezekiel Polk and other political news. |
| 28 Aug | From Isaiah Rynders. ALS. DLC–JKP. Informs Polk of his election to honorary membership in the Democratic Empire Club of New York City. |
| 28 Aug | From James M. Williamson. ALS. DLC–JKP. Writes from Somerville that Frederick P. Stanton probably cannot meet his appointments in Middle Tennessee. |
| 29 Aug | From John P. Chester. ALS. DLC–JKP. Encloses letter mistakenly addressed to Polk at Jonesboro, Tenn. |
| *29 Aug* | *To George M. Dallas.* |
| 29 Aug | From Samuel Darling. ALS. DLC–JKP. Solicits Polk's views on slavery and Texas annexation, both of which issues are of particular public concern in Livingston County, N.Y. |
| 29 Aug | From Boling Gordon. ALS. DLC–JKP. Agrees to join George S. Houston at Lawrenceburg and to accompany him until relieved of this emergency duty. |
| 29 Aug | From Cave Johnson. ALS. DLC–JKP. States that he is |

still too ill to ride, but that he hopes to recover sufficiently to meet Levin H. Coe at Pleasant Exchange, Tenn., on Monday next.

29 *Aug* *To Herschel V. Johnson.*

29 Aug From William J. May et al. LS. DLC–JKP. Enquire whether or not Polk holds any property in slaves.

30 Aug From Alexander O. Anderson. ALS. DLC–JKP. States that he will leave Washington City in ten days and will send a large supply of Charles Elliot's speeches for distribution in Tennessee.

30 Aug From John Edwards. ALS. DLC–JKP. States that the Whigs in Fulton County, N.Y., are circulating a story that Polk opposed pensions for the soldiers of the revolution; requests that Polk send a statement of his views on that question.

[30 Aug 1844] From Gideon B. Frierson. ALS. DLC–JKP. Advises that James W. McClung cannot tour the eastern part of Tennessee; estimates that a crowd of between twelve and fifteen thousand people attended the Democratic mass meeting in Shelbyville.

31 Aug From Francis B. Barclay. ALS. DLC–JKP. Relates details of a mass meeting of Democrats in Bedford, Penn., on August 29.

31 Aug From Israel Brown, Jr. ALS. DLC–JKP. Requests Polk's views on the Texas annexation question; anticipates a Democratic victory in Hamilton County, Ohio.

31 *Aug* *From Auguste D'Avezac.*

31 Aug From James Garland. ALS. DLC–JKP. Anticipates a six-thousand vote majority for the Polk electors in Virginia and thinks that William C. Rives' defection has done no harm.

31 Aug From Charles O'Hara. ALS. DLC–JKP. Explains that he had been a supporter of Henry Clay until Polk's nomination; details why he has changed his political preference; and claims that the Democratic ranks in Geneva, N.Y., are swelling in numbers.

31 Aug From N. Ramsey. ALS. DLC–JKP. Warns against putting Thomas H. Benton in the cabinet should Polk win the election; worries that Benton may be returned to the U.S. Senate, despite his opposition to Texas annexation.

# INDEX